Journey into
America

"Ahmed's media profile is now as high as that of any living cultural anthropologist. One does not have to agree with all his positions to recognize that, in the specific but crucial field of Islam and relations between Muslims and non-Muslims, his life's work has done much to advance the values of anthropology. His celebrity should be welcomed as a gift to the discipline."

JONATHAN BENTHALL, *former Director of the Royal Anthropological Institute, in* Anthropology Today

"My friend Professor Ahmed came to America in the great tradition of Alexis de Tocqueville: a perceptive foreigner affectionately looking at America and American identity. This important new book advances his heroic, even dangerous, 'five minutes to midnight' effort to save us from our foolish mutual animosities. Pray his efforts are not too late."

TONY BLANKLEY, Washington Times *and Heritage Foundation*

"In the tradition of Alexis de Tocqueville, Professor Akbar Ahmed has had a conversation with and about America which illuminates an important part of our national identity."

AMBASSADOR CAROL MOSELEY BRAUN, *former United States Senator and presidential candidate*

"A timely and stimulating contribution to a critically important issue: the West's (and especially America's) relationship to Islam."

ZBIGNIEW BRZEZINSKI, *former National Security Adviser*

"*Journey into America* is an essential pillar in the effort to build the interfaith bridge of understanding. It will inform, provoke, and inspire Americans of all colors, cultures, and faiths."

U.S. REPRESENTATIVE KEITH ELLISON *(D-Minn.)*

"An absolutely riveting journey into an America most Americans have no idea about. As the U.S. faces up to the tensions within its own Muslim communities, it could not be more timely."

CHRISTINA LAMB, *Washington Bureau Chief,* Sunday Times

"*Journey into America* is a journey ensuring that we can see all of our American brothers and sisters, and see that they are indeed created in the image of God."

SENIOR RABBI BRUCE LUSTIG, *Washington Hebrew Congregation*

"What a wonderful, wonderful work! Akbar Ahmed has written an important book on Islam in the United States today. With the refreshing perspective of both Dr. Ahmed and his bright young traveling companions, this book presents great insight into the diversity and vibrancy of American Islam and its potential to help achieve the American promise."

EBOO PATEL, *Founder and Executive Director of Interfaith Youth Core*

"One of the most exciting and readable accounts not only of Muslim life in the U.S., but of the context of American history more broadly. I have learned a great deal about my own country through Akbar Ahmed's eyes."

LAWRENCE ROSEN, *Princeton University*

"Profound, commanding—simply brilliant. This is a powerful piece of writing."

TAMARA SONN, *College of William and Mary, former President of the American Council for the Study of Islamic Societies*

Journey into America

THE CHALLENGE OF ISLAM

AKBAR AHMED

BROOKINGS INSTITUTION PRESS
Washington, D.C.

Library of Congress Cataloging-in-Publication data

Ahmed, Akbar S.
    Journey into America : the challenge of Islam / Akbar Ahmed.
        p.   cm.
    Includes bibliographical references and index.
    Summary: "Examines American identity as influenced by its founding and history and the diverse Muslim experience in America, as well as the experience of other religious groups, and how each has affected the other"—Provided by publisher.
    ISBN 978-0-8157-0387-7 (hardcover : alk. paper)
    1. Muslims—United States—Social conditions. 2. Muslims—United States—Ethnic identity. 3. Muslims—Cultural assimilation—United States. 4. Islam and culture—United States. 5. Cultural pluralism in Islam—United States. 6. Islam and civil society—United States. 7. United States—Religious life and customs. 8. United States—Social life and customs. I. Title.
    E184.M88A39 2010
    305.6'97073—dc22   2010014051

9 8 7 6 5 4 3 2 1

Printed on acid-free paper

Typeset in Adobe Caslon

Composition by Cynthia Stock
Silver Spring, Maryland

Printed by R. R. Donnelley
Harrisonburg, Virginia

For Anah,
who traveled with me on my journey into America
even before she was born,
with love

CONTENTS

Journey into
America

ONE

Muslim Odyssey

I HAD WALKED into an ambush. An aggressive sniper was positioned directly in front of me, with two equally effective sharp-shooters to my left and the obvious leader of the group facing me from the back row. Having been in charge of some of the most battle-hardened tribes in Afghanistan and Pakistan, I knew something about war tactics. One lesson I had learned was to keep cool under fire.

Showdown in a Mosque

Where does one begin a search for American identity and its Muslim component? The answer seemed obvious: in the nation's heartland. But what could be learned about America's founding principles of freedom of speech and religious tolerance in a nondescript, almost shabby mosque in Omaha, Nebraska, where I now was? Especially in the midst of a verbal ambush by an African American man wearing a typical Arab red-and-white checkered headdress, or *kufiya,* who looked as if he had come straight out of an orthodox mosque in Saudi Arabia.

Hearing my call for interfaith dialogue with Jews and Christians, the man stood up in a startling breach of mosque—not to mention Muslim—etiquette to challenge my interpretation of Islam. "Good Muslims" could not talk to nonbelievers, he almost shouted. The salvos continued, despite my well-founded explanation: Muhammad, the holy Prophet of Islam, had himself paved the way for such dialogue. He had urged Muslims persecuted in Mecca to migrate to Abyssinia, a Christian country, because he

1

anticipated they would be well received there once the natives of that land had met them and learned about Islam. But, the man in Arab headdress snapped back, the Prophet had really intended those Muslims to convert the Abyssinians by force.

To me, that seemed an unlikely scenario. This was a small group of destitute refugees, I explained, about a dozen men including their wives, seeking refuge in a large country. And why would the Prophet have sent his own daughter, Rokaya, to join such a group, essentially a war party in this man's interpretation? And why, on the death of Abyssinia's king, did the Prophet lead the funeral services if not out of respect? My remarks fell on deaf ears. By now highly agitated, the man turned his back on me and strode out of the room, only to return within minutes to undertake his prostrations in prayer even while I was still talking. On rising, he approached a bookshelf on my left and noisily browsed among the volumes, keeping his back to me.

I ignored him and continued talking to the congregants seated in front of me. They were a microcosm of Muslim society in America—African American Muslims, Arabs, and South Asians, with one or two white converts. Their conversation also faithfully reflected the range of Muslim thinking in America: some wished to live in contemporary times, and some would have nothing to do with modernity.

My host, a Pakistani lawyer from Karachi and acting president of the Islamic center running the mosque, did not remain with me at the pulpit once the harsh words began to fly. He had felt intimidated by those eager to challenge me and had quietly left. He had invited me with my team of research assistants to participate in the *iftaar*, the opening of the fast, in September 2008, as it was the month of Ramadan, but did not feel compelled to defend his guests. Meanwhile, the challengers, now numbering four, pressed on, disputing my claim that *ilm*, or knowledge—a central feature of God's message in the Quran—encompasses all knowledge, even if it comes from Western sources. For them, the only knowledge relevant to a Muslim arises from *shariah*, or Islamic law—never mind that in his famous sayings, or *hadith*, the Prophet had exhorted Muslims to acquire knowledge even if it meant going to China, which for a Muslim in the seventh century was a distant and forbidding non-Muslim land. It did not take long to grasp the "defensive" subtext of the debaters' argument: Islam must be defended at all costs, even to the point of martyrdom.

I replied with one of my favorite hadiths: "The ink of the scholar is more sacred than the blood of the martyr." The truth of this hadith, I added, was abundantly apparent throughout the Muslim world, which during all my

At the main mosque in Omaha, the Pakistani host prepares to leave while another man stands up to protest as Akbar Ahmed continues his talk.

travels there exhibited a primarily open-minded and compassionate Islam, even under trying circumstances.

The older, more portly challenger in the back row, wearing a colorful shawl and a black velvet cap, shot back accusingly: "How could you take two white kids with you to the Muslim world and hope to explain Islam?" He was referring to my former students Frankie Martin and Hailey Woldt, who were present and had helped me gather data for *Journey into Islam: The Crisis of Globalization.*[1] But he had overlooked my main research assistant for that project—a Muslim. Particularly unsettling was his reference to the color of my students' skin. Islam prides itself on being emphatically color-blind in this regard.

The rebuke I had received was rooted in antipathy not only to other religions and the idea of knowledge as I saw it, but also to other races. On this and subsequent stops on my new journey, this time through America, I found that color continues to be a defining factor for Americans, affecting status and authority and echoing tensions of past eras. It was clearly a subject that needed to be explored further as we continued our fieldwork on a project that would take us across the length and breadth of the United States studying Muslims in the context of American society.

To my team's chagrin, our interviews had begun on shaky ground. We were being met with suspicion, paranoia, and fear fostered by the news media, particularly by reports of infiltrators—of secret agents pretending to be Muslim converts. When Frankie, always sensitive to mosque culture, tried to politely distribute our questionnaires to the men in Omaha's mosque, one congregant balked: "Believe me, you don't want to hear what I have to say." Hearing everyone's views was essential to our investigation, replied Frankie, but he quickly backed off upon receiving a "chilling look" that made his hair "stand on end." Some of the men gruffly asked whether we were working for the FBI. Their rudeness and open hostility surprised both Frankie and Hailey, who had not experienced "anything like this in the Muslim world," a remark they would utter several times on our new journey.

Celestine Johnson, another former American University student accompanying us in Omaha, was crestfallen. Her excitement at the prospect of visiting a mosque for the first time was squashed when she tried to take some pictures of us with the congregants. They angrily waved her back behind a sheet erected to segregate the women from the men. For Celestine, a young, white, middle-class American girl, the experience unleashed a fear lurking in the minds of many white Americans—a fear of Islam and aggressive non-white males. Some would call this America's nightmare.

The next day the team interviewed people about Omaha's Islamic center and community. The four who had challenged me, they learned, had posted a *fatwa* (pronouncement) in the mosque before 9/11 calling for the killing of Jews and Christians and praising the deeds of Osama bin Laden. All four were converts to what is known as Salafi Islam in the United States, a fundamentalist version of the faith influenced by Saudi Arabia (see chapter 5). It purports to be an unadulterated and "pure" form of Islam that is incompatible with any modern Western ideas. The Salafis believe Islam is under attack throughout the world and consider themselves champions of the faith. While most lead peaceful, isolated, and austere lives, some are prepared to take aggressive action in standing up for their beliefs. According to many informants in Omaha and elsewhere, Salafi Islam attracts the young by inspiring them with a sense of identity and of pride. It was estimated that roughly 50 percent of the Muslims in Omaha were Salafi or those inclined toward a more fundamentalist interpretation of Islam, a figure that cropped up again and again on our journey.

Salafi teachings are a far cry from those of Muslims such as Imam W. D. Mohammed, who has had a monumental impact on Islam in America, especially among African Americans (see chapter 4). He advocated acceptance of others and interfaith dialogue.

Just before our visit, the Salafi members of this congregation had sent waves of fear through Omaha's Muslim community when they brutally attacked some of their Muslim opponents in the parking lot of the mosque. Understandably, many congregants were vague about the incident but did hint that the Saudi government was filtering money into such groups through umbrella and student organizations.

Resurfacing after the talk, my host, the Pakistani lawyer, drew me aside to commend me for standing up to this group. Others, men and women alike, also came up to me and in hushed tones voiced their approval of my words. They could do little else in the face of the aggressive measures being taken to impose Salafi views on their congregation. Such a group can have an enormous impact on a small mosque. In this instance, its Salafi members had successfully blocked the appointment of any imam who was not of their thinking, leaving the Islamic center without an imam for six months. According to the community's mainstream Muslims, the previous imam had been fired because the Salafis claimed that he was not conservative enough.

Two days later, I delivered a public lecture on Islam at Omaha's Creighton University, and who should be sitting in the audience but the African American who had heckled me in the mosque from the back row, again strikingly attired. This time, however, he kept his peace, even when I again called on Muslims to participate in interfaith activity. Here, information gleaned during Frankie's conversation with the man's wife cast a different light on this individual. Apparently the state had removed their grandchildren from their home at the behest of government lawyers arguing they were a bad influence on the children because they were Muslims. The experience had left the family angry, distressed, and defensive.

Yet another scene presented itself three days later at an interfaith breakfast hosted by the inspiring figure of Rabbi Aryeh Azriel at Temple Israel. About sixty of the leading Jewish, Christian, and Muslim leaders of Omaha were present, including the Pakistani lawyer from the Islamic center. More vocal in this forum, he spoke of the Muslim community's struggles to become established. As first-generation Americans, they needed time, he explained plaintively, sounding a little lost and unsure.

Some Jewish leaders were not buying this argument, even in the temple's welcoming atmosphere, preferring to think that the Quran teaches violence and that Muslims have failed to integrate into mainstream U.S. culture. One said Americans "mistrusted their Muslim neighbors" for not speaking out against Muslim terrorists: "If I knew a Jew who would want to harm America, I would report him. I wonder if a Muslim would do so. Most Americans believe that Muslims are out to do us harm as Jews and Americans."

By contrast, Rabbi Azriel, a Sephardic Jew, understands and even sympathizes with Muslim culture. As the leader of the Tri-Faith Initiative, a project to create a temple, church, and mosque on the same site, he is dedicated to promoting true interfaith understanding. Despite his energetic efforts, some members of his congregation remain opposed to the project, and like many Americans they consider the Muslim community an impenetrable and alien entity.

These and other encounters at the outset of our own project laid bare the social patterns, problems, and dilemmas of Muslims living in America today. I also realized that the three models of Muslim society I developed following my previous travels to the Muslim world—the mystics who believe in universal humanism, the modernists who attempt to balance modernity and religion, and the literalists who adhere strictly to tradition—were not easily applicable to the American Muslim community, and new ways of studying it were needed. Take the Omaha group. For one thing, this tiny midwestern mosque has had to deal with external problems common throughout the country: non-Muslim neighbors objecting to plans for expansion and overflow parking on the street or young white men intimidating Muslim women. Within the mosque itself, the community's narratives of American identity differed widely, with some overlapping and others in conflict. An intense ideological struggle was under way in the mosque concerning the nature of Islam and the directions it would take in the United States. To complicate matters, the mosque's leadership was in crisis, and scholarship was being marginalized. In addition, ethnic differences were creating conflict between the major Muslim groups in America—African Americans and immigrants. Islamic *adab*, or traditional etiquette, was disappearing. These heartland Muslims needed to reach out to other faiths to become better integrated into American society yet were uneasy about doing so. As we soon came to recognize, all of these factors were among the multiple strands of culture and history that have shaped American Muslim identity.

The Challenge of Islam

Muslims are for Americans what the Russians were for Churchill: "a riddle, wrapped in a mystery, inside an enigma."[2] Yet it is urgent for America to comprehend Islam, not only for the sake of its ideals (which include religious tolerance) but also for its geopolitical needs and strategy. American troops are in several Muslim nations, including Iraq, Afghanistan, Pakistan, and Somalia; five of the nine states that analysts consider "pivotal" for American foreign policy are Muslim; 6 million to 7 million Muslims live in the United States (our field estimates weigh in on the higher side); with about 1.5 billion Muslims worldwide, one out of every four people on the planet is a Muslim. Furthermore, Muslims are beginning to make an impact on all levels of American society—even as members of Congress. Another reason to learn about Islam is the long list of its followers who want to harm the United States—from Osama bin Laden to the new phenomenon of the "homegrown terrorists" (see chapter 9).

America's attempts to grapple with Islam reflect some rather misguided views of the faith's tenets and its followers. These have led some, including so-called experts, to ridicule Islam's holy book, mock its Prophet, and reject its teachings. Some also believe that the teachings in Muslim holy texts promote violence and terrorism, that these ideas exceed the boundaries of religious tolerance, and that Christianity and Islam are on a collision course.[3] Needless to say, American Muslim identity has been greatly affected by the aggressive hyperpatriotism following 9/11, which pointed to Islam as the antithesis of all that was good and worthy in America and led many to ask whether Muslims could be good Americans.

Media and even government figures compounded the hostility: TV commentator Bill O'Reilly has compared the Quran to Hitler's *Mein Kampf,* and Representative Tom Tancredo of Colorado has advocated the nuking of Mecca. Comedians, whose traditional role has been to make fun of everyone regardless of race or religion in order to underline their common humanity, now also single out Muslims. In a 2006 Comedy Central special, *Carlos Mencia: No Strings Attached,* for example, the Mexican American comedian demonstrates his American patriotism by attacking Muslims more crudely and viciously than anyone else. Demeaning portrayals are also common in films like *Witless Protection* (2008), in which Larry the Cable Guy insults a Muslim motel keeper in a pointless sequence, or *Observe and Report* (2009), in which a "Mideast-looking" character called "Saddamn" functions as a punching bag for the main character.

These and other treatments suggesting Muslims are crude, inherently violent, and not to be trusted have now pervaded society, painting them as un-American. In the wake of growing American suspicion, fueled by terms bandied about in the media such as "jihad," "fatwa," "female circumcision," and "honor killings," the gap between mainstream Americans and the U.S. Muslim community has grown ever wider since 9/11.

Muslim actions have not helped. Every new case of violence involving a Muslim like that of Major Malik Nadal Hasan's killing spree at Fort Hood, Texas, pours salt on the still-raw wounds of 9/11. Commentators in the media and on blogs have been angrily warning of the dangers of homegrown terrorists. Such demonization robs Muslims of their dignity and humanity.

Cognizant of this problem, America's top military field officers—such as General David Petraeus, General Stanley McChrystal, and Colonel David Kilcullen—have emphasized winning the hearts and minds of Muslims.[4] In September 2009 General McChrystal warned Americans against being "arrogant" in the ongoing war in Afghanistan and called for the protection of Muslim civilians, asking that they be treated with "respect."[5] Otherwise, he feared, Americans would have greater difficulty maintaining security at home and safeguarding the troops abroad. He repeated this theme when launching the largest military operation against the Taliban in February 2010.

Who, then, is right—those who advocate the bashing of Islam or the field commanders who urge that it be treated with dignity and respect? The fact of the matter is that many Americans on both sides, as well as others throughout the country, have an incomplete knowledge of Islam. Many are also unaware of Islam's role in U.S. history. The first nation to recognize the newly formed United States was Muslim Morocco, and the first recorded man to visit the North American continent with a Muslim background was a North African Berber who arrived almost a century before the landing of the *Mayflower* in 1620.[6] Scholars speculate that 15 to 30 percent of the male slaves and 15 percent of the female slaves brought from Africa were Muslim, although Muslims believe the figures could be higher (see chapter 4).[7] Thomas Jefferson owned a copy of the Quran, with which he taught himself Arabic, and hosted the first presidential iftaar. The Founding Fathers acknowledged Islam with cordiality.

Our journey revealed some interesting cultural contributions of Islam to American identity.[8] In Houston, Texas, Father Donald Nesti was describing the special features of the beautiful church on the campus of the University of St. Thomas when the bells began to ring. Were they the equivalent of the Muslim call to prayer? I asked. "That's right," he replied.[9] "Saint Francis of Assisi started the bell after his visit to the caliph, the sultan; he came back and figured we have to have some kind of call for prayer, so he took the bell." Considered a mystic figure close to God, Saint Francis was widely respected in the Muslim world, even by the Fatimid sultan. Islamic principles echo in the works of Ralph Waldo Emerson, the father of American Transcendentalism, and of Walt Whitman, to name but two literary figures influenced by the Quran and by the great Muslim mystic poets, including Ibn Arabi and Jalaluddin Rumi, whom Whitman echoes in his well-known poem "Salut au Monde!":

I hear the Arab muezzin calling from the top of the mosque,
I hear the Christian priests at the altars of their churches, . . .
I hear the Hebrew reading his records and psalms, . . .
I hear the Hindoo teaching his favorite pupil. . . .

Even that most quintessential American icon, the Statue of Liberty, France's gift to commemorate the centennial of the signing of the Declaration of Independence, has an Islamic connection. The inspiration for this colossal representation of republican virtue came from sculptor Frédéric Bartholdi's plans for a giant lighthouse to be patterned after the Roman Goddess Libertas, veiled in Arab fashion, with light beaming from a headband and a torch held upward at the entrance of the Suez Canal.[10] The United States even has its Muslim "superstars" in Muhammad Ali and Malcolm X; and Rumi is America's best-selling poet. In other words, there are sufficient reasons for Americans to know and appreciate Islam.

The negative "normative" definition of Muslims imposed from outside their circles clearly burdens Muslim community leaders with a monumental task: they must cope not only with intrinsic forces arising from the diverse nature of the Muslim community but also with extrinsic ones arising from a culture vastly different from that of their countries of origin. Both sides— the American Muslim community and mainstream Americans—need to recognize the nature of these forces and their implications for the future.

An Anthropological Approach to America

"Foreigners can't write about America," pronounced a colleague when I outlined plans for a study of contemporary American society with a focus on the Muslim community. Before I could respond, he had added a postscript: "especially a Muslim." It was the fall of 2007, and we were living in post-9/11 America. This was not the best of times for a Muslim to be out in the country asking about American identity and distributing questionnaires enquiring about threat and security.

Moreover, I was not a scholar of America, although I had read diverse works about the country, historical and otherwise, and had traveled to many of its parts. But my trips had been brief, to give a lecture or to visit with relatives. Still, I was amused at the rich irony of my American colleague's comment because his job at a leading think tank was to study and travel to the Muslim world. It was ironic also that he was questioning someone who has grown up inspired by the traditions of the earliest and greatest travelers and ethnographers, such as Ibn Khaldun, Ibn Battuta, and Al-Beruni.

Together, these Muslim scholars laid the foundations for what centuries later would be called the science of anthropology. Besides, I thought, if a Frenchman such as Alexis de Tocqueville could do it, I saw no reason why a Pakistani could not.

For some early insights, I turned to de Tocqueville and was immediately struck by his remarks about American hypersensitivity to perceived criticism:

> There is nothing more annoying in the habits of life than this irritable patriotism of the Americans. A foreigner would indeed consent to praise much in their country; but he would want to be permitted to blame something, and this he is absolutely refused. America is therefore a country of freedom where, in order not to wound anyone, the foreigner must not speak freely either of particular persons, or of the state, or of the governed, or of those who govern, or of public undertakings, or of private undertakings; or, finally, of anything one encounters except perhaps the climate and the soil; and still, one finds Americans ready to defend both as if they had helped to form them.[11]

And there I was, about to deal with the most sensitive of subjects for Americans: race, religion, and politics. Any remarks touching on these subjects, especially before television cameras, have the potential to be blown out of proportion or to destroy a career under the gaze of the entire American public. Hence I knew I had to tread carefully yet believed in the importance of my proposed study, not least because it was long overdue. I could not back away from it, even if my name was Ahmed.

How then, I asked myself, would Americans react to a Muslim perspective on American society? More to the point, how should the Muslim go about eliciting their answers? My training as an anthropologist showed me the way: to get the full story, it would be necessary to look at the psychological, economic, and religious dimensions of American society in the context of its history. Anthropologists believe that society consists of interacting parts, and that anthropology is therefore the only discipline attempting to study society as a whole. The history of the group, social organization, leadership, and rites of passage are of particular interest. Anthropologists interview individuals, spend time with their families, and follow them as they go about their daily business. Their principal tools include face-to-face interviews and questionnaires, diaries, and notes. They are thus immersed in society through "participant observation."

I vowed to faithfully record what I saw and heard as objectively as possible. I hoped the study would conform to scientific principles as far as possible, and that by engaging a tried and tested team in the endeavor, I would balance any tendency to error and present a fairly accurate picture of the society in question. To ensure that our methods established trust and allowed for counterchecking, we also sought to maintain objectivity throughout the interviews. The team had been trained to remain neutral, respectful, and nonargumentative during interviews. They were not on this journey to change people's opinions but to give them a chance to talk and share their views. This is the only way to achieve the anthropological objective: namely, to hold a mirror up to society fairly and steadily.

Any doubts I may have had about the sheer size of the project or about a foreigner trying to comment on America were quickly dispelled by the enthusiasm of my team (which, incidentally, was composed mainly of Americans) and the people we met on the journey. We encountered so many good and decent people who prayed for our success and academics who were enthralled by our project that I was sure we were on the right track.

A central message of this book, then, is that scant information and knowledge are to blame for the stereotypes and prejudices that Muslims and non-Muslim Americans have of each other. For those critics of applied anthropology who may believe I am suggesting the use of knowledge to better assist in invading Muslim societies or torturing individual Muslims my answer is no, not at all. On the contrary, by presenting Muslims in the context of larger society, I aim to humanize both and therefore make it more difficult for either to inflict cruelty and pain.

In a 2007 Department of Homeland Security (DHS) video in which I participated, I explained why a Muslim woman arriving at an American airport may be nervous and disconcerted if a male official has spoken to her loudly and aggressively, has looked directly in her eyes, or come too close to her. He would be violating the rules of modesty for this woman. She would be nervous not because she was hiding a bomb, but because her culture tells her that men must respect women and maintain boundaries between them. The video was distributed to thousands of DHS agents, and I was told it helped them to receive visitors at airports with more courtesy and understanding.

For Muslims and non-Muslims alike whose professional interest is to look at or comment on Muslim society in America, the sociological reality is that they cannot do so without also looking at the context of larger American society. It is the interaction of the two that shapes Muslim society. That is why a study of the Muslim community needs to be placed within the frame of American identity.

Why Societies Maintain Boundaries

Identity, a subject of long interest to social scientists, is clearly taken seriously in American society. Although I use simple labels to categorize complex identities for purposes of discussion in this book, they are nothing more than a sociological device and should not be taken to suggest that I accept the stereotypes and prejudices that are implied in normative attitudes. Rather, I am merely trying to explain the boundaries that ethnic groups establish to ensure their "purity" and to confer certain rights, privileges, and obligations on their members. Boundaries also establish a pool for leadership, which is required to look after the interests of the group and to perpetuate its values, attitudes, and beliefs. The stakes are high in the creation of boundaries because they provide access to political, economic, and social power.

Anthropologists, in particular, have been preoccupied with the way in which communities define themselves, maintain their uniqueness, and are defined by others.[12] A group sets itself apart through its language, genealogical charter, historical traditions, cultural patterns, special rites of passage, or a combination of these factors. An individual is thus born into a web with some or all of these features, which define his or her identity. This identity confers security and stability. That is why those living in societies with a strong sense of identity have few problems in defining themselves. By contrast, those living in societies with less sense of identity, perhaps because traditions have been disrupted by high urbanization, rapid change, or migration, are more unsure of their identity and even troubled by its murkiness.

Yet social boundaries are never as rigid as they may seem. They are made permeable by different strategies adopted by a society's less privileged groups. Intermarriage is one such strategy, education another. The dominant group may also broaden its definition of who can be part of the group. In time, the differences between ethnic and religious backgrounds fade as the minority or weaker groups are accepted and they are allowed to maintain their particular identity without compromising it. Many Americans have told me that they are a mixture of ethnicities, their ancestors coming from different European countries. An American could be a descendant of Polish, Scottish, Hungarian, and French ancestors, and also have some Native American blood.

The Question of the Muslim Minority

Americans tend to have mixed views about how to approach minority cultures. For decades they considered the country a "melting pot" in which all immigrant cultures eventually became blended into the larger American culture. Now they see it as more of a "salad bowl" in which immigrant communities maintain a sense of their own identity within the context of the larger American culture. This raises important questions for studies such as ours: how, then, is one to define a minority community, and how does such a community maintain its particular identity in the face of a powerful centralizing culture?

An Iraqi may consider himself or herself a Shia or Sunni, and a Pakistani a Punjabi or Pathan. In other words, identity for Muslims living in the Muslim world is based on sect or ethnicity, each of which is associated with a distinct code of behavior. Underlying sectarian and ethnic differences is a common bond arising from worship of the same God, reverence for the same holy book (the Quran) and the same Prophet Muhammad, and adherence to the Five Pillars (core beliefs) of Islam.

To add to this complexity, the American Muslim community is not a monolith but is roughly divided about one-third each between African Americans, Muslims from the Middle East, and those from South Asia. There are also a small but growing number of white and Latino converts. These groups in turn differ markedly in historical background, lifestyle, attitudes, and values. Muslim life is also affected by location. New York's Muslims remain traumatized by 9/11 and the changed attitudes toward them as a result. By contrast, West Coast Muslims are much more confident, relaxed, and only occasionally reminded of 9/11 through the media. Communities having a strong religious leader such as Imam Hassan Qazwini in Dearborn, Michigan, or Muzammil Siddiqi in Los Angeles, California, appear to be more cohesive, with rituals and festivals, rites of passage, and social activities focused on an Islamic center and its leadership. On the other hand, some of the newly formed Islamic centers in medium-size towns are having leadership problems owing to the community's ethnic or sectarian divisions, as in Omaha, yet do not have a large enough population to support more than one center.

Amid the many contradictions witnessed by our team—vitality and confidence here, disunity and despair there—some interesting patterns emerged. For one thing, Muslims promoting interfaith activity tended to be at odds with the more orthodox members of their communities; we saw such clashes in centers and mosques ranging from Honolulu to New York, and Dearborn to Omaha. Those in favor of literalist interpretations of Islam emanating from Saudi Arabia are the most vocal and aggressive in rejecting or ignoring "corrosive and corrupting" American culture. They believe Muslim energy and commitment should be focused on reeducating Muslims or converting Americans to "true Islam." Some of their barbs are also directed at female leaders and those who practice Sufi Islam. Complaints of another sort surfaced among African American Muslims who balk at immigrants' displeasure with American culture and their air of superiority, particularly before 9/11. Muslim rapper Quadir "Q-Boogie" Habeeb of Buffalo, New York, explained that immigrants were not as effective as blacks in the white media because "they say 'Allah Subhanatallah,' while we say 'God'—they are seen as un-American."

The immigrants had reasons to celebrate their Americanness. Many proudly said that America was the "best place to be a Muslim" (see chapter 5). Arriving from Pakistan destitute, Munir Chaudry in Chicago and Hamid Malik in Los Angeles became prominent and successful citizens who are now gratefully living the "American dream"; a century ago, the Lebanese grandfather of activist Najah Bazzy came to work in a Ford factory in Dearborn and established a family of achievers; out of loyalty to his new land, Imam Qazwini, originally from Iraq, publicly supported the U.S. invasion of Iraq and faced the wrath of his own community. Perhaps the most poignant sentiment from individuals across the land was summed up by the woman from Cairo who, abandoned by her Egyptian husband, took the opportunity to educate herself and now lives a successful life in Paterson, New Jersey: "America saved my life."

However successful the lives of these immigrants, a fundamental question that propelled our investigation remains: whether Americans, on the one hand, could overcome their fear (commonly appearing in the guise of patriotism) and reach out to Muslims, and whether Muslims, on the other hand, could correct the distortions and misunderstandings about Islam enough to demonstrate that they, too, are fully "American." The first logical step of our project—and one expected to ultimately foster mutual understanding—was to uncover concerns common to *both* communities and to see how each perceives the other.

Everywhere we traveled we saw that the problem of accommodating Muslims in American society poses a challenge to American identity itself. With their different appearance, different religion, and different values, Muslims create a complexity for mainstream Americans. Their presence and treatment by Americans test the limits of pluralism. Indeed, torture in secret prisons, wiretapping, and policies in Guantánamo Bay have seriously damaged the nation's core values. The enormity of the challenge lies in its dual effect: first, on American self-perception in the future, and, second, on the relationship with the Muslim world, which will also determine the political trajectory of the United States as a global power. Therefore any attempt to analyze America's predicament needs to begin with a discussion of its identity.

Dr. Sadiq Mohyuddin, center, greets Ahmed and members of the team, Frankie Martin on the right and Madeeha Hameed and Jonathan Hayden on the left, on their first stop at the airport in St. Louis. Throughout their journey team members traveled to unique and the most representative communities in the country using many modes of transport, including cars, SUVs, planes, trains, and even boats.

Fieldwork Methodology

Our greatest methodological challenge lay in the geographic boundaries of the community under study, which is spread across a vast nation. Some might be inclined to forgo traveling across its breadth and to draw conclusions from the works of others, brief discussions with elites, or mass polls. None of these approaches could yield the mine of information from face-to-face encounters in places of worship, homes, and recreation centers, which we endeavored to reach by all possible means of transportation.

As in my previous study of the Muslim world, the project was a social science experiment encompassing history, religion, and political science. In preparation for these encounters, my team and I dug into works of American history, society, and culture written from a wide range of perspectives.

Fortunately, there are excellent books on American history, many of them written recently, for example, by Joseph Ellis, David Hackett Fischer, Jon Meacham, Walter Russell Meade, and Sarah Vowell.[13] There are also insightful books on contemporary American society by Morris Berman, Diana Eck, Chris Hedges, and Samuel Huntington.[14] In addition, I read the works of scholars like Howard Zinn and Noam Chomsky for whom American history is soaked in blood and tears, as well as of those whose

America is forever drenched in sunshine like Larry Schweikart and Michael Allen.[15] For the former, white people are unrelenting villains providing little worth or value; for the latter, they are the triumphant embodiment of God's vision on earth. I do not find either view entirely convincing.

Our constant and most reliable companion was de Tocqueville's *Democracy in America*.[16] We were invariably surprised at the detailed nature of the analysis and its contemporary relevance for a book written almost two centuries ago. De Tocqueville takes in the entire range of American society. He found American democracy a "superabundant force" that can "bring forth marvels" but was not impressed by the general level of political understanding in America. Because "the majority draws a formidable circle around thought," he did "not know any country where, in general, less independence of mind and genuine freedom of discussion reign than in America."[17] He was "struck by the vulgar aspect of this great assembly [House of Representatives]," members of which "do not always know how to write correctly" and warned of the "effects of the omnipotence of the majority on the arbitrariness of American officials."[18] As for the health of the nation, he found that due to the ever-weakening federal government, "the sovereignty of the Union alone is in peril."[19] He admired Thomas Jefferson, "the most powerful apostle that democracy has ever had," but disliked Andrew Jackson, "a man of violent character and middling capacity," whose actions forced de Tocqueville to contemplate "evils that would be impossible for me to recount."[20] De Tocqueville was not hopeful of the fortunes of the slaves and the Indians: "The servility of the one delivers him to slavery, and the pride of the other to death."[21]

In addition, we consulted various works on Islam in America and interviewed both Muslim and non-Muslim scholars of the subject. In spite of the obvious need, there is a surprising dearth of reliable and good books on American Muslims. We read and met respected Muslim figures like Sheikh Hamza Yusuf and Imam Hassan Qazwini, those well-meaning but controversial Muslims who would be adventurous with Islam in America like Irshad Manji and Asra Nomani, and the authoritative non-Muslim scholars of Islam like John Voll, John Esposito, Tamara Sonn, and Lawrence Rosen. We also read the work of those authors, like Steve Emerson and Daniel Pipes, whose combined corpus conveys the impression that Islam is inherently a violent religion.

Of the excellent books that are available, those by Jane I. Smith and Karen Isaksen Leonard provide scholarly and useful overviews, but neither is based on fieldwork.[22] Many others are limited in scope: Paul Barrett's book is based entirely on interviews with seven Muslims; the Hafiz family's popular book is based on data gathered from 150 questionnaires sent to high school students; Yvonne Yazbeck Haddad, Jane I. Smith, and Kathleen M. Moore and Jamillah Karim have studied Muslim women; Evelyn Shakir's book is about Arab women; Abdo Elkholy writes of Arab Muslims in Toledo, Ohio, and Detroit, Michigan; Alia Malek and John Tehranian of immigrant Muslims; and Robert Dannin and Sherman Jackson about African American Muslims.[23] Aminah McCloud has written two books on African American and immigrant Muslims.[24] Several books by Muslims are of an autobiographical nature, notably by Imam Qazwini and Asma Gull Hasan.[25] Some works on Islam in America are marred by the ideological stance of the author who wishes to project Islam in a specific way, as in the books by Steve Emerson and Robert Spencer.[26]

Our team spent a year on the background work for the project and starting in September 2008 about nine months in the field. We visited over 75 cities and over 100 of the estimated 1,200 mosques, some of which are little more than a room or two. Following the anthropological techniques just mentioned, we endeavored to engage in participant observation to the extent possible. This meant that we often stayed with Muslims to see how ordinary Muslims live their lives. We spent time with their families, opened the fast with them, observed them at prayer. Our strategy of having males speak to the men in the mosques and females to the women was very effective. Working within the culture of the respondents in this manner, the team gained unique access to the community and obtained important data. With a trained and motivated team, it was possible to maintain a frenetic pace and ferret out significant facts and figures on Islam in America over nine months. We approached the fieldwork with humility, bent on learning and listening. Thus we were able to collect the wide range of opinions and ideas needed to paint an accurate picture of the American moment that we wished to study.

The typical procedure on arriving in a city would be for me to address a large congregation on the first day in its main mosque, followed by an interfaith gathering, if possible, or reception. This would swiftly open the doors of the community, enabling the team to follow up leads. In addition, we would also research a city beforehand to determine what community members would be important sources of information. In Atlanta, for instance, we were welcomed at a dinner on our arrival by some thirty of the city's leading Muslim figures, consisting of Bosnians, Turks, Arabs, Pakistanis, Indians, and Ethiopians, representing Sunnis, Shias, and Ismailis. Through contacts made at the dinner and research on the city, we were able to successfully arrange interviews and meetings. This was anthropology on speed—but still anthropology.

Our work has had several outcomes besides this book. By filming our interviews and anything that caught our interest in the context of the project, we collected valuable film material. With the help of my son, Babar Ahmed, a professional filmmaker, we produced the documentary *Journey into America* in time for the Islamic Film Festival organized by the Islamic Society of North America in Washington, D.C., on July 4, 2009.[27] Since then, the film has been shown in France, Australia, Pakistan, and other countries and in the United States at venues including the National Cathedral. We also maintained a popular blog, www.journeyintoamerica.wordpress.com. For more information on the project, see the Berkley Center's Knowledge Resources page "Understanding Islam in America and Around the World" at http://berkleycenter.georgetown.edu/.

Questionnaires

Altogether, we gathered about 2,000 questionnaires from people of all ages, races, religions, and classes across the country. The questionnaires were designed with two objectives in mind: to capture the views and social circumstances of a particular individual at a particular time in his or her life, and to penetrate that subject's personality. We presented open-ended questions and included ample space for the interviewee's responses. Many people complained about the time it took to answer the questions and the level of difficulty it posed, but this approach produced considerable insight into and details about the community that no multiple-choice question could provide.

Our first question asked about the interviewee's role models. Through many years of fieldwork, I have found this to be an effective way to get people talking, even though the question by implication asks about their identity or beliefs and thus makes some people uncomfortable. This was followed by questions about American identity, the books that respondents read, the media that informed their opinions, and what they saw as the greatest threat to America. Some of the answers to the last question were particularly surprising. Expecting to be told "terrorism"—which for the majority of Americans is implicitly associated with Muslims—we found lack of education, ignorance, and the compromising of civil liberties most frequently cited as the greatest threat. At times, respondents misunderstood the question or were offended by it. The answer to "What does it mean to be American?" seemed obvious to many and offensive to others.

Two major organizations, with vast budgets and large staffs, have conducted surveys on American Muslims in the past several years. The Pew

Research Center Poll, "Muslim Americans: Middle Class and Mostly Mainstream," released in 2007, polled 1,050 people, while Gallup's "Muslim Americans: A National Portrait" released in 2009 sampled 946. Our sample of 2,000, of which about half were Muslim, was not only larger but also provided a more in-depth survey. Unlike the multiple-choice questions common in other surveys or a telephone call, our open-ended questions conducted in face-to-face sessions gave us better access to people's emotions and passions. It is impossible to learn "what Muslim women really want" without getting to know them in their living rooms and kitchens and chatting with them for hours, or shopping with them, or meeting their families. Similarly, one cannot determine "who are the extremists" without meeting them face-to-face in their isolated mosques. In short, no study of Islam in America can be complete without the use of the anthropological method.

The Team

A great deal of our success in rapidly getting to the heart of a community was due to our team. As Frankie pointed out in an interview with Al Jazeera on the *Riz Khan Show,* "I think people realize that we travel as a family ourselves. Professor Ahmed is like a father to us. We have known each other for four or five years, so we are traveling as a unit. When we traveled in the Muslim world and among Muslims here in America, we were welcomed as a family by Muslim families. It builds relationships that we need for the study."

Inasmuch as this book is about American identity, it is correct to disclose the background of my team. Four are white and Christian. Jonathan Hayden, from Alabama, is a Protestant of mainly Anglo-Saxon descent, and one of his ancestors was a general with George Washington. Frankie Martin comes from a Catholic background, part Italian and part Irish, but was raised Episcopalian. Hailey Woldt, a Texan, is partly descended from travelers on the *Mayflower,* was a Protestant, and is now a Catholic. Craig Considine is an Irish-Italian Catholic from Boston. While studying at the College of William and Mary, Madeeha Hameed, who is of Pakistani background and a Muslim, joined us for three months. Two of the team are therefore descended from America's earliest white settlers.

Although they all had video and still cameras, I designated Craig the film director and Hailey the photographer, in addition to their other tasks. Celestine Johnson, a good friend of Hailey's, also joined us intermittently. Various friends and relatives contributed to our fieldwork as well. My wife, Zeenat, joined us on the northern leg of our journey, and Amineh Hoti, my daughter and fellow anthropologist, with her two children, Mina (thirteen) and

Ibrahim (ten), came in on the southern leg. Amineh was pregnant with Anah, but this did not deter her from participating in fieldwork with the rest of us.

Each member had a different talent that in combination made for a cohesive, fast-moving, perceptive, and dedicated team, whatever the circumstances. At times we had to sleep on the floor in the house of a friend or drive six hours in pouring rain or the dark of early morning to keep an appointment. While we occasionally enjoyed the luxury of a Hilton Hotel, we usually checked in at more modest accommodations. The Hampton Inn became our second home. The women on the team slept in one room and the men shared another.

Although the road travel was long, it permitted us to compare experiences and discuss theoretical issues. Cramped in a van, we found these peripatetic seminars exhilarating, with ideas flowing freely and being dissected vigorously. The drive from Las Vegas to a Hopi reservation in Arizona and back, when we spent fourteen hours in the van, then had to rush to board a plane to San Francisco, is an example of our long road journeys.

Pressures were constant and often arose from unexpected quarters. In Honolulu, Frankie and Celestine were taken to a police station and threatened with arrest (see chapter 3). Craig sustained so many injuries and accidents that we jokingly compiled a "Craig's list," which included an allergic reaction to peanuts in Los Angeles that sent him to the emergency room, a sleepwalking accident in Miami warranting another hospital visit, and the theft of his driver's license by a taxi driver in Washington, D.C., the day before we left for Florida. But even technical difficulties with his camera failed to dim his enthusiasm. At one point in Chicago, a computer glitch threatened to keep him from producing the DVD I needed for the next morning's meeting. Pulling an all-nighter, with no thought to his health, he had the DVD in hand at 7 a.m., the problem solved.

In Atlanta and Dallas our rental car was broken into, and in New Orleans and Boston the car was towed away. In Atlanta, Hailey's expensive camera, with shots of some significant moments of the journey, was stolen. When I fell ill in freezing Nashville in winter, the team bundled me up and we climbed into the minivan early in the morning for our next stop in Memphis. Miraculously, we somehow kept to our busy schedule. Over these long grueling months away from home, the team never complained.

American Journey

To learn what America means to Americans, why they are so passionately attached to the land, and how they express this affection, visit Monticello and see it through the eyes of its owner, Thomas Jefferson. Monticello sits atop a small mountain reaching 850 feet, and in the distance one can see the Blue Ridge Mountains, which in Jefferson's youth marked the furthest extent of the new nation, beyond which lay the unknown.

Spread over 5,000 acres, Monticello is surrounded by undulating green fields with dense thickets of trees. Scenic views extend across miles of valleys, giving the landscape a secure and serene look, far from the grasping reach of monarchs or the prying eyes of government officials. It speaks of an America of endless possibilities, with even greater ones lying beyond the mountains. Jefferson's America is what many still see today—a land of hope and optimism, of boundless opportunity, and the promise of a bright tomorrow. As de Tocqueville remarked, "In the United States they rightly think that love of one's native country is a kind of worship to which men are attached by its observances."[28]

What America meant to Jefferson—architect, philosopher, founder of a university, ambassador in a foreign land, author of a document that would trigger a revolution, founder of a new country, president of the nation— was a host of fine and noble things that still stir the imagination. Even so, Monticello is also a reminder of the canker at the heart of American society: slavery, which Jefferson himself called America's "original sin."[29] But this did not deter him from keeping and using slaves, behavior that has raised charges of hypocrisy, especially in the case of his relationship with Sally Hemings. Although Sally was related to his dead wife, mostly of English descent, and alleged to have given birth to several of his children, Jefferson did not free her. Jefferson had promised to free Sally's children, and she was paid wages when she accompanied him to Europe, but the reality was that slaves did help maintain his estate. Yet their graveyard is but a small patch of rough land without markers, cordoned off by a rickety wood fence. Those caring for the estate at present have been sensitive to notions of political correctness, and signs now point to the "African American graveyard" without mentioning the word "slave." Stripped of their ancestral identities and without the courtesy of markers, they seem never to have even existed.

Having grown up in the foothills of the Himalayas, the most majestic mountain range in the world, I know something of the beauty and grandeur of nature. Yet America's landscapes never fail to take my breath away. Who does not marvel at the splendor of New England in the autumn, with leaves aflame in crimson, red, and gold, or the awesome spectacle of the Grand Canyon, the thundering roar of Niagara Falls, or the sun slipping over the Pacific horizon in Honolulu? Landmarks that we visited were equally evocative: the Statue of Liberty in New York, Plymouth Rock in Massachusetts, Jackson Square and the French Quarter in New Orleans, the Alamo in Texas, the arch in St. Louis, and Pearl Harbor in Hawai'i. At various stops, we participated in some of the country's key cultural events: a Sunday service in Houston at the largest church in the United States, a parade during Mardi Gras in New Orleans, and prayers at the Mormon holy sites in Palmyra, New York, and Salt Lake City, Utah. And at Chicago's Wrigley Field, I went to my first baseball game and saw the Cubs in action.

Our travels also brought home the astonishing affluence of America and its highly visible position as the engine of what is known as globalization. Coming from Pakistan, I could not imagine such a high standard of living was possible for so many people. The endless shopping malls were bursting with colorful products and throngs of people. Hotels offered cheap meals, and people were invited to eat as much as they wanted. There was excess everywhere, and in its midst, shocking pockets of poverty. Almost everywhere we went the comfort zone of a suburb or town awaited us, often of a generic type now dotting the landscape of modern America. On one long road trip from Houston to Dallas, we saw a former desert and scrubland covered with unending urban sprawl, with all the familiar logos visible from the road. I thought of the resources required to maintain the affluence and was reminded that America's population alone, not even 5 percent of the global total, was using up about one-fourth of the planet's energy.[30] How long could this disproportionate consumption last?

Overriding all the negatives, however, was the basic goodness of the American people, reaffirmed again and again in our travels. Rabbi Susan Talve blessed us as we began our journey in St. Louis at a breakfast hosted by our friend Susan Zuckerman, the mother of my former student Lauren. Geitner Simmons, an editor at the *Omaha World-Herald,* went out of his way to welcome us. Leona Kalima of Hawai'i arranged a week of visits to homes of native Hawaiians and treated us like one of her own. Herb Goodman and Bapsi Sidhwa of Houston took time off from their busy schedules to make sure we met a cross section of their friends. Our Pakistani American hosts, both husbands and wives, were especially hospitable: Sadiq Mohyuddin in St. Louis, Kamran Khan and Munir Chaudry in Chicago, Hamid Malik in Los Angeles, Shaukat Fareed in New York, and Faizan Haq in Buffalo. Relatives of the team—the parents of Craig and of Hailey, the brother and sister-in-law of Jonathan—also opened their homes to us and treated us like family. Many spiritual leaders prayed in support of our journey and efforts, including Senior Rabbi Bruce Lustig of Washington, D.C., Rabbi Hillel Levine of Boston, former Archbishop

Joseph Fiorenza and Father Donald Nesti of Houston, Reverend Bob Norris of Palm Beach, Florida, Jeffrey Clark, the president of the Mormon community in Palmyra, and too many imams to name. Muslim rappers spent time with us in Buffalo, observing that although we were "not an all-Muslim team," we were an "all-righteous" one. Archbishop Fiorenza said we were "doing God's work."

We also interviewed prominent Americans like U.S. Representatives Keith Ellison and André Carson, Sheikh Hamza Yusuf, Imam Qazwini, the Reverend Jesse Jackson, comedian Maz Jobrani, Judea Pearl, Maya Soetoro-Ng, former governor Bob Holden of Missouri, Joanne Herring, Sheriff Lee Baca of Los Angeles County, former secretary of the Department of Homeland Security Michael Chertoff, and Noam Chomsky.

Another of America's astonishing features, we discovered, is the infinite variety of its population and the cultural paradoxes it engenders. Sometimes the juxtapositions were jarring for us as we traveled from place to place and event to event: destitute lives in Detroit next to the affluent gated community of nearby Grosse Pointe; puritan ways of Salt Lake City next to the bright lights of "Sin City," Las Vegas; the Hopi settlement in Arizona, where there is no electricity, next to high-tech Silicon Valley, with its young dot-com entrepreneurs and scientists talking of settlements on Mars; hope and faith of the rap music of African American Muslims in Buffalo next to the anger and despair of Mexican gang members in a jail in Los Angeles; the universal love of the Sufis in New York alongside the abuse hurled at the Muslim Day parade on Madison Avenue.

We interviewed the heads or representatives of major Muslim organizations, such as the Islamic Society of North America (ISNA), Council on American-Islamic Relations (CAIR), Islamic Circle of North America (ICNA), Muslim Public Affairs Council (MPAC), and Muslim Students Association (MSA) (see chapter 5). We met Muslims with different ethnic and sectarian backgrounds. Our impression of America's rich cultural variety was further heightened by our visits to its Muslim communities and their mosques. We went to the largest mosque in New York, to the oldest mosque in the United States in Cedar Rapids, Iowa, the westernmost mosque in Honolulu, the only mosque in Vermont, and perhaps the most magnificent mosque in the United States in Dearborn. We found mosques even in unlikely places. An amiable TV chat show host in Memphis, Tennessee, was surprised to learn that a Muslim like me would be interested in seeing Elvis Presley's Graceland, and that Memphis has six mosques, which we planned to visit. On our trip to Hawai'i, a *Honolulu Weekly* reporter chuckled when he heard of our visit's purpose.[31] Did Hawai'i even have

Muslims? Indeed, it has at least 4,000 Muslims and a flourishing central mosque where we said our Friday prayers. In Houston, we were surprised to learn that this sprawling city has some 120 mosques.

Even the tiny Muslim community of Gadsden, a small town in Alabama, had its mosque. There were no signs of its identity outside, but we found a small buoyant group waiting to welcome us with a traditional Pakistani lunch. The wife of the Pakistani president of the mosque committee told me shyly how much she enjoyed seeing *Jinnah,* the movie I had made with Christopher Lee. One of the congregants, an Arab man who had been in the region for decades and had married a local woman who remained a Christian, summed up his American identity in a notably southern accent as "Muslim by birth, Southern by the grace of God."

The optimism and hospitality of our hosts made this a memorable visit. Then I heard the call to prayer. I stopped and joined the few worshippers. At the end of the prayer, the man leading us said a special prayer for the success of our project. Moments like this reconnected me to the purpose that had prompted me to launch this project in the first place.

Survival of the Fittest in America

In *Democracy in America,* de Tocqueville states: "Peoples always feel [the effects of] their origins."[32] These are the "deep structures" that anthropologists believe shape a society's character and values. America's deep structures go back to the seventeenth-century settlements at Jamestown and Plymouth (see chapter 2), when a white population arrived from England and over the years consolidated its hold on America. Some clues to American identity rest there and in that population's demonstration of Charles Darwin's famous thesis espoused in *On the Origin of Species by Means of Natural Selection, or the Preservation of Favoured Races in the Struggle for Life.*[33] My interest here is not the relevance of these theories to the creation of the world or to humanity's random or predictable evolution, but their influence on the organization of societies, specifically American society. Darwin argued that it was not the strongest of the species that survived, nor even the most intelligent, but those most adaptable to change. This principle he called "natural selection," also known as "the survival of the fittest." The idea of favored races and the struggle for life came to imply a belief in evolution or a movement toward "progress."

Those who succeed in the competition to survive are said to be the "favored races." Along with their genes they will pass on memes, the cultural equivalent of genes, which are the ideas, behavior, style, or usage imitated by succeeding generations. If the favored races are defined by a certain religion, language, and culture, these will be imitated, preserved, and passed on. Because in America the English—and later by extension the white race—emerged on top in the competition, their characteristics have become the standard, as explained in chapter 2. In time, all others—African Americans, Mexicans, Native Americans, and Asians—were forced to imitate the dominant ethos if they wished to succeed. Barack Obama is a good example. He has dark skin and a Muslim father from Africa, but as president, he sounds, dresses, and behaves like other politicians from the dominant white race.

For Darwin, the world was not created in six days, and all races were related by blood. Therefore being white or black was no indication of any special status. On the contrary, Darwin found the whole business of slavery abhorrent and hoped his work would help terminate it. Darwin's ideas undermined two pillars of American society: literal belief in the Bible and the notion that the white race was innately superior to all other races and therefore destined for greatness. Although the theories of Darwin have resonated throughout American history, they have generated more heat than light. Even today they evoke intense passion in the United States, either in their defense or opposition.

Darwin versus Jesus

A debilitating tension between Darwin and Jesus lies at the heart of American identity. It is not so much about *how* society originated and evolved but *what* defines and motivates it. The core principles of the Darwinian thesis and Christianity are diametrically opposed and cannot coexist simultaneously in one society without causing severe friction. Darwin represents adaptability and survival, Jesus compassion and universal love. Darwin acknowledges that those who cannot adapt will not—indeed must not—survive; for Jesus it is precisely the least privileged members in society who are deserving of support. For Darwin, the concepts of "morality," "compassion," "humility," "austerity," "poverty," "shame," or "honor" are irrelevant in the struggle for survival; for Jesus, these are what define a good Christian.

Darwinian principles rest in notions of a struggle to survive. In this struggle, the ruthless will to succeed, strength, speed, stamina, and force determine success. In turn, success generates pride and arrogance, the chauvinism of being on top, and a belief in the superiority of the dominant group. The Abrahamic faiths, on the other hand, advocate austerity and humility in a greater cause. They encourage selfless love, care, and concern for the dispossessed and the needy. They advocate proper moral behavior, even at the cost of suffering.

For me as a Muslim, Jesus is the embodiment of compassion, humility, and love for all humanity. For Muslims, there is no figure quite like Jesus in the Quran. His birth was miraculous. He can breathe life into clay figures. He is an inspiration to the Prophet of Islam himself. To Christians, Jesus is *the* figure of love. Even in the face of aggression, they will emphasize Jesus' sayings about turning the other cheek. But in what Darwin described as a "struggle for existence," the weakest are eliminated. Only the fit survive. The survivors will pass on their characteristics to the next generations, and in time a new species will form. It is a depressing thought that existence is reduced to a meaningless struggle for survival, that there is no larger cause to live for than self-preservation, no inspiration on earth or in the heavens except self-interest. Because it is unpalatable in its implications for human society, Darwinism is often cloaked, disguised, and confused with terminology borrowed from religion.

As a direct consequence of the dominance of Darwinian thinking, Americans remain in a state of anxious competitiveness that creates insecurity and engenders fear and anger. In the context of the number of guns available to Americans and their inclination to use them, it is well to keep in mind the frequent episodes of violence reported in the media. The anger combined with fear is a ready-made formula for tense individuals to commit acts of violence.

I have always found American fear and anger surprising. Why should the most powerful people on earth be fearful? And why should the richest people be angry? If there was more true Christianity and less Darwinian thinking, I am convinced, there would be far more calmness in American social life.

American Christianity should thus be viewed through a prism inspired by French sociologist Emile Durkheim, who argued that a society's notions of God reflect its predominant ideas and ethos. Kurt Vonnegut's observation in *A Man without a Country* encapsulates the struggle between these two diametric forces in the Christian tradition: "I haven't heard one of them (vocal Christians) demand that the Sermon on the Mount, the Beatitudes, be posted anywhere. 'Blessed are the merciful' in a courtroom? 'Blessed are the peacemakers' in the Pentagon? Give me a break!"[34]

From the seventeenth century on, Christian preachers used the Bible to justify slavery (see chapter 4): Ham, the ancestor of the black race and son of Noah, they taught, was cursed by his father and along with his descendants doomed to servility. Blacks, as Saint Paul had admonished the slaves, therefore needed to accept their subordinate position and obey their masters, the colonists argued, conveniently ignoring the teaching of the Gospels that "ye are all one in Christ Jesus." As good Christians, white colonists felt obliged to care for slaves, though "lesser" beings, as they would their property. Using religious scripture, the favored races ensured their own preeminent position by denying blacks any rights to education, ownership of property, or even citizenship. Slaves existed only as an extension of their owner. Miraculously, in spite of several centuries of brutal subjugation, the black population itself devised means to preserve learning and humanity. When one reads the works of African Americans like Frederick Douglass or W. E. B. Du Bois, one is moved by the clarity and moral power with which they convey the nightmare of legalized slavery. These works stand as a challenge to the idea of the favored races.

Also competing for survival in colonial America were people of other faiths. Notions of universal compassion or kindness did not enter into early American theological thinking. Battles with the Native Americans were therefore fierce and conducted in a spirit of a fight to the finish, wiping out some 60 to 80 percent of the native peoples of New England within half a century of the first white arrivals.[35] Other Christian sects like the Catholics and Mormons were treated with prejudice (see chapters 2 and 8), as were members of the Jewish community (chapter 7). From this fundamental tension emerged a white majority that considered itself superior to minority peoples, who in turn devised special monikers for those they viewed as soulless aggressors. Mexicans, for example, called white Americans *gringos* because of the color of the uniforms worn by the soldiers who came to kill and capture territory, or *gueros,* possibly from *guerra,* the Spanish word for war. To Hawaiians, they were *haole,* or those without a breath or spirit, while to Native Americans, they were *eankke* (cowards) or *yankwako* (snakes). The African slaves called them *buckre,* or someone who cannot be trusted. The Nation of Islam would hold up a mirror to white people and reverse the prejudice, calling them white devils (chapter 4).

The consequences of the uneasy fusion of Darwinism and Christianity are not limited to America. The excesses inspired by Adolf Hitler are a stark, if extreme, example. Hitler melded Darwinism and Christianity in the concept of the "Aryan Christ." His "feeling as a Christian" led him, like Christ, his "Lord and Savior," to recognize "these Jews for what they were": a "poison," a "brood of vipers and adders," to be driven from the land. That is why, Hitler claimed, Christ "had to shed His blood upon the cross." Jesus, he said, was "greatest not as a sufferer but as a fighter."[36]

Perhaps the answer to racial hatred is the very same Jesus so misunderstood by Hitler. We need to heed the commandment of Jesus to love one another. Or to look at the example of the Prophet of Islam, who in his last address at Arafat categorically rejected the division of society on the basis of race, "Arab and non-Arab," or color, "black and white." Dividing societies into superior and inferior members on the basis of race is not only morally wrong but also makes little sociological sense. Morally, the Abrahamic faiths espoused by most Americans reject divisions based on color and would say that in the eyes of God humans are to be judged by their actions and beliefs. Biologically, the DNA of the vast majority of the world's population is nearly identical. Moreover, history shows that the rise and fall of different cultures and civilizations have nothing to do with race.

Cherchez la Couleur

Stephen Colbert, the popular television satirist, is fond of telling guests, especially those who are non-white, that he "does not see color." In the guise of a conservative who means precisely the opposite of what he says, Colbert is implying not only that he sees color, or race, but also that it is everywhere. He is right. While many Americans doggedly do not want to see race, they cannot ignore it. Many feel threatened by what they see as potential challenges to the ethnic composition and normative ideas of American society.

My journey confirmed that color functions as an important factor separating social groups in America, just as tribal identity does in Muslim societies and caste in Indian society.[37] The lobbies and dining rooms of many hotels we stayed in invariably had an overwhelmingly white clientele. They were mostly husbands and wives, sometimes with families, touring America and enjoying its sights. A few visitors might be black, but almost none were visibly Latino. In some cases, reception staff were black, while those who cleaned the rooms and tended to the grass and garden were Latinos who spoke little English.

America's ethnic hierarchy is apparent not only from direct observations. Even more telling are its social symbols. The color white, for example, is associated with goodness, nobility, virtue, and purity, whereas black conjures up negative or bad images. Think of expressions that are widespread both in America and other Western cultures, such as the "white knight" or "pure as snow," on the one hand, and the "dark side," "black mark," or "black magic," on the other. Villains in film and drama dress in black to depict their black hearts, while heroines wear white to symbolize purity.

Color discrimination and segregation have marked American identity with a legacy of tears, bloodshed, and violence.

Color-created boundaries gave the WASPs (White Anglo-Saxon Protestants) a dominant social position over the "red" (Native Americans), the black (African Americans), and the yellow (Chinese and Japanese) groups. This tradition persists. On our journey, some referred to Muslims as "sand niggers."

One could easily argue, however, that the category "white" is quite diverse in itself, with its different languages, customs, religions, and regional and historical characteristics. White populations, quite different from the English settlers, also came to America's shores bringing with them diverse religious and social traditions, all now lumped in the category "white." America's "black" category is just as diverse in its linguistic and cultural origins, which range from light-skinned communities of North Africa to dark-skinned tribes along the equator and to the south. This rich diversity has also been compressed into that all-too-simple label, "black." And, of course, before the "white man" arrived on its shores, America, north and south, had a native population of some 112 million people, 18 million of whom lived in what is now the United States.

What does all this mean when it comes to defining Muslims? The Muslim community represents the entire spectrum of the world, because it, too, is not defined through any one racial or ethnic group. But, accustomed to categorizing people by race, Americans are befuddled by the great variety of Muslim ethnic backgrounds and skin color. When the first Muslims from the Middle East arrived in the late nineteenth century, there were too few and their backgrounds too varied to warrant a label. They also posed a "color problem." Being brown, with a range of skin color within the communities, they were neither quite white enough for the white category nor dark enough for the black category, nor would their features qualify them for the Asian category, as it is understood in America. In time, those from the Middle East and Iran would be called Arab and those from South Asia, Indian.

The importance of color in defining American identity was recognized over a century ago by Du Bois. His observation that the "problem of the Twentieth Century is the problem of the color line" still holds true, except that today "Muslim" could substitute for "Negro." Du Bois argued that African Americans are separated from the mainstream white culture not by a wall but a "veil"—a metaphor that also has great resonance for Muslim Americans.

Du Bois was right to sound the alarm. By the time America achieved its independence, the structure of white male power was already in place.

For the next two centuries, the men who ran the country—the president, vice president, the head of the armed forces, the Supreme Court judges— would be white and male. The legislative arm of government would be dominated by whites. If a black man was arrested, he would invariably have been apprehended by a white sheriff, then would have faced a white judge and white jury, and in jail white officials. The leading business tycoons, entertainment figures, and scholars would also have been white except in sports and entertainment, where blacks began to emerge in the twentieth century. Where it mattered in terms of making the law, interpreting it, and executing it, America was a white country for most of its history. And its philosophy toward race, formulated early in its history, was summed up in the motto "zero tolerance."

The American "Club"

From the seventeenth century onward, then, being American was like belonging to a club with membership based on the criteria of race and color. The leadership, organization, values, and attitudes of the club formed the basis of what came to be loosely and widely referred to as "the system." Its definition remains amorphous and intangible, but people who refer to it do so as if the system is as concrete as the U.S. Constitution. Furthermore, the English had appointed themselves the guardians of the club. Even white immigrants from places like Ireland or Italy who had become legal citizens were not automatically accepted as full-fledged members. As others arrived, their faith, if not Protestant, would keep them from becoming full members.

Jewish immigrants posed an interesting new challenge. Although Eastern European, Irish, and Italian Catholics were outside the Protestant pale, they were still white and Christian. It would take the Jewish immigrants a century or two to become fully accepted. Non-white communities like African Americans and Mexicans were only permitted to provide "services" to the club, the former as slaves and the latter as hired help. Meanwhile, Native Americans, many of whom had been forced into separate communities far from urban areas, had no association with the club whatsoever and were reduced to an anthropological curiosity.

After 9/11 immigrant Muslims also posed a problem. Although they arrived throughout the twentieth century, especially from Egypt and Lebanon, the largest number appeared from the 1960s onward, many coming as students, others to take on a professional life. Many moved into professional jobs and assumed they were part of the club. On 9/11, however, they found themselves out in the cold. In an address to South Asian leaders in Chicago after 9/11, Jesse Jackson reputedly admonished them for ignoring African Americans and noted, "Before 9/11 you thought you were white but now you realize you're black."[38] Lawrence Rosen of Princeton University explained the problem of "placing" Muslims in America: "It is not so much that Muslims in America are out of category, but that they were never clearly in a category, and now, people aren't sure which category to put them into." Rosen, too, recognizes the defining force of color: "Race in America is literally skin deep. When somebody passes for white, it's not really an issue. When somebody is visibly different, then Americans historically have not known what to make of that person. They are out of their category."

Perhaps the elderly Muslim we talked to in Al-Mahdi Foundation Mosque in "Little Pakistan" in Brooklyn, New York, captured the dilemma best (see chapter 3). White colleagues in his office repeatedly shoved him against the wall and tried to choke him—or as he put it, "to kill him"—because they thought he was a potential terrorist. But he was also a target of the black community, which saw him as a "Jew or a Christian," meaning a white man. "I am in much trouble," he ruminated dolefully.

Obama's election in 2008 and inauguration in January 2009 unleashed euphoria in the United States among those who wished to see America moving beyond race—or becoming a club open to all. The *New Yorker* had Obama dressed up as George Washington, white wig and all, on its cover. *Newsweek*'s cover showed a reflective Obama with the title "Obama's America: Who We Are Now." The *Atlantic* cover with the new president asked, "The End of White America?" While these magazines reflected an exuberance felt by millions of Americans, they failed to appreciate that there were limits to what had actually changed and what could be changed. Demographic changes are seriously challenging the white population's hold and alarming many of its members. The Latino population has topped 50 million, and in a few short decades whites will actually be in the minority for the first time. Samuel Huntington, who borrowed the idea of the Clash of Civilizations from Bernard Lewis and popularized it, thus shifted his focus from Muslims to Latinos, who, he argued, were threatening the white Protestant way of life.[39] In short, issues of identity trumped even those of terrorism and security.

Many white Americans, already feeling threatened, believe that the natural order has been further disturbed by Obama's presidency. Extreme hysteria built on absurd arguments marked the first counterpunch in the media following the Obama inauguration. In the forefront of the onslaught were media heavyweights such as Rush Limbaugh, Sean Hannity, Bill O'Reilly, and Glenn Beck. Obama was compared to Hitler and called a Muslim Marxist. Beck questioned Obama's "Americanness" and called him a "racist" who "hates white people" and "white culture." Crudely and explicitly, the attacks on Obama suggested that he hated the very foundations of the country of which he was the president. Through innuendo, Islam, widely demonized in certain media outlets, was associated with Obama. Later in the year, Beck vented his fury on those Europeans who were responsible for awarding Obama the Nobel Peace Prize because, he warned, they were "dismantling America." It was a dangerous game because the passions generated by discussions of race have frequently triggered violence.

A Facebook poll asking if Obama "should be killed" was only removed after the Secret Service discovered it.[40] In late September 2009 columnist John L. Perry, a former top official in the Lyndon Johnson and Jimmy Carter administrations, wrote in the online edition of *Newsmax* that a military coup may be necessary to "restore and defend the Constitution" and stop Obama from turning America into a "Marxist state."[41] Some people even seemed to be calling for Obama's assassination or unconstitutional dismissal in a very public way and getting away with it. Matters reached such a point that two former presidents, having emerged as wise and respected international statesmen since their days in the White House, felt they needed to comment publicly on the tone of these assaults: Jimmy Carter said he detected racism, and Bill Clinton suspected a "vast right-wing conspiracy."

Racial ideas obviously continue to shape American identity. How do we make sense of its complex nature and the relationship its different parts have to each other? In order to probe further, it would be useful to go back to the Greeks—the source of Western culture.

Greek Philosophers, Viennese Psychiatrists, and Pakistani Anthropologists

What is more fundamental to Western thinking than the notion that the human mind can be divided into three parts, or the use of color as a metaphor for virtue and vice, or the importance of "shame" in defining character and controlling passion. It is said that Freud discovered the mind's tripartite division, the Ku Klux Klan (KKK) invented color prejudice, and Japan's Samurai created the code of shame and honor. Yet all these ideas are reflected in Plato and Socrates.

The concept of the tripartite division was introduced in Plato's *Republic*, Book IV, in which the Greek philosopher explained the Socratic approach to the human soul as being divided into three parts: *logos* (reason), which seeks truth and knowledge; *thumos* (spirit), which desires honor; and *alogon* (irrationality), which lusts after the objects of passion, including drink, food, sex, and especially money. The just man sets these three parts together as "chords in a harmony" and controls his passions in pursuit of balance, philosophy, and truth.

These three parts of the individual soul correspond to the components of an ideal society, says Socrates: at the top are the "guardians," whose concern is philosophy and just governance, and not money or property; then come the "auxiliaries" such as the military, who keep the peace, protect the city, and implement the directions of the guardians; and the productive class, including various businessmen, craftsmen, and artists, who are concerned with money and the passions.

In another Platonic dialogue, the *Phaedrus*, Socrates compares the soul to a charioteer with two horses, one representing reason and the other passion, that he must steer and control through life:

> The horse that is on the right, or nobler, side is upright in frame and well jointed, with a high neck and a regal nose; his coat is white, his eyes are black, and he is a lover of honor with modesty and self-control; companion to true glory, he needs no whip, and is guided by verbal commands alone. The other horse is a crooked great jumble of limbs with a short bull-neck, a pug nose, black skin, and bloodshot white eyes; companion to wild boasts and indecency, he is shaggy around the ears—deaf as a post—and just barely yields to horsewhip and goad combined.[42]

Plato reveals that the notion of "shame" is enough to keep the white horse in check, but something much more violent is required to control the black horse. When the charioteer tries to restrain the black horse by whipping it and pulling on the reins, causing blood to gush from its mouth, the horse has the ability to taunt the charioteer with insults and accusations of cowardice and unmanliness. The black horse, writes Plato, is "without any shame at all."

One can see, then, that Freud's analysis dividing the human mind into three parts was not entirely original. Freud described the "psychic apparatus," which is the function of every individual's mind, as being divided into an ego, super-ego, and id. Ego means I, or myself. Ego is anchored in reason and common sense and aims to be organized and realistic. The super-ego is critical and moralizing, aiming for perfection. The id is uncoordinated and based in instinct.

In some ways, nations are like individuals. The character of both reflects a constant internal struggle between various forces that invariably pull in different directions. External forces also influence and shape them. Under such pressures, nations change over time, yet try to remain true to their character. The challenge for social analysts is to understand society and identify these pressures and their effect on its character. As an anthropologist, I approach the task through ethnicity and identity in pursuit of the principles that define and determine the behavior of a particularly diverse society: that of the United States.

Using an anthropological framework in the following chapters, I delineate the three basic identities that define American society: primordial, pluralist, and predator. These three American identities overlap and derive from the same source—namely, the first white settlers at Plymouth, and to an extent those at Jamestown. In terms of Plato's allegory, one might loosely equate the charioteer to primordial identity, the well-behaved horse to pluralist identity, and the wild horse to predator identity. Or following Freud's classification, one might equate ego to primordial identity, superego to pluralist identity, and id to predator identity. The story of America may be read as the story of these identities and their struggle to form the dominant narrative.

Structure of the Book

This book is about how people of different religions, cultures, and skin colors can live together at a time when their communities have become more jumbled and juxtaposed than ever before in history. This subject cannot be fully explored without discussing pluralism (the concept of accepting others not like us); integration, if not assimilation, of freshly arrived immigrants; and ways in which people have adjusted to and live with one another when events in other parts of the world disturb and disrupt life here. In short, the book is about some fundamental concerns to all societies and nations in this difficult and turbulent time.

The book is divided into three parts. The chapters of part one define American identity and present the ethnography to support that definition. Part two focuses on the ethnography of Islam in America—African American Muslims, immigrants, and converts. Part three compares Muslims to other minorities and suggests ways to improve understanding between them.

In chapter 2, I examine the different events, ethnic strands, and ideas that form American identity, as well as the sources of its dynamism and tension. I also explore the creation and development of distinct identities that have emerged from the original American identity. While the boundaries by which American society maintains itself are defined by white Americans, several other well-defined ethnicities have been maintained by Native American, African American, and Latino communities, and I also refer to them.

The book will not retell American history. That has been done well and many times in the past. However, episodes from history illuminate the broader arguments in the book about American identity and its formation. Chapter 3 presents the findings of our field trip that corroborate the outlines of my interpretation of American identity, revealing its three components in the actions and words of the people we met on our journey. African American leadership in forging an American Muslim identity is discussed in chapter 4. Muslims who migrated from the Middle East, South Asia, and other regions of the world are the subject of chapter 5. The social and cultural factors behind the conversion to Islam of white and Latino Americans are explored in chapter 6, while chapter 7 turns to the history and role of the Jewish community in shaping American identity and its relations with Muslims. Chapter 8 compares Muslims and Mormons, both at times persecuted and controversial minorities in the United States. Chapter 9 draws on our fieldwork findings to suggest ways to help resolve the tensions within American society and improve relations between America and the Muslim world. It also throws light on the "homegrown terrorist," a subject that had assumed urgency by the time we were ending our fieldwork.

Every society has a vision of the ideal community, which is challenged by the different pulls and strains within it. America's ideal was formulated by its Founding Fathers. If this book succeeds in reminding the reader of that ideal, it would have served its purpose, particularly since questions of American identity and the meaning of America have never been of greater importance than today.

PART ONE

American Identity

TWO

Defining American Identity

WE WERE IN Plymouth on a freezing October day. The Atlantic heaved angrily and a light drizzle hit our faces like pinpricks. As we boarded the *Mayflower* tossing about, we wondered how it had survived the journey from England. It seemed so fragile, as if put together by little more than nails and a hammer. Standing on board the tiny *Mayflower*, or more accurately its replica, I thought of the momentous train of events the perilous seventeenth-century crossing had set in motion, a historical trajectory carrying diverse peoples toward collision, among them Native Americans, Spanish, French, Africans, peoples of the British Isles, and through them my own people from South Asia.

I also thought of what was happening in my part of the world at the time. The Muslim Mughal Empire, one of the richest and most powerful in the world and covering what are now Afghanistan, Pakistan, India, and Bangladesh, was at its peak. Two centuries later, the kinfolk of America's English settlers would abolish the Mughal Empire and capture its capital, Delhi. India would become "the jewel in the crown." Relations and perceptions between the Western and Muslim worlds would change dramatically. Muslim lands and peoples would be seen as backward, while the West would consider itself the beacon of world civilization defined by words such as "progress," "science," "freedom," "democracy," and "liberty."

Grandma's Tea Set from the Mayflower

The *Mayflower* has assumed such mythic proportions for most Americans that once below deck you are taken aback by the cramped quarters. How

39

In Plymouth, Massachusetts, Akbar Ahmed poses in front of the replica of the Mayflower *with two descendants of Dr. Samuel Fuller, the ship's surgeon—Hailey Woldt and tour guide Paul.*

could it have accommodated 100 men, women, and children, desperate to take this journey to seek a better life? This surely was a test of the survival of the fittest.

As we explored the *Mayflower*, we spoke with an actor playing Dr. Samuel Fuller, the ship's deacon and surgeon. Fuller's primary incentive to take the voyage had been economic. "Where in Europe," asked the actor, "would a man be given 50 acres of land by the king that would belong to him after seven years? Besides, there are no taxes to pay."

As I disembarked, I asked our amiable and knowledgeable guide, Paul, about the ship's history and his connection to the site. Our ears pricked up on learning he was descended from Dr. Fuller because Hailey was a descendant of the same Dr. Fuller.

Paul said he was a direct eleventh-generation descendant. The lineage meant a great deal to him, and his great-grandmother had urged him to pass this knowledge to the next generation so the memory would not be lost. The Fuller cradle was exhibited in the Pilgrim's museum at Plymouth, he added, and as a child his grandfather was taken there to be rocked in it. The cradle was like a covenant bequeathed to the museum on the condition that all Fuller offspring could use it. At this point, Hailey could not contain herself. "Could I rock my kids in the same cradle?" she asked, anticipating the day she would have children. Paul welcomed the idea of Hailey maintaining the tradition.

I asked Paul how Fuller and his small band, if alive today, would react to modern society? "They would be shocked. Quite horrified to see what has come about from their original thoughts," he said. "How horrified?" I asked. "It would be so totally alien, totally heathen, that they could not respect it," he answered, mentioning disapprovingly the "indulgences" of people today (see chapter 6).

For Americans like Hailey who trace their descent to the English settlers, Plymouth Rock and those who came on the *Mayflower* have special significance. "Every nation has its myths and heroes, and the myths of Plymouth Rock and the Pilgrims are almost divine," said Hailey. "I grew up with my grandmother placing the figurines of Pilgrims around the house every year in November for Thanksgiving and reverentially looking at a white tea set with pale pink flowers that she believed had come over on the *Mayflower* with my ancestors."

According to a recent estimate, approximately 35 million Americans, or about 12 percent of the population, are descendants of the *Mayflower* passengers.[1] Their offspring are everywhere, it seems. So many Americans claim the *Mayflower* in their patrimony that this may well be the case. Or perhaps Americans, like people everywhere, are simply identifying with their founding origins. In South Asia, for instance, the number of Muslims who claim to be a Sayyed, or a descendant of the holy Prophet of Islam, is so large that there is now a saying, "Last year I did well economically and became a respectable elder of the village; this year if the crops are good I will become a sheikh; and next year if I can get my crops to the bigger markets I will become a Sayyed."

Anthropologists believe that people's memory of their ancestors is notoriously fickle as to how they view those who have gone before. A social group may be tempted to create a "fictitious genealogy" containing links to influential individuals or groups, or to "telescope genealogy" that fuses past generations in order to highlight the importance of certain ancestors, or have an "amnesiac genealogy" that simply drops individuals embarrassing to the family line. American society provided ample examples of all three processes throughout our study.

The *Mayflower as Mythology*

On this journey, I found myself appreciating and agreeing with Alexis de Tocqueville many times. In his *Democracy in America,* the description of "Plymouth Rock," the actual rock on which the *Mayflower* reportedly landed, is accurate. It is not particularly remarkable either in size or in shape except for the date 1620 chiseled in it. Not surprisingly, however, the rock is covered by what looks like a Greek temple, complete with columns. For most white Americans, Plymouth Rock is an inspiring symbol of American mythology. For most non-white Americans, it is an equally powerful negative symbol, as depicted in Malcolm X's widely quoted phrase, "We didn't land on Plymouth Rock, Plymouth Rock landed on us."

The legend of Plymouth Rock began in 1741 when ninety-five-year-old Thomas Faunce visited the Plymouth waterfront and, too infirm to walk to it, asked to be carried there. With tears in his eyes, he recalled his father, who had arrived in Plymouth in 1623, telling him that this very boulder was where the original Pilgrims had landed. Faunce had heard that a pier was to be built over the rock that would obscure it forever.[2] Moved by his story, local citizens shifted the rock inland in 1774 and would move it again several times over the years. In 1921 it reached its present location, and a temple-like structure was built over it, confirming its iconic status in American mythology.

Both Plymouth Rock and the *Mayflower* quickly became central to the founding myth of America, which moved all Americans, including the Founding Fathers. John Adams, a descendant of the *Mayflower* travelers, burst into tears when he recalled the ordeal of his ancestors on a visit to the church of the Pilgrims in Leyden. Like Thomas Jefferson and Benjamin Franklin, Adams believed that the arrival of the Pilgrims was providential, to be regarded, as Adams wrote, with "reverence and wonder."[3] In time the *Mayflower* and its passengers became popular in works such as the 1856 "literary sensation," *Of Plymouth Plantation*, which had been based on the journal kept by Governor William Bradford, who had arrived on the *Mayflower*. Two years later Henry Wadsworth Longfellow further romanticized the hardy Pilgrims through his best-selling poem, "The Courtship of Miles Standish."[4] Then in 1863 President Abraham Lincoln proclaimed the holiday of Thanksgiving to bring a fractured nation closer together through the mythology of a common origin. The day would be officially established and celebrated as a national holiday in 1941 under President Franklin Roosevelt. Not all Americans were satisfied with the Thanksgiving celebrations. Native Americans in 1970 declared Thanksgiving a National Day of Mourning and selected Plymouth as the natural place to observe it.[5]

The problem with mythology is that it dramatizes and simplifies complex events. Those first settlers arriving on the *Mayflower* faced a desperate situation. Terror permeated every aspect of their lives. They were fearful of the native inhabitants and unsure of their intentions. Earlier European visitors, they knew, had not met a happy fate. The crew of a French vessel marooned in the bay had been killed or enslaved by local inhabitants.[6] Food was scarce and the winter ferocious. Reinforcements would not be forthcoming from England since the settlers were in a state of self-willed exile. Half of them perished in that first winter of 1620.

In this case, the myth paid due respect to the hardship at Plymouth but bypassed an English settlement started thirteen years earlier, at Jamestown in what is now Virginia. Why, I wondered, is Plymouth and not Jamestown so often thought of as the first English settlement in America? According to President Taylor Reveley of the College of William and Mary, in Williamsburg, Virginia, Plymouth receives greater recognition because of the fortunes of the Civil War. When the North won, it wrote the history of America and the mythology of Plymouth was born, explained Reveley, who is from the South. Because Jamestown happened to be in the defeated South, it was relegated to second place in historical memory. Another factor in Plymouth's favor, I suspect, is that it was founded by mostly "ordinary folk" seeking a new life and therefore was closer to the spirit of democratic America, whereas Jamestown was settled by members of the English aristocracy and ruled directly by the king.

The myth also tends to overlook non-English settlements that predate Plymouth. Saint Augustine, Florida, was founded by the Spanish in 1565. The first Christian service held in a permanent settlement on American soil was a Catholic mass celebrated there. The Spanish had established even earlier settlements, including the one at Pensacola colony in West Florida in 1559, but they had failed. Nevertheless, the Spanish left their mark, which is evident even today in the South and the West.

Today, the founding mythology of the nation is reflected in the annual Thanksgiving holiday and its story is allegorical: the feast marks the end of hard times and glows with interracial harmony. The settlers and natives are metaphors for the virtues Americans invest in them—friendship and hospitality on the one side, innocence and purity on the other.

Native American Identity

Not far from Plymouth, we visited the re-creation of an early Native American village, but here the central actor, a young Native American dressed as a Wampanoag, appeared almost bored with his assignment. After he had hammered away at some wood, he walked off for no apparent reason, leaving us alone, along with several tourists from Germany and small-town America.

We tracked him down for an interview to learn what he thought of American identity. His quick response—"That question is offensive; I am not an American"—generated a brief exchange that brought us no closer to an answer. He insisted he belonged to the Cherokee tribe. That, he said, was his identity, and he refused to carry a government-issued ID card. He spoke bitterly about "being forced to give up our faith and become Christian. Within a few years of their coming, the white settlers had wiped out 80 percent of our people in New England."

By now, some white tourists had gathered around him, looking somewhat uncomfortable with the conversation. This was not the script of a "civilized" Indian. He noted cynically: "Do you know why time is set here in 1627? Because if it was set any later we would be in a state of war with the white man."

When Frankie pressed him again on the question of identity, he replied with some hesitation this time: "I would consider myself indigenous, native. We were here before anyone named it America. We prefer to be called whatever nation we are from, Wampanoag, or in my case, Cherokee. My people have lived here for 15,000 years, and it has a lot of spiritual significance." The *Mayflower*, by contrast, was a "very romantic story." He elaborated: "That's what our history books tell us, about how the natives and Pilgrims sat down and had Thanksgiving dinner like it was kum-ba-ya. What really happened here, not in the beginning but later on, was conflict, betrayal, and broken trust."

The young man spoke bitterly of the forced conversions to Christianity imposed on the Wampanoag. Those who did not convert were sold into slavery and sent to the Bahamas, he said, while black slaves were brought to this land. But he also noted, "Forty years ago you couldn't mention you were native. If you spoke the language you hid it. Today people are so interested in us as a culture. We are beginning to name our children with indigenous names, hold our ceremonies out in the open." Asked about the total indigenous population, he replied, "Let me give you a shocking number. Five hundred years ago, we made up 100 percent of what is the United States today. Today we make up 1 percent of the entire population."

The Formation of American Identity

As we journeyed through America's bewildering mixture of races, religions, and cultures, we asked thousands of Americans, as we did the young actor in the Wampanoag village, what it means to be an American today. Their answers confirmed the complicated nature of American identity and its historical, ethnic, sociological, and emotional dimensions, which I am distilling into three distinct but overlapping identities—primordial, pluralist, and predator.

Primordial identity is rooted in the seminal landing at Plymouth and provides the foundation of the two other identities. The aim of the early settlers was to survive and create a Christian society. While some of their actions were the result of excessive religious zeal and fear, others, who still clung to their Christian faith, hoped to create a society in which everyone could live according to his or her faith and under the rule of law. The majority of the Founding Fathers in the next century would subscribe to this latter view, which I call pluralist identity.

As primordial identity was taking shape at Plymouth, new trends were already emerging. The more zealous of the settlers argued that the land was given to them by God, and they were to occupy it regardless of who was living there. With time, the colonists grew confident, built new settlements, and began to prey on the weaker natives with impunity. Every kind of depredation was justified in the violence that followed. Immoral acts were committed in the name of protecting the community. Compassion was seen as weakness and compromise as defeat. This aggressive impulse generated an arrogance that did not encourage self-reflection but made it easy to demonize and destroy the enemy. In short, this marked the birth of a predator identity.

Even as the latter two identities emerged to assume distinct traits of their own, they still sought inspiration, genealogical reference, affirmation, and continuity from primordial persons and events such as the Pilgrims and the Plymouth landing. Curiously, Americans of all identities relate to, and even champion, the values of primordial identity. Although pluralist identity derives from primordial identity, it remains diametrically opposed to predator characteristics. Each one is authentic in its own way, but together they form an organic whole that sheds light on American history and character. American society can therefore only be understood as constantly changing, expanding, and adapting to new circumstances within the context of its identities. The central dynamic of American society is the tension between these identities.

Of course, I hasten to add that these identities are little more than an aid to understanding American society. They are what sociologists call "ideal types"; they approximate reality but are not a substitute for it. Ideal types are formed on the basis of aggregates of how people behave. They are rarely watertight and, as already mentioned, often overlap.

Early Exemplars of American Identity

This discussion of the three main American identities is based on the actions, words, and beliefs of actual individuals at the very start of modern American history. Men like Edward Winslow and John Winthrop, the first governors of the Plymouth Colony and Massachusetts Bay Colony, respectively, and John Cotton, the head cleric of Massachusetts Bay, provide the basis for primordial identity. Roger Williams, who spent time in both colonies but was essentially forced out to establish a new settlement, Providence Plantation, can be said to be the first to fight and sacrifice for the vision of a genuinely pluralist society in America. Edward Winslow's son, Josiah Winslow, also became governor of Plymouth like his father, but his actions and attitudes were of a more predator variety. His harsh treatment of Native Americans, tolerance of slavery, and curtailment of religious freedom were the first clear expressions of the predator identity emerging from primordial identity. The debates, tensions, and conflicts between these individuals are the precursors of the interplay between the three identities throughout American history.

Winslow, Winthrop, Cotton, and Williams—these were impressive men by any standard. They were not desperate, starving immigrants arriving destitute, having escaped famine or unbearable persecution. They came from comfortable middle-class backgrounds and had the best education England could give. They were leaders of men who would have done well anywhere. They were not revolutionaries either. They did not want to overthrow their religion and traditions from home. What they wanted was something even more ambitious. They wanted to create a new society in a new world built and improved on the old. They would shape the future according to their "pure" version of Christianity and were therefore "Puritans."

They had a definite idea of the role and boundaries of Christianity, as reflected in the Puritan Connecticut Code of 1650: "If any man shall have or worship any God but the Lord God, he shall be put to death."[7] But Christianity promised the world to these Puritans. Their community was to consist of God-fearing, hard-working, law-abiding individuals eager to practice free enterprise and trade. The Puritan aim was to produce a prosperous and ordered society. The message was one of hope and optimism. It promised the future. In time, sociologists like Max Weber would term this the "Protestant work ethic," which drove the spirit of capitalism. Given the colonists' respect for learning and knowledge, it is no coincidence that the great American universities were established early in American history: Harvard University in 1636 and the College of William and Mary in

1693. Universities like Yale and Dartmouth followed in the next century. It was not long before they were producing scholars and scholarship of international renown. The links with English culture can be seen in the architecture of these older American universities, which is patterned on that of Oxford and Cambridge Universities.

Primordial Identity

The archetypal primordial American is Edward Winslow, who was born in Worcestershire, England, and arrived in 1620 on the *Mayflower*. Winslow's family background had ensured his admission to one of Britain's older public schools, the King's School in Worcester. I am familiar with the school because my younger brother studied there in the 1960s. It is a beautiful part of England, and I enjoyed my visits and walking about the school by the banks of the River Severn.

Winslow oversaw the signing of the Mayflower Compact on November 11, 1620, endorsed by nearly half of the *Mayflower*'s passengers. Here was America's first social contract: the signers agreed to abide by the compact's rules and regulations in order to survive. While acknowledging allegiance to the king, the compact also established the principle of majority rule. The idea and practice of incorporating the will of the people were thus established at the very founding of America. The Declaration of Independence and the Constitution would be the culmination of what began at Plymouth.

Winslow served as the governor of Plymouth Colony for several terms. When delegated by the colony to negotiate with the Wampanoag, he established cordial relations with Chief Massasoit. Winslow attended to Massasoit when he fell ill, and their friendship ensured peace between their peoples. Winslow returned to England to serve Oliver Cromwell and later died at sea in the West Indies. Winslow's son, Josiah, would become governor of the colony in 1673.

John Winthrop is another seminal figure in American history who embodies primordial identity. Educated at Cambridge University in England, he went on to become a lawyer in London. An ambitious and practical man, he set his sights on the new land across the Atlantic and arrived a few years after Winslow with other Puritans on the *Arbella*. Winthrop was elected governor of the Massachusetts Bay Colony several times.

In Winthrop's vision, God had granted America to Christians so they could build an ideal community patterned directly on the teaching of the Bible. In his famous sermon, "A Model of Christian Charity," also known as "The City upon a Hill," Winthrop outlines a vision of Puritan settlers arriving in the New World as part of a special pact with God to create a holy community. Commentators have seen this speech as the forerunner of the concept of "American exceptionalism," the idea that America was ordained and created by God as a special nation in order to do extraordinary things. Like other Puritans, Winthrop viewed Roman Catholics as heretics and believed the dispossessed or disadvantaged were somehow to blame for their lot: "God Almighty in His most holy and wise providence, hath so disposed of the condition of mankind, as in all times some must be rich, some poor, some high and eminent in power and dignity; others mean and in subjection."[8] Unlike the elder Winslow, Winthrop gave the native inhabitants short shrift, arguing that they had not "subdued" the land and therefore had no "civil right" to it.[9]

While early settlers espoused a free society administered by the will of the majority, Winthrop delivered strident tirades against democracy, calling it "the meanest and worst of all forms of government," a "manifest breach of the Fifth Commandment," and pointed out that "there was no such government in Israel."[10] Contemporary figures like Ronald Reagan have been inspired by John Winthrop, his "City upon a Hill" sermon, and his primordial identity. In his farewell address in 1989, Reagan praised Winthrop as "an early freedom man" and extolled his vision of the "shining city."

Pluralist Identity

If Winthrop had a nemesis, it was Roger Williams. A gifted linguist educated at Cambridge University, Williams had collaborated with the great English poet John Milton. After university, Williams was offered attractive posts in the Church of England and at university. Had he accepted either, he would have been condemned to obscurity and his genius lost. Ever the restless intellectual, he refused.

Having spent over a decade at Cambridge, I can appreciate a man like Roger Williams in the intellectual and cultural context of that institution. I can imagine Williams in the rooms of a fellow student savoring Chaucer one moment and arguing about the nature of the soul and God's purpose in creating man the next. Without complete freedom of worship, he might add, man could not truly understand God. Like Winthrop, also a Cambridge man, Williams was an intellectual and an idealist. He dreamed of translating his ideas into action. This would not have been possible in the England of his day. America, however, was a different matter. It was a clean slate—or as the classics scholar would have put it, a *tabula rasa*.

Williams had no sooner arrived in America in 1631 than he was engaged in the major debates of the age, almost single-handedly laying the foundation for future civil rights and liberties. He argued boldly that the Puritans who had escaped the tyranny of England were themselves behaving as tyrants in their new land. He challenged the laws of the Massachusetts Bay Colony and the magistrate who could convict people for committing religious infractions, maintaining that every individual should be free to follow his personal convictions in religious matters. He defended the rights of natives, excoriated the practice of slavery, fought for the separation of church and state, and demanded complete freedom of worship. On each of these points he challenged and enraged the church and administrators of Plymouth Colony. What they found particularly maddening was that he could match them biblical verse for biblical verse. In a letter to John Winthrop, then governor of Massachusetts Bay, Williams quoted thirty biblical passages, yet again leaving an opponent at wit's end.

Williams also came under sharp criticism from John Cotton, another Cambridge alumnus and a prolific writer. Cotton had been a vicar of a church in Boston, England, but dissatisfied with the Anglican Church, he crossed the Atlantic with other Puritans inspired by Winthrop's "City upon a Hill" vision. In Boston, Massachusetts, part of the Massachusetts Bay Colony, Cotton accepted a key paying position in the church hierarchy (refused earlier by Williams), which made him the most influential cleric of his time.

Williams and Cotton clashed over the treatment of Native Americans. Williams had learned their languages and visited their homes. He noted that, unlike Europeans, native communities did not suffer from rape, murder, or robbery, and their wars incurred less bloodshed. He pronounced it an outrage that on the authority of the king the colony could take Indian land whenever it pleased. Echoing the sentiments of Winthrop, Cotton provided moral cover for the illegal actions of settlers who were acquiring Indian lands by force. Cotton used the Bible in support of his arguments: "Multiply, and replenish the earth, and subdue it" (Genesis 1:28). He then concluded: "If therefore any son of Adam come and find a place empty, he hath liberty to come, and fill, and subdue the earth there."[11]

Cotton also opposed Williams's views on democracy, which he found inappropriate for governing commonwealths and churches. In response, Cotton compiled New England's various laws into a single document to be called the Mosaic Code. It was judged too stringent and was rejected by the Massachusetts authorities, but the New Haven Colony in what is now Connecticut would base its legal system on Cotton's work.

Eventually, Williams's opinions were deemed too disruptive for the colony, and Winthrop ordered his expulsion. Warrants were issued to forcibly put Williams on a ship back to England. The relationship between the two was a complex one, however, and appears to have been based on mutual respect. Winthrop apparently had tipped off Williams, allowing him to escape capture. Later in life, Williams would say that Winthrop had "personally and tenderly loved me to his last breath."[12]

Narrowly escaping deportation, Williams led a small group of supporters in establishing a settlement named Providence Plantation, which would become Rhode Island. Williams divided the land into equal 11-acre plots. In 1637 these settlers signed what is known as the Providence Agreement, whereby only "civil things" would concern the community and religion would be left to private conscience. The state, said Williams, should allow all religions, including the "Turkish" (Islamic).[13] More than a century before Washington, Jefferson, and Franklin were advocating religious freedom, Williams was opening America to all, including Muslims.

In matters of slavery, too, where even the towering Jefferson would stand faulted for his ambiguity, Williams was two centuries ahead of his time. On May 18, 1652, Rhode Island passed the first law in America making slavery illegal. In word and deed, Williams defied the power of civil and religious authorities when he thought it transgressed individual liberty. Williams described the treatment of the native population as a "national sin," and this notion was later reflected by Jefferson who called slavery the "original sin." Jefferson also echoed Williams when he called for a "wall of separation" between church and state.[14] Williams was an Enlightenment figure before the Age of Enlightenment.

Curiously, American history has not given Roger Williams due credit for laying the foundations for America's pluralist identity. John F. Kennedy, for example, in Boston a few days before his inauguration in 1961, cited Winthrop rather than Williams. Other presidents who advocate pluralism, such as Bill Clinton and Barack Obama, also overlook Roger Williams, although he has been acknowledged briefly by politicians Mitt Romney and Ted Kennedy, who, as a Mormon and an Irish Catholic, respectively, probably found inspiration in Williams's religious tolerance. On the other hand, had their campaigns won the presidency, perhaps both men would have cited Winthrop, in keeping with primordial identity. The challenge for those who believe in American pluralism is to revive the memory of Roger Williams and bring him into mainstream politics and society as a seminal and inspirational figure in history.

Predator Identity

Perhaps the prime example of the predator identity among the first white settlers is Josiah Winslow, the son of Edward Winslow. Whereas his father had been a friend of Chief Massasoit, as governor Josiah would fight Massasoit's son, Metacomet, also known as King Philip, and be brutal to the natives. In what came to be known as King Philip's War, Winslow organized an attack on the main stronghold of the Narragansett tribe in Rhode Island. Despite the pleas of his captains, he ordered the destruction of the entire camp. Three hundred native warriors and an equal number of women and children were killed.[15] Josiah decapitated King Philip and had his head impaled on a pole and his limbs strewn across the land. Philip's nine-year-old son and other natives were shipped to the Caribbean as slaves on vessels including the *Seaflower*. Plymouth under Josiah declared that "no male captive above the age of fourteen years should reside in the colony."[16] Josiah was equally brutal to those natives who surrendered. When several hundred approached the authorities in Plymouth and Dartmouth after being assured amnesty, Josiah and the Council of War ensured that they would meet the same fate as the others shipped abroad as slaves.[17]

Indians who had converted to Christianity and pledged their loyalty to the English, known as the Praying Indians, were deported to a concentration camp on Deer Island in Boston Harbor where hundreds died of starvation and exposure to the harsh elements. Missionary John Eliot was threatened with death for educating the Indians, and there was talk of attacking Deer Island and exterminating all the Praying Indians. William Hubbard, a contemporary Puritan historian of English background, declared that Indians were "the children of the devil, full of all subtlety and malice."[18]

Profit or religious and racial hatred were not the only motives behind Josiah's cruel actions. The white population lived in constant fear of natives wiping them out, and this emotion embedded itself deep in their psyche, leading them to demand a solution that would remove the threat permanently. Thus was born the concept of zero tolerance. Within half a century of the *Mayflower*'s landing, the native tribes would be decimated in New England. They would be killed by the settlers and their descendants, ravaged by disease, or sold into slavery.

The Triumph of the English

American identity had been profoundly shaped by the English. But the dominance of the English was not a foregone conclusion. In the early seventeenth century, the North American continent was the stage on which several European nations and native populations were locked in a struggle for survival. The original inhabitants ranged from Eskimos in the north to Seminole in the south. Those from Europe included not only the English but also the Spanish and French. The Spanish settled in the American South and Southwest, and throughout Central and South America, while the French were prominent in the southern and northern parts of what is now the United States. It would be the clash between the French and the English that would rage across North America into the eighteenth century. After the French and Indian Wars, the English dominated much of the eastern United States, making English the lingua franca for that part of the continent and thus warding off other contenders for the national language, such as that spoken by the large numbers of German immigrants settling in the region in the eighteenth century. In the end, English became the language of America shared by every other ethnic group.

In dominating America, the English settlers marginalized and ignored the rich history, culture, and languages of the Native Americans and the Africans transported to America as slaves. They would force the land from the former and use the latter to work it. English names were given to towns like Boston and Plymouth and states such as Georgia and Virginia. So strong was the impression that those first English settlers at Plymouth made on the nation that even two centuries later American leaders would proudly identify with them. In 1850, on the anniversary of the Pilgrims' landing at Plymouth, Daniel Webster, the famous American orator and senator, spoke about the importance of English ideals and culture in America—in a Freudian slip substituting "English" for "Anglo-Saxon American": "It is our duty to carry English principles, I mean, Sir, Anglo-Saxon *American* principles, over the whole continent; the great principles of Magna Carta, of the English Revolution, and especially of the American Revolution, and of the English language. Our children will hear Shakespeare and Milton recited on the shores of the Pacific."[19] The British imperial poet Rudyard Kipling paid the ultimate compliment to America when he included it among those called by destiny to "take up the White Man's burden—Send forth the best ye breed" to "serve" peoples who were "half-devil and half-child."[20]

Why did the English come out on top in North America? I believe the first English settlers had an advantage from the beginning: they were coming from a country bursting with new ideas and confidence. The previous century had seen unprecedented developments in England and created a conviction that everything was possible: King Henry VIII had challenged the Roman Catholic Church and forged a new version of Christianity, which came to be known as the Church of England; the mighty Spanish Armada was defeated, and Queen Elizabeth I ruled over a prosperous England that saw merchant ships sail to far realms, returning with fantastic goods and stories, while other vessels set off to explore distant coasts and to establish settlements; and English literature reached new heights through the masterful works of William Shakespeare, who would draw from the traditions of many nations for inspiration. Finally, as an island race, the English developed a sense of national uniqueness.

The English had also introduced the idea of limiting the authority of the ruler—be it a king or lord—through the Magna Carta Libertatum, the Great Charter of Freedoms issued in 1215. It explicitly protected the rights of all the king's subjects, most notably through the writ of habeas corpus, allowing appeal against unlawful imprisonment. The influence of the Magna Carta can be seen in many constitutional documents, including that of the United States.

Many analysts are of Samuel Huntington's view that the original English identity of Plymouth and Massachusetts Bay settlers is apparent in Americans today. Huntington associates American identity with Anglo-Protestant culture, which he thinks "has been central to American identity for three centuries."[21] Even those not of English descent or Protestant faith can be assimilated into this identity (as can be seen in the case of Professor Robert Kraynak in chapter 3).

Broadening of American Identity

The story of Plymouth and its English settlers overshadows that of other immigrants from the British Isles. There were in fact four distinct and large waves of immigration during the seventeenth and eighteenth centuries.[22] The first occurred early in the seventeenth century, bringing settlers from eastern England mainly to Massachusetts; the second, a few years later, brought royalist elite to Virginia; the third wave, in the late seventeenth and early eighteenth centuries, came from the north Midlands and Wales to the Delaware Valley; and the fourth consisted predominantly of Scots from the border areas between England and Scotland and Northern Ireland who settled in the Appalachian back country. Today, four centuries after the first settlers landed at Plymouth, millions of Americans claim British ancestry that may date to any one of these groups.

The immigrants disembarking on the shores of America were aware that they had left behind the comfort and shelter of their villages, extended families, and clans. While some still retained respect and loyalty for the British crown, most had said goodbye to their country and their king. In America, they would be judged and tested as individuals. Even their links with the church would loosen and weaken. In their new homes many were tempted to join a new church or even abandon formal religion altogether. Many found themselves expressing loyalty to a new identity for which they had crossed an ocean, that of being American. On our journey, many Americans spoke of their intense love of American symbols. They told us that they cried with emotion at the very thought of "The Star-Spangled Banner." It was a new kind of religion, what sociologists like Robert Bellah have called a "civil religion."[23]

To understand the self-perception of ethnic purity among the English settlers, one must forage back into the past of the British Isles, which themselves had seen wave upon wave of foreign invaders and settlers—Roman, Saxon, Viking, Norman—stretching over a period of a thousand years. Even the Saxons, who are perceived as the ethnic base of English society, were foreigners. By the time the Norman invaders crossed the English Channel, the Saxons had been living in England long enough to be considered natives. The blood of the invaders and settlers intermingled with ethnic groups constantly migrating within Britain, such as the Scots, Welsh, and Irish. It was only a few generations before the *Mayflower* left its shores that a distinct English identity and a United Kingdom had taken shape.

For all the emphasis on English racial purity in early America, a similar mingling took place there, first among the English, Scots, and Welsh settlers and subsequently among their progeny and later immigrants. Now most Americans are a mixture of different ethnic groups. Take Elvis Presley. Presley's father's side had a Scottish background. His mother's ancestry can be traced to French Normans who married into the Scots. From there they went to Ulster in Northern Ireland and then migrated to the United States. One of Presley's ancestors married a full-blooded Cherokee on the frontier and subsequently served with Andrew Jackson. His son would marry a Jewish woman, also on the frontier.[24] Presley's lineage reflects the greater frequency of marrying outside the group on the frontier than in New England.

"True Blue American Originals"

Dreaming of a new society in which they would maintain their independence and preserve their rights, the early white settlers from England had laid the foundations for American primordial identity. The next wave of immigrants to assume this primordial identity and become its torchbearers were the Scots. They were mainly from Ulster in Northern Ireland, where they had been transplanted from Scotland. The English followed a policy of divide and rule, playing the Protestant Scots against the Catholic Irish.

In time, they came to be known as the Scots-Irish and saw themselves as "true blue American originals." The main waves of Scots-Irish immigration to the United States occurred during the eighteenth century.

The Scots were profoundly tribal, saw the English as effete and dishonorable, were fiercely independent and resisted the state, and adhered to codes of honor, revenge, and clan loyalty. Who better to define the Scottish code of honor than the famed eighteenth-century Scotsman Rob Roy, explaining it to his son in the 1995 film *Rob Roy*:

Son: Father, will the MacGregors ever be kings again?

Rob Roy: All men with honor are kings—but not all kings have honor.

Son: What is honor?

Rob Roy: Honor is what no man can give you, and none can take away. Honor is a man's gift to himself.

Son: Do women have it?

Rob Roy: Women are the heart of honor—and we cherish and protect it in them. You must never mistreat a woman, or malign a man. Or stand by and see another do so.

Son: How do you know if you have it?

Rob Roy: Never worry in the getting of it. It grows in you and speaks to you. All you need do is listen.

By contrast, the English saw the Scots-Irish as a backward and unruly mob of tribesmen who rejected codified laws and churches that imposed order and organized society along "civilized" lines. These immigrants arrived with a different understanding of Christianity and central authority than the English. While they had been called "the scum of both nations" at home, in America they found an equally hostile reception.[25] An Anglican clergyman expanded the metaphor, calling them "the scum of the universe."[26] John Cotton's grandson Cotton Mather fumed that the Scots-Irish represented "the formidable attempts of Satan and his Sons to unsettle us."[27] Charles Woodmason, an English clergyman visiting the Scots-Irish in the South, was horrified at their "gross Licentiousness, Wantonness, Lasciviousness, Rudeness, Lewdness, and Profligacy." They would, he complained, "commit the grossest Enormities, before my face, and laugh at all Admonition." In contrast to even the "Vulgar" in England, who "delight in Historical Books or in having them read to them," Woodmason found "these People despise Knowledge, and instead of honouring a Learned Person, or any one of Wit or Knowledge be it in the Arts, Sciences, or Languages, they despise and ill treat them—And this Spirit prevails even among the Principals of this Province."[28]

Undeterred by the contempt of the English, the Scots-Irish were determined to make their own life in America. Their Calvinist Christianity was emphatically egalitarian, gave priests minimum authority, and kept their churches and services spare. Even the distinctly democratic Presbyterian Church was considered too hierarchical and centralized for some, and they joined a myriad of denominations such as the Baptist. The Christianity practiced by these Scots-Irish was colored by the notion of individual salvation and a direct relationship with Jesus, who they saw more as a warrior chief leading them on to battle than as a loving messenger of peace and humility. In time, the Scots-Irish would provide fertile ground for the evangelist movement in America.

For the most part, the Scots-Irish settled not in the plantation region of the South or in the bustling cities of New England, but in the harsh wilderness of the frontier, where they provided a buffer against Indian tribes. They were prominent in the settling of Texas, for example. There, as elsewhere, their society was governed by few rules. More often than not, the arbiter of right and wrong was the lynch mob. The place names indicate the nature of Scots-Irish society: Tickle Cunt Branch, Fucking Creek, Cutthroat Gap, Killquick, Lynch's Creek, and Bloody Rock.[29] Subsequent settlers of English background discreetly changed those names when they could. Fucking Creek, for example, became Modest Creek.[30]

Not long after the Scots-Irish arrival in America, they began to think of independence for themselves. In 1732 those in Maine attempted to form their own colony, but their request was rejected by Massachusetts magistrates.[31] In 1787 they rioted against the U.S. Constitution.[32] And in 1794 President George Washington personally commanded the U.S. Army to crush Scots-Irish rebels who were torturing and mutilating federal officials attempting to levy a tax on whiskey.[33]

For the Scots-Irish, the right to be free had to be earned and fought for. The famous Scots-Irish vice president, secretary of war, and U.S. senator John C. Calhoun articulated this point of view succinctly in 1851: Liberty "is a reward to be earned, not a blessing to be gratuitously lavished on all alike; a reward reserved for the intelligent, the patriotic, the virtuous and deserving; and not a boon to be bestowed on a people too ignorant, degraded and vicious to be capable either of appreciating it or of enjoying it."[34]

The Scots-Irish urge for independence would surface again in the South's push to secede from the Union and plunge the nation into the Civil War. While the popular understanding of that war is primarily about slavery, for the Scots-Irish it was an expression of their wish to live as independent and free people. It is no coincidence that the Confederate flag adopted Scotland's heraldic symbol, St. Andrew's Cross, as a reminder of the Scottish lineage of many Southerners. Although some Scots-Irish fought for the North, the majority fought for the South.

The Scots-Irish would say, as indeed they did to our team in West Virginia, that they had been the "slaves" of the English and would refuse to accept bondage in America under anyone (see the Benton Ward interview in chapter 3). Such was their contempt for, and rejection of, central authority that poverty-stricken Scots-Irish living in the area were going hungry rather than accept government food aid. They had little sympathy for the blacks, as they themselves "had nothing." Freedom for the Scots-Irish goes to the heart of one of America's eternal political battles: gun control. Guns are a symbol of protection and guarantee of independence, and the Scots-Irish we met said they are prepared to challenge President Obama himself if he attempts to take their weapons.

Of all the descendants of European immigrants, the Scots-Irish have remained perhaps closest to their original values, ways, and attitudes while fully and completely identifying with, and embodying, an American identity. As Senator Jim Webb, one of the most distinguished of the community, wrote, "The Scots-Irish did not merely come to America, they became America."[35] The Scots-Irish way of life rests on devotion to Christianity, on the one hand, and social freedom, on the other. To many Americans, however, the Scots-Irish in these remote valleys and mountains are backward, illiterate, and coarse hillbillies. Indeed, the English referred to them in derisive terms such as "redneck," "cracker," and "hoosier." The poverty of the regions they inhabit in the South and their patriotism encourage the Scots-Irish to join the military in large numbers. It also makes them least willing to accommodate Muslims, who threaten not only their beloved America but also their fiercely guarded way of life.

Locating the Scots-Irish in America today is sometimes difficult because unlike the Irish or the Italians, they frequently do not identify themselves as Scots-Irish and therefore do not feature on the ethnic map provided by the U.S. Census Bureau.[36] According to its map, the most populous ethnicity in America is German, encompassing most of the Midwest. However, a group called "American," colored in light yellow on the legend, is dominant from central Texas to North Florida in the South and to Indiana, West

Virginia, and Ohio in the North. These are the Scots-Irish who over the years have developed so strong an American identity that they have erased all previous ethnic lineages in their collective memory. Many are today unaware of this descent or claim to be simply Irish, or a mixture of ethnicities, and therefore a "mutt."

The Founding Fathers, Pluralism, and Islam

The late eighteenth century was an exhilarating time both in Europe and in North America: a time of hope, of dreams, of change. Poets like William Wordsworth captured the mood of that period in verse: "Bliss was it in that dawn to be alive / But to be young was very heaven!"[37]

A new country was emerging in North America, and its identity would be a hotly contested subject. It was the sheer personality, vision, and extraordinary character of America's Founding Fathers—figures like George Washington, Thomas Jefferson, James Madison, and Benjamin Franklin—who would forge a pluralist identity and direction for the new nation. These were sophisticated, land-owning gentlemen influenced by the intellectual debates of the Age of Enlightenment in Europe. The talk at their dining tables was of freedom, liberty, and democracy. But even these sophisticated and genuinely open-minded individuals could not countenance the contradictions posed by the treatment of the Native American peoples and those of African origin. Although these problems were set aside, the framework the Founding Fathers erected enabled leaders in succeeding generations to promote rights for disenfranchised Americans.

As much as the Founding Fathers were inspired by the early white settlers, they did not always approve of the Puritans' conduct. "They cast their eyes on these new countries as asylums of civil and religious freedom; but they found them free only for the reigning sect," Jefferson observed trenchantly.[38] Emphasizing the principle of freedom of worship, he condemned Plymouth's policy of putting to death religious dissenters and Jamestown's persecution of Quakers (the English mystic movement) and Presbyterians, the majority of whom were Scots. Much later, near the end of his life in 1822, Jefferson warned against the "growth of Presbyterianism" prevalent among the Scots-Irish, which represented "a threatening cloud of fanaticism, lighter in some parts, denser in others, but too heavy in all."[39]

Franklin also rejected the early English settlers' intolerant attitude toward other faiths. When consulted by the Vatican following American independence, Franklin put forth the name of John Carroll, a Jesuit priest, to become America's first archbishop. (Carroll would go on to found

Georgetown University.) The Founding Fathers embraced even Islam, which surely at that time would have been considered exotic and alien. Outlining his vision of America in 1783 and foreshadowing words now associated with the Statue of Liberty, George Washington wrote, "The bosom of America [was to be] open to receive . . . the oppressed and persecuted of all nations and religions; whom we shall welcome to a participation of all our rights and privileges. . . . They may be Mohometans, Jews or Christians of any sect, or they may be atheists."[40] Late in his administration, Washington reconfirmed his firm belief in a pluralist state in a treaty stipulating that the nation's government "is not in any sense founded on the Christian Religion." The treaty, which was signed by President John Adams in 1797, pertained to Tripoli and assured that the United States "has in itself no character of enmity against the laws, religion or tranquility of Musselmen."[41] Even the Prophet Muhammad was praised by the Founding Fathers; John Adams called him one of the world's "sober inquirers after truth" alongside such figures as Confucius and Socrates, and Franklin cited the Prophet as a model of compassion (see the next section).[42]

Jefferson's copy of the Quran, now in the Library of Congress, was used during the swearing-in of the first Muslim member of Congress, Keith Ellison, in 2007. An uproar followed that ceremony, and during a television interview, Glenn Beck challenged Representative Ellison to "prove to me you are not working with our enemies." Another hint of Jefferson's pluralism appears in Virginia's colonial legislation, written in 1777 "to comprehend, within the mantle of its protection, the Jew and the Gentile, the Christian and the Mahometan, the Hindoo, and infidel of every denomination."[43]

A visual tribute to Jefferson's pluralism stands outside the entrance to the University of Virginia, which he founded near his estate at Monticello: a statue of an angel carrying a tablet inscribed "Religious Freedom, 1786." Underneath is the name "Allah" along with that of God and Jehovah, as well as Brahma, the Hindu god. Adding this non-Abrahamic deity is true evidence of Jefferson's pluralistic mind.

Jefferson's views on religious freedom were derived from philosophers like the English John Locke, who, unlike other Enlightenment figures such as Voltaire, was a believing Christian. The true Christian's duty, Locke wrote, was to practice "charity, meekness, and good-will in general towards all mankind, even to those that are not Christians."[44]

The Founding Fathers, particularly Washington, Jefferson and Madison, were passionate about defending the rights of the minority in their new country, be it ethnic, religious, or gender-based, against the tyranny of the majority. With "every barbarous people," wrote Jefferson, "force is law.

The stronger sex therefore imposes on the weaker. It is civilization alone which replaces women in the enjoyment of their natural equality. That first teaches us to subdue the selfish passions, and to respect those rights in others which we value in ourselves."[45]

The Founding Fathers were not only upholding the principles of American pluralism but also self-consciously providing examples of leadership to their new nation. Washington asked people to address him as plain "Mr. President," rejecting any more grandiose title. Once in office, even the president bowed to the principles of democracy, serving for limited terms and thus creating a healthy precedence. Such a limit was revolutionary at that time, when Europe's rulers were still advocating the divine right of kings, and the notion of despotic rulers prevailed in the Muslim world.

Of all the glittering speeches spoken on behalf of democracy and freedom in the United States, none have had quite as powerful and far-reaching an impact as Jefferson's thirty-five words that open the Declaration of Independence: "We hold these truths to be self-evident, that all men are created equal, that they are endowed by their Creator with certain unalienable Rights, that among these are Life, Liberty and the pursuit of Happiness." (To the end of his days Jefferson complained that the delegates had "mangled" his document because of what had been left out, including his comments on slavery.)[46]

The pluralism of the Founding Fathers was in part informed by their ethnic backgrounds. Some of the most famous Founding Fathers, and the ones who spoke most eloquently about pluralism, were not purely English—Jefferson was of Welsh, Scottish, and English descent, Madison was Scottish, Welsh, and English, John Jay was French Huguenot, and Alexander Hamilton was Scottish and French Huguenot. Even Adams was of English and Welsh descent. The man who wrote much of the Constitution, Gouverneur Morris, was Welsh. Significantly, one of the signatories to the Declaration of Independence was an Irish Catholic, and two from that faith signed the Constitution. Clearly, the Founding Fathers were shifting away from the exclusive interpretation of Christianity that the Plymouth settlers had so vigorously maintained.

Clues to this change are evident even in the decade between the writing of the two key documents of the United States, the Declaration of Independence and the U.S. Constitution. Of the fifty-seven signatories of the Declaration of Independence, twenty-nine had higher education, of which twenty-four had been educated at English, Anglican-dominated universities such as Oxford and Cambridge, the law colleges in London, or at American institutions that emulated them, such as Harvard, Yale, and William and Mary. Additionally, two received honorary degrees, including Benjamin Franklin from Oxford in 1762. Yet by the time the Constitution was signed, the English dominance was not so pronounced. While seven Harvard men and three from Cambridge University had signed the Declaration of Independence, only one of Harvard background and none from Cambridge signed the Constitution.

It is those with a Scottish background, with their ideas rooted in Presbyterian teaching and a belief in independence and freedom from central authority, who are prominent in the signing of the Constitution. Among the thirty-nine who signed the Constitution twenty-one had higher education and six, including one with an honorary degree, were educated at Princeton, a Scottish Presbyterian university, then called the College of New Jersey. Of the sixteen who left early or refused to sign, five had been educated at Princeton. These Princeton alumni were inspired by the impressive figure of John Witherspoon, the president of Princeton and a clergyman from New Jersey, who had lived in Scotland until the age of forty-five. Witherspoon succeeded Jonathan Edwards, one of the founders of the evangelical movement in America. Witherspoon had begun preaching immediately following the Jacobite Scottish rebellion against King William of England and was a proponent of populist Calvinism against the perceived hierarchy and corruption of the Anglican Church. Such was the power of Princeton that alarmed Anglicans, along with the Archbishop of Canterbury, established Columbia University in nearby New York City to contest its influence. The Anglican first president of the school, then called King's College, denounced Princeton as a "fountain of nonsense."[47] The sectarian differences between Presbyterian and Anglican overlaid and sharpened the ethnic animosity between the Scots and English.

While these documents represented an effervescent American pluralism, those who spoke for predator identity on behalf of the English were not pleased with them. James Winthrop, the direct descendant of John Winthrop, was blistering in his criticism of the pluralism he saw in the Founding Fathers, the Constitution they had drafted, and the city of Philadelphia, which had hosted its signing. He singled out Rhode Island for criticism, thereby continuing the hostility of his ancestor who had expelled Roger Williams, the founder of Rhode Island. Writing from the ivory towers of Harvard University in the *Massachusetts Gazette* in December 1787, Winthrop argued for the need to "keep their blood pure" as the Puritans had done in the past.[48]

Franklin Condemns "Christian White Savages" and Applauds Islam

Franklin expressed his respect for Islam when he wrote he was pleased that his financial support had led to the construction of a large new hall that would provide a pulpit to members of all faiths, "so that even if the Mufti of Constantinople were to send a missionary to preach Mohammedanism to us, he would find a pulpit at his service."[49] But not all Americans were as open to those of other cultures and faiths, as can be seen in the following case.

On December 14, 1763, a group of about fifty Scots-Irish frontiersmen attacked a community of peaceful Christian Indians in present-day Lancaster County, Pennsylvania. The Indians had earned a living "raising hogs, hunting deer, tending to their gardens, and making and peddling brooms and baskets to their settler neighbors."[50] The Scots-Irish had heard that Indians in the settlement were helping Indians in the West attack Scots-Irish settlements and accused one particular Indian of murdering whites. They found six Indians there that day, murdered all of them, and burned their cabins.

Colonists rummaging through the smoldering remains found a bag containing the tribe's most cherished possessions, including a treaty made in 1701 with William Penn, one of America's founding pluralists, pledging that the Indians and colonists "shall forever hereafter be as one Head & One Heart, & live in true Friendship & Amity as one People."[51] Penn's son John, the governor of Pennsylvania at the time of the attack, was outraged and ordered the fourteen remaining Indians who were absent at the time of the massacre to be put in protective custody. Two weeks later the perpetrators returned to torture, mutilate, and murder the Indians in custody. A man from the town reported that two children's heads were split open with tomahawks, appendages severed, "scalps taken off," and a rifle discharged into a male Indian's mouth after his arms and legs were hacked off "so that his head was blown to atoms."[52]

When the Scots-Irish gang learned that English Quakers were rounding up vulnerable Indians to protect them from another massacre, it was enraged that the Quakers seemed to care more for Indians than for the Scots-Irish who had been suffering from Indian attacks for nearly ten years, and the group, now numbering over 200, headed for Philadelphia. As they marched through Germantown, Pennsylvania, they thrust "the muzzles of their guns through windows, swearing and hallooing" and grabbing locals "without the least provocation; dragging them by their hair to the ground, and pretending to scalp them."[53] Even some of the Quakers, a community that practices nonviolence, armed themselves, convinced the Scots-Irish were about to capture the city by force. The conflict was averted when Benjamin Franklin negotiated with the group and promised to raise their grievances with the government.

This did not deter Franklin from writing a scathing essay in 1764, in which he called the frontiersmen "CHRISTIAN WHITE SAVAGES" and attacked their logic: "If an *Indian* injures me," Franklin asked, "does it follow that I may revenge that Injury on all *Indians?* . . . The only Crime of these poor Wretches seems to have been, that they had a reddish brown Skin, and black Hair."[54] The frontiersmen's claims to be acting according to God's word were a "Horrid Perversion of Scripture," Franklin wrote; they pretended to be Christian while ignoring the command of the "God of Peace and Love" that "*Thou shalt do no Murder.*" Even if an Indian present had attacked the Scots-Irish, Franklin asked, "ought he not to have been fairly tried?" The frontiersmen were more barbaric than "*Heathens*" over whom they claimed to be superior, including "Turks, Saracens, Moors, Negroes, and Indians." They had not an iota of the compassion shown to prisoners by the Prophet of Islam, as "recorded in the Life of *Mahomet,*" who applauded the humanity of soldiers who refused to massacre their captives, saying, "*If thou possessedst a Heap of Gold as large as Mount* Obod, *and shouldst expend it all in God's Cause, thy Merit would not efface the Guilt incurred by the Murder of the Meanest of those poor Captives.*" Franklin even cited Saladin, the legendary Muslim ruler, who retook Jerusalem from the Crusaders, as a compassionate and just ruler.

Had the Indians been living in a Muslim country, Franklin was certain, they would have been treated justly and would have been safer "if Faith had once been pledged to them, and a Promise of Protection given. But these have had the Faith of the *English* given to them many Times by the Government, and, in Reliance on that Faith, they lived among us, and gave us the Opportunity of murdering them.—However, what was honourable in *Moors,* may not be a Rule to us; for we are *Christians!*"

The Scots-Irish were quick to defend their actions in a pamphlet released in the same year titled "A Declaration and Remonstrance of the Distressed and Bleeding Frontier Inhabitants." In it, they claimed to be an oppressed people in constant danger of frontier attack whose concerns were being ignored by those controlling a government that did not represent them. Casting themselves as country people struggling against out-of-touch "city Quakers" dominating the administration in Philadelphia, they argued that they were forced to challenge authority out of "Necessity," because of "the Villany, Infatuation, and Influence of a certain Faction that have got the political Reigns in their Hand and tamely tyrannize over the other good

Subjects."[55] They swore to uphold their right to "Life, Liberty, and Security," even if it meant killing members of a "Perfidious" race.[56]

As a footnote to history, Franklin's grandson, Benjamin Franklin Bache, joined Jefferson to oppose the Alien and Sedition Acts passed under President John Adams, which allowed the government to arrest, imprison, and deport immigrants, foreshadowing legislation such as President George W. Bush's Patriot Act. William Cobbett, publisher of Philadelphia's widely read *Porcupine's Gazette,* suggested that Bache be treated "as we would a TURK, a JEW, a JACOBIN, or a DOG."[57] Bache was arrested and charged with "libeling the President & the Executive Government."[58] Crushed by the arrest, destitute, and the victim of yellow fever, he died shortly thereafter.

Jackson and the Rise of Predator Identity

Every president who took office in the nation's first half-century had been a member of the exclusive and august group called the Founding Fathers. Ever conscious that they had created in the United States something unique in history and were in a position to implement their vision, they were driven by grand ideas and ambitious ideals. Yet in the main they remained faithful to the principles of democracy and equality: they were merely the first among equals.

All this began to change when the Scots-Irish Andrew Jackson became president in 1829. He had already shown his contempt for the Founding Fathers when, as a member of Congress, he refused to participate in the glowing farewell tribute prepared in the House of Representatives to honor the departing president George Washington. Jackson accused Washington of being soft on Britain and indulging the Native Americans against the rights of white settlers.[59] Jefferson, who had been observing Jackson, was "alarmed": "He is one of the most unfit men I know. . . . He has had very little respect for laws or constitutions. . . . His passions are terrible. When I was President of the Senate he was a Senator; and he could never speak on account of the rashness of his feelings. I have seen him attempt it repeatedly, and as often choke with rage . . . he is a dangerous man."[60]

Jackson's early life was unsettled; he was barely literate, and found little appeal in history or philosophy. Though far removed from many of the thoughtful and erudite Founding Fathers, Jackson nonetheless cut a heroic figure as the archetypal American frontiersman, a self-made man, a fearless commander, successful general, and victor of New Orleans in the War of 1812. Affectionately called "Old Hickory," Jackson personified the tough frontier spirit of the age of expansionism, when an impoverished orphan boy could become the president of the United States. This larger-than-life character suited the mood of Washington with its brawling and dueling legislators and vice presidents.

Predator Identity and the Native American

During his two terms as president, from 1829 to 1837, Jackson implemented a policy toward American tribes not unlike Stalin's dismantling of entire tribes through forced transport to far-flung outposts in the Soviet Union—except in the United States it was done under the fig leaf of the law. In a move some called legal chicanery, tribe after tribe was uprooted from its ancestral land and marched hundreds of miles to a bleak new destination, without regard to justice or humanity. Thousands died on the way, and those passages came to be known as "The Trail of Tears." Perceptive as ever, de Tocqueville did not fail to notice that America's dealing with the Indians "breathes the purest love of forms and legality," which allowed Americans to take an Indian nation "like a brother by the hand and lead it to die outside the country of its fathers."[61]

Beaten, killed, and driven from their lands, the Indians were still capable of attacking settlers, especially in isolated communities. Their practice of scalping the victim created a loathing among the white settlers. Both sides knew that no quarter would be given. During the 1812 wars with the British, the Shawnee chief Tecumseh organized an attack on Fort Mims, where some 400 settlers were massacred. In retaliation, Jackson led an army of militia that defeated the Creeks in 1814, slaughtering 800 of their number.

Following the battle, Jackson oversaw the mutilation of all 800 Indians, cutting off their noses and slicing long strips of flesh from their corpses to be tanned and turned into bridle reins. Tecumseh's skin became razor straps.[62] For Jackson, it was God's design that the Indians of Horseshoe Bend had "disappeared from the face of the earth. In their places a new generation will rise who know their duties better." Jackson also attacked the "Philanthropy" that is "devising means to avert" the "fate" of the Indians. The "true philanthropy," Jackson argued, is rather to reconcile the "extinction of one generation to make room for another."[63]

Jackson's policy toward the Indians, whom he described as "cannibals" threatening white "female innocence,"[64] is best summed up in his own words: "Build a fire under them. When it gets hot enough, they'll move."[65] Indians who had allied with Jackson in the hope of being spared found themselves treated like those who had fought against him. A Cherokee chief who had saved Jackson's life in a major battle against the Creeks lamented: "If I had known that Jackson would drive us from our homes, I would have killed him that day at the Horseshoe."[66] Once spread across the state of Alabama, the Creeks were now forced to cede 23 million acres to the Americans. This was high-handed and cruel, but it is well to keep in mind that the British were using the Creeks to destabilize the newly formed American government. There was no sympathy from any quarter for the Creeks.

Jackson next turned his energies to subduing the Seminole in Florida. President James Monroe charged Jackson with pursuing the Seminoles, who had been staging raids into Georgia, whereupon Jackson followed them into Spanish-held Florida, captured St. Marks and Pensacola, and ordered the execution of two British citizens suspected of aiding the Indians. His actions shocked many in Congress but were defended by Secretary of State John Quincy Adams, an early believer in the idea of America's God-given right to expand its power and territory, or "Manifest Destiny." Hence Adams used Jackson's conquest and Spain's weakness to get Spain to cede Florida to the United States in 1819.

The encroachment of white settlers on Cherokee lands in Georgia caused further turbulence. In 1823 Chief Justice John Marshall decreed that although Cherokees had rights to land in Georgia by virtue of "occupancy," these were outweighed by white rights of "discovery." Congress was thus persuaded to pass the Indian Removal Act of 1830, giving Jackson the authority to negotiate treaties to that effect. Georgia was then in the throes of a gold rush and sought the widespread removal of its Indian population. Upon Cherokee appeal, however, the U.S. Supreme Court ruled in the tribe's favor, arguing that the state could not impose laws in Cherokee territory, since only the national government had authority in Indian affairs. Jackson scoffed at the Supreme Court ruling: "Well, John Marshall has made his decision, now let him enforce it."[67] U.S. Army and militia personnel rounded up some 20,000 Indians from Georgia and placed them in concentration camps in Tennessee, then marched them along the Trail of Tears to Oklahoma reservations, an ordeal that claimed the lives of almost half the total number.[68] This would be just one of many such ordeals the Native Americans endured.

The Native Americans understood all too well what was happening to them at the hands of the white man. Who cannot grieve upon hearing Tickagiska King, a wise and respected Cherokee chief, eloquently chronicle their plight. Having given up most of their land, they pleaded for pity, asking that no more be taken away without their consent, for "we are neither birds nor fish; we can neither fly in the air, nor live under water" but "we are made by the same hand, and in same shape with yourselves."[69] These words are as moving as Shylock's famous speech in Shakespeare's *The Merchant of Venice* describing the plight of the Jews in the face of Christian persecution in which he asks, "Hath not a Jew eyes? . . . If you prick us, do we not bleed? . . . If you poison us, do we not die?"

Their cries fell on deaf ears, however, as Jackson forged ahead with his ethnic cleansing. So intense was his hatred of Indians that his tobacco pouch was said to be made of the skin of an Indian woman's breast. Jackson prided himself on being the terror of the Indians: "We bleed our enemies in such cases to give them their senses."[70] To the Indians, Jackson was the personification of the devil. He was not averse to turning a profit from his policies either. Indian lands were quickly converted into valuable property.

Jackson's policy could not have been further from that of the Founding Fathers. Leaders like Washington and Jefferson were determined to protect their citizens, and in specific cases where British-backed Indians attacked Americans during war, their policies were aimed at capturing prisoners of war, not killing civilians.[71] During the 1812 wars, for example, Jefferson regretted that the "cruel" actions of the British-backed "tribes within our neighborhood" forced Americans to "pursue them to extermination, or drive them to new seats beyond our reach" to protect American "women and children" who had settled on the frontier.[72] Yet the Founding Fathers wished to educate and absorb the Indians, whom Jefferson declared in major presidential addresses were "brothers" possessing the "rights of men."[73] Jefferson's policy was to de-emphasize the military in favor of economic development and commerce with a goal of living "in perpetual peace with the Indians," providing them "justice," and giving them "effectual protection against wrongs from our own people."[74]

Jackson's Legacy

Jackson's presidency was a watershed in American politics, society, and culture as it helped release the energy and imagination of America's white population in a race to settle and acquire land westward across the continent. The period marked the ascendancy of the Scots-Irish and the unambiguous glorification of the new America that was forming on the frontiers of the original colonies. It was an America imbued with and driven by the idea that God's hand favored and directed Americans, who now looked forward to seeing their country stretching from "sea to shining sea" and fulfilling its Manifest Destiny. Minorities such as the Mexicans were powerless "to impede the march of our greatness," boasted an influential political journal in 1846: "We were Anglo-Saxon Americans; it was our 'destiny' to possess and to rule this continent—we were *bound* to do it! We were a chosen people, and this was our allotted inheritance, and we must drive out all other nations before us!"[75]

The American acquisition of one-third of Mexican territory by force confirms the predatory nature of the age and contrasts with the doubling of the U.S. in size through peaceful, legal means in the preceding pluralist period. The confrontation with the Mexicans is part of Jackson's legacy that gave rise to one of the most significant symbols of American spirit, the Alamo, another stop on our journey. Not as large as one might expect, the former fortress compound is now a museum dwarfed by tall buildings. Inside, we found almost all the visitors were white, their manner hushed and reverential, as if at a sacred site. A discreet sign requested that "gentlemen remove hats," and a vigilant guard stood nearby to ensure that they did so. A large portrait of John Wayne from the film *The Alamo* (1960), in which he plays Davy Crockett, looked down on us with his characteristic wry smile.

The 189 defenders of the fort in 1836 have come to represent American resolve to stand and fight for one's beliefs, as reflected in the rallying cry, "Remember the Alamo." The small band of Texans who died there rather than surrender to the 1,500 Mexican soldiers surrounding them believed they were fighting for independence from Mexico. The words of Colonel William Travis in a letter written to all Americans just before he died are engraved at the fort's entrance. They contain an expression that has become part of American identity: "victory or death."

The defenders of the Alamo were almost all white Protestants, mainly of Scots-Irish descent or born in Britain, with some recent European immigrants among them. To Mexicans, these "defenders" were illegal occupiers of their lands who had arrogantly insulted the rightful owners. Yet death turned them into martyrs and provided a pretext for acquiring more Mexican land. The Alamo again exemplifies the thinly veiled use of legality to take away land. It is no coincidence that the heroes of the Alamo were protégés of Andrew Jackson. While Davy Crockett lost his life there, Sam Houston went on to become the first president of Texas in 1836. Supporting their cause would be President James Knox Polk, the Scots-Irish Jackson acolyte known as Young Hickory.

With its indelible Scots-Irish character, Texas remained an independent republic until it joined the Union in 1845, with the clear understanding that it had the option to leave. Polk also encouraged Texas to fight in the

Mexican-American War of 1846, which brought vast swaths of new territory to the United States. The state's feelings toward the Union changed, however, once Lincoln became president and the Civil War erupted, whereupon Texans declared their support for the Confederacy.

Rarely mentioned in the history books is the fact that some of the heaviest casualties taken by the Scots-Irish–dominated U.S. Army during the Mexican-American war were inflicted not by Mexicans, but by St. Patrick's Battalion, a unit within the Mexican army composed primarily of American Irish and German Catholic deserters seeking revenge against American primordial and predator identity. They were joined by Italians, Poles, French, native Mexican citizens, and African Americans. They are still remembered as heroes in Mexico.

The Great White American Century

The white Protestant march to greatness in the nineteenth century, briefly interrupted by a bitter Civil War, resumed in the next decades and beyond into the next century. This period stretches from the 1830s—which marked the end of the Founding Fathers' era—to the 1930s and the start of World War II, which would change America once again. During this span, more people outside the English-Protestant lineage became accepted as Americans. Confident of a future in which anything was possible and of their nation's Manifest Destiny, Americans made it a century of spectacular success, with countless stories of rags to fabulous riches made possible by their drive, boldness, hard work, and ambition. With breathtaking speed, they would transform a collection of colonies on the eastern seaboard into a major industrial and military power. Not only did the nation's entrepreneurs and industrialists create products that would change the world, but they also established a sophisticated communications network across the land, as well as prestigious centers of learning. Most significant, they were able to show that democracy can work in a large, sprawling nation.

For many, however, especially the white settlers pouring westward, society was rough and lawless. The strong survived by taking the law into their own hands. Government was either distant or overlooked the fine points of law and more often than not was represented by military personnel. Whether a white man looking for justice, an Indian hoping for a semblance of humanity, or a native of Hawai'i wishing to appeal a decision, they had to turn to the soldier in uniform and carrying a gun. In contrast, colonized peoples under British rule during the same period could appeal to an educated civil administrator who usually understood their language and culture (see chapter 9). It was a model envisioned by Washington, who sought the "employment of qualified and trusty persons to reside among [the Indians] as agents," which would contribute to the "preservation of peace and good neighborhood."[76] Unfortunately, Washington's vision remained unrealized.

The fictional heroes from this period reveal much about life in the Great White American Century. Probably the first major character of American literature is James Fenimore Cooper's Natty Bumppo. Known variously as Hawkeye, the Pathfinder, or the Deerslayer, Natty is the wise, noble, and courageous frontiersman, in harmony with nature and the native tribes (he is adopted by them). In time, Natty Bumppo would become the role model for succeeding generations of cowboy heroes in the Wild West. *The Last of the Mohicans*, in which Bumppo is a leading character, is a Hollywood favorite.

Mark Twain's Tom Sawyer and Huckleberry Finn exude irresistible optimism and irrepressible exuberance, capturing not only the essence of youth but also the mid-nineteenth-century American spirit. Tom and Huck cross over into each other's stories and are friends. The boys cannot read and have no wish to go to school, are not restricted by any boundaries—neither family, nor church, nor state—and inhabit a gray area reflecting an unflattering view of the adult world. Grownups are generally depicted as untrustworthy and unkind. Huck's drunken father, Pap, kidnaps him for ransom money.

Tom Sawyer Abroad, narrated by Huck Finn and the least known of the boys' adventures, is the most relevant for the purposes of this discussion.[77] Tom hatches a scheme to launch a "crusade" in the Holy Land to take it back from the Muslims. Huck thinks it is a crazy idea and asks what Muslims ever did to deserve aggression, a sentiment that the slave Jim agrees with, arguing that Muslims are just like anyone else, and if the three were hungry, the Muslims would be hospitable. The friends make their way abroad across the Sahara to Cairo in search of adventures.

The three American identities can be applied to the three friends. Huck represents primordial identity, arguing it is useless to try to understand Muslims or Native Americans, and they should just be left alone as there is "no money in it." Jim represents pluralist identity, backing Huck in arguing that Muslims should be left alone, but unlike Huck imbues them with humanity and expresses his desire to live "as good a life as he could, so he could see them again in a better world." To Tom, however, though a Presbyterian like Jim, "they was only Mohammedans." Tom represents American predator identity, advocating a war against Muslims and using the derogatory word "paynim" to describe them. It does not matter to him that the Holy Land belongs to Muslims— actually arguing that it does. He still wants to take it by force, dismissing Huck and Jim as "idiots" for their tolerance and acceptance of Muslims.

In spite of the assertiveness of predator identity, pluralist voices were well represented in American thought. Transcendentalists, many of English background like Ralph Waldo Emerson, found the Prophet of Islam an inspiring figure and were influenced by the Sufi poetry of Rumi and Hafiz. They were roundly attacked as "Socialists" by the Scots-Irish Edgar Allan Poe, who opposed their views on social reform and slavery.[78] The Transcendentalists also included women who challenged their place in primordial identity, among them Margaret Fuller, who in 1845 wrote *Woman in the Nineteenth Century,* considered America's first work of feminism.[79] Elizabeth Cady Stanton, a close confidant of Emerson, opened the landmark 1848 Seneca Falls Convention promoting women's rights in New York by echoing Jefferson in her cry, "All men and women are created equal." As pluralists, Fuller and Stanton joined the Transcendentalists in condemning both slavery and the Mexican-American War.

Although now joined by other white groups, the Scots-Irish were the ones spearheading the drive to the Pacific and to the gates of world power. Nothing would stand in their way, neither man, nor animal, nor nature. They would finally finish the Indians, slaughter 45 million bison to near extinction, and blast through mountains and valleys to create railways and settlements. They would not be stopped by the Pacific Ocean either. American sailors landed in Japan under Commodore Matthew Perry (descended from the legendary Scottish hero William Wallace) and by the end of the century had occupied Hawai'i and Guam. Small bands of Scots-Irish even conquered countries for themselves: William Walker declared himself president in Nicaragua in 1856 before he was removed and killed. Nor did the Philippines escape American attention. The Scots-Irish President William McKinley was inspired by God to help the Filipinos by making them Christian: "The next morning," McKinley declared, "I sent for the chief engineer of the War Department (our mapmaker) and told him to put the Philippines on the map of the United States."[80] (American occupation troops would meet their stiffest resistance there from the local Muslim population.) By the end of the next century, a thousand American military bases were straddling the globe.

Early in the twentieth century, the United States had become the world's leading industrial power. Its major developments in weaponry, transport, photography, and the production of oil and other natural resources would have far-reaching ramifications—not always beneficial—both for Western civilization and for the entire world. These developments enabled

American identity and its internal tensions to leave their mark on ensuing ages, eventually paving the way for environmental catastrophe, asymmetry in wealth, and the threat of mass destruction of life and property.

Hollywood glamorized the image of the cowboy and the Wild West from the start, especially in comparison with the bumbling, timorous, and out-of-their-depth visitors from the eastern coast. It was as if a culture now dominated by the ethos of the Scots-Irish was taking its revenge on those like the Reverend Woodmason who had once mocked it. The title of the film *Man of the East* (1972) does not refer to an Asian but a man from Boston. He has a magnifying glass hanging round his neck, roams around in his bathrobe, carries a tennis racket, and in a pronounced English accent frequently says, "My dear chap!" Kenneth More plays an earnest eastern visitor to the Wild West with comical results in *The Sheriff of Fractured Jaw* (1958), as does Bob Hope, who is of English background, in films like *The Paleface* (1948), *Son of Paleface* (1952), and *Alias Jesse James* (1959). The rough and tough cowboy glorified today continues to reflect country/city and Scots-Irish/English cultural tension. The division is reflected on campus, between the admired "jock" and the mocked "nerd." In this social environment, even the revered Founding Fathers would have risked ridicule. Benjamin Franklin, with his bald head, bifocals, paunch, and library, is, after all, the classic nerd, while Jefferson, with his books, French tastes, and love of abstract ideas, is suspiciously more nerd than jock.

Even if Americans were not saying so, in the nineteenth century they were already behaving like imperialists. In their towering architecture, they defined themselves just as the pharaohs of Egypt had through their pyramids, the Mughal emperor of India through the Taj Mahal, and the emperors of China through the Great Wall. The skyscrapers in New York and Chicago proclaimed the confidence, strength, and power of the new nation. The Statue of Liberty, with its face to the Atlantic Ocean, also held high the nation's ideals before the world.

For me, a more telling image of American self-perception is a statue of George Washington commissioned by Congress in 1832 on the centennial of his birth. When the statue (see next page) was unveiled in its designated place in the rotunda of the U.S. Capitol building, it drew widespread criticism and had to be relocated—eventually to the Smithsonian Institution's National Museum of American History in Washington, D.C. It was not quite what people expected. Based on the classical Greek statue of Zeus, it depicted Washington with a muscular naked torso, his right hand pointing to the heavens and his left hand holding a sword symbolizing world power. Here the father of the nation becomes the embodiment of arrogance and

This statue of George Washington fashioned after the Greek god Zeus greets visitors at the Smithsonian Institution's National Museum of American History and symbolizes the power and vision of America in the age of expansion in the 1830s, when it was commissioned.

militaristic power reflecting the country's hubris to match that of the Greek gods. Washington, a modest man who eschewed exalted titles, would no doubt have had reservations about the statue.

The same American spirit is evident at Mount Rushmore where, early in the twentieth century, the heads of four presidents were carved on the cliff face of a mountain. The sheer technical effort this entailed rivals the achievement of the Sphinx in Giza. It is a bold, grand, almost vulgar exhibition of a nation's ego proclaiming to the world: "Look on these faces and wonder, these are our gods, and we have carved them in stone for eternity."

As significant as the size of the heads is the choice of the four presidents. Washington, the founder of the nation, and Lincoln, in many profound ways its savior, preserving the union and resolving the issue of slavery, are the expected presidents. Jefferson and Theodore Roosevelt are the interesting choices. Jefferson is the pluralist, whereas Roosevelt is the champion of primordial and predator identity. They represent two diametrically opposed views of America, yet indicate that America's vision of itself encompasses wide-ranging opinions.

Roosevelt and the Consolidation of Predator Identity

Like Andrew Jackson, President Theodore Roosevelt (1901–09) helped redefine primordial identity by fusing it with predator identity. If Jackson is the military commander of predator identity, Roosevelt is its philosopher-king. All the presidents who lie between the two were but pale shadows in comparison, except for one other towering figure, Abraham Lincoln, who by contrast was so out of tune with the spirit of his times that he would enrage and fall victim to a murderous fellow countryman. Lincoln, of English Quaker background, kept the flame of pluralism alive by freeing the slaves and protecting the rights of Jews and Mormons (see chapters 7 and 8). His aversion to the century's spirit was evident from the start of his political career. In the first speech of his presidential campaign, he reversed the motto of the age, transforming "might makes right" into "right makes might."[81]

Like Jackson, Roosevelt had a great restless frontier spirit, was of Scots-Irish background (with Dutch blood), and bore a fierce chauvinistic love for his nation, but unlike him had a formal education (which included studies at Harvard) and wrote books defining America. There is another fundamental difference between the two: Jackson loathed the English, while Roosevelt admired them as founders of American identity. A man of enormous energy and imagination, Roosevelt vigorously reinforced the iconic mythology of the first white settlers at Plymouth. Standing on the presidential yacht, the USS *Mayflower*, in December 1907, he launched a world tour of the ships of the U.S. Navy. The name of the formation, the Great White Fleet, underscored the purpose of the mission, which was to demonstrate the nation's might and new status as a world power. As the iconic image of Roosevelt brandishing a sword in the charge at San Juan in Cuba suggests, he had a vision for American society and the physical will to implement it. He and Jackson alike were living examples of the Roman maxim *mens sana in corpore sano*—a healthy mind in a healthy body.

In the spirit of the century, Roosevelt fused Christianity and Darwinism in his definition of America, an exercise in which he was aided by his friend, the Reverend Josiah Strong. The Reverend's widely influential 1885 book, *Our Country: Its Possible Future and Its Present Crisis*, identified seven "perils" facing America: Catholicism, Mormonism, socialism, intemperance, wealth, urbanization, and immigration.[82] The way to rid the nation of these perils, argued Strong, was to encourage progress, which could only be achieved through the propagation of the Anglo-Saxon race. It was America's destiny—and God's will—for the white race to spread out across the world until it had "Anglo-Saxonized mankind."[83] Strong believed that the world was facing "a new stage of its history—*the final competition of races, for which the Anglo-Saxon is being schooled*," and that before long the American race would "move down upon Mexico, down upon Central and South America, out upon the islands of the sea, over upon Africa and beyond. And can any one doubt that the result of this competition of races will be the 'survival of the fittest'?"[84]

Reverend Strong encouraged white Protestant Americans to breed a new American super race that would outshine the "mixed races" of the Egyptians, Greeks, and Romans.[85] Americans were already taller and stronger, he noted, than the Scots or English of the United Kingdom owing to natural selection, which Charles Darwin also credited for "the wonderful progress of the United States, as well as the character of the people . . . for the more energetic, restless, and courageous men from all parts of Europe have emigrated during the last ten or twelve generations to that great country, and have there succeeded best."[86] Strong draws additional support from the English philosopher Herbert Spencer, who coined the phrase "survival of the fittest" and who inferred from "biological truths" that "the eventual mixture of the allied varieties of the Aryan race . . . will produce a more powerful type of man than has hitherto existed, and a type of man more plastic, more adaptable, more capable of undergoing the modifications needful for complete social life."[87] Roosevelt wholeheartedly agreed with Strong and believed American supremacy depended on "a mighty race, in its vigorous and masterful prime," with "the physical and moral traits which go to the makeup of a conquering people."[88]

Seeing the Catholic and Jewish immigrants from Europe as a threat to America, Roosevelt pleaded with Anglo-Saxon Americans to have more children to avoid committing "race suicide."[89] Roosevelt was not alone in feeling that the roots of his treasured America were under attack. As minorities became more prominent and began demanding their rights, millions of white Americans aggressively reaffirmed their primordial identity. White chauvinism, abetted by dubious racial theories and scientific experiments, enlisted the full authority of the state in its efforts to suppress the minority. Pluralist America was clearly in retreat.

This version of American identity bore little of the philosophic sweep of the Founding Fathers or the influence of European intellectuals. Not surprisingly, Roosevelt drew inspiration from Jackson, "emphatically a true American" in his eyes. "With the exception of Washington and Lincoln," he wrote, "no man has left a deeper mark on American history." With his eye for military strategy, Roosevelt appreciated Jackson's "instinct for the jugular" and ability to "recognize his real foe and strike savagely at the point where danger threatens."[90]

Roosevelt reserved special vitriol for Jefferson, denouncing the "evil" policies of his political party, which caused "serious and lasting damage" to the United States. Through the "cowardly infamy" of Jefferson and James Madison and their neglect of the U.S. military during the War of 1812, said Roosevelt, the British had been able to invade the homeland and cause America "shame and disgrace."[91] Roosevelt was outraged that Jefferson and Madison refused to take "full revenge" and never faced "sufficiently severe condemnation" by the American people.[92] Such a patriotism that did not wish to see the nation "prepared for war" or to uphold the "honor of the American flag" was merely "lukewarm" and even dangerous.[93] Jefferson could certainly not be considered a benefactor of the frontier because of the Louisiana Purchase, which Roosevelt felt was an accident, and he was "too timid and too vacillating" to be a match for the likes of Napoleon, the "greatest warrior and lawgiver."[94]

In his book series *The Winning of the West*, written before he assumed the presidency, Roosevelt spoke glowingly of the predominantly Scots-Irish frontiersmen, who would lead the way in carrying "civilization" from the Atlantic to the Pacific Ocean. Praising the contributions of that "bold and hardy race," he believed the Scots-Irish, as the "leaders of the white advance," provided the impetus and energy for America's extraordinary rise and development in this period.[95] These men were not barbarians, but the "outposts of civilization" against the Indians and were instrumental in settling the West.[96] Since the Indians were not going to yield their land, and the white settlers were not going to stop their rightful advance across the continent, war was the only way to settle their differences. According to Roosevelt, the U.S. government tried to reach a "friendly understanding," but this failed because of the "treachery and truculence of the savages," who could only be cowed by a "thorough beating."[97] He criticized any notion the Founding Fathers may have had of imparting, as did Washington's secretary of war, "our knowledge of cultivation and the arts to the aboriginals of the country," whose interests were incompatible with those of the white settlers. If anything, "the question of their clashing rights had to be settled by the strong hand."[98] He ridiculed the fashionable "theory of universal and unintelligent philanthropy" and "love of natural science" of the Founding Fathers' age and was astounded that the Jefferson-backed expedition of Lewis and Clark attempted to make peace with the "wild savages" they encountered.[99]

But Roosevelt was not the only primordial standard-bearer of his age. A long list of other white Protestants were leaving a similar mark on American identity—now increasingly associated with scientific invention and industrial prowess—and transforming the world. Some called them "robber barons," others saw them as living examples of the American dream. Among the most notable were Andrew Carnegie (1835–1919), who built America's libraries on his "empire of steel"; John D. Rockefeller (1839–1937), said to be the richest man in the history of the world, who founded an oil empire and supported charitable causes; Samuel F. B. Morse (1791–1872), inventor of the telegraph and Morse code; and Henry Ford (1863–1947), who pioneered the automobile and invented the assembly line.

In the spirit of the age, however, their success did little to diminish their prejudices. Morse was unabashedly and vocally anti-Catholic, and Ford an anti-Semite. Articles from the Ford-owned weekly paper, the *Dearborn Independent*, were published in book form under the title *The International Jew*, which appeared in Germany as *The Eternal Jew* and became a bestseller. It argued that Jews posed a threat to America's Anglo-Saxon Protestant culture. The *Dearborn Independent* printed Ford's anti-Semitic screeds and published *Protocols of the Learned Elders of Zion*, a Russian forgery claiming to be the minutes of a secret meeting of Jewish leaders plotting to take over the world. All Ford dealerships were required to subscribe to the paper. One of Ford's most ardent admirers was Adolf Hitler, who had a well-worn copy of *The Eternal Jew* and lauded Ford in *Mein Kampf*, the only American mentioned in the book: "Every year makes them [the Jews] more and more the controlling masters of the producers in a nation of one hundred and twenty millions; only a single great man, Ford, to their fury, still maintains full independence."[100]

But dangerous intolerance and greed were not the only driving forces of the Great White American Century. Some Americans were more like John Chapman (1774–1845), widely known as Johnny Appleseed. Early in his life Chapman decided that he would dedicate himself to spreading apple seeds he had patiently dried from the residues at Massachusetts cider mills. He was said to be so poor that he could not afford shoes. According to legend, that did not deter the shoeless Chapman from marching across the continent to give his seeds and apples to farmers and individuals he met along the way. Tales are told of him handing a bag of seeds and a gleaming apple to a gangly, tall young man called Abe Lincoln. By the time he died in 1845, Chapman had helped promote apple orchards on thousands of acres of land. His life as a Christian preacher living in humility and poverty and befriending animals echoes that of Francis of Assisi, who won the hearts of Christians and, when he visited Egypt, Muslims alike.

Catholics Negotiate American Identity

It was the flood of Irish immigrants and their large families that sounded the alarm for Protestants, especially those whose Scottish forebears were from

Northern Ireland. They did not want to be confused with the Irish who still pledged allegiance to the pope, seen as a foreign power. As mentioned earlier, relations between the Scots-Irish and the Catholic Irish had long been strained. Perhaps their only bond lay in a common hatred of the English. Otherwise, their history, religion, and society pitted them against each other.

Between 1845 and 1854, 2 million Irish flooded into the United States, pushed out by a catastrophic potato famine in Ireland and oppression by English overlords. By the time of the Civil War, they numbered 5 million and formed one-tenth of the U.S. population. Today some 40 million Americans claim Irish descent. What sustained the Irish was their strong Christian faith, which predated that of the English and Scots and was introduced to them by St. Patrick in the fourth century. Loyalty to their faith endured and intensified in response to the brutalities of British invasion and occupation. Neither Henry VIII's penal laws against Catholicism nor the devastating famine of the nineteenth century served to weaken their faith. Arriving in America, they encountered the same racial and religious prejudices they had faced at home. Here signs said "Irish and dogs not allowed," there were lynchings, their churches were attacked, and their people ridiculed.

In 1844 mobs in Philadelphia burned a Catholic seminary, two churches, and entire blocks of Catholic buildings. In 1855 on "Bloody Monday" in Louisville, Kentucky, 100 Irish and German Catholics were killed and their homes and businesses burned to the ground. Catholic leaders, citing fanaticism and intolerance, accused Protestant leaders of preparing to "wage a war of extermination against infidels and Roman Catholics."[101] Still the Irish did not lose faith. Their greatest strength lay in having come to America with their identity fully formed: they were ethnically Irish and devoutly Catholic.

While speaking to the largely Irish Catholic Knights of Columbus at Carnegie Hall on Columbus Day in 1915, former president Theodore Roosevelt warned that the Irish and other "hyphenated" Americans would turn the United States into "a tangle of squabbling nationalities" and would "bring the nation to ruins . . . there is no such thing as a hyphenated American who is a good American. The only man who is a good American is the man who is an American and nothing else."[102] President Woodrow Wilson was of a like mind, cautioning that "any man who carries a hyphen about with him carries a dagger that he is ready to plunge into the vitals of this Republic whenever he gets ready."[103] He was playing on the prevalent stereotype of the dangerous knife-wielding poor Catholic immigrant.

Confirming the strength of pluralism in America, not to mention the resilience of the Irish, the Kennedys would see one of their own in the highest office of the land within a century of arriving destitute, half starved, and without employment. Widely admired, John F. Kennedy came to represent the best of American culture. Recognizing the contribution to pluralism of this Irish American and his two brothers, the nation gave them the unprecedented distinction of being buried side by side in its sacred burial ground, Arlington Cemetery.

Italian Americans, the nation's other major Catholic immigrant community, encountered deep prejudice as well before finally being accepted as Americans. One of the biggest lynchings in American history, in New Orleans in 1891, involved Italians. Following the assassination of the city's Mafia-assailing police superintendent, its mayor, Joseph Shakespeare, had ordered the police to arrest "every Italian you come across," whom he had already branded as "idle," "vicious," "worthless," and "from the worst classes of Europe."[104] When the men charged with killing the superintendent were either acquitted or released because of a mistrial, an enraged mob of 10,000 burst into the police station where the Italians were still being held and hanged, shot, and clubbed 11 to death. Several Italians had their heads blown off. Mayor Shakespeare praised the lynchings, vowing to "wipe every one of you from the face of the earth."[105]

No charges were brought against those who carried out the lynchings, with a New Orleans grand jury declaring it a "spontaneous uprising of the people."[106] Many in the national press approved of the mob's actions: the *New York Times* wrote that the chief's death had been "avenged" by killing the "Italian murderers."[107] Later, notorious criminals like Al Capone were used to stereotype Italians as being predisposed to commit crime. Mario Puzo's book *The Godfather* and the subsequent *Godfather* films fed into the stereotypes, as did the suspicion surrounding Italians after Mussolini allied with Hitler in World War II. Half a million Italians were put on the "Enemy Alien List," thousands were arrested, relocated, and interned along with Japanese, Germans, and even some Jews fleeing from Hitler's Germany. But 1.2 million Italians fought in the war, and by its end they had become "Americanized." As their hyphenated status faded, some of the more prominent members of the community became beloved national icons after changing their names: Giuseppe Paolo DiMaggio Jr. became Joe DiMaggio and Dino Paul Crocetti became Dean Martin. No longer a barrier to Americanness, an Italian background was now considered an additional dimension to American identity.

Engineering American Supermen

The idea of racial superiority enflamed by European immigrants took a dark turn with the growth of a eugenics movement committed to selective breeding and supported by major universities like Yale and Harvard and philanthropic organizations such as the Carnegie Institution and Rockefeller Foundation. As a scientific attempt to develop American supermen who would dominate the world, the movement was largely embraced by America's white Protestant community because it promised the "social salvation" of the world through the perpetuation of Christian ideals such as charity, education, and poverty alleviation. Some "New Light" Scots-Irish Protestants saw little use in improving society, however, and focused on personal salvation instead.

These ideas were coming from the English and nourished American primordial identity. The eugenics movement took its inspiration from Charles Darwin and Herbert Spencer. Darwin's cousin Sir Francis Galton had coined the term "eugenics" (from the Greek for "good in birth") to indicate human beings could take control of human evolution: "What nature does blindly, slowly, ruthlessly, man may do providently, quickly, and kindly."[108]

For Christian support, the movement drew on the notions of H. G. Wells, who wrote that the world's non-white population, including the Jews, would "have to go," in keeping with "God's purpose." An ethical system "shaped primarily to favour the procreation of what is fine and efficient and beautiful in humanity," argued Wells, would "check the procreation of base and servile types, of fear-driven and cowardly souls, of all that is mean and ugly and bestial in the souls, bodies, or habits of men," giving these types "little pity and less benevolence" and society "an ideal that will make killing [them] worth the while." Like the prophet Abraham, wrote Wells, members of this society must have the "faith to kill." In this society, Wells envisioned a time when men will "naturally regard the modest suicide of incurably melancholy or diseased or helpless persons as a high and courageous act of duty rather than a crime."[109]

As the movement took hold, scientists and researchers endeavored to identify "defective" family trees and subject them to segregation and sterilization programs to end the bloodlines of those deemed weak, inferior, and unfit. Eugenicists successfully lobbied for laws against interracial reproduction: in 1926 the state of Indiana forbade marriage between a white person and any individual more than one-eighth black. Between 1910 and 1963, 64,000 Americans had been subjected to forced sterilization to "purify" the American gene pool, and by 1940 nearly thirty states had such laws on the books.[110] Many Americans thought they had simply undergone a routine procedure and could not understand why they were unable to have children. In 1924 the state of Virginia mandated sterilization of the mentally retarded, a decision upheld in an 8-1 ruling by the U.S. Supreme Court in 1927. In the Court's majority opinion, Chief Justice Oliver Wendell Holmes found sterilization ethical for those who "sap the strength of the State . . . in order to prevent our being swamped with incompetence." Sterilization benefits society, he argued, inasmuch as "the principle that sustains compulsory vaccination is broad enough to cover cutting the Fallopian tubes."[111]

Other prominent Americans believed that execution was a more efficient way of combating "feeble-mindedness" among Americans. The U.S. Army's Paul Popenoe, a descendant of *Mayflower* Puritans, the leader of the eugenics movement in California, and the coauthor of the widely used college textbook *Applied Eugenics,* originally published in 1918, emphasized the value of execution "in keeping up the standard of the race," especially from a "historical point of view."[112] In a chapter in *Applied Eugenics* titled "Differences among Men," Popenoe, with his coauthor Rosewell Hill Johnson, wrote of the need to combat Thomas Jefferson's "utopian" claim that "all men are created equal" and lamented that Jefferson's ideas are "by no means dead" in America.

According to American physician W. Duncan McKim, a "gentle, painless" means of executing those whose heredity was "the fundamental cause of human wretchedness" would be gas chambers. "In carbonic acid gas," he noted, "we have an agent which would instantaneously fulfill the need" to prevent reproduction among those deemed "unworthy of this high privilege."[113] Adolf Hitler was impressed by such ideas and wrote that he had "studied with great interest the laws of several American states concerning prevention of reproduction by people whose progeny would, in all probability, be of no value or be injurious to the racial stock."[114] Hitler closely followed the American eugenics program and had a special affinity for the scientist Madison Grant, who, in *The Passing of the Great Race,* argued for the need to preserve the "Nordic races" against the Jews and others by "the obliteration of the unfit" and against the "sentimental belief in the sanctity of human life" and American "altruistic ideals." Hitler called the book, which was a sensation in the United States, selling 1.6 million copies, his "Bible."[115]

For the proponents of American Anglo-Saxon racial superiority, concepts such as "Social Darwinism" and "eugenics" provided a convenient way of defending primordial identity against familiar antagonists, such as Native Americans, blacks, Jews, and even "Neanderthal" Irish Catholics, with their "considerable mental defectiveness."[116]

The Ku Klux Klan

As the South's whites wrestled with a sense of honor lost after the Civil War and the accompanying uncertainty, anger, and fear, some banded together in hate groups to restore the honor of the white race (see the interview with Pastor Thomas Robb, the Ku Klux Klan's grand wizard, in chapter 3). Gangs of robed men calling themselves the Ku Klux Klan (KKK) began terrorizing blacks, using violence to protect their so-called white rights. The name Ku Klux derives from the Greek *kyklos*, meaning "circle." The term "Klan" was added because the first Klansmen, according to one of their founding members, were "all of Scottish descent."[117] Chief among the founders was the Scots-Irish Confederate general Nathan Bedford Forrest. According to *The Clansman,* first published in 1905 and the inspiration for D. W. Griffith's *The Birth of a Nation* (1915), Hollywood's first epic film, the Klan's cross-burning arose from the ancient practice among Scottish chieftains of summoning their clans on an errand of life and death with a "Fiery Cross, extinguished in sacrificial blood, . . . sent by swift courier from village to village."[118] In any case, this was part of the KKK's strategy of fear, which might begin with intimidation and economic boycott, then culminate in physical violence.

The Klan's methods were terrifying—cross-burning at night, lynching, bombing, and arson. Although its targets were initially blacks, it freely included Catholics and Jews—accusing the former of betrayal for taking orders from the pope and the latter of "blood libel" in causing the death of Jesus.

Ideas of racial superiority found particular expression in the treatment of African Americans. Whereas Native Americans could be brought to the brink of extinction, African American slaves were needed to run plantations and their owners' homes. Many African Americans converted to Christianity and through the church found a means to improve their social position. Some overcame large hurdles to acquire an education, as illustrated by W. E. B. DuBois, whose determination and intelligence enabled him to rise to a position where he could argue the case of his people.

Those hurdles remained high even after Emancipation. Despite the rights granted under the Reconstruction Act of 1867, such as voting and employment, the black population still felt the stings of the white population's primordial fear and anger. White outrage was fed in part by stories of black men raping and molesting white women, as depicted in the film by Griffith, of Welsh descent and son of a Confederate colonel. In *The Birth of a Nation,* the Klu Klux Klan saved the white women from a fate "worse than death." The film incited violent race riots throughout the United States and a bitterness that did not evaporate for decades. A similar theme can be seen in *Gone with the Wind* (1939), the classic film about the Civil War.

By the 1920s, with 4 million official members and countless more supporters, the Klan had become an enormously powerful and influential force. Sheriffs and their deputies, lawyers, judges, and politicians, even churches, sympathized with its aims. Preachers of that ilk quoted the Bible extensively to justify the Klan's activities, which they said were intended to protect their American identity and Christian faith, both under threat. The influence of the KKK reached the president of the United States. Not only did Woodrow Wilson, the Scots-Irish son of a Confederate chaplain, screen *The Birth of a Nation* at the White House, but the film featured his writing, which praised the Klan. In short, the KKK represented an authentic and enduring strain in American society, one echoed in Hitler's racist views across the Atlantic, which would lead to the deaths of 10 million Jews, gypsies, homosexuals, Poles, and political opponents.

The KKK's message is being propagated in the present day by the likes of Pastor Richard Butler, head of the Aryan Nations/Church of Jesus Christ Christian in Idaho, who called Hitler a biblical prophet and claimed the white race is descended from Jesus, whereas the Jews originate with Satan and are therefore deserving of extermination.[119] The United States, says Butler, of English and German descent, was "made for" the white race, and the annual July 4 celebration is exclusively for the white Christian Aryan race. Proof of membership in the Aryan Nations is skin color. Members also give the Nazi salute and wear T-shirts bearing the swastika, which also adorns their flags. Citing the Bible and *Mein Kampf* as its two most important sources of inspiration, the organization represents a fusion of European fascism and Christianity.

The Aryan Nations had teeth. One man who shared its philosophy was a former Scots-Irish U.S. soldier, Timothy McVeigh, who blew up the federal building in Oklahoma City leaving 168 people dead. The first media reports of the bombing suspected Muslim terrorists. Butler called McVeigh, who had once signed up for the KKK, a "volk hero of our race" and "good soldier who gave his life."[120] Though Butler's camp closed in 2001 and he died in 2004, the movement remains potent, if under the surface of society.

Before 9/11 white supremacists like the Aryan Nations targeted mainly African Americans and Jews, but since then their focus has shifted to the Muslims, with reports of burning crosses outside mosques. In my many conversations with African American taxi drivers after 9/11, they expressed relief that the pressure was now on "you guys"—adding that no one knows how long this might last and whether hostility might turn on them again. They could not be hopeful, many said, because of the past 400 years of history.

The Black Struggle for Humanity

Until the middle of the twentieth century, any black man in America who happened to be in the wrong place at the wrong time could find himself the victim of blatantly false accusations leveled by a white press and police and leading to conviction by a white jury. In many cases, racial and social prejudices mingled with that most sensitive of issues: the fear of black men attacking white women with lewd intent. Even those who tried assiduously to become like the white man faced rejection, strengthened and hardened to such an extent that it condemned them to "a life-long and hereditary bondage from which they could not claim exemption even if they embraced the religion and culture of their masters."[121] Castration as a legal punishment dated back to the colonial era and reflected male sexual anxiety provoking racial injustice.[122]

In Puritan belief, women were susceptible to sin and therefore needed to be protected from the dangers posed by the black man. While the insidious argument about black men being physically well endowed and therefore proving a temptation to white women had circulated among whites before the Civil War, afterward it gained further currency in white society. The subject touched a deep nerve because blacks were now free and therefore had access to white women. The imagined threat of the black man had sociological and theological dimensions. This explains the absolute intolerance toward miscegenation and the brutality exercised when it occurred.

American society's relationship with slavery is nowhere better set out than in Harriet Beecher Stowe's *Uncle Tom's Cabin*.[123] Indeed, upon first meeting Stowe, Lincoln reputedly remarked: "So this is the little lady who made this big war." Uncle Tom, Stowe's "noble hero," represents pluralist identity at its finest. Tom will not give up his Christian faith or his wish to acquire knowledge even at the cost of displeasing his slave master and being punished with a brutal whipping. By forgiving his murderers with his dying breath, he not only confirms his compassionate understanding of Christianity but also transcends the slave-master relationship. In contrast, Simon Legree, a greedy northerner transplanted in the South who rapes and kills his slaves in violent fits of rage, represents the worst side of American predator identity.

The sexual insecurity among white males explains their fury when in 1910 Jack Johnson became the first black heavyweight boxing champion of the world. The challenge to white manhood lay not only in this victory but also in the public flaunting of his relationship with white women. The worst fears of the white population were now unfolding: a black man who was physically stronger than any white man was publicly humiliating white women sexually. Johnson had to be defeated. A search was launched to find the "Great White Hope" who would redeem white honor. That phrase resurfaced in August 2009, when Representative Lynn Jenkins of Kansas used it to emphasize her desire to see a strong Republican challenge Barack Obama. At best, she was ignorant of its connotations; at worst, she was being racist.

For the white population of Tulsa, Oklahoma, life was imitating art in 1921. Like the black characters of *The Birth of a Nation*, a local African American boy was accused of molesting a white girl, Sarah Page, a teenage elevator attendant. In the following days, the *Tulsa Tribune* ran inflammatory headlines such as "To Lynch Negro Tonight"—but with a larger target in mind, Tulsa's wealthy and influential black community. This affluent neighborhood of 15,000 was known as the Black Wall Street, although Tulsa's whites referred to it as Little Africa or Niggertown.[124]

America's wealthiest black neighborhood infuriated many whites in Tulsa, so the elevator incident was just what they had been waiting for, and they launched a coordinated and deadly mass attack on Black Wall Street. The National Guard was mobilized to protect white areas in case of trouble and rounded up about half the black population, herding it into cattle and hog pens.[125] A white mob of 10,000 then descended on the neighborhood and set it aflame. The oil for the fires was provided by men in uniform. Members of the mob walked into black homes and shot dead their inhabitants. Airplanes dropped incendiary bombs and opened fire from the air.[126] Official figures claimed 39 people lost their lives, but estimates ran as high as 300 and even 3,000 as homes, churches, shops, and schools were all burned to cinders.[127] Photographs of the Black Wall Street devastation are reminiscent of Hiroshima or Nagasaki. This was by no means the only such instance of the era. Five years earlier riots had led to the deaths of an estimated 500 blacks in St. Louis and over 800 blacks in Arkansas in 1919, according to contemporary journalists.[128]

The 1930s also saw the beginning of the Tuskegee Experiment conducted by the U.S. Public Health Service on hundreds of black men in the late stages of syphilis. These were illiterate and poor sharecroppers from Alabama who were misled by doctors into believing that they were receiving medical attention, whereas the purpose of the program was to study the ravages of the disease following a patient's death. Perhaps most chilling, the men were deliberately denied penicillin, the first real cure for syphilis, when it was discovered in the 1940s. In treating these human beings as laboratory animals, the experiment proved to be not only dubious science but also racist.

It was not until the early 1970s that the Tuskegee Experiment gained public attention and was forced to close down in the wake of comparisons with the Nazi experiments on the Jews in Hitler's Germany. With the ensuing loss of credibility between the administration and the black population, a major 1990 survey found 10 percent of African Americans believing that the U.S. government had created AIDS as part of a plan to wipe them out, with a further 19 percent indicating that it "might be" so.[129]

Centuries of such brutal treatment created anguish and anger against the whites among African Americans, as voiced by James Baldwin, one of the leading writers of his day:

> Who has not wanted to smash any white face he may encounter in a day, to violate, out of motives of the cruelest vengeance, their women, to break the bodies of all white people and bring them low, as low as that dust into which he himself has been and is being trampled; no Negro, finally, who has not had to make his own precarious adjustment to the "nigger" who surrounds him and to the "nigger" in himself.[130]

Such sentiments sometimes led to violence against whites, especially in urban areas where blacks found themselves locked in a bitter Darwinian struggle for survival with Catholic immigrants who were also below the white Protestants in the social hierarchy. Catholics, especially the Irish, could treat blacks brutally, as in the 1863 New York Draft Riots, depicted graphically in the film *Gangs of New York* (2002), and the 1919 Chicago Race Riots, in which 38 people were killed and 1,000 left homeless, the vast majority of them African American. Attacking blacks could also facilitate the adoption of American identity among Catholics, as with the "All-American Raiders," a Chicago gang with Italians among its leaders, whose main activity was starting "fights with niggers."[131]

It is this troubled history that helps explain contemporary black anger against whites, especially in urban areas. In a 2009 article in the *Washington Examiner*, the African American journalist Gregory Kane lamented the continuing racism against whites among black youth: "How do we account for black teens in this day and age, who've seen little to none of the racism and segregation that their elders have seen, harboring such a sense of racial grievance and dudgeon?"[132] He pointed to a case in which a young white couple who had ventured into a black neighborhood in Baltimore was shot dead by a black teen. The teen was arrested after a policeman, acting on a tip, discovered a text message in the teen's phone which read: "I shot 2 white people around my way 2day and one of them was a woman."

White students at Temple University in Philadelphia told Frankie in 2010 that they were terrified to walk off campus lest they be shot, robbed, or caught in a "flash mob" where large numbers of black youths, some brandishing firearms, take to "running wild, jumping on cars, knocking over shoppers, and starting random fights"[133] In an African American mosque in New Orleans, the men on our team were warned by several people not to step outside the grounds of the mosque lest they be "shot" by African Americans.

It is the burden of hateful history that provides sociological insight into the unfortunate statistics on violence and rape in America today. According to FBI data, blacks are 39 times more likely to commit a violent crime against white people than vice versa, and 136 times more likely to commit robbery.[134] We found startling—as they reflected stereotypes—the statistics on rape in America provided by the U.S. Department of Justice. In 2006, for example, 32,443 white females were raped or sexually assaulted by a black man, whereas 0–10 black females were similarly assaulted by a white man.[135] The corresponding figures for 2005 were much the same: 37,461 white females sexually attacked by black men and 0–10 black females attacked by a white man.[136]

I suspect that these numbers may reflect the inherent bias within the system against minority groups, and it bears keeping in mind that the majority of crimes against blacks are perpetrated by blacks and against whites by whites, and that there are clearly more factors in any situation involving crime than race. Still these are official government statistics and relevant for anthropologists attempting to explain society. Discussion of interracial confrontation is generally avoided in America as part of being politically correct. As a result of the unresolved ambiguities, questions surrounding the subject continue to circulate and create fear and doubt about each other. Our ethnography from the field and the alarming statistics presented here reflect the tragic history of race relations in America and the need to close the gaping wounds and move ahead.

Enter the South Asians: The Case of Bhagat Singh Thind

South Asians did not fair much better in being accepted as fully American than African Americans until the middle of the twentieth century, as seen in the landmark case of Bhagat Singh. Singh had come to the United States in 1913 seeking education, joined the U.S. Army to fight in World War I, and was quickly promoted to the rank of acting sergeant. When the war ended, Singh received an "honorable discharge" and his character was described as "excellent."[137] When Singh applied for citizenship, however, the Immigration and Naturalization Service (INS) insisted that U.S. citizenship was reserved for "free white persons," classifying him as a Hindoo or Hindu, as it did all Indians in North America, even though he was a Sikh. Singh's lawyers argued that his "Aryan blood" made him racially "pure" and therefore met the stipulations for citizenship. In 1923 the Supreme Court ruled unanimously that U.S. citizenship was reserved for whites only and that while Singh may have been born in Punjab, India, and claimed "purity of the 'Aryan' blood" and "high-caste" status, the Indian caste system was not sufficiently stringent in preventing "intermixture." This meant that Singh could not be included in the "statutory category" as a white person, and in any case was not Caucasian in the "understanding of the common man."[138]

As a result of the Supreme Court's decision to reject Singh's claim, the citizenship of A. K. Mozumdar, who was of Indian origin, was revoked. Singh, however, persisted, and through a loophole in New York state law allowing veterans of World War I to obtain citizenship, he eventually overcame the objections of the INS.

Japanese Internment

The Japanese, like the Chinese, had already experienced the barriers to citizenship that Bhagat Singh had to face. But during World War II, matters deteriorated rapidly for the Japanese. They were initially encouraged to move away from the West Coast in case they acted as agents for Japan, but many either did not wish to leave or were not welcome elsewhere, as Idaho governor Chase Clark noted: "The Japs live like rats, breed like rats, and act like rats. We don't want them buying or leasing land or becoming permanently located in our state."[139]

The eventual solution was to forcibly remove those of Japanese descent to ten large concentration camps in the western, mountain, and plains states, one of which was Idaho. More than 120,000, two-thirds of them American citizens, were relocated and spent the war years behind barbed wire under the watch of armed guards, cut off from their homes, their jobs, and their lives, without regard to their constitutional and legal rights. They were a "dangerous element," announced General John L. DeWitt, the head of Japanese internment: "American citizenship does not necessarily determine loyalty. . . . we must worry about the Japanese all the time until he is wiped off the map."[140]

The War That Realigned American Identity

World War II was a turning point for America, which emerged from it as the leader of the Western bloc against the Soviet Union. Within the United States, the war acted as a catalyst for social and political change. In particular, it altered the way America viewed itself, including its Catholic population, thereafter fully accepted. African Americans also played a significant role in the war, which eventually led to a desegregated military. These and other developments eventually gave rise to the civil rights leaders and movements of the 1960s.

Even so, the structure and ideology of primordial identity remained in place, causing confusion and uncertainty in the land and enabling men like Senator Joseph McCarthy to anoint themselves as witch hunters on the lookout for communists. The guardians of the republic in the State Department crumbled before McCarthy's gaze and ordered forty books removed from American libraries around the world, including *The Selected Works of Thomas Jefferson*.[141] Some books were burned. The spirit of this age is reflected in the film *The Good Shepherd* (2006). When a Mafia boss pointedly asks a white U.S. intelligence officer: "We Italians, we got our families, and we got the Church; the Irish they have the homeland; Jews, their tradition; even the niggers, they got their music. What about you people, Mr. Wilson, what do you have?" Wilson coldly responds: "The United States of America. The rest of you are just visiting."

John F. Kennedy's presidency pricked the balloon of the political invincibility of the Anglo-Saxon "American race." His immigration bill, which was signed by President Lyndon Johnson, allowed millions of people from all corners of the earth to share in the American experience. By then, revelations about the horrors of the Holocaust had dealt a death blow to the eugenics movement and Social Darwinist engineering. In short order, another war, Kennedy's assassination, and the deaths of leading activists would spark a civil rights movement that would tear the nation apart yet eventually bring equal rights and human dignity to the nation's black population, which it had to fight for every step of the way. Fortunately, enough white individuals lent support, companionship, and leadership in this struggle to uphold the universal principles of the right to employment, dignity, and human rights and to confirm that pluralist America was alive and well.

Camelot and the Return of Pluralist America

John F. Kennedy made a large impression on people across the world in the brief time he was president. I was one of them. Like most people hearing of Kennedy's assassination on November 22, 1963, I can recall where I was at that moment. The news reached me on the radio in my student rooms in England, and in a state of shock I hastened through the winter evening to the student's union. A gloom as dense as the fog had descended on me. The usually boisterous union was also silent. Some students had tears in their eyes.

Even then I was taken aback by the strength of my emotions. I had no direct link with Kennedy. I had not even been to the United States. Yet Kennedy was everything a young man could look up to—bold, articulate, humorous, wise, a visionary, and most important, a leader who embraced everyone regardless of their race or religion.

Kennedy inaugurated a new flowering of pluralist America, aptly captured by the term "Camelot." To me, America was then a land of giants, a land of John F. Kennedy, Robert F. Kennedy, and Martin Luther King Jr. fighting for equal rights for all citizens. These men were not speaking for Americans only. They were speaking for all of humanity. When President Kennedy spoke of putting a man on the moon, I did not hear him say a man of his nation or his religion. As a Muslim I looked up to America's great Muslim figures who achieved world superstardom in the 1960s, Muhammad Ali and Malcolm X, who was to be known as El-Hajj Malik El-Shabazz (see chapter 4). All these figures in their own ways would change the United States and the entire world. They all argued passionately for peace and pluralism. All except Ali were killed for their beliefs.

With the election of John F. Kennedy, American politics reached a watershed. For the first time in the country's history, a non-Protestant was president of the United States. The fact that he was an Irish Catholic would have been enough to enrage anyone affiliated with America's primordial and predator identities. Kennedy's championing of immigration and civil rights would have been the final straw for them. His overhaul of immigration policy, implemented in the Immigration and Nationality Act of 1965 (also called the Hart-Celler Act after the Catholic senator and Jewish representative who sponsored it), tends to be overlooked alongside his other far-reaching accomplishments: averting nuclear war with the Soviet Union during the Cuban Missile Crisis, launching America's space mission to the moon, implementing the Peace Corps and international development programs to assist the world's poor, and providing the impetus for the Civil Rights Act of 1964 and Voting Rights Acts of 1965, which greatly expanded opportunities for African Americans and minorities. The Immigration and Nationality Act reversed decades of immigration policies designed to block non-whites from the United States and granted millions of Asians, Africans, and Latin Americans the opportunity to experience the American dream. Kennedy, who was writing a book about immigration at the time of his death, did not believe the existing U.S. laws were in keeping with the ideals of the Founding Fathers. I have called Muslims coming from overseas, who benefited from Kennedy initiatives on immigration, "Kennedy's children" (see chapter 5).

Before Kennedy, it was almost impossible for Asians to get citizenship, as in the case of Bhagat Singh. Following the Immigration and Nationality Act initiated by Kennedy, the Asian component of immigrants arriving in America changed markedly: from 6 percent in the 1950s, compared with 53 percent for Europeans, to 31 percent in the 1990s, compared with 15 percent Europeans.[142] The percentages of Latin American and African immigrants also jumped significantly.

Muslim immigrants—doctors, engineers, students—took advantage of the act as well, arriving in the thousands from towns and cities in the Middle East and South Asia to participate in the unprecedented prosperity of the next decades. Though few realized it, these immigrants had an opportunity to become part of the American dream because of Kennedy. One beneficiary of this act was President Obama's father, who arrived from Kenya.

Kennedy idealized the Founding Fathers. In 1962 he told forty-nine Nobel Prize winners, "I think this is the most extraordinary collection of talent, of human knowledge, that has ever been gathered together at the White House, with the possible exception of when Thomas Jefferson dined alone." In a state dinner for President Ayub Khan of Pakistan held at Mt. Vernon in 1961, Kennedy remarked the two were the guests of George Washington, one of the "extraordinary group of men" who created the United States. He felt Ayub Khan understood what Mt. Vernon stands for, and he "hoped" the United States was living up to those ideals, which go beyond independence.[143] Tellingly, he did not refer to Plymouth or the *Mayflower*. He also said that Pakistan, too, had its own founding ideals that it was striving to live up to (for a comparison of the founding fathers of America and Pakistan, see chapter 9).

Trusting in Pakistan's ideals, Kennedy took the bold diplomatic step in 1962 of dispatching his wife to Pakistan as his envoy. It was a calculated risk to send his wife alone to a patriarchal and male-dominated society, where women were segregated in public. Pakistan had never seen anything

Jackie Kennedy, here with President Ayub Khan, was enthusiastically greeted by welcoming crowds in Lahore when she visited in 1962.   (John F. Kennedy Presidential Library)

like this high-profile female visitor, young, glamorous, and affable. When the queen of England visited Pakistan the previous year, the reception was cordial enough, but memories of British imperial rule still colored people's views: senior British officials and their wives were widely perceived by the South Asian elite as imperious and stiff and their gestures hinted at racial superiority. In contrast, Jackie Kennedy's easy charm and manners spoke of a pluralist America, quickly winning over the Pakistanis, who saw in her visit the expression of an alliance of friends, with respect and dignity on both sides. A photo from that time shows Jackie in Lahore standing alongside Ayub Khan in an open car, with smiling Pakistanis showering the visitor with rose petals.

Despite Kennedy's assassination, many of the causes he championed were pushed through Congress and enjoyed the support of the public for a few years. His brother Robert, who had already demonstrated his commitment to civil rights and school integration in the post of attorney general under his brother, now took on the mantle of pluralism, focusing intently on poverty and injustice at home and abroad and decrying the war in Vietnam. In 1968 Robert decided to run for the presidency. Not everyone was thrilled by this prospect: the associate director of the FBI, Clyde Tolson, hoped "someone shoots and kills the son of a bitch."[144]

In one election speech, delivered not long before he died in 1968, Bobby Kennedy stressed that a battle was being waged for America's very identity, that the dangers sprang "not just from foreign enemies; but above all, from our own misguided policies and what they can do to the nation that Thomas Jefferson once told us was the last, best, hope of man."[145] During the campaign, Bobby Kennedy became hugely popular among America's poor and disadvantaged. Shortly before his death, he had confidently predicted: "There is no question about it. In the next forty years, a Negro can achieve the same position that my brother has."[146] American society was, he recognized, making progress and would no longer "accept the status quo."[147] Four decades later, Barack Obama was sworn in as president.

Martin Luther King Jr., too, found inspiration in the Founding Fathers and frequently cited "that great American," Jefferson.[148] By using Jefferson's phrase "All men are created equal," King argued that civil rights was an inherently American imperative: "When the architects of our republic wrote the magnificent words of the Constitution and the Declaration of Independence, they were signing a promissory note to which every American was to fall heir," King said in his famous "I Have a Dream" speech in Washington, D.C. It was time, King said, for African Americans to "cash" the check written by Jefferson and others.[149]

Some, however, like the Nation of Islam, found King's emphasis on reconciliation ineffective (see chapter 4). For Malcolm X, whites were "devils," and the Founding Fathers "artful liars" who created "one of the most criminal societies that has ever existed on the earth since time began," and who wrote a document about freedom yet neglected to mention "they still owned you. . . . Who was it wrote that—'all men created equal'? It was Jefferson. Jefferson had more slaves than anybody else."[150] President Kennedy's assassination, he declared, was "chickens coming home to roost." Later Malcolm X would move toward Sunni Islam and adopt a much more conciliatory attitude toward America and its white population.

Following a similar path, Muhammad Ali initially rejected pluralism. "Integration is wrong," Ali said in 1964 upon joining the Nation of Islam. "We don't want to live with the white man; that's all."[151] By 1975, however, he had entered into Sunni Islam, realizing "there comes a time in every person's life when he has no choice but to forgive or he will be consumed by bitterness." Ali's journey to reconciliation, dialogue, and pluralism through Islam is contained in a Sufi message he quotes in his autobiography: "A heart enlightened by love is more precious than all of the diamonds and gold in the world."[152]

Nothing captures the spirit of Camelot better than Neil Armstrong's words on stepping onto the surface of the moon: "That's one small step for man, one giant leap for mankind." It was a triumph not for America alone, but for the human race. The same spirit was reflected in *Star Trek*, the popular television series, whose main assortment of characters, including aliens, explore the universe, not to colonize and conquer but to promote their ideals. The spaceship's crew included a Russian during the height of the cold war, an African woman (one of the first prominent black TV characters), and most recently a Pakistani captain. *Star Trek* might also be said to illustrate the successful transition of Scots-Irish primordial identity to pluralist identity. Here the Scots-Irish truly come of age and blossom into sympathetic global leaders. Captain James T. Kirk, a farm boy from Iowa, is named after the explorer Captain James Cook, the son of a Scottish farmer. *Star Trek's* tagline and mission statement come from one of Cook's journal entries: "Ambition leads me . . . farther than any other man has been before me."[153] The other tagline, "the final frontier," is from John F. Kennedy's "New Frontier" administration. Montgomery Scott, the lovable engineer who will do anything to give the captain warp speed and frequently enjoys a stiff drink, is also Scottish. The almost certainly Scots-Irish Leonard McCoy, the southern "country doctor," is frequently bigoted toward aliens such as Spock, making slurs about his appearance, physiology, and cultural heritage. Yet the Scottish elements in *Star Trek* give ship and crew their drive, energy, and emotion and help pluralist identity to triumph. America's real space program has also had its share of Scots-Irish: Alan Shepard, the first American in space, John Glenn, the first American to orbit the Earth, and Neil Armstrong, who wore a kilt while leading a 1972 parade though his ancestral home of Langholm in the Scottish border areas.[154]

Clinton and the Era of Excess

America by the 1990s had become the sole unchallenged superpower of the world and the "end of history" seemed on the horizon.[155] Bill Clinton, also Scots-Irish, embodied pluralist America in the last years of the twentieth century. He captured the ethos of the time: entitlement, indulgence, and excess (see chapter 6). Clinton is the American Bacchus, a Big Mac in one hand and Monica Lewinsky in the other, with the Stars and Stripes wrapped around him. It is also a time of change, with pluralism permeating society. Some of the biggest superstars—Michael Jackson and Denzel Washington— were or are black. But people seem to live in a bubble of deception, with little attention to the meaning of America or its alignment with the vision of the Founding Fathers. Noble objectives like liberty, freedom, and democracy are reduced to the right of individuals to indulge themselves in consumerism. The asymmetry between the very rich and the poor population struggling to survive is greater than ever before. One percent of the population is said to "control" more wealth than the bottom 90 percent of the population.[156] No one seemed to be particularly concerned about the poor and the homeless.

Gordon Gekko, the successful trader with slicked-back hair, dead eyes, and a cold heart in *Wall Street* (1987), captured the zeitgeist of the age with his mantra "greed is good." This is precisely the philosophy prevalent in the nineteenth century, except that now it shows little traces of philanthropy. Instead it favors consumerism, hedonism, and excess.

Beneath the surface of the new ethos, dark and dangerous currents were flowing through American society. Small bands of violent white men, intent on preserving their racial purity and independence, were willing to go to any lengths in this direction, even it if meant confronting the government and its law enforcement agencies. The 1990s brought the Oklahoma bombing, the Aryan Nations' plans for ethnic cleansing, Ruby Ridge, Idaho, and Waco, Texas.

The growing rage of whites is depicted in the film *Falling Down* (1993). The protagonist's encounters with society's crass commercialization, poverty, greedy Asian shopkeepers and aggressive Latino gangs in Los Angeles, alienation from his family, the loss of his comfortable job—all push him over the edge into a homicidal rage that ends with a killing spree. The final straw is the threat to English, his language, posed by those around him. He tells the Latino gang that if they communicated in "fucking English" instead of Spanish he would have understood them.

Popular culture glamorized vacant consumerism. Television's highly successful *Friends* and *Seinfeld* of the 1990s were about a seemingly endless succession of trivial day-to-day occurrences and temporary affairs. According to one of its characters, *Seinfeld* was actually about "nothing." Although ostensibly pluralist in nature, as just about everyone was being accepted on these shows, they lacked the gravitas, confidence, desire for knowledge, and willingness to push to new frontiers of the classic pluralist identity.

Homer Simpson is another product of the American consumerist age. Every American male can see something of himself in Homer, and that explains his immense popularity. If Huck Finn represents primordial identity, Hawkeye pluralist identity, Kirk a combination of the two, and Tom Sawyer predator identity, then Homer is a composite of all three American identities. He is primordial in his love for America and his family; pluralist in counting Carl, an African American, and Apu, an Indian immigrant, among his best friends; and predatory in being consumed by chauvinism, rage, envy, and greed, all of which can lead him to violence. The dizzying transformation from Hawkeye to Homer in just over a century is as good a metaphor for change and identity in American society as is possible.

Muslims and the Reassertion of Predator Identity

On September 11, 2001, Muslim immigrants from the Middle East and South Asia who had been attracted to and invited in by pluralist America, woke to find they had tumbled from their comfortable positions in the professional middle class. These Muslims had not studied enough history to know that this was but another side of American society. From the time of the earliest settlers, Americans have reacted with ferocity to any threat. The policy of zero tolerance is embedded in the deep structures of their society. Muslims saw that their friendly pluralist America had morphed into a minatory predator and were baffled.

In the wake of 9/11, George W. Bush and his kitchen cabinet of half a dozen white, Protestant males twisted the law to their predatory vision for the next two presidential terms. Co-opting enthusiastic but token members from the minorities and small groups of vocal commentators to join their bandwagon, this cabal seemed to advocate an all-out war with Islam, vigorously defending its right to use torture to keep the nation secure and to invade a Muslim country suspected of stockpiling weapons of mass destruction (see chapter 9). The terrorist threat provided the pretext for the Patriot Act. The spirit and content of the Bush administration's harsh actions were in keeping with the old predator identity of the Josiah Winslow and Andrew Jackson eras, except that now the targets would be Muslims. Dick Cheney, with his unsmiling face, cold eyes, and advocacy of torture, became the poster child for predator identity. Like their predecessors, these Americans did what they did while arguing that their actions were within the law.

In terms of the arguments presented here, it is relevant to point out the strong identification with contemporary Scots-Irish culture developed by Bush and Cheney. While Cheney has a Scots-Irish background, Bush, who has English and German blood and a background in New England and the Episcopalian church, chose to behave as if he was Scots-Irish from Texas. Born to privilege in Connecticut, the son of a sophisticated and well-educated president, Bush studied at Yale and Harvard, but everything he said and did in his political life was almost a conscious rejection of his Ivy League persona. Those who mocked him and mimicked him in the media depicted him as a Neanderthal man; he was characterized as the classic jock. Having met him at dinner at the White House on two occasions, I can vouch for the fact that he was far from the witless moron depicted in the media. He may have got many things wrong after 9/11, but the man I saw had the capacity to laugh at himself and make intelligent conversation. His strategy paid off: of the ten states with the largest

The "Terror-Free Oil" gas station outside Omaha displayed a prominent sign stating "Your Money → Non-TFO Gas Station → Oil company → Unfriendly Nation → Islamic Terrorism."

Scots-Irish population, Bush won all but one in 2000 with an average of 55 percent of votes cast.[157]

For Americans after 9/11, being patriotic meant invoking the memory of events on that day, which in turn meant remembering those who were responsible for the attacks. Just as 9/11 stirs anger, vengeance, a sense of unity, and outrage at being unfairly struck—the name Muslim conjures up images of the terrorists. Many people interviewed on our travels compared Muslims to Nazis, just as media commentators have done on numerous occasions.

The site of Ground Zero in New York City, which we visited, spoke to us of the challenges to American pluralism and the resurgence of predator identity. We found the entire location sealed off and vacant, still not reconstructed almost ten years later. The vacuum says something about America today. A cloud of uncertainty, of lack of confidence and hesitation, hangs over the epicenter of the 9/11 tragedy. There is no visible reminder of those who died on that day.

Just a year after the attacks, the United States declared September 11 Patriot Day, a national holiday honoring the victims of the terrorist strike. Even the celebrated Statue of Liberty now bears a plaque reminding visitors of 9/11. And of the hundred potential questions officially asked of new immigrants, one asks what 9/11 refers to. We were frequently reminded of 9/11 on our journey as well. The logo of the Museum of Patriotism in Atlanta showed the Twin Towers alongside the Statue of Liberty and some Washington, D.C., landmarks. A gas station in Omaha advertised "Terror-Free Oil" as a marketing ploy, and Steve Emerson's Islamophobic documentary *Jihad in America* was on constant loop inside. The gimmick proved successful for the store's Russian owners. A recent U.S. naval ship was named the USS *New York* and made of steel from the World Trade Center. "When it was poured into the molds on Sept 9, 2003, 'those big rough steelworkers treated it with total reverence,'" a widely circulated chain e-mail quotes U.S. Navy captain Kevin Wensing as saying. "It was a spiritual moment for everybody there." The foundry operations manager, Junior Chavers, says that when the steel first arrived, he touched it and "the hair on my neck stood up. It had a big meaning to it for all of us." The ship's motto, "Never Forget," is to be used for operations targeting terrorists.

With 9/11 now firmly entrenched in the American psyche, a chasm of fear separates the American and Muslim communities. That fear has turned 9/11 into a national symbol on one side, and Islam into a force of evil on the other. Prominent psychologists have diagnosed this national mindset as the "September 11 syndrome," noting that many Americans have an innate fear of anyone resembling the terrorists and that instead "people of all faiths—including Middle Eastern/Islamic groups—should fear the prejudices that have been aroused by the events of September 11."[158]

Pluralist America was rocked on its heels and unsure of how to proceed. Yet it worried about the excesses of the Bush administration, its incompetence, and failures in Iraq and Afghanistan, as it demonstrated at the polls with the election of Barack Obama. Although Obama appeared to represent pluralist America, he did little, in effect, to end the surveillance, extradition, and wars in Iraq and Afghanistan, or to close Guantánamo Bay, as promised during the election campaign. Yet Obama's capacity for bold action and high resolve were evident in his making health care reform a reality.

Clearly, America's different identities continue to vie for position in today's society. The white male, warns one commentator, is still a majority and yet to be reckoned with: "If you keep pushing this country around, you'll find out that there's an ugly side to the white male that has been suppressed for probably 30 years right now, but it really has never gone away."[159]

This chapter has set out the historical and social parameters of American identity. Now it is time to examine that identity through individual Americans. Chapter 3 introduces Americans of diverse backgrounds from across the land as they reveal their attitudes, values, and views of their Americanness and as they relate to one or other of the American identities. I intend to show that these different identities affect views about Muslims, as well as Muslim responses to American identity.

THREE

Searching for American Identity

"THESE ARE THE best and brightest in Los Angeles," said Madeeha Hameed, the Muslim member of my team. "I would say in all of California," she added, beaming with pride as a bright young Muslim herself. "This is the new Muslim leadership, young and dynamic."

It was a tough choice. I was in the third month of our fieldwork. Several other events were scheduled in different parts of the sprawling city, and I already had a packed day. I now hoped to attend a session of evocative South Asian Sufi music known as Qawwali, but Madeeha persuaded me to meet this group.

We had been to mosque after mosque and met imam after imam, so perhaps it was time to see this other face of the Muslim community. We might even find the future leaders of Islam in America, and where better to do so than in California, the self-avowedly most progressive state in the country, always embracing new ideas and searching for new horizons. Besides, I liked the name of the group, Hikma, which meant wisdom.

I wished to visit with offspring of immigrants to the West, often dismissed by people from the Muslim world for the way they represent Islam. Western culture, many say, is too strong and therefore influences young Muslims in America, turning them into an ABCD, or American-Born Confused Desi. (Desi, meaning "native," is a term South Asians use to describe themselves; for a fuller discussion see chapter 5.)

As we settled in the conference room, I saw a group of some twenty-five mostly young, smartly dressed professionals. The women all wore *hijab*s and some of the men had trimmed beards. Although the event had been organized in an office of the Council on American-Islamic Relations (CAIR), this was not a CAIR event.

As was standard, we distributed our questionnaires and showed some documentary footage we had been filming on our journey in order to get feedback. The footage covered two contrasting aspects of American society: Plymouth Rock and the *Mayflower,* and the Muslim Day parade in New York, with fierce anti-Muslim protests, including a smattering of Islamophobic remarks.

"How dare you? How dare you!" a young woman shouted, turning toward me as the video ended. Taken aback, I wondered who she was addressing and looked over my shoulder to the right and left. She was a convert of African American and white parentage. Another girl, of Native American and African American background, asked if the Plymouth video was a joke. "This is offensive! I'm outraged!" she yelled at me. The members of my group were baffled, especially Hailey, who not only considered Plymouth Rock and the *Mayflower* sacred symbols of America but also claimed descent from the ship's surgeon.

Plymouth Rock had triggered a cascade of angry emotions: "Who are you?" and "Where were you educated?" "Who is funding you?" Surprisingly for a group concerned with Muslim issues, no one mentioned the derogatory language in the footage of the Muslim Day parade, especially the abuse of the holy Prophet of Islam.

It quickly dawned on me that they had no information about my background. Worse, they assumed I was being funded by some conspiracy to propagate the image of Plymouth, which in their minds meant white Christian racial superiority in America. In vain, I tried to impress on them that a cardinal rule of anthropology is to depict society in all its hues, to hold a mirror to it, and that Plymouth was very much a part of the founding of this, their country, and therefore could not be ignored. Although it may have been uncomfortable, even offensive for some, I could not shy away from the importance of the first settlers at Plymouth in American mythology.

The conversation took an even more bizarre turn when for no apparent reason a Pakistani mentioned Jesus, one of the most revered and loved figures in Islam. Calling Jesus "the first terrorist," he mounted a scathing criticism of America: "America is nothing but the Jerry Springer Show. Only Muslims have morals, Americans have none. We reject American culture. Everyone has tattoos. This is rock-and-roll culture. They are all crazy."

At this point, a South Asian couple to my left launched an anti-Semitic tirade: "Why were 4,000 Jews missing from the World Trade Center on

9/11?" Jews, they said, had organized the attacks. "All Muslims in the United Kingdom want shariah for that country," said the husband of the half Native American and half African American girl. "So do we in the United States." The tension heightened when a bearded Pakistani who was married to the half Native American and half African American, remarked sarcastically, "Hand all your questionnaires to the white people." There was a spluttering of nervous laughter. The discussion was going nowhere. Everything I—or my team—said seemed to inflame them further until everyone seemed to be shouting at everyone else. After the discussion, one of the leaders of the group sounded apologetic: "You have to understand, we are all on the defensive. We hate that everyone thinks we are terrorists, and we have to answer for all that. They keep asking us to renounce terrorism; it makes us angry."

The Mad Hatter's Tea Party

When the team later compared notes, we all felt that we had just come from the Mad Hatter's tea party. Madeeha was crestfallen. It was difficult to make sense of the confusion, anger, and prejudice, especially alongside the exaggerated confidence. We could not help looking at the experience here in light of what we had witnessed in the Muslim world. From Damascus to Deoband, one of the most prominent centers of orthodox Islam, we were invariably received politely and in many cases warmly, whether in mosques or madrassahs. Even though Damascus, the proud capital of Syria, had recently been excoriated by the Bush administration and we faced some agitated questions about American foreign policy, the tone was neither menacing nor personal. In every case, adab informed the proceedings.

Adab was also present in L.A. at the largest Islamic center in California, where its director, Imam Muzammil Siddiqi, received us with courtesy, mentioned us in the *khutba* (sermon) at Friday prayers, and asked me to speak to the congregation. Afterward, dozens of enthusiastic Muslims wanted to support or help us in any way they could. Even the boys at the Islamic high school welcomed us and invited Craig to join them in their soccer game.

The adab tradition alone would have led us to expect the young Muslim leaders in Los Angeles to be more cordial, but their anger in the context of Muslims in America did not make sense either. One would have thought they would be helping their community chart a way to the future by building bridges with the majority around them. Instead, by attacking Plymouth and its symbolism, the young Muslims of L.A. were failing to understand not only the American temperament but also the formation of its identity.

Plymouth is a powerful symbol of American identity, evoking strong positive or equally strong negative responses (recall Malcolm X's statement, mentioned in chapter 2)—and must be taken into account by informed Americans claiming to be community leaders, for they need to know how that identity was shaped and defined. Only then will they—and Muslim leaders, in particular—be able to work out their community's location within American identity.

American Primordial Identity

Taken together, our interviews and encounters with Americans of diverse backgrounds provide an authentic and coherent picture of modern American society. To project and preserve the authenticity of these voices, editing and commentary are kept to a minimum. Many of them reflect primordial identity, and perhaps no one better illustrates its meaning than Sam Bailey of Florida.

Personifying Primordial Identity

So strong are Sam's feelings for his cherished America that he has felt compelled to express them in verse. Sam may not be in the ranks of America's great poets, but his patriotism comes shining through in his poems, some of which he read to the team. One titled "The 2009 Administration" was written to honor the change of guard in Washington, D.C., and the following lines provide its refrain:

> I love my country, as most of us do,
> So let's get together for the red, white, and blue. . . .
> By working and helping wherever we can.
> So let's all be true Americans, to the last man.

Sam talked to Frankie, Jonathan, and Craig in the general store he owned on Sanibel Island off the western coast of Florida near Fort Myers. Sam is known as the grandfather of the island and is somewhat of a local celebrity. Sam's family, which is Methodist, is credited with making the island a popular resort and owns its oldest hotel, which is reminiscent of the Old South, long gone but nostalgically preserved. We ate our first meal there in the atmosphere of a bygone charm.

Remarkably fit for his advanced years, Sam still carried himself like the National Football League (NFL) player he once was and reflected a pride in America in almost everything he said: "Well, I thank God every night that I am an American. We're the best country in the world. . . . And people want to come here, the immigrants. Someone who really wants to be here and wants to be an American, I'd welcome. But there's too many of them comin' here smuggling drugs and doing all kinds of things that are illegal. In the first place, anyone who really wants to come here, however long you think it takes, you must learn the English language." Sam has little patience for what is generally called the multicultural approach to diversity: "This crap they're saying that everything has to be written in German and Spanish, whatever, you know. And I hate this business calling people Afro-Americans. They're either an African or American. Goddamn it, if you're an African go back to Africa. When you come here and become a citizen, you are an American."

Sam had much to say about Muslims in America, which we found reflected a common perception of Muslims among proponents of primordial identity: "There are Islamics in our country that are American. And they're good people. I think they should speak the English language. They have a different image of God. Of course, I would prefer not to have the Muslims in here, unless they completely divorce themselves and become true Americans, not Afro-Americans, not Chinco-Americans, or whatever. In all those [Muslim] countries over there, some of those guys are complete idiots. They think nothing of blowing themselves up. We need to keep those kind of people outta here." Sam summed up the cardinal philosophy of primordial identity toward minorities: "You can marry and do whatever you want, and join any church, you can go anywhere you want to go, as long as you abide by the rules."

For Sam, the 1920s were the golden years, when society was affluent and America isolated. It reminded him of the more recent Clinton era before 9/11: "Things were rosy; everybody thought everything was going good. And then all of a sudden, somebody comes in and blows up two of the biggest buildings in New York City and kills 4,000 people."

Like most Americans, Sam was not only shocked but also furious at the attack on his country. He wanted a strong response and felt he got it in President George W. Bush's actions: "You can criticize Bush all you want, but if you think about it—they blow up two of the biggest buildings in New York City—there is not a great deal of security around is there? The FBI and the CIA . . . were just a bunch of Mickey Mouses . . . with their thumb in their ass, and Bush did something. He wasn't gonna be pushed around. And I hope this guy [Obama] has a similar attitude."

The most effective way to improve relations with the Muslim world, emphasized Sam, is to exercise America's military might. Though he conceded that it is a difficult situation, he believed what Will Rogers said— "You got a man and he's puny and people are gonna pick on him. And the guy who's strong, nobody's gonna mess with him." And he went on, "That is why battleships and weapons are essential: You don't wanna use 'em, but you got 'em. That's one of the problems we had with Jimmy Carter. I loved Jimmy Carter, I voted for him, but he's probably the worst president we ever had. His idea of doing something was, 'Naughty, naughty, naughty. Don't do that.' And then Ronald Reagan came in and said, 'You sons of bitches, if you don't straighten up, I'm gonna blow your Goddamned head off.' And we straightened out a few things overseas with Reagan."

Preserving the Purity of Primordial Identity

When the grand wizard of the Ku Klux Klan, Pastor Thomas Robb, and his daughter Rachel walked into my office at American University, they were not aware that they were going to be talking to a Muslim. Hailey, who had arranged the meeting, thought it better to focus on the subject of American identity rather than my identity in case they backed out. It had been difficult enough to confirm dates, and she did not wish to risk losing the interview. At one point, we had planned to drive from Memphis to Harrison, Arkansas, where Robb has his headquarters, but the interview was canceled because of an ice storm. But Hailey persevered. Interviewing the head of the KKK was an important part of the jigsaw puzzle of American identity. If Robb had qualms about meeting me, he did not show it.

While Sam Bailey represents mainstream American primordial identity, Pastor Robb represents one extreme version of it. His position highlights the conflict and contradiction that are inherent in primordial identity between the Darwinian principle of survival of the fittest and the ideas advocated by Jesus Christ. In Bailey's case, Darwin and Jesus are in balance, whereas in Robb's case, Darwin has prevailed. Robb was not even prepared to concede the one great virtue so directly associated with Jesus—compassion. For Robb, compassion is reserved for the white race, but white liberals show too much compassion, especially toward African Americans, and thereby compromise the interests of the white race.

Unlike his predecessors, Robb does not often call himself the grand wizard, preferring the title national director of the Knights of the Ku Klux Klan. An acknowledged leader of the Klan, he frequently refers to its other leaders, such as David Duke, as colleagues. We found him to be an unimposing man in an ordinary suit, and with a mild, even amiable air about him. He grew up in Detroit, Michigan, has a doctor of theology degree from the Rocky Mountain Kingdom Bible Institute, and has written approvingly of the politics of Joseph McCarthy. He is an ordained Baptist minister. His children have followed in his footsteps.

While Craig filmed our conversation, Rachel had set up her own camera to capture us filming them. Rachel is blue-eyed and blonde and speaks with passion on behalf of the Klan. She said little at first, but when she intervened later, her intensity contrasted with her father's more seasoned statements. Rachel runs a blog and is active in Klan affairs. Robb claims to head a gentle, upbeat, and friendly organization and to preach a message of "love not hate."

Robb has been a powerful spokesman for the Klan for thirty years and has been featured in local and international media. His website posts several concessions to his talents, including this quotation from London's *Sunday Times:* "An accomplished and charismatic speaker, Robb is viewed by civil rights experts as the most dangerous of the new breed of white supremacists because of his communication skills, political ambitions and his impressive ability to cloak the underlying message of hatred and intolerance in an avuncular garb of reason and logic."[1]

The website unfurls the Klan's new approach combined with the old prejudices, all too apparent in the heavy symbolism of its logo. The Stars and Stripes is visible, but the Confederate flag is prominent, with a Confederate sword and pistol superimposed on it. Behind, radiating light, is the Capitol dome. The heads of the presidents at Mt. Rushmore appear on the right—except that of Lincoln, who has evidently not been forgiven for emancipating the slaves. The website offers a catchy jingle, appealing to the Aryan race fighting for survival all over the world to defend the bloodline. The website also advertises small ceramic statues of a Klansman fully hooded in white, with his left arm outstretched in the familiar salute of the Nazis. One posted headline reads: "Obama LOVED by Communist Party, USA: They Are Thrilled at His Win!"[2] The "Communist Party," the post continues, is working through the "Socialist Media" in "portraying white people who love their Race as Evil Monsters! Don't forget the 22 Million White Christians Killed in the Marxist/Communist Revolution of Eastern Europe." The website accuses communists of infiltrating America through "Propaganda in the Schools," "Modern churches," and the "Liberal Entertainment Industry . . . ask why has God allowed this to happen. Could it be because America has turned its back on its white Christian foundation? We believe the answer is a resounding YES!"

For Robb, who is English, Scots-Irish, and German, his role models are Thomas Jefferson, Thomas Paine, Thomas Edison, and Patrick Henry. He believes Plymouth Rock is an icon in American history, symbolizing

America's foundation in Christianity: "The rock stands for the faith. Moses had the rock in the wilderness and so did Jesus. So this rock in our national history, our racial history, has deep meaning."

Robb believes America has two identities: the "old" and the "new" identity. The old identity extends from the settlement of Jamestown and Plymouth to the late 1960s. The old identity, he explained, was white. "No people of color in the Mayflower Compact or the drafting of the Declaration or the state constitutions. No people of color in the Constitutional Convention. Right up until the Civil War, thirty-seven states were in the Union, and thirty-one said in their state constitutions that the only way to be an American citizen was to be white. So you may think that's horrible—that's not the point—but that was the identity."

The 1960s marked the beginning of what Robb calls the new American identity. The crucial change was the passage of the Hart-Celler Act of 1965 by President Lyndon Johnson, which shifted the focus of U.S. immigration policy from mainly Europeans to people from other nations: "With that the demographics began to change and the new identity emerged. The old identity was white and Christian; the new identity is not what we wish it to be. . . . One of the signs of insanity is multipersonality disorder, and since 1960s we have been approaching this—we don't know what our personality is anymore." As Robb sees it, the only way to build strength is through unity, not diversity: "Diversity weakens the element, destroys the rock."

Quoting a *Time* magazine article of April 9, 1989, Robb asserted that as recently as 1967, 92 percent of Americans were white. With pain in his voice, he stressed their unfair treatment in history, at the same time noting the Supreme Court's support in the 1923 landmark case *United States* v. *Bhagat Singh Thind* (see chapter 2): "The identity was that the Supreme Court said you aren't white enough. That was the identity. There are many countries in the world that are exclusively black, there are Asian countries. There isn't one single white nation."

He was not sure that American pluralists like Martin Luther King Jr. and John F. Kennedy should be recognized as great Christians and great Americans, although they would be recognized as such in the new American identity. As for the Pilgrims and how they fit in, Robb was unapologetic: "I have a certain right to this nation on the law of inheritance. So my mom and dad pass on and are extremely wealthy, I have the right to it—not you, because you didn't earn it. We have a right to inheritance to what our forefathers created. The architects of America are those in Jamestown, at the Mayflower Compact, in Philadelphia in 1776, at the Constitutional

Convention in 1787. They were the founders of this republic. We receive it because of what some people did; nobody else contributed to it. The architects created the republic."

By fusing the first white settlers and the Founding Fathers, Robb was removing the distinction between primordial and pluralist identity. Yet evidence failed to support his simplistic conflation of the links between the two—though the former was the precursor to the latter. For Robb, American identity was frozen in time. He was not prepared to recognize the American pluralists of the 1960s and onward. As for American predator identity, Robb refused to even acknowledge its existence.

Explaining the origin of the Klan's name, Robb said Ku Klux comes from the Greek word for circle. Robb was reluctant to answer a question about membership numbers but did emphasize wide support: "The number of people who sympathize and join are two different figures, but they lead the same and bleed the same. We have a common concern about our nation."

Robb kept coming back to the subjects of slavery and anti-Semitism in the interview. He explained the freeing of the slaves after the Civil War in these terms: "Suppose you had a kennel and had 100 dogs, and you love those dogs, you pet them all the time, and someone told you one day that they were going to take those dogs, what would you say? Who is going to feed them? Who is going to take care of them?"

"Mr. Robb, but these are human beings . . . ," I replied, dumbfounded. Robb flashed back: "I understand that, I understand that, but you have to put yourself in the position of these people, those people. According to *Time on the Cross*, the concept of blacks being whipped didn't exist."

"Why weren't the African slaves shown Christian compassion?" I pressed. Robb gave what I suspect is a standard answer, without a trace of irony: "There is a historical element among white people that is a benefit to us—the element of compassion. White people have a greater sense of compassion in people, and so you find a need to help everybody that they can, even to their own detriment."

To further justify slavery, Robb gave the example of a black professor at George Mason University who is happy that he was brought here because he is better off than he would be in Africa. "There isn't a single nation in Africa that treats its black citizens as good as we treat black people right now, or from the beginning—housing projects, aid to children."

Rachel now intervened with possibly another standard argument: "We don't condone slavery; whites were held in slavery by blacks, blacks were held in slavery by other blacks throughout the South. Jewish people held blacks in slavery."

When I asked why Robb dismissed as a total myth four centuries of suffering endured by African slaves in America, Rachel interjected: "A slave lived better than the average free white person." Robb added, "The average slave had better health care, better working conditions, than the average urban white dweller as late as 1890. . . . It's terrible. I'm not endorsing it."

Did they know that many of those slaves were princes and chiefs and scholars picked up and brought here, I asked. Rachel was unrepentant: "Well, some blacks sold blacks into slavery, sold by their own people." But, I reminded them, "No good Christian would accept these kinds of conditions; no good Christian can endorse this." Robb agreed: "I'm not defending slavery. We should just try to separate myth and reality. The slave ships were horrible, lined up there; it's not good, it's horrible. What I'm saying is we have all these facts."

At this point, Hailey interjected with some acerbity: "So what about reparations?" Robb was dismissive: "We are not responsible." I repeated the question, as I thought it was important. He again denied responsibility. When pressed to at least acknowledge the pain and suffering of slaves, Robb would have none of it: "Acknowledge? I just gave them acknowledgment right here: they had pain and suffering." But the old was still better than the new: "I'm from Detroit, Michigan. I can't even go there anymore; it's not safe. I can't even go to the home I was born in because it's a ghetto, a major ghetto. My dad used to sell insurance, and practically all of the crime was found in African American communities. In the older America, these African Americans were safe. In the new America they are not. . . . An article by James Meredith in the Chicago *Star* said the worst thing to happen to the blacks were the white liberals."

Both father and daughter called the Klan's violent tactics a Hollywood creation and that "you need to go back twenty-five years to find a record of Klan violence." They blamed the Jews for depicting mainstream Americans and their values in a way that tarnished the image of Christians. Quoting a founding member of the Klan, Rachel explained: "In this state of chaos, we are trying to maintain law and order regardless of white or black and whether they are victims of black and white."

Several times, Robb and Rachel tried to shift the conversation to anti-Semitism. I suspect they assumed that any Muslim would harbor anti-Semitic sentiment. They were victims of their own stereotypes. Frustrated at my reluctance to go along with them, they returned to the subject of Hollywood, "which promotes promiscuity and drug abuse and trashes Jesus Christ and Christianity at every opportunity," the subtext being that Jews ran Hollywood.

But they saw traditional values being assaulted elsewhere as well: "There is this element that trashes Christianity that we as Americans once held dearly to, and these are the same people that trash the Klan. If you believe in home schooling, you are a potential terrorist. If people believe in the sanctity of marriage, then they are terrorists. If you oppose illegal immigration, then you are a potential terrorist. If you believe in the Bible, you are a potential terrorist. So this hatred is growing against everyone that espouses traditional values."

Even ordinary young white people have begun to raise doubts about their cultural legacy: "White kids are told to hate their past. Those who are telling us that are hypocrites. I can go across this country and name many organizations that are created around a person's identity, like Black Doctors Associates, Black Lawyers. You find many organizations like this, but any group that is white that is trying to create an organization on an identity is scrutinized."

Up to that point, the grand wizard had remained composed during the interview—but he seemed to lose his cool when asked about the Klan's hooded white robes: "I'm going to answer that in two ways. First I'll say I don't know its significance. It's like me asking you, 'Why are you wearing a tie?' Do you know why?" "As a matter of fact," I replied, "I'm wearing a tie because I was colonized by the English." He had no reply.

If our team assumed that Klan prejudices would automatically encompass Muslims, we were all surprised to hear Rachel's remarks about a Muslim friend of her husband's living in Arkansas: "He loves what we do, but it's a polite agreement to agree to disagree on faith." When asked what he thought of Muslims, Robb said, "They're all out there trying to kill us," adding that he meant this as a joke. Pressed to indicate what steps Muslims and mainstream Americans could take to bring their communities closer together, he reacted as though given an electric shock: "I'm not trying to bring them closer together. I don't want to. As long as they are here, fine, but I don't think a Muslim has the right to dictate our national policies, to construct our national personality."

As trained, my team sat impassively throughout the interview, knowing that any disagreement or disruption on their part would have defeated the purpose of our fieldwork. Yet I could sense their discomfort with Pastor Robb. Immediately afterward, Jonathan, who is from the South, recorded his emotions: "Meeting the grand wizard of the KKK was an unreal experience. I was shocked and nearly fell out of my chair when he made the statement about releasing dogs and comparing that to freeing the slaves. He said that other races should be separated, adding, 'The white man is destructive to their culture, just like the Muslim culture is destructive to ours.' Everything he said was exactly the opposite of what I was raised to believe. I've heard hate speech, but to be spewed in such a polite manner made it all the more sickening. He was a true silver-tongued devil."

I, too, was experiencing a storm of emotions. Had I been born in Africa rather than Asia and at a different time, I could have been one of the slaves brought across the Atlantic to be treated like a dog. The conversation with Robb triggered memories of racially abusive letters I had received at Cambridge University after appearing on national television. Most of the mail was positive, but periodically it would contain an anonymous exhortation such as "Go home, you black bastard!" To some in England, anyone who is not white is black.

Defending Primordial Identity in the Mountains of West Virginia

We saw yet another version of primordial identity in Benton Ward, a large, grey-bearded, Scots-Irish coal miner in his early sixties. Benton grew up in a log cabin in the West Virginia wilderness where life was a struggle. He toiled for years in a coal mine before saving enough money to start his own mining business, which is now successful. Despite this, he has refused to move out of his modest home. Benton is more inclined toward a quicker, less forgiving, and more aggressive response, including advocating torture, to any Muslim threat. Although representing primordial identity, Benton's words and actions suggest an affinity with predator identity.

Jonathan and Frankie spent a day with Benton outside the town of War, West Virginia, and then spent several more exploring the environs. At one point, I lost touch with them and grew apprehensive because of the cultural stereotypes in the American media about this region, particularly as portrayed in a film I had recently seen called *Wrong Turn* (2003), about a young group lost in this very area who are captured by inbred, illiterate hill men, dismembered, and thrown into cooking pots. Fortunately for the team, these really are stereotypes about a decent, hardworking, well-meaning, if rough, society. Benton was the embodiment of hospitality.

Having studied tribes for decades, I found the tribal character of this region and the adaptations to broader American culture particularly interesting. Benton's views made perfect sense in this context—age-old clashes between traditional tribesmen and central authority, certainly evident in the historical confrontation between the Scots and the English. In Benton, Scots-Irish ethnicity had become fused with a larger American identity to the point where it had become one and the same. Benton's ancestors may have come from the British Isles several centuries ago, but he still proudly carries their memory in his talk of revenge, honor, fighting, community loyalty—the basic tribal laws of Scotland. Benton's case proves that you can take the Scot out of tribal culture, but you cannot take tribal culture out of the Scot.

In the Darwinian thesis, fear ensures survival, and Benton talked about the role of fear in his society, which is a characteristic of primordial identity: "Fear controls every aspect of your life. If you don't have no fear, you don't have no control. You have to have a certain amount of fear. Usually it is instilled in you when you are a little kid, and that controls the rest of your life—you are afraid of the law, you are afraid of your wife, you might be afraid of your neighbor. You might be afraid to ride a motorcycle or drive a fast car. It's still fear and it controls what you do."

It is for this reason, Benton said, that he is concerned about Muslims: "The fanatics in Islam, they don't have fear, they don't care to die. To me, life is the most important thing there is. The last thing to go is your life, and that's the end. They might think there is something in the future; I basically don't; that's the end. Your soul may go on, but your body is gone."

Benton supported Dick Cheney's widely publicized advocacy of torture: "He's just saying what needs to be said." After 9/11, Muslims had perplexed and angered people like Benton. Muslims had unfairly attacked America out of the blue, and the code of revenge was uppermost in Americans' minds, which he explained thus: "If you kill one of my brothers, I'll kill one of yours, or kill you. If you rape my sister, I'll rape yours. It goes back to biblical times, an eye for an eye and a tooth for a tooth." Benton believed that the Ten Commandments should be the law of the land, the only law that America needs.

Benton said his ancestors came to America in the early nineteenth century, just after the major waves of Scots-Irish immigration. When asked why so many of today's military recruits come from Kentucky and West Virginia, he again tied it to the people's Scots-Irish background: "Around here kids grow up with parents that teach them that the price of liberty is to fight for liberty: don't let nobody take your liberty. They are free people. It goes back to their Scottish-Irish descent, where they were servants, subclass people."

Once in America, the Scots-Irish did everything they could to preserve that liberty, even if it meant fighting unconventionally. Benton revered Andrew Jackson because "he defeated the British, didn't he?" Jackson's often brutal tactics were of no concern to Benton: "I mean look at what Sherman did to the South; they burned it out. There ain't no fair way to fight a war. There's only one way to fight it, and it's full blast. There ain't no such thing as a fair fight."

When asked how best to improve relations between the United States and the Muslim world, Benton cited the example of George H. W. Bush, who wanted to keep things even. "The best thing to do is to set your agenda, say 'I'm going to do this right here, then I'm going to get my ass out,' and tell them, 'Look, if this shit happens again, I'll come back and do the same thing.'"

Benton was convinced that Obama's number one objective was to take everyone's guns and that the government's first step toward this goal will be to register their weapons: "That's where I draw the line from being a law-abiding citizen," he exclaimed, vowing to take on the government by joining an armed movement if it tried to register guns. "Look at what Hitler did to the Jews when they didn't have any weapons."

Thousands from this social and cultural milieu, like Lynndie England of Abu Ghraib notoriety, joined the army to escape poverty and express their patriotism. In the summer of 2009, the BBC interviewed Lynndie in her hometown in West Virginia. She had grown fat and bitter since pictured in the news as a slim girl, torturing and sexually humiliating Iraqi prisoners with a cheerful smile on her face. She had no remorse, no self-reflection to share. Speaking of the torture, Lynndie said, "It was nothing . . . compared to what they would do to us," not much worse than hazing at American universities. "If it helps get whatever information they might have, sure." In her view, she was doing what she had been brought up to do, which was to stand up for the group, defend its honor, and wreak vengeance on the enemy. Muslims were therefore fair game.

Pig Races in Texas

Another man with a Scots-Irish cultural background roused my curiosity because in 2006 he had started organizing pig races next to a mosque in Katy, Texas. The fact that he held them on Fridays, the day Muslims gather for the special congregational prayer, seemed to be a deliberate attempt to provoke the community. I was keen to hear his reasons for these actions and also to learn of the Muslim response.

When Hailey asked him for an interview, the man, Craig Baker, declined because he had already had enough attention in the national media, including a segment on *The Daily Show*. He agreed to correspond with her, however. Baker saw himself as an unwitting and innocent victim of an advancing Islamic civilizational front. He said he had read some fifteen to twenty books about Islam, including the Quran: "Anyone with a brain & an open mind that reads & learns about this religion will know first hand what America is facing in the coming years. Take a look at France or the Netherlands, or even England. During the time when I was having problems with my neighbors I received thousands of emails from all around the world. People just can't imagine the kind of things people were telling me about experiences with Muslims around the world."[3]

Baker warned Hailey that as he saw it, "Muslims will attempt to make inroads one step at a time. Take a look at what is happening in Dearborn Michigan, or how about Minnesota cause this is happening already right under our noses. Yes you can go right ahead and be complicit with them and someday and mark my words one day you will come to realize that their sole goal is to rule the world."

But Baker's problems were of a more personal nature, confronted as he was by the presence of a large, recently opened Islamic center next to his property where his family had lived for generations: "My grandmother who is 92 years old has lived in the same house for 60 or 70 years. Matter of fact my family roots go back before the civil war, actually while Texas was still part of Mexico my family was right here on Baker Rd." Relations between the new arrivals and Baker had got off to a bad start. At a public meeting "these same Muslim men called me a liar. So I got pissed off, they were f__ with my reputation, my livelihood, what do u expect me to do?" Baker's sense of honor was outraged, and he devised a plan to take revenge: "So I fought back by putting pigs on the property line, & put up a big sign that I would hold pig races." The Muslims retaliated by alerting the media and hiring lawyers. Baker even accuses them of "taunting my children" and trying to "run over one of my daughters. They started harassing my family, threatened to kill me, & my family." However, good sense eventually prevailed: "Now we have not had a pig race in a couple of years & things have settled down except for last week a Muslim man dressed in Middle Eastern garb tried to snatch my 12-year-old son."

Baker wrote again to Hailey, explaining his improved relations with a new group that has moved into the mosque, the Muslim American Society. Baker noted that one of the members of the previous group came and apologized to him for "calling him a liar." He took down his American pig race website. He says, however, that he still receives hate mail and feels he is a scapegoat for much of the anti-Islamic rhetoric targeting his organization. After receiving a letter from the mosque's attorney demanding that he take a derogatory website down and accusing him of being the creator, Baker denied it, "'cause anything I do I am always more than willing to put my name on it."

Baker said he still receives hate mail from the Muslims and that his son was almost kidnapped by one of them, an accusation the mosque categorically denies. Baker sent Hailey a copy of an email his brother received from an email address called "Football Players" with a request to forward it to him. The message called Baker "a fool. . . . What he is doing with the pigs and the signs and all his angry shit is doing ABSOLUTELY nothing to the Muslims in Katy. Every time he does something stupid like that, we just sit and laugh at how angry he is." The writers of the message proclaimed defiantly: "We are not going ANYWHERE! and i bet that makes his blood boil with anger, but the sooner he realizes that and that he is nothing but a laughing stock to us the better things will be for him. We will always be in Katy on Baker Rd, and no matter how many pigs he races, no matter how many Jewish/Christian signs he puts up." The message ended with the traditional Muslim greeting for peace: "Salam!"

To get the other side of the picture, Jonathan and Frankie tracked down the Arab spokesperson of the mosque in Katy, Yousef Allam, who saw the matter differently. Allam said that a member of the mosque had gone over to Baker's house to give him a clock as a gift. Allam denies outright that anyone wanted to kidnap Baker's son or had asked him to move off his land because the mosque has eleven acres and "we don't need any more." Unfortunately, Baker's antics became an excuse to abuse and speak out against the Muslim community. When the team asked Allam what he thought about Baker's motives, he replied, "I don't think it was the hatred at all. I'm not going to say it's prejudice. I'm not going to say it's racism. I think it's just ignorance."

Baker is not the only neighbor to be upset about the mosque moving in. One neighbor still blasts religious rock music at night and has hung Christmas lights that read "Jesus is Lord." Baker caught onto the idea too and put up a sign of the Star of David and a large cross. The most offensive manifestation of the backlash was a website carefully disguised with a website address almost identical to that of the mosque, meant to promote suspicion and antagonism toward the Katy Islamic Association. There was extensive use of hate material with language and cartoons that would be highly offensive, not only to Muslims, but to anyone with a sense of respect for religious pluralism.

When asked how best to improve relations between Muslims and mainstream Americans, Allam surprisingly took his own community to task. He did not seem to reflect any bitterness or hidden anger against Baker. For him, the Muslim community needed to be better informed and educated: "There's enough ignorance in the Muslim community that needs to be fixed, such as how you are supposed to act in a non-Muslim land." Allam also alerted his community to the necessary method of talking about Islam: "It shouldn't be an aggressive thing, because then people will think, 'Oh, they're trying to convert us.'"

Confronting Primordial Identity in Alabama

To see how it felt to be black in America, John Howard Griffin, a white man, darkened his skin medically and disguised himself as an African American for just over a month and traveled in the South. He documented his findings in *Black Like Me*.[4] That was a half century ago. Americans now have a black president. Much has changed, but some things remain the same. We, too, conducted a similar experiment in the same region. But in this instance, Hailey adopted a Muslim identity and did so with the simplest of operations—by wearing an *abayya,* a full black Arab dress.

Where Griffin experienced hatred, Hailey found curiosity and a mild antagonism. It seemed that while America was adjusting to Muslims after 9/11, tensions and misunderstandings between them had not entirely dissipated. Our anthropological exercise allowed us to take society's "temperature" through the instant reactions of people at airports and restaurants.

As we walked through Miami airport, we asked Hailey to walk ahead of us so that we could observe and film the reactions. A few people turned around fully to watch in disbelief, at times with a look of scorn. We then stood self-consciously in a security line winding its way around a small room. Overhead a sign stated that it was an FAA-rated best airport for security and customer service. As we passed through the X-ray machine and metal detector, Hailey was asked to step aside for a special check, although no one else on our team had been asked. She found the personnel friendly and considerate, and they explained that an additional check was required because her clothes were so loose. With a name like Ahmed, I thought I was the obvious choice for special scrutiny, but in this case Arab dress seemed to have trumped everything else.

The female official at the boarding gate was visibly agitated when we handed her our boarding cards. She suddenly announced that the plane could not take the extra weight of another five passengers—curiously, the exact number of the team. We stepped aside and watched four other passengers board the plane. We protested, but the official was unmoved. On seeing Craig with his camera rolling and our mounting concern, she had second thoughts, perhaps out of fear of a lawsuit or losing her job. She finally relented, and we boarded the plane without further incident.

If Miami, with its diverse ethnic communities, reacted so negatively to Hailey's Arab dress, what could we expect in Alabama? Jonathan, who is from Huntsville, had suggested we look for the answer in a small all-white town called Arab—pronounced AY-rab locally—because it met our requirements. The town was reputedly not too welcoming to outsiders and especially non-whites, he warned.

The team was pleasantly surprised by the welcome received in Arab, Alabama, pronounced "AY-rab" in the local twang. Hailey Woldt wore traditional Middle Eastern dress during the "cultural experiment."

We decided to have Sunday brunch at a barbecue restaurant on the main street. The restaurant was filled with families, groups of men in camouflage (perhaps just back from hunting), and older people. It was an entirely uneventful meal. Our waitresses were friendly in the typical southern style. As we left, we ran into a pleasant young couple coming from a nearby church. We stopped them and asked if they knew what Hailey was wearing. "I don't know. I wouldn't want to say something just to stereotype because I'm not that educated about it," the young woman said. When asked how many Arabs lived in the town and where to find them, the man quickly explained that the town was supposed to be called Arad after a man named Arad Thompson, but the name was misspelled.

It had been a brief and uneventful visit despite Hailey's dress. Yet the community was the embodiment of American primordial identity—all were white and Protestant. For Hailey, even the visit to the restaurant reaffirmed her faith in southern culture: "All eyes fixated on me for a solid five seconds. I gave a sheepish smile, and all went back to eating their meals. After that no one else stared, whispered, or asked me any questions. I was totally ignored. I walked into the adjoining room to go the restroom and had the same reception there, except one woman with big hair and big jewelry gave me a big smile. Being from Texas, I know the hospitality for which southerners are famous, but I also know that southerners may smile to your face, but think otherwise privately."

The media, said Hailey, suggest that all Americans are hostile to Islam and Muslims, and that the most prejudiced of them are southerners. She felt highly encouraged to hear the Muslims we interviewed in the South say they were by and large happier than those living in places like New York City.

Some of the criticism of our project and the team, in reaction to the CNN story about our visit, made it appear that "all we were trying to do," as Jonathan complained, "was to make the United States look bad. We were labeled as liberal egghead Yankees out to besmirch the South, which could not be further from the truth."[5] Yet the newspapers of Arab and Huntsville both wrote that our visit had been a positive experience for the town and that these types of exchanges were most welcome. They did wonder, noted Hailey, "whether I could have gone into the Muslim world wearing American clothing. What they apparently had not done was to look further into our project to see the visit we took to the Muslim world in which I did wear American clothing as well as traditional Muslim clothing and was welcomed warmly."

Hailey felt the incident with the flight attendant in Miami was not simply security or safety related but was in response to the clothing she was wearing: "We had bought tickets, checked in, and others were behind us boarding. Walking through the airport my fears were confirmed. People were turning around with open mouths and intense, hostile stares." Yet Hailey found that wearing the abayya also created a sense of defiance and confidence in going against the norm (see also chapter 6). It made her feel protected and secure, something she thought should not be dismissed lightly because in her usual clothes she often found men staring or acting as if they might touch her at random: "I also felt that a Muslim woman would be given a lot of peace in knowing that her identity was solidly and publicly declared, that the abayya had given her an identity and a feeling of uniqueness."

Adopting Primordial Identity

It is a sociological truism that the most fanatical believers in a cause are its recent converts, as can be seen among those who identify with American primordial identity but are of neither Protestant nor British descent. For those with a Catholic background like Sean Hannity, Glenn Beck, Bill

O'Reilly, Laura Ingraham, and Ann Coulter, this sociological association poses interesting challenges. They all noisily advocated war in Iraq, including Beck, who in the meantime had become Mormon, and paid no heed to Pope John Paul II's disapproval of the American invasion as a "crime against peace." Coulter, described as "Rush Limbaugh in a miniskirt," argued for an invasion of Muslim lands, the killing of Muslim leaders, and a mass Muslim conversion to Christianity.

Those who are neither white nor Protestant often bang the drum of primordial identity the loudest. Michelle Malkin, who has been called the "Asian Ann Coulter," enthusiastically endorses the World War II internment of the Japanese and demands the same for Muslims.[6] Geraldo Rivera, a colleague of hers on Fox News, finds her "the most vile, hateful, commentator I've met in my life, who actually believes that neighbors should start snitching out neighbors, and we should be deporting people. It's good she's in D.C. and I'm in New York—I'd spit on her if I saw her."[7]

Without indulging in pop psychology, Malkin's background may have something to do with her obsession with being considered fully American. Her birth name is Maglalang, her parents are Filipino immigrants, and she was subjected to racial abuse growing up in a small town in New Jersey. Ironically, those like Pastor Richard Butler of the Aryan Nations/Church of Jesus Christ Christian, who base American identity exclusively on being white and Protestant, would have difficulty accepting either Michelle Malkin or the Catholic Irish Sean Hannity. This may be a case of reductio ad absurdum, but it is sound logic for Butler and those who think like him.

Another example of someone who has adopted primordial identity but is of neither Protestant nor British descent is Robert Kraynak, director of the Center for Freedom and Western Civilization at Colgate University, in Hamilton, New York. Kraynak is a frequent contributor to the *Claremont Review of Books* and has written extensively on Thomas Hobbes, John Locke, and Alexis de Tocqueville. He said he was Catholic and of Czech descent and, at dinner with us, identified himself as a conservative.

Kraynak believes America had two foundings, one beginning with the *Mayflower* and the Puritans and the other with the Founding Fathers. The Puritan identity was English and Christian, and the founding identity was universal, humanist, and influenced by the Age of Enlightenment and ancient Greece and Rome. Both foundings had their roots in English common law. For Kraynak, true American identity is based in the English Protestant heritage. When pressed about color in America, he replied, "It's not white, it's English." But color and race were not sufficient to assume American identity; playing tennis and golf, attending a liberal arts college in New England, and learning to be a "gentleman with a conscience" were also essential requirements. Kraynak does not conceal his infatuation with the English and told us he felt a stronger affinity for Winston Churchill than for any Czech leader.

The *Mayflower* and the Founding Fathers were almost sacred symbols to Kranyak, and he drew on them to define Anglo-Protestant American identity, which would prevail even if African Americans and Mexicans became a majority in the United States; he was confident that they too would adopt the culture. Catholics like himself, he maintained, would become Protestant in their beliefs, and in three generations the Mexicans would have assimilated. This was the time it took his Catholic Czech family to assimilate into Anglo-Protestant culture. Furthermore, young Mexican children do not care about Mexico and wish for nothing more than assimilation, he claimed. Confident that there was no racism in America ("although you couldn't put that on the cover of the *New York Times*"), Kraynak pointed to the wide acceptance of interracial dating: "It is in the suburbs, where the assimilation to American culture is taking place."

Muslims, too, would assimilate by "becoming Protestant" upon interpreting the text for themselves, said Kraynak. "The American electorate's lack of knowledge about Islam is immaterial in a democracy. Americans are bound to confuse Muslims for terrorists because some Muslims are like that," a remark spiritedly protested by the Egyptian studies professor at our table, who said only a tiny percentage are disposed to terrorism.

Color, Kraynak acknowledged, is a reality in American society, but it is "perfectly normal for birds of a feather to flock together." It is understandable for people to reject a Muslim or a black leader such as Barack Obama because they feel such a person will not have their interests at heart or represent their values. Kraynak also felt "ordinary people" tend to be ill informed and most are inherently irrational. Two professors across the table, including the faculty dean, objected to Kraynak's arguments and implicit dismissal of American public education. As we stood up after dinner to leave, Kraynak shook Hailey's hand. Knowing how much he was in thrall of the *Mayflower*, I could not resist saying, "Bob, I'm sure you won't wash that hand tonight!"

Failing to Connect with Primordial Identity

Kraynak may have overestimated America's capacity to assimilate its minorities, as Frankie found on his visit to Chicago. Minority groups there, including the large Mexican population, were so destitute and still so "foreign" that culturally and psychologically they were living in their countries of origin and had explicitly rejected American primordial identity. The Mexicans lived in a cultural cocoon that extended block after block in Chicago's South Side. Frankie was looking for the house where his family had lived from the 1940s until his grandmother moved out in 2000. Over the years more and more of the old European Catholics moved out to the suburbs, and more Mexicans began to move in. What Frankie discovered was startling: "The neighborhood was now entirely Mexican and the signs were in Spanish. My family's house was boarded up, with broken windows and trash strewn across the yard. Mexican children playing near the house next door told me it was the 'gangsta' house. Other than the children, who spoke to me in English, everyone else spoke only Spanish."

When Frankie asked six children who had followed him to the steps of the house if they wanted to move to Mexico or remain in America when they grew up, "five out of six—in perfect English—replied that they wanted to move to Mexico. People said they had no problem with American culture but that the dominant white ethnic group 'hated Mexicans,' in the words of one teenager."

Frankie asked a bald Mexican man in his thirties wearing no shirt about race relations in the neighborhood: "With the whites things are good, with the blacks things are not good," he replied. When asked what he thought of American society, the man, who only spoke Spanish, looked at Frankie quizzically: "I don't know the culture of the U.S. One lives more or less as one would live in Mexico. We live here separate from the Americans."

Walking around the neighborhood, Frankie found some people were suspicious: "A pickup truck full of tattooed Mexican men circled the area trailing us and then pulled up on the curb beside us. 'You should ask *them* what they think of America,' snickered a teenage Mexican boy. I asked their group what the greatest threat to America was, and a girl, glancing across to the men in the pickup, whispered 'gangs.'"

For Frankie, "It was an emotional visit to my family's old neighborhood. I was left wondering if the Mexicans I met would 'assimilate' as my family did, or whether that was even a relevant question."

Meeting Native Americans

The first people to feel the full negative impact of American primordial identity were the Native Americans. Not only were they herded off their lands onto far-off reservations, but their very culture and character were reduced to a caricature, especially as depicted by Hollywood. Projecting the broad white Protestant narrative of American history, films glorified the idea of Manifest Destiny and the divine right of whites to settle the land. *Stagecoach* (1939), considered one of the classic westerns of all time, portrays white men as paragons of civility, addressing women as "ma'am" and tipping their hats to them. The women are the embodiment of loyalty and virtue. By contrast, the Indians are irrational, untrustworthy, and cowardly "savages" or "rattlesnakes," who attack the stagecoach because violence is in their blood. The film depicts Indian leader Geronimo as a supernatural terror who can strike at will anywhere and any time. But at the time the story takes place in the late nineteenth century, Geronimo and his Apache community had already been dislocated and confined to a reservation. *Stagecoach* distorts history by giving the erroneous impression of two equal powers in a fair combat with an uncertain outcome. In reality, the fate of the Indians had been sealed.

Andrew Jackson's view of the Indians as "savage dogs" to be exterminated had become the philosophy of the age. Not even the near-total demise of the native population by the turn of the century was able to quench the thirst of American predator identity, as illustrated in this 1890 newspaper piece by L. Frank Baum, the Scots-Irish and German author of *The Wonderful Wizard of Oz:* "The Whites, by law of conquest, by justice of civilization, are masters of the American continent, and the best safety of the frontier settlements will be secured by the total annihilation of the few remaining Indians. Why not annihilation? Their glory has fled, their spirit broken, their manhood effaced; better that they should die than live the miserable wretches that they are." Baum shortly after reiterated his call to "wipe these untamed and untamable creatures from the face of the earth."[8]

U.S. commanders who had fought the Indians became denizens of the new imperial America and carried their philosophy onto the world stage. The Scots-Irish general William Rufus Shafter, whose nickname, Pecos Bill, later became immortalized in American folk tales, expressed the philosophy of predator identity in reference to democracy and progress in the Philippines while discussing America's acquisition of the country: "It may be necessary to kill half of the Filipinos in order that the remaining half of the population may be advanced to a higher plane of life than their present semi-barbarous state affords."[9]

The desire of predator identity to remove the Indians from the face of the earth persisted well into the twentieth century. In the aftermath of a 1973 firefight in which U.S. marshals killed two Indian activists at Pine Ridge Indian Reservation, South Dakota attorney general candidate William Janklow exclaimed that "the only way to deal with the Indian problem in South Dakota is to put a gun to the [American Indian Movement] leaders' heads and pull the trigger."[10] Janklow, a former U.S. Marine, would go on to serve as South Dakota's attorney general, governor, and representative in Congress.

The plight and character of the Indians were all too evident on our visit to the Hopi reservation, deep in the state of Arizona. We drove for hours through spectacular desert landscapes enveloped in silence and devoid of shops or neon signs. Far from the sights and noises of modern America, everything here seemed authentic and of the soil, giving us a therapeutic feeling—especially after driving straight from the bright lights, constant noise, and artificiality of Las Vegas. The views at sunset are unmatched for the grandeur of their vistas. Once the sun goes down, the stars glittering above in the clear black sky seem so close that you could reach out and touch them.

Our destination was the village of Oraibi, which sits on a plateau overlooking a large plain. Oraibi is said to be almost a thousand years old and the oldest continuously inhabited settlement on the continent. It seemed as though we had stepped back in time.

The material poverty of the village took even me by surprise, accustomed as I was to seeing such sights in rural Pakistan. It was hard to believe I was in America. The mud and brick houses were crumbling with rubbish scattered around them. Oraibi has refused any signs of modernity, so there was no electricity, plumbing, or telephones. And we were not allowed to take photographs. Cars were permitted, but the one or two we saw were dilapidated models standing on cinder blocks. Subdued dogs slunk around sniffing the rubbish heaps. Some men wearing worn clothes tried to sell us shoddy local crafts.

We visited the modest house of Myrtle, a matriarch born in 1934. In the main room—which served as bedroom, kitchen, and living room—she proudly displayed pictures of her grandchildren. She had twenty grandchildren and fourteen great-grandchildren. "See, I'm rich," said the tiny old woman, now blind and barely able to walk. Two of her children were serving in the American army in Iraq. As we left, she cried out, "I hope you come again!" Our Navajo guide George, or Sun Turtle, tried to give her twenty dollars to help out, but she refused to take it. Myrtle's hospitality and dignity in the face of infirmity and poverty confirmed the spirit of her people—now in a state of impoverishment while clinging tenaciously to their identity. The government had deliberately settled their ancient enemies, the Navajo, in barren land around the Hopi to finish them off, but the two tribes "did not play the white man's game."

George "Sun Turtle," a Native American, was the team's guide on the Hopi reservation outside Flagstaff, Arizona, where anthropologist Akbar Ahmed saw firsthand the struggle between a native population and modernity.

On the way back, George expounded on the devastation brought by the Europeans. Words like "sad" and "sorrow" permeated his stories of the white man's dealings with the Indians, with the trails of blood, blankets infected with smallpox and distributed among the tribes, and entire tribes wiped out. George knew American history only through the actions of the military toward the Indians. Americans, said George, deliberately demeaned Indian women by calling them squaw, a word derived from Indian languages and commonly translated as a woman's genitalia. Hollywood made sure that "squaw" became part of the American lexicon.

George talked of the ravages brought by "fire water," or alcohol, and it was not uncommon for Hopi we met to immediately tell us they did not drink it. George was bitter about the Indian schools where children were forced to "assimilate" into American culture, mentioning with sorrow Lieutenant Richard Henry Pratt, who developed the first such institution in Pennsylvania. The U.S. government dragged children from their homes and took them to these schools, said George, and "if we got caught speaking our language we were whipped, punished. They cut our hair and said 'Christ loves you.'" It would not be until the 1960s that the Hopi would be allowed full voting rights in American elections.

As an anthropologist studying tribes, I saw among the Hopi a native population making a desperate and heroic effort to hold back the tidal wave of modernity at great cost. What impressed me was their integrity. They were prepared to live on the margins of American society rather than compromise. I wondered how long they would last before they, too, were absorbed into mainstream American culture.

American Pluralism

American pluralism encompasses a wide range of people: whites, African Americans, Asians, Protestants, Muslims, Catholics, Jews, Mormons, and more. If Benton Ward represents primordial identity veering toward predator identity, some rooted in primordial identity can also veer toward pluralist identity. One example is Joanne Herring, a philanthropist from a prominent Texas family, who figures prominently in the film *Charlie Wilson's War* (2007), in which she is played by Julia Roberts. Together with Representative Charlie Wilson, she worked tirelessly to arm Afghan resistance fighters during the Soviet invasion and occupation of Afghanistan and therefore helped to expedite the collapse of the Soviet Union. Her husband was chair of Houston Natural Gas, which later became Enron (she says he had nothing to do with the company's later debacle).

As a Pakistani, I found Joanne particularly sympathetic because of her role as honorary Pakistan consul general in Houston in the 1980s. It was an unlikely choice, but a shrewd one. This intelligent and charming petite southern belle brought a rare devotion and passion to her post.

Ambassador of American Pluralism

We were invited to meet Joanne in her elegant apartment in Houston. The meeting had been facilitated by our mutual friend, the renowned novelist Bapsi Sidhwa, who also lives in Houston. Bapsi had given a dinner in our honor and told me that the film should have been called *Joanne Herring's War* because she was the brains and drive behind Charlie Wilson.

Joanne has a confident grasp of world affairs and can reduce complicated events to simple ideas. She recounted her frustration in the 1980s as she watched events unfold in far-away Afghanistan. Although Jimmy Carter called the conflict a tribal war and did not want to get involved, Joanne was determined to show Americans the significance of the Soviet invasion. She recounted the geopolitics of the Soviet invasion: "At that point, the Soviets were even flying over the border and shooting Pakistanis. President Zia-ul-Haq of Pakistan couldn't do anything to protect the Pakistanis because the minute he retaliated in any way, that was exactly what the Soviets wanted him to do and then whack! And of course what the Soviets were interested in was not Afghanistan or Pakistan. They were interested in the Straits of Hormuz. They wanted the warm waters and they wanted those straits. They could be effective, you see—two tankers at that point sunk in the Straits of Hormuz and the energy to the United States was cut off."

Joanne could not conceal her disappointment that the Americans left so abruptly following the Soviet withdrawal from Afghanistan: "It is such a terrible tragedy that we just walked out and left these wonderful people with a ruined country and no money. You can't rebuild. It was terrible. When you leave empty shoes, they are rarely filled by the good guys, and that's what happened with the Taliban." She compared the Taliban youth to young men plucked from their homes in conquered countries and raised to be loyal infantry like the Ottoman Janissaries: "And they became top fighters. . . . That's what the Taliban are. They're the children, taken into these schools, and taught only to be loyal to one another, and the Muslim religion—but in a bad way. And how else are they like the people in America? They're no different in Pakistan and Afghanistan than on our street corners. What are street gangs? Disenfranchised children whose parents have abandoned raising them correctly. And who are they loyal to? The drug lord and each other. See, this is the same all over the world."

Joanne admired Ronald Reagan as president. At the time she was working with Representative Wilson to fund the mujahideen, I was a Pakistani administrator on the border with Afghanistan. In Pakistan we believed that we could rely on Americans and that they would stand by their friends. The picture of Reagan honoring the mujahideen in the White House captures the president's respectful relationship with the Muslim world. He called them "the moral equivalents of America's Founding Fathers"—the greatest compliment an American can give.[11]

Like Benton, Joanne was a fierce patriot. When I asked her what it meant to be American, she smiled: "You are asking me some questions that I have never thought of before in my life. They require thought." Joanne was "a southerner first, then a Texan, and then an American," adding, "We're all a little tribal." Unlike Benton, who felt Muslims lack honor, Joanne saw a great deal of honor among them and even similarities between Muslims and the southern ethos, especially pride in family. Joanne said that this sense of honor was still very strong in the South, and that southerners do not speak about it except to each other.

Joanne did admit that southerners lose their temper too often and could learn from Pakistanis: "I never saw any Pakistanis lose their composure or their temper. It's the most beautiful quality." Yet manners are still valued in

President Ronald Reagan receives Afghan mujahideen at the White House in 1985, declaring, "These gentlemen are the moral equivalents of America's Founding Fathers."

the South: "We must be ladies and gentlemen. And that is very important. And you try to cultivate that in your children. The North does not cherish that as much."

Benton and Joanne also differed in their choices of role models: Andrew Jackson versus George Washington, whom Joanne claimed as a great uncle many generations back, calling him Uncle George: "He continued to do what he thought was right for our country and then he changed the world when he turned down the crown. No one ever thought that one would turn down being a king, but he did, and in doing that he changed the thinking of the world. He continually tried to be what he said he was, which I believe is the Christian way."

Joanne was an unapologetic defender of the Christian nature of America and thus of primordial identity. She found a great deal of discrimination against Christians today, whereas other religions have greater freedom in practicing their traditions and prayers: "We would never expect to have a Christian prayer said at a Muslim event, in a Muslim country in front of their Congress. If you want a Muslim prayer, you should have it. It's your country. We consider ourselves a Christian country and now there's pressure to take Christian prayer out of our Congress. Throughout America's history we've always had prayer in Congress, and this is sad for us."

Joanne had warmed to us quickly and spoke frankly about Islam, "a lovely religion that teaches many wonderful things . . . but sometimes, you are not as forgiving as Christians are." She also shared some amusing anecdotes from her experiences in Pakistan to illustrate the cultural challenges she faced. Knowing little of Pakistan's traditions, she made "every mistake in the book," but Pakistanis overlooked them as she was trying to do her best. During a state dinner in her honor, "we sat down to enjoy this fabulous dinner and placed in front of us was soup. But no one lifted a spoon! We sat, and we sat, and we sat, but no one started eating. In our country, the hostess lifts the spoon first. In your country, the guest of honor does. After five minutes, I said, 'Oh, I hope that this is what I should do.' So I picked up my spoon, and then everybody picked up their spoon."

Joanne's interactions in the Muslim world were not restricted to Pakistanis. Female members of the Saudi royal family saw her as a potential convert to Islam and even persuaded her to join them in Muslim prayer. Affable as ever, Joanne went along to please her hosts while not intending to compromise her own faith:

"I had a marvelous experience one afternoon with three Saudi princesses. They were the daughters of King Faisal. They picked me up in a beauty shop and they invited me to come home. This was the first family of King Faisal, and they decided they were going to convert me to being a Muslim that afternoon, and it was the most beautiful experience of my life. We couldn't speak to each other. They would talk to me in Arabic and I'd talk to them with my hands. And what we all ended up doing is talking very loudly. . . . Then, in came the prayer rugs. So I said, 'Okay, Lord, you got to understand that I am here and I can't explain to these princesses, so I'm going to do my best to be a good Christian. I'm certainly not converting to being a Muslim, but I respect this religion and I love these ladies, so I'm going to do my best.' So the ladies pull me down on the prayer rug and squished my nose into it, and it was just lovely. And I said now, I'm really very glad to do this, and I think it's a beautiful thing that you do." Joanne reiterated that she had never seen "anything but goodness in Muslims."

Joanne's intelligence and charm were infectious. Craig, for one, felt that Hollywood had not done her justice by portraying her as an American socialite interested in lavish parties, the latest fashion line, and capitalistic endeavors: "The Joanne I met in Houston came across as a much deeper person concerned with the general well-being of not only the ideals of her country but also the people of Afghanistan. She surprised me with her intelligence, her depth of knowledge in tribal codes, and the critical steps that must be taken to defeat the Taliban in the current war." Craig's preconceived perception of her as a conservative, hard-liner Republican proved wrong: "Rather, she represents the best of America— the compassionate, inquisitive, and curious citizen concerned with justice and human rights."

Hailey found Joanne especially inspiring as she reaffirmed Hailey's own sense of identity by demonstrating that she could be Texan, Christian, and yet an authentic ambassador for different cultures: "Most people assume a beautiful, blue-eyed, blonde Texan could not put together a visionary and near-impossible scheme that helped to bring down a superpower. She also overcame the stereotypes of Muslims. She saw them as humans with dignity, grace, and intelligence and saw them as equals. Joanne has shown that incredible things can happen when Muslims and Christians work together and that anyone from any background can do it, too."

The Fugitive from Fox

Professor Jane Hall of American University is another charismatic woman rooted in primordial identity whose experience at work, where she rubbed shoulders with some of the most famous of those associated with American predator identity, forced her to rethink her own. A noted American journalist, Pulitzer Prize finalist, and former associate editor of *People* magazine, she made a spectacular exit late in 2009 from the Fox News stable of contributors after working with the network for eleven years as a regular fixture on Bill O'Reilly's show. She had started receiving hate mail for her views, which to her colleagues and viewers sounded suspiciously pluralist. Her exit came after intense soul searching and anguish. She is moving along a path that, I suspect, will lead her to pluralist identity.

Hall is a Texan of German Catholic and Scots-Irish Baptist background but was raised Episcopalian by her parents as a compromise. She was emboldened in her decision because she sees herself as coming from a history of Texas pluralists. To Hall, American identity is "citizenship" as well as a "shared mission that we are all in this together," of "certain values and traditions," a "patriotism and love of country and a sense of optimism." "You can make it here," Hall said, summing up the definition of American identity. As a Texan, however, she also acknowledged the "lost history" that occurred with "western expansion."

From her vantage point at Fox, she noticed "the definition of America changing" after Obama's election, giving rise to a "scary nativism driven by people's fears about the economy, the government, and internal threats." She found voices like hers marginalized and the language of others, such as the "demagogic" Glenn Beck, becoming "vicious and incendiary." She made the decision to leave: "The people at Fox were shocked that I was walking away, because Fox had never had that happen before."

Hall's decision made headlines, and she was predictably singled out by Beck, who had emerged as the raging bull of American predator identity and towered like a colossus in the media. Beck was outraged that Hall, whom he dismissed as an "idiot," had called his language scary, when, he said, he was only "speaking the truth, pointing out facts, and asking simple questions" in the tradition of the Founding Fathers. Why was he being called dangerous, he asked, when "there are communists, Maoists, socialists, Marxists, anti-free market people in and around the United States government who are redesigning our government."

Despite the enormous personal cost, Hall is happy she made her decision. She warned of the levels of hate she found in the media: "The climate is rewarding people who are fringe. It is ugly, especially with the first African American president in office. People are profiting from this hate speech. People like Rush Limbaugh are demonizing Obama in a way that is frightening. They should not be saying things that will drive some borderline person to do something."

Here, we turn to de Tocqueville, who, once again, seems so current in his observations, this time on the state of the American media. American journalists, he wrote, "attack coarsely, without preparation and without art, the passions of those whom it addresses, to set aside principles in order to grab men." He adds, "Their education is only sketchy," and "the turn of their ideas is often vulgar."[12]

The Compassionate Christians and Pluralism

In the wake of 9/11, the Muslim community in America became isolated and misunderstood, yet this landscape began to change with the help of Bishop John Chane of the National Cathedral in Washington, D.C., and Ambassador Doug Holladay, who served as President Reagan's special ambassador to South Africa. Both are of English and Episcopalian background, and I met them separately not long after 9/11 to see what could be done to reach out to the Muslim community. They had never met a Muslim before, and we quickly became friends.

The bishop worked with Senior Rabbi Bruce Lustig of the Washington Hebrew Congregation to create the First Abrahamic Summit (see chapter 7). The bishop, the rabbi, and myself formed a partnership to promote Abrahamic understanding and goodwill. We have spoken at the National

Press Club, the National Defense University, and the National Cathedral to large audiences. Every year on or around September 11, we lead a Unity Walk down Massachusetts Avenue that links synagogue, cathedral, and mosque. In 2005 the three of us received the First Annual Bridge Builders Award given by the Interfaith Conference of Metropolitan Washington.

For me, two of Bishop Chane's initiatives confirm his true spiritual boldness and compassion: a Christmas card he sent out in 2003 and the 2004 Evensong at the National Cathedral dedicated in my honor (see the Epilogue of *Journey into Islam*). Bishop Chane's card was the perfect Christmas gift. In it, he unequivocally acknowledged Muslims as part of the Abrahamic tradition: "The Angel Gabriel was sent by God to reveal the sacred Quran to the Prophet Muhammad."

The bishop's acknowledgment of the sacred nature of the Muslim holy book and the prophethood of Muhammad constitutes a theological earthquake. Consider the cultural context of the time. The Reverend Franklin Graham, who offered the invocation at President George W. Bush's inauguration, called Islam "a very wicked and evil religion." Islam's God was not the God of Christianity, he said. The Reverend Jerry Vines denounced the Prophet of Islam as a demon-possessed pedophile. For Jerry Falwell, the Prophet was a terrorist; for General William Boykin, Muslims were idol worshippers.

Not everyone was pleased to see Bishop Chane's hand of friendship stretched out to the Muslims. He was flooded with hate mail, some of which he showed me. The abuse and anger were frightening, but he remained strong in his conviction that he was doing exactly what Jesus would have done in a similar situation.

Jesus inspires Ambassador Doug Holladay as well, but in a different way. Some of Doug's thinking and many of his friends are influenced by evangelism. I certainly owe him many thanks for bringing Jonathan Hayden to my attention. Several years back, when I desperately needed an assistant, Doug mentioned the son of his good friend Neb Hayden. I had asked for a responsible, hardworking young assistant, and Jonathan has lived up to expectations.

Doug and I wrote editorials together and appeared in many forums after September 11. We cofounded the Buxton Initiative, which in the next few years generated seminars, conferences, and publications reaching out to hundreds of influential people in the country. Buxton was supported by two of Doug's remarkable friends who also became mine—Steve and Jean Case. Their social and religious background was similar to Doug's, and, like him, they were eager to promote understanding. The Reverend Billy Graham, America's most famous evangelist leader, presided over their wedding.

When I asked Doug what American identity meant to him, he replied, "E pluribus unum," one out of many. The Founding Fathers, Doug believes, were very clear that America was not a Christian nation but one that allows diversity and freedom of expression and worship. Even so, as America is becoming more textured and diverse, he thinks some are feeling threatened, that these Americans perceive the United States as once a Christian nation, but it no longer is. In his view, "It never was a Christian nation, but the general populace was Christian. Now that things are changing, I would say that . . . you should not resist the change, embrace your own faith, but reach out to this wonderful salad bowl called America."

Doug's own faith is Episcopalian, which, he said with a chuckle, some refer to as religion in its mildest form, although he identifies more with people like C. S. Lewis, the Oxford scholar, "who really saw his faith as practically engaging, very personal orthodoxy. For me, it's less about the denomination and more about the bigger themes; for me, it's seeing the scriptures as the source of authority; for me, it's understanding a personalized relationship with Jesus Christ; for me, it's saying that everyone, *everyone* on this globe is made in the image of God, and I have a responsibility to lay my life down for them."

On our journey we were often asked if Muslims, Christians, and Jews worshipped the same God, and I asked Doug for his thoughts on this question: "The more I'm on this journey, the more I'm comfortable with mystery. . . . Theologically, in the Abrahamic faiths, I must say I'm very comfortable with our monotheistic approach, that there is one God, the true God. I think where we differ is the expression: you know, you would see Jesus as a great prophet, I would see him as the incarnation. But I believe at the end of the day, the God of Abraham is the one that we all cry out to, and He is making sense of our lives."

The bishop and the ambassador had shown us how those who embody primordial identity can in fact become the best representatives of pluralist identity. At a critical time in their nation's history, John and Doug had stepped up to provide much needed leadership and direction. I also count my young team—both the Catholics and the Protestants—in the ranks of compassionate Christian pluralists. Like John and Doug, they were at once the best of Americans and the best of Christians.

When I meet such Christians, I appreciate the wisdom of a Quranic verse well known to Muslims: "And you will find the nearest in love to the Believers

[Muslims] are those who say, 'Verily, we are Christians.' That is because among them are priests and monks, and they are not proud" (Surah 5:82).

Although some Christians and Jews are not prepared to accept a relationship between Islam and their religions, Islam has always seen itself in a direct line from the Abrahamic faiths. The Quran, sacred to Muslims, says this about Jews and Christians: "We believe in God, and in what has been revealed to Abraham, Ismail, Isaac, Jacob, and the tribes, and in [the books] given to Moses, Jesus and the prophets from their Lord: We make no distinction between one and the other among them, and to God do we submit in Islam" (Surah 3:84).

An American Pluralist Sheikh

Muslims, too, are adapting to and citing American pluralism as *the* identity for them. Sheikh Hamza Yusuf, a white convert and star of the Muslim community, reflected on American identity in San Francisco when my team and I spent the evening with him at his home. When we arrived, Hamza showed us his extensive collection of books on Fiqh (Islamic law), literature, philosophy, and American history. He joked that unlike human beings, books seem to have no problem in sitting side by side, despite the very different ideas inside them. He said he had been reading Plato that very morning for inspiration.

With his sharp Western features, thick dark locks, and shaped beard, Hamza cuts a debonair figure. His parents were scholars of Greek origin, and Hamza was brought up in an atmosphere of ideas, books, and free thought. The family thrived in the intellectually exhilarating atmosphere of San Francisco. He is the Western media's poster child for an Islamic scholar who also represents American pluralism.

We were seated on carpets by a comfortable fire, and a faint smell of musk and incense permeated the air. Like Socrates with his disciples or a desert chief holding court, the sheikh sat in our midst supported by a high-backed cushion with his back to the fire. The sheikh's Mexican wife, wearing the hijab to indicate her conversion to Islam, had prepared dinner for us. Their young son watched the proceedings quietly but with interest.

When asked what being an American meant today, Hamza smiled, his eyes twinkling. "Fear and stupidity," he replied. But he also gave us a more philosophical answer, that America was "an experiment" in an attempt to break from the past, from the political decadence and tyranny of Europe. The idea of the Founding Fathers, he explained, "was to have a country in which religion was not forced upon people, but was something they could choose for themselves. Religious tolerance is something rooted in freedom of speech, which is really the freedom to criticize your politicians and is articulated profoundly in the Bill of Rights. I don't think they envisioned things like pornography in the definition of freedom of speech." He went on to note that the United States was still evolving as a government by the people and that groups who were not necessarily considered by the Founding Fathers in time became part of the democratic process: "That's what I think is deeply extraordinary about the American experiment. The founding principles are so perfectly articulated. I think for me, the political ideals of America have completely changed the world. Even the Iranian constitution, despite the fact that it arises out of an Islamic ethos, is nonetheless very much influenced by the American Constitution. So even in an Islamic society that's trying to formulate an Islamic state, they're relying on tools from the American experience."

Hamza's pluralism even accepts the *Mayflower* and Plymouth Rock as part of the "enduring story of America" for they represent "the beginning of religious freedom and the democratic impulse." At the same time, alternative narratives—like Malcolm X's version—are possible, and for Hamza one of the exciting aspects of modern America is that these alternative narratives are gaining strength and are challenging and even eroding the dominant narrative of an American mythology: "I think a lot of people do not accept them in the ways they were accepted by the Norman Rockwell version of America, which is a very white-washed version. And that's being true to ourselves. Jung talks about embracing the shadow; for America to live in that kind of denial about the atrocities and those dark aspects of our culture and our history is to deny people the possibility of transcending them. You live in a melodramatic universe of comic book heroes and villains."

Hamza believes the Muslim experience, too, is challenging America, just as many immigrant experiences did in the past. But this is not a bad thing for either party: "It's also good for the Muslims because resistance is what makes you stronger. If you want to build your muscles you have to have resistance, but when there's no resistance there's nothing gained so I don't see this as necessarily a negative thing—it's a challenge. But obviously there are certain aspects to the post-9/11 world in America in particular that have challenged this country to the core. I don't have any illusions about the fact that torture has been used by the CIA. I think Abu Ghraib was an opportunity for us to take a look at ourselves because Abu Ghraib is not an anomaly—there have been many Abu Ghraibs in American history."

To those who would justify such measures for security reasons, Hamza would say that the United States did not even torture Soviet spies during the cold war, when the threat of nuclear war was much greater and our own citizens were being tortured over there. He wondered if race might be an element now: "Noam Chomsky has said that racism toward Arabs is kind of the last acceptable bastion of racism, you know. Nobody seems to really care much about the Arabs, and I think that goes for Muslims in general because Muslims have been demonized. Our history is a history of a thousand-year war with Islam. We tend to forget that."

Even so, Hamza still saw a bright future for the melding of Muslims and Americans. If anything, he saw a new West emerging: "The old West will not die, but it's going to change, it's going to transform. And that's the nature of language, the nature of culture. Everything changes. That's the very nature of the world we're in. Trying to preserve what is precious from the past and yet relevant in the present, to prepare us for the future—those are challenges."

Lee Baca, the Sheriff of Los Angeles County

Lee Baca is that rare policeman who combines a philosophic curiosity about humanity with a compassion for it. I had met him on an earlier visit to Los Angeles with the help of Hamid Malik, who had arranged the meeting for me and my friend Judea Pearl. Baca presides over what is said to be the largest sheriff's office in the world and the nation's largest jail system. I was impressed by the sheriff's quiet thoughtfulness and on this trip was determined to talk to him about American identity. This time we met in the sheriff's office, along with deputies of Muslim background. In their appearance, language, and values, they looked like any other senior police officer. After our official meeting, all of us continued our discussion over lunch.

In 2004 Hamid had helped to arrange Lee Baca's visit to his hometown of Peshawar at the mouth of the Khyber Pass in Pakistan, a trip discouraged by both American and Pakistani authorities because of the security risks. But Baca, accompanied by Hamid, enjoyed the visit and identified with the Pashtun tribesmen of the region, thereby earning the affection of the Pakistani community in L.A. In his conversation with us, he added the words "peace be upon him" whenever he mentioned the Prophet of Islam, illustrating his attempts to be culturally sensitive to the Muslim community.

A Catholic of Mexican background, Baca is understandably a strong advocate of American pluralism. He associates American identity with the Founding Fathers: "That is a very important historical fact, and those of us who are interested in the first definition of the American society must respect the Founding Fathers of the country; otherwise the paradigm of change is going to move us into an area where we are not America anymore." Baca named Jefferson as his favorite Founding Father but also cited John Jay and James Madison.

The key to our society, Baca emphasized, is that we have a Constitution that protects religion, protects all people, regardless of race, color, creed, or religious background: "Anybody who is an American who does not respect the history of the immigrant is not truly an American in the pure sense of the word. In other words, there has to be a respect for the vision of the Founding Fathers of America, and that vision has to be brought up to date with the current realities of America."

Recalling the country's immigration history, he noted that the poor of all nations were welcomed, from European countries such as England, Ireland, Italy, and Poland, and from Mexico, and the Indians of course were already here. So America is not a country born of wealth, but people created wealth: "That's why we are the wealthiest nation in the world, because we have hardworking people who know how to create an economy that I think will always be a very strong one because of the kind of people that are attracted to the United States."

Baca's own ethnic background, he said, had no effect on his identity as an American. His mother was born in Mexico, his father in Albuquerque, New Mexico, but he does not identity himself as someone who is loyal to Mexico: "If we call someone Italian American or Polish American or Muslim American or Egyptian American, the fact is that they're an American of Egyptian descent, or Mexican in my case. If I was Muslim, I would want people to know that I am an American of Muslim faith."

Baca had a distinctly positive view of Muslims: "Muslims have not done anything to America to warrant anything but the highest respect." Unfortunately, radical speeches in some mosques have left a bad impression, so he advocated a campaign by Muslim Americans within their communities about being an American: "I have a Hispanic background, but I am a patriotic American, and would put my life on the line for America. So there needs to be discussion among the Muslim society asking whether they are willing to put their life on the line for America."

In his faith, Baca felt motivated by the idea of God, "because I think that God has created all of humanity. I've heard the same from Muslim believers, Jewish believers, and Christian believers. What religion are you going to practice in heaven? Will you practice Islam? Or Judaism? Or Christianity? Do you think God cares about these things?" Hence he finds the Quran as much a source of inspiration and wisdom as humanity's other great sacred books—the Bible, the Old Testament, the writings of Confucius. For Lee Baca, the major threat American society faces today lies in poverty and violence. Throughout the United States, the poor are getting poorer, and the behavior of their children is becoming more problematic. This is a bigger threat than anything from outside the United States, Baca admonished: "There has always been too much crime in the United States. Think of all the guns that we have in the hands of people. We have over 300 million guns."

By embracing the Muslim community, Baca himself has become a target, as when he was accused by a Republican member of Congress in Washington of "giving legitimacy to organizations that fund Hamas," referring to Baca's meeting with CAIR. Baca was not intimidated, objecting to the challenge to his patriotism and calling the member's comments "scary." LA Muslim leaders appreciated his stand: "Sheriff Baca is our champion and is our hero in defending against McCarthyism in this era."

Allan Lichtman, the Pluralist Professor

Allan Lichtman, outstanding scholar at American University and media commentator on American politics, has argued in *White Protestant Nation: The Rise of the American Conservative Movement* that the base of the Republican Party today is white Protestant society.[13] Lichtman, who is Jewish and a staunch believer in American pluralism, is also a political practitioner: he ran—unsuccessfully—for the U.S. Senate.

Lichtman agreed that the *Mayflower* and the arrival at Plymouth were very important in shaping American identity: "After all, the Mayflower Compact was, in a sense, our first move toward democracy, toward government by the people. And, of course, the Pilgrims were fleeing religious intolerance. I think if there is one great hallmark of America, it is tolerance. It is the acceptance of our differences. Otherwise, America would not work as a society. We would be engaged in a war of all against all if we did not recognize that principle of the toleration and, indeed, the celebration of our diversity, while at the same time we're united by a common set of principles and beliefs and a common government."

Lichtman therefore disagreed that non-whites and non-Protestants were aspiring to join the American primordial identity defined by white Protestant culture, as suggested by Samuel Huntington, Bob Kraynak, and others. Rather, he considered this one of "the many cultural streams that have enriched this country," and by no means the only cultural stream. In Lichtman's view, one of the greatest threats to America is the enormous disparity in wealth and income. He also finds the war on terror "a totally inappropriate metaphor," comparing it to the war on drugs—both of which are impossible to win.

When asked about Latino immigration, Lichtman felt the alarm bells raised by people like Huntington were "way overblown," that it was not challenging American identity and values. He pointed out that America has experienced wave after wave of immigration throughout its history, and each wave was accompanied by alarmists worried that America would be ruined by the new entrants. But "every time, the new waves of immigration only strengthened our country, and showed the value of our diversity and the power that comes from being a diverse nation and tolerating diversity rather than trying to make everyone conform to some narrow set of cultural values that don't apply to everyone."

Pluralist versus Predator

On our journey we witnessed the ideological opposition between American pluralist and predator identities several times. The latter appeared to remain strong because of its resilience and capacity to be reborn in every generation, if in a different form and replenished by new leaders and new enemies. Today's Ku Klux Klan, though a mere shadow of its former self, with membership down to about 5,000, is still active. Many of its prejudices, stereotypes, and even methods can be seen in the words and actions of people who have no connection with the KKK. A new target has been added to the Klan's list since 9/11. Mosques have been vandalized and crosses set afire outside them.

We learned of a firebombing that destroyed a mosque in Columbia, Tennessee, from Jonathan's brother, Josh Hayden, who lives in Nashville. Further details surfaced when we arrived for a reception at the Nashville Islamic Center and met Daoud Abudiab, director of the Islamic Center of Columbia. He invited us to Columbia to tell us the story of the attack, see the mosque, and have lunch with the community. The mosque's community of some fifty-five people had purchased the building, paid for it in full, and were gratified that they had a home in the idyllic small town of Columbia in southern Tennessee. The mosque was the only one within miles, and Muslims from small towns in the area came to worship there.

On February 9, 2008, almost a year before our visit, Daoud was awakened by the fire department at 5 a.m. He arrived in time to see the entire mosque engulfed in flames and the roof collapsing. Someone had broken in, vandalized the inside, and then set the building on fire with Molotov cocktails. Several swastikas and "White power, we run the world" had been spray-painted on the walls.

Because of the sensitive nature of the crime, eighty agents were on the scene within a few hours to investigate. That same day three individuals were arrested. When questioned, the culprits claimed that what was going on in the mosque was against God's law, according to the Bible.

Daoud was devastated. "Is being a Muslim a liability in this town?" he asked himself. He was especially upset for his children, who were asking if all Christians hated them. They had lived in Columbia for over a decade and had considered it their home but now wondered if they were welcome at all. Daoud's white wife, a native of Arkansas who had converted, found it "a bit disturbing that people do not talk to her about it. They hear people say on television or on the radio that Muslims should get a boat back to where they came from." Daoud interjected, "I don't think you can get a boat from Tennessee to Cabot, Arkansas."

A few days after the firebombing, neighboring Muslim communities held a vigil that was open to the public. People from all faiths came, but only a few from Columbia. One of those was Reverend Bill Williamson of Columbia's oldest Christian congregation, the First Presbyterian Church, which was established by the Scots-Irish in 1811 and once included President James K. Polk's wife among its members. Upon hearing the news of the attack, he had collected money during a service at the church and provided Muslims with a set of keys to his church so that they could worship there. He set aside a room for them to use for meetings and prayers and even offered to remove any Christian symbols that might offend them. Williamson was accused by some of using church money inappropriately to fund "illegal activities."

Daoud spoke of Williamson as of an admired brother. "I was impressed with the clarity in which Williamson interpreted 'love thy neighbor,'" he said. Daoud's message to non-Muslim Americans was also unequivocal: "We are not here to establish an Arab or Palestinian or a Gulf community. We are here to establish an American community."

In November of 2009 it was announced that one of the three men involved in the attack had been given a fourteen-year prison sentence. Although Muslims tend to criticize the American system as biased, cases like this illustrate that the wheels of American justice may grind slowly but they grind surely.

The thinking that all Muslims are terrorists is ironic, lamented Jonathan: "As Daoud said, they were now the ones attacked by terrorists. His child had been mocked in school, called a terrorist, and teased mercilessly, as children often do to one another. It was a hard thing to hear—a child, the victim of terrorism, being called a terrorist." Jonathan, who comes from this region and is sensitive to interfaith understanding, was particularly incensed by the lack of protest from within the Christian community: "Americans commonly faulted Muslims for not speaking up after 9/11, but in this community Christians failed to condemn the terrorists in their midst. Some Christians failed to speak up in this case because they saw the attackers as non-Christians or misguided individuals so felt no reason to apologize or speak out against it. The people who did this to the Columbia Islamic Center no more represent Christianity than Osama bin Laden represents Daoud and his community."

The visit reminded Frankie of his conversation with two officials at Brentwood Oaks Church of Christ, in Austin, Texas. Frankie could not believe his ears when one of the men said that "pluralism" was the biggest threat to America. The man was dismissive of the Founding Fathers: "I don't necessarily think they reflect being followers of Christ."

This was not idle chatter. A year after the conversation in Austin, in the spring of 2010, the Texas Board of Education voted to change the state's school curriculum, dropping Thomas Jefferson from a world history section on great political thinkers who influenced America and replacing him with other figures, including John Calvin. More emphasis was to be placed on American presidents Richard Nixon and Ronald Reagan. The board also announced that Texas students will read Confederate President Jefferson Davis's inaugural address alongside Lincoln's speeches, study the "vindicated" Joseph McCarthy and new evidence proving that the U.S. government was infiltrated by communists during the cold war, question the doctrine of "separation between church and state," and learn of the "unintended consequences" of civil rights. An infuriated Latino board member stormed out of a board meeting, accusing the body of trying to "pretend this is a white America." In the actions of the Texas Board of Education, we were once again reminded of the contested nature of American identity and the challenge pluralist identity faces from the more aggressive predator identity.

The Predator on the Prowl

The true character of an individual or nation is best judged under duress. Whereas the Founding Fathers passed the test with flying colors, the leaders of post-9/11 America floundered and failed. While the former personify grace under pressure, the latter embody gracelessness compounded by arrogance, which is puzzling because it was based on neither talent nor wisdom.

In the end, the former won a nation, the latter almost destroyed the nation's reputation in the world community while challenging its core principles.

Laws were passed and existing laws bent after 9/11 to permit American predator identity to exert its will on anyone, anywhere, and at any time. Faced with the predator on the prowl, Muslims felt vulnerable and unsure.

"Don't register," warned Joan Greenbaum, who is a family friend and an associate of the Washington Hebrew Congregation. She was alerting Zeenat and me to the dangers that lurked in the new official order requiring all Muslim males from twenty-four Muslim nations—and North Korea—to register with the government. Her voice somber and her eyes clouding over, she described events of another time and another land. She talked of her mother, a charming and intelligent Holocaust survivor, whom I had met in Kansas, and her mother's narrow escape from Hitler's gas chambers and crossing to America. Her mother's younger brother was sent to what her family thought was a safe home in Holland. When the Nazis demanded registration in Holland, her brother complied, was captured, and taken to Auschwitz. He was never seen again. "But this is not Hitler's Germany," I protested. "No, I have a bad feeling about this," Joan insisted.

Despite Joan's urging not to trust governments that demand that its people register, my South Asian upbringing told me it was all right. I had been a member of Pakistan's civil service and knew that if a government implemented an action for its citizens, it must have their interests at heart. At the same time, my instincts developed as an officer working in one of the most dangerous parts of the world, the tribal areas of Pakistan, set alarm bells ringing. There were too many unanswered questions and too little information about the procedure—not to mention the many stories circulating about the miscarriage of justice.

Not for a moment was I concerned about myself. I would go and register, even if Zeenat and Joan thought it unwise. As a precaution, I mentioned it to my dean at American University, Louis Goodman, who had alerted the provost, Cornelius Kerwin. Both said that they would follow my progress that day closely, and if anything happened, they would be down there immediately to ensure justice and fair play.

What worried me was my son Babar. If something happened to him, God forbid, who would I turn to for help? Who would listen to a father who loved his son and admired him for his integrity and character, who had never ever broken the law? How would I explain that this boy belonged to a well-known royal family of my country, had been educated at the finest schools in Pakistan and England, and had dedicated his life to filmmaking after winning an award at the New York Film Academy because of his love of American cinema?

But I knew he was exactly the kind of person who would arouse suspicion in the minds of the security agencies. He was young, male, a bachelor, a Muslim, and his name was Babar Ahmed, the same name borne by a man picked up and charged under terrorism laws in the United Kingdom. I knew the authorities were capable of confusing two unrelated individuals living on different continents simply because they have the same name. Stories like this were being reported daily and causing fear and panic in the community. As it turned out, neither Babar nor I had to register.

Other Muslims were not so lucky: 83,000 Muslims were labeled high national security concerns, and 14,000 were detained or deported.[14] Not one of these Muslims was charged with a terrorism-related crime. Muslims went underground, fled the country until better times, or were detained. Entire Muslim neighborhoods disappeared. The large Pakistani population living in the neighborhood nicknamed "Little Pakistan," in Brooklyn, New York, was one of them.

The Decimation of Little Pakistan

Many worlds live side by side in the generous heart of New York. From one street corner to the next is like passing from one world to another. When we went to meet scholar David Shasha in the Jewish quarter of Brooklyn, we entered into "Little Israel" (see chapter 7). It was the Jewish holiday of Sukkot, and makeshift huts adorned with branches, fruits, and vegetables lined the streets in celebration. Many male Orthodox Jews wore the traditional hats, women were in black, signs were in Hebrew (some not even translated), and food stores were kosher. David took us to a restaurant for dinner where we were given menus in Hebrew. The male customers wore traditional long flowing black coats and their heads were covered, some had long beards, and they spoke in Yiddish. It was as if we were in Tel Aviv.

Then, as we crossed the street, we were magically transported to Lahore and we were in "Little Pakistan." The shops went from knish and challah to kababs and curry. The signs were now in Urdu, and people were wearing Pakistani clothes and speaking in Pakistani languages. It was as if two cultures from different parts of the world were juxtaposed neatly with all the glory of their languages, clothes, shops, and food intact without any overlap or interaction.

But unlike the festive environment on the Jewish side, the atmosphere in the Pakistani community was heavy with fear and uncertainty. We visited the small Al-Mahdi mosque on the main street and were received by the imam himself. He had asked some thirty worshippers to remain after the evening prayer and talk to us. We sensed a heightened anxiety in this mosque, whose Shia community feels particularly vulnerable because the American media associate its sect with Iran and Hezbollah militants. Zeenat and Hailey could hear and see everything but, observing mosque protocol, did not join in the conversation.

The imam's welcoming statement emphasized that we were in a "humble" place, not a big mosque. He lauded my work in promoting the understanding of Islam, which encouraged the worshippers to speak frankly. Soon they were pouring out their hearts. They told me that some 40 percent of their community had left after 9/11, that it was devastated. In the old days, someone said, when you went to Coney Island Avenue a lot of people would be about, even at midnight. Now the place is deserted by 9 p.m.

A frail, old bald man with glasses was agitated beyond measure: "What is the very root of this 9/11? What is the background of it? Who are responsible? They are making us responsible. Few people did it, but an entire nation has been involved in it. We have to distinguish that we are not terrorists. Now the definition of Muslims in the dictionary has changed totally. In the dictionary of America, Muslims mean terrorists. This is very dangerous." Everywhere he turned, he felt physically, mentally, and financially victimized. He had been assaulted at work and choked until he thought he was going to die. His daughter has a master's degree but is not being hired despite her qualifications. They have been subjected to "a hundred questions and deprived of all their rights."

A small boy of ten sitting in the front row talked about his experiences at school: "Well, they say, you Muslim people are like terrorists. You don't have a life. But then, I say, well, you'll see, like in the future you'll see how big we are. We're not bad people; we're peaceful people. We don't want to hurt; we just want peace." He went on to explain that the towers in New York must have fallen because of explosives at their base, as demonstrated through a computer simulation he had seen, not because of being hit by planes. A man in a red shirt then talked about a pattern he saw in world events involving Muslims that appeared to be "a conspiracy." He compared the attacks in France, the United States, Spain, and London to a chain of events in which "Muslims all over the world have been framed" and are being associated with all of these acts of terrorism. As a result, peaceful people living over here, working hard to support their families, are afraid to go out: "We are all isolated in our own community."

Members of the mosque were particularly sensitive to negative depictions of the Prophet of Islam, lamenting the many negative things being associated with his name. One of them said, "He's not that personality that you see in the media. This is international propaganda coming from Jewish papers to totally distort Islam. It's out of proportion." When asked how this issue should be addressed, he felt that someone informed about Islam, "who knows of our culture, who's from our country, who's from Saudi Arabia, who's from the Middle East . . . should be able to represent themselves in international media." Unfortunately, the community is unable to represent itself because "we are an uneducated people," with only about 25 to 30 percent being educated. "How can we project ourselves in the international media and the international community?" he sighed. "We don't have the muscle."

The mosque's members also felt it was essential to clear the community's name. They complained that most of the experts on international relations, Muslims, or Middle Eastern countries commenting on the community in the media are non-Muslim. Another man agreed: "They are not representative of the communities. They are Americans with no knowledge of our culture and our background. And they are always saying wrong things about us and about all the Muslim world."

The imam mentioned that someone from the community who had joined the U.S. Army was killed in Afghanistan fighting the Taliban—"He preferred to be killed rather than surrender to the Taliban." The imam felt his death "will make some difference to the community in America. And America will feel that Muslims are of the U.S. and are not disloyal; they are not selfish. Their children, their youth, are ready to get killed against the terrorism. As we know, Islam is not the religion of terrorism. Muslims are not and they were never terrorists. But some of the so-called Muslims, they are defaming us in Afghanistan, Iraq, and Pakistan. We should draw a line of differentiation that we are not from those who kill the innocent people." Then to improve relations between Muslims and non-Muslims, the mosque's members said, it would be essential to open "dialogues with the government, the FBI, IRS, and the police."

Another boy spoke in a low measured voice that belied the trauma he had experienced. He had been sitting at home watching TV when the police arrived, and described the episode this way: "I was like, what, are they going to arrest me or something? They're like, we're looking for something. And they search our whole house, and I'm like, Oh my God. And then they leave, and I'm like, Mom, what did they do? She's like, nothing."

These stories were sad enough, but nothing prepared us for what one of the two young boys sitting politely in the front row was about to relate (also see chapter 5). He was repeatedly called a terrorist by his classmates, and we were later informed that his mother had been killed by the Taliban in Pakistan. His predicament was that of his immigrant community—caught between two opposed civilizations in conflict.

In the Belly of the Beast

In the film *Harold and Kumar Escape from Guantanamo Bay* (2008), there is a scene that is crude but makes its point. Rob Corddry, who plays the aggressive, ignorant, white senior Department of Homeland Security official, is interrogating two Jewish friends of Harold and Kumar to ascertain the location of the two escapees. He employs a stereotyped object, a small bag of gold coins, and empties it noisily on the table before the two boys, who look nonplussed. When they invoke the Fifth Amendment, which protects them from incriminating themselves in testimony, Corddry orders the U.S. Constitution to be brought to the room, rips out a page, sticks it into the back of his trousers, rubs it noisily and energetically between his buttocks, and then thrusts the filthy page at the boys, and declares, "This is what I think of the Fifth!"

In terms of the discussion in this book, Corddry's character is a stand-in for predator identity. As is well known, the predator uses—or misuses—the law in dubious ways to justify actions. The experience of Abdulrahman Zeitoun is a case in point (see also Dave Eggers's recent book, *Zeitoun*).[15]

We met Zeitoun, a Syrian American who owns a construction business, in New Orleans. He had courageously faced the wrath of Hurricane Katrina to rescue countless stranded residents in his canoe. After days of saving people, including an old woman, and dogs from the crushing floodwaters, Zeitoun returned to his home. Because of his house's construction on high stilts and its location, he was spared the most devastating effects of the floodwaters. His wife, a white convert named Kathy, had fled with their family, but he had remained in New Orleans. While he was visiting one of the rental properties he owns with two white men and a Muslim friend, a boat appeared carrying a group of men and one woman dressed in military fatigues and armed with machine guns.

The boat's occupants approached Zeitoun and asked if he needed any help or food supplies. He declined, saying that he had everything under control. Then they took a closer look at him. "What are you doing here?" they asked. "This is my property," Zeitoun replied, whereupon they jumped out of the boat and asked for his identification. When Zeitoun complied, the men ordered him into the boat, without any explanation. Zeitoun asked if he could at least retrieve a piece of paper from the house with his wife's number on it. "If you step inside," warned one of the men, "I'll shoot you." Forced onto the boat at gunpoint, Zeitoun watched his house recede into the distance.

Zeitoun now entered a twilight world of deceit, torture, and uncertainty. He was allowed no phone call, given no notice of his crime, and denied medical

Abdulrahman Zeitoun, far left, in front of a mosque damaged by Hurricane Katrina in New Orleans. After Katrina, Zeitoun stayed behind to help friends and secure his house when he was inexplicably picked up on suspicion of terrorism and imprisoned under grueling conditions. Charges were later dropped after an ordeal of twenty-three days.

attention for a nasty cut on his foot that had become infected. He recalled his ordeal with a trembling voice: "From there they got us to the bus station that was designed exactly like Guantánamo Bay, that has very high security there, guys with a machine gun sitting around, one in almost each corner and one on the roof. So I started thinking that this was the start of something not good because there is no system, we don't know what happened."

The makeshift jail inside the bus station, built by other prisoners, was nicknamed Camp Greyhound. It held about 1,200 prisoners, who were given ready-to-eat meals, bottles of water, and bare facilities. While the authorities, and military contractors like Blackwater, were busy building jails such as this and picking up looters around the city, thousands of people were still trapped in the Superdome, the football stadium of New Orleans, with no water, food, or protection. Meanwhile, Zeitoun's wife, Kathy, was beside herself with anxiety and their children terrified.

Upon arriving at Camp Greyhound, Zeitoun was asked to strip: "They made me take all my clothes off and made me bend down to see if I had anything hidden." It was, understandably, "the most humiliating thing," for dignity and respect are central cultural features of Muslim society.

On the first day, Zeitoun described guards walking by and calling inmates Taliban, terrorist, and other such names. "The second day," Zeitoun described with pain in his voice, "we don't have no blanket, no place to stay. The worst torture was at the bus station. I had a train engine next to my head for three days, no sleep. The ground is full of oil; you know with the bus and the oil dripping, it was full of grease. I used to hang on the pipe like that just to get off my foot. We couldn't touch the wire of the cage, and we could not move."

Even more disoriented, Zeitoun was then transported to the Elayn Hunt Correctional Center, a maximum security prison. Zeitoun described Hunt as "a jail inside the jail inside the jail." Kathy told Hailey the center consisted of a concrete slab with six men to a cell containing one thin rolled-up cot and a toilet in the middle. At Camp Greyhound, they had had Porta-Potties, but without doors.

Zeitoun was then interviewed by the FBI, CIA, and Department of Homeland Security. He was initially charged with terrorism, but when they found no evidence, they changed the charges to looting. Eventually, all charges were dropped. Kathy cannot forget how hard it was for both of them. With haunted voice, she recounted Zeitoun's appearance after he emerged from prison twenty-three days later: "He was so short, so short— his beard was so overgrown because normally he keeps it very trimmed, it almost looks like razor stubble. And his hair was so, so white. It was like that prison aged him. He looked like an old, short man."

Although Zeitoun was singled out for being Muslim, others were treated just as unfairly and brutally, in one case for the suspected looting of sausages from a convenience store. The story of the seventy-three-year-old, diabetic, African American church elder Merlene Maten became nationally known. Merlene was arrested for alleged looting, with bail set at $50,000, and was taken to the maximum security prison for women next to Hunt. She was released two weeks later with the help of lawyers, the American Association for Retired Persons, and the media, which proved her innocence.

Zeitoun saw a man in a neighboring cell at Camp Greyhound treated badly as well. Obviously mentally disturbed, the man would call out for his mother and tell everyone to wash their hands. The guards got tired of his shouting and moving about in the cell against their orders. They dragged him into the hallway, doused his entire body with pepper spray, and then threw a bucket of water on him to prevent permanent damage. Watching this brutal behavior, Zeitoun learned to hold his silence and avoid a similar fate.

It was this brutality accompanied by unchecked power that shocked Zeitoun. This was, after all, America, not his homeland, Syria, Zeitoun kept reminding himself. He came to the sad conclusion that the America he loved may have changed beyond redemption: "Not just me. I think every Muslim, doesn't matter what you come from or where you are, you don't have no rights. You are being watched. I see many stories worse than mine. You feel like you are in a circle, and the circle gets closer and closer to you, gets tighter and tighter."

Senseless Sadism of the System

Perhaps nothing is crueler than the physical victimization of a patient by the very people charged to take care of him or her. It signifies not merely administrative but also moral collapse. A case of this nature was brought to Hailey's attention by Farhat Chishty, whom she met in Dallas, Texas.[16] Mrs. Chishty was in the middle of a legal battle regarding the neglect and torture of her son Haseeb, who was in a mental health institution called Denton State School, spread over 200 acres of wooded, rolling hills.

Although Mrs. Chishty is a Pakistani, she had raised Haseeb in Saudi Arabia, where they had lived for eighteen years. Haseeb was born there in 1973 and at the age of ten months was taken to Pakistan for a visit, where he contracted pneumonia. Because of complications, Haseeb suffered permanent brain damage. When Haseeb was about twenty, they moved to Dallas, where he was sent to the Denton State School. He was at the institution for barely a month when he fainted during one of his mother's visits. Some of the staff rushed him back to his room but would not let her see him. Although she sensed something was amiss, she returned home.

Her mother's instincts were right. A kindly nurse called her in the middle of the night to report that Haseeb was in very poor condition. When she arrived, she found him in a pool of his own urine and blood. She demanded that an ambulance take him to a hospital.

Mrs. Chishty later learned that on that day two of his caretakers—Kevin Miller and an accomplice—had gone into Haseeb's room, and that Miller, in a drug-induced rage, had mercilessly beaten Haseeb while his accomplice held the door shut to prevent anyone from entering. Haseeb was beaten so badly that he had boot prints on his stomach and groin area, his intestines were ruptured, and his lungs damaged. After emergency surgeries, he was kept in the intensive care unit for six months. He was paralyzed from the shoulders down. The doctors told Mrs. Chishty that his chance of survival was less than 1 percent.

To her horror, Mrs. Chishty discovered that this was not the first time that Haseeb had been viciously beaten. Miller and his accomplice had been beating him because they believed he was an Iraqi, she said. They had overheard him speaking Arabic and seen the Arabic writing on his birth certificate. It was one year since the attacks on September 11, and emotions were still running high. A distressed Mrs. Chishty lamented that her son had had to pay for a crime that was not his.

Initially, the facility staff attempted to cover up the story, saying that Haseeb's condition was the result of his seatbelt in the ambulance going awry and the vehicle stopping abruptly. The hospital doctors refuted this, and Miller later discredited that account himself.

Unfortunately for Mrs. Chishty, Texas has a law known as sovereign immunity that prohibits any state-run facility from being sued. She was therefore not allowed to bring legal action against Miller and his accomplice. It was only her perseverance in hiring a private investigator that extricated a confession out of Miller.

Tragically, the abuse was not limited to Haseeb. The *Houston Press* described the facility as an "Abu Ghraib for the retarded."[17] Miller later broke down and confessed to other crimes, which he blamed on his abuse as a child and psychological deficiencies. Miller said in a statement that it got to the point where it was fun, beating, hitting, and torturing the patients. Ironically, he is now confined to a mental institution.

In the meantime, the state gave Mrs. Chishty further bad news: the only place that Haseeb could be treated is the same institution in which the incident occurred. Terrified of sending him back, she quit her job to take care of her son, who is now thirty-five years old. He cannot feed himself or go to the bathroom on his own. Mrs. Chishty told Hailey the lesson she learned from her ordeal was that while individuals can be evil, unfortunately even the system in America has become corrupted. Various lawyers and institutions have helped Mrs. Chishty in her struggle for justice, among them the Muslim Legal Fund of America. Even so, she has lost both her job and her home. She has become bitter about American justice, comparing it to Saudi Arabian justice, under which no one takes responsibility. In May 2009 she finally received some good news: in her case alone, sovereign immunity would be waived. Seven years had passed since her nightmare began. Though emotionally and financially exhausted, Mrs. Chishty refuses to give up and is now involved in a bigger battle: "Whatever happens, I will keep fighting. Not just for Haseeb, but for the other people here. I have to make sure what happened to him never happens again."

Seeing Enemies Everywhere

It was not just individual Muslims who faced the wrath of American predator identity after 9/11. Muslim organizations and charities across the land were also subjected to special scrutiny and investigation. One of the better-known cases, because it was so much in the news, centered on the Holy Land Foundation for Relief and Development (HLF), based in Richardson, Texas, and once the largest Muslim charity organization in the United States. Concerned with Palestinian refugees in Lebanon, Jordan, Gaza, and the West Bank, the foundation was committed to funding and implementing practical solutions for human suffering through humanitarian programs for the disadvantaged, disinherited, and displaced peoples suffering from man-made and natural disasters.

Yet in the immediate aftermath of 9/11, no one challenged the presidential executive order issued in December 2001. The order shut down the HLF, which it labeled a specially designated global terrorist group, finding it guilty of providing material support to the Hamas movement, classified as a terrorist group. It also charged the defendants with providing "financial support to the families of Hamas martyrs, detainees, and activists knowing and intending that such assistance would support the Hamas terrorist organization." When the case came to trial, the Department of Justice accused the HLF of intentionally hiding its financial support for Hamas "behind the guise of charitable donations" in the amount of "approximately $12.4 million in support to Hamas and its goal of creating an Islamic Palestinian state by eliminating the State of Israel through violent jihad."[18]

The Department of Justice argued that money in the hands of a terrorist organization—even if for so-called charitable purposes—supports that organization's overall terrorist objectives. Furthermore, the HLF defendants were deemed guilty by association: for example, Ghassan Elashi, HLF's former chair of the board, had a cousin who was married to Hamas's political chief, Mousa Abu Marzook.[19]

The case caused consternation and controversy among Muslims because charity, or *zakat*, is one of the five compulsory "pillars" of Islam, and the HLF was considered a premier organization for its charitable work in Palestinian refugee camps and homes. Recognizing the importance of the case, we sought out Khalil Meek, the president of the Muslim Legal Fund of America, who represented the HLF defendants. Meek is a bearded white Texan who converted to Islam in 1989, although at one stage he had planned to become a Baptist preacher. Meek felt that initially 9/11 motivated the Muslim community to become more involved in and more serious about being American. It all fell apart, however, when legal and immigration forces began targeting Muslims. As a result, Meek argued, the best way to prove your patriotism now is to show how much you hate the Muslim community.

Meek stated there was no judicial process in the freezing of HLF's assets. Though the authorities indicted no one, they claimed the HLF was the largest source of funding for Hamas in America. From 2001 to 2004 the government tried to find a connection between the foundation and Hamas, said Meek, but was unsuccessful. In 2004, in a change of strategy, it contended that the HLF provided material support to Hamas through donations to nonprofit organizations in Palestine. The theory, Meek said, was that if the HLF was able to send money to Palestinians through non-profits and the people of Palestine knew that it was coming from Hamas even indirectly, this could draw them to Hamas. Though none of the non-profits that the HLF worked with are on the list of specially designated global terrorist groups, they were used in evidence against the foundation. The Muslim community in Texas was dismayed. "Feeding kids became a crime," Meek said. "Insane."

In 2004 a federal grand jury in Texas returned an indictment against the organization, charging it with conspiracy, providing material support to a foreign terrorist organization, tax evasion, and money laundering. The government's criminal case against the individuals involved began in 2007. In Meek's view, the government had released a list of unindicted cocon-spirators illegally. It contained 306 names and organizations, including the Council on American-Islamic Relations, Islamic Society of North Amer-ica, and almost every other mainstream Islamic group. It took the govern-ment three months to present its case, at the end of which it drew no guilty verdicts and thirty-one acquittals. The rest of the charges were undecided because of hung juries.

Undeterred, the government launched an appeal in order to try the undecided cases. This time the government called secret witnesses; one was an Israeli soldier described as an Israeli defense expert, who Meek con-tended could not have known about any of the transactions. Even the U.S. consul general in Palestine testified on the HLF's behalf. After a drawn-out trial, the court found the HLF guilty of all charges. The defendants were incarcerated immediately and were held pending an appeal.

In May 2009 five defendants were given sentences ranging from fifteen to sixty-five years in prison. When asked why the government would do this, Meek responded that it was the influence of Israel on the U.S. political process. The HLF was a sacrifice to the war on terror. He called the trial a

witch hunt and considered it persecution: "All the HLF was doing was giving money to kids and widows, which the government does not even dispute.
They just think that it helps Hamas," he said, calling it "a scary precedent."

After the meeting with Meek in CAIR's Dallas offices, Jonathan was
disturbed by the lack of evidence against the HLF: "America's Muslim
community is really in trouble because the justice system seemed so much
against it. We knew that we were hearing only one side of the story, but the
evidence seemed so flimsy, and even looking through the official government statements, the deck seemed stacked against the defendants. Regardless of the guilt or innocence of these particular defendants, it seemed that
any Muslim individual or organization could be picked up, convicted, and
branded a terrorist with just a smattering of circumstantial evidence. This
could have happened to anyone. We knew exactly what the defendants and
lawyers probably knew from the beginning: they had no chance."

"I felt badly for the Muslim community in America," Frankie observed.
"It broke my heart to see the suffering traveling in the Muslim world, especially among groups such as the Somalis in East Africa's refugee camps. But
how is a Muslim who wants to give aid to Palestinian civilians in Gaza, for
example, supposed to do it? In Omaha, I spoke to a middle-aged Pakistani
man who said he was 'terrified' to give zakat: 'I will donate, but I only give
cash. If you donate to any charity you are called by the U.S. government.'"

Jonathan Benthall, the British scholar who has spent the last decades
studying Islamic charities, had this to say about their role in the United States
when asked to comment:

> *Zakat,* the Islamic tithe, is a vital part of the Muslim commitment.
> In my country, the United Kingdom, a sympathetic government has
> facilitated the growth of some major relief and development agencies,
> led by Islamic Relief Worldwide, based on *zakat* and other Islamic
> prescriptions. I argue that in addition to all their good work overseas
> they are a powerful force for social integration in Britain itself. In the
> United States, with five times the population, one would expect a
> larger and equally important Islamic charity sector to have developed.
> This is not the case, because all the major US Islamic charities have
> been closed down since 9/11.
>
> Abuse of the privileges of charities does regrettably happen all over
> the world, but this has been an overreaction. In my view, the attack on
> Islamic institutions by the US Government—underwritten by the new
> profession of terrorology, woefully lacking in intellectual rigor—is as
> regrettable, in this most legalistic of countries, as the better known

provocations of Guantánamo and extraordinary rendition. Yet the United States has such a strong tradition of civil rights advocacy and religious freedom that it will surely correct this aberration and encourage Islamic charities to flourish. After all, the McCarthyism of the 1950s, with its attack on allegedly "unAmerican activities," is now regarded as a blot on the country's history. World politics are now more complex than during the Cold War, but the urgent war against Al-Qa`ida is not helped by branding the provision of medical services and the care of orphans as tantamount to terrorism.[20]

The Predator Turns on Itself

Muslims may be the latest victims of the predator identity, but they are not the only ones. Those representing predator identity through its security forces will set out to prove that anyone targeted is guilty until proven innocent. In the following case, members of our own team who are white were at the receiving end of American predator identity and felt the heat of reverse racism.

Frankie, Celestine, Jonathan, and Craig were on Waikiki Beach late one night after fieldwork in Honolulu, looking at the stars and listening to the breathing of the ocean when they noticed a man stumbling around drunk. Concerned that he might fall into the water and drown, Celestine and Frankie went to get help. They crossed the street and approached a policeman who was a native Hawaiian. As they began reporting the situation on the beach, he gestured for them to follow him into the station. Rather than helping, he perfunctorily informed them he was going to write them up for jaywalking and threatened them with arrest when they protested.

At the station, matters deteriorated even further as the officer made disparaging comments about "students on vacation." Frankie found the officer intimidating and irritable: "His voice quivered when he spoke, and he stared at us intently with bloodshot eyes. His demeanor suggested we had not jaywalked but had just stabbed someone with a knife." When Craig and Jonathan arrived, they were rudely told to leave the station.

We had heard that the native Hawaiians have a reverse prejudice against the white minority, referring to them as *haole,* a derogatory term meaning those without a spirit. Both Frankie and Celestine were traumatized. They had never experienced this kind of situation before, especially at the hands of an authority figure. Frankie received letters from Hawai'i in Washington, D.C., telling him that if he did not pay a $130 fine, a nonbinding warrant would be issued for his arrest.

There Will Be Blood

In Houston, Texas, we met representatives of American predator identity at a different level of society from the policeman encountered in Hawai'i. Well-known oilman Herb Goodman had invited us for lunch at the Petroleum Club located on the top floor of the ExxonMobil building. The scholarly and genial Herb had been introduced to me by my oilman cousin Mahmood Mushtaq, who also lives in Houston (see chapter 5). The building's state-of-the-art architecture and technology proclaimed the importance of oil to the city. The view of the city was spectacular. Goodman had also invited a dozen of his other successful oil friends so that we could talk around the table as we ate. They had been educated at Harvard and Yale and talked of Jesus and Winston Churchill as role models.

Far removed from the archetypically uncouth and demonic oilman Daniel Plainview of the film *There Will Be Blood* (2007), these were polished and successful men of the world who had lived in foreign lands. While abroad they tended to live in their own social and cultural cocoons, meeting few ordinary locals. They did not seem to fully understand Islam or feel sympathetic toward it. Their opinions on Islam, mainly derived from the media, were negative.

Steve Koh, who is from Singapore and of Chinese descent, identified strongly with the American predator identity. He was more American than the whitest of white Protestants and was living proof of Huntington's and Kraynak's theories about American identity. Koh aggressively and frequently proclaimed his Americanness, boasting that "we are the most charitable country ever known. Others take advantage of the generosity of Americans. Americans put their blood and treasure on the line. They are blamed if they do or if they don't. We need to make others around the world understand us better. The greatest threat to America is the jealousy that others have of us."

Koh saw a sharp contrast between American generosity and openness and Muslim societies in general. Muslim madrassahs, he claimed, taught little else but how to hate America. To him the clash with Islam was over global values. Christianity taught belief in law and order, justice, and compassion. Islam taught the opposite.

Another oilman elaborated on that train of thought: "There will be terror and war in the Middle East as long as those people hate enemies more than they love their children. They have an unwillingness to negotiate. Muslims are consumed by hatred of the enemy. It's frightening. It's really frightening. We are headed for extermination." In contrast, he remarked, hate is not a cultivated emotion in the United States. When we mentioned television's Sean Hannity and his anti-Muslim tirades, the oilman said that Hannity speaks out of fear, not hate: "People who watch Hannity are thinking people. We don't burn flags or strap bombs to ourselves."

Herb produced an article about a Muslim man in Buffalo, New York, who had beheaded his wife. He lamented that the mainstream media had not reported the story. He found the incident in keeping with the spirit of the Quran, "where the Prophet Muhammad said to be good to your wife, but beat her if she's not." Herb also told Frankie the Saudis drink a lot and that a Saudi told him alcohol was invented in Saudi Arabia. He confided that the Saudis made wine in Mecca basements. He attributed this to a Saudi split personality, saying he knows the Saudis well, having worked with King Faisal and conducted many oil deals there.

A Cuban executive who spoke with a Texas accent nostalgically recalled the days of the British Empire and blamed the poor condition of the Muslim world on the historical fact that the British gave them independence. Business was much easier in those countries when they were under colonial rule: "It may sound like a cliché, but the best way to run a city and country is where the leaders of businesses get together in smoke-filled rooms." He said this is what they did in Houston: "The captains of industry were part of a group called the City Fathers. The government can't do it all, so we'll do it in the government's place. In Houston the City Fathers at one point included the mayor of Houston and also county judges, but we kicked them out! We didn't want politicians in our inner discussions. We decide, not them—and it works." Frankie asked them if alternative energy would replace oil in the near future. Every one of them said absolutely not.

From Sam Bailey on Sanibel Island to the oilmen of Houston, the people in this chapter illustrate the interplay of America's different identities today. American primordial identity remains flexible in adjusting to Muslims, as long as they acknowledge and adhere to it, while American pluralist identity, which once welcomed them as a celebration of its own character, now, with some honorable exceptions, has reservations. Predator identity, on the other hand, has created problems for Muslims and in doing so has compromised some of America's founding principles.

The following chapters look more closely at the different Muslim communities within the context of American identity. The next chapter is about African American Muslims, who I am calling "the first Muslims" because in profound historical and cultural ways, Islam first came to America with them.

PART TWO

Islam in America

FOUR

African Americans as First Muslims

ONCE UPON A time, a thoughtful man named Muhammad lived in a town in the middle of a desert. The town attracted many visitors who spent their time gambling, drinking, and womanizing. The people worshipped idols, replacing them with new ones when they saw fit.

Muhammad was unhappy. He was a spiritual man searching for answers to the purpose of life, and the society around him had little to offer except brawling and debauchery. So he talked to sages who told him stories of past prophets; and he contemplated the traditions of his ancestors. He withdrew to the mountains, looked at the night sky and the distant stars. He was forty years old and a soul still on a quest.

Then, in a flash, he found his answer: *submission,* bowing his will to that of God, and this was Islam. Having discovered the moral clarity and vision that he craved, Muhammad set forth rules and principles by which to live. Islam gave him the balance he had sought all his life, that between the next world and this—between what Muslims called *deen* and *dunya.* Through the practice of Islam, he had also discovered the key to Paradise in the next world. Muhammad had become the Prophet of Islam, a man whom Muslims bless with love and reverence every time they mention his name.

Miracle in the Desert

This story of Muhammad, the Prophet of Islam, echoes in the story of another man, an African American living in Las Vegas. Imam Mustafa Yunus Richards discovered Islam around the age of forty and named himself Mustafa, another name of the Prophet. That the Prophet never compromised his compassion, in spite of the cruel attacks on him, touched Mustafa. The Prophet's constant refrain—to attend to the needs of the orphan, the widow, and the poor—moved him. The Prophet's message went straight to his heart, unlike the arguments and discussions of religious scholars and jurists who appeal to the head.

Imam Mustafa identified with the circumstances of the Prophet's life and through them made sense of his own. By taking his Islam directly from the Prophet, without the heavy cultural and political baggage that Muslims preaching Islam from the Middle East and South Asia carried with them, he could be inspired by the true spiritual message of the faith.

We first met Imam Mustafa, an affable, heavyset man, at the Sahara hotel, where we were staying in Las Vegas. We received him, neatly dressed in a well-worn coat and trousers, at our hotel with its ersatz Arabian desert lounge, arabesques and arches, date palms and plastic camels (veering to the ridiculous). The décor and structure of the Sahara were "oriental" in a brave, if futile, attempt at Las Vegas's exuberant embrace of the world's most recognized sights, competing with others there that mimicked the Egyptian pyramids, the Eiffel Tower, and a Roman palace complete with a coliseum.

We heard Imam Mustafa's remarkable life story over an all-you-can-eat buffet dinner. He had come from a poor background in the embattled city of Detroit, but even as a young man, he yearned for spiritual solace. He read about different religions and asked questions. As he grew older, he studied with rabbis and, not satisfied, spoke with Catholic priests. He even spent time with the Nation of Islam, but its members' hostility to whites was not to his liking. Finally, looking for employment, he ended up in Las Vegas. Here, in "Sin City," he became a card dealer in a casino. All around him he saw gambling, drugs, nudity, and prostitution (see the story of Liza in chapter 6).

Then one day it happened. He picked up a copy of the Quran at a bookshop and, after reading a few of its pages, said to himself, "This is it, I have found my answers." From that moment on, Mustafa was consumed by a passion to learn about Islam. As a first step, he gave up his job as a card dealer for a more respectable position. Taking the Quran to work each day as a bellhop, he would read it riding up and down the elevator. "People say you shouldn't read the Quran in a hotel," he explained, "but this was the only place I could read. I had two children, we lived here for thirty-something years, and there is a lot I drew from Vegas that is happy. As a bellman, I saw myself as helping travelers who are confused and trying to find their way. I thought of it as doing a good deed for someone." He went on, "These people who work here are just trying to do the best they can for the families, to provide assistance to people who need it, so I don't disrespect Vegas. But the gambling is a cancer that has spread across the country." The imam is critical of the social trends and bemoans the damage it has done to children, questioning "a society that lets you go out late at night and have intimate relationships, and there seems no way to check it, or the level of drinking among college students, the sexuality of young children, the alcohol and drugs."

While he disparages gambling and drinking, he is grateful to Las Vegas because that is where he discovered Islam: "Vegas has a lot of negatives— the highest drop-out rates, highest home foreclosures, highest bankruptcies. There is a lot that hides behind this stuff, but I never knock it because this is where I studied the Quran."

This humble man, who barely finished high school, taught himself Arabic, memorized the Quran, and went on to become a respected imam. For Imam Mustafa, Islam brings the perfect antidote to the sins he sees around him. While prohibiting drug use, alcoholism, and prostitution, it also rejects the idolatry of entertainers and celebrities on prominent display. And he notes that Islam has a wider application than just for those souls exposed to the temptations of Las Vegas. He believes that African Americans who fall prey to the deliberate attempt of the "white man" to destroy their moral caliber through drugs, alcoholism, and prostitution, which has led to divorce, teenage pregnancy, early deaths, and often despair, can be saved by Islam, just as he was saved by it.

We saw Imam Mustafa several times during our stay, and I was impressed by his thoughtful gentility and manners. He is the imam of the Masjid Haseebullah in Las Vegas, a small unpretentious center of worship, barely more than a room and a veranda, but in which he takes great pride. The imam looks after it with the tenderness of a lover. His faith gives him an aura of calm unshaken by the centuries of difficult history that his people have suffered. He has found peace in Islam; his is the perfect *submission*.

Imam Mustafa told us about a video presentation and booklet that he had spent years preparing titled "The Missing Pages of History," which document the history of the black community. We quickly organized a viewing, and the team was riveted.

The presentation opens with events in the Middle Ages "when Europe began to emerge during the fourteenth and fifteenth centuries [and] began a program of colonizing most of the world's land and minerals . . . accepting the hospitality of the world's peoples; they then enslaved their host and destroyed their history and culture." A section on Native Americans asks,

"When did these people, who were the oldest residents of North America, cease to have land rights and were only good when dead?"

Another section, on Africans, asks, "When did these people become subhuman, fit for use only as slaves?" Referring to the sophisticated and complex cultures of Africans unknown to most Americans, the presentation notes, "Merchants, librarians, teachers, and *hafiz* [those who have memorized the Quran] were seized. Fulani, Wolof, Yoruba, and hundreds of other tribes were carried into the wilderness of North America."

The imam's presentation was particularly critical of Christian missionaries and their use of the Bible to suppress the black population: "Whether the Bible teaches or condemns racism is not the issue at hand. But without doubt, millions of those who have studied it, interpreted it, and taught from it have been and are racist. And no part of the Europeans' (white race's) curriculum has for us been more damaging than those distortions which have been passed on in the name of God [quoting Carter G. Woodson]."

In a scathing indictment of slavery, the imam writes, "The house Negro knew the alcoholic master and the abused wife . . . the incestuous relationships, battered wives, insanity, and war. More than any other slave, they knew of the master's low character and bestial nature. . . . But they also knew something else . . . they learned a lesson which remains a part of the Negro psyche to this day. They learned that there was nothing that a Negro could do for them[selves] and that their fate was controlled by the Master. They might pray to Jesus for a cabin in the sky, but they knew that heaven or hell on earth was in the hands of 'the Man.'"

Even African Americans such as Imam Mustafa who have made their peace with the past find the weight of those lost centuries of slavery and brutality difficult to contemplate. He blamed many of the ills of his community on its subordinate position under the whites, believing that whites encouraged the use of alcohol, heroin, and crack cocaine among African Americans to create depression and disintegration. "Crack cocaine," he said, "had the impact on the African American community that the atom bomb had on the Japanese. It destroyed families and generations." The imam believed it was possible to transcend these challenges with his religion. "Islam saved my life," he told us several times. It was a refrain we were to hear from many African Americans throughout the journey.

"I Love That Brother"

The identity of African American Muslims is rooted in the most basic and simplest of Islam's tenets: that the Prophet himself is an inspiration and a model. This admiration for the Prophet of Islam is so strong that many African American Muslims have taken the name Muhammad or derivatives as their own, including some of the most prominent members of the community: Wallace Fard Muhammad, Elijah Muhammad, Muhammad Ali, and W. D. Mohammed are examples. And many African American imams are named after the Prophet. We have just met Mustafa, but there were also Imams Muhammad Ameen in Memphis and Mustafa Carroll in Dallas, as well as Minister Abdul Hafeez Muhammad of the Muhammad Mosque No. 7, a Nation of Islam mosque in Harlem.

African American Muslims, like other Muslims around the world, invariably told us the Prophet of Islam was their greatest role model, from the Muslim rappers we spoke with in Buffalo to Imam Abdul Karim Hassan of Los Angeles, who said, "The Prophet is life to me. Without him, I would not have a full life." Imam Hassan noted that the Prophet gave Muslims "guidance for human behavior" and "laid the groundwork for people who claim to be Muslim. There are a lot of times we don't live up to that."

Imam Fateen Seifullah in Las Vegas explained that he felt the Prophet is "the example everyone should follow, a simple example, a blueprint, a model for my life. He offers common sense, a simplified religious life. He demonstrated it for me." Perhaps the most moving tribute came from the prisoner we interviewed in Los Angeles, who said: "I love that brother" (see below).

Their direct affiliation to the Prophet makes African American Muslims authentic followers of Islam. At the same time, their community cannot be easily placed in one of the three specific models of Muslim society that we found in the Muslim world. Although some individuals are inclined toward mysticism, most African Americans are concerned with the here and the now, with issues relating to housing, education, drugs, and employment. Modernism implies an acceptance of, and working within, the "system," with its white values, attitudes, and ethos. And while some may indeed veer toward literalism, as in the case of the Salafis in Omaha mentioned in chapter 1, the distrust of immigrant Muslims is strong enough to encourage a more local development of Islam based in the African American historical experience.

African American Muslim identity is therefore a complex matter. These are thinking individuals who, in many cases, made life-changing decisions to convert to Islam. They also carry with them the memory and culture of their African American background and the larger one of American society itself. Negotiating between these identities has always been a challenge. The community therefore requires a different frame of analysis.

For this reason, I explore the African American Muslim community from the time its first members landed in America and see how, almost four centuries later, they are rebuilding their Islamic persona on the basis of scholarship, memory, and instruction. It is an exciting experiment in the rediscovery of a lost identity. Unlike other scholars looking at the African American Muslim community, who see an evolutionary trajectory from the Nation of Islam to what they call "mainstream" or Sunni Islam and view the two as mutually exclusive, I take into account the entire range of experience that is common to African Americans. This legacy includes influences such as the earliest stirrings of Islam in the United States, the Black Nationalist Movements, the Nation of Islam, the inspiring leadership of Imam W. D. Mohammed, and the myriad directions in which his followers have taken his message. I believe that any African American Muslim, regardless of sectarian or ideological affiliation, has inherited this legacy and now represents a truly authentic and unique African American Muslim identity that is still evolving and growing.

African American culture predisposed individuals to talk of "reverting" to Islam rather than "converting." Imam Al-Hajj Talib Abdur-Rashid of Harlem told us that almost 50 percent of Africans brought as slaves were Muslim, and it is true that most slaves were from the continent's west coast, where Islam was the predominant religion. In spite of those terrible centuries of slavery, the community miraculously clung to the memory of Islam, however tenuously. In order to discover how much, if any, of their original Islamic culture or tradition survived, we traveled to remote Sapelo Island, off the coast of Georgia.

"Christian by Day, Muslim by Night"

A bitterly cold Atlantic sea spray hit my face like a thousand razors, and our speeding boat seemed about to capsize, yet I was excited. We were approaching a tiny community said to consist of descendants of former slaves with a common Muslim ancestor who was captured in Africa and brought to the United States early in the nineteenth century.

We had traveled a long distance from Miami to rendezvous with our boat on the sparsely populated Georgia coast. We had stopped a few miles away at what appeared to be the only shop in the entire area. The reception was frosty. The African American owner wore an Obama T-shirt on his muscular chest and curtly refused to be interviewed, saying, "Me and cameras don't get along." Some items in his shop like the pickled pig's ears, pig's feet, and pork rinds made members of my team from the North queasy. We drove off looking for the pier where our boat was supposed to be waiting but saw no signs to direct us, and the side roads we took were basically dirt tracks. Now and then a deserted-looking house would appear, its yard filled with junk.

When we finally found the right spot, we saw neither a boat nor anyone to ask for help. To add to our consternation, our cell phones were out of reception range. As we waited around, a van with two or three African Americans stopped a distance away and then drove off. This happened several times with different vehicles, and we were not sure what that meant. As the day wore on, the darkening landscape of huge old live oak and cypress trees draped with diaphanous Spanish moss began to look sinister. This was swamp country—could large reptiles be lying in wait for unsuspecting visitors? As we shivered in the Atlantic winter wind amid the "creepy" surroundings, as Frankie put it, our boatman suddenly appeared as if from nowhere, and we were on our way.

Peering across the dark and watery vista, I wondered what answers we might find to a question of vast importance to an anthropologist: how long might religious custom and tradition survive among individuals dislocated from one society and transported to another where people deliberately set out to obliterate them? Would these customs even be recognizable after a few generations?

Sapelo Island held the answer. Our guide on the island was the sagacious Cornelia Walker Bailey, a direct eleventh-generation descendant of Bilali Muhammad and an author and lecturer on the history and culture of Sapelo. She believed her ancestor Bilali was originally from North Africa and possibly studying Islam or preaching when he was captured. He was first taken to Middle Caicos and then to Sapelo Island, where he became the head "enforcer" over the other slaves.

Glimpses of Bilali Muhammad's life and thought are to be found in the "Bilali Diary," a manuscript he wrote entirely in Arabic characters, although the language he used is not standard Arabic.[1] Bilali begins his manuscript with the phrase used as a benediction throughout the Muslim world: "In the name of God, the Beneficent, the Merciful." This is followed by "God's prayers upon our master, Muhammad and his family and his companions." The manuscript describes various Islamic activities such as the *dua* (the direct prayer calling upon God for assistance and mercy), the *adhan* (call to prayer), and *wudu* (ablutions). Bilali's emphasis on the washing of the arms, elbows, and feet would be passed on to the following generations.

Bilali's manuscript reveals a scholarly, pious, and intelligent man who clung to his identity and dignity. This pride was shared by the larger

Cornelia Walker Bailey with Akbar Ahmed on Sapelo Island, Georgia. She is an eleventh-generation descendant of an Islamic African scholar, Bilali Muhammad, who was enslaved and brought here in the early nineteenth century.

African American community. Imam Abdur-Rashid in Harlem told us Bilali was one of his role models—along with Muhammad Ali and Malcolm X. His legacy was kept alive through the generations by his descendants, like Mrs. Bailey.

Mrs. Bailey, dressed in jacket, trousers, and cap to protect her from the bitter wind, took us into Hog Hammock, where her tiny community lived, and to our lodgings in her quaint, if austere, house turned hotel—with its possibly haunted rooms, muttered one team member with a slight shiver. Over a long interview late into the night, Mrs. Bailey allowed us glimpses into her community.

For Mrs. Bailey, the *Mayflower* meant "nothing"—if anything, mention of it irritated her because it was "the beginning of us coming to America as slaves. It turned out to be not so good." The coming of white people in their lives did not augur well for Mrs. Bailey's people. They called the white race "buckre," meaning "white people who leave a bitter taste" or "those who were not to be trusted," although she was not sure of the origin of the term.

She painted some graphic images of the brutality that slaves suffered—that of a pregnant mother's belly being slit open and the fetus trampled under the boots of the slave owners was particularly disturbing, especially as we had heard this several times on our journey. She said black ministers talked of "forgiveness" constantly, but "sometimes I don't feel like being so Christian. Sometimes I want the Old Testament, an eye for an eye." In the middle of this long, depressing conversation, Mrs. Bailey said something that I almost missed but that forced me to sit up as I absorbed its significance. She said she would like to "reverse the ships." For a moment, I thought she meant that the descendants of the Africans should be allowed through some magical process to go back in time to Africa and prevent the ships from landing in the first place. Her meaning was entirely different and more sinister: she would like to enslave whites, she said, to put them in "shackles" in order to do to them what they had done to the Africans. The team was stupefied as the implication of what she was saying sank in. There was a moment of complete silence that seemed to stretch for a long time, only interrupted by the howling wind outside.

For Mrs. Bailey, history amounted to a constant battle to preserve as much of her people's identity as possible. Her African Baptist Church, for example, was a response to the mainstream Baptist Church dominated by white people. It was established to assert the congregants' unique identity and distinct ancestry from Africa, including some possibly Islamic roots, she said. Even though worshippers were Christian, once they entered the church the men went to a section on the left and women to one on the right. They also took their shoes off, and the men and women covered their heads. The church was called a "prayer house" rather than a church, an echo of the meaning associated with the term "mosque." Churches face the east, she explained because the sun rises in the east and the "devil" resides in the west. Clearly, the east was originally perceived as good, and the west, because of its association with slavery, was seen as bad. Even as Christians, they said their prayers facing east. Perhaps the significance of facing the east comes from the fact that Mecca, which Muslims face to pray, lies in that direction.

Mrs. Bailey remembered a long tradition of washing hands and feet, which comes directly from the Muslim wudu. Modesty was pronounced among women, and after puberty arms and legs were covered. She recalled her grandmother not eating pork, although it slowly entered their diet out of necessity, but still in small, reluctantly eaten, quantities. She mentioned stories of her ancestors and grandmother praying five times a day. Divorce was strongly discouraged, and even today men and women are not allowed to "live in sin."

The memory of elders having real authority reflects both African and Islamic tradition. A recognizable authority resting in elders gave stability to a slave community that was often dislocated as it was moved around. The elders also helped to keep traditions alive. As part of the rites of passage, young men and women were told to go into the wilderness and meditate for an hour or so at night and required the approval of the council of elders before being confirmed in the church.

Although all slaves were expected to convert to Christianity, Bilali clung to his identity as far as possible, passing some inherited beliefs to his children, who in turn passed them on to theirs. As Baptist preachers only arrived once a month to teach Christianity, Sapelo's residents were largely left to continue their Islamic practices.

Mrs. Bailey recalls her grandmother telling her, "We were Christian by day and Muslim by night." Mrs. Bailey was not the only one who told us of a grandmother keeping Islamic custom alive. Imam Fateen of Las Vegas remembered his grandmother in Tennessee not eating pork, not eating with her left hand, and covering her head. He talked of tombstones with crescents on them.

With each generation, however, the links with Islam faded. Even the meaning of the seminal and eponymous name, Bilal, after whom her ancestor was named, was lost. When I recounted the story of Bilal and his devotion to the Prophet—and the reason why Mrs. Bailey's ancestor would be called Bilali in the first place—she confessed she had no idea what I was talking about.

Hazrat Bilal—*hazrat* is a term of respect—was an Abyssinian slave, I told Mrs. Bailey, who converted to Islam and was then tortured to force him to abandon his faith, yet refused. The Prophet had a special love for Bilal and appointed him the first *muezzin* in Islam, or one who performs the call to prayer. Bilal's voice was legendary for its soothing and exquisite quality. It is the subject of a popular South Asian folk story immortalized by the Sufi musicians, the Sabri Brethren in their Qawwali. The Arab aristocracy, objecting to this appointment because Bilal was an African slave, prevented him from saying the adhan. When the people of Arabia awoke the next morning, they were shocked to find the sun had not risen. The angel Gabriel appeared to the Prophet and with due respect said, "God loves to hear the beautiful adhan of Bilal and has decreed that the sun shall not rise unless Bilal gives the call to prayer." The Prophet then requested that Bilal give the adhan, and with that, the rhythm of nature was restored.

With eyes glistening, Mrs. Bailey absorbed the significance of the story relating Bilal's central role in Islam. Up to that point, she had been businesslike and even curt with us, but now a gentler, more personal side crept into view as she said softly: "I love my Muslim background; ignoring it would be like cutting off an arm."

We woke on Sapelo Island to a historic day. Barack Obama was being sworn in as president. A smiling and cordial Mrs. Bailey met us for a visit to the local cemetery, emphasizing that this was a rare concession as the community discouraged outsiders from disturbing the sleep of those buried there. Such permission, I noted, was also in the Islamic tradition, as was the practice of burial on the day of death. The dead were buried facing the east in the belief, Mrs. Bailey told us, that when people rose on Judgment Day they would be "facing the right way."

It was soon time to leave, but no boat was available because of the holiday. Working her magic, Mrs. Bailey asked a relative to help us, who turned out to be none other than the man who owned the store. The idea of ferrying a group of strangers across the freezing Atlantic when he could have been watching Obama's inauguration on television had not improved his mood.

As we skimmed over the water, Hailey moved closer to him and asked sweetly, "So what do you think of the *Mayflower* and Plymouth?" My team was relentless in pursuing interviews under any circumstance, but Hailey had not recognized him as the same man from the store. "Lady, ask your ancestors," he replied testily. Not deterred, Hailey pressed on: "Can we film you?" To which he repeated his earlier rebuff: "Me and cameras don't get along."

An awkward silence descended on the boat as the situation dawned on Hailey, so I leaned over to him and said loudly in a mock-serious tone, "We all look alike to her." He glanced at me and then gave what was the first faint smile in our brief acquaintance. Everyone relaxed, and we were soon on land and on our long drive to Atlanta.

What came home to me yet again was the power of the subject of slavery in every corner of American society. Contemplating the enormity of what happened over the centuries to those Africans can silence the most garrulous and eloquent of people. Even Barack Obama appeared subdued in 2009 when, during a visit to Ghana, he emerged from what was called the "Gate of No Return" in a holding castle on the coast where Africans captured as slaves had been kept in the basement. The floor was raised several feet by human excrement. The marks on the walls are still visible. The women were separated and regularly raped. Centuries later, the stench of blood, urine, and feces still hangs in the air. If there was ever a place where Dante's dictum "Abandon hope, all ye who enter here" held true, it was here.

Obama noted that a church stood just above the basement and was dismayed that a faith based on compassion and love could be involved in something as degrading as slavery. Michelle Obama, who is descended from slaves, looked drawn and lost.

Mrs. Bailey's wish to "reverse the ships" has to be understood in the context of the slave ships from Ghana, which marked the first step toward robbed dignity, stripped identity, and negation of the self. Her thoughts echoed those of countless other African Americans we met on our journey.

A Pre-Columbus Muslim Discovery of America

Throughout our travels, we heard of Muslim explorers who discovered America before Columbus. For Chris Lovelace, a young imam we met at the Muslim Center of Detroit influenced by Imam W. D. Mohammed, proof of this discovery lay in the nation's name: *Ameer* means "leader" in Arabic, he told us, and in time, "Amiraca" became "America." He saw further evidence of Islam's influence in the name "California," which he traced back to caliph, meaning a leader of the Muslim community, and in "Tallahassee," derived from "tell Allah hussey," perhaps meaning "pray to Allah, girl." He thought New Orleans was nicknamed the Crescent City and police badges bear a crescent because Muslim pirates and sailors once dominated the port. His evidence included other places, such as New Medina on the Mississippi, Koran in Louisiana, many named Mecca (such as Mecca, Texas), and Honolulu, which comes from "Hon-Allah-hu," an invocation of God.

"Muslims were trading with Native Americans long, long before the discovery by Columbus," Lovelace told us. "In fact, on Columbus's ship, the lead sailor was a Muslim, he was a Moor. They call him Moor in history because that sounds a lot less intimidating than a Muslim—we can deal with that. . . . In Pennsylvania, there is a Civil War memorial dedicated to the people of Algeria. The Union had brought some of these soldiers in to defeat the Confederate Army. Also there are stories of Muslims who the U.S. Cavalry brought over to train in how to use camels in warfare like Hannibal used the elephants."

When I told Representative Keith Ellison about Lovelace's beliefs, he said: "There are a great number of links that I really hope our historians dig into. . . . But sometimes today pundits try to represent Islam as hostile, foreign, not a part of us, but some of the names are irrefutable. But I think it merits investigation. The young imam might be right; he might not be right, but it's worth digging into."

In an article titled "We Came Before Columbus: The Pre-Columbian Presence of Muslim Africans in America Is No Myth" available on his mosque's website, Imam Abdur-Rashid, known as the "hip-hop imam," argued that a growing body of evidence points to a Muslim pre-Columbian American (and Caribbean) presence and that "those who study the evidence and continue to deny the obvious, reveal themselves to be rooted in old, racist, European renditions of American history. . . . Muslim explorers came to the land of the Original Americans, met them, peacefully interacted with them, traded with them, intermarried with them, and perhaps even gave another relative handful of them *dawah* [invitation to the faith]."[2] He contrasts their purportedly peaceful actions in North America with those of white Europeans who "stole" land from the continent's "indigenous inhabitants" and "committed genocide against [the continent's] true people, stole the 'Black Man' from Africa and brought him to the stolen land against his will, and . . . populated the land from Europe."

Charging that America has robbed native Africans and Muslims of their heritage, Abdur-Rashid wrote: "Many of the people kidnapped to this country and sold into slavery were already Muslims. And then, we suffered psychic and blunt-force trauma to the head, and forgot everything, including who we are and what we are. We were told, 'Your name is not Ahmed. Your name is Charlie. You don't worship Allah. You worship Jesus.'" Pointing to violence toward people of color, he views the United States as a nation permeated with injustice and derides its annual celebration of "so-called Thanksgiving."

Early Muslim Awakenings

Upon their arrival in America in the late twentieth century, immigrant Muslims were disapproving of what had been passing for Islam among African Americans. They found un-Islamic the hatred of white people, the number of daily prayers, the rituals, and the references to Wallace Fard Muhammad as Allah, and Elijah Muhammad as "the Prophet." What they failed to appreciate was the community's struggle to reach toward a distant vision of Islam in difficult if not impossible circumstances. Without the foundations laid by these early Muslims, there would have been no Islam in America among African Americans. Imam W. D. Mohammed is a direct beneficiary of their legacy, however radically he changed its character and direction.

Black movements and black Muslim movements ran parallel, often overlapping and invariably drawing from each other. The leaders across the board felt mutual empathy and together gave African Americans a sense of common aspirations and dreams. Their broad objectives were the same—to better the condition of the community. Some chose the civil rights route, some religion, and others political activism.

Both Muslim and non-Muslim African Americans emerged from a culture that had denigrated and rejected them. As de Tocqueville observed bleakly,

> The Negro makes a thousand useless efforts to introduce himself into a society that repels him; he bows to the tastes of his oppressors, adopts their opinions, and in imitating them aspires to intermingle with them. He has been told since birth that his race is naturally inferior to that of the whites, and he is not far from believing it, so he is ashamed of himself. In each of his features he discovers a trace of slavery, and if he could, he would joyfully consent to repudiate himself as a whole. . . . The law can destroy servitude; but God alone can make the trace of it disappear.[3]

Even in the nineteenth century, which I have called the Great White American Century, African Muslims clung to Islam. Bilali Muhammad and Abdul-Rahman, the famous "prince among slaves" at the turn of the century, struggled valiantly not to lose their connection with the faith they had brought from Africa, a task that became more difficult with each succeeding generation as Islamic custom, practice, and terminology faded.

But the story of Islam in America was far from over. It rallied in different ways and in different places. It was recalled and imagined in items of clothing and names—a fez, later a crescent on a cap, baggy trousers, a sash. These efforts in the early part of the twentieth century vaguely conveyed an idea and impression of the Muslim "Oriental." Names associated with Islam were plucked from history, one being "Moor," a name applied to Muslims on the Iberian Peninsula. Leaders even called themselves "Allah" and "the Prophet." It would take the best part of the twentieth century before the momentum generated by this "Islamic identity" would be realigned with and move toward orthodox Islam.

The slow but sure path to the rediscovery of Islam goes back to the founding of the Moorish Science Temple of America in 1913 by Noble Drew Ali. Settling in Chicago, which Ali believed would become the second Mecca, he claimed to have been sent from Allah to instruct African Americans to return to "Islamism," which he took to be the Moors' original religion at the time Ali believed the Moors dominated the world. The Moorish Science Temple urged its followers to assert their true identity, to shed names like "black" and "negro," and call themselves "Moorish Americans." Members added "El" or "Bey" to their American names to make them sound more "Moorish," prayed facing the east, and dressed in elaborate "Turkish" attire complete with fezzes, turbans, silk robes, and curved swords.

As the movement became firmly entrenched in Chicago and Ali was acknowledged as a religious leader, Moorish Science Temple members took to the streets, confronting whites and singing the praises of their leader, Ali, who had "freed them from the curse of the Anglo-Americans."[4] Arrested for causing racial disturbances and allegedly beaten by the Chicago police, Ali died on July 20, 1929, under mysterious circumstances. His death triggered a struggle for leadership, his driver claiming that he was Ali reincarnated.

Another who made the same claim was Wallace Fard Muhammad, known in the movement as David Ford-El. When he was rebuffed, he formed his own group, which in 1930 would become the Nation of Islam. Despite the splits within the Moorish Science Temple, it continued to show steady growth, mainly because of its prison ministries. During the Great Depression it attracted the attention of the FBI after a special agent found a temple flyer denouncing money as the "root of all evil" and reported the leader of the local temple chapter as a "fanatic on the subject of the equality for all races."[5] The FBI soon infiltrated all Moorish chapters around the country and during World War II accused it of aiding the Japanese, but no evidence was ever found to support these claims. The bureau then shifted its attention from the Moorish Science Temple to the Nation of Islam.

The frail, slight figure of Elijah Muhammad, born Elijah Poole, took over the Nation of Islam when Fard disappeared in 1934, never to return. Elijah Muhammad remained the head of the Nation of Islam until his death in 1975, by which time it was a flourishing economic and political organization. Born to a Baptist pastor in Georgia, Elijah moved north with his extended family in what is called the Great Migration, which saw thousands of African Americans journey north in search of work. As a young man, he had witnessed three lynchings of blacks and had "seen enough of the white man's brutality . . . to last me 26,000 years."[6] Elijah found work in an automobile factory in Detroit, where he came into contact with the Moorish Science Temple.

At a temple meeting in August 1931, Elijah was so moved by its speaker, Wallace Fard Muhammad, that he became his disciple and converted with his wife and family, changing his name at Fard's instruction to Muhammad. Fard handed over leadership of the Detroit followers to Elijah, and the temple changed its name to the Nation of Islam. Shortly after, Fard vanished, and Elijah was declared the successor. Elijah now pronounced Fard divine, an incarnation of God, and predicted his eventual return to earth.

Plagued by power struggles and fearing for his life, Elijah moved from Detroit to Chicago. During World War II, he was arrested several times for refusing to serve in the military and was imprisoned. When the war was over, Elijah emerged to lead a movement that now gathered support with impressive speed. Members like Malcolm X, who converted in prison, became charismatic speakers and brought their oratorical and organizational skills with them.

Elijah Muhammad had accomplished what "generations of welfare workers, and committees and resolutions and reports and housing projects and playgrounds" failed to do, wrote novelist and essayist James Baldwin, which was "to heal and redeem drunkards and junkies, to convert people who have come out of prison and to keep them out, to make men chaste and women virtuous, and to invest both the male and female with pride and a serenity that hang about them like an unfailing light. He has done all these things, which our Christian church has spectacularly failed to do."[7]

While undoubtedly creating an Islamic awareness and passion, Fard and Elijah had also confronted the Muslim community with a theological predicament, having taught them that Wallace Fard was "Allah" and Elijah his anointed messenger on earth. This belief posed a fundamental challenge to Islam, despite the community's many acceptable customs, such as abstinence from eating pork, from smoking and drinking, from the use of drugs, and gambling. In addition, the Nation of Islam followed a black separatist doctrine of reversed prejudice, teaching that the white race was intrinsically evil and shaped by the devil. Elijah preached that Allah would destroy the "white devil" while the followers of the Nation of Islam would emerge as the conquerors and settlers of the New World. Believing in its community's total independence, the Nation of Islam sought its own state or territory within the United States. Strangely, the KKK was rumored to be providing funding for the Nation of Islam as it shared the Nation of Islam's interest in keeping the two races separate. We learned of at least a strategic meeting of interests from Pastor Thomas Robb, who cited Marcus Garvey and Elijah Muhammad as the best leaders for African Americans. The worst thing to happen to the African Americans, said Robb, was the "white liberals," with their misdirected attempts to bring all religions and races together.

Pastor Robb's views were not shared by his predecessor, Grand Wizard J. B. Stoner. In the Atlanta Masjid of Al-Islam, we came upon a letter Stoner had written to a Chicago conference of Muslims in 1957 in which he rants against black Muslims. Addressed to "Infidels," the letter warns blacks to "repent of Mohammedanism or burn in hell forever, throughout eternity." The text clearly reflects a definition of American identity infused with racial hatred as it refers to Islam as "a nigger religion" that has "only been successful among Africans and mix-breeds and never among the white people never. . . . Islam is a product of the colored race. Islam is a dark religion for dark people. I don't know why Africans would support Islam for any other reason except of race."

The letter's prejudice is the product of religious indoctrination that drew on Christian narrative, such as the story of Noah and his three sons, to rationalize race relations in America. Noah was said to have passed out drunk and naked one night and been discovered in this condition by Ham, one of his sons, who told his two brothers of it. With eyes averted, the brothers covered their father, who upon waking was furious to learn that Ham had seen him naked. He cursed Ham, saying that "a slave of slaves shall he be to his brothers," as a result of which the sons of Ham were dark in color.

The gentle and reserved Imam Fajri Ansari of Masjid Nu'Man in Buffalo, another mosque affiliated with Imam W. D., became impassioned during our interview over the depiction of a blue-eyed, blond, and white Jesus, which allowed white preachers to say, "We are like Jesus, we are close to him; you are descendants of Ham and therefore cursed." The images of Jesus suffering on the cross, continued the imam, were interpreted as "You black people must learn to suffer for your sins." This theological notion reinforced the master-servant relationship and locked it in place. Local officials, politicians, and the educational system supported the philosophy of the church, together creating America's normative attitudes toward color.

Countering the Ham symbol, the Nation of Islam used the figure of the ancient black scientist Yakub to explain the intrinsic evil and worthlessness of the white race. The doctrine was based on a series of genetic breeding experiments conducted by Yakub, who was guided by Allah to create the white race by grafting "the devil (white man) from the black."[8] This race was described as "blonde, pale-skinned, cold-blue-eyed devils—savages, nude and shameless; hairy, like animals, they walked on all fours and they lived in trees."[9] From the day they were grafted, the doctrine states, the "devils were doomed, or limited."[10] Malcolm X later criticized Yakub's place in the Nation of Islam's theology.

The Great American Reformer

Although cross-cultural references can be misleading, it seems fitting to compare the impact of Imam W. D. Mohammed on Islam among African Americans with that of Martin Luther, who radically altered the course and content of Christianity. Like Luther, the imam took on the entire establishment of what was normatively seen and accepted as Islam and gave it a new direction.

I had met Imam Warith Deen Mohammed, affectionately referred to as Imam W. D. by his supporters, at an iftaar dinner given by President George W. Bush at the White House not long after 9/11 and kept in touch with him. I was hoping to interview him for this project when I learned in Detroit that he had just passed away. We were visiting Imam Abdullah Bey El-Amin at the Muslim Center of Detroit and found its congregation in mourning. Imam W. D. was truly beloved of the community, "the greatest imam that ever lived," said Imam El-Amin in his eulogy.

The genius of Imam W. D. was that he single-handedly moved the African American community toward identifying with pluralist American identity while moving away from Black Nationalist Islam. Today, millions of African American Muslims are comfortable with being as strongly American as they are being devout Muslims, demonstrating the two are not incompatible. This achievement is due entirely to Imam W. D.

It was not easy. He had broken ranks with the Nation of Islam and suffered every kind of calumny. He was "excommunicated" several times for denying the divinity of Wallace Fard Muhammad, considered the founder of the Nation of Islam. The excommunication was particularly painful because it was executed by Elijah Muhammad, his own father. But he would not relent. He was finally allowed back into the Nation of Islam in the early 1970s and after his father's death was declared its leader.

Imam W. D. now set about instituting a major overhaul of the Nation of Islam to align it with orthodox Sunni Islam. To start with, he rejected the literal interpretations followed by his father and other Nation of Islam members. He also rejected black separatist views that reflected racism and reverse prejudices, removing references to Yakub, which in the Nation of Islam's lexicon depicted white people as devils. This act alone removed the theological justification for a negative perception of whites. On the contrary, the imam argued, whites are fellow worshippers. He also encouraged the learning and recitation of the Quran in the community and laid the foundations for an entire generation of Islamic scholars.

Emphasizing the personality and history of Hazrat Bilal, Imam W. D. introduced the word "Bilalian" to refer to the African American community to draw strength and pride from Bilal's analogous experience during the Prophet's time. This direct link with the origins of Islam imbued the community with a sense of history and honor. The focus on Bilal also allowed Imam W. D. to avoid falling under the cultural and theological

At the Detroit Muslim Center, a mosque influenced by Imam W. D. Mohammed. Imam W. D. had died earlier on the day the team met with Imam Abdullah Bey El-Amin, second from right, and mourned his loss with the congregants.

influence of contemporary Arab Islam, which he did not find particularly attractive.

Imam W. D.'s other great contribution was his interfaith initiatives, especially with Jews and Christians. In 1978 he became the first Muslim to address a large gathering of Jews and Muslims at the Washington Hebrew Congregation, then headed by Rabbi Joshua Haberman. Over the years, he continued his interfaith initiatives and in 1998 spoke at Auschwitz in Poland. Imam W. D. also reached out to the Catholics, meeting the pope on several occasions and addressing a gathering of 100,000 at the Vatican. In addition, he kept a busy schedule within the Muslim world, meeting its leaders including King Fahd Bin Abdulaziz of Saudi Arabia and President Anwar el-Sadat. He led several delegations of Muslim Americans to Saudi Arabia. In 1977 he led the largest delegation of Muslim Americans—some 300 strong and consisting largely of former Nation of Islam members—on a pilgrimage to Saudi Arabia.

Imam W. D. was not only a visionary but also a practical leader. He headed the Mosque Cares, an Islamic dawah project, and a business entity called the Collective Purchasing Conference. His videos, audiotapes, and television programs ensured that his message was reaching the community.

By the 1990s mainstream America had begun to acknowledge Imam W. D.'s stature as a great American in the best pluralist tradition. In 1992 he was asked to give the first invocation by a Muslim in the U.S. Senate. In March of that year, he became the first Muslim to deliver an address on the floor of the Georgia State Legislature. The next year saw him offering the Islamic prayer at the inaugural interfaith prayer service hosted by President Bill Clinton.

Imam W. D.'s faith sustained him in a life filled with personal turmoil. In his twenties, he was sent to prison for over a year for refusing induction into the U.S. military as a conscientious objector. Spending time there studying the Quran in depth, he developed an approach to Islam that caused him to become estranged from his father, although their relationship thawed toward the end of his father's life. However, relations remained strained between the imam and Louis Farrakhan, who led what remained of the Nation of Islam.

Imam W. D. had his Muslim critics, most commonly among immigrant and African American Muslim literalists, many of whom had been part of his movement at some point but decided that it deviated from the "straight path." Literalist mosques are often located within shouting distance of W. D.'s mosques, as in Denver and Dallas, and invariably in the less affluent areas. Many literalist African Americans accuse Imam W. D. of the grave sin of "innovation" and claim he disliked immigrant Muslims, especially Arabs, and was therefore a "racist." They also say he preferred to cite the U.S. Constitution rather than shariah, or Islamic law. In Memphis's Masjid Al-Noor, an African American Muslim in traditional Islamic clothes, a beard, and kufiya told Jonathan and Frankie that "W. D. Mohammed was a government agent" because "he always kept Muslims off the right path" and didn't have the people's best interest at heart: "This is why the U.S. government is scared of the true Islam," he said. "Islam makes you God-conscious in a land where you are free to send yourself to hell."

Imam W. D.'s supporters in Memphis and elsewhere would argue otherwise. Responding to Frankie's account of our experience with the African American Muslims in Omaha, an assistant imam commented: "These Salafis don't know what they're talking about. They say that everything has to be exactly like the Prophet Muhammad, but what do they do in the winter? Do they wear sandals when it's freezing outside?"

Imam Mustafa from Las Vegas commented on the pride that Imam W. D. engendered in the community: "Today the descendents of the slaves join their brothers and sisters not as African American Muslims, nor as

Negro Muslims or as Moorish Americans, colored Muslims or any other such thing. But rather as Muslims who strive to be *mumineen* [believers] and are bound to Islam."

Imam Fateen Seifullah, also of Las Vegas, said that Imam W. D. is the reason that he and many other African Americans "are not on the street selling drugs, hangin' with the gangs. People don't understand what he did for America in taking African Americans to mainstream Islam. We could have been gangbangers; instead we live the best life we can." We heard this sentiment repeatedly—that Imam W. D. saved peoples' lives, kept them off the streets, inspired many to work in the community instead of helping to destroy it.

Sulayman Nyang, a prominent Islamic scholar in the United States originally from West Africa, spoke movingly of Imam W. D. in an obituary, citing in particular his efforts "to keep his people away from all of those things that make African Americans the butt of jokes or religious bigotry and extremism. This side of him was evident in his decision to remind his father's followers that they were Americans and that their knowledge of Islam should never be seen as a false mixture of racism and religiosity."[11]

In an interview with Frankie at Imam W. D.'s memorial service in Chicago, the imam's grandson Kevin Walker, a college student at the time, remembered especially his grandfather teaching him "different things about the religion, and how I should pray and be kind to people. When I was little I used to kill bugs 'cause I didn't like them, and he used to tell me that everything was equal, and why is my life more important than the bug's life, so I should care for the bug and let it outside, so it could be where it belongs." Tariq Mohammed, Kevin's younger brother, loved his grandfather, both a teacher and a hero to the boy: "When my great-grandfather, Elijah Muhammad passed, he [Imam W. D.] built the bridge for mainstream Islam."

Frankie asked one of Imam W. D.'s followers at the service to describe the imam's legacy. "Because of Imam Mohammed," came the reply, "I don't hate you. We were taught to hate whites. He changed our mentality and led us in embracing the true Islam." Such remarks were commonplace among African American Muslims—they would often tell Frankie how racist they once were but how different they had become now because of Islam and Imam W. D.'s leadership. "As we traveled," said Frankie, "I began to grasp the enormity of what the imam was able to accomplish, and I was dismayed that as a history major in college I had not even heard his name before."

Malcolm X: The Voice of Islam

Americans like Frankie would have certainly heard the name Malcolm X, who was the trailblazer even before Imam W. D. The impact of Malcolm X on African American Muslims, America, and the rest of the world makes him a key figure in modern history. He had a genius for translating complex issues into a few words, as is evident in his saying about Plymouth Rock. His autobiography and the film *Malcolm X* (1992) offer fascinating glimpses into his life and conversion to Islam.

Born Malcolm Little, he was frequently in trouble with the law as a junkie, a pimp, and a convict. A turning point came in prison, when he was told by another inmate, a member of the Nation of Islam, "You are nothing, less than nothing." That simple statement led him on a quest to discover himself. He learned of Elijah Muhammad, of how the "blue-eyed devil" had robbed the black man of his humanity, and of Islam as salvation. He became a Muslim and took the name Malcolm X, the "X" replacing the white man's name of Little.

A pilgrimage to Mecca was another turning point: "This was the only time in my life that I felt like a complete human being." Malcolm X described the experience: "There were tens of thousands of pilgrims, from all over the world. They were of all colors, from blue-eyed blondes to black-skinned Africans. But we were all participating in the same ritual, displaying a spirit of unity and brotherhood that my experiences in America had led me to believe never could exist between the white and the non-white."[12] Malcolm's journey is reflective of the journey of his community. Within a few years, he was transformed from a man living on the margins of the law to a religious leader pushing for acceptance and compassion in society.

The tragic assassination of Malcolm X in New York in 1965 was a turning point in the history of the Nation of Islam, which some suspected of having a role in his death. While many members felt that Malcolm X was getting too much publicity and was too ambitious, his brilliance and eloquence were making a mark not only in the United States but also abroad. Many were also disturbed by Malcolm X's conversion to Sunni Islam and movement away from the Nation of Islam. They were enraged by his outspoken criticism of the Nation of Islam's ideas about whites and his explicit criticism of Elijah's teachings on the subject, especially his suggestion that the story of Yakub "infuriated the Muslims of the East."[13] As if this was not enough, he now wished to work with other civil rights leaders.

Malcolm X had dreamed of finding a balance between Islam and America: "America needs to understand Islam, because this is the one religion that erases from its society the race problem. . . . I have never before seen *sincere* and *true* brotherhood practiced by all colors together, irrespective of their color . . . . With racism plaguing America like an incurable cancer, the so-called 'Christian' white American heart should be more receptive to a proven solution to such a destructive problem . . . in time to save America from imminent disaster—the same destruction brought upon Germany by racism that eventually destroyed the Germans themselves."[14]

Jonathan and Frankie spoke with a follower of Malcolm X at the mosque that commemorates him, Malcolm Shabazz Masjid, in Harlem. The man pointed to another there, Khalil Islam, who had been Malcolm X's driver and bodyguard and was alleged to be one of his assassins. "He was in prison for twenty-two years," the man said, "but he didn't do it." Previously known as Thomas 15X Johnson, Khalil Islam had embraced Sunni Islam while in prison after a visit by none other than Imam W. D. Ironically, the man accused of assassinating Malcolm X for moving away from the Nation of Islam toward Sunni Islam was traveling the same spiritual road.

Meeting the Nation of Islam

Though now somewhat marginal to the African American Muslim community, the Nation of Islam retains a distinct identity. It is often maligned in the media, and many white Americans remain fearful of its allegedly violent nature. Whenever I have had the occasion to meet its members, I have found them courteous. Its leader, Louis Farrakhan, has a national presence and is frequently in the news, often for some fresh controversy. Relations between followers of the Nation of Islam and Imam W. D. are affable, if complex.

On a visit with the homeless population in inner-city Detroit, Frankie was approached by a man who aggressively identified himself as a former U.S. Marine and member of the Nation of Islam and responded to Frankie's attempts to talk with an ominous "I could stab you right now." Not one to be easily discouraged, Frankie, accompanied by Jonathan, visited the main Nation of Islam mosques in Chicago and in New York. Frankie found the headquarters in Chicago an impressive building, a refitted Greek Orthodox cathedral with the distinctive star and crescent extending above the dome. The two were met by burly security guards in leather jackets and earpieces, "who gave us a more thorough search than most airports I've visited. Jonathan's pen was completely disassembled to make sure it wasn't a bomb."

Although Nation of Islam members were courteous to the two visitors, they were cold and suspicious of the team's project and motives. The racial tension was palpable as they waited to meet with Larry Muhammad, the director of education of the Muhammad University of Islam, which is situated next to the mosque. Wearing a meticulous white suit, he discussed his school and the position of the Nation of Islam, which, he said, remains popular in the black community but has also experienced recent growth among Mexicans and Puerto Ricans. The curriculum is based on the teachings of Elijah Muhammad and Louis Farrakhan, but some Sunni practices have been introduced, such as fasting for Ramadan. Although Muhammad spoke "exceedingly carefully and apprehensively," he was cordial with Frankie and Jonathan and tried to arrange a meeting with Louis Farrakhan, but it did not materialize.

In New York City, Frankie and Jonathan visited Muhammad Mosque No. 7 in Harlem, once headed by Malcolm X before his split with the movement. Unlike Chicago's mosque, the one here welcomed them warmly, although Jonathan's pen was once again examined. The building was grand but decaying and creaky, with a large portrait of Elijah Muhammad at the entrance. Frankie and Jonathan chatted with the friendly Minister Abdul Hafeez Muhammad, who invited them to Friday prayers. They observed that the large hall was almost empty and there were only fifteen worshippers although this was the main prayer of the week.

Hailey had her own encounter with the Nation of Islam in Washington, D.C. She was in a taxi headed for American University when the African American male driver asked whether she was a student or worked there. She said she was "doing research." He then spoke of his trips to Ghana, which he had visited in order to trace his ancestors who had been brought over in the slave trade. He proudly told Hailey he had been to Ghana five times and that she needed to go there to see "what your people did. Everything was fine until whites started dividing people based on race."

Hailey was inured to this argument, having heard it before, and veered the conversation to the broader interests of the project by asking what Plymouth Rock meant to him. He said the real history of America did not start with Plymouth Rock but was the result of the work his people had done as slaves as they built this country. "Without us, you would be nothing," he said, almost daring her to challenge him. Throughout Hailey never once felt threatened, although she "was aware of the level of anger he had."

He then asked her if she had read or seen *Roots*. When Hailey said yes, he appeared mollified and told her Kunta Kinte was a Muslim and did not eat pork. He asked Hailey if she had ever heard these things before in "snowflake land," a term he used to describe a place where white people live segregated from blacks. She said that she had. He calmed down a little, but remained agitated.

As they drove up Massachusetts Avenue toward the university campus, he mentioned that Christianity was used to keep slavery in place. Asked if he was a Christian, he declared, "Absolutely not!" As a member of the "Islamic faith," he did not associate with that "white" religion. When asked if he followed the teachings of Imam W. D. Mohammed, he said that he did not follow a man who had "committed incest," preferring the teachings of Elijah Muhammad and the Nation of Islam. He said that he was aware of the Moorish Science Temple and revered its founder as one of the great prophets. When Hailey asked for clarification on the "mad scientist Yakub," he explained that Yakub had banished the "white freaks" to the caves and forests of Europe, adding, "You know you are only albino black people, right?" He explained that Europe was so named because "you roped in: Eu-rope, you rope."

When Hailey indicated that she had been working with a Muslim scholar studying the Muslims of America, he asked abruptly: "Is he a foreign brother?" When she told him I was from Pakistan, he shook his head disapprovingly: "No, they study the Muhammad of 2,000 years ago. I study the Muhammads of America. You need to study us." He felt foreign Muslims wanted to be white and ignored the African Americans, something his people resented greatly: "Where were the Pakistanis when we were being hosed in the South and under the Jim Crow laws?" Not to be cowed, Hailey came back with, "This scholar was under British colonial rule." He seemed satisfied, adding that they, too, had had their fair share of "white people."

"The System"

Predator identity and its instrument of power and authority, known as "the system"—that baffling, amorphous, ominous, all-pervasive web of the administrative and power structures that surround and entrap the individual in America—are the bane of the African American community, although ideas about the system and its harmful effects varied among those we interviewed.

In Miami, we heard complaints about Cuban policemen who had adopted the ideas and cultural prejudices of white people. They called it the system and said once a person is in the system, there is no way to escape. Minor offenses or merely suspicious activity can land you in jail for months, with no proper representation and no one to listen.

Frankie and Jonathan interviewed a group of African Americans bar-
becuing outside a convenience store on a Saturday afternoon. One named
Sweet, aged fifty-eight, who had never been in prison and had honored his
country when he fought in the Vietnam War, defined the system: "They got
new ways to mess you up now. They ain't whupping you, they ain't hanging
you, they ain't tarring and feathering you—they doing paperwork on you.
Mess up your whole life. You can't never be nothing once they put that
paperwork on you. It's just a messed up deal. But believe me, the Ku Klux
Klan is all over the world. They in the military, up in the White House,
they're everywhere. It's hard to straighten things, but it is getting better."

Sweet complained that "the rights we have are not the same. . . . We
sit here in the neighborhood and barbecue and the police will come. They
don't come to any other neighborhood. They arrest us for having an open
container of alcohol, for drinking a beer. We're not driving. Any excuse to
arrest us they will take. We're desperate—our get-togethers are the only
thing that keeps us going. They come up here like we done killed somebody. Catch robbers and killers, not us."

Another veteran, E. L. Randel, who would not speak to Frankie until he
saw his ID because he was so suspicious of talking to a white person asking
questions, said he was "absolutely not" proud to have served in Vietnam
and "wanted no part in that bullshit." When asked to name the greatest
threat to America he replied "white people."

To black Mardi Gras revelers on Bourbon Street in New Orleans, the
system meant the police and prison. When asked to name the greatest
threat to America, one young man replied: "The biggest threat right now?
Is the police comin' and messin' with me for no apparent reason, that's the
biggest threat to me right now." His companion was even more forthright:
"The police fucking wit ya. The Feds, you heard me? They locked me up
for like three months, you hear me? Man, fuck the motherfuckin' police,
fuck the system, fuck Orleans, fuck New Orleans."

For Dawud Walid, the African American director of the CAIR chapter in Detroit, the system has something to do with the legacy of slavery
in the black community. He wished blacks appreciated this history more
fully and "how it helps explain current problems." He felt the nation's only
foreign policy goal is "oil." He blamed the media as an agent of the system that incites hate "everywhere." "The media is a puppet," he said, that
"has become part of the political establishment" full of "Zionists and anti-
Muslim bigots," and he gave the example of Fox News. He considered the
war on terror and attacks on Muslims the system's way of turning attention away from substantial issues such as poverty and education in places

like Detroit. Walid joked bitterly that he has committed the double sin in America of "driving while black and flying while Muslim."

Indeed, a frequent complaint we heard was that the system portrays Islam in a negative way through the media. As a result, noted Imam Abdullah Bey El-Amin of Detroit, Americans tend to be misinformed about Islam, and he urges them to read the scripture and see that "Allah doesn't say anything about Jews are monkeys in there. . . . Allah doesn't say kill the Christians in there. It says if they hurt, come at you, kill them, and I don't see anything wrong with self-defense. But . . . right after that it says 'But if they desist,' then leave them alone because Allah is forgiving and peaceful. They don't put that part in."

Racial prejudice was another constant theme of those talking about the system. When asked on our questionnaires if they had ever experienced racial prejudice, African Americans thought the answer was obvious, with replies of "On a daily basis," "Duh, I'm black," and "What do you think?" An African American Muslim male in Harlem at the Mosque of Islamic Brotherhood said the greatest threat to America is "its unwillingness to part with the notion of white privilege and racism." A twenty-one-year-old woman in Iowa of mixed white and black ethnicity said she experienced both religious and racial prejudice: "I wear hijab so people judge me every day. Some days are worse than others. I am African American and white, so people think I am Arab or not 'American.'" A female African American Muslim convert in Atlanta said, "YES. YES. YES. All of my life, I've had to endure racial prejudice."

Even followers of the more pluralist Imam W. D. remain suspicious of the system. An African American woman in her thirties in charge of organizing a Ramadan dinner in Detroit's Muslim Center told Frankie that despite the advancements of the past forty years, African Americans remain in "perpetual slavery." Cradling her child as she cleaned up in the kitchen, she said she refuses to let her children join the military because it is another way of enslaving blacks. She does not have a credit card because card companies are another form of enslavement. In fact, she maintained, the entire system keeps "moving the bar back on blacks. . . . First, you needed a high school diploma; then blacks got high school diplomas. Then you needed BAs, and blacks got them; but now you need an MA to succeed. Blacks can't keep up."

Imam Luqman Ameen Abdullah, a Muslim convert in an elaborate turban who had served in Vietnam and was a member of the same mosque, lost his life to the system one year after meeting us at the Muslim Center of Detroit in September 2008. He had said to us, "Allah tested people with races, languages, and differences. It's hard for somebody to be different from someone else and be able to accept them as their brother or sister. Islam has given me a level playing ground."

Imam Abdullah ran a mosque and clinic in Detroit, a city that was making headlines during our fieldwork owing to the desperate economic situation of its citizens and the near apocalyptic deterioration of its infrastructure. Over a Ramadan dinner of spaghetti and canned string beans, Frankie asked Abdullah if the people he worked with still had hope for the future. "They don't think that way," the imam said; "they're only focused on subsistence, getting by hour by hour." His criticism of the system was unsparing, and he defined American identity as a "Hollywood movie" and the Constitution as a "theory": "People say America the beautiful, America is this and that. But when you get into the cities, you see what America really is."

To Jonathan, Craig, and Frankie's surprise, they again ran into Imam Abdullah at Imam Seifullah's Masjid As-Sabur in Las Vegas months after meeting him in Detroit. Abdullah was traveling around the country teaching in various mosques, and here his lecture compared the tribulations of Muslims in America with those faced by the Prophet, whom he called "the reality of Allah manifest through a man." He again railed against the system but said that despite the oppression, Muslims should follow the Prophet, who "cared about people, helped everyone, no matter their religion or color—that is Islam."

When our questionnaires were distributed in the mosque, the immediate response was one of displeasure. One man approached Frankie and asked for my e-mail address in order to protest: "No Muslim would ask these questions—there is something going on here," he said suspiciously. He was wearing a skullcap and a stylish tan T-shirt that read "Islamic Revolution" and had the white outline of a man in five stages of prayer. He demanded to know if Frankie had read the Quran and asked how he could possibly be working on a study involving people from a religion he "believed was false" because of Frankie's Christian background. Frankie said his only purpose was to learn from him and others in the mosque.

Imam Abdullah defended the team to the Las Vegas worshippers, pointing out that they were working for "understanding." Abdullah took Frankie aside and said he wished him well, although "the system" was sure to oppose "Journey into America." Islam is being targeted, he said, and spoke of the past when Muslims had rallies for their causes, such as Bosnia, which are now impossible. He also mentioned his problems with the U.S.

government, which he said kept arresting him and had confiscated his passport. His cynicism about law enforcement was pervasive, and he claimed to have been offered grenade launchers by the FBI for use in a nefarious plot. He was dismissive of Obama, calling him the "great black hype." And he remarked, "The system remains in place, but people in power are right to fear Islam because Islam is a threat to what they want to keep, and what they want to keep is garbage. Islam is bad for business."

One year after talking to us, Imam Abdullah was killed in a shootout with the FBI in a Dearborn warehouse. According to initial news reports, he opened fire on FBI agents after refusing to surrender and was killed in the ensuing exchange of gunfire. It soon emerged that he had shot an FBI dog that had been released on him. Although the FBI claimed in its federal complaint that Imam Abdullah was a "highly placed leader of a radical fundamentalist Sunni group" called the "Ummah," whose aim was to establish a separatist Islamic state within the United States governed by shariah law, they did not charge him with terrorism. When asked why the imam was not charged with terrorism, the U.S. attorney for the Eastern District of Michigan said that the "charges speak for themselves."[15]

In February 2010 Imam Abdullah's autopsy report was released to a storm of controversy. According to the county medical examiner, the imam was found handcuffed and shot twenty times, including once in the back. His face was covered with cuts and bruises and his jaw smashed by something other than gunshots. There were reports that an undercover white informant, who had disappeared moments before the FBI turned up, had played a key role in the case. The man who had had a premonition about the system in the end fell victim to it.

Shortly after, Imam El-Amin issued a public statement in the Muslim Media News Service in which he claimed that the goods Imam Luqman was accused of stealing were "supplied by the FBI" in a case of "intentional entrapment" and "murder." The imam wondered whether there were larger forces at work "to further discredit Islam" or "put more emphasis on African American Muslims because since 9/11, most of the spotlight was on Arabic and Asian Muslims, and now the campaign has spread wider." Imam El-Amin warned the Muslim community that "everyone that says As Salaam Alaikum and prays five times a day is not necessarily your friend. . . . The case of Imam Luqman is a good example of how the Satan works." The imam's relating the "devil" to the FBI's actions and comparing their use of dogs to those unleashed on civil rights protestors is a throwback to the wounds of the past.[16]

African American Imams

We met many other imams who were more at peace with themselves and American identity than Imam Abdullah. Imam W. D. had unleashed a pent-up energy and force in the community, which was now under the direction of these dynamic religious leaders.

The History of African American Islam in One Man

The story of Imam Abdul Karim Hassan in Los Angeles is the African American Muslim story: his ancestors were slaves, he was raised on a sharecropper's farm, and he saw his family embrace Black Nationalism with Marcus Garvey, then the Nation of Islam with Malcolm X. Hassan moved to Sunni Islam with W. D. Mohammed, and since 9/11 has become a key leader in the local Muslim community. Jonathan and Frankie sat down with the tall, thin Hassan in his mosque, Masjid Bilal, in South Central Los Angeles for several hours and were fascinated by what he had to say.

Masjid Bilal opened in 1973 as a Nation of Islam mosque and moved to Sunni Islam just two years later. It is located on a historic piece of land, the site of a former African American Elks Club. Duke Ellington and Louis Armstrong performed there, and Joe Louis was a frequent guest, the imam said proudly. The mosque is now both a place of worship and a charter school for Muslims and non-Muslims with an enrollment of 200. He said that he decided to build a school instead of a new mosque because "the school serves more people," citing Elijah Muhammad's focus on education.

Imam Hassan's father was a sharecropper in South Carolina during the Great Depression. His family had come from slavery and knew how to work the fields. One day his father reached his breaking point. He disobeyed the plantation owner by refusing to use a mule that was exhausted and in need of rest to remove a tree stump from a planting field. Furious at this insolence, the plantation owner, carrying a whip in his hand, threatened to "beat the black off you." Hassan's father did not budge, responding defiantly, "You come down here and get into these arms and you're going to hell."

The infuriated owner walked away in anger, but Hassan's father knew that he would return to punish him. Even young Hassan was aware of the punishment for disobeying and threatening a white man: "They would kill you and bury you in the field." That night three full carloads of white men showed up to kill Hassan's father, but he had escaped that afternoon with the understanding that his family would join him later in Connecticut.

Hassan told the team he still remembers with fear the huge, bright headlights lighting up the dark night.

In the North, his mother became active in Black Nationalist movements—in Marcus Garvey's Pan-African movement in the 1930s, and in the Moorish Science Temple in the 1940s, with Hassan at her side wearing his "little red fez." His mother then became a member of the Nation of Islam and knew Malcolm X personally. In 1956 she took Hassan to hear him speak, and Hassan was dazzled by Malcom X's "fiery speech," which drew him instantly to Islam. Signing up as a "laborer," Hassan was dispatched to Los Angeles by Elijah Muhammad himself, who changed the spelling of Hassan's Muslim name, Abdelkarim (after a North African Muslim insurgent leader who fought the French), to Abdul Karriem because he thought it was more in line with what the Nation of Islam's founder, Wallace Fard Muhammad, would have wanted. With the death of Elijah Muhammad in 1975, Imam Hassan followed Imam W. D. in leaving the Nation of Islam. Imam W. D. now changed the spelling to Abdul Karim to coincide with the Arabic spelling and therefore to be closer to "pure Islam." Throughout his family's many tribulations, Hassan found peace in Islam and the example of the Prophet, whose ethical standards should bring compassion to all Muslims.

Hassan felt both blacks and whites had a problem because of slavery: "The slave masters and their children had mental problems, by reducing us to something less than human, and we had a mental problem by being reduced to something less than a human, thinking that we were inferior." He did not hesitate to criticize even the Founding Fathers, singling out Thomas Jefferson: "I don't think they even knew what they were doing when they put in the Constitution that every man is born with inalienable rights. They didn't have us in mind when they did that. We were chattel to them, when they wrote that." Thomas Jefferson, Hassan believes, proved the inescapable fact that African Americans are human beings by fathering children with a black slave, proving black and whites were the same species. But Jefferson "didn't care one bit about that child he produced." Hassan contended that a mixed race child of someone like Jefferson "became the whippin' boy for his own white child. And that meant that if the white son got in trouble, he wouldn't get in trouble, his guardian would get in trouble. The half-white one would have got the whoopin'. So we had a lot of things going here that were very destructive to both people—the African descendant and also the European descendant."

He went on to say that while the Muslim world was affected by September 11, things did not change for African Americans unless you were flying.

"They already knew our history," he said; "big brother was watching us all along. There is a historical dislike of African Americans, but it doesn't come from anything we did, except be freed from slavery. What have we done?" In Hassan's view, terrorism and Muslim resistance to the West sprang from social factors connected with oppression and had nothing to do with religion: "To deliver yourself from oppression takes some violence. Violence overthrows violence to enjoy peace. Anyone who is oppressed will try to relieve that oppression. You can't judge them by their situational behavior. I can sympathize with them, but that's not me."

"Radical Muslims," said Hassan, "don't live up to those high standards of the Prophet Muhammad. They ought to be ashamed of themselves. Islam itself, in its definition, is a beautiful way of life, if you can attain it, if you can follow it. But there are a lot of people out there who aren't following it. Yet they call themselves Muslims. Some Christians give a bad impression of what Christianity represents. During the days of slavery in America, the ignorant Southern preachers cleared the consciences of the slave masters, to make them feel that what they were doing was right—consciously right and just. Christianity didn't teach that. They interpreted it wrongly, and they interpreted it at the expense of millions and millions of African captives that were brought here and made slaves. You can search the Bible up and down and you won't find the Bible approving of that condition that they put upon those African captives."

According to Hassan, African American Muslims are the best bridge between the Muslim world and the West, and as a patriotic American, he sees no threat to America beyond itself: "We are our own worst enemy and we create enemies sometimes. If America is less in stature, then it has done it to itself—we commit suicide. Nobody can conquer America; America will conquer itself." At the same time, he disapproved of those who criticize America, who thereby reveal their ignorance of the rest of the world's problems: "There is nothing better over there. Don't paint a rosy picture of other countries—I've been there."

Islam in "Sin City"

Imam Fateen Seifullah heads the Masjid As-Sabur, the oldest mosque in Las Vegas and a haven for celebrities like Muhammad Ali and Mike Tyson—the latter, we were told, helps to vacuum the mosque's prayer rugs as an act of piety. Tyson donated $250,000 to the current building, which amounts to more than half of the total cost, and Muhammad Ali helped with fund-raising. With the mosque welcoming ten to twelve converts every month, the Muslim community is growing rapidly and includes doctors and lawyers.

The name of Imam Fateen's mosque reflects the trajectory of African American Muslims and that of his own life. Founded in 1971 as Muhammad Mosque No. 75, it was part of the Nation of Islam until the congregation joined Sunni Islam in 1975 under the leadership of Imam W. D., whereupon it became Masjid Muhammad. In the 1980s the name was changed to Masjid As-Sabur. Its congregation is about 50 percent African American, and the leadership is mixed.

Imam Fateen has an easygoing charm and radiates energy in his dedication to changing society around him. Islam provides him the perfect platform. Like Imam Mustafa, he seemed a thoughtful man living in the desert on a quest for spiritual answers. Growing up in Los Angeles's Compton neighborhood, one of the most impoverished in America, the imam identified with Black Nationalism and joined the Nation of Islam because Farrakhan's rhetoric blaming white America for all the ills of the world appealed to his own anger. In 1988, now in trouble with drugs and gangs, he discovered that blaming the whites had left him "nothing but the underworld." A desire to come closer to God overcame the hatred in his heart, and Fateen turned to Sunni Islam. He gave up wearing Muslim clothing following a trip to Morocco with some other African Americans. The sheikh they had come to visit, upon seeing them, asked "Where are the Americans?" "Right here," they responded. "Then why are you dressed like Moroccans?" the sheikh asked. "Bring your uniqueness to the table. . . . Be American." It was not that easy for Fateen because "it was a challenge to remember our history here in the U.S. as African Americans. . . . We have a genetic memory of slavery. It is sometimes triggered, but we must remember we are Muslim first."

When I visited Imam Fateen in his mosque in Las Vegas, my heart warmed at seeing him in cordial conversation with a local bishop, R. E. Lee, also African American. I felt I was in the presence of spiritual brothers. They pointed out that the wall of the mosque is shared by the church next door and emphasized the power of their different faiths in bringing them together in the worship of the same God. The bishop even referred to God as "Allah." Together they have launched a vigorous program to look after the homeless and provide medical support to the needy, irrespective of faith or color.

Bishop Lee told me: "The imam and I, we have forged a relationship. He's my brother, my brother in the Lord, and my brother just in general. And what we're trying to do is to distill the myths that a lot of people have

Imam Fateen Seifullah, on the right, and Bishop R. E. Lee in Las Vegas at Masjid As-Sabur, with Ahmed. These religious leaders' mosque and church share a wall and more. They, along with their congregants, enjoy a strong friendship and do charitable work among the poor.

about Islam, and even about Christianity. And you know, I believe there's one Allah, and many prophets, and we're trying to bridge the gap together. He has a heart for mankind. That is the only way you can do it." "Which doesn't see color or religion?" I interjected. "No, no, color-blind," affirmed the bishop. "Absolutely, that's the only way you can do it." Was that the true message, I asked the bishop. "Yes sir," he replied.

As we walked about, people would come up to the imam, embrace him, or whisper some confidence in his ear. He had a smile and hug for everyone.

He confided that he was constantly short of funds: "Every week is a fund-raiser of some sort to sustain this. Because people, they want to give to the building of a mosque, but Muslims have not come to understand the value of this kind of service, you know." Muslims, he felt, tend to spend more money building new mosques than helping the poor, which was against the true spirit of Islam: "Oh you can get money for building mosques here all the time, you know, the physical structure. And our Prophet, peace be upon him, that wasn't his example. Service to humanity was far more important than luxurious properties."

In the imam's mosque, with the famous Las Vegas skyline visible behind it, I saw the paradox of modern civilization. Juxtaposed with the wealth and extravagance of the revelers were the poverty and squalor of the homeless. Las Vegas hotels threw away tons of food daily rather than give it to the hungry and needy. "They have health regulations," remarked the imam, "at least that's what we're told, that prevent them from giving food that has been sitting in the buffet for a couple of hours to feed the homeless. We run into a challenge with that kind of wastefulness . . . in a society, not only in the hotels but in the fast food places, the McDonalds, the Burger Kings. We'll see them throw stuff in the garbage cans."

As the imam showed me around the neighborhood, we passed a van with the word "Hanifa" on its license plate. The owner, he explained, was Hanifa Abdul Kareem, an African American who had painted the mosque. "I hope he's not stopped twice, once for being African American and once for being Muslim," I said jokingly. "Well, you know, generally it works so different, once you're stopped as an African American, and they find out you're a Muslim, they ease up a little bit!" "They ease up?" I asked. "Yeah," the imam said with a hearty laugh.

Imam W. D. Mohammed's Right-Hand Man

At the Atlanta Masjid of Islam, Jonathan, Frankie, and Craig met Imam Plemon T. El-Amin, W. D. Mohammed's long-time assistant who traveled the world with him. Attesting to its good relations and integration in the larger community, the Masjid is the only mosque we found on our trip that broadcasts the adhan on loudspeakers in the neighborhood, calling Muslims to prayer as in a Muslim country. The imam is a prominent leader of interfaith dialogue in Atlanta and has been a close associate of the city's mayors. Numerous African Americans throughout the country had told us we had to meet this embodiment of American pluralist identity, who had won his spurs in the turmoil of the civil rights movement and gone on to embrace the vision of the Founding Fathers. Dressed in a suit and small cap, he spoke with the team in his office following afternoon prayers.

El-Amin was born and raised in Atlanta in a family descended from slaves. His parents went to black colleges, but he attended Harvard University on a Reserve Officers' Training Corps (ROTC) scholarship, which he gave up in protest of the Vietnam War. In 1974 he converted from Christianity to the Nation of Islam for "social and political, not spiritual" reasons, hoping to make a difference in the African American community. He believed that the Nation of Islam would be the vehicle for that change.

Imam El-Amin's belief in dialogue and engagement came directly from his mentor and role model, Imam W. D., about whom he spoke with reverence and passion: "He is the greatest inspiration to us; he inspired us to accept our obligations and responsibilities as Americans. Since 1975 we have identified as Muslim Americans. We have rights, duties, and responsibilities as Americans. We have to support good wherever we see it." Indeed, Imam W. D. always encouraged him to think of himself as an American. "Islam overseas is different," Imam W. D. told him once. "If it was presented to me in the way they do it overseas only, it would not be as attractive to us [African Americans]." Other role models included Frederick Douglass, W. E. B. Du Bois, Booker T. Washington, President Barack Obama, the motivational speaker Stephen Covey, and Martin Luther King Jr.

The imam's pluralism was inspiring, encompassing "anyone who believes in goodness . . . including Hindus and Buddhists. In the Quran it says God created us in different nations, different tribes so that we would know each other."

Waving the Islamic Flag in New York

Imam Siraj Wahhaj of Masjid At-Taqwa in Brooklyn, New York, is one of the country's most famous Muslim leaders. Wahhaj is vice president of the Islamic Society of North America (ISNA), chair of the Muslim Alliance in North America (MANA), and the first Muslim to lead a prayer before the start of a session of the House of Representatives. Yet he has also become one of America's most controversial imams and remains a frequent media target.

Interviewed by Jonathan and Frankie, Wahhaj said he joined the Nation of Islam shortly after the assassination of Martin Luther King Jr., taking the name Jeffrey12X because, as Jeffrey Kearse, he was the twelfth Jeffrey to join the Nation of Islam in New York. He became a minister in the movement but then followed W. D. Mohammed into Sunni Islam.

After studying in Mecca in 1978, he decided not to rely on one person's interpretation, as he had earlier with Elijah Muhammad, and pored over the Quran.

In 1981 Wahhaj founded Masjid At-Taqwa with only some two dozen people in attendance; today, about 1,300 come for Friday prayers. At that point, the mosque was situated in the middle of a bleak, crack-devastated African American ghetto. In the winter of 1988, he worked closely with community residents and the New York police to stake out drug houses for forty days and nights. The effort was successful, and now the neighborhood is home to more than forty Muslim businesses. He has maintained good relations with the city and non-Muslims in the neighborhood, noting that an African American woman came to the mosque not long ago to tell him that she used to hate Muslims but now loves them because of their work in the neighborhood.

Imam Wahhaj believes that the police and non-Muslims treat African American Muslims better than immigrant Muslims, but he is still harassed at the airport every time he travels. He said when "randomly selected" by security, he tells himself sarcastically, "Yeah, I know. I've heard that before. I suffered through being an African American second-class citizen, and we got past a lot of that, but now we get the Muslim hits, so here we go again."

Speaking about some of the controversies surrounding his activities, he blamed the media for sensationalizing them and taking his words out of context. For example, he was put on a list of "unindicted," "may be alleged," "co-conspirators" in the case of Sheikh Omar Abdel Rahman, known as the Blind Sheikh and convicted in the 1993 World Trade Center attack. While the label has cast a shadow over his reputation with Americans, it has also made him something of a celebrity, especially with those Muslims who feel he is being victimized for standing up to America. Just as controversial are Wahhaj's statements on Israel. Wahhaj pointed to "our misguided foreign policy, especially toward the state of Israel. It's horrible. We have a right to be allies with everyone, even Israel. That's not the issue. The issue is: are we going to hold everyone accountable, including the state of Israel? I'm not doing anything different than I always do. I speak what I think is the truth. If I can criticize the president of the United States of America, if I can criticize the policy of the United States of America, why can't I criticize the policy of Israel? Why am I now this pariah because I criticize Israel?"

Wahhaj was unsparing of the "corruption of values, morality and the evolving standard of decency" in America. People are overindulged and spending more money on drugs than food, he said, in exasperation: "What are we doing?"

Despite the controversies, Wahhaj spoke affectionately about America. It is his home, and he is part of American culture. He loves baseball and is frustrated when his favorite team, the New York Mets, loses a game. To him, America is a "place of freedom and opportunity" where he can talk to people about his religion, can convince people that "this is the correct religion, it is a good religion." He refused to "damn America," he said, and instead honestly prayed for it because he and his community want America to thrive: "This is what I think most Americans don't understand. So when President Bush says something simplistic like 'they don't like us, they hate our freedom,' you're crazy. It has nothing to do with hating your values. We don't like the corruption, admittedly. We don't like places like Sin City, prostitution, admittedly. We don't like homosexuality, admittedly. We don't like the corruption, just like Christians and Jews don't like it either, but we don't hate America. We don't like some of the policy of our government toward Muslims around the world, but we don't hate America. Not at all. I love this country. This is my country as much as it is anyone else's."

To explain one of his community's traditions, Imam Wahhaj drew on a story told by the Prophet in which a number of people are in a boat and someone starts to drill a hole. The Prophet said that if you stop that person, you save him and everyone else, including yourself. The question for Muslims, then, is "What can we add to make America better?"

Jonathan observed that whereas the imams who revered W. D. Mohammed dressed "mostly American" with some Islamic attire, Wahhaj was in full Arab dress with a skullcap and large white beard. "If I didn't know any better," remarked Jonathan, "I would think he was East African. He came over to Sunni Islam with W. D. Mohammed but then followed a different path in embracing Arab Islam and culture that other African American Muslims tend to shun. I think his Arab credentials enabled him to assume his leadership roles in ISNA and MANA, where he is frequently invited to speak. This is in contrast to other African American imams, who are rarely featured in these larger gatherings."

Frankie, too, saw something different in Imam Wahhaj. While appreciating Imam Wahhaj's interfaith commitment, Frankie still felt "he lacked the Zen-like quality of other African American imams we met and didn't talk about W. D. Mohammed at all. While talking to me about how to speed-read, a talent he is proud of, he exclaimed 'You know who doesn't read? *Your* President,' which I thought was odd as George W. Bush was the president of the entire United States at the time."

Rappers, Editors, Prisoners, and Members of Congress

Today, African American Muslims are part of the fabric of contemporary American culture and are prominent in many fields, especially music and sports. Well-known popular figures include musicians Michael and Jermaine Jackson, Snoop Dogg, the Wu-Tang Clan, Akon, Lupe Fiasco, Mos Def, Busta Rhymes, and T-Pain. Songs by T-Pain and Akon, in particular, were constantly broadcast on our car radios as we traveled across the country. African American Muslim sports superstars include Kareem Abdul-Jabbar, Shaquille O'Neal, and Mike Tyson. In addition, Dave Chappelle, who converted to Islam in 1998, is one of America's most popular comedians and television personalities. African American Muslims are contributing not only in music and sports, but also in other fields such as journalism and politics. While the following sections detail conversations with prominent African American Muslims, I also wanted to highlight the problems surrounding the American penal system, and I have included a synopsis of interviews with Muslim prisoners who reflect on the importance of Islam in their lives.

The Muslim Rappers

My meeting with Muslim rappers came about by chance. Imam Fajri Ansari had invited me to speak after his Friday sermon at the all-black Masjid Nu'Man in Buffalo. A scholarly and thoughtful man, he had impressed Zeenat, Hailey, and me with his comments and insights about Muslims in America. Hailey was the only white person there and found the women welcoming.

After prayers, the imam introduced the small congregation, and I found myself talking to two young brothers who were professional rappers. The Habeeb brothers were polite, amiable, and of imposing height, reaching almost 7 feet each. The older brother was named Arleym and the younger Quadir, who goes by the name Q-Boogie or Da Poet.

I invited them to join us that Saturday night at the house of my friend, Faizan Haq, where we were staying. It was an insightful evening for all of us, and I was instructed in American hip-hop and African American history. After receiving a Division One scholarship to Howard University to play basketball, Quadir Habeeb became a lyrical poet and hip-hop artist and performed on ABC *World News Now* in February 2007 in a tribute to Black History Month. Today he works with the renowned disc jockey

Green Lantern. Arleym Habeeb is a successful business entrepreneur, who focuses on "giving back" to the community through educational initiatives to ensure that children with few opportunities have good role models and programs to help them grow and achieve.

As we began filming and interviewing the Habeeb brothers, I asked the older brother what his name meant because I thought I heard the word *alim*, which in Arabic means a scholar. He said his name was derived from alim, but "they kind of messed it up, because during that period of time they didn't really know the Arabic correctly so they spelled it A-r-l-e-y-m."

Arleym and Quadir were fifth-generation Muslims, "which is unique for African Americans," said Arlyem. I recalled Imam Ansari telling me that these two were the most regular congregants attending Friday prayers and two of the most devout. "*Alhamdulillah* [blessings be to God], our family has a long Islamic tradition."

When asked about American identity, Quadir exhibited a flash of anger, which would appear intermittently throughout his conversation: "As an African American I feel slighted being descended from slaves, that our identity has been stolen and replaced with just an 'X' for slave. A lot of African Americans' last names—Jenkins, Jacksons, Smith—should be African names. . . . We don't have Dashikis, Grambobas, Grababas. We don't have that, so American identity for us as being younger African Americans will be more likely close to hip-hop. I dress hip-hop because that's all I know—that's it."

Asked to define "hip-hop," he described a music form with easy rhymes interspersed with profound truths about life and death, pain and sorrow. But the pain and sorrow did not take the form of an elegy or mournful poem. Hip-hop had vitality and energy that linked it to Islam.

Quadir began to sway with the rhythm of his own beat and voice as he demonstrated how Quranic verses he has translated loosely are adapted to hip-hop. "Oh help me, help me find a way," Quadir sang to God, "to take the pain away every day I struggle with."

When I asked them about the symbolism of the *Mayflower* settlers landing at Plymouth and what it means to them, Quadir, citing the famous Malcolm X quote, said, "It wasn't a choice for us to be here. . . . We celebrate Christopher Columbus who killed a lot of people, put smallpox in blankets, infected so many hundreds of Native Americans and raped and pillaged." And he raised the question of reparations for slavery, asking if victims of the Holocaust could be compensated, why not those whose ancestors had been brought over as slaves: "Americans need to recognize our suffering. You know what? If I hit your car, I recognize I hit it then—'zoom, bye.' Or I make an attempt to ease your pain and say, 'Hey, let me fix this.' This has not been done."

Quadir also felt that Christianity had damaged the psyche of his community: "Noah in the Bible said to his grandson, 'You will be cursed black.' Then you show a picture of Jesus, *alay-salaam* [blessings be on him], and he's white, blond hair, blue-eyed. That's psychological slavery." Even so, Quadir did not feel antagonistic toward Christians, emphasizing that Islam teaches that "a good Christian is a good Muslim, and a good Muslim is a good Christian because they believe. But African Americans came to Christianity as slaves and were taught that the Bible says you will be cursed."

Arleym interjected with equal passion: "You talk about the *Mayflower*, and you know the ship we came on was the *Amistad*." He recited a poem he had written:

We were led into the bowels of the ship,
The smell of bowel movement and piss,
Just a whiff could leave you nauseous from this,
Lost to the gift of sunlight, just like a solar eclipse,
Some swollen from hits, bruised from the stroke of the whips,
All 'cause of my skin and the size of my lips,
I'm eyeing my missus, she's getting dragged to the top of the ship,
She got raped, beat, and then killed, and she was fed to the fish.
I'm fed up with this.

The enormity of human suffering expressed in Arleym's hip-hop poem silenced us for a moment. It explained in part why Arleym could not relate to the *Mayflower*. However, he could relate to the *Amistad*, a slave ship that has been the subject of books and a film (1997). But he also expressed some optimism about the future: "I see the potential for America to be amazing, especially right now as we look at Barack Obama. Little children in the urban cities will be able to say, 'You know what? I want to go to Harvard.'" He then became agitated, remembering four young men who had been killed before his very eyes in the past two years. Islam, he kept repeating, had saved his life.

The team was moved by the brothers' discourse and saw these young men not as African Americans but simply as Americans. Clearly, the brothers' experience and life works set an example of a black cultural phenomenon that could influence young whites. For Craig, the experience was particularly illuminating: "Many American citizens see Islam as a serious threat to mainstream American culture in the post-9/11 world. But what I learned through the Habeeb brothers is how practicing Islam can relieve young Americans from the threats of violence, guns, drugs, and gangs. Instead of watching and believing in the media's negative portrayal of Islam, American citizens should be aware of the 'Habeeb case.' The Habeeb brothers are living examples of how Islam saves lives."

The Editor

We met Tayyibah Taylor, a graceful and impassioned advocate of women's rights and editor of *Azizah* magazine, at the dinner given in our honor by Soumaya Khalifa, a prominent Arab American Muslim in Atlanta. Although Tayyibah was busy, she spent some time with us during the next few days, and we got to know her. Of African descent, Tayyibah was born in Trinidad but has spent most of her life in Atlanta. She currently attends the Al-Farooq Masjid but remains open to other interpretations of Islam and is active in interfaith dialogue.

Tayyibah and Hailey struck up a friendship and soon became inseparable as we visited the main Bosnian mosque in Atlanta's suburbs and attended the Friday prayer together. Hailey learned that Tayyibah had a privileged life. Her father was a chemical engineer for Texaco, and they moved often. When she was still a teenager they moved to Canada. They were devout Christians, but to her the trinity of God, Jesus, and the Holy Spirit as one and yet separate was confusing. When in her tenth-grade class, she began learning about world religions and visited a mosque. She loved the simplicity of the structure of Islam and its theology. She took the *shahada* (declaration of belief) there and then.

Describing how her faith grew with time, Tayyibah said her conversion to Islam was initially "academic" but later "became a search for a way to connect with the universe." In her biology lab at school, she looked at a microbe and said to herself, "There *is* a God." The mystery and beauty took her breath away in what was both a spiritual calling and an awakening.

Later, after becoming Muslim and while visiting her parents' home in Barbados, Tayyibah found herself lying on the beach in a bikini and felt uncomfortable. She had done this many times before, but it was different now, and she was not happy about being so exposed. After that, she "realized that Islam was the answer and saw it as a formula for inner peace through self-mastery." Tayyibah began grappling with the meaning and degree of covering for Islam. She noticed that in today's world, being covered is considered backward and bareness in women is "modern," something she calls a strange concept. But even the matter of covering her hair reflected her strong and independent character. She wore the hijab as many African American women do, as a turban-like headdress rather than the Arab version.

Tayyibah moved to Saudi Arabia with her first husband, a National Basketball Association (NBA) player for the Houston Rockets. He was also a Muslim and was invited to coach a team there. Tayyibah calls that her "formative period" in Islam. She took Arabic classes and learned a great deal more about Islam. What fascinated her most was discovering the various interpretations of the Quran. "It's OK to think differently about the Quran," she noted.

In comparing U.S. and Saudi attitudes toward women, Tayyibah observed that in America women are encouraged to undress as much as possible and are used to "sell excitement" on billboards, cars, and every other possible venue, while Saudi women are required by law to cover themselves. Yet these two extremes end up producing the same result—"the objectification and extreme sexualization of women." Freedom is a responsibility, and a person must be "spiritually and intellectually capable." At the same time, she believes everyone needs spiritual guidelines, but the choice is up to the individual.

Azizah—which can mean "dear," "beloved," or "strong" or can be a woman's name—is an eclectic, glossy magazine containing thought-provoking articles; it reflects Tayyibah's own personality. Launched in 2000, it has been featured in the *Boston Globe* and *Newsweek* and, according to Tayyibah, is the first magazine devoted to all Muslim women, not just those of one ethnicity. Although meant as a forum for various points of view on Islam, an Arab woman in Atlanta found the magazine too focused on African Americans. Tayyibah feels otherwise, noting that while each issue may explore a specific subject, it will vary widely and may cover bold topics that most Muslims are embarrassed or unable to talk about, such as birth control and domestic violence.

Hailey was overjoyed at meeting Tayyibah, seeing her as the wave of the future for Islam in America: "She represents what could be the contribution of American Muslims to the world of Islam—seeking knowledge, encouraging debate and freedom of thought, and yet remaining Islamic."

Muslim Prisoners

God moves in mysterious ways. Though misunderstood and the subject of controversy, Islam has taken root in that most unlikely of soils, the American prison system, where it has always had a tinge of glamour since the story of Malcolm X captivated the world. Islam's spirit of brotherhood, egalitarian ethos, clear-cut theology, and structured life are attractive to inmates looking for meaning and direction in what can be a brutal environment. Converting to Islam also gives the prisoner what he craves most: dignity and self-confidence. Not surprisingly, some 80 percent of prisoners who convert to a religion that was not their own become Muslim.

The nation's prison system seems to be heavily tilted against its Muslim population. Although they constitute about 2 percent of the total U.S. population, Muslims make up about 20 percent of the prison population.[17] There are about 350,000 Muslims in prison, a number that increases by about 40,000 each year. Most of these are African Americans.[18] About the same number of African American men are in jail as in college.[19] In 2000, 32 percent of African American prisoners in New York State were Muslim, a microcosm for the rest of the country.[20] If there are about 7 million Muslims in America, and I must emphasize that these figures are estimates at best, then about 5 percent of all Muslims in America and 15 percent of all African American Muslims are in prison across America.

These statistics take on greater significance when one sees the dramatic impact of prison on the prisoners' communities, as we did one Saturday morning when we attended the Reverend Jesse Jackson's sermon at the Rainbow Push Coalition headquarters in Chicago's South Side. He noted that Jesus was born impoverished, "in the slums," and it was the poor who would inherit the kingdom of heaven. After describing the cycle of poverty and injustice in the black community, Jackson asked women whose sons were in prison to stand up, whereupon a large number rose, their faces clouded with despair and hopelessness. I am sure they were thinking of the misery of their loved ones lost in the prison system of America.

Given the tension between African American Muslims and immigrants, it would be logical to assume an unhappy fate for an immigrant who landed in a prison dominated by African Americans. One shudders to think what might happen to a frail, bespectacled, bookish Asian financier with an English accent who had been convicted of brutally beating his wife. Yet it seems that Islam trumps ethnicity, as I found in the case of Aftab Islam when he landed in jail. I had known Aftab Islam at Karachi Grammar School, and although both of us attended Cambridge University, our paths had not crossed and we lost touch. I had heard stories of his success as a high financier in New York. He owned a country house with sixty rooms and an estate of 135 acres in North Salem in Westchester County, New York. He had a townhouse off Park Avenue. All of this was lost when he pleaded guilty to brutally attacking his Jewish wife. He said he did not stand a chance in court after 9/11 with a name like Islam, a Jewish prosecutor, and a jury inclined to imagine the worst of Muslims.

Yet when I spoke with him in late 2008 after he had just completed a seven-year prison sentence, he was not bitter. He spoke with animation about the African Americans who provided him friendship and protection. He had developed a respect for his fellow inmates, and his easygoing and pleasant personality obviously disarmed his new companions. Many would ask him what he was doing in a place like this. He took this as a compliment.

In one of his earliest encounters, he was playing Scrabble with a large African American when he broke off momentarily to buy a package of cookies. Half a dozen men came up to him at that point, asking whether someone was blackmailing him. Obviously, they had a prison code, and Aftab was now lodged within its confines. His protection became a matter of honor for his companions.

Aftab's story reminded me how important it was for purposes of this study that we talk to Muslim prisoners. We were able to do so thanks to the good graces of the sheriff of Los Angeles County (see chapter 3), who is in charge of some 20,000 inmates in Los Angeles County, many of whom are Muslim. We arrived at the main prison to see long lines of visitors waiting to meet with their family members locked inside. They were almost all African Americans or Latinos. The deputies who met us, most of whom were white, were polite and smiling, but we detected a distinct trace of resentment. Not only could they not fathom how we had managed to get visitor permits within a day or two of our arriving in L.A., but they suspected that no good could come of academics carrying notebooks and talking to inmates.

After some rigorous security checks, we passed through several slow-opening, heavy-barred doors into a large green and white room. Signs all around the room demanded that visitors not touch or have any contact with the prisoners. When we finally met the prisoners, a large number of deputies watched us like hawks, their hands on their hips an inch or two away from their pistols and Taser guns. The prisoners wore orange jumpsuits and were tightly shackled as they were escorted by a warden one at a time and asked to sit opposite us for the interview.

One Muslim prisoner (whom I will call Mike) was in his fifties, slightly built, and soft-spoken. He wore small glasses and had a graying beard. He shuffled in, slightly hunched. His somber appearance and unsmiling face conveyed the air of a man resigned to his fate and ran counter to our stereotyped preconception that we would encounter a rambunctious Mr. T with angry eyes, booming voice, muscular arms, and Mohawk haircut.

As Mike walked in, I looked at him and said, "*Salaam alaykum*" or "peace be upon you," the traditional Islamic greeting. Taken aback, Mike replied "*Walaykum assalaam.*" When I told him I was a Muslim and an author, his demeanor changed. He sat up and his conversation became animated. I found him to be a thoughtful man wrestling with ideas about the purpose of life and human existence.

He spoke of how he had begun reading the Quran in prison because it spoke to him. He talked about the importance of books to him, and I surmised that in another time and place he could have gone on to be a scholar or useful member of society. But here he seemed caught up in the notorious system, and the system had won.

Originally from Arkansas, Mike said his cousin had been an imam with the Nation of Islam and had tried to convert him, but he resisted. First imprisoned at age eighteen, he had been in and out of jail for the past three decades, this time for stealing a car. After a few years in prison he began "seeking methods to rehabilitate myself" and became a Muslim. A film about Ahmed Deedat, a South African Muslim who often spoke out strongly against Christianity, had been influential. For Mike, Islam represented "honesty, compassion, and an education." He had read the Quran and many works on Islam since his conversion and shared my favorite translation of the Quran by the Indian Muslim scholar Yusuf Ali. The other authors he savored were al-Bukhari, who collected the hadiths and the works of Imam Malik, an Islamic law scholar who founded one of the four major schools of thought in Islam. His favorite works were *The Autobiography of Malcolm X* and books about African holistic health, and he wished to read much more. After I told him I was a scholar of Islam, he requested some of my works, noting "there is not much about Islam in the library here."

Although he spoke softly and calmly, his anger about the past history of the United States and slavery was easy to detect. And his understanding of Islamic theology was a conflation of several strands in African American Muslim thought. Mike spoke of Iblis, the Islamic name for Satan, and said Satan "manipulated genealogy" and used "scientific methods of applying evil." He referred to Yakub, the scientist in Nation of Islam theology who experimented with black genetics to make an "evil" white race. But, he said, this white lineage is part of humanity, and Islam "does not want you to be bitter and angry." The Day of Judgment, he warned, is coming.

Mike's role models were Gandhi and Malcolm X, the former for his "sacrifice" and the latter for his ability to "evolve out of hate." Mike was forgiving of America, although he had been through a great deal in the prison system. America for him was "a wonderful place. . . . You can become anything you want to be, like President Obama." He philosophized that to improve relations between Muslims and non-Muslims, Americans need to follow the example of the Prophet, who had been abused and attacked by non-Muslims but remained compassionate and fair to his enemies. Mike's affection for the Prophet was captured in his simple but powerful phrase "I love that brother."

Our conversation about Islam had awakened something in Mike. To the surprise of everyone, when the interview was over, Mike stood up and despite his chains and the presence of the guards and the signs that forbade it walked directly toward me and extended his hand. I took it. Mike thanked me for the conversation, and walked out with his chest held high and an air of dignity about him.

The other prisoner we interviewed presented a quite different demeanor, and he was not a Muslim. Let us call him Dan. He appeared hard and cold throughout the interview, and even his smile appeared forced and somewhat sinister. In his twenties, short, and with a shaved head, Dan was a member of a Mexican gang and was in prison for murder. He said his gang was called the "P's." Dan made a hand sign to indicate the letter of the alphabet that was his gang sign. Dan said he was raised a Catholic, although he did not indicate his faith was a big part of his life. Dan thought that American identity was "to get a job, work 9 to 5, and raise a family." He said when he saw the Stars and Stripes he felt "nothing."

While he knew of no Muslim gangs, he did know many Muslim inmates. One man incarcerated near him, he said, would pray five times a day in his cell. He thought that in order for America to deal with its problems with Muslims, America should "listen."

Dan reflected the conversations we had at a rehabilitation center for teenagers in L.A. that catered to a mainly Latino population (see chapter 6). He was so sure of his own world that he had neither the time nor the patience for anything outside it, and it was American predator identity he was most familiar with. Because Dan represents an increasingly large and significant Latino population in the United States, already outnumbering the African American population, it will be well worth the effort of those interested in more harmonious relations not to ignore men like Dan.

Muslim Members of Congress

Keith Ellison and André Carson, from Minnesota and Indiana, respectively, are the nation's first Muslim members of Congress. Both are

African American, and they quickly captured the imagination and support of the Muslim community. We interviewed them separately on Capitol Hill early in 2009.

Being the first Muslim member, Keith Ellison has always been in the spotlight. At times, it was uncomfortable as some in the media saw the arrival of a Muslim in Congress as the first step toward the destruction of "civilization as we know it." The calumnies of the media knew no bounds. It is to Ellison's credit that he met this media blizzard calmly and with an easy charm. His many years as a top civil rights lawyer no doubt helped in his new role.

Ellison invited us for breakfast at the congressional members' dining room to answer questions pertaining to our project. Responding to our first question about his role models, Ellison cited his mother: "I mean obviously my mother was a tremendous figure in my life, a very strong powerful woman. My mother to this day is a practicing Catholic. I embraced Islam and took shahada at the age of nineteen, and you know it was never an issue in my household, but she is still very devoted to her faith and I'm very devoted to mine."

His conversion to Islam, he said, was part of a process. He started life as a Catholic, went to Catholic grade school and an all-boys Jesuit high school in Detroit, but somewhere around the age of sixteen, "the faith I was practicing stopped making sense to me. It was something I didn't have any energy for. My mother would say, 'Well I'm going to church,' and I would say, 'Well have a great time, Mom. See you when you get back.'" In addition to not feeling any spiritual attraction to Catholicism, he had some unpleasant experiences with religious figures at his high school involving religious tolerance: "The school was a great school, I was honored to have gone there, but there were some individual cases where people who I admired said some things. . . . Actually it's funny because it impacted the way I view my religious identity. . . . I think it's important for adults to know that how they treat a high school kid may affect that person and alter the trajectory of that person's life."

This experience got him thinking and reading. One book that captivated him was about Muhammad Ali: "I thought he was the most fabulous figure around, and I really admired how he was able to sacrifice his world champion belt for the sake of his principles against the Vietnam War. It was an amazing display of conscience." That led him to read about Malcolm X, and after reading everything he could find about Malcolm X, he became interested in Islam. However, he noted, "I didn't know any Muslims at the age of sixteen. In my world, there were Catholics and Baptists and

Methodists and other forms of Christians, and there was a small minority of Jews in my neighborhood. I cut their grass and knew them, but didn't know any Muslims."

Ellison converted to Islam in 1981 as a result of a conversation with an African American friend at Wayne State University who took him to Friday prayers. Asked if this was a black mosque or an immigrant mosque, he said it was actually the Muslim Students Association, "so it was everybody." He was given a Quran, which he started reading. Then one day as he was driving to school, he saw "this place called the Muslim Center right on the west side of Detroit. I started talking to those guys. . . . Next thing you know I took my shahada, and I've been Muslim ever since. It's been a great experience." He said that he had had a Muslim wedding and that his children were all born into the faith.

Inevitably, during our conversation the question of Ellison's swearing in came up because he used the Quran owned by Jefferson for the ceremony, rather than the Bible. The copy was borrowed from the Library of Congress, where it is on display. He had not given much thought to what book he was going to use, much less Jefferson's Quran, until one day he received an "innocuous, hand-written letter" from a constituent pointing out that with "all this controversy that is going on about you swearing in on the Quran, you should swear in on the Quran owned by Thomas Jefferson." The writer even mentioned its location in the Library of Congress and the reference number, whereupon Ellison said, "Snap. That's it."

I asked him who signed the letter. "Well that's the thing," he replied. "They asked that I not reveal their name." "Was it a Muslim name?" I inquired. "The name was not Muslim," he replied. "I mean my name isn't Muslim. . . . So I really don't know." "So it could have been a Christian who simply wanted to reinforce pluralism?" I asked. "It certainly could have been," he replied. "I think the individual was a person with a keen sense of history. I didn't come up with the idea, but I know a good one when I see one."

Because of all the attention he was getting, Ellison was not sure how the Democratic leadership was going to react to him. Any worries he had about the Democratic leadership and his use of the Quran quickly faded "when Speaker Nancy Pelosi reached her hand out in a handshake and pulled me close in, and said, 'You swear in on anything you want.'" He mentioned that Pelosi had asked him to give the opening prayer before a dinner in honor of all the incoming freshmen before the big day. "And she made the point, 'Well, here Keith Ellison is giving the prayer, and it's just like any prayer we might hear anywhere.' And I have to say, though it was fraught with controversy, it was a welcoming environment because Speaker Pelosi made it that way, and I thank her for that." He also recounted the excitement of the day the oath was administered, January 4, 2007, with a wall of reporters all clicking their cameras and chattering.

Ellison had some hopeful observations about the delicate subject of relations between African American Muslims and Muslim immigrants. He was quite certain that he could see the cultural walls "beginning to really thin." In his experience visiting mosques across the country, while there may always be a "predominant ethnic group," there will also be "a few from Pakistan, a few from Africa, a few African Americans. There are other people who are there who are welcome, and you don't get the sense that they can't be there." He felt "it's been a tension over the years, but it's never been a bad tension."

Even the vexing subject of Plymouth Rock did not throw the self-possessed Ellison off balance, although I added he must not cite the quote from Malcolm X because so many African Americans had done so. In reply, Ellison questioned the truth of the notion that American identity springs from Plymouth Rock or the *Mayflower,* because "America didn't arrive suddenly at a multicultural reality—it's always been that way." In 1619, he pointed out, twenty Africans came to Jamestown, Virginia, one year before Plymouth Rock: "So before Plymouth Rock and the big celebration whose heritage we honor ever occurred, twenty Africans who came to America indentured, not enslaved, were standing in Virginia being American, and their first baby born there was an African American." He noted that a law prohibiting miscegenation was promulgated in Virginia around 1680.

Ellison also mentioned another early law, one concerning the criteria for servitude, which was a condition distinct from slavery. When many Muslim Africans brought over as servants converted to Christianity, the authorities "had to pass a law that it was blackness that made you a slave because they used to have a law that said you can enslave anyone who is a non-Christian. . . . So they had to change the criteria from religion to color."

A concern for him was the present shabby treatment of Muslims in general, with females having their hijabs pulled off at airports, for example: "These incidents help us understand how important civil rights are for everybody. There is nothing to make you a convert to civil rights like having your civil rights denied. And it's a sad way to learn a lesson, but at least the lesson has been learned."

Ellison's colleague, Representative André Carson, the second Muslim member of Congress, met us in his office. A big man, Carson greeted me warmly with a bear hug. His role models, he said without hesitation, were "certainly my mother, most importantly my grandmother, the late and great Representative Julia Carson, and Barack Obama, of course, is someone who motivates me, and I probably have to say Judge David Shaheed, . . . the first Muslim judge from Indiana and one of the first in the country, absolutely." He admired "George Washington, Abraham Lincoln, Dwight Eisenhower, Frederick Douglass, Malcolm X, Martin Luther King Jr., Sojourner Truth, and JFK—so many great leaders who are born from the womb of this great country, the United States of America, the true land of opportunity."

When asked why he converted to Islam, Carson went into some detail, beginning with his early years when he was raised a Baptist but spent seven years in a Catholic school. An altar boy for several years, he had serious thoughts about becoming a priest "until puberty hit, and then things changed a bit, but during those times I had deep discussions with the priests at school, and they always encouraged me to study different faiths, different religions, and so that led me to study Rumi." As a teenager, Carson was "into hip-hop": "I was a rapper . . . and the artists in the late eighties and early nineties were into Islam, through the Five Percenters, through the Hive, through Imam Mohammed's community. So I was motivated by their language. I read the Quran, and I said this is for me. It was a personal journey that was encouraged definitely by my grandmother . . . she had Qurans. Also there were Muslims who would come over regularly. During that time, it was the height of the crack cocaine epidemic, so you had Muslims policing the neighborhoods, pushing out drug dealers, and I was greatly influenced by that." Although he saw a similar commitment in the church, he found Islam's approach to the poor "to be particularly unique . . . because I saw the kind of firepower that Islam brought intellectually as well as spiritually."

Before coming to Congress, Carson sat on the Indianapolis City Council, was also a police officer for nearly a decade, and was assigned to Indiana's Department of Homeland Security, which worked with the FBI, the Secret Service, and other organizations: "I was a supervisor over a counterterrorism unit, and so as a Muslim it was especially important because it helped humanize Muslims, and it sent a message that America will not win the war against terrorism without the help and cooperation of Muslims."

As for the greatest threat facing the United States, Carson found it difficult to single out one thing but did name several of great concern: the still-lurking poison of racism, terrorism, national security threats, the economic downturn, and increasing crime. At the end of the day, however, it was important "to unite as Americans across racial divides, across religious divides, across social divides, and address the issues that affect all of us."

A question about American identity provoked a burst of patriotic fervor, which was as complex as it was genuine: "Oh wow, it means so much because I'm a very proud American. Most important, I'm a proud Hoosier, and more important than that, I'm a proud Muslim. And so you can be a proud American and a proud Muslim at the same time. Most Muslims want the best for America. Most Muslims are proud Americans."

"Why Can't They See Us As You See Us?":
Relations with Immigrants Today

We caught a glimpse of African American Muslim attitudes toward Muslim immigrants during a visit to Masjid al-Islam, the oldest mosque in Dallas. Hailey, who is from Dallas, had shown us Dealey Plaza, where Kennedy had been assassinated. That image of hatred and violence was what the world associated with Dallas, not the warm, open spirit of the mosque and the people who welcomed us there.

As we drove to the mosque past empty warehouses and desolate buildings, Hailey pointed out that this was the "bad part" of town, a blighted neighborhood with a reputation for homelessness, violence, and drug dealing. Although she was a Dallas native, Hailey had never been to this part of the city, and the very idea of her visit there and unnecessary exposure to danger drew gasps of disbelief from her family and friends later that night, who behaved as if she had just returned from the deepest and most dangerous jungles of equatorial Africa. She met with exactly the same reaction when she described her visit to her former teachers at Greenhill, her old high school located in a suburb of Dallas.

Yet we felt not a hint of danger in that section of Dallas. On the contrary, we were greeted warmly by Imam Mustafa Carroll, another charismatic African American follower of Imam W. D., and some ten women and fifteen men, including several imams from neighboring mosques. They appeared excited to host us. After my talk, the group responded with intelligent questions. The first two were about American foreign policy in Pakistan and Iraq. Then they asked how African Americans can help Muslims in America and around the world (this was the first time we had been asked that question). One young man commented on relations with Muslim immigrants, expressing a sentiment by now familiar to us: "Why can't they see us as you see us? They see us through white eyes."

The last word was with "Grandma Ruby," an old woman who had converted to Islam very early in her life. Her husband, Brother Antonne X, had converted under the guidance of "Brother Malcolm," that is, Malcolm

X, at the Nation of Islam Temple No. 1 in Detroit. She spoke lovingly of Brother Malcolm and of the pain that his death had caused her.

We were then led to a table with a large vanilla cake with "Welcome to Dallas" written on top. When I asked what the special occasion was, they replied, "You!" I was asked to cut the cake and I invited Grandma Ruby and Imam Carroll to help me. They filmed the entire event, having hired a professional photographer. I felt at home in the mosque, a brother among brothers and sisters. Even Hailey, who was the only non-Muslim and white American there, was received with respect and addressed as "sister."

But it is the larger problem between African American Muslims and the immigrants that I felt needed to be addressed. Too often Muslim leaders brush this issue under the carpet as they feel it will impair the unity of the Muslim community. In Dallas and elsewhere, the African American community complained that immigrants behaved as if they had a monopoly on understanding Islam, viewing African American Islam as a "secondhand" version, despite the efforts of individuals like Imam W. D. to promote orthodox learning and scholarship in the community.

Imam Hassan of Los Angeles traced the problem to 9/11. Before then, the immigrants were "invisible" and "blended in." Afterward, "they were seen as worse than African Americans, and they began to identify with African Americans. People began calling them camel jockeys and sand niggers. This drove the immigrants toward African Americans, but not on the social level. They still think they are superior. Immigrants haven't accepted themselves as Americans yet, so they don't get involved in social issues. They feel they have a superior culture, and that it would be diluted somewhat if they were to socialize with other cultures. But everything mixes. You can't bring a piece of Egypt, a piece of Tunisia, a piece of Saudi Arabia here and keep it. At some point, that piece has to be American. They don't realize that their children will need them, that the problems will come home. They have to see themselves as part of the social structure and social fabric." One of Islam's great contributions, Hassan said, is to build bridges to other societies, and "the most successful Muslims at doing this are African Americans."

During an evening in Memphis with a charming African American Muslim couple, Imam Muhammad Ameen and his wife, Constance, we again heard some critical comments about immigrant Muslims who put pressure on African Americans to adapt to their cultural norms. In her voluntary work at the central mosque, Constance had several immigrant women tell her to wear the hijab in a certain way, but she replied that the style of hijab "reflects your culture, not mine." She also found irritating the immigrant assumption that America and Islam are somehow incompatible. Immigrants often criticized African Americans for doing certain things that are considered "American" and not Islamic. Constance had an answer for this: "I *am* American," she said with pride and some attitude.

The next morning Jonathan, Craig, and Frankie arrived at Imam Ameen's mosque to interview him, but to their surprise, no one was there. Not sure where to go, Frankie pulled out his notebook and began jotting down some notes when someone tackled him from behind. Startled, Frankie lurched forward into a wall, too confused to register what was happening. He turned around to face Imam Ameen. "Hey it's the team!" the imam exclaimed, grinning from ear to ear. "We're thrilled you're here, welcome!"

The imam invited the three team members into the prayer room for a discussion with two older African American Muslims and one younger man in his twenties. Frankie found them "bursting with enthusiasm and affection for Dr. Ahmed and our project. It was obvious they had really connected with him and joked several times about how Dr. Ahmed had told them that in England he was seen as 'black.'"

Even the genial Imam Seifullah of Las Vegas found the immigrants irritating. They had accepted an "America for the wealthy" and did not want to deal with problems of racism, inner cities, and the like. These Muslims "didn't care about the common people." By contrast, African Americans understood the "inner workings" of American society, just as "Moses had understood the Pharaoh."

Imam Abdur-Rashid, who is leader of the Harlem Shura, a coalition of seven Harlem mosques, commented on the different types of immigrant Muslims and the "baggage" some bring to the community. Their backgrounds alone can complicate relations: "African American and Spanish-speaking Muslims live in a different world from Arab and South Asian Muslims. They . . . have a different identity, history, and different destiny." Interpretations of Islam are another source of friction, said the imam, especially between those who favor a rigid interpretation and those following a more open one.

Imam Abdur-Rashid gave us a sustained and honest comment on relations between immigrant and African American Muslims, beginning with a criticism of several initiatives immigrants have taken to ingratiate themselves into the American political process without consulting the African American community: "There is a colleague of mine, the founder of the American Muslim Taskforce on Civil Rights and Elections, Dr. Agha Saeed, a South Asian Muslim immigrant. . . . They decided they were going to back George W. Bush for the presidential race at that time. They are entitled, but they made the decision without any consultation whatsoever with indigenous Muslims, and then they publicized it throughout the country as 'Muslims support George W. Bush for president.'"

The imam found this upsetting: "You could imagine the friction that that created. Now we have forgiven them for that faux pas. But we live in very different worlds from Arab and South Asian doctors and engineers. They arrive here, as Dr. Saeed says, with 'their own sense of destiny.' But we have a sense of destiny that is completely different from theirs, and it creates tension and flashpoints. The 2000 election was one of them."

Imam Abdur-Rashid felt immigrants had a naïve understanding of the American landscape and tended to "fall for Uncle Sam's plan, which encourages division among oppressed people. They are in denial. We are trying to find ways to work together." He also blamed some of the younger generation's thinking on notions that Arab Muslim immigrants bring with them: "Even some of our sons are going to different countries, particularly the Arab countries, and some of them come back with a very rigid understanding of Islam that doesn't really sit well in the American context."

An African American woman in her thirties at the Muslim Center of Detroit claimed that African American Muslims and not Arabs were the "best Muslims, the indigenous Muslims." She was upset that through globalization stereotypes of blacks in America are beamed around the world, and even fellow Muslims "don't want anything to do with us." She had traveled to Egypt and was dismayed to find the same view toward blacks as in "mainstream America." The Arabs avoided blacks until 9/11, when they finally showed up to ask the African Americans for advice. This was due to the fact, she said, that the FBI only targeted Arabs, believing that the African Americans were "poor ignorant people with no passports." The Arabs "would come to us and ask for assistance on civil rights and how to communicate with the government, how to have our children go to school without being persecuted. Since we have been on this continent for a few hundred years, we pretty much know how to move around and to survive here." Despite the problems between the communities, the African Americans obliged, because "as Muslims, we help one another."

Activist C. B. Hanif and his wife, Aneesha, interviewed at their home in West Palm Beach, Florida, stressed the importance of African American Muslims embracing their own culture and not trying to be Arab. Aneesha, who wore a colorful headdress and donated an abayya to Hailey for our social experiment in Arab, Alabama, urged African American Muslims to resist pressure from immigrants and avoid all their baggage: "All these things about 'infidels.' I have four translations of the Quran and nowhere does it say anything about infidels! You have to go to the authentic sources of Islam, the Quran and the sunna. As W. D. Mohammed said, 'Think, question me! Would the Prophet be riding a camel when he had a car?'"

Most African American Muslim leaders spoke of the Arabs in a detached manner, but a few, joined by non-Muslims, were sharply critical, complaining in Detroit, for example, that they are "taking from the community" and "never putting anything back." Described as the "new Jews," the Arabs are perceived as greedy and selfish. According to Jesse, a homeless African American man in Detroit, "They look at you like dirt. Black, white, green, I don't care. They treat a black person like dirt. And pretty soon, people gonna get tired, and there's gonna be a riot. Oh, I guarantee you. There's so much violence here, so much anger. People are full of hatred."

The poisonous feelings toward Arabs in Detroit's African American community were echoed by Sweet and E. L. Randel in Miami. Randel, who kept pointing to a convenience store in disgust, grumbled that the "Arabs are taking our wealth and our black women while they keep their women covered in rags and to themselves. These black women, damn dirty bitches, they give away their pussy for money. Our young people will do anything for money, it's so humiliating."

The gaps between the communities exist even at a higher level. In their style, conversation, and culture, the African American imams differed from immigrant imams. The former generally tended to be outgoing, amiable, and ready to receive us with a big smile and embrace. They shook hands with the women researchers of our team. They talked with the confidence and awareness of being American. In contrast, the immigrant imams tended to be defensive because they saw the community as being under attack. They were not prepared to shake the hands of the women, nor were they speaking as Americans. They appeared to be preoccupied with trivia. In some cases, they were surly and rude to members of my team when they were trying to fix appointments. I appreciated the challenge these imams faced after 9/11, but I was also aware that it was precisely this challenge that underlined the importance of their job. If they were not ready to reach out, how would they be able to explain their religion? In several cities, immigrant imams insisted on being contacted ahead of other imams. In Las Vegas an immigrant imam was so abusive to a female member of my team that it reduced her to tears. He blamed her for arranging my meetings with the African American imams before we called on him, and he refused to see us. It showed an immigrant leadership out of touch with social reality. Post-9/11 America was not the time to behave like prima donnas.

Let me give the last word to the inimitable Malcolm X, who recognized the characteristic hospitality of the Arabs, but was nonetheless critical of their failure to promote the true teaching of Islam in the West. As a result, all kinds of charlatans—and he referred to Elijah Muhammad specifically for propagating the myth of Yakub—could claim to speak on behalf of Islam: "I reminded them that it was their fault, since they themselves hadn't done enough to make real Islam known in the West. Their silence left a vacuum into which any religious faker could step and mislead our people."[21] Oddly enough, considering the rich potential for leadership due to their wisdom and experience, African American Muslims do not get the attention they deserve in discussions of Islam in America. President Obama's main Muslim appointees advising him on Islam are immigrants, as was the case in the Bush administration. It is high time that the importance of the African American community be acknowledged.

Meeting African American Muslims has allowed me to see my own faith in a new and hopeful light. There are few stories as inspiring in the annals of history as that of the rediscovery of Islam in America and the success, grace, and ease with which African American Muslims have come to embody it. Through them can be built an authentic and viable bridge between Muslims and non-Muslims in America.

FIVE

Immigrant Muslims: Living the American Dream/American Nightmare

JUST AS THERE is no *Hamlet* without the prince of Denmark, there can be no study of Islam in America without the Muslim immigrant community. The same underlying doubt, neurosis, energy, and fear drive both the play and the community. And because its members represent such a wide range of cultures and nationalities, dominate Muslim organizations, and are directly influenced by the politics of the Muslim world—as evidenced by the phenomenon of the homegrown terrorist and the number of refugees—I spend more time on this chapter than any other.

While Islam unites African American and immigrant Muslims, each group expresses it quite differently. For African American Muslims, Islam means tackling issues of health, education, violence, drugs, and poverty. For immigrants, by and large better educated and more prosperous than African American Muslims, Islam is about uniting the *ummah,* or the global community of Muslims, and rallying the world behind the suppressed Muslim minorities in Palestine, Kashmir, and Chechnya.[1] For African American Muslims, Islam is a simple and functional way of life, directly related to the example of the Prophet Muhammad as a social reformer. For immigrants, Islam is a complex, grand, overarching historical experience initiated by the Prophet and the inspiration for splendid empires and dynasties. African American Muslim role models are mostly contemporary American figures such as Muhammad Ali, Martin Luther King Jr., Malcolm X, and Imam W. D. Mohammed. Immigrant role models are mainly Arab and lived in the distant past, such as the Prophet of Islam, Umar, Ali, and Saladin.

The Islam of African Americans is arrived at through personal choice, a process of trial and error, and is valued for its own sake. The Islam of immigrant Muslims is part of an unbroken line passing through the generations and is their inheritance. The latter therefore take possessive ownership of Islam with an air of superiority over other Muslims, which African American Muslims find arrogant and irritating.

The past creates certain burdens as well as aspirations for American Muslims. African Americans were enslaved, the immigrants colonized. The former have little memory of their past before the time of slavery; for the latter, the past is vivid and alive. Because the two communities relate to the past differently, they also have different views of the future. African American Muslims wish to build a future based on an imagined society; immigrants wish to build on what they have salvaged from their culture and traditions in the Middle East and South Asia. What the immigrants have retained in one form or another are the three Muslim models: mystic, modernist, and literalist. And we ran into them early in our fieldwork in Buffalo, New York.

The Three Muslim Models in Play

If New York is ground zero for Muslims, Buffalo is a war zone. Its Muslim community believes it is under attack, still haunted by the memory of the conviction of local Muslims—known as the Lackawanna Six, five of whom were Yemeni—for providing material support to al Qaeda in 2002. The episode hit the community hard because it believes that the accused were unfairly treated, that the evidence was tenuous, and that the men were condemned even before the proceedings began. Buffalo's Muslims tend to see undercover law enforcement officials in every stranger asking questions.

George W. Bush and Dick Cheney wanted to send in the army to round up the young Muslims.[2] Immediately after 9/11, the administration overreacted to any suspicion of a Muslim-associated threat, using not the proverbial sledgehammer but helicopter gunships to kill a fly. Everything Muslim was exaggerated and fed into America's fear and anger of what it saw as a threatening minority rooted in its deep structures. After all, Bush had declared that the country was involved in a war on terror, a not-so-subtle code for war on Islam for many Americans. He had described it as a "crusade." Before the invasion, Christian preachers like Franklin Graham and the Southern Baptist Convention, America's largest Protestant denomination, prepared to send their missionaries to Iraq with millions of Bibles to convert Muslims to Christianity, as well as to carry out aid work.[3]

Erik Prince, the head of Blackwater, now known as Xe, had a much more aggressive and militaristic approach to Muslims. In an affidavit lodged with a court in Virginia, a former Blackwater employee said that Prince "views himself as a Christian crusader tasked with eliminating Muslims and the Islamic faith from the globe." He also stated that many Blackwater employees "used call signs based on the Knights of the Templar, the warriors who fought the Crusades."[4]

Such American activity abroad generated hostility toward American Muslims at home, which translated into abuse and physical attacks. Muslims were contemptuously referred to as "ragheads," "towelheads," "sand niggers," and "Arabs" (despite the fact that only some 20 percent of Muslims in the world are from Arab lands). In addition, Islamic centers and mosques were attacked, and there were reports of burning crosses outside mosques. Everything about the immigrant Muslims—their foreign accent, a front-row seat on a domestic flight, charity organizations for the needy, a gathering at home to celebrate a Muslim festival—was viewed with suspicion and subject to possible investigation. In a spirit of goodwill, some Muslims would wish that one day America "would become Muslim"—meaning they hoped that Americans would in time benefit from Islam's compassion and balance. But such a statement was misunderstood—and to most American ears suggested the imposition of shariah or Islamic laws that called for beheadings—and it only fomented more fear and hatred. Yet the Founding Fathers had insisted that any American is free to express any religious opinion as long as it does not violate the law. But these were not ordinary times.

The act of immigration in itself rearranges identity in dramatic and unexpected ways. For Muslim immigrants in America, these challenges increased multifold after 9/11. In Buffalo, as elsewhere in America, each of the three Muslim models of society that immigrants brought from their homeland responded differently to expressions of American identity. The mystics were content to accept American identity in its entirety and to teach even its predatory aspects the ways of love. The modernists were attracted to pluralism. But the literalists, who saw themselves as the true champions of Islam, rejected American identity altogether as irrelevant to their lives. In this atmosphere, many a tongue wagged about Darul-Uloom Al-Madania in Buffalo, a boarding school for boys that trains imams.

Darul-Uloom: Creating American Imams

Darul-Uloom is where Charles Dickens meets *24*. Run by tense, bearded, and silent men, the school is housed in a forbidding grey complex of buildings with dark and dank corridors that were once part of a juvenile detention center. A high wall topped by heavy wire netting protects the 6-acre compound and reinforces the image of a fort preparing for a siege. "It sent a chill down my spine," recalled Hailey, with a shudder.

Having heard so much about the Darul-Uloom Al-Madania, I was particularly keen to visit it in October 2008 on our trip to Buffalo. Our host, my friend Faizan Haq, had promised to do everything he could to get us an interview with Mohammed Ismail Memon Madani, its president and author of several books, including *Hijab: Islamic Commandments of Hijab.*[5] In view of some uncertainty about the communication between Faizan and Ismail Madani, we decided to turn up at the school unannounced. The two men in the administrative office were unhelpful and would not respond to our simple questions. We stood around awkwardly as they spoke with Faizan in Urdu. They did not even ask the women to sit as a matter of ordinary courtesy. I felt that these young men had lost their traditional South Asian manners and not quite acquired the American etiquette of greeting visitors with a smile and openness. They seemed suspended between two cultures.

Darul-Uloom and its separate sister school for girls had a total enrollment of some 350 pupils. The boys were dressed in an approximation of Islamic clothes: most wore skullcaps, others black turbans and long white shirts over baggy trousers; some wore American sweatshirts over these clothes to keep warm. They spent their time learning Arabic, Islamic law, and the Quran. We entered a class of about 100 students seated on carpets and memorizing the Quran in the traditional way by swaying vigorously. An amiable African American convert then allowed us to talk to his class of about twelve third-grade boys. The walls displayed several maps of the United States and the world, along with student drawings of the Kaabah in Mecca. Almost all the students said their life's goal was to be a *maulana, mufti,* or *alim*—the names for different types of religious scholars. When asked to define these words, one of the boys replied, "They give fatwas and are someone who knows everything." Students said they wore this kind of dress outside of school and could not name a favorite cartoon or movie character.

Most of the boys were born in the United States, but their parents were from Pakistan, Egypt, Yemen, and other Muslim countries. When Zeenat asked those who had any non-Muslim friends to raise their hands, only one boy from Kenya put his up. It is not all work and no fun for the boys, however. Outside there was a basketball court and soccer field.

When I asked the office staff how these students coped with the "outside world," one replied curtly, "We teach them deen [religion] only. As long as they keep deen, they will be okay on the outside." Improving relations

The forbidding gate of this former juvenile detention facility in Buffalo, New York, frames Zeenat Ahmed as she walks in the parking area. It is now the gateway to Darul-Uloom Al-Madania School, which trains imams in America. Many Muslims across the country defend the school as being vital to their community.

between Muslims and other Americans, they said, "is really not our line of work. Our major concern is within this compound." They were also evasive about American identity: "We don't think about it." When we asked for the schedule, it was given reluctantly and was in Arabic. All of the announcements were in Arabic and Urdu.

Not discouraged, we pressed for answers in the interest of our study. Their role model was the founder of Darul-Uloom in Buffalo, Ismail Madani, whom they reverentially called *hazrat sahib,* a term used in South Asia for respected religious figures. A role model for one was his teacher of Islam, and for another it was the Prophet of Islam. These two may have submitted a negative report about our visit because our interview with Ismail was later canceled.

Debating the Three Models of Muslim Leadership over Dinner

Faizan gave a dinner for us at his home on the last night of our visit, which allowed us to see the three Muslim models in the behavior and talk of his guests, numbering about thirty. Faizan himself is an example of the confluence of all three Muslim models. Educated in a madrassah in Pakistan, he defended the need for Darul-Uloom in the community; but he also believed in the modernist M. A. Jinnah, while quoting the Sufi verses of Rumi and Iqbal with relish. Ideological strains quickly surfaced that night. Matters were complicated because of the different ethnic backgrounds of the guests, a mixture of South Asians, Turks, Arabs, and African Americans, including Imam Fajri Ansari, a leading local religious figure. At one point, the Turk became so exasperated that he accused the South Asians of being "racist."

After we finished eating, we all sat on carpets in the living room as the family's furniture had not yet arrived, but Faizan's Pakistani hospitality demanded we stay at his house. He handed me a microphone to address the guests and answer their questions. I gave two examples of how minority communities were projecting themselves: the Mormons in Palmyra were well organized and receptive to visitors, going out of their way to make a Muslim like me feel welcome (see chapter 8); Darul-Uloom made no attempt to explain its institution or objectives to visitors and was not helpful, an observation that generated an immediate and heated debate.

Farooq Maududi, a retired medical doctor, launched an attack on Darul-Uloom and its teachers. When Faizan suggested it was similar to Deoband in India, Maududi countered, "Deoband is enlightened, dedicated, and educated, whereas Darul-Uloom is a 'criminal cult.'" Privately, he claimed that the male instructors were preying on the young students in their charge. He called school founder Ismail a "rogue" who had spent time in a Saudi Arabian jail and was released early only because he was a hafiz, someone who has memorized the Quran.

This was no ordinary voice. Farooq Maududi is the son of Maulana Maududi, the founder of the Jamaat-i-Islami Party, which plays a significant role in South Asia, especially in Pakistan. The Jamaat-i-Islami is the South Asian equivalent of the Muslim Brotherhood in the Middle East, and the Maulana was a contemporary of Hassan al-Banna, founder of the Brotherhood. The Maulana died in his son's care in Buffalo in 1979.

Maududi's words, as much as his appearance, took me by surprise. He did not have a beard, nor robes, nor a turban. Light-skinned, small, and neatly dressed in dapper Western clothes, Maududi carried himself well for his years and looked like a country gentleman who had retired after a successful professional career. He told me of his son who led a rock band, and I thought of how Maulana Maududi, who loathed the West, would have reacted to that news. Maududi's presence that evening generated a buzz as he was considered something of a local celebrity—several guests whispered that he did not usually attend community events.

But even Maududi could not get away with his criticism of Darul-Uloom. Many guests, including our host, argued that Darul-Uloom provided a real service to the community, offering "purity" and the training of popular imams who are now involved in interfaith activity. In response to the argument on behalf of purity, Imam Ansari suggested that Islam in America was more about "fighting oppression" than about purity. Some of the women were excitable supporters of Darul-Uloom and emphasized its "uniqueness," explaining the institution needed to draw boundaries around itself, so did not require public relations.

As if this was not excitement enough, another drama was being played out in the next room. A prominent Pakistani physician who believed in modernist Islam pleaded with me to talk to his two sons who were being "dangerously influenced" by the literalist approach of the Darul-Uloom. The situation became complicated for me because the older son had approached me earlier, after my lecture at the University of Buffalo where Faizan taught. I could not fail to notice him. He had a big, bushy black beard and was wearing a white *shalwar-kameez* (traditional South Asian loose-fitting shirt and pants). He was supportive of our project, telling Hailey that "your work is equal to 1,000 Iraq wars to help America." Though willing to share his innermost reasons for supporting the Darul-Uloom, he did not want me to mention them to his father, or he would have a difficult time at home.

At Faizan's dinner, however, the young man was a transformed person. He was defensive and nervous. Perhaps his father's presence and guests had intimidated him. He begged to have his younger brother included in the conversation, and I went looking for him. Dressed in a smart Western suit with a neater and shorter beard than his sibling, the younger brother was in a corner rocking gently while he recited the Quran to himself. He seemed oblivious to his surroundings and not particularly concerned about joining the discussion, leaving his brother to talk on his behalf.

Just when I thought things could not get more interesting, the doctor's wife joined in, speaking passionately for Darul-Uloom, while he stood by looking miserable. Then the wife of the older son, a white American convert to Islam who works at Darul-Uloom, spoke. There was no need to mix with other Americans, she said, but only with good human beings inspired by the Quran. When Zeenat suggested the Darul-Uloom might issue brochures describing the school's work, she replied, "There is no need to worry about anything because everything is decided by Allah Subhanatallah." She wore the hijab, calling it a "noble concept," though her mother thought anyone wearing it was a "terrorist" and dressed for Halloween.

Darul-Uloom was a public relations disaster waiting to happen. I wondered what people like Steve Emerson, the terrorism czar of American media, would have to say if some controversy erupted around it. Seen as a combination of Torquemada and Joe McCarthy by his critics and as the oracle of terrorism by others, Emerson would condemn it without hesitation. Yet the goal of the Muslim community to create cadres of trained imams to run the mosques of the United States is not only timely but also crucial if the community is to have a coherent framework within which to conduct its religious practices (see chapter 9).

In its training of imams, Darul-Uloom represents a distinct literalist philosophy rooted in the Muslim world. The training at some of the other centers we visited was designed by people who know American culture. The Islamic Association of North Texas schools in Dallas, run by the Turkish imam Yusuf Kavakci, endeavors to train American imams, while in the Bay Area of San Francisco, Sheikh Hamza Yusuf (see chapter 3) is building America's "first Islamic university" dedicated to the same mission. Such efforts should help to address the complaints of many young American Muslims who find it difficult to seek advice from immigrant imams and teachers because they fail to understand what it is like to grow up in America.

An enthusiastic class at the Universal School in Buffalo, New York, interacts with the author. On the blackboard is a lesson plan on the origins of America at Plymouth, Massachusetts.

In contrast to Darul-Uloom, the Universal School of Buffalo had a lively and cheerful atmosphere, with an enrollment of about 100 boys and girls who are Muslim by birth or the children of converts. The building was modern and airy and surrounded by lawns and landscaped grounds. Faizan, a board member, explained the need for such an establishment. The board had deliberately selected a name for the school that would not appear threatening to Americans and avoided using the word "Islamic" in it. The school aimed to educate children to become good Muslims as well as good Americans, and the teachers and principals told us they hoped that one day the school would be perceived as another educational option, just as Jewish and Catholic schools are today. We visited many such schools across the United States, including in Chicago, New Orleans, Los Angeles, Patterson, New Jersey, and Atlanta, which offer traditional subjects such as history, math, and science, along with courses in Islamic study.

At the Universal School it was a relief to find an Islamic institution free of tension. I spent a whole period talking to a group of about thirty boisterous students in grades 6 to 8. Half of them were girls, all wearing hijabs. Their backgrounds were Somali, Egyptian, Yemeni, and Indian.

The children's enthusiasm knew no bounds, and while we went through our standard list of questions, they asked us whom we would vote for in the presidential elections. When I asked them the same question in return, all except one girl said Barack Obama. From the affectionate way they chanted Obama's name, I suspected that they thought he was a Muslim.

As good Muslims, they all "wanted to go to *jannah*," or paradise. They also wanted shariah in the United States. Their role models, for both girls and boys, were the Prophet of Islam, the first four caliphs of Islam, and Saladin, the legendary ruler of Egypt during the time of the Crusades. They defined American identity as "freedom." One boy with a Somali background said it meant "money grows on trees" and told us his relatives in Somalia expected his parents to give them money as if they had unlimited amounts. Many even had a response to Plymouth Rock and the *Mayflower*, describing it as "extremism." For them, Plymouth was associated with the killing of Native Americans and enslavement of the Africans. In their minds, all three American identities were one and the same.

Mystic Muslims

Buffalo is a microcosm of the Muslim community in America. It provides a glimpse of the scale and scope of the larger community's leadership, ideological, and social issues, which are best understood in the light of the three Muslim models: the mystics, the modernists, and the literalists. Let me begin with the mystic model.

Hollywood has long had an affectionate idea of what a Muslim mystic looks like. In the popular romantic thriller *The Jewel of the Nile* (1985), for instance, the Sufi Al-Jawhara is a likable and exuberant character with an unkempt beard, ragged turban, and loose Arab clothes. His fire-walking, flame-juggling, and gravity-defying tricks make the Hollywood Sufi a felicitous cross between a Hindu yogi and a circus performer. In real life, however, Sufis are elusive and difficult to locate and define.

On our journey, many people told me casually, "I am a Sufi," but I was never sure what they meant and how serious they were about mystic Islam. Actual Sufis remain focused on their own devotions through the practice of quiet piety, humility, and advocacy of universal acceptance and compassion. Their position on the ideological map of Islam clearly distinguishes them from both modernists and literalists. The former see them as remnants of an embarrassing past, the latter as dangerous heretics who have strayed from the orthodox path and, like the Barelvis of South Asia, go so far as to elevate the Prophet to near-divine status. Sufis are also accused of saint and shrine worship and of indulging in drugs, alcohol, and ecstatic music at their shrines.

Sufism in America, which has both men and women adherents, is most dramatically represented by Shaykh Hisham Kabbani.[6] With his twinkling eyes, fair complexion, long white beard, high turban, and loose, flowing robes, Kabbani looks as if he had just auditioned for a sequel to *The Jewel of the Nile.* After 9/11, when America associated Islam with angry young Arabs from the Middle East, Shaykh Kabbani was a welcome contrast, speaking through many media outlets of peace and interfaith dialogue and denouncing the "ideology of extremism and violence" as promoted by the Saudi-influenced Wahhabis and Salafis. Many Muslims complained, however, that Kabbani was using the community's predicament to promote himself.

Seeing this concern, the U.S. government found itself in a quandary. If it listened to Kabbani, it would alienate the major Muslim organizations that represent the bulk of the country's Muslim population. If it worked with the Muslim organizations, it might find itself falling into the trap that Kabbani warned against. In the end, the administration failed to enunciate a coherent policy and adopted a piecemeal approach that was not particularly effective, although it did have the appearance of dialogue (see chapter 9).

This was a pity. Kabbani was a Sufi master with a pedigree in Islamic mysticism. Born in Lebanon in 1945, he had grown to prominence in the Naqshbandi-Haqqani Sufi order. For half a century, he had been a disciple of Nazim al-Qubrusi and had married his daughter. At his mentor's behest, Kabbani came to the United States in 1991 to promote the peaceful message of Sufi Islam. He opened several Sufi centers, spoke on many campuses, and wrote a number of books with titles like *Angels Unveiled, Pearls and Coral,* and *Illuminations,* which provide considerable insight into Sufism.[7] He is the chairman of the Sufi Muslim Council and is said to have several thousand disciples across the United States.

I met Kabbani's spiritual guide, Shaykh Nazim, in the mid-1990s at his north London headquarters, a large church converted into an Islamic center. The ruler of Brunei, one of the richest men in the world, was rumored to be Kabbani's disciple and benefactor who had bought the property for him. Shaykh Nazim wore a large green turban and green silken robes. He was a grand sheikh of the Naqshbandi order, and whenever I called on him, I saw a large gathering of respectful middle-class British converts, men and women, around him. He mentioned that I should meet with Kabbani on my next visit to America.

The Gülen Movement in America

In contrast to Kabbani, another prominent Muslim mystic, Fethullah Gülen, does not have a beard, dresses in Western suits, and promotes interfaith understanding and education. Gülen's books include collections of mystic verses, many in praise of the Prophet of Islam. He has successfully brought a mystic form of Sunni Islam from his homeland in Turkey to America. He won the title of world's top public intellectual by a landslide in a poll conducted by *Foreign Policy* and *Prospect* magazines in 2008, though he remains controversial in Turkey, as many there consider him a threat to the secular state.[8] He lives in exile in Pennsylvania, and his followers have wide and influential networks throughout the United States. Clean-shaven, attired in grey business suits with white shirts and ties, and invariably smiling, they are the modern face of mystic Islam. They promote more than interfaith dialogue and world peace. They are actively involved in education, business, charity, and the media.

On our journey, we visited the recently opened Turquoise Center in Houston, a bright feather in the Gülen cap. Spread over a large estate, it was formally inaugurated by Madeleine Albright in 2009, and I was asked to address the large gathering of Muslims and non-Muslims. A cordial atmosphere permeated the proceedings, and many of the Muslims could be identified as mystics and even Sufis, although none wore turbans or long black and green robes.

The Barelvis of America

In Houston, Jonathan and Frankie visited the Barelvis, who also harbor mystic inclinations. The two had been cautioned by a modernist Muslim from Pakistan, Aziz Siddiqi, head of the Islamic Society of Greater Houston, an organization to which most of the city's mosques belong. Siddiqi complained that the Barelvis "elevate the Prophet too high." Entering the Al-Noor Masjid, my researchers came upon a scene they had not encountered before on their American trip: a prayer room filled with twinkling colored lights and awash with the smell of incense. A man in a leather jacket was singing verses from the Quran in honor of the Prophet into a microphone, in what Frankie described as an "exquisite voice." At certain words, the 200 or so congregants joined in, chanting the words and rocking back and forth. They were asked to recite these verses with pride, as they would "The Star-Spangled Banner." Most were wearing traditional Islamic dress, and the men and women were separated. There were Arabs, Iranian Shia, and South

Asians present, along with refugees from Somalia. It was a special occasion honoring the founder of the Barelvi movement, Imam Ahmed Raza Khan. The young congregants spoke about their love for him and his wisdom.

Our team talked to a small group of men, including two prominent Houstonians, Imad Gire, a Tanzanian of South Asian background wearing a greenish-tan shirt and slacks who has a printing business, and Iftikhar Khan, an Indian wearing a shalwar-kameez who is the president of an insurance company. Both described themselves as Sufis. The men said that more than 1,000 people come to Friday prayers at Al-Noor Masjid, but soon they will be accommodated in "the biggest mosque in America" being constructed next door. All said that they "loved America" and claimed the country as their own.

Reacting to criticism from other branches of Islam, Khan retorted, "If we want to put up a few lights and burn incense, how are we hurting anyone? . . . Every time we celebrate one of our festivals like the Prophet's birthday, we hear from the Wahhabis. We love our Prophet so much, what trouble is it to anyone if we want to celebrate his birthday? It is just like Christmas." He felt it was the Wahhabis who failed to understand the Prophet or to follow his message, even if they pray five times a day. Several in the mosque dismissed the Islamic Society of Greater Houston as having "Wahhabi connections." Khan left the organization because it started receiving money suspected to be of Saudi origin. "If the Wahhabis spent 10 percent of what they earn, they could cure hunger," claimed Khan. "They live like Las Vegas. The Bedouins now have all this wealth. They are arrogant."

A few days later, over dinner at Houston's Bijan Persian Grill, Gire and Khan told the team Houston now has 5,000 to 10,000 Persians and 50,000 Pakistanis. Khan, who had been in Houston since 1971, had witnessed the exponential growth of the Muslim community from just five families in 1978. There was no denying his commitment to America: "We're Muslims, but we're American. We have to help each other. America is the greatest country in the world—the whole world wants to be American." Both men said that the Sufis of Al-Noor Masjid were among the first to drive truckloads of groceries, water, and supplies to New Orleans after Hurricane Katrina. In his role as teacher of the young at the mosque, Khan describes an American as someone who is "decent, polite, and healthy. I tell my children if alcohol and partying makes you American, then you are not American." To Khan, the problems between Islam and the West will only change when "Jesus returns to earth." The best way forward, Khan said, was to follow the example of the Prophet, Rumi, and the message of Sufism, which, he said, was "love."

The Sufi of Atlanta

Imam Salahuddin Wazir of Atlanta, originally from Ethiopia, is an American Sufi of the old school. He radiates humility and gentility yet does not go about parading his mysticism. He is defined by his love of God and the kindness in his dealings with people. We first met Imam Wazir at a dinner for us in Atlanta attended by the city's top Muslim leaders. Imam Wazir was seated on my right, and I was struck by the personality of this slightly built, middle-aged man with a perpetual smile and twinkling eyes. He wore prayer beads on his wrist, with a kufiya and scarf around his head. With his long robe flapping around him, he had the air of a friendly magician at a children's birthday party.

Nothing tests the compassion and patience of an individual more than a crisis late at night, in the deep of an American winter, and involving strangers. As we came out of the restaurant to drive home, we found that our SUV had been broken into, its windows smashed and contents stolen. Imam Wazir, without prompting, stayed with us throughout the ordeal and even helped us patch the windows for the cold drive ahead. Over the next few days, Jonathan, Frankie, and Craig spent time with the imam, attending Friday prayers, meeting him at his business, having lunch with him, and visiting the school that his mosque helps run. The team interviewed him in his store, Global Express Mail, where a CD played a continuous recitation of the Quran in the background. Some customers, he said, ask him about the recitation, but they are only curious and in the end they like it, because it sounds "peaceful."

Imam Wazir's role model is the Prophet, who is his "number 1, 2, up to 100." He praised the Prophet's "love and compassion," which are also the foundation of the imam's mysticism. While he rejects the materialism of America, he realizes that he does not have the luxury of living in the past and that he must adapt to the present. He feels that his culture and traditions can help "America be a brighter and more diverse country. I chose America; I believe that this is a role model country, best country in the world."

Modernist Muslims

Modernist Muslims are often successful and leading members of the community, as in the case of physician Hassan Bukhari, who insisted that I "come right away" when I talked to him on the phone. I had just described a wound on my calf that was looking ugly, one of those cuts that appear mysteriously during a long journey. This one, I suspected, had been inflicted by the low, steel-tipped tables at the ultramodern AT&T Hotel and Conference Center in Austin, Texas. We had been on the road for several days since I first noticed the cut, and I had hoped that the body's natural healing powers would deal with it.

But on our arrival in Dallas, my team urged me to see a doctor. The problem was that it was a Sunday. Ghulam Bakali, a friend who was visiting me, immediately rang Bukhari, a Pakistani surgeon in Dallas. We drove to his house in a posh suburb alongside White Rock Lake.

A model of efficiency, Dr. Bukhari had prepared the necessary gauzes, ointments, and prescriptions and was waiting for us outside his house. In the meantime, his wife had laid out tea with savories. Frankie was impressed with the surgeon's hospitality and availability to a patient he had never met, going so far as to host us in his home on a Sunday without charging a fee, and saying, "It was an honor that you came." Frankie could not imagine an American doctor doing the same.

Apart from working at the hospital, Bukhari was also a prominent member of several national Muslim organizations, including the 12,000-member Association of Pakistani Physicians of North America (APPNA) and the Pakistani American Public Affairs Committee (PAKPAC). His wife, Talat, and son, Rizwan, are both doctors, and just a glance around his house confirmed the impression that Bukhari was living the American dream, but with a distinctly Pakistani flavor. The coffee-table books of Lahore and Islamic architecture, furniture, carpets, and paintings on the wall all reflected Pakistan. Even the photographs on display were of prominent Pakistanis such as the former military dictators Zia-ul-Haq and Pervez Musharraf. It seemed his aim was not to make this a small part of Texas but to preserve it as an outpost of Pakistan.

Arriving four decades ago with a degree from King Edward Medical College in Lahore, Bukhari had worked hard and was now enjoying the fruits of his labor. He came to America with his personality intact and ideas well formed, easily associating with American pluralist identity. He spoke English fluently, albeit with a distinct South Asian accent, and he flourished professionally in an environment that was welcoming to educated immigrants. But his support of and identification with the military dictators of Pakistan suggested that his appreciation of true American pluralism rooted in democracy, human rights, and civil liberties was incomplete.

When asked to assess the relative strength of the American Muslim community in terms of the three models, Bukhari estimated that 99 percent of Muslims in America are modernists and perhaps 1 percent Sufis. He dismissed the literalists with a wave of his hand, saying they could be squeezed into that 1 percent with the Sufis. This was contrary to our findings, which indicated that the modernists are about 40 to 50 percent and the literalists about 30 to 40 percent, while the mystics make up the rest in terms of their numbers in the community and in the mosque.

Bukhari's lack of knowledge about and contempt for the literalists was commonplace among modernists. At a dinner for us in Chicago, individuals reflecting the different Muslim models lapsed into a heated exchange when Kamran Khan, a leading Pakistani businessman, reacted to some vociferous remarks on behalf of literalist Islam. At this point, Jonathan leaned over to Kamran and joked that he was giving the literalists a hard time. "These guys are useless," Kamran replied, adding colorful and choice expletives, "a bunch of ignorant, tribal hillbillies who make us all look bad."

By minimizing the presence and impact of the literalists, both Bukhari and Kamran were not seeing the full picture of the Muslim community. If these modernist Muslims failed to recognize one of the major Muslim models, how could they engage with and influence it? And how could they explain the Muslim community to mainstream America?

Kennedy's Children

As noted in chapter 2, Muslims like Hassan Bukhari owe their presence in America to John F. Kennedy. The United States was not open to non-white and specifically Asian immigration until the passage of the Hart-Celler Act in 1965 under Lyndon Johnson, legislation inspired by John F. Kennedy and vigorously supported by his brother, Ted Kennedy. Subsequently, immigration from Western Europe declined significantly, while the numbers from the Middle East and Asia increased, with more than half from these regions being Muslim.[9]

Muslim immigrants of this period were attracted by pluralist America and reflected a Muslim world in which modernism seemed to be ascendant. Most of the leaders in their home countries were aligned with either the capitalist West, as was Ayub Khan of Pakistan, or with the communist bloc, as in the case of Gamal Abdel Nasser of Egypt. Whatever their political leanings, the emphasis in those countries was on "modernization." By the 1970s, however, the Muslim world had begun experiencing a significant shift from modernism to a more literalist version of Islam, the symbols of which even crept into Egypt's "Ramadan War" with Israel in 1973. One of the staunch promoters of an Islamic agenda was King Faisal of Saudi Arabia, who withdrew his country's oil from world markets in protest of the West's support of Israel in that war. By the end of the decade, two other major political figures were asserting Islam's place on the world stage: Ayatollah Khomeini, who led the Islamic Revolution in Iran, and General Zia-ul-Haq, who set out to Islamize Pakistan.

In 1979 the Soviet Union invaded Afghanistan. American, Saudi, and Pakistani intelligence services found the perfect weapon to make the Soviets bleed: jihad, or holy war as decreed by Islam. Overnight it became fashionable for young Muslim men to pack their bags and head for Afghanistan to fight for Islam. One of these was Osama bin Laden. After the defeat of the Soviet forces in Afghanistan, confident Muslim literalists would turn their sights on the United States. The literalists also condemned the modernist leaders for their corruption, dictatorial methods, and role as foreign puppets, and worked to remove them in favor of traditional Islam. Muslim modernists in America were as surprised as mainstream Americans at the emergence of literalist Muslims. By then many Muslim modernists in America had achieved professional success, which enabled them to drive expensive cars and live in large suburban homes, kept clean by Latino staff with dubious immigration status.

Some, like Munir Chaudry of Chicago, are living proof of the American rags-to-riches story. During our stopover in Chicago, we stayed with the Chaudrys, and both husband and wife looked after us like family. Chaudry proudly recounted his climb to success after arriving in the United States from Pakistan's Punjab in the 1970s with only $100 in his pocket. Through hard and honest work, Chaudry slowly accumulated enough capital to open up his own business, which eventually developed into a beauty products firm employing 200 people. Chaudry now lives in the affluent Chicago suburb of Falling Water surrounded by the latest and most expensive amenities, along with photographs of himself with leading American politicians like Hillary Clinton and Barack Obama, who had attended a fund-raiser in Chaudry's home.

We accompanied Chaudry to a service at Reverend Jesse Jackson's headquarters in Chicago. The two were friends, and Jackson asked Chaudry to speak from the podium. Chaudry announced ten jobs for the congregation at his factory and a $1,000 donation to the church. Later we interviewed Jesse Jackson for our project.

At a dinner he hosted for us, Chaudry invited some fifty of the leading Chicago figures, including the Pakistan consul general and former president Pervez Musharraf's brother. The biryani and karai dishes were superb, and the welcoming atmosphere encouraged our appetites. The team threw restraint aside and made several forays to the serving table.

Munir Chaudry stands in front of his luxurious home outside Chicago. He came to the United States as a young man from Pakistan with $100 in his pocket and now runs a lucrative cosmetics company and lives the "American dream."

Elsewhere, we met immigrants who had been equally successful, including Shafqat Chaudry of Washington, D.C., who began with one taxi and eventually expanded the business into a limousine company named Sunny's, after himself. The company now owns some fifty vehicles in Washington and about the same number in New York. With the contract for major corporations like CNN and the BBC, Sunny's is one of the most successful limousine services in America.

These modernist Muslims make valiant, if futile, attempts to fuse the interests of Islam and America, as in the case of Taufiq Raihan, a Bangladeshi businessman whom Frankie and Jonathan met at the Colorado Muslim Society, the largest mosque in Denver. Raihan runs Royal Bengal Mechanical in Aurora, Colorado. Born in Bangladesh to Yemeni parents, Raihan had been in the United States for twenty-five years. He wore a Pittsburgh Steelers hat, blue jeans, and sunglasses with a Bluetooth headset and spoke of the controversy surrounding his mosque because the accused Afghan terrorist Najibullah Zazi "might have prayed" there.

Raihan said his e-mail and phone were monitored by the FBI, but that he "was not bothered by it. They try to buy me as an informant but I tell them, 'You don't have to buy me. *I'm* an unpaid citizen; *you* are paid. It's my duty.'" Raihan's advice to Muslims was not to be as concerned with matters of "power and control" as these things are transitory. This philosophy was shaped by his experience in 1971, when he fought "bunker to bunker" against the Pakistani army for the liberation of Bangladesh, then called East Pakistan. Within a few years, Raihan said, "the leaders of both Pakistan and Bangladesh would be dead." Raihan further advises Muslims, "Don't fear the FBI. Your biggest protection is Allah. If you obey Allah, you obey the FBI. Muslims should live according to this rule."

For all their keenness to be accepted as Americans, "Kennedy's children" did not fully understand the American view of what it means to be American. They assumed that professional success was sufficient for social and cultural acceptance, so failed to tap into those symbols of American identity instantly understood by Americans—whether it was celebrating the Fourth of July, watching a baseball game, or cheering the armed forces. In our interviews and at functions in our honor, I would make a point of asking Muslims how much American history and culture they had absorbed—whether, for instance, they had read anything by Jefferson, Franklin, or even de Tocqueville—and invariably found that no one had. For all their professional education, it seemed immigrants were not really interested in American history and culture.

Muslim leaders also fell back on the habits of their countries of origin, where sycophancy in dealing with figures in authority was a cultural fact of life. They repeated "Islam means peace" in every forum they could, and when they met prominent Americans, they gave them gifts and made sure they took pictures with them, which they displayed prominently in their living rooms.

I call this the "deputy commissioner syndrome," being reminded of the South Asian practice of giving gifts to, or endeavoring to be photographed alongside, the deputy commissioner, once the most important official in the district. Seeing pictures of a host and his wife grinning from ear to ear next to a member of Congress in the living rooms of South Asians confirmed for me that the deputy commissioner syndrome had been transported across the oceans to the United States. Any thought that such gifts and pictures guaranteed immunity and protection in times of trouble was disproved after 9/11.

Although some immigrants like Hassan Bukhari, Munir Chaudry, and Shafqat Chaudry still live the American dream, many others have been living the American nightmare since 9/11—recall the experience of Abdul-rahman Zeitoun described in chapter 3. As a result, the modernists have become foreigners in important cultural and psychological ways, both in America and in their homelands.

Modernist Muslims Running out of Steam

Modernist Muslims are partly to blame for their problems. They have provided neither leadership nor the critical mass needed to change the Muslim community. Everywhere we went, Muslim modernist leadership was divided and in disarray. Even the biggest mosque in New York, on East 96th Street at 3rd Avenue, which routinely attracts 3,000 to 4,000 worshippers, was having its problems. Mohammad Shamsi Ali, its smiling and gentle imam from Indonesia, complained sadly about attacks by literalist Muslims, especially from South Asia. These attacks occurred largely because of his interfaith initiatives, he speculated (see photo on next page). After prayers, he and I talked to a group of men who started asking each other, "Where are you from?" A Turk, I believe, interjected irritably, saying that only one word "unites us—it's Islam." When I asked this group whether they had heard of or seen the DVD documentary *Obsession,* which depicts Islam so negatively, they all shook their heads. How could Muslims explain Islam without even knowing about attacks on them such as in *Obsession?* An Arab imam visiting from Detroit ruefully answered: "There is no unity here; that's the problem, you know."

Muslim modernists do not even follow up on the opportunities that American society offers for dialogue and understanding, as the following case involving my cousin, Mahmood Mushtaq, illustrates. Mahmood, introduced in chapter 3, is the embodiment of South Asian modernist Islam. Educated at Cambridge University in the early 1950s, he attended, like his father before him, Peterhouse College, the oldest in the university. Mahmood married a German and settled in Houston after retiring from a successful career in oil.

When Father Donald Nesti, the director of the Center for Faith and Culture at the University of St. Thomas, asked me to represent Islam in a high-level interfaith event in Houston, Mahmood promised to invite the Muslim community. Contacting a self-proclaimed Muslim leader, he was told enthusiastically, "No problem, not only will I come, but I will bring at least a thousand guests." Impressed, Mahmood cautioned the Muslim leader that even a hundred would be more than enough. The event was a success, but neither the leader nor his friends turned up. Mahmood felt

Zeenat Ahmed, Craig Considine, and Akbar Ahmed with Imam Shamsi Ali of the largest mosque in New York City after Friday prayers. Imam Ali has been an outspoken advocate of interfaith dialogue and Muslim outreach, at times attracting criticism from the Muslim community.

betrayed and was livid: "It is typical of these people. They live in cocoons. They have no interaction with Americans. They only compete with each other. They will say, 'Look at my new car, my new house.' They will not help one another. If they tell you they are in America for freedom and democracy, that's bullshit. They're here for the money only."

The rifts in the community often spill into violence, as we heard in the case of a newly wed couple, Farhan and Sofia Latif in Dearborn, Michigan. Personable, educated, and successful, they believe in interfaith dialogue and are secure in their identity as Americans. Farhan's antagonists were members of the Hizb-ut-Tahrir, a literalist Islamic organization known for intimidating other Muslims, especially modernists and Sufis.

Farhan had just become president of the Muslim Students Association (MSA) at the University of Michigan–Dearborn when 9/11 occurred, and the media descended on the community. He wished to condemn the violent acts of that day and to say that Islam had been "hijacked." But he noticed some Muslims were saying just the opposite, "things like 'Let's celebrate the atrocities' and 'Let's pray for the destruction of Jews and Christians.'" Farhan was troubled to hear fellow Muslims say things he disagreed with and condemned them, wondering why they were speaking on his behalf. "This is not what Muslims believe; as a matter of fact, we have been taught that if you take one life, it's like taking the life of all of humanity, and here was a person speaking on Islam. He had a beard, but he had so much hate. So our group decided to counter the hatred and ignorance," he told us.

In quick response, threats began arriving by e-mail and in person, and Farhan's car was vandalized three times. Then in September 2004 he was attacked by two people and sustained heavy injuries, including cracked ribs, but that was not the end of it. His assailants tried to run him over in a car. He had to be taken to the hospital. Recovering from his injuries, Farhan had time to think about his predicament and how it reflected on his community: "The ironic part of this whole thing is that the case lingered for four years, and the individual that attacked me and almost took my life was fined $400 for what he had done and then let go. I know friends who have paid speeding tickets that are more than $400."

The fine had little effect on his assailants. At the time of our interview in September 2008, Farhan and his wife were still being threatened by these same men. Her car had been vandalized, and one of the men intimidated her personally. Both husband and wife live in constant fear.

Farhan's case raises an important concern for Muslims in America—that when a Muslim takes the initiative to counter extreme views within his own community, he or she may be attacked for it, with little support from the justice system. In Farhan's case, when justice did prevail, the penalty was so meager as to be almost meaningless. The conclusions are inescapable: the modernist Muslim finds himself maligned by the critics of Islam for not countering extremism, yet when he does take action, no assistance is forthcoming from those whose job it is to uphold the law and promote harmony in the community. And one can speculate as well that had a Muslim assaulted a white man under similar circumstances, he would have been accused of terrorism and, depending on the severity of the assault, would have received a swift and long jail sentence.

We had been introduced to Farhan by my friend Saeed Khan, a cheerful and articulate face of modernist Islam and professor at Wayne State University. His Muslim and non-Muslim students appreciated his easygoing style and pop culture references. With Saeed as our guide in the Dearborn Muslim community, we found doors opening to us. This enabled us to gain deeper insight into the community than others might who have had to rely on non-Muslims to guide them.[10] As we drove around parts of Detroit that looked as though they had suffered aerial bombing, Saeed described the city's historic importance as a thriving commercial and industrial center. This was once the heart of the automobile manufacturing world, where Ford made the cars that would define the industry that attracted workers from around the world, including the Middle East. That is why Detroit came to have the densest Arab population in America.

Saeed appeared uneasy in both the poor and rich non-Muslim neighborhoods. African Americans, many of whom live in the former areas, would treat him as an immigrant and therefore a possible target of their anger, while the mostly white residents in the latter would consider him an unwanted "man of color" in an area with tight security. When we decided to stop outside a home in Grosse Pointe, the affluent part of Detroit guarded by police checkpoints, Saeed preferred to stay in the car. We were attracted to the house because of its many imaginative lawn ornaments of Uncle Sam and American flags. The owner, Mark, who looked eerily like President George W. Bush, came out to talk to us. His family had come to the United States from Germany in the 1930s. "Muslims," he pronounced, "are free to live here as long as they think like us and act a certain way."

Modernists in Distress

Modernist Muslims like Farhan or Saeed are aware of their predicament in being under attack from literalists who see them as compromised Muslims and from non-Muslims who identify them only as Muslims and thus potential terrorists. Modernist Muslims feel not only the injustices of the world around them, but also their powerlessness to do much about it. At the same time, they continue to cling to their modernist identity, however tenuously. Their situation reminded me of the modernist Muslims we met on our journey to the Muslim world. There, too, modernists lived in a state of despair and uncertainty, desperately trying to create a world in their vision and yet acutely aware of the forces ranged against them. Modernists are therefore in a state of distress.

I met modernist Muslims whose lives have been so disrupted since 9/11 that they have been pushed out of their comfortable, middle-class existence and are now left searching for answers and direction. I heard countless heartbreaking stories from Muslim taxi drivers, many of them limousine chauffeurs. These men had lost both their jobs and position in society, as in the case of a former professional pilot whose license was revoked after 9/11 and who now barely makes a living. His only "crime" was that he happened to be a Muslim. There were others: a businessman whose small company collapsed because of a minor infraction, people who were fired or forced out of their jobs, qualified graduates unable to find employment. Whereas many of the middle-class Muslims took a passive view of their changed circumstances, those like the taxi drivers were furious, believing their plight was a direct consequence of a larger conspiracy against Islam itself.

The theme of powerlessness and frustration loomed large in our conversations with these Muslims. "We have no leaders, no unity," they complained, or "We only talk," or "We are divided by ego problems." Anti-Semitism was widespread among them. They accused the media of constantly ridiculing and fomenting a fear and hatred of Muslims. They blamed American foreign policy, which they said had destabilized the Muslim world. They even accused Americans of having created rifts between Shias and Sunnis in order to destabilize Muslim society. Divide and rule, they said, is the old policy of the Western powers.

These modernist Muslims are suspended between several identities. It is an uncomfortable and dangerous position to be in. Some will veer toward literalism, and some, like the homegrown terrorists discussed in chapter 9, may even be guided toward a violent expression of their frustrations. Yet others may move away from religion and adopt a more overtly "American" identity.

Modernist Muslims Morph into American Pluralists

The debate about cultural boundaries rages in Muslim communities throughout America. One might have assumed that modernist Muslims working for Google in Silicon Valley, California, would have laid the debate to rest, but when I was invited to give a "Tech Talk" at Google's main headquarters, I discovered this was not so. The talk was preceded by a luncheon with about twenty Muslim employees, mainly Pakistani engineers born either in the United States or in Pakistan. One young American-born woman was in marketing and wore a hijab. It was early November, so when asked about American identity, the group gravitated to the issue of Halloween and a heated discussion quickly ensued.

The younger American-born Muslims argued that Halloween was a cultural tradition and not incompatible with Islam. If Americans are Christians who are in the Abrahamic tradition as well and have no objections, then why not join them? Others were opposed to Halloween on both religious and cultural grounds. An older bearded engineer from Karachi insisted that Halloween had nothing to do with Islam or Christianity and was in fact rooted in pagan ritual. Furthermore, if Muslims began to celebrate Halloween, where would this end? Would they begin to celebrate Christmas, and then something that is most incompatible with Islam, Easter? "If I don't stop my kids now, where would it stop? Do they begin to drink alcohol and eat pork later?" he asked.

One young man argued in favor of cultural adaptation: "American culture is changing all the time. Why not take some of their culture and add ours?" The older man retorted that Halloween was all about drinking and sex and asked whether the young man supported this. "We should not impose our religion on them," replied the young man.

Others across America, like Khaliq Baig, a Pakistani physician in Las Vegas with orthodox views, also saw American holidays as cultural traps: "When you try to integrate, you disintegrate." He warned Muslim children to stay away from Halloween and Christmas because "these things do not belong in our religion."

Some Muslims have moved away from their own identity perhaps because of the controversy surrounding Islam. We came upon an example in Honolulu, that most pluralist of American cities. Hawai'i has a small Muslim community of between 3,000 and 4,000, which I was asked to address after Friday prayers at the main mosque. Hakim Ouansafi, the Arab head of the mosque committee, and the president of the Muslim Association of Hawai'i, welcomed us but warned us not to be in touch with Saleem Ahmed, someone we were anxious to meet. Hakim said irately that Saleem reputedly gave interviews in the media and talked to interfaith communities claiming to represent Islam, which he did not. Indeed, according to Hakim, Saleem was not even a true Muslim.

Hakim, who was from Morocco, kept a tight control over the affairs of the mosque. His protégé, Imam Ismail El-Sheikh, who gave the khutba at Friday prayers, was fresh from Al-Azhar in Cairo. The imam wore long black robes and delivered the khutba in painfully halting English, offering generalities about loving one another before switching to Arabic, which he spoke beautifully.

Hakim's number one role model was the Prophet. Khadijah, the Prophet's wife, was another of his role models. He thought "America was the best country in the world to live in," although its reputation has been dented by some "bad people." He could not resist bringing up the perfidy of Honolulu's Saleem Ahmed again, whom he blamed for "diluting our religion."

When we finally met Saleem, we saw a jovial and energetic man who was well liked in Honolulu. Like others encountered on our travels, Saleem seemed to have erased the "Muslim" from his identity, replacing it

In Honolulu, team members Hailey Woldt, Madeeha Hameed, Jonathan Hayden, and the author gather with Hakim Ouansafi, in the middle, and Imam Ismail El-Sheikh, on the far right, at the main mosque after Friday prayers. Hawai'i's diverse Muslim community numbers roughly 4,000 and hails from Morocco to the Philippines.

with what he understood to be an American one. Saleem's Thanksgiving dinner, which he generously hosted at his home on November 27, 2008, was American pluralism, Hawai'i style. Saleem said a prayer before dinner, asking all of the guests to hold hands, and referred to Allah, Bhagwan, God, the Hawaiian wind and sea gods, and some other deities I did not recognize. He also mentioned a "Supreme Being." The variety of dishes for dinner that night was as colorful and eclectic as his theological reference to divine beings. His guests hailed from India, Pakistan, Bangladesh, and the United States mainland, and included Sikhs, Christians, and Hindus. All seemed to be doing well professionally and were grateful for what America had done for their lives, while recalling their homes in South Asia with despair. For all their joy about being American, most did not know the origins of Thanksgiving or the meaning of the *Mayflower*. One woman thought it was a spring festival. Since 9/11, suspicion and distrust have crept into the island's various communities, we were told. The Sikh doctor, who wore the traditional turban and had a beard, complained that he was now subjected to extra scrutiny every time he flew on an airline.

During an interview over breakfast, Saleem referred to "Muhammad" several times before I realized he was talking about the Prophet of Islam, whom Muslims usually mention with a blessing, especially if they are talking to other Muslims. It was ironic that a non-Muslim like Sheriff Lee Baca added the words "peace be with him" every time he mentioned the Prophet as a gesture of respect to the Muslim community, whereas a Muslim leader seemed to show him disrespect.

Sporting a colorful Hawaiian shirt usually seen on tourists, Saleem described himself as a Muslim who practices Islam in the broadest and loosest of ways. Although he comes from a Muslim family, his attitude toward the Muslim community and its Moroccan leader was unambiguously critical. He believed the community is responsible for its current problems, finding its members "too locked in ritual" and unconcerned about being "better human beings." He objected when his wife, a fifth-generation Japanese American who converted to Islam and took the name Yasmin, was not allowed to pray in the main hall of Hawai'i's only mosque unless she covered her hair. More controversially, he showed us the manuscript of *Islam: A Religion of Peace?* in which he points to the "negative" verses in the Quran and argues for their removal.[11] "We should reject the earlier part of the Quran and only use the end part," he told us, noting that the community calls him a *kafir* (non-believer).

Saleem's number one role model was Mahatma Gandhi. The Prophet of Islam was second, but only in his teachings toward the latter part of his life. His other role models included Guru Nanak, the founder of the Sikh religion, and Martin Luther King Jr. Saleem declared that he would "want racial profiling" that involved Muslims because "the next attack is going to come from people like me." Furthermore, he "supported the war on terror wholeheartedly."

When Saleem invited us to attend an interfaith gathering at the Jewish Temple Emanu-El, we found him sitting forlorn in the last row of the meeting hall. No other Muslims were present. Either he had not invited them, or they had refused to join him. I was not entirely surprised that other Muslims were not responding to someone who advocated editing of the holy text they believe is divine. Saleem has effectively cut himself off from the community. He no longer goes to the mosque even for Friday prayer.

Granted that Saleem's role model is Gandhi and Hakim's the Prophet of Islam, other factors may account for their differences. As Saleem is South Asian and Hakim an Arab, their communities throughout the United States are engaged in a similar, if not always so explicit, rivalry for leadership. Saleem is an academic, a PhD, working in a university environment and dealing with ideas. Hakim is a businessman concerned with practical problems as he goes about his daily routine of constructing hotels and hiring and firing people. I tried to persuade them to talk to each other in the spirit of civility and dialogue, and they appeared to be listening, but I suspect the rift was too wide to bridge.

Chris Lovelace, the young African American imam mentioned in chapter 4 who talked of Islam's early contributions to America with such animation, would have been pleased to hear Hakim's remarks about Arab sailors reaching the Hawaiian Islands before any Americans. By way of proof, Hakim said the names Hawai'i and Honolulu come from Arabic. Hawai'i derives from *hawa*, or the trade winds that brought the Arabs, Honolulu from *huni*, which means "here," and *lulu*, which means "pearls," or "here are the pearls," a phrase associated with the islands because of the abundance of pearls there. A wise elder in the native language is called *hakim*, the Arabic word for a ruler or leader.

Along our way, we met many people like Saleem who are trying to reach out to other faiths. Ghalib Begg, a Pakistani in Dearborn who calls himself "Victor," the English translation of Ghalib, the name of a celebrated Urdu poet of South Asia, is an example. Having been involved in interfaith activity, Begg had assembled a large gathering of Jews, Christians, and younger Muslims, including his daughter Sofia and her husband, Farhan, to meet us.

People seemed keen to have a dialogue with Muslims but were not sure how to proceed. One Jewish lady said that her community was suspicious of Muslims. A Christian man asked, "Why don't Muslims speak up when atrocities are committed by other Muslims?" He mentioned that his Christian neighbor had bought a gun as he feared that Muslims were taking over America but was now ready to face them. Other Christian guests quoted Steve Emerson and political commentator Daniel Pipes to warn the guests of the dangers that lurked in the Muslim community.

Because Muslims like Saleem and Begg are disconnected from the mainstream Muslim community, their efforts at interfaith dialogue leave participants unaware of the real issues in the community and their forums do not attract its members. While well-meaning and tireless, they appear too eager to ingratiate themselves and therefore are exposed to the charge of "dancing for whitey," as Jonathan put it.

The reluctance of the Muslim modernists to stand up for and explain their culture and traditions with confidence was noted by Bapsi Sidhwa, a novelist from Pakistan, who told us at her home in Houston: "I'm very often invited to conferences, big humongous things on Islam like 'Lifting the Veil.' They always ask me to talk about Islam, and usually there are other Muslim women with me, or men, and I find them a little apologetic. They will say, 'You know I'm not a practicing Muslim,' or something like that, because they feel so intimidated or threatened. Being a Zoroastrian and not a Muslim, I feel like I can give a voice here, a much stronger voice, and what I really emphasize very often is the similarity between Islam and Christianity and Judaism."

Joe of Cedar Rapids

"Hello, I'm Joe," said a smiling man with a ruddy white complexion and blue eyes, speaking in a midwestern American accent. He was wearing a short-sleeved shirt and a pair of well-fitting jeans, looking like a typical Midwesterner. Curious, because we were standing outside the main mosque in Cedar Rapids, Iowa, I asked tentatively, "Are you a Muslim?" "Of course," he smiled. "But your name . . . ," I said. "It's the equivalent of Yusuf," he replied with a grin. Joseph, or Yusuf, figures prominently in the Quran and the Bible.

Joe's older brother was called Bill, although his Muslim name was Yahya, another prophet in the Quran. Though accepted to law school, Bill heeded John F. Kennedy's call to join the Peace Corps in 1963 as the organization's first Muslim member. In Senegal he hand-dug wells that provided a more sanitary water supply and, being an Iowa wrestler, also coached what would become that country's 1964 Olympic wrestling team. His company, Midamar, currently exports *halal* (lawful) food to some thirty-five countries.

For all their outward appearance, both Bill and Joe Aossey were proper Muslims and fasting because it was the month of Ramadan. Joe talked excitedly of the time he spends on his Harley-Davidson and especially of going through a religious phase a few years ago. He had grown a beard, which made him fit perfectly with his motorcycle gang as they sped across the continent. A friendly sort, Joe invited Jonathan, Frankie, and Craig to join him in Arizona later in the year with his gang.

Joe was born and grew up in Cedar Rapids. His father had come to America from Lebanon at the turn of the century and made his way up to Cedar Rapids searching for work. "Iowa was a very open place then," explained Joe, "because there were people here from everywhere, so it wasn't like New York City where you had ghettos of Irish, of Scots, of English, of German. Here you had almost a totally open relationship with everybody because the population was spread out across the countryside." By 1925 about twenty-five Lebanese families had settled in the area. Many of the men from these families, he said, would go on to fight in World War II.

Joe was comfortable in his identity as a Muslim and as an American: "I don't consider myself to be a Muslim in an American society; I consider myself an American who believes what the Quran teaches us, which isn't that alien from the way I read it from Christianity and from Judaism." Like his brother, Joe was alarmed, though, at some of the recent trends toward literalism, which promoted the fundamentalist version of Wahhabi or Salafi Islam beginning in the 1980s. He attributed this to Saudi funding and an influx of Saudi ideas, recounting bitterly that the Saudis had banned his community's traditional Lebanese cultural dance because it was deemed "un-Islamic." The Wahhabis, Joe fulminated, "they always have plenty of money to spend. That's when it all started changing. The Wahhabis don't represent us; it's such a disgusting idea. The Wahhabis and the Saudis are like the Spanish government during the Inquisition, like the priest and the conquistador." Wahhabi influence in the community was soon reflected in the politics of the mosque, with Saudi-trained imams moving into the community and, much to the dismay and frustration of Joe, "telling us what Islam is."

To Joe, they were moving away from both their true Muslim identity and loyalty to America. "This illusion or argument about what comes first, country or God, is a created argument. There is a chapter in the Quran, chapter 90, that states very clearly that you are responsible for the land that you are living in, and it states very clearly that you are supposed to be involved in the society. So this is a bogus argument created by the propaganda system here," he explained. Islam and America "are one," in his view: "I've lived here for seventy-one years, and my ideals of what America is and what Islam is blend beautifully."

We met Joe after Friday prayers at the Islamic center, where its Cairo-trained imam, Ahmed Nabhan, asked me to give the khutba. The imam had not been particularly communicative when we tried to set up the visit, so I thought I would speak for only a few minutes. As he led me to the microphone, he whispered, "We expect you to speak for forty-five minutes." Taken aback, I had to improvise and fell back on my favorite theme for Muslim audiences, the importance of *ilm,* or knowledge, in Islam. I talked of knowledge as a way of understanding non-Muslim communities, citing one of my favorite sayings of the Prophet, which emphasizes the importance of scholarship over martyrdom.

Imam Nabhan then took us to the site of the real purpose of our visit to Cedar Rapids, the oldest mosque in America, built in 1934. The date, he explained, was "misleading" because Muslim families were already present in the area in the late nineteenth century but could not build a mosque until they had a critical mass of worshippers. Called the Mother Mosque of America, it is a modest structure resembling most other houses in the town and was under repair after the region's extensive flooding. Seated on a threadbare carpet, Imam Nabhan spoke of the importance of interfaith dialogue, but with a shaky command of English and poor knowledge of American culture. The small community was obviously under some pressure from neighbors complaining about the mosque. The story seemed a familiar one until a charming but tense-looking young girl wearing a hijab and jeans and introduced as the media spokesperson for the mosque interjected with a surprising remark. She thought the main symbol of America and its culture was the Holocaust Museum. When asked to elaborate, her reply surprised us even more. She alluded to who was really running things in America, namely the Jews. The team had heard such sentiments in the Middle East and was now hearing them in America.

Modernist Muslim Women

We met so many extraordinary modernist Muslim women on the journey that it is difficult to give adequate space to them all. Perhaps two good examples are Amra Tareen and Najah Bazzy because they not only hold leadership roles in their communities but are an interesting study in contrasts. Although both are modernist, Amra wears fashionable but modest Western clothes without a hijab, while Najah chooses to wear a hijab and more orthodox apparel. Amra's background is Pakistani and Najah's is Lebanese. Amra lives in San Francisco and moves easily among the high-tech and dot-com entrepreneurs of Silicon Valley, while Najah lives in Dearborn and works among ordinary women facing the daily pressures of prejudice, poverty, and ignorance. I also share my sister Rani's story below.

Amra grew up in Islamabad, Pakistan, and after finishing high school moved to Australia. She came to America for her master's degree at Harvard Business School, where she met her husband, Steve Ackroyd, a white Christian American. Steve converted to Islam in order to marry Amra. We interviewed them in San Francisco after Amra had just returned from a conference in Monaco. Like many others, she had found that before 9/11, "no one knew what a Muslim was," and that being a Muslim was "a private affair." Being a Muslim was important to her because her "values are very

The Mother Mosque of America, built in 1934 in Cedar Rapids, Iowa, is the oldest mosque in the United States and was constructed by Lebanese immigrants, whose descendants are now fourth- and fifth-generation Americans.

Muslim," which she thought were not much different from American values in that they stress standing up for justice, and "if there's something you don't believe in, you find an answer, you solve a problem."

Amra and Steve decided to raise their children as Muslims, but, Amra said, "after 9/11, I felt that the environment changed. I consider being Muslim the new black for the United States, that being Muslim is considered worse than being black. During the election, you saw with Barack Obama, everyone saying he is a Muslim, so people should not vote for him. My biggest disappointment was he should have said 'Why does it matter if I'm a Muslim? I'm not saying I am, but why should it matter if I was a Muslim?'"

This pressure pushed Amra to develop a company in Silicon Valley called AllVoices, which is a public news website where anyone can post political, cultural, or other news emanating from any country in the world. Her role model is Christiane Amanpour of CNN. When asked if she had ever faced discrimination, Amra responded with her usual big smile: "I may have, but I don't know. I don't dress up like the stereotypical Muslim. You know, I don't cover my hair, I don't act like a Muslim; they expect Muslim women not to speak about what's on their mind. Even being in Silicon Valley, I don't think I felt it. But just to be very honest, there is discrimination against women themselves. Only 3 percent of women founders get funded. So I don't think I myself have felt discrimination, but I've felt that just watching TV, media, watching other people talk about the Muslim faith, that it is considered a little demeaning to be a Muslim in the United States."

Hailey and Madeeha spent a great deal of time with Najah Bazzy, whom they considered an ideal role model as both American and Muslim. After meeting Najah, Hailey insisted that I meet her. "I promise, you will not be sorry," she cajoled me. She was right.

Najah Bazzy described herself by fusing her identities: "I am a devout Arab, a devout American, and a devout Muslim." She described what the Prophet meant to her with tears welling in her eyes and voice trembling in a whisper, "I love him. He is my oxygen, the air I breathe. Every year I go to Medina, to his final resting place." Thomas Jefferson was another hero and represented the best of America. For Najah, Jefferson was a Muslim at heart, although it would be "sacrilegious" to say so. The spirit of the Declaration of Independence, she argued, was Islamic because of its emphasis on the universal values of equality, justice, and tolerance. The Arab world, and its politics, did not practice these values, she remarked. For Najah, "American Muslim identity produces the best Muslims in the world because the values of America and Islam are congruent."

"Dearborn," Najah said with a sigh of contentment, "is a place of tremendous pride." She took Madeeha and Hailey to the meat shop, Ronnie Berry's, where the tradition of halal butchery has been practiced by that Arab family for generations. Ronnie, however, is completely American, with a crew cut, hunting trophies proudly displayed around the shop, and participation in his "fifty-and-over" baseball team.

Najah was born and raised near the Ford factory just outside Detroit where her father and grandfather worked. Most of the other families had moved there from Lebanon with her grandfather's generation. Her grandfather, who arrived in 1905, was one of the first workers at the factory. "That's why the family's been here over a hundred years. They were working hard and building America right in front of you," she said. "We didn't eat pork, we were supposed to pray and fast." There was "generational respect." Her grandmothers lived with her family, and her family showed hospitality to everyone. The community, she explained, had retained traditional notions of shame and honor, which were considered "very big" among them. As they grew older, most of the men went to Saudi Arabia to perform the *hajj* pilgrimage. For Najah, a critical factor defining who was an American in the community was his or her burial site. "I would prefer to be buried in the courtyard with the Prophet of Islam in Medina," she said, but her second choice was Dearborn. Until the 1960s, those who could afford it in her community preferred to be buried in Lebanon.

The early immigrants maintained certain cultural traditions, Najah said, while their children became fully American. They all went to the local public school, participated in the sports teams, and lived with other immigrant groups whose children were also becoming "Americanized." Everyone celebrated Thanksgiving, the Fourth of July, and even Christmas. One of her earliest memories was of her mother crying as she pulled a turkey out of the oven on Thanksgiving in 1963, while her father watched continuing coverage of John F. Kennedy's assassination of the week before. "It was a traumatizing moment for my family," she remembers.

The most dramatic changes in Dearborn were set in motion, particularly among the Shia, with Iran's Islamic revolution of 1979, which shook the Muslim world. They were suddenly confronted with questions of identity. Were they Muslim, Lebanese, Iranian, or just plain American? Overnight, Najah said, America's Muslims faced an "existential crisis" over their previously comfortable acceptance of both traditional Arab and American culture, which had led many to adopt a more secular lifestyle and forsake much of their Muslim identity without even realizing it. After 1979, they reverted to their Islamic identity. That trend has progressively increased with the large influx of immigrants into Dearborn, especially from Yemen. Najah's treasured South End no longer resembles the Dearborn of her childhood, and she is saddened and frustrated at the changes.

The South End—with its Arabic signs, women in *niqab*s (veil covering the full face), and traditional black dresses, coffee shops, billiard halls, halal meat shops, and mosque—is "re-creating Lebanon." There are more signs in Arabic than in English on Warren Avenue. And the houses, landscaped with roses, fig trees, and grapevines, she pointed out, are like "the Arab world." The other stores on Dix Avenue all have signs in Arabic, some even without an English translation, and bearded men walk about in traditional Muslim clothes of their homelands. Modernist Muslims like Najah accuse recent Muslim immigrants of "seeing America as a giant ATM machine." They are usually unable or unwilling to say what it means to be an American and have no interest in America or in having American friends.

Discussing racial prejudice in Dearborn, Najah recalled the white National Guard beating up her cousins during the race riots and civil rights movement because they saw little difference between young Arab men and young African American men. For the Arabs, this was as baffling as it was paradoxical for they, too, had their own form of racism. Many of the Lebanese Arabs have light skin, blue eyes, and blond hair. "If we do not have a hijab," Najah told me with a confident smile, "we look like Hailey." The Lebanese see themselves as "Arab whites" and are "very bigoted." For her, Arabs have a distinct prejudice against blacks. Arabs call blacks *abid*, meaning "slave," a term that dates back to the time when Arabs kept African slaves. Najah confirmed that even today's Arabs use the term. Arabs, Najah told me, place blacks in two categories: converts to Islam, whom they find acceptable, and non-Muslims, whom they distrust. Arabs take credit for the conversion of the African Americans to Islam. Arabs, she said, find the black community a victim of drugs and criminal behavior and consider them lazy and their young men irresponsible for fathering babies and then abandoning them. Najah described Dearborn as the "South" of the North, a significant phrase in the context of American history.

Race also divides the Arab community, Najah remarked, for the Lebanese see the Yemenis as "dirty" and "dark," "as just one notch above the blacks." She herself was indignant at the Yemeni custom of covering women with the niqab, which she said was not Islamic. Even the hijab was not really mandatory, Najah stated. African American women who believed in the Salafi version of Islam were also wearing the niqab. The niqab, Najah reflected philosophically, "almost negates the notion of the hijab," which is to save a woman's beauty for the eyes of the husband only.

Showing Hailey and Madeeha around the mosque, Najah mentioned that her grandmother had been a driving force in its construction and was annoyed when told to enter from the back. Najah did not understand why Muslims expect women to enter from back doors and relegate them to small rooms when, at the same time, Islam calls on them to take prominent roles in society: "What's that about? I don't think the Prophet would be happy about that at all. What's strange is that my grandmother helped to build this place, and they never had this segregation. This segregation came much later."

For some, Najah is a controversial figure. Debbie Schlussel, described by Najah as a "Zionist lawyer in Detroit who was part of Daniel Pipes's network, which routinely attacks Muslims," has accused Najah of committing Medicare fraud. Schlussel's blog has also juxtaposed pictures of Najah with known Muslim terrorists, calling her an America-hater and accusing her of promoting an "Islamo-fascist invasion of America." A particularly virulent comment advised Najah to "get out of my country! You're not wanted here. Fuck her! GO BACK TO IRAN (Or wherever the fuck you're from). Shalom!"[12]

Rani's Story

The story of my sister Rani provides another example of a modernist Muslim woman while giving a glimpse of the Muslim life cycle. Rani was born in Karachi and died in Los Angeles; born a Pakistani, she died an American. The most gentle of souls, her life was dedicated to her students at the Montessori school in Los Angeles where she taught. Her friends represented a variety of religions and cultures. Her sons, Ali and Yusuf, were born in L.A., went to school there, spent time with their friends in malls and on basketball courts, and Ali was married there. Rani's family celebrated Christmas and the Fourth of July as much as the Muslim festivals.

Rani had fallen ill in January 2008 and was taken to the hospital. I was busy with my classes in the new term and was also preparing for my project on America, but I kept in touch with her husband, Alam. When I asked whether I should come, he said Rani would be home soon, and that might be a good time to visit. Shortly after came the message from my friend Hamid: "Come immediately. Please understand what I am saying." It was the last phrase that sent a chill down my spine. As I put the phone down, I tasked Zeenat with booking the next flight to the West Coast. Zeenat and Rani had been in school together at the Jesus and Mary Convent in Murree and had remained good friends.

We arrived from Washington, D.C., late at night on Thursday, planning to drive straight to the hospital. Alam, who was by her bedside since Rani had been admitted, said the best time would be early in the morning so we went to Hamid's house to spend the night. Not long after midnight I heard a desperate knocking on my bedroom door. "Get ready," Hamid said. From the tone of his voice I knew something had happened.

Rani had passed away. Zeenat and I had missed seeing her alive by a few hours. As we ran into the hospital and I saw her lifeless body, I almost fainted in grief. But I was not too distraught to notice the plight of Ali and Yusuf. They had fallen apart, and their condition forced me to pull myself together. Courteous, energetic, and intelligent young men, they were favorites of their mother. They were especially close to me. Yusuf, the younger boy, in particular, had collapsed. He sat by himself on the floor in the corridor, his head buried deep in his hands. He looked lonely and lost. I asked his father whether he had eaten anything, and I was told he had not eaten for several days. I forced him up and took him down to the cafeteria to get him hot tea and croissants.

Dawn was breaking as the news of Rani's death spread. Her unexpected passing created sorrow in the community, which was heightened among those who knew that her first grandchild, Ali's son Rayaan Khan, had been born the day she was admitted to the emergency room and that she did not live to see him. Within hours her funeral had been arranged, and we headed for the main Islamic Center for the Muslim rituals and burial afterward.

The funeral services at the mosque were impeccable: they combined American efficiency with Islamic compassion. The Friday prayer, the main Muslim prayer of the week, was designated *namaz-e-janaza*, or the funeral prayer, and that day it was one of the largest possible gatherings. The director and imam, Muzammil Siddiqi, asked the congregation to pray for Rani's soul, after which we departed for the burial ground. As if to complete the perfect Muslim burial, a light rain had begun, which is considered a sign of God's blessing in Islam. From a Muslim point of view, the signs had been auspicious: Rani's death took place early in the morning, when Muslims believe God listens to the prayers of people, and it was Friday, the holy day of the week.

Too much was happening too quickly, and I could not even begin to comprehend the scale of the loss. As I drove back to Rani's home and sat down on her sofa in the living room, I fully expected her to walk up to me and, in her cheerful manner, quietly ask if I was ready to eat a favorite dish that she had specially prepared. The response to her death showed me the variety of people who had been touched by her kind of saintliness. If her grandson

Rayaan Khan was anything like his parents or grandparents, he would grow up to be a decent and charming man with integrity and one at ease with his American identity. But not all Muslims are prepared to concede so much of themselves to American identity, as we see in the next section.

Literalist Muslims

In the popular imagination, literalist Muslims see themselves as the champions of Islam, have beards, wear a headdress and robes, and noisily proclaim jihad against the infidel. In real life, however, some are clean-shaven, wear Western suits and blazers with ties, and talk of interfaith dialogue; others sound like modernists, and still others can be said to be shifting their position. Some may be working as doctors and engineers, while others popularly known as Salafis will eke out an existence as laborers or taxi drivers in order to avoid contact with the system. The former literalists are active proponents of Islam but wish to interact with mainstream America, while the latter wish to be left alone to their prayers and devotions.

The Challenges for the Champions of Islam

Imam Mohamed Al-Darsani, originally from Syria and now living in Fort Myers, Florida, is an example of a literalist Muslim who looks and sounds modernist. When Jonathan and Frankie first met him at his Islamic Center for PEACE (an acronym for Progress, Education, Awareness, Cooperation, Enlightenment) in Fort Myers, the imam talked of defending, explaining, and spreading Islam in a land he felt was hostile to it. He appeared to be a man under pressure. One of the center's concerns was reflected in the words "Pray for our families in Palestine" written on a white board mounted in the prayer room. The imam said he produces DVDs to educate people about Islam, but they have been rejected by television networks like PBS because "we all know who owns the media." His wife—a white, self-described former "Evangelical Christian" convert from West Virginia named Paulette—wore the hijab in the center but said she did not do so in public.

Arriving from Syria in 1982 to continue his studies, the imam had been a student of Syria's grand mufti, Sheikh Ahmad Kuftaro. He named Kuftaro one of his role models, along with the Prophet of Islam, Thomas Jefferson, Abraham Lincoln, and Hugo Chavez. Although he did not agree with Chavez's "theology," Al-Darsani praised his "dedication." He called

America the "symbol of freedom, prosperity, and dreams" and said he "couldn't believe I was actually here" when he first came. "But the more you know about America," he said, "the more disappointed you get," pointing to other less appealing values of American "hypocrisy and democracy." The imam felt that "America needs Islam for its own salvation. All the corruptions of the last three decades have come to fruition. Christianity has failed in the West. Even this masjid used to be a church. We must offer people a way out. You bring water to people, but if you don't drink, you die of thirst."

Al-Darsani confessed he was in the eye of the storm in Florida's debate about Islam, especially with Tom Trento of the Florida Security Council, an organization that distributed the DVD *Obsession* and warns against the "sinister dangers of radical Islamism." The "campaign of fear" against Islam is "worse now than after 9/11," lamented the imam and spoke of recent shootings at mosques: "After 9/11 we only received one negative call. Women would call us in sympathy and escort us around for our protection. Now some of the same people are scared to say hello—they hate you. Our next-door neighbors used to be nice; now they shun us. 'Your god is the moon god,' they tell us. 'You're nothing but terrorists.'" The imam gave George W. Bush credit for "reaching out to Muslims" but said in the 2008 election neither candidate visited a mosque: "Within four years everything has changed. I've been here for twenty-six years. I can't make myself blond and blue-eyed. I came here by choice. I had to take an oath. These Americans who hate Muslims never took an oath."

The imam participates in interfaith dialogue and finds the priests "friendly," but when he speaks in their churches, he can "feel the congregation's hatred." People challenge their priests for inviting him to speak to them. "How dare you!" they say. The imam thought the greatest threat to America is the "ignorance of the American people. They are letting go of their own freedom by allowing this Zionist Christian religion to dominate. Soon America will be a Nazi country. The United States is in decline. America is hated in the Muslim world."

In plotting a course ahead, America should "change its foreign policy and military industrial complex," urged the imam. These are currently based not on morals but on self-interest and "build prosperity on the misery of others." It was also important to "honor the American Constitution," which he felt was "totally Islamic," although "Islam offers even more to people."

The next day, the imam attended my public lecture on Sanibel Island with his son, a large muscular man who had been in the U.S. Army and who accompanied his father reluctantly. The imam hoped his son might learn something from listening to an Islamic scholar. The imam sat next to Frankie, who thought he looked "a bit uncomfortable as the only Muslim in a sea of WASPs as we talked about some of the people who live on the island, like Porter Goss, former head of the CIA." In my speech, I stressed the need for Americans to understand Islam and for Muslims to engage fully with American society. The imam insisted that we have breakfast with him in an example of traditional Arab hospitality before we drove across the state to Palm Beach.

At a Perkins restaurant in Fort Myers the following morning, the imam seemed a different man from the one my team had described. Some tension had obviously developed between father and son after the previous night's lecture. The son confronted his father over hash browns, eggs, and coffee, and neatly turned his father's argument that he should heed me against him: "You said I should be listening to Dr. Ahmed. Don't you think it's correct that you should be too?" The imam agreed that the way forward should be marked by efforts in interfaith dialogue different from the kind he had conducted so far. Up to now, his work had been aimed at "defending" Islam in a combative manner and launching "counterattacks" against Christianity and Judaism, but the way forward was mutual respect and understanding. The team members were surprised at the turnaround in the imam's attitude. After breakfast, he blessed our journey: "It's the message of Christianity, it's the message of Judaism, which is to bring peace and harmony among people, among each other, and between them and God. May Allah bless you, may Allah reward you, and make your journey and mission an easy and blessed one."

In Atlanta we discovered the complexities of literalist Islam in action in its imposing and ornate Al-Farooq Masjid, said to be the largest mosque in the city. We had met Khalid Siddiq, the mosque's public relations official and number two man on its board of directors, at a dinner given for us on our arrival. Siddiq is from Pakistan, and from his views and his appearance—the cropped beard and hair, the neat grey Western suit—it was obvious that he was a member or supporter of the Jamaat-i-Islami. We were told Siddiq was the main community leader, and we had to interview him to really understand what was going on in Atlanta. He "likes to keep an eye on everything" that other Muslims are doing, community members told us. Siddiq invited us to interview him and join him at Friday prayers. The interview was not memorable, but the visit to the mosque provided some insights.

CNN wished to do a story on our visit to the Atlanta mosque, and Siddiq said it was fine with him, but he needed to check with the president of the board, who was Syrian and very orthodox. I then learned CNN had been refused permission. When I pressed Siddiq, he asked me to speak to the president, who I found courteous—he called me "brother" throughout—but he was unwilling to have anything to do with American media owing to the Muslim community's bad experience with this "enemy," which was innately hostile to Islam. In the end, my pleas that Muslims needed to seize such opportunities to project themselves failed to persuade the president.

We attended Friday prayer with more than 1,000 men and women, according to Siddiq. I estimated that 30 percent of the congregants were South Asians, 30 percent were Arabs, and the rest African Americans and others. Mohammad Khalid and Muhammad Sajid, the two young imams who had just arrived from Deoband, spoke in succession. Khalid gave a long-winded sermon in English about abstract ideals and Islamic history of a thousand years ago. Sajid spoke in Arabic, which the majority of the audience did not understand. In the adab tradition, the mosque leadership invited me to lunch and asked the imams to join us. We marched off to an appropriately "Muslim" restaurant in the neighborhood, the imams in their flowing shalwar-kameez and turbans. They had little to say, however, and appeared to know nothing of American culture. When I asked them for their best advice to the Muslim community in America, they said it was to "become walking Qurans."

Not everyone in the community was impressed with the mosque's leadership. Some were cynical about the "good-cop, bad-cop" way the Pakistani and the Syrian conducted affairs. An imam from another mosque felt Siddiq was "totally out of touch with the rest of the community," noting that Al-Farooq appoints imams that the board wants and that will do its bidding, a familiar problem in many mosques in America. If the imam steps out of line, the board will remove him, as it did with the previous Al-Farooq imam, who was asked to leave under mysterious circumstances a few months before. The board usually sets the agenda for the mosque. We found many boards would not allow our team to distribute our questionnaires or film interviews if they had not cleared it first, despite the imam's approval.

Lifting the Veil of the Salafis

Mystery surrounds the Salafis, variously known as Wahhabis, Deobandis, or Islamists. The majority in the United States are immigrants, many of them freshly arrived. Their newness combined with their determination to cling to their beliefs and traditions ensures that it will be a long time, if ever, before they become fully American. African Americans who convert to this version of Islam adopt the Saudi-influenced ideas, dress, and behavior of the Salafis and are prominent among them. For most people in the United States, Salafis are the embodiment of Islamic extremism, and Americans continue to sleep uneasily, still dreaming of men with long unkempt beards, wearing shalwar-kameez and carrying explosives.

Western commentators such as Gilles Kepel have popularized the double-barrel name Salafi Jihadists for these Muslims, considered the embodiment of "political Islam." Federal agencies have uncovered little information about the Salafis, and their efforts have been clumsy: agents turned up at the wrong mosques, asking the wrong questions, of the wrong groups. This bull-in-a-china-shop approach was doomed to failure. Our own estimates from the field suggest that as many as 40 percent of American Muslims are inclined toward literalism, but we must emphasize that not all of them adhere to Salafi philosophy. It is difficult to say what percentage of the literalists would be Salafi, but they remain a substantial and significant part of the community.

I was determined to penetrate the world of the Salafis during our journey, but the problem was how to approach them. Although I normally led our investigations personally, in this case a better strategy was to observe Salafis in their mosques without disturbance by sending in the team's male representatives, by now veterans of our fieldwork methods. I had been to every kind of mosque and madrassah in the Muslim world, but my experience in the Omaha mosque had alerted my anthropological sensibilities to the fact that my visit could compromise the neutrality of our fieldwork if I was drawn into a discussion about the nature of Islam. Given the background of the Salafis, there was a strong possibility of this happening.

Approaching them was not an easy task. They live largely isolated lives, worshipping in their own mosques. They are not on the Shura councils or in the high-profile Muslim organizations spread throughout the United States. They will not be seen at interfaith conferences. Even Muslim leaders who claim to speak on behalf of the Muslim community have little knowledge of who they are, where they live, and what they believe in.

Salafi mosques tend to be located in small, humble rooms in rundown or unlikely locations: strip malls, warehouses, basements, and apartments. Their light investment in the building infrastructure allows them to move frequently. Even if other Muslims have some idea of the mosque's location, they are nervous about sharing the information. We were often told that the Salafis are nonexistent or were advised not to speak to Salafis because they do not represent "true Islam." The Muslim community considers

Salafis reclusive and protective of their privacy. In San Diego, a representative of the Council on American-Islamic Relations (CAIR) who knew the location of a Salafi mosque pleaded with the team, "Please don't tell them I told you where it is," advising the group against going there because the Salafis "won't ever talk to an outsider." Remarked Jonathan, "We often raised eyebrows when other Muslims would find out that we had spent long periods with the Salafis in their mosques."

The team's experience in Atlanta is a good example of our fieldwork strategy. Following our dinner with Muslim leaders from different ethnic and sectarian backgrounds, the team split up, with Jonathan, Frankie, and Craig pursuing leads with Imam Wazir and Hailey organizing visits with women. Imam Wazir invited the three male team members to a feast of roasted goat in a local Somali restaurant. He mentioned his constant theological battles with the local "Wahhabis," or Salafis, who were seldom able to carry on a discussion without getting angry. The Wahhabis, the imam told them, believe in violence and "shedding the blood of the nonbeliever." Though they try to intimidate and slander him in public for being a Sufi, he refuses to be intimidated by them.

Despite his reservations, the imam agreed to show the three the Salafi mosque, but only on the condition that they not speak his name to anyone they met there. As they drove past a strip mall, the imam pointed solemnly, "There it is." Frankie said he saw only a group of stores. "Right there," insisted the imam. Frankie spied a store with a sign reading "East African Halal Meats." "The meat store?" he asked. "No, behind it," the imam replied. When they returned later that evening and went around the back of the strip mall, they found the usual dumpsters and beige-colored backs of stores. Just then, said Frankie, "we noticed cars driving up with people wearing kufiyas, staring intently at us. We noticed a small building with a door and a small sign on it reading 'Masjid At-Tawheed.' Another sign read 'No weapons.'"

Team members' reception at Masjid At-Tawheed was typical of their visits to Salafi mosques across the country. On entering the mosque, they were welcomed as is customary, but the Salafis were suspicious and acutely aware of the controversy surrounding them. "How do you have so much confidence to walk into *this* masjid and start talking to *us?*" they would ask. In spite of this, Jonathan found their welcome surprising "for a group that had built such a mystique and fear in the minds of both the intelligence agencies and the Muslim community."

The worshippers in Salafi mosques tend to be cab drivers and laborers for the most part, but a few professionals attend as well. The walls are frequently lined with bearded Muslims slowly rocking back and forth recit-ing the Quran. "Look at this carpet," said one Somali worshiper in Atlanta. "It is worn, torn up. People come to pray all the time, every day. It is not like these other masjids where they have these expensive carpets that are brand new where people only come on Friday," he mocked.

The Salafis met my assistants with openness and entered into long discussion with them about topics ranging from theology to America, to Osama bin Laden and the potential for terrorism in the United States. This was partly because the Salafis felt duty-bound to talk to my team and answer all of their questions in the hope they could preach to them and possibly convert them. Sometimes subtly, sometimes aggressively, my team was asked to convert to Islam. My assistants were seen as "ignorant blank slates" and therefore ripe for conversion. An imposing African Ameri-can man aggressively confronted Craig in the Salafi mosque in Atlanta on being told that Craig was raised a Christian, which the man called a "hypocritical" religion. "When our conversation was ending and we rose up off the prayer rug," said Craig, "the man grabbed my arm, looked me in the eyes with a determined look and said, 'Embrace Islam before it is too late.' He had a scary glint in his eyes."

"You must have seen that the truth lies in Islam," Jonathan was told by Salafis in San Diego. "You've met many Muslims and been to many masjids, how could you not have embraced the truth yet? There must be a reason why you are doing this project. You will see the light soon!"

The team also faced some tense moments regarding Islamic interpreta-tions. Craig tried to establish rapport with an African American Salafi by talking about our Harlem visit with the "hip-hop imam," Al-Hajj Talib Abdur-Rashid. The man's face soured: "Hip-hop is not permitted in Islam. Even music is not permitted in Islam." When Craig asked if he could film him for our documentary, he replied, "Images are not permit-ted in Islam," although there was some disagreement among the Muslims there on this point.

How Salafis Define Themselves

The term "Salafi" has been defined ad nauseam by commentators. Salafis are known to emphasize *tawhid,* or the unity and sovereignty of God over everything; reject *bid'a,* or innovation; and believe in the necessity of *tak-fir,* or the declaration of heresy, which is punishable by death, and in the notion of the centrality of jihad. When the team asked the Salafis them-selves to define the term, the imam of a small Salafi mosque in Dallas said:

"Salafi or Salaf means predecessor or ancestor. The Prophet is my number one teacher. He was a true Salafi. But Abraham was Salafi. Moses was Salafi. Jesus was a Salafi." Another man in the same Dallas mosque also defined Salafi as predecessor. "I am a Salafi but I'm also Ameriki, meaning I come *from* America," he said. They call themselves Salafis because they seek to live exactly by the example set by the Prophet and his companions.

The majority of Muslims, myself included, would have no objection to being inspired by those early Muslims: the Prophet, Abu Bakr, Umar, Uthman, and Ali. They were indeed remarkable figures—both men and women such as Khadija, Aisha, and Fatima. Scholars, jurists, warriors, and rulers—their emphasis on justice, compassion, and knowledge made them visionaries for a new society. The problem for other Muslims is that Salafis insist on imitating *every* aspect of the early Muslims' standards, words, and behavior, including the way they dressed, kept beards, and performed their daily tasks. Their definition of Muslimness is not an academic one involving the quest for knowledge. According to the Salafis, anyone deviating from the standard set by the early Muslims is not a good Muslim—indeed, not even really a Muslim. Some Salafis may be encouraged to express their disapproval of those whom they see as wayward Muslims by using intimidation and force. Yet many Salafis dismiss terrorism and violence and feel betrayed by other Salafis, such as Osama bin Laden, who they say are guilty of "innovation."

In Atlanta Frankie asked one African American Salafi if he was also a Wahhabi. "Some have called us Wahhabis," he said, "but I reject this term. It is a slur. But we do adhere to the teachings of Abdul Wahhab, may peace and blessings be upon him. He only returned Islam to its rightful path, the path of the Prophet of Islam." Referring to the sects of the four imams popular in Saudi Arabia at the time, this man said that Abdul Wahhab "cleared the confusion and we will follow his example." Another African American Salafi, this time in Dallas, commented, "People who say they are Wahhabi are actually Salafi." He allowed that the negative opinions of Wahhab have arisen because "many people were hurt" when "order was restored" to Saudi Arabia under the Wahhabis and the royal family.

The Salafis the team met were conscious that the name is ascribed to many militant groups, frequently by the militants themselves, and one of them explained it thus: "These groups that you're seeing, like Salafia Jihadia in Morocco, may claim to be Salafi, but they're not. They go against the actual text they claim to uphold. Bin Laden is an example of this because he kills innocent non-Muslims—this is against the Quran. Even in war, killing innocents is prohibited." In Atlanta a Salafi Somali imam named Khalifa condemned the actions of al Qaeda, describing members as Kharijites, after a violent seventh-century breakaway sect. "The bin Laden group was very happy with 9/11," the imam said, "but they don't speak on behalf of Islam. They have a misconception. By no means can you kill children, females, or people worshipping in church, unless they are fighting you." The attack on the World Trade Center was unjustified, he said, because it contained a "prayer room."

Bilal, a literalist African American man in Denver wearing Islamic dress, including a kufiya, declined to be described as a Salafi, although Jonathan and Frankie believed the mosque was dominated by the Salafis. Bilal lamented the presence in his community of "extreme" and "hard-core" people saying "crazy stuff" who came from places like New York and Philadelphia. They speak of violent martyrdom, but he tells them "a *shaheed* [martyr] is not just someone who fights but someone who dies protecting another person, who saves someone's life, by drowning even."

Salafis around the country gave the team reading material—almost all of it from Saudi Arabia—that condemned bin Laden and described his followers as Kharijites and *takfiri*s (apostates). Those in Dallas noted that some Muslims who believe in "killing unbelievers" are not followers of Wahhab but of the Egyptian writer and activist Sayyid Qutb, and gave the team a book titled *The "Wahhabi" Myth* to prove their point.[13] While many Muslims, especially the literalists, may agree with Qutb's vision of American society as "a reckless, deluded herd that only knows lust and money," most would not accept his solution, which was to correct the immorality of America through violence.[14] (For a more general Muslim perspective on American society, see chapter 6.)

The role models the Salafis cited consistently were the Prophet and his companions, but they frequently included the former mufti of Saudi Arabia, Abdul Aziz bin Baz, and Muhammad ibn 'Abd al-Wahhab. Significantly, all of them were from the Arabian peninsula, now dominated by Saudi Arabia. Ibn Taymiyya, another role model, has inspired Saudi Islam. The tracts given to the team around the country were identical, and people spoke about bin Laden and other topics using identical phrases. As Frankie said, they seemed to be working "from a script." In Atlanta an African American assistant imam of Salafi persuasion explained the position of his mosque to the team: "We welcome you to this masjid. But we want you to understand what it is . . . a part of a network of masjids in the United States linked to the Middle East. We teach the only Islam, the true Islam."

Salafi View of Women

Salafi mosques insist on a strict separation of the genders, usually by a curtain or wall. In many Salafi mosques, the male members of our team found no evidence of women and otherwise had no contact with women, although the few they did see outside wore the niqab. In Atlanta Frankie asked a Somali man about the place of women in the mosque. "The women pray in a room at the back," he explained. "We want the women to learn and to pray, but their place is in the home. I myself am planning to take a second wife; it is our obligation in Islam. In Islam there is no gender equality."

We gained further insights into the literalist male view of women through our questionnaires. A thirty-two-year-old Sudanese male student in Omaha was also opposed to gender equality, albeit with a slight difference: "There is no gender equality in Islam, except some points for the benefit of the woman." A forty-seven-year-old Jordanian man from New Jersey said it was "unfair" and "unjust" to speak of gender equality: "You cannot compare apples with oranges. So there is no justice when you try to make people equal because people are not equal in their abilities, and treating them equally is not fair. For example, when a woman is pregnant, she is not to fast during Ramadan. So she is not treated equally, but it is fair and better for her. So obligations are based on abilities. Justice is better."

Salafi View of Other Muslims

The team observed strains in the Muslim community throughout the country, each group accusing the other of being "extremists." Two groups in particular were a rich source of information about Salafis as both were victims of Salafi wrath: the Sufis and the Shia. These Muslims have to often defend their "un-Islamic" style of beard, dress, ritual, and theology from the Salafis. In San Diego, Jonathan heard two people debating whether it was permissible to pray in the same room as a Shia and finally deciding it was definitely not. If you happen to pray next to a Shia, they agreed, you must say your prayers again. A twenty-year-old Pakistani college sophomore in Cedar Rapids had a similar opinion of the Shia: "Eighty-five percent of Muslims are Sunnis, the 'calm' Muslims, yet the other 15 percent, Shiites, are showcased—they are the loonies." In Austin, Texas, a Syrian man in his late thirties told the team, "The Shias are not Muslim. If I saw one in the same mosque as me, I would leave immediately." He was not happy with Sufis either: "The American media is so biased, always talking about

Islamic extremists," when they should focus on the Sufis—"They are the real Islamic extremists."

Salafis judge other Muslims by the extent to which they follow the "original Islam" of the Prophet. The relationship between Salafis and Sufis, in particular, is complicated and reflects some of the changes and current conflicts in the Muslim world. In places like Somalia and Afghanistan, the land of Rumi, Sufi Islam was once prominent but has now been marginalized in favor of a literalist interpretation. This means that some of the literalists who have immigrated to the United States may once have had Sufi backgrounds. Sufis are also widely criticized for lacking practical answers to the problems Muslims face—poverty, absence of justice, and foreign military interventions.

Imam Khalifa in Atlanta, who had worked and studied at Dar Al-Hijrah, the controversial Northern Virginia mosque, condemned the Sufis "for deviating when you deny what is clear in Islam." He surprised the team by revealing that he had been a Sufi before he "came to the straight path . . . back to the Quran" after being confronted in Mogadishu by a man who told him he was "worshipping saints," an un-Islamic practice in the same category as worshipping the grave of the Prophet.

The Salafis also condemn "political activists" for being influenced by other belief systems and thus tainting their Islam. Imam Khalifa was angry with Hamas, for example, for "having contact with Shia" and with the Muslim Brotherhood for getting involved "in political conflicts" instead of "collecting different sects together" and correcting "those who deviate." In Dallas the team was given literature discouraging anyone from following bin Laden because of Sufi tendencies arising from association with the "Sufi Deobandi movement." This came as a surprise to Frankie, who had spent time in Deoband and "thought it was anything but Sufi."

Among African American literalists, it was common to condemn Imam W. D. Mohammed's movement. Bilal, whom Jonathan and Frankie met at the Masjid Shuhada'a off Martin Luther King Boulevard in central Denver and just down the street from a W. D. Mohammed mosque, told them that Imam W. D.'s followers have a "pro-American ideology" that favors the U.S. Constitution over shariah law. For Bilal, however, "it is forbidden to give an oath to any but Allah. We're not supposed to mesh with society. We take the example of the first three generations alone."

Bilal said that he converted to Islam while attending college in Louisiana. He was the president of his fraternity and spent several years indulging in nonstop parties and womanizing. One day at a frat party he stumbled into his friend's room and spied a Quran on his bookshelf, along with holy books from several other faiths. As the party became wilder, Bilal read thirty verses and converted to Islam on the spot.

Unlike other literalists, Bilal defined himself as an American who believed that Islam, which he called the "real reform party," was the way to save the country. When asked to name the greatest threat to America, he replied, "believing in something other than Islam." He went on to cite aspects of American culture that he felt were extremely dangerous, such as music, which he described as *haram* (prohibited). "One of the signs of the end of times is people saying that music is permissible."

A conversation with an African American Salafi imam in Atlanta had its awkward moments for Frankie but also provided insights into how Salafis see other Muslim scholars. Frankie was talking about his experiences in India and Pakistan, when the imam began to shake his head in disapproval: "The Muslims of India are not good Muslims. Everywhere, even here in Atlanta, there are those who claim to be Muslim but aren't. Don't listen to them." He worried that as potential converts, the team would be exposed to the "wrong Islam," which seemed to Frankie to be any Islam not coming from Saudi Arabia. "You may have heard about the Shia Ahmadinejad of Iran making statements against the West," said a man from Djibouti, "but don't listen to him because he is not a Muslim. Imagine, the Shia hate Sunnis even more than they hate Jews!"

An African American then looked Frankie in the eye and pointedly asked: "This scholar you're traveling with, is he a Sunni?" "Yes," replied Frankie, breathing an inward sigh of relief, given the company. He later observed: "Although I had traveled with Dr. Ahmed to some of the most conservative mosques in the Muslim world and seen the warm manner of his welcome, I was not sure if my Pakistani professor would pass the test of these American Muslims. They did not have a high opinion of scholars in general, saying these persons often knew the true Islam and then chose not to follow it and accused them of 'innovation.'"

Salafi Views of America

America, like our team, was a blank slate for Salafis. It was merely a backdrop for their practice of Islam: they could be on the moon or Mars. When an African American in Atlanta was asked what it meant to be American, he replied "nothing": "The three most important places in the world for me are Mecca, Medina, and Jerusalem. America might as well be any other country." A Muslim from Djibouti claimed that he had ended up here almost by accident after enrolling in the U.S. visa lottery system. "Bush means nothing to me," he said, "and Obama means nothing to me." A Yemeni imam in New York City said that George Washington and Karl Marx meant the same to him.

Some were not happy about being in America at all. "We Muslims should not be here," said a Somali man in Atlanta. "It is better to be in a Muslim country." When asked to name the greatest threat to America, the man from Djibouti replied "Islam." An African American agreed, saying "America will become Muslim." A Salafi Somali saw an inevitable clash between Islam and America: "There can be no coexistence."

This was not unexpected, as literature on their mosque's website warns, "The Jews and Christians are waging a war upon Islam," and one method is "democracy," which it describes as a "criminal path." Muslims, listening to "educated" and "evil scholars" do not see this "calamity" as they are in a state of "negligence, heedlessness, slumber, sleep, and amusement." Any Muslim who participates in democracy, an approved scholar declares, has renounced Islam and is to be condemned as a heretic. "If the Muslims were to establish the punishment of apostation," he writes, they would need to heed the Prophet: "Whoever changes his religion, then kill him." The literature calls for "hatred and enmity" against all non-Muslim faiths.[15]

Imam Khalifa in Atlanta was opposed to the American justice system: "America should adopt some of the practices of Islam for the punishment of criminals. In Islam, they cut off the hand of criminals. If someone intentionally kills someone, they can be killed. This is from God. It works." The United States, he said, has "too many murders" because of "soft laws." By way of example, the imam cited the case of a Somali cab driver in Minneapolis who was brutally assaulted and subsequently murdered by his assailant when the latter was released following a short prison term and sought out the cab driver for testifying against him. In Islam, the imam claimed, the assailant would have been properly punished, and the cab driver would still be alive.

Other literalists voiced their unhappiness with certain aspects of American culture. An Egyptian imam in his thirties in Blacksburg, Virginia, becomes livid with anger when he sees old people working at Walmart: "Why do people let this happen? Where are their families? If one of them dies, no one will care." He would sacrifice everything to ensure this did not happen to his mother: "I would die to preserve respect for my mother and the elderly so that they may stay at home. I hate that Americans don't have a place for emotions; they don't feel."

Bilal in Denver condemned the treatment of animals in America: "The slaughterhouses in America are horrible. There are millions of animals being killed cruelly, and we could care less. In Islam we believe that by turning a blind eye to suffering on such a mass scale we are held responsible. Instead we spend so much more time on our house and fancy stuff, we forget what our great responsibility is. We can help the whole world. This is like the people in the North who turned a blind eye to slavery, but they were still responsible; that was the time to use your intelligence and submit to what is good."

In Omaha a Palestinian businessman said that he had information about Saudi-linked networks in the United States that were just waiting to be activated to commit terrorist acts, a claim repeated to us by Muslims and non-Muslims alike. These networks included Muslim student associations, Islamic schools, and mosques connected through an intricate web of Saudi funding and influence.

The team caught glimpses of possible future terrorist attacks when an African American Salafi in Dallas told Jonathan that violence was "very possible" in the United States: "Bin Laden has his followers in the U.S. They are not Salafis but followers of Sayyid Qutb, the man who inspired bin Laden. They are here in America, and I have spoken to them—mostly foreigners. At any minute they could strike. They are waiting; I don't know for what. But most Muslims here? No, they'll be civil. They love money too much."

Al-Farooq Mosque's Yemeni imam in New York City, speaking in Arabic with the mosque's African American assistant imam translating, referred to terrorism in a way that made Jonathan and Frankie uneasy. His comments, which reflect the philosophy of Qutb, could only be understood in the context of the Salafi tendency to speak with the aid of metaphor and allegory. The imam described a man with a cancerous leg: "The doctors decide that the only solution is to amputate his leg to save the patient. If a video of the doctors cutting off this man's leg is shown on TV without any context, people will think that the doctors have cut off the leg for no reason." The public, the imam said, will side with the patient because "they don't understand the whole story." "The only sense Frankie and I could make of it," wrote Jonathan, "was that he was explaining terrorism to us. The attacks on 9/11 were the surgery required to remove the cancer of immorality from the patient, which was the United States." At the end of their interview, the imam switched to English and addressed the team directly: "You don't mess with us and we won't mess with you. Justice will always come around to those who deserve it."

Atlanta's Salafi from Djibouti said that "people have gotten up and argued for suicide bombing and killing the nonbelievers. We do debate that. I believe that killing nonbelievers is against Islam. And the Quran says you cannot commit suicide. September 11 has made it hard for the Muslims in America. I did not agree with that."

Jamal and Abdullah, two African American Salafis in the South Dallas mosque, spoke candidly when asked about the concept of a "just war." Jamal noted that Islam demanded strict conditions for it: "Basically, a ruler of the Muslims must call out for war if it is just. But Muslims must *never* kill innocents. Today, people are indeed fighting against Islam. But it isn't a *war*. This is a misunderstanding on the part of some Muslims. It is difficult, though. When children are being oppressed and women raped, how does one react? If I was in Palestine, what would I do? Should I fight? Based upon the situation, I think it is justified for the Palestinians to defend themselves. But this emotion produces ready recruits for bin Laden. These Muslims are blinded by emotion."

Abdullah intervened: "But we *can't* be trapped by emotion. I remember what it was like here after 9/11. People were going around saying, 'Kill the Muslims.' I was angry. I could have easily jumped up and called for a war inside of America. We could have launched one. But I didn't because I would have been acting on emotion, and this is not Islam." The Salafis are aware of what is happening around them and are mildly amused, as reflected in this remark by Jamal: "It's funny—the Homeland Security and FBI put us under surveillance, always asking people 'Where are the terrorists?' Did they think to ask the Salafis? We know exactly where they are!"

The team met an unlikely, but inspiring Salafi in the same South Dallas mosque—Issa Gisesa, the former grand mufti of Rwanda. His birth name is Edward, and he was once a Christian priest, so it is befitting that his Muslim name is Issa, or Jesus. Islam is spreading in Rwanda, Issa told the team, and 2,000 to 3,000 people convert to Islam there every month, partly because the 1994 genocide of Tutsis was conducted in Christian churches. "Before I was a Muslim," said the imam, "I was a Tutsi."

Issa's views on America refuted the common assumption among experts that Salafis hate America: "I am an old man, and I've been to every country on earth but Japan. America is in a special situation. It is a big country and a rich country. I respect America. Actually I can say that I love America. Allah can test you, he can give you everything you want. But having everything is dangerous. The first danger is wealth. In America, we have the sickness of envy. Look at Cain and Abel: one killed the other because of envy. We need people who know the different religions, who can quote from them. Look, here is my Bible, I carry it around with me." Saying this, he removed a battered, ancient-looking red book from his bag and called for a "United Nations of religions."

The young Americans on my team, even those from a strong Christian background in the South such as Jonathan, found much to respect and admire in the Salafis and took issue with the experts: "The Salafis' detachment from the material world and dedication to the holy book did not pose a threat. True, some could be convinced to do something stupid if they believe that their religion is under attack," Jonathan admitted. "But this can happen among the modernist Muslims as well. Some may find it suspicious that many Salafis have no attachment to America and want to be left alone, but we found the same detachment from America among another religious sect of bearded men and covered women believing in a strict adherence to God's law, the Mennonites in Texas. Salafis can be allies. There is no reason for us to fear or suspect literalist Muslims, be they Salafi or any another interpretation."

While Jonathan may be right, Salafi leadership needs to be more responsible in what they say and do. Salafis are playing a dangerous game, even if unwittingly, by the ambiguity around their discussion of jihad, which can be easily misunderstood in the heated environment of Islamophobia in America today. Similarly, their attacks on interfaith acceptance and dialogue are neither helpful to the Muslim community, nor calculated to win them support for their faith with Americans.

Literalist Muslim Women

Literalist women believe in strict notions of "modesty" and "gender segregation" and therefore are reluctant to talk to anyone who is not in the family. Even Madeeha, who is a Muslim, was received frostily in New York's Al-Farooq Mosque, perhaps because the women, all attired in hijabs, niqabs, and abayyas, thought she was immodestly covered with an ordinary shawl. She felt out of place.

Hailey and Madeeha met many literalist women who reflected some of the cultural strains they saw at the office of the Arab Community Center for Economic and Social Services (ACCESS) in Dearborn, an impressive enterprise serving the entire city, offering both Muslims and non-Muslims health care, job placement, and language training. They noticed that the women in and around the office were dressed in full abayyas and niqabs. They interviewed about ten Muslim women (mostly Arabs) from Yemen, the Palestinian Territories, the United States, Austria, and other countries.

The women had difficulty responding to questions about American identity because half of them did not speak English well enough to understand what was being asked. Those who did answer said that America was the best place to practice Islam because of the freedom of religion. One woman spoke in favor of America because "Americans are really open. We think that because we wear the hijab we can't get a job, but it's only paranoia." Although the women were not consciously trying to become American, they were incorporating small aspects of American culture into their lives. Interestingly, when they visit their country of origin, people expect them to have become "Americanized," meaning "corrupted" by the excessive freedom in America's hedonistic society. On the contrary, the women said they end up becoming even more religious.

One Palestinian woman, who had been in the United States for twenty years and had lived in Alabama, Texas, Pennsylvania, and Michigan because of her husband's assignments as an engineer, recounted that "everywhere we moved, I would find the nearest mosque, and we would buy a house in that neighborhood. There was always one near and I never felt out of place." Another woman had lived in the United States for five years but was unable to say much about American identity. Ironically, she taught the American citizenship exam for ACCESS, which requires applicants to master 100 questions about American history.

An Egyptian woman named "Sister Mona" interviewed in Masjid-ul-Mumineen, the central Islamic center for Nigerians in Greater Houston, said she used to be a physician, but after 9/11 became a female imam, traveling from mosque to mosque. A class the team witnessed was on how Muslim women could lead a better life. "Guard your eyes, sisters," Sister Mona instructed her students. "Have only the best manners; follow the right path because all your senses will be used against you on the Day of Judgment. Wake up, be healthy, work, have a husband, stick to the basics. Islam is in need of Muslims with good manners. A Muslim's priority is self, family, community, and humanity. Today in America we don't appreciate anything. Everyone is lonely, there is no warmth. There is no feeling. We must clean out our hearts all the time. We must forgive."

From our questionnaires we learned some women literalists felt that Islam is under attack. Asked how her community would react to a terrorist attack on America, a sixteen-year-old Palestinian in New Jersey said, "They would love it!" Responding to the same question, a twenty-nine-year-old Indonesian female in Omaha said, "Some think the U.S. should feel what the Muslim world felt every day when they lost their family because of war." A twenty-one-year-old Afghan American woman born in

Sacramento commented: "I have been spit on for wearing the hijab and told to take it off." An Arab Muslim female of the same age in Detroit said that when others look at her religion, they "probably think it is violent and evil, and that women are like slaves and have no rights." A nineteen-year-old Michigan-born sophomore media arts student at Wayne State University in Detroit whose parents are from Syria said she has experienced prejudice "many, many times. The worst was when a guy followed me home in his car and called me a towelhead." By contrast, she sees gender equality in Islam: "As a Muslim woman, I feel more liberated and respected than the half-naked women 'sex objects' on TV."

The concerns of these women reflect those of not only literalist Muslims but also many modernists and mystics. While these divisions define Muslims, some issues also bring them together. It was precisely with this in mind that Muslim organizations were formed in America, some of which have now gained national prominence.

The Role of Muslim Organizations

My first encounter with a major American Muslim organization was in New Orleans in 1997. It was the annual gathering of the large and influential Association of Pakistani Physicians of North America (APPNA), and I was the keynote speaker. After the working session, our hosts had arranged for a boat ride on the Mississippi.

The *Mississippi Queen* slid smoothly over the choppy waters of the dark Mississippi. It was late in the evening, and I sat by the railing of the top deck looking out across the water at the rapidly fading lights on shore. The gentle rhythm of the engines lulled me into quiet contemplation. A century earlier, I thought, perhaps Mark Twain's Huck Finn and Tom Sawyer would have sneaked on board. I began to think of famous names associated with the land dominated by this mighty river and their rich contribution to culture—author William Faulkner, country singer Faith Hill, rock and roller B. B. King, talk show hostess Oprah Winfrey, and author Tennessee Williams.

From somewhere, floating above the gentle noise of the engine, I thought I heard the sound of the Muslim call to prayer. Was I dreaming? Then the call became louder and closer. I stood up and went searching for it. The sight on the main deck startled me. The Pakistani doctors, some thirty men wearing shalwar-kameez, were confidently forming lines for the evening prayer. There was an air of smugness about the Muslims, as if they had just taken a small bastion of Christianity for Islam. I glanced at the other passengers, who were mostly white men and women. They did not look surprised or curious, or even angry, but impassive as if the scene had not registered with them.

I had just flown in from England, where I had been in the thick of the debate about Islam's relationship with the West. Salman Rushdie, the Gulf War, the Muslims in the Balkans, and the emergence of obscure figures like Osama bin Laden, who talked of violence, had occupied the passions of the media for the past few years. I feared a storm was brewing that would engulf Muslim communities throughout the world. I had written about this extensively in the hope of alerting people and prompting them to start building bridges.[16] I had argued that both Muslims and non-Muslims needed to be much more aware of each other's cultural sensitivities than before.

That is why on board the *Mississippi Queen* many questions raced through my mind that night: Did these Muslims know of the area's troubled history concerning race and religious relations? Of the great battles fought for civil rights? Of the leaders who had laid down their lives in the struggle?

What made me increasingly uneasy as I lined up to join the prayer was the passivity of the Americans. While the Muslims assumed that it reflected American acceptance of their ways, I was not so sure. No community confronted by something so foreign could remain indifferent for long. I knew then I was witnessing a mutual lack of appreciation of different cultures. Muslims were behaving like carefree children dancing around a gnarled old log and prodding it with sticks, not realizing it was a deadly alligator. The beast struck with lightning speed and viciousness after September 11, 2001.

Before and after September 11

From the 1970s onward, Muslim organizations—apart from APPNA, whose leaders were Pakistani—were mostly controlled by Arabs who oscillated between modernist and literalist Islam. Among them were the Islamic Society of North America (ISNA), the Muslim Students Association (MSA), the International Institute of Islamic Thought (IIIT), the American Muslim Council (AMC), the Muslim Public Affairs Council (MPAC), the Islamic Circle of North America (ICNA), and the Council on American-Islamic Relations (CAIR). They appeared to exist in a cultural cocoon and were intoxicated with a sense of triumph because they believed they had brought Islam to America. In doing so, they were ignoring both the contribution and presence of African American Muslims. These organizations were the creation of the first wave of Arab and South Asian immigrants, many of them arriving via the United Kingdom. Most members were engineers, doctors, and architects. They were supported by Arab businessmen and governments in the Middle East. The Saudi royal family promoted one kind of Islam, Muammar Qaddafi another.

The dynamic between Arabs and South Asians in the Islamic organizations reflected the realities of the Muslim world. The Quran was in Arabic, the Prophet was Arab, and the Arabs had oil and therefore money. The South Asians, committed to Islam and ambitious to be its leaders, nonetheless accepted a role, even if reluctantly, as lieutenants to the Arab captains, who thus retained control over the direction and strategy for the ummah. Even the physical attacks on the West—leading up dramatically to 9/11—were led by Arabs, but it was not long before the center of gravity shifted and South Asians entered the fray.

After 9/11, these Muslim organizations became an immediate target of aggressive investigation by U.S. law enforcement agencies, a move the media supported blindly and loudly as a patriotic duty. People were picked up for questioning, offices were raided. Anyone with any connections to Palestinians was automatically a suspect. Because the majority of Muslims have deep sympathy for the plight of the Palestinians, and many happily donated to Palestinian charities, the law-enforcement agencies felt they had found concrete links between American donors and the politics of terror in the Middle East (as in the case of the Holy Land Foundation discussed in chapter 3). The more generous the donor, the more questions raised in the mind of the agents. Every organization felt the heat. The IIIT, for example, was raided and all its files removed by the FBI. Some of its senior figures left the country in disgust, never to return. To date nothing has been found to incriminate this group, but the cloud of suspicion created by the investigations still hovers over it.

I had several interactions with Muslim organizations both before and after 9/11, which gave me a close view of the problems Muslim leaders faced. After my keynote address at the annual convention dinner organized by the Association of Muslim Social Scientists at Georgetown University in the fall of 2000, I was surrounded by two dozen young Muslims who objected to my promotion of Jinnah's vision of a modern Muslim society based on women's rights and human rights over ideas espoused by bin Laden. How could I criticize bin Laden, the Islamic warrior, in favor of Jinnah, who drank whisky? How could I talk of interfaith dialogue with the Jews and Christians when Muslims were suffering in Palestine?

And the following summer, when asked to address the annual dinner of the American Muslim Council in Arlington, Virginia, I was again struck by the vast gulf between the Muslim community and mainstream Americans.

The event took place at a large hotel in Arlington, and I was impressed by the vitality of the event but also uneasy with the triumphalist tone of the conference. Hundreds of people were there, many of them obviously very successful in their businesses and enterprises. The leaders of the AMC had invited some members of Congress and saw this as proof of their success with the American political machine. They felt confident enough to make anti-Semitic references. In their self-congratulatory style, they were representing themselves as the standard-bearers of Islam overlooking African Americans and their contributions to the faith.

When it was my turn, I spoke about the challenges facing the Muslim community, the need to be self-reflective and versatile, and to reach out to non-Muslims. But I also talked about the contributions of African Americans to Islam in America. Spotting Ali Mazrui, a distinguished immigrant scholar from East Africa in the audience, I asked him to stand up and take a bow. My speech was not particularly well received, judging by the smattering of applause.

After 9/11, the community launched a desperate search for strategies to reach out to America. This time, when I gave the keynote address at the annual ISNA convention in Washington, D.C., in November 2002, I noticed not only sympathy for but also interest in my theme of interfaith dialogue. Muslim organizations were now exploring interfaith dialogue and adapting it to their understanding of Islam.

Interview with the Ameer of the Islamic Circle of North America

Khurshid Khan is the *ameer,* or head, of the Islamic Circle of North America, which sees itself as the flagship Sunni orthodox organization in America. Khan proudly stated, "I am American, but first I am a Muslim." On the whole, however, Khan thinks Americans are "very nice people" but are "brainwashed." He believes the Quran influenced Jefferson and the U.S. Constitution, that what the Salafis are doing is "extremism" and haram, or "wrong" in his mind. He proves that one can be a Muslim literalist and still claim to be American, that one can be both optimistic and gloomy about the future, and, finally, that one can face Islamophobic attacks with calm.

Born in Delhi in 1937, Khan migrated to Pakistan when it was founded ten years later and came to the United States in 1971, specifically with the aim of spreading Islam. In 1973 he obtained a Ph.D. in education from the University of Pittsburgh; then, together with members of the Jamaat-i-Islami, helped found some of America's major Muslim organizations, including the Muslim Students Association and the Islamic Circle, the latter formed in response to Muslim demands for a more orthodox, more Sunni, and more "Islamic" identity.

A thoughtful man with a clipped beard, Khan looks trim and alert, dresses neatly, and wears a skullcap. He has the style and manner of the old South Asian aristocracy steeped in adab. Not only did he cancel three appointments to meet me but agreed to come to where I was staying in New York so as not to cause me any inconvenience. Khan's role models could be that of any other Muslim: the Prophet was number one, followed by the first four caliphs. Among contemporary figures, he named M. A. Jinnah, the founder of Pakistan, first. The name he gave next provides a clue to Khan's identity: Maulana Maududi, the founder of Jamaat-i-Islami.

As *ameer*, or head, of the Islamic Circle, Khan carries the full weight of one of the most important Muslim organizations of America on his slim shoulders. The organization's main goal, as posted on its website, is to establish "the Islamic system of life" as "spelled out in the Qur'an and the Sunnah of Prophet Muhammad." Some 2,000 to 3,000 members across the country are part of the group, which is run by an elected *shura*, or council, of 400 persons, who in turn elect the ameer. The Islamic Circle's governance structure was deliberately patterned after the political system at the time of the Prophet. Khan said they all "work for the pleasure of Allah Subhanatallah."

While the Islamic Circle focuses on *dawah*, or dialogue, and invitation to learn about Islam, it has also an active outreach and training program, especially for the young. It has also reached out to non-Muslim victims of Hurricanes Katrina and Ike through its charity, Helping Hands. Its members also helped victims of the earthquake in Pakistan and the tsunami in Indonesia. It provides shelter for the homeless, especially homeless women in Detroit and New York.

During his interview, Khan expressed particular interest in the role of the young in society. Many with excessive freedom are exposed to numerous temptations—drugs, alcohol, and sexual promiscuity. Some come from broken homes and do not receive adequate love. Among Muslims, Khan saw contradictory trends. Young Muslims born in America now memorize the Quran in droves, which entitles them to the title hafiz. Unfortunately, the vast majority, perhaps as many as 95 percent, are in the "melting pot." If this trend continues, Khan observed gloomily, Islamic values and culture may disappear in three to four generations. He complained about the "vacuum of Muslim leadership," about Muslims falling prey to extremism despite Islam's emphasis on "balance," about the lack of think tanks among Muslims, and about Muslims "falling far behind" and being "asleep." Khan also presented several arguments to support the idea of "a Zionist con-spiracy" against Islam that included 9/11.

To meet the needs of the young in the context of American culture, the Islamic Circle has started arranging mass family outings such as trips to Six Flags for the Eid festival. Khan called this "halal fun," emphasizing that "Islam is a happy thing" and his is not the terrorist organization depicted by Fox News and commentators like Steve Emerson and Daniel Pipes, who focus on ICNA's links to the Jamaat-i-Islami, which supports Hamas. Such attacks are the irresistible force to Khan's immovable object.

The Islamic Center of America, Home of Shia Islam

The preeminent leader of Shia Islam in America is Imam Hassan Qazwini, a refugee from Iraq and from the tyranny of the secular Saddam Hussein. In addition to the difference in their sects, Qazwini and Khan are quite different in personality, style, and the generation that produced them. How Americans view them is also different. President George W. Bush embraced Qazwini when he supported the Iraq War and welcomed him as a visitor to the White House. In contrast, many Americans view Khan and his Islamic Circle with suspicion. Muslims, on the other hand, saw Qazwini as "selling out," while they admired Khan's loyalty and integrity.

A descendant of the Prophet, Imam Qazwini was born in 1964 in Karbala, Iraq. Imposing in his formal turban and flowing robes, he smiles a great deal and meets guests with an embrace. Qazwini embodies the notion and practice of Muslim adab. He received us warmly outside his office in Dearborn, patiently answered our questions on camera, and hosted an iftaar dinner with traditional Arab food. He presented me with a copy of his book, *American Crescent,* and gave souvenirs of the center to each member of the team.[17] At dinner we met a range of Muslim leaders from the area who worked closely with the imam. Among these were Najah Bazzy, who is half Shia and half Sunni (a "sushi" as she calls herself), and Dawud Walid, a prominent Sunni leader and executive director of CAIR in Dearborn.

The imam also gave us a guided tour of the mosque, considered the largest in the United States and probably the grandest in terms of its deco-rations and architecture. Verses from the Quran emphasizing learning and knowledge and written in exquisite calligraphy adorn the circular prayer hall. Impressed by their beauty, I asked Qazwini about the artist. Smil-ing, he said the artist was an Arab Christian who came from the Middle East especially to work on the mosque. It took the artist two months to complete the work, and he refused to take any payment as a gesture of interfaith friendship. I noted that the names of the Prophet of Islam and his son-in-law, Ali, were given the same prominence in that they were written alongside each other. The fact that Ali was thus elevated confirmed the Shia identity of the mosque. Although Sunnis revere Ali as one of the greatest of Islam's rulers, they would unambiguously place him below the Prophet. I also noted that three of the main halls at the center were dedicated to the holy Prophet, Ali, and the Prophet's daughter, Fatima, who was married to Ali. The words "peace be upon him or her" followed after their names.

The grand mosque reminded me of mosques in the Muslim world and reflected how its worshippers thought of themselves. It contrasted sharply with the majority of Sunni mosques and almost all of the African American mosques that we saw on our journey. Those mosques have little or no calligraphy and no ornate pictures or flowers; their walls are often bare and the carpets worn. Sunnis may support their mosques just as passionately as Shia, but they see their character and position in society differently.

Imam Qazwini's role and the organization around him underlined the difference between the Shia and Sunni communities. Shia social, religious, and political leadership revolves around the status and organization of its religious clerics, who are judged by their seniority, wisdom, and scholarship. There is a clear-cut hierarchy of leadership up to the ayatollahs, considered the most learned members of the community. While some Sunni imams that we met are bravely creating leadership roles for themselves as well, few can match the confidence of traditional authority that Qazwini exudes. None wore robes as resplendent as his.

Other Shia Centers

We visited several other Shia communities, including the Ismailis and the Dawoodi Bohras. Although each has a distinct identity, both are actively involved in and promote business, and both have a clearly defined hierarchy and organization, which is headed by highly revered figures whose leadership derives from a sacred lineage claiming descent from the Prophet of Islam. Both communities also identify wholeheartedly with America and venerate it. Their gratitude to be in America stems in part from the persecution some face in Muslim countries with a Sunni majority.

The Ismaili hierarchy is currently headed by the charismatic Aga Khan, who lives outside Paris. A Harvard-educated Muslim, he overhauled the community's image and organization upon assuming leadership. Its other

At the main Dawoodi Bohra mosque in Houston, the author, with his daughter, Amineh Hoti, and her children, Mina and Ibrahim, and team member Hailey. The Bohras are a small sect of Shia Islam and ardent supporters of America.

leaders are invariably well educated, speak good English, dress smartly in Western clothes, and are successful businessmen. Those we met in Atlanta and Houston were typical of the community.

The leader of the Dawoodi Bohra community, Syedna Mohammed Burhanuddin, is ninety-nine years old, wears traditional clothes, is somewhat of a recluse, and lives in Mumbai. We were invited to meet leaders of his community in Houston at their central mosque, Muhammadi Masjid. The entire high command had turned out to welcome us and presented us with traditional shawls as a gesture of respect, and we were able to talk to both the men and the women, all in traditional dress.

Invariably, their number one role model was the leader of their community, whose saying, "You must become part of the country you live in," they repeated several times. Remarkably, the Bohra members have a 100 percent literacy rate. Children in a classroom we visited welcomed us and sang religious songs for us. The word "ilm" featured in Islamic sayings was displayed on the classroom walls.

The community took pride in being able to wear traditional clothes and yet be accepted as part of American culture. The women reeled off their professions: teacher, pharmacist, real estate agent, medical doctor, financial analyst with ExxonMobil Corporation, and a caterer. One of them said, "I love America and I love the fact that they allow me to wear this dress at school. It just helps me show how much I'm proud of my religion."

When Sheikh Nooruddin Yamani, one of the elders, expressed his ardor for America, he obviously reflected the sentiments of the community: "All these girls, they wear the same dress as they do here, in the school, public school. And they are proud to be a Muslim and they are proud to be American. We love America because we have freedom of speech, freedom of religion."

Community Critics of Muslim Organizations

Muslims tend to close ranks behind their organizations and communities. They are reluctant to criticize them, especially in public, as we saw in Dallas when I asked Frankie to interview Ghulam Bakali, a mild-mannered Muslim professional from India with an orthodox, trimmed beard. But Frankie found Bakali's answers deliberately evasive and vague. When he reported this to me, I took Bakali aside and explained why Muslim leaders must speak out openly if they hoped to improve the community and its relations with the rest of America. This was not the time to be timorous or diplomatic. He said he was too frightened to talk about what was really going on in the community. I challenged him to be a true Muslim and a true American. That seemed to work. He apologized and agreed to a frank conversation on the record.

Part of the reason Muslims do not speak out, he said, is that they are intimidated by other Muslims, which is precisely why he himself "stopped speaking out twenty-five years ago." He confessed that this was a mistake and that he "should have not been intimidated." Bakali complained that Islamic organizations in America are not effective, as he knew firsthand from earlier work as a conflict resolution specialist for the Islamic Society of North America. Politics, civil rights, and relief for Muslim countries drive the agenda of many of these groups. When these agendas are imposed on local mosques, conflicts break out. Many groups also want to convert non-Muslims to Islam, whereas he believes Muslims at a local level should simply "lead by example."

Bakali had much to say about internal friction within the Muslim community, which is "plagued" with poor leadership and internal struggles for power. Internal conflicts are only settled when one group leaves and starts another mosque somewhere else. Some of what Bakali saw was ugly. When Salafis, predominantly Arabs as well as Latino, black, and white converts, attempted to promote their approach to Islam in their El Paso, Texas, mosque by bringing in their own imam from Syria, a physical fight broke out with others, including South Asians. The police had to be called in to restore order. The same thing happened in Arlington, Texas, and this time the police shut down the mosque.

Bakali also complained about the young intellectual Muslims who are moving toward groups such as the Zaytuna Institute run by Sheikh Hamza Yusuf. Instead of addressing the community's real problems, these young Muslims only want to "improve their souls." This creates a leadership vacuum for the next generation, Bakali concluded, and the problem will only get worse in the future.

Singling out CAIR for criticism, Bakali said the organization uses a "litmus test" in "making alliances" that assesses the degree of one's pro-Palestinian sentiments. "But Muslims in America can't always be concerned about Palestine," he said. Other issues are of more immediate relevance to them, such as dietary restrictions, prayer, travel, discrimination, and so on. "I need to worry about America first," said Bakali. "I need to ask myself, 'How can I better the situation of the Muslims in America first?'" The goal should be to "get my neighbor to accept me as a Muslim and as an American."

The best way to do this, suggested Bakali, is to "give gifts in the hospital, play football, play baseball, show kindness to people, and contribute to causes like the fight against breast cancer. There are poor in Dallas we must feed, kids in hospital without parents, hunger, homelessness, a nursing shortage, senior citizens. Muslims need to work on these common issues. The Prophet did not say 'care about your neighbor only if he is a Muslim.'" Bakali noted that "if you don't want to talk about religion, sex, or politics, it is okay; offer to grab a latte with someone, or give them a free pass to the health club. Show how you live your life as a Muslim but do not dictate to people. I don't use the word 'non-Muslim.' I am an American. I just happen to be Muslim."

Muslim Refugees

A substantial section of the Muslim community in America is here not because of having been born in the United States or having come on their own volition once the Hart-Celler Act made them welcome, but because they were escaping the turmoil of their homes. The first waves of refugees fled the Islamic revolution in Iran in the late 1970s. Then came those displaced by the wars of the 1980s and 1990s in Afghanistan, the Balkans, Somalia, and Iraq. Other smaller Muslim refugee groups include the Cambodians and Burmese. Acutely aware of the reasons they escaped from their war-torn homes, they identify with and appreciate America. These refugees tend to live together in the community and are therefore able to maintain a cultural identity, but they are not easily categorized in terms of my three Muslim models. In their case, tribal and ethnic identity vies with the Islamic one.

Iranian Refugees

Jonathan, Hailey, and Madeeha spent an evening in St. Louis with a group of about twenty Iranian Americans at the home of Bahar Bastani and his son Parsa, who helped arrange the evening. All were successful, well dressed, mostly middle-aged business owners, professors, and doctors who had built a new home for themselves since their move to America three decades ago.

Having been here for so long, they had a lot to say about establishing their community and becoming part of America. Most had mixed feelings about their new country and their place in it. One man said that he has not assimilated, but his wife has. A teenage female found "some communities really are segregated," yet all felt relations with people of other faiths are by and large good. Another woman stated plainly that she is an American and does not like being treated as an outsider: "It's not like I'm living a separate life. There is no 'them' and 'me.' I don't know who 'them' is."

Most also saw much stereotyping and anti-Muslim sentiment in the United States: "We will not hear a positive word about any Muslims in America," said one man. When he came here to study at a university over thirty years ago, people would associate a camel with Muslims. Now it is an "armed militant." "It's the same as the portrayal of blacks," he continued, "they have—Tarzan, jungle, monkeys. This is all necessary to suppress a certain part of society. They've done that with blacks, . . . and now with Muslims."

A young female doctor who used to live in Europe felt people there are more curious and more open: "They might not be as kind and polite as Americans are, but they at least come to you and say, 'Hey, I heard that you guys eat cockroaches and it was in a book back in the eighties.' But in the United States you do not talk about politics, you do not talk about religion, you do not talk about culture." Once in a while a patient will ask her if she is from India, to which she responds, "No, I am from the axis of evil," because "when I start joking about it, they open up." Usually, however, they remain reserved, "because they are all nice midwestern people, and they do not want to offend me. That's why they are afraid to ask questions. And I think that is why the majority of them are so ignorant."

The doctor also recounted her family's experience with suspicion and stereotyping when they moved into a new neighborhood. Her neighbors "had this picture that I am sitting home, taking care of the child, don't go out. Then we had our first neighborhood meeting. I intentionally sent my husband out to change the diaper so that they could see, okay this is a Muslim woman and she is ordering the husband to change the diapers."

President Mahmoud Ahmadinejad's various inflammatory statements have kept Iran in the news for some time, conjuring up images of attacks on Israel and stockpiles of nuclear weapons. One man in particular, the owner of a sandwich shop, became animated on this subject. Muslims are too often on the defensive about Israel and too ready to apologize, he complained. "We are the victims here, so we don't have to apologize. The number one threat for the Muslim world is Israel. That is my opinion. It has attacked every neighbor except the sea. It would if it could. And I think the number one threat for the United States is Israel too."

As the conversation grew more heated, the man defended President Ahmadinejad's comments on Israel, particularly a statement made in 2005 to the effect that "Israel must be wiped off the map," insisting that "what he said is absolutely right." He continued: "It's an illegitimate state over there; it has occupied other countries for forty-five years. . . . the Soviet Union was wiped off the map without using nuclear weapons. That is what Ahmadinejad means." Although the group had varying opinions on Israel, all agreed with the woman who said, "When we talk about Israel, there's a separation between Israel and its policies and Judaism. They are not one, so when we are talking about Israel, it has nothing to do with anti-Semitism, with all of those things that come attached when you talk about it here in the States."

Toward the end of the evening, the most animated man in the group launched into a tirade against America, to laughter throughout the room, even among my team: "This is an arrogant attitude—that anything that happens in the U.S. is constituted as the world. The World News Tonight? Maybe three minutes of the world and twenty-seven minutes of U.S. news. In the World Series, we only play with each other. The World Series? There's no world involved with that." Hailey could not resist being provocative: "Well, if you don't like it so much, why don't you leave?" Without missing a beat and with a sly twinkle in his eye, he replied: "Because we can have conversations like this." As they were leaving, several people told Jonathan that political arguments and intense discussions are a favorite pastime for Iranians—and that they could talk like this all night.

Bosnian Refugees

Like many Muslim communities in the United States, Bosnians feel a mixture of gratitude that America has provided a refuge but also concern that some Americans express hatred and distrust of them. In St. Louis, Missouri, Muhammad Hasic is the most prominent imam of a Bosnian community with 60,000 to 70,000 members, said to be the largest concentration of Bosnians in the United States. When they began arriving in the 1990s to escape persecution at home, the U.S. government resettled them in St. Louis, where they moved into decaying and crime-ridden neighborhoods and opened businesses. Today they are widely credited with vastly improving neglected areas of the city. We were able to interview the imam as well as several other Bosnians and visited them in their homes and main mosque.

With their fair complexion, and in many cases blue eyes and blond hair, the Bosnians seem to be integrating more readily than other Muslim refugees. Many of them now have comfortable jobs in hotels and businesses in the city. They are interested in integrating into American life and remaining invisible as much as possible. There are limits to their full assimilation into American society, however. At a lunch hosted for us by the manager of the Ritz-Carlton in St. Louis, we talked to two Bosnians working for the management. In their smart grey business suits and clean-cut midwestern appearance, they were the perfect advertisement for the upscale luxury hotel. They were grateful to be there at all, yet admitted to some problems they faced almost daily. Although they are white Europeans, they have Muslim names such as Muhammad and Mustafa. The relationship invariably changes when people hear their names. "Right color, wrong religion," they said ruefully, repeating a phrase we heard several times from Bosnians.

Imam Hasic is active in interfaith dialogue and invited us to join him at the Friday prayer. In his khutba, he spoke of kindness as an Islamic duty. In my address to the congregation, I expanded on his theme of kindness, an obviously critical factor in the community's life because it was prominently missing in the refugees' former homeland. The Bosnians went to great lengths to express how accommodating Americans had been, and how lucky they felt to be in America and to have the opportunities it afforded. After Friday prayers, a man in his fifties told Frankie that Americans must surely be Muslim without knowing it because they "treated the Bosnians with such compassion."

Yet the prior experience with genocide in the Balkans was never far from the minds of the Bosnians. Imam Hasic has posters and pamphlets with pictures of corpses in his office depicting the 1995 Srebrenica massacre.

The Bosnian mosque's large minaret, he said, drew a hostile reaction when word got out that it was going to be built. A website suddenly appeared threatening that pig's blood would be poured on it and sounding the alarm that the Muslims were taking over. In an instance of globalization at work, the website was picked up by Hindu and Serb nationalists, who have their own problems with Muslims, and who jointly warned Americans that Muslims would take over if not stopped, and their "Christian daughters would soon be wearing the headscarf."

Imam Hasic talked of the steady dose of hate that the Serb media served daily, depicting Muslims as barbaric and violent, as if they were lowly insects. The imam felt uneasy about the American media's constant criticism of Islam, because this brought back memories of violence and hatred that made him fear for the future. His young son, not yet ten, constantly asked him why people hated them. Feeling besieged, some of the young Bosnians have begun identifying with literalist Islam, as indicated in responses to our questionnaires. Kenan Kadil of St. Louis, a twenty-four-year-old Bosnian male who listed his race as "white," said that the war on terror was a "war against Islam," adding that the best way to improve relations would be for the United States to "stop killing the Muslims."

In Atlanta the Bosnian leaders Imam Ismet Zejnelovic, head of the religious community, and Abdullah Kapic, a community spokesman, fretted about this trend: about 50 percent of this Muslim community was now Salafi, and many young Bosnians, especially those who made the pilgrimage to Saudi Arabia, found Salafi doctrines attractive. Both Bosnians were really worried. Imam Ismet, in particular, aroused Salafi fury because he was suspected of Sufi leanings. Abdullah was called a kafir for advocating interfaith dialogue. The rest of the community was too divided to stand up to the Salafis.

Imam Ismet and Abdullah had invited us to the Bosnian Islamic Cultural Center in Snellville, Georgia, on the outskirts of Atlanta and promised to show me a copy of my book *Living Islam* in the Bosnian translation.[18] They said it had helped them through difficult times in Bosnia in the 1990s by giving them hope and pride. When we did visit them and were running late, we found a large and eager congregation patiently sitting in the prayer room, the women at one end but not segregated. And yes, a copy of *Living Islam* was reverentially placed on a lectern in the center of the room.

Somali Refugees

We met our first Somali refugees also in St. Louis. It was the first day of the month of Ramadan, and Madeeha was able to open the fast with

Team members spent some intense time interviewing Muslim refugees from Somalia. Here Madeeha Hameed speaks to Zaynab, one of fifteen children living in a one-bedroom apartment in St. Louis with their mother, who supports the family by housekeeping and picking up trash.

a Somali family. She found it a moving experience: "They all lived in a one-bedroom apartment with about fifteen children sleeping on the floor. The decorations of the house and the smell of African food gave the illusion that I was sitting right in Somalia." Acting as her mother and aunt's translator, a seven-year-old Somali girl named Zaynab said her mother had left her father in Kenya and moved to America with her children and sister only two years ago. The mother was currently supporting her entire family by housekeeping and picking up trash around the area.

Zaynab's cousin Mana, aged thirteen, said that the only thing she liked about America was her school. The other girls agreed with her. Mana said that she does not like living in America because people make fun of her for her traditional Muslim attire. They ask her why she wears a hijab and a dress covering from head to toe during the scorching summer heat. With her eyes glued to *Hannah Montana* on the TV, she told Madeeha that she just wanted to go back to Somalia to reunite with her older sister and friends.

Mana's mother explained the deterioration in Somalia, where she saw houses blown away before her very eyes. Her family split up and fled in different directions just to ensure the safety of the children. Madeeha was touched when "Zaynab pulled me down, gave me a kiss on my cheek, and said, 'I really really love you. I just want you to come back and see me again.' Tears started trickling down my eyes as Zaynab held me tight in her feeble arms for a couple of minutes. I realized that for the first time in twenty-one years I had truly understood the spirit of Ramadan. The essence of Ramadan and Islam—the word 'compassion'—could never have been taught to me in a better light."

The Somali refugees seemed to be finding it difficult to settle into American life, both in large cities like St. Louis, Seattle, and Minneapolis, and in smaller towns like Grand Island, Nebraska. On our visit to Omaha, Nebraska, not long after our stop in St. Louis, we read that 200 Somali workers had been fired from their jobs at a meatpacking plant run by the JBS Swift Meat Company in Grand Island. The workers had demanded time to pray and break their fast at sundown because it was Ramadan but were refused. Somalis had also been fired in a similar fashion at other Swift plants in Colorado and Texas, and the influx of Somalis in places like Shelbyville, Tennessee, and Lewiston, Maine, had caused friction with the local population.

Frankie met Abdi Mohamed, a member of the Somali community in Omaha, to discuss the controversy at the plant. A refugee himself, Abdi had recently been granted U.S. citizenship and works in the Nebraska public school system. He said he knew some people in Grand Island and graciously offered to take Frankie and Craig there. Having just the day before heard my lecture at Omaha's Creighton University, he agreed with the mission of our project and the issues I had spoken about, namely, the need for improved relations between Muslims and non-Muslims.

Abdi, Craig, and Frankie set off on the nearly three-hour drive across the state to Grand Island. Upon arrival in the town, Abdi stopped briefly to pick up a Somali worker, hoping he could direct them to the workers. A white woman from across the road saw the group and yelled, "Welcome to America! Get moving!"

They conducted their interviews in a rundown place the Somali community uses as a center with an old sign in the window that read "Carmelita's Restaurant." It was a small structure just off the main street and served as a prayer room, restaurant, community center, and place of business all rolled into one—a Somali enclave hidden next to the train tracks of "Main Street, USA." Six workers were present, one of whom had been fired that very day. They did not speak much English, so Abdi served as the translator. As the conversation proceeded, more workers who had been fired came in to share their story, which unfolded in the following way.

During Ramadan the Somali workers often took the opportunity to pray during their government-mandated break times, but other workers, mainly Latino, did not approve. The final straw came when a manager, also Latino, grabbed two Somali women who were praying and removed their prayer rugs from under them. For the Somalis, who observe strict gender separation, this was an affront to their sense of modesty and honor. As Abdi explained, "It would upset any man with a sense of dignity." The management fired those suspected of praying during their breaks. Many others simply walked off the job when threatened with dismissal if they prayed.

Frankie, who has lived in Kenya, where many Somalis took refuge from the war in their homeland, is especially interested in the community in the United States. He was struck by the devout and humble spirit of these workers. With so many illegal immigrants working in the United States, he found it hard to believe that legal residents such as these were having so much difficulty here: "These workers had fled the hell of civil war in Somalia as refugees, languished for years in camps in Kenya, and finally made it to the U.S. There they journeyed to small midwestern towns to work in a dangerous job, living in apartments packed full of people. Craig and I visited their plant later that day and it had a foreboding prison-like atmosphere with an almost unbearable stench—a pretty rough place to work."

Hundreds of Somalis had been left jobless and found themselves without resources in a strange land. They seemed light-years away from the Muslim community in Omaha and its wealthy and educated professionals. To Frankie they looked "lost and dazed." They had no one to represent them because it takes money to hire lawyers. Nonetheless, the Somalis maintained a sense of dignity and confidence. When asked how they felt after losing their jobs, they responded as many traditional Muslims would: "This is not a loss for us; it is a win." In their minds they had preserved their culture and their religion.

Asked what they would do now that they were left with nothing, one worker replied: "According to Islam, if your religion is being oppressed in one place, you can leave and go someplace else. That is the meaning of *hijra*." Plants elsewhere were accepting Somalis and were letting them pray, the workers told Frankie.

Before the incident, the Somalis had not experienced any conflict between practicing their religion and living in the United States. Most said they were happy living in Nebraska, a place far from their violence-plagued homeland, although now they were confused and hurt. "America has freedom of religion," one man said. "I don't understand what is happening here."

Supporters of the Somalis argued that the firings violated the Civil Rights Act of 1964, one of President John F. Kennedy's initiatives passed in the wake of his assassination. The act forbids employers to discriminate on the basis of religion and stipulates that they must "reasonably accommodate" religious practices that do not cause "undue hardship" to the company's business interests. Though the case of the Somali meatpackers in Grand Island was a labor dispute between immigrant groups, in the American media it was often cast as a straightforward matter of Islam versus America, wherein Muslims were not adapting to American values in the workplace. Thus, the case needed to be seen in the context of American identity itself. "We don't get time to pray at work," said one white Grand Island woman in her fifties. "Why should they? I'm not prejudiced or anything, but they should go the American way." Sam Bailey of Sanibel Island, introduced in chapter 3, was so "disturbed" by the case of the Somali meatpackers in Colorado, which mirrored the situation in Grand Island, that he wrote to Colorado's governor and the attorney general complaining of the immigrants and their demands. In a front-page article in the *New York Times,* Grand Island's mayor, Margaret Hornady, to whom the Somali workers had appealed for justice, said she found the sight of Somali women in hijabs "startling" and suggestive of female subjugation. The Somalis made her think of Osama bin Laden and the 9/11 attacks.[19] In August 2009 the U.S. Equal Employment Opportunity Commission did find that the Somalis faced "unlawful harassment" because of their religion.

Craig's video of Frankie's interview with the Somalis in Grand Island was submitted to CNN and broadcast just as news of the firings was breaking. While some of the reactions posted on CNN's website reflected American pluralism, the majority echoed primordial and predator attitudes. One posting, from "Amusa1," all in capital letters summed it up: "SCREW EM LET THEM GO BACK TO SOMALIA OK JUST LET THEM GO AND WHILE WE ARE AT IT SEND BACK THE DAMM MEXICANS AND THE REST."

Proponents of American primordial identity have formed organizations to oppose the influx of Muslim refugees, including Refugee Resettlement Watch, run by Maryland farmer and Yale-educated activist Ann Corcoran, who was angered by the Somali meatpacker episode and our team's role in covering the story. On her organization's website, she accused Frankie of bias in an article he wrote on the controversy for the *Huffington Post*. She was livid about the workers' remarks to Frankie, stating their firing was not "a loss" but "a win" because they preserved their Islam.[20] It was, she wrote, a "set-up," a strategy adopted by Muslims and the American "Left" aimed at "wearing us down."

A Somali response to a white commentator on CNN's website who told the Somalis to "assimilate" as his family had done, and change their names, reflected American pluralism: "Well I am proud to be somaliamerican, besides that the constitution didn't say I should change my name. I have a beautiful name which was given to me by my parents if you are not comfortable with that sorry. Again this is not about being an immigrant, we all know this is the land of immigrants. I am legal immigrant who is paying tax but not ready to be slaved. Therefore let's stop the fear among us which is not safe for the community."

The Kurds of Nashville, Tennessee

The United States has been good to the Kurds. It has given them what every Muslim country has denied them: a chance to be themselves. Nashville has the largest concentration of Kurds in the United States, now numbering some 10,000 to 15,000 out of about 100,000 in the country. Those we met in Nashville had a distinct and coherent Kurdish identity, now radiating a security that contrasted with the community's troubled history in the Middle East. Fleeing from persecution in Turkey, Syria, Iraq, and Iran, where they form unhappy minorities, Kurds sought refuge in the United States. Here their plight was widely known because of Saddam's brutal massacre of their community in 1988. The Iraqi dictator had used chemical gas to slaughter thousands, yet failed to break their spirit. Through their tribal pride and clannishness, they were able to withstand the oppression of the Middle East's dictators.

In the Middle East, ethnicity matters almost as much as religion in defining identity. Because the Kurds are not Arab but have always been surrounded by a strong Arab cultural environment, it has been a struggle to maintain their identity. Ironically, one of the greatest heroes of Islam, Salahuddin Ayubbi, or Saladin as he is known in the West, was a Kurd. Muslims throughout the world take pride in Saladin's legendary exploits as the leader who took back Jerusalem from the Crusaders. He allowed the Jews to return to Jerusalem, where they had been banned by the Christians, and freed numerous Christian prisoners from slavery, paying for many from his personal estate. Keeping his memory alive in Nashville, the Kurds have named their center the Salahadeen Islamic Center, which also houses the main mosque in Nashville.

Mir Ahmed and Mwafaq Mohammed, the leaders of the Kurd community, hosted a lunch for us with a group of other Kurds, allowing us to gain some insight into a traditionally closed community. Ahmed was on the board of the Salahadeen Center and spokesman for the community, and Mwafaq, originally from Kirkuk in Iraq, was director of the youth program. Mwafaq said the community provides him with a sense of security, with its seventy or so Kurdish businesses and the center: "They provide outreach, social services. I have my brother-in-law here. We have a sense of unity here." His friend Mir Ahmed noted that "the weather in Nashville is very close to northern Iraq. We kept the same [tribal] structure in Nashville that we had in Iraq, these family ties, even in marriage."

Mwafaq talked about the tension between the "two generations" of Kurds in the United States—those who arrived as adults and those who have grown up here. At times, conflicts arise because "in some of the houses you have two cultures." The children are soaking up American culture, he says, and the parents are not aware of or able to understand the changes.

Such conflict was causing turmoil in young refugee and immigrant communities across the country. We heard of gangs forming among Somalis in Minneapolis and "Persians" and Pakistanis in Los Angeles, many of whom, although "involved in drugs and violence," according to a CAIR representative in Los Angeles, wore medallions that read "Allah."

Young Kurds in Nashville, too, had problems with gangs, as Mwafaq explained: "The gang is not part of the Kurdish life; it's not part of our system," he explained. "We are very hospitable, very gentle people. Back in the 1980s these kids were harassed, and I think that part of it is also having Islamic identity—you know, having the name Muhammad, Ahmed, Hussein, which associates them with 'you are violent, you are a terrorist.' What happened is that the kids came together to defend themselves and the genie went out of the bottle. Eventually it evolved into formal gangs. Some of these kids are good kids who have made wrong decisions, the wrong choices."

To counter the trend toward gangs, Mwafaq is operating a program in association with the YMCA called the Kurdish Achievers: "It is educational blended with the sports activities with some lectures to intervene and prevent that violent lifestyle. Every community in this country has a gang problem. If you look at history, every immigrant community goes through those who are the strong beating the weak, the mafia system, this gang system." He was "100 percent confident this issue that tarnished our name will eventually go away. These kids will evolve."

Mwafaq had unkind words for the media, which he found selective in their news. By projecting stories about Kurdish gangs, it tended to paint the entire community in a negative light: "There are close to 10,000 Kurds in this community, and the gang number could be less than 100, so 1 percent. Associating 10,000 with 1 percent of the population is absolutely wrong."

Muslim girls from a tribal background, whether Kurds from Iraq or Pashtun from Afghanistan, are able to maintain their sense of identity and defend it with customary vigor. This is illustrated by the story a young Kurdish girl named Kasar Abdulla told Hailey at lunch with Muslim women in Nashville. She had come to America in the 1990s and had absorbed much of American culture but remained strongly Muslim. Inspired by the Prophet Muhammad, she decided to wear the hijab during her senior year in high school. Her family was completely against it and ridiculed her.

At school one day, two American girls stood behind her in the lunchroom. One said, "I dare you to pull that off of her," and the other one replied, "I dare *you*." Kasar, whom Hailey called a "regular spitfire," turned around and said, "I dare both of you!" With that, they began rolling around on the floor, punching one another. The teachers decided to stand back, saying they saw nothing, knew nothing. Kasar then went to the principal, telling him, "This is unacceptable and I won't stand for it." But he would not do anything and suggested she see the school counselor. The counselor, an African American, advised her, "Maybe you should rethink your wardrobe." Kasar quickly responded, "Well, maybe you should rethink being black. What if someone in the 1960s asked you to bleach your face instead of standing up for yourself—how would you feel?" Although she regretted her comment, said Kasar, the damage had been done. At the same time, she persevered in her decision to wear the hijab throughout that last year of high school and later in college. Since graduation from college she has been much in demand for jobs, panel discussions, and documentaries, and has generated an overall feeling of respect in others because of her stand. Kasar was now director of advocacy and education at the Tennessee Immigrant and Refugee Rights Coalition.

Because she was so determined to wear the hijab, Kasar's story encouraged the other women present to share their own experiences and also discuss modesty in American culture (also see next chapter). Della, a professional Tae Kwon Do instructor, is often asked to teach self-defense classes. The first line of defense is how you dress. The hijab, she said, was her defense in a way, since more rapes occur during the summer when women wear short shorts and small tops.

Suzanne, a white American convert, said she was ready to scream if any-one else asked her if she was hot wearing the hijab and full-length clothes during the summer. She normally wears an abayya, a "self-contained air conditioner that helps keep you cool in 120-degree heat in the desert or in Tennessee summers." She finds tight clothing is even hotter "because it does not let the body breathe."

Kasar then said that her "heart goes out to Christian girls" because they are being commodified, objectified, and used by men and society. She had a Christian friend who had been dating a man for several years, even lived with him, and still he had not proposed. When the friend puzzled over this behavior, Kassar said, "If I were him, I wouldn't propose either. What does he not have that he would if you were married?" She advised her friend to abstain from sex with him until he decided that he either loved her and wanted to marry her or he left her, which would in the end be better for her. Within six months he had proposed and asked her friend's father for her hand in marriage.

Kasar said that she gets much respect and positive attention for wearing the hijab. Her Kurdish friend used to wear "cute clothes" and "short skirts," but this drew such unprofessional remarks from men at work that she now wears the hijab. People accept her for herself, she said, not her looks, and do not try to make her feel inferior. Kasar told Hailey that women in this country are not allowed to be women because they are competing with men all of the time. They are not able to take time for their pregnancies or care for their children without getting behind or being looked down upon. All of the women at the table agreed and said they wanted to start wearing hijabs, especially for the respect it inspired in men.

Just as our blogs on the Somalis provoked a flood of comments, our account of the meeting with the Kurdish community triggered a similar outpouring of negative feelings. "Dirk Diggler" summed up the sentiments of many when he wrote on February 9, 2009, "They do not assimilate, and use the freedoms granted by our Constitution to subvert our way of life. The ultimate goal is the imposition of shariah law, and any Muslim who denies this is lying through their teeth. If they don't wish to assimilate, I say send them back to where they came from."

Afghan Refugees

Learning that San Francisco was home to one of the largest concentra-tions of Afghans in the country, estimated to number 40,000 or more,

Frankie and Jonathan showed up at the large and beautiful Masjid Abubaker Siddiq for Friday prayers, hoping to speak with the imam afterward. The mosque has more than 10,000 members, mostly Afghan refugees who arrived in the 1980s.

The team approached the tall, bearded Afghan imam and introduced our project, saying that they had traveled to the Muslim world and throughout the United States, discussing a wide range of subjects, including globalization, Islam, American identity, and politics. When they mentioned politics, the imam immediately cut them off: "No politics. We do not discuss politics in the mosque." He was happy living in America but urged Americans to "let us pray and be Muslims, and there will be no problem." He resisted any further conversation until the director of the mosque arrived and invited them to join him, the imam, and the rest of the board in the conference room for a discussion. Just before heading to the conference room, the team had asked the imam what it means to be American. He stumbled and went completely blank, offering no answer.

On entering the room, Jonathan overheard a group of board members discussing what their answers should be to the same question. "Just say that it is a melting pot," urged one in a low voice. When the question was finally posed, this is exactly what they said, "a melting pot," as if their answers had been rehearsed.

In Omaha the team met a full-bearded Afghan youth leader who considered the mujahideen "heroes." He was dressed theatrically, sporting a denim jacket with the Afghan flag sewn onto it. He told Frankie the Arabs were embracing "being American" more than Afghans and Pakistanis, who tend to be more conservative, adding that many young Muslims were following the Salafi creed, which he called the "most American" of Islams.

In Fort Myers, Florida, we spoke with an Afghan man in his fifties, bald, wearing a buttoned shirt, and looking professional. Apparently depressed, he complained about his job and his boss, who would not let him off work to attend prayers. He also found fault with U.S. foreign policy and with the lack of morals in America. He saw injustice everywhere and blamed the United States for violence in Israel and Palestine. The United States today, he said, is what Russia was in the 1980s.

He said he could not return to Afghanistan "as people there hate me because I've been living in America. Here in America people hate me because of my religion." He called Hamas a "legitimate government" and Israelis "terrorists." He maintained that the "U.S. used to stand for truth, but look at what happened in the UN Security Council and Gaza—the U.S. pushed for the killing to continue." Recently the United States has killed "millions of people," he complained. Soviet forces "killed millions of Afghans," and now their nation is gone, he shrugged. "The same thing will happen to America."

Other Refugees

A rough, predominantly Latino neighborhood in Santa Ana, just outside Los Angeles, is an unlikely setting for one of the biggest concentrations of Cambodian Muslims in America. That did not deter my team from tracking down a Cambodian guide who would show them the community. This man seemed to be in charge of the mosque's administration, and he explained that the community was poor and plagued by gang violence. The Cambodian Muslims, he noted, came to America in the early 1980s after fleeing the Communist Khmer Rouge under Pol Pot. The Cambodians live in an apartment complex that consists of five small buildings with a courtyard in the middle growing banana trees, sugar cane, and lemon grass. A modest mosque is housed in the complex, which consists of two apartments joined together to provide space.

The complex is populated by Muslim and Buddhist Cambodians, as well as Latinos. Describing the neighbors, the guide pointed at various apartments, indicating who lived there: "Muslim, Muslim, kafir, Muslim, kafir." The kafirs, he explained, were both the Cambodian Buddhists in their community and the Latinos. There had been tension between the Muslim and Buddhist Cambodians, he said, but they were getting along better lately. The guide's journey to America had been hazardous, beginning with his family's flight across Cambodian minefields. Using a long stick, they had tapped the ground checking for mines. If they hit one and it blew up, they knew they could walk on safely. The group finally reached Thailand and then traveled to the United States for refugee resettlement.

Of the mosque's 400 members, some were Vietnamese, but most were Cambodians who had fled the persecution of the Khmer Rouge, splitting up after they first arrived in the United States, but later resettling in Southern California because of the weather. A good number of Cambodians also settled in Olympia, Washington.

Gang violence was a problem, said Imam Salim Ghazaly, joining the team inside the mosque, with shootouts taking place even on the building's front lawn: "At first, we wouldn't walk around at night, but we got used to it." Because the youth badly want to be American, this causes conflict between them and their parents. He asks the youth what kind of American they want to be: "doctors or gangs?" American culture poses morality problems for the young Cambodian Muslims, he lamented: "If we have no modesty, we have no shame." The marriages he performs now are more of the "emergency" kind, he added. Some imams refuse to perform these, but he sees so many cases that he feels obliged to do so.

"Islam is not a threat to America. Islam is peace. Islam is a religion for the world. You can be a Muslim anywhere you want. It is not hard to be a Muslim in America, not compared to Khmer Rouge," said the imam, offering somewhat of a backhanded compliment. He predicted that Islam would spread in the United States and hoped the country would become Muslim one day. His role model was the Prophet: "I look to him for everything." He felt the best way ahead was to "open our minds. We should use the basic teaching of Jesus and the Prophet. They said the same thing—love your neighbor."

The Next Generation

The children of Muslim modernists who arrived in the United States during the latter part of the twentieth century face a dilemma. Having parents who wanted to work within the American system but still guarded their heritage jealously and drummed its importance into the heads of their children, many of this new generation are caught between past and present, between here and there. Many are confused and unsure of their identity, not to mention their relationship with both America and Islam.

ABCD

For these young American Muslims, balancing the different identities is a difficult, if not almost impossible task. American culture aggressively seeks to integrate and assimilate, and its expressions can easily seduce young people eager to belong to a peer group (for a fuller discussion see chapter 6). More traditional Muslims with Middle Eastern and South Asian backgrounds who still retain a nostalgic attachment to their homelands have given young American Muslims the pejorative label ABCD, meaning American-Born Confused Desi (see chapter 3). Granted, this is said in a semi-humorous way, but it is still unkind and unfair. In retaliation, American Muslims call their more traditional compatriots FOB, or "fresh off the boat." They consider FOBs crude, semiliterate, backward, and narrow minded, and worst of all, they do not understand American culture.

ABCDs know America firsthand and accept American values but sometimes give the impression in what they say and do that they do not fully understand the culture. At the same time, they see themselves as the most enlightened and capable leaders of the Muslim community. They even criticize their parents' generation for its ignorance of "how it's done" in America. Some goodheartedly, or even cruelly, mock their parents' accents or poor understanding of American slang or expressions. In the highly charged atmosphere after 9/11, many were desperate to be "accepted," so they behaved in a manner they thought Americans would find familiar and therefore appealing. This would also draw a clear cultural line between themselves and the practices of their parents. For example, I overheard a young Pakistani who has grown up in the United States boasting to young American women at a party in Washington, D.C., how modern his people were back in Pakistan. As I passed by, I caught the words, "The girls wear frontless shirts at parties in Lahore," and could not resist intervening to ask exactly what "frontless shirts" were and which Pakistani girls wore them. My intervention seemed to have frustrated his amorous initiative. These American women may not have been to Pakistan, but they were not totally ignorant of its culture.

In another conversation with students at the College of William and Mary while discussing *Girls Gone Wild*, a male Muslim immigrant wishing to demonstrate his broad-mindedness said he saw nothing wrong with women lifting up their top and showing their breasts. When I asked him if he would allow his sisters to do this, he said, "Of course." I asked him where he was from. "Pakistan," he answered. "Who are your parents?" I queried. It turned out that I knew his father. I could not resist teasing him with, "Son, knowing your family, if you were to say this in front of them, especially your sisters, you might be in trouble."

Our questionnaires, too, reflected a sense of confusion and frustration among young Muslims. For them, their parents' generation and clerics do not always provide the religious and cultural answers they are looking for, which means they are often out on their own, like so many American teenagers. As a nineteen-year-old female Egyptian student at Detroit's Wayne State University wrote: "For us, advice on religious matters is not really accessible. A lot of the imams are immigrants and have recently moved to the U.S. They don't understand youth culture, and what we already have to give up in being Muslim. For this reason I may go to the Internet." Freshta Sahaqr, an eighteen-year-old female Afghan student born in Kabul, says she would go to a "Muslim website" for advice on a religious issue because "we can't just rely on the mullahs, because their advice makes you think you won't be able to manage Islam in America."

Matters are exacerbated for young American Muslims because they believe that Islam is under attack. An Indian Muslim male in Cedar Rapids said others view his religion as "weird, scary, and despicable." A female Indian Muslim in Salt Lake City wrote: "It's very hard to answer the question 'is violence justified' because I want to defend Islam, but I disagree with the way the extreme Muslims make the headlines. It is hard to speak up when we are in the minority." At Wayne State University, a twenty-year-old male Palestinian predentistry student, who said his favorite TV show was *That '70s Show,* named Osama bin Laden his number one role model, because "he is cool and stepped up to Americans, even though I don't think he did it." His other role models included Hamas's Ahmad Yassin, because "he got his legs, half his body paralyzed from Israelis and he still fought till they killed him," along with "the president of Iran," who is "amazing," and Saddam Hussein, whom he described as "my man," noting "my dad worked for him." When asked to name his favorite books, he admitted he "doesn't read any." He said that he was working in a convenience store in Canada after 9/11 and was "beaten up" and his "glasses broken" in the anti-Muslim backlash. When asked how his community would respond to a terror attack, he replied, "Scared, unless they did it, then happy."

For young American Muslims with roots in foreign conflict zones like Palestine, the sense of persecution was acute, whichever of the Muslim models they identified with. A nineteen-year-old Arab Muslim female whose role models included the Prophet and rapper Eminem praised Hezbollah's Hassan Nasrallah and wrote that "if you are supporting your religion and fighting for your country, then it's an eye for an eye." A twenty-one-year-old Iraqi male student in Dearborn told us, "It's stupid to justify killing for no good reason, unless a country is killing my people, then let them do what they want." A fourteen-year-old Arab male in a Muslim school in New Orleans defined the U.S. war on terror as a war to "kill all Muslims in Palestine. I think American government and Israel are the enemy." Another fourteen-year-old male in the same New Orleans school asked: "Man, what do Jews want with us? Man, I swear, only if we had weapons, let's see them try to pick on another country. But just wait, we're gonna mess over them one day. Those one-hit wonders. They just got lucky because the U.S. is supporting them. And 9/11 was an insight [*sic*] job. The U.S. planned it all the way. They just tried to make Muslims look bad. And thanks for letting us speak."

Answers to our questionnaires also revealed Muslim frustration with the American media's portrayal of Islam. A nineteen-year-old Lebanese Muslim female at Wayne State University in Detroit named her role models as Barack Obama, Martin Luther King Jr., and Abraham Lincoln. She listed her favorite movie and television show as *Sex and the City* and wrote of her enjoyment of *Friends* and *Grey's Anatomy.* Yet she is upset that Islam is portrayed as a "terrorist religion," saying "the media make Islam seem evil." Karima Al-Absy, a nineteen-year-old Arab female student at Omaha's Creighton University, whose favorite TV shows included *Project Runway* and *Seinfeld*, felt that even shows attempting to show Islam in a more positive light, like *Little Mosque on the Prairie* and *Aliens in America*, "get things wrong."

Muslim leaders cannot help but worry that children of immigrant Muslims will collapse under the weight of the two cultures, as I discovered at several gatherings when only Muslims were present and they spoke freely. On one such occasion, at the home of the prominent physician and community leader Sadiq Mohyuddin in St. Louis a year before our journey began, some fifty Muslim men and women of different ethnic backgrounds—including Imam Hasic—had come to meet Zeenat and myself after my talk at the World Affairs Council. Outwardly, these Muslims appeared to be living the American dream, yet the atmosphere, talk, and prognosis for the future were gloomy. After initially painting a rosy picture of their lives, the floodgates of their emotions opened, and we were inundated with stories colored by Islamophobia.

Some of this was not unexpected in the aftermath of 9/11. What surprised me, however, was the problem between the generations. Lines of communication had broken down. The new generation was no longer listening to or following the older generation. Parents were unsure and worried about who was influencing their young. If the young did something reckless, the parents sighed, everyone would suffer.

The parents complained that the young responded to all this by saying they were angry and not at all convinced they were to blame for any of the ills that had befallen Muslim society. They were also more inclined to follow the sacred Islamic text for information on their religion rather than their parents, who tended to rely on their culture. The Quran, the young believe, forbids them to talk to Jews, for example. Many found it difficult to get jobs and faced racist and religious prejudice daily. The anger, warned the parents, was mounting. Some even predicted that another incident like 9/11 was inevitable and would ensure that all Muslims are locked up in internment camps. "We are helpless," they said over and over again.

Yet the young are the direct victims of the failure of their parents' generation, which has neglected to change its strategy and direction for the community in any noticeable manner. Muslim leaders continue to emphasize material standards for themselves and their children. A good job is one that earns the maximum amount of money. In the rush to become lawyers and doctors, the community has bypassed academia and the media. Academicians earn good incomes and are respectable members of society, although it is the media types who form public opinion and define the community. While others were defining Muslims, the community itself was not investing in any systematic or urgent way in producing scholars and commentators. The negative stereotypes of Muslims that have circulated in American society for the past few years have thus remained more or less unchallenged, while the Muslim leadership continues to moan about feeling helpless and Muslim children remain confused and unsure.

Finding a Balance

Not all young Muslims born in the West are confused and unsure. Although many Muslim girls do not wear the hijab, for example, our interviews and other surveys indicate a developed sense of modesty, which is also reflected in the popular book *The American Muslim Teenager's Handbook.*[21] Its cover shows a male Muslim teenager with a guitar alongside a girl with a ponytail and T-shirt texting on her cell phone. However "modern" they appear, the authors stress that Muslim teenagers must not succumb to the "Four Ds"—dating, dancing, drinking, and drugs. Avoiding the Four Ds may help Muslim teenagers preserve their identity, but challenges and dangers still lurk at school and at university (see chapter 6).

We met many younger American Muslims who were balancing their Islam with their Americanness and had a good grasp of both—Sofia and Farhan Latif, mentioned earlier, are but two examples. Another is my daughter Nafees, who was born in Cambridge, England, but has grown up in America and is currently a sophomore at Georgetown University. Hailey interviewed Nafees on campus. As Nafees's father, I thought it would be more appropriate if Hailey spoke with her alone. That way, Nafees would be a legitimate source of information for our project and not feel constrained by our relationship.

Nafees believes that the Muslim community, like American Jews, will eventually find a balance in its identity. At present, Muslims are reacting to the perception of being attacked, she says, which has led some to revert to more orthodox practices and others to reject or move away from Islam. Yet another group is seeking to negotiate a path between these two positions. She herself identifies with the third group.

For Nafees, who does not wear the hijab, Islam is the best of all religions because it "encompasses all aspects of life—religious, cultural, political, and social." Muslims are facing many challenges because their societies have not fully emerged from the effects of Western colonization or America's foreign policy mistakes. These factors robbed Muslims of "hope." In their desperation, some began resorting to violence.

But Nafees did not let the Muslim leadership off the hook either. On a visit to Pakistan in the summer of 2009, she was appalled by the selfish, corrupt, and cynical behavior and ideas of the elite.[22] She found Pakistanis more interested in making plans to abandon the country than in reforming it. Paradoxically, she felt she could be a much better Muslim in America because of its developed notions of justice, civil liberties, and freedom. These made her more confident about her identity and optimistic about the future. In Pakistan she felt "really American." Even family members living in Pakistan saw her as American and felt the need to vent their anger against Americans in her presence. "I feel like I need to defend Islam in America, and defend America in Pakistan," she told Hailey. "I feel like I'm fighting a battle on both fronts."

When 9/11 happened, Nafees was eleven years old. It had a big impact on her, encouraging her to "learn more about my religion and culture to see if it was really to blame. It made me more aware of my identity as a Pakistani and a Muslim." She felt her classmates at Walt Whitman High School in Bethesda, Maryland, had many questions about Islam but were too shy or too polite to ask them, so she started an interfaith club, which quickly became popular.

Nafees observed that the Muslim community in America is not as cohesive and welcoming as it is in France, where she studied for a summer. In America, she could not name a single Muslim religious leader she admires and has little to do with the campus MSA, although her number one role models are the Prophet of Islam and Muslims who strike a balance between living in the West and remaining strong Muslims.

As with any immigrant group, a large cultural divide often separates Muslim parents and their offspring. But Nafees told Hailey that was not the case with her. She and her parents shared common interests such as television shows like *The Office*. She also noted, "My parents were really trusting of me, especially in high school. The only thing was that I could not explain how my American friends would have boyfriends or something like that. They thought that was really bad, but it was hard to explain American culture to them that way."

Hailey found Nafees to be an example of Muslim youth "who have been able to balance their faith, culture, and home life with the wider American culture." Hailey saw the same qualities in many young Muslims she knew at Georgetown University and in others we met on the trip. Bright, well-rounded, engaged, Muslim, and American, they provided "many hopeful examples of the best of America and the best of Islam."

The Soldier's Story in Silicon Valley

In Silicon Valley, Hailey's friend Celestine invited Frankie and Craig to a "hackers' conference," called SuperHappyDevHouse after a *Saturday Night Live* skit and organized for the elite of the valley. Computer whizzes met there once a month to discuss their projects and ideas for changing the world. Most of the participants were startlingly young considering what they had already accomplished, and a few were already multimillionaires, having created applications for Facebook, for example. Lee Felsenstein, who helped develop the first personal computer for Apple and whose work is now in the Smithsonian Institution, was on hand to give advice. Almost everyone was either white or Asian. The meeting was held in "Rainbow Mansion," the house in which Celestine lived with several tech-oriented friends. The name, adopted from the street it was on, evokes color, light, possibilities, science, and pluralism, not to mention the current association with gay rights. Tellingly, the flag outside the home was not the American flag but that of the United Nations. "Obama" signs adorned the kitchen.

Amid the talk of colonies on the moon, robots, or possible new dot-com businesses, Newton, a Filipino scientist of Catholic background who said he had been involved in experiments to clone humans, turned to the team with a most unexpected question, given the company: "My uncle in the Philippines was beheaded by a Muslim. Is there anything in the Quran that would justify this?" Just then a tall, young Pakistani man, whom I will call Tarik, joined the conversation with an impassioned defense of Islam. He said he was a Silicon Valley web developer born in Karachi, who at the age of three moved to California, where he grew up. After high school, he joined the U.S. Army, one of 3,500 Muslims out of a total force of 1.5 million. He described a harrowing experience as an infantryman near the end of boot camp that forced him to think about his "own identity."

He had completed his training with high marks on the physical fitness tests and was to graduate from boot camp in two weeks or so. One day, the drill sergeant instructed about 500 soldiers to come down to the barracks and line up together, then told them to raise their machine guns, M-16s, in the air. "He was really passionate about this," recalled Tarik. "He had spit coming out of his mouth, his face was red, he was really into it." Tarik continued: "He says, 'Raise your machine guns in the air!' He made us do this like 100 or 200 times until our arms were so tired we couldn't raise our machine guns anymore. And then he said, 'Repeat after me.' He instructed us to say, 'We will kill all the Muslims in the world!' And then he said, 'Those god-damned bastards over there want to kill you.' So we had to say this over and over. I didn't say it. I'd never really thought of myself as a Muslim, I always thought of myself as an American first, because I was so Americanized, growing up in the United States. So it just didn't seem right and I didn't do it. I got into a fight with the drill sergeant. I was able to get out eventually."

Some soldiers, added Tarik, came up to him afterward and said, "That's not right, that's not right, he shouldn't have said that," or "That drill sergeant's an ass." But at the same time, Tarik observed, they did not stop or object and obeyed all the commands. "These same soldiers who were taught to hate Muslims for absolutely no reason at all," Tarik realized, "are the same soldiers who have been released into Iraq and Afghanistan today where the population is largely Muslim. And then you see stories about thirteen-year-old Muslim girls being raped by U.S. soldiers and them killing civilians. Well, what do you expect? You train someone to hate a whole race and then release them into that population. How do you think they're going to react?"

Following 9/11, Tarik had faced another crisis. A construction worker spotted him walking home from work in Pittsburgh, where he had moved, and yelled, "Are you from Afghanistan?" The worker attacked Tarik, kicking and punching him "in a rage" before others intervened and stopped him. The construction worker was now screaming, "I want to kill you all. Go back to where you're from!" Tarik managed to duck most of the punches, except for one kick. A young Korean girl then stepped in the middle, which "amazed" Tarik: "I was able to dodge him long enough that his coworkers finally came over and grabbed him away. It was interesting because the coworkers didn't come initially. They waited, watched, and then came over and said, 'Let's go.' Then the cops came over and said, 'Well, what do you expect?' which really shocked me."

When asked the best way to improve relations between the United States and the Muslim world, Tarik appeared unsure and confused: "You can't have stuff like Guantánamo Bay and imprisoning people. You can't have secret police, and you can't have stuff that happened in Iraq when all those pictures came out with the army and the military abusing and torturing prisoners. You have the U.S invading Pakistan, the Pakistan government saying this isn't right. The U.S. just says we're the U.S., what are you going to do? And really what can a small country like Pakistan do against the U.S.? It can't do much."

Tarik thought that today, after 9/11, many younger Muslims felt as he did, that they just do not have an identity: "They're not close with their roots, they don't really understand much about their culture. At the same time, you have a lot of this propaganda against Muslim people going out that makes them feel like they're not really wanted, or feel like they're not really citizens of the U.S. So you're left in the middle of nowhere."

Ten, American, and Muslim

A generation of Muslims even younger than Tarik will be coming of age in the next few years. They still live under the dark shadow of 9/11. It is not difficult to imagine this generation harboring resentment and anger as young men and women. In St. Louis, Imam Muhammad Hasic told us that whenever his family travels, his young son, not yet ten, who was born in the United States, wants to know, "Why do they always stop *us* at the airport?" During one flight security check, after asking the father and son to step aside, an officer separated them and asked the little boy if the father had given him any money. The boy was quiet, and the officer kept aggressively questioning him to the point of harassment. The boy finally screamed and threw the three dollars that his father had given him to the floor. The father told us that he is frightened for his son and tries to teach him why officials are so scrupulous in their security checks. They are meant to provide security and safety for all passengers. But his son remains unconvinced. He is becoming bitter and angry.

In Chicago we had dinner with an Egyptian father who expressed similar concerns for his young boy. As a part-time professor at DePaul University with a young family, he was struggling to pay his rent. He lived in a predominantly African American neighborhood, which can be quite dangerous, he said. Arsonists, most likely his neighbors, he thought, had attacked his house. He guessed the reason for the attack was that the African Americans considered him white, but being an Egyptian immigrant, he was not even American.

His son has had to face similar challenges at the local school where he is beaten frequently for being "white." When he goes to summer camp with mostly white children, they beat him up for being a "terrorist." Although the boy was born in the United States, he asks his father to "go home." His father can only say, with resignation, "This is your home."

One of our most painful stories comes from our visit to a small, rundown mosque in "Little Pakistan," Brooklyn (referred to in chapter 3). One man had his son, who was about ten years old, sitting on his lap. They looked endearingly similar, with their big glasses, jeans, and loose-fitting shirts. The father was in the insurance business and one day shortly after

9/11 was stopped by the police for a minor traffic violation, his first ever. He was arrested, hand-cuffed, and brought before the judge. "I felt humiliated," he said. He was released after a few hours, but badly shaken. Some days later, the police knocked on his door and searched the house, and their rough questioning traumatized the boy. The father had apparently also been suspected of having ties to the Taliban, but it was established that he did not. However, the experience left a scar on the father and his son.

Another boy, also about ten, articulate and dressed in a polo shirt looking like any other American kid, then spoke up: "People in America, they think they have a right to push us around. Well, like in the New York Constitution, it says that all people have a right to practice religion, right? So, we can practice our religion in peace, but other people, they're gonna do something like attack us and then they're not gonna go to jail for it. When you call the police, they're not gonna do anything because they think we're bad people and then they're gonna blame us for doing something. Well, when I was going somewhere, I saw this guy, he was beating someone up and I was looking at him saying, 'Why is he beating him up?' And then later, when I thought about it more, I found out the guy was Muslim, and he was beating him up because of the race he is." He especially wanted to tell us that "I was searching on the Internet and I believe 9/11 was planned by the Jews. I saw a video about how the towers fell, and they fell like there were explosives in the bottom, not because of the planes. There were no Jews in the tower that day."

This little boy also talked about being beaten up at school by classmates calling him a terrorist. His father, who could barely speak English, told Zeenat a story in Urdu about the boy's mother. She was in a bus in Pakistan near the Afghan border when it was blown up by terrorists. "The irony and pain broke my heart," said Hailey, "for the injustice of what had happened to this little boy."

Gender is no barrier to the prejudice some of these young children experience. In Buffalo, while staying at the home of Faizan Haq, we became friendly with his family. We asked his niece Aisha, who is seven years old, what it meant to be an American. She was puzzled by the question. "I can't be an American," she replied, her brow wrestling with the question, "I'm dark."

A New Chapter?

Of all the immigrant communities in the United States, the Muslim one poses the greatest challenge to American identity. American pluralism, which had initially attracted Muslims to this country, now treats them with distaste and indifference. The cultural role of women and Muslim commitment to democracy, progress, and peace are all under scrutiny. Mostly non-white and entirely non-Christian, Muslim immigrants cannot be part of American primordial identity; and because immigrant Muslims were identified with the terrorists of 9/11, they have become the magnet for negative attention from American predator identity. The Muslim immigrant community's resulting uncertainty and anger and the media's unrelenting hostility have created the impression that dangers to national security do indeed lurk within it. As a result, experts now seek to uncover plots against America, including homegrown terrorist schemes among Pakistanis, Somalis, and others.

The discussion of Muslim immigrants in this chapter will benefit if one reflects on the American experience with other immigrants, like the Catholic Irish and Italians in the nineteenth century and the Jewish immigrants at the turn of that century. Unlike those other immigrants, however, Muslims arrived with the cultural baggage of bad history between Islam and the West. The Muslim immigrant community, as this chapter confirms, is also the most diverse and complex of America's newcomers because it includes individuals from Morocco to Indonesia. And, of course, 9/11 created a completely new dynamic. For this reason, the ethnography in this chapter may appear gloomy and even pessimistic, but it also highlights the greatest challenge posed to religious and racial relations in America today.

Yet this very community holds the key to better connections with the Muslim world. Unlike African American Muslims and converts, immigrants have links with their countries of origin in the Muslim world and therefore have the potential to play a vital role as bridge builders on behalf of America to that world. Unfortunately, too often the process works in reverse, as horror stories from the United States confirm in Muslim minds elsewhere that America does not care for Islam. If not for the vision of the Founding Fathers or for the sake of humanity, but for its own security, foreign policy, and diplomatic considerations, America needs to have a better understanding and appreciation of Muslim immigrants.

SIX

Muslim Converts:
Shame and Honor in a Time of Excess

RELIGIOUS CONVERSION IS a dramatic event in anyone's life, no less than it was for Saint Paul on the road to Damascus. It changes everything. Fashion photographer Nicole Queen of Dallas had arrived at just such a turning point, paradoxically, at the pinnacle of her career. She was standing next to Justin Timberlake, one of pop music's icons, with cameras flashing. The glare seemed to illuminate the world of vacuous celebrity Nicole was part of. Wasn't there more to life than this? At the suggestion of a Muslim friend, she watched motivational videos on YouTube and was impressed by Yusuf Estes, a white Muslim convert from Texas who was once a member of the Disciples of Christ Church. Shortly after, she converted to Islam.

One of the reasons for her conversion, Nicole explained, was the excessive behavior of women who appeared to be without shame or modesty, especially in front of a camera: "Girls took off their tops, exposed their breasts, they were making out with each other—and they aren't lesbians, but if a camera's there 'I'll do it if you put it on TV.' . . . Do you think parents are proud of that? . . . They want to show that stuff because that's what people want to see. How low can a girl go? That's what sells here. They know what everybody likes; everybody likes to see the lowest point that someone can go. People just want to make a dollar out of it; these are the morals of our nation, whether we want to face that or not."

Who Is Converting to Islam and Why?

Nicole's conversion touched a raw nerve in American society. While the idea of the clash of civilizations between Islam and the West is often cast in terms of theology and history, another area of contention is culture. People on both sides are zealous about defending their customs and traditions. It is in this context that the conversion of some 30,000 Americans, only a tiny fraction of the country's population of 300 million, assumes significance.[1] Matters are exacerbated for both sides because of the gender ratio of the converts, which stands at four females to one male.[2] In this chapter I explore what is attracting people in the West to Islam in spite of the controversy surrounding it, and why so many more women are converting than men. The subject is still largely uncharted, with few accurate statistics or extensive case studies.

Like African American converts, white and Latino converts are difficult to typify as mystics, modernists, and literalists. Appearances can be misleading. A woman in a hijab or a man with an orthodox beard quoting the Quran and speaking loudly on behalf of the ummah, or the worldwide Muslim community, may turn out to be a modernist or mystic, and not the suspected literalist. What does seem indisputable is that converts come to Islam with an open mind and invariably adhere to the text without the cultural baggage of immigrant Muslims, although they do carry over some of their own Western culture. Thus one might talk to a woman in a hijab and not be too surprised to hear about her favorite baseball team, movie, or TV show. These are committed Muslims but still profoundly American. Just as African Americans bring one kind of richness to the Islamic texture in America, white and Latino converts are bringing another.

Western converts to Islam have interested me ever since Roger Boase converted to Islam four decades ago when he married my sister Aisha after they met at Cambridge University. Roger found Islam through the guidance of the grand Sufi master, Sheikh Nazim, introduced in chapter 5. The sheikh gave him the name Abdul Wahhab, which means "servant of the one who gives." Roger is an example of not only a good Muslim but also an upstanding member of Western civilization. Roger's father was a distinguished academic, and he himself has become a renowned scholar of Muslim Spain. Converts such as Roger provide anthropologists with insights into two societies simultaneously: the one they seek to leave and the one they adopt.

For Westerners like Roger and Nicole, Islam is both a foreign and a familiar religion. They find in it the notion of God and the great prophets such as Abraham and Moses and see that Jesus and Mary are highly loved and revered figures. People also have some idea of Islam's contributions to art, architecture, and culture: they recognize the Taj Mahal as a Muslim monument and Ibn Arabi and Rumi as Muslim mystic poets. Islam's territory is therefore somewhat recognizable to the convert, and the leap to it not so forbidding.

Many American converts we interviewed are distressed by the soul-destroying materialism that dominates society and turn to Islam for a spiritual alternative. Some are attracted to the strongly developed sense of justice and compassion in Islam. Others are riding the unprecedented wave of curiosity and interest in Islam following the 9/11 attacks. Since then Islam has been very much in the public eye. Many imams told us that conversions went up after 9/11, and Quran sales skyrocketed.

Islam's clear-cut structure and boundaries appeal to many in search of order and discipline in their lives: it has fixed times for prayers, fasting, and festivals. It is unambiguous about the dangers of alcohol and drugs. It is a simple religion unencumbered by a complex theology centered on the Holy Trinity and Original Sin or a priesthood acting as interpreters of and intermediaries to God. Many are also attracted to the Islamic idea of the ummah, which by definition rejects racial and national barriers. Those searching for complete answers to their spiritual needs find Islam's holistic approach attractive and satisfactory. It offers a guide to every aspect of daily living, expecting the follower to be Muslim twenty-four hours a day, seven days a week. For many Americans, the idea of going to church once a week and being left to do whatever they please the rest of the time is spiritually unrewarding. Furthermore, they find Islam to be a religion of "balance": it seeks to keep the other world, deen, and this world, dunya, in a state of harmony and equilibrium.

Some are motivated by economic reasons, others by matrimonial ones. The intended Muslim spouse may insist on conversion before marriage, as in the case of Steve Ackroyd, a white Bostonian living in Silicon Valley and the husband of Amra Tareen (see chapter 5). Although a scholarly individual, Steve explained his conversion in one sentence: "You never know who you're going to fall in love with, and I fell in love with a Muslim." Steve needed to convert to Islam to marry Amra because Muslim societies are patrilineal, and the children are expected to follow the father in his religion and custom. The rules are more flexible for a Muslim man marrying a non-Muslim woman because the children would follow his religion in any case.

Muslims cherish these converts. When Pastor Rick Warren, founder of evangelical Saddleback Church in Lake Forest, California, and one of America's most recognized preachers, agreed to speak at the annual Islamic Society of North America (ISNA) conference in 2009, the organizers fielded three white converts to respond to him: Yusuf Islam, Hamza Yusuf, and Ingrid Mattson. Islam has come of age in the West, and its converts are playing a role as bridge builders.

White Female Converts

A sociological conundrum lies at the heart of American female conversion to Islam. Why should a woman who has every freedom available to her convert to Islam, known in the media as oppressive and cruel to women, and henceforth lead an alternative style of life? Alexis de Tocqueville gives us a clue to the answer. More impressed with American women than any others he had met in his travels, de Tocqueville wrote: "Nowhere is the girl more promptly and more completely left to herself." He believed this freedom empowered women: "Far from hiding the corruptions of the world from her, they wanted her to see them right away and to exert herself to flee them; and they would rather safeguard her honesty than respect her innocence too much."[3]

Although each story of conversion my team and I heard is unique and could only be understood in its specific context, the women have one thing in common: all were reacting to some aspect of American society. They had come of age in a time of unprecedented affluence and indulgence. Materialism and consumerism permeated society. Nothing represented the excess more than sexual promiscuity, which was not only widespread but was also reaching younger and younger people. Men and women prowled bars and clubs to pick up partners for one-night stands, relationships were reduced to momentary sexual acts, naked women were used in the media to sell products, pornography flourished like an out-of-control weed—all this and the frequently reported cases of child abuse had struck a nerve in these women. Perhaps it was an atavistic Christian memory of purity and virtue, perhaps plain common sense that was being awakened. Whatever the case, they found that in Islam notions of modesty, shame, and honor were not extinct.

The more these American women learned of Islam, the more they were attracted to it. As early as the seventh century, Muslim women could inherit property, initiate divorce proceedings, be poets and scholars, or lead armies or businesses. Besides, they could do all this with their sense of self and dignity intact. When asked three times the best shortcut to heaven, in each case the Prophet of Islam replied: "Paradise is at the feet of the mother." He was underlining for society the importance of being kind to and respecting women. Numerous verses in the Quran and other examples from the Prophet's life—the two sources that define Islam—reinforce the Prophet's saying about women.

In addition, converts found that Islamic role models were a perfect antidote to their predicament. The women of the Prophet's household—Khadija, Aisha, and Fatima—were strong and intelligent role models. Khadija, the first convert to Islam, was a widow and successful businesswoman. Her example illustrated that a woman did not have to compromise her modesty to be successful or happy. That is why several of our respondents had taken the name Khadija after conversion.

Becoming Muslim also means becoming a spokesperson for Islam, which constantly demands attention and answers to the questions people have about that religion. The role is both challenging and empowering. With their conversion, these women become cultural mediators between their new faith and their original community.

Women often dramatically proclaim their conversion by adopting the hijab or abayya. There is no concealing their transformation. Their clothing has become a recognizable symbol of Islam in the West. That is why women are easier to target than men and therefore bear the brunt of prejudices and stereotypes about Islam. The attacks are invariably couched in foul sexual language. The woman who converts is thought to have betrayed the community. By contrast, men who convert do not necessarily want to advertise their new faith. They continue to wear their regular clothes, and many prefer to use their original name. Apart from an occasional wispy beard, it is difficult to tell them apart from the rest of the population.

Nicole Queen

Nicole Queen, now wearing a black abayya after her conversion, applies her natural vivaciousness and confidence to explaining her new faith. We met her when she was assigned to photograph Hailey for a feature article in the Turkish daily *Zaman*. Hailey had been grappling with some of the issues that had troubled Nicole, and the two Dallas natives developed an immediate rapport. Both had been attractive "party girls" who had grown up in a permissive culture but were intelligent enough to observe that people in Dallas were obsessed with their looks and making money. "A soul-destroying black hole," Hailey called her hometown. The two reacted by finding comfort in other faiths: Nicole in Islam in 2006, and Hailey in Catholicism two years later. It was their way of saying "enough." Henceforth, they would draw moral boundaries around, and demand respect for, themselves.

Showing an American confidence in her Muslim identity, Nicole kept her own name after conversion, explaining that "Islam is my religion, but it's not my name." The Quran, she noted, nowhere commands people "to start changing their identity to mimic that of an Arab by taking on a Muslim name, which is really just an Arabic name. God wanted me to be born in America, to an American family, and I have an American name. My ethnic background is Caucasian. My family is Deep South on both sides; their generations are from Mississippi, Tennessee, and Louisiana. I am a southern 'white' girl who converted to Islam."

Nicole had had a difficult childhood. Her Baptist parents had been drug addicts, and she had grown up with different family members in small towns in Texas. When she was older, she left for New York to pursue her dream of becoming a fashion photographer and eventually returned to work and live in Dallas. In New York, she realized that women were dressing to attract the attention of men in order to feel accepted, and she hoped to find a different lifestyle in Dallas. But nothing changed. After a year of partying, drinking, and wearing clothes with "the look," she felt worn down: "When that's all your life is about, when those are the only kind of people you are around—greed, party, this whole lifestyle—after a while you start to see what people are like behind the mask. It's kind of scary. You don't want to be on the inside anymore. I kind of went into a transition, a pit where you hit the bottom."

Nicole vowed not to dress to please other people: "You can't do that, you can't show enough skin, you can't look good enough, so I'm not going to do it anymore." She also questioned the individual's relationship with God in Christianity. She felt that in Islam no one stood between God and herself. There was no need to explain one's sins to someone else and then have them passed on to God: "It's just you and God. I felt that before I had to create my own religion because everyone had something that I wasn't interested in; this religion was just you and God. I felt like it was what I needed in my life."

Wearing the abayya was the full symbolic act of conversion for Nicole and gave her a new self-confidence and self-respect, "like a nun" whom "everyone respects because she lives her entire life for God, in the way she dresses—she isn't showing anything of her body. They can't look at you as a piece of meat. I went to different places, to Starbucks or Walmart, wearing the hijab. It was so cool. Girls would say how pretty the scarf was, people felt like they had to compliment you because they knew that you were facing a challenge, that you were a little bit stronger than they were, that you took yourself out of the materialistic world." When people asked her why she started wearing the hijab, she had many reasons, but "the first one is God. . . . It would be a nightmare if I took it off."

While talking to Hailey as the two walked about in a Dallas mall, Nicole pointed to an advertisement for Guess jeans and said, "Look good, show your body while this guy puts his hands all over you—is that what you want?" This prompted her to raise a host of questions: "So where are the morals? Are we raising our daughters to think that 'I'm a jewel, that I need to cover myself up? Does the man I'm going to spend the rest of my life with deserve what everyone else hasn't seen yet?' Do they even have anything left to show their husbands when they get married that they didn't show Johnny at Starbucks or every bozo at Walmart?"

While Nicole found peace and a new meaning in Islam, she also faced a variety of challenges, not least from people who felt this local Texan had become an alien: "You kind of get angry because they are looking at you like you aren't one of them anymore. I don't understand that. If I was a Baptist and I switched over to Catholicism, Catholics live a different life. A true Catholic would dress differently, follow a different life, spend time at the church, and time at the school. Your life would change, you would think differently, but you wouldn't look like you are from another country. So people kind of accept you, but you're still an American. I changed my religion, I still believe in the same God, I still live by the same rules—do the right thing, live for God, don't be this menace to society. But Americans look at me like I'm not American anymore, and it hurts. I'm proud of who I am, I'm proud to be American. This is my land, this is what I love, and it hurts to feel like you don't belong."

Did Nicole think that she had given up something many young American girls dream of doing—being a photographer in New York, meeting celebrities in famous bars and clubs? If anything, she looked back on her past with a shudder of relief: "TV isn't real, nothing is real, and many of the people involved aren't real. It's a vicious circle where everyone is alone and they keep on living their lives for temporary satisfactions and temporary pleasure. It's self-indulgence." People like that cannot move forward, she said. "They just stay there," with no one to pull them out even though they want to get out: "They don't want that life, they are miserable, they are having divorces, they are having affairs, everything that can go wrong will, and you don't have anything to live for. You are never going to have enough money, you will never be beautiful enough, you won't have enough clothing, or you won't look as good. It's always going to be that way. It's not enough, you are never at the top and you will never be there, so why don't you just get out of the whirlpool, why not get out? . . . I think that

God is the only way to do that. That's why when people are at their worst they are saved by God."

Nicole is now happily married to a Jordanian and continues to practice her profession, although she is particular about what and who she will photograph in order to preserve her modesty. She spreads her message to others by using the social networking site MySpace to reach out to help people with Islam, life, and the challenge they are facing. Blogs on her page cover "about everything," including her transition and who she was before.

Nicole's conversion triggered a storm of controversy. She became an online sensation. One interview with her posted on YouTube has received more than a million hits and 55,000 comments. While Muslims were heartened that someone of her caliber had joined their beleaguered ranks, Nicole's countrymen were not so pleased. In the wake of 9/11, the conversion of a young, glamorous, white Christian woman from the South made Islam's challenge appear covert and insidious. It touched Americans in complex psychological ways that were not only religious but also racial. Her conversion had touched a nerve connected to the deepest fears of interracial sexual relations in American society. Many commentators made crude remarks and felt she had betrayed her white American inheritance in order to literally sleep with the "enemy."

A typical comment attacked her sexuality as well as her new religion: "Can't wait for her to release her 'girls beheading gone wild' video"; "hot radical islamic chicks cutting off the heads of the kicking screaming nonbelievers. sweet"; "she's a brainwashed cunt." The shock waves of her conversion crossed the Atlantic: "I am an Eastern European Christian. She said she was a Christian before? And she was drinking, night clubs, etc. Then let me tell you something. She wasn't a Christian. True Christians don't do that."

Meeting Nicole in Dallas, I did not have the impression of a woman under attack or pressure. On the contrary, she appeared remarkably poised and intelligent. She was proud to be a committed Muslim as well as an American. No one could take that away from her. It is well to remember that Nicole is a daughter of Texas, whose famous symbol is the Alamo, which stands for independence of spirit, strength of character, and fighting for one's beliefs.

Living in one of the freest societies in the world, Americans are free to choose their religion from the different denominations within Christianity to "lifestyle choices," which in turn range from New Age spiritualism to the green movement. As a result, about half of all Americans practice a religion outside the one in which they are born.[4] The test for the new Muslims would be in the future. Would Nicole assert her Western prerogative and abandon Islam to go on to some other faith, or would she remain, as Islam designates its followers, part of the faithful?

We met dozens of white females across America who became Muslim for reasons similar to those of Nicole. Some, like Suzie Smith, who had recently converted and asked Hailey that her real name be withheld, were less confident and articulate than Nicole. From a conservative Christian community in Nashville, Suzie has only told her devout Christian son, who thinks the greatest threat to America is "the Devil and sin." He supports his mother but finds it difficult, especially when he sees her wearing the hijab. He expressed Suzie's predicament bluntly: "I feel that she's worried that she's gonna be disowned, basically." Others like Kathy Zeitoun of New Orleans, the wife of Abdulrahman Zeitoun (see chapter 3), are determined to raise their children with proper respect for Islamic principles and have placed them in local Muslim schools to protect them from America's "corrupt culture." Because Kathy lives in New Orleans, she commented on Bourbon Street during Mardi Gras: "These women downtown, they'll go and they'll show their breasts for beads—for plastic and string, plastic and thread! Is the body not worth more than plastic and thread? Islam frees me. We have limits as Muslims. It's not oppression; it's respect for yourself."

Sheikha Fariha

We also encountered white women who converted for other than sociological reasons. In New York we called on Sheikha Fariha Fatima al-Jerrahi, a Sufi mystic who became a Muslim after a decade-long search for God. Whereas Nicole Queen, in her black Arab abayya, used Islam as a protective wall, keeping out the life she had rejected, Sheikha Fariha expanded the boundaries of Islam, including traditions of other faiths and absorbing her Americanness and Christianity into Sufism. She spoke in the language of universal mysticism, and it was impossible to tell where her American identity ended and her Islamic identity began.

In the mid-1960s the sheikha began feeling that the hierarchy and doctrines of her Catholic church obscured her ability to worship God. Ten years later, she took up studies under Sheikh Muzaffer Ozak in Istanbul, Turkey, becoming the first female leader of the Nur Ashki Jerrahi Sufi Order or, more correctly, the Halveti-Jerrahi Order of Dervishes.

When we visited her on a Thursday in the fall of 2008, the sheikha permitted us a private audience in her dressing room, where we sat on carpets, drank tea, and talked at length. With her back perfectly straight, she looked

Sheikha Fariha Fatima al-Jerrahi in her mosque in New York City talking with the team.
The sheikha is a convert who has brought a Western sense of feminism to her interpretation of
Islam, which follows the mystic path.

the picture of physical discipline. Being an American mystic, she had no
reservations about shaking hands with us and even embracing us. She was
modestly dressed in an eclectic ensemble, with a loose covering on her head
and a tie-dyed scarf around her shoulders and sleeves.

The sheikha brought a Western sense of feminist confidence to her
interpretation of mysticism. She prophesied a coming "feminine age of
Islam," noting that women were more for the "spirit" than the "letter of
the law" and "better at dialogue." And as Sufism emphasized the heart, not
the intellect, women were natural leaders in the movement. When asked
whether she would lead the prayers, as some women in the United States
wanted, she declined, "I don't feel that is my calling," but added, "I do lead
prayers when I am among dervishes."

Every time the sheikha referred to Isa, or Jesus, she added the title of
respect, hazrat. She called Jesus and the Prophet "brothers." She reminded
us that at the Kaaba in Mecca when Islam triumphed and some Muslims
wished to break the statues of Jesus and Mary because of the laws forbidding idolatry, the Prophet protected the images. Early Christians, she

noted, wept with emotion when they heard recitations from the Quran, and the mystics of both religions loved one another.

The sheikha's primary role model was the Prophet, followed by his daughter Fatima, his son-in-law Ali, and his two grandsons Hassan and Hussein. (Her name, Fatima, testifies to her devotion to the Prophet and his family.) Her greatest role model among the mystics was Sheikh Ibn Arabi, who said there are twenty-seven interpretations of the Quran, every one of them correct. Every letter of the Quran has a different meaning, she continued, making it an "infinite ocean." She rejoiced in the Western acceptance of scholarship, which allowed Ibn Arabi and Rumi to be welcomed as "great heroes of the heart."

Turning to relations between Islam and the West, she complained of the "ignorance on both sides." For its part, the Islamic ummah should embody the "light of mercy," she said, and when it fails to do so, it misrepresents the "light of the Prophet," so "we have to take primary responsibility." She talked of "infinite love," of everyone meeting in "one vast ocean," summing up her mystic advice in two sayings: "Let the soul fly to the Lord," and "Merge into unity."

She also spoke of the need to ask forgiveness for what had been done to Native Americans and African Americans. For the sheikha, American identity means "friendship, fundamental goodness, and creativeness." For me, the most interesting part of the evening related to the larger thesis of this book. When asked what the *Mayflower* meant, she described it as the "living Rumi": "It was an approach to God; it was love."

The sheikha's followers, disciples, and friends gathered once a week on Thursday night to perform the *dhikr,* or recitation of the names of God, and we joined some forty others representing a mixed ethnic and religious background. There were Zen Buddhists, many Jews, and some Christians.

When we moved to a larger room where the other visitors joined us after we interviewed her, the sheihka was careful to preserve a hierarchy in the seating, placing us in the inner ring closest to her. A young white woman arrived midway into the dhikr and was warmly embraced by the sheihka. It was difficult not to notice her outfit, which consisted of a robe that barely concealed a silk tank top and silk shorts and allowed an ample view of her legs. She also wore a red alpine hat. We chanted the wondrous names of God, sitting, kneeling, and standing. We also chanted in praise of the Prophet.

Her repetition of the phrase "*la ilaha il allah* (there is no God but God)" floated over the expectant crowd, softly at first, and then more strongly as people joined in. The sheikha broke off into "AL-lah, AL-lah, AL-lah."

The effect was hypnotic and intoxicating. After about thirty minutes, she stood up and asked everyone to hold hands, continue chanting, and rotate in a circle.

Although the sheikha constantly referred to the Prophet of Islam, the eclectic and syncretic nature of the evening was almost neutral to Islam itself. "It didn't feel Muslim at all," said Jonathan, somewhat like a disgruntled customer on the verge of demanding his money back. After all, he was accustomed to spending late hours in Salafi mosques discussing the Quran and the boundaries of faith with earnest bearded men inspired by Saudi texts.

The American Hijab

American women have taken to the veil like ducks to water for it makes them feel, as several told us, "special." Men do not leer at them, and even treat them with respect, as Nicole Queen remarked. They no longer feel like "a piece of meat." But wearing the hijab is not easy; it evokes friction and anger. It is more than a foreign mode of dress. It reminds most Americans of a different, even hostile, world that threatens their way of life. Many think that women who wear the hijab are oppressed. Thus the hijab represents a critique of social behavior for Americans as much as a challenge.

Yet millions of Muslim women who strongly identify with Islam cover themselves modestly without wearing the hijab. Three generations in my own family—my mother, wife, and daughter—do not wear the hijab. But for Muslim converts, this covering is an important symbol not only of their wish to identify with what they see as the most literal expression of modesty in Islam but also of their need to assert this new identity.

Many white female converts told us of their struggles wearing a simple article of clothing that remains so controversial in American culture. At Houston's Masjid-ul-Mumineen, a white female convert in her thirties, the daughter of an oil company vice president, said no one bothered her at her office job until she began wearing the hijab. Then everything changed. Management offered to allow her to resign, but she refused. Her hours were drastically cut, and still she stayed on, finding unobtrusive places to pray. When management found out she was praying in a closet, they took away the key. But today, she said, "*Mashallah,* by the grace of God, I work for a wonderful company that lets me pray."

Ingrid Mattson, first female head of ISNA, the largest Islamic organization in North America, gives those who meet her the impression of a caring nun with her hijab and low-key, attentive manner. Originally from

Canada, Ingrid became a prominent figure in Islamic studies in America and converted to Islam. Reading the Quran, she said, "was like connecting with God." After converting, Ingrid did not feel it was necessary to adopt the hijab, but her work with Afghan refugees in Pakistan persuaded her to do so, to "fit in with the culture." There she experienced the benefits of the head covering: it "took away undertones of sexual tension," and many things were left unspoken in her presence that previously would have been expressed. The hijab released her from the pressure of attention. A leader in America's Muslim community, Ingrid now serves as a role model for many young Muslim women, as confirmed by our questionnaires.

White Male Converts

The road to Islam for Sheikh Hamza Yusuf started from the site of a near-fatal car accident when he was a young man. It got him thinking about religion, life, and mortality: "I really wanted to look at all these different religions and see which one had the most convincing arguments. Islam was like the last on my list, but when I did get there finally, it just resonated in a way that I think led to my conversion and ultimately taking it very seriously and studying it." Initially, part of the reason was to make sure he did not make a mistake: "In Californian culture, especially, we're allowed to dabble, so there are a lot of dabblers. People will try something out, see how it fits, but the more I studied, I think, the stronger my faith got. It didn't get less, which was the case with Christianity. Christianity caused a crisis for me."

The sheikh was baptized and served as an altar boy in the Greek Orthodox Church. His great-grandfather built the first Orthodox Church west of Chicago, in San Francisco. Although his father was a devout Catholic, Hamza was encouraged to be open-minded, his mother making it clear that "religion is largely arbitrary . . . that people generally follow religions of the families that they are born into, and there's something very arbitrary about that. That if I was born in Sri Lanka I would be a Buddhist or a Hindu. So that really struck me. Heidegger calls it thrownness. You are kind of a historical product and most people don't ever challenge their thrownness, the fact that they're just thrown into an environment that determines how they view the world, what they think, and how they worship."

Asked about his family's reaction to his conversion, the sheikh thought his mother was very accepting, perhaps because his older sister had married a Jewish man and converted to Judaism. His mother's uncle, George Fields, who had opened up a metaphysical bookstore in San Francisco in 1932, was also very interested in Buddhism, Sufism, and Gurdjieff's Fourth Way. His

Sheikh Hamza Yusuf, a Muslim convert and leader in the American Muslim community, hosts a dinner in traditional Arab style. Born a Greek American, Hamza was raised and lives in the San Francisco area where he hosted the team.

father, on the other hand, seemed "very perplexed by it; bemused is probably a better word. I think that he had the hardest time with it. But he has of late begun to study [Abu Hamid Al-] Ghazali and got very impressed. Because my father loves Thomas Aquinas and he saw a film that I was involved in about Ghazali, he started reading him in translation. Now he's really convinced that Ghazali is one of the great religious thinkers of all time."

Cat Stevens Becomes Yusuf Islam

Yusuf Islam also converted because of a near-fatal event in his life. Then known as Cat Stevens, he had gone swimming in the Pacific Ocean. Close to drowning, he felt the only thing saving him was a divine power, which did so for a purpose. Even before his swim in California, Yusuf was struggling with the greed, competitiveness, and frustration permeating the music world. A child of the 1960s—when drugs, alcohol, and sex were freely available, especially to a pop star—Yusuf admitted to Alan Yentob in a 2009 BBC documentary on his life called "The Artist Formerly Known as Cat Stevens," "I indulged as much as I could."

Once he became a Muslim, Cat chose the name Yusuf, Arabic for Joseph. Like himself, Yusuf in the Quran had faced immense challenges in his life and in the end survived because of his faith. Because Yusuf Islam associated his guitars with his previous life, he decided to give them away and never perform again, but he agreed to one last farewell concert as Cat Stevens in London's Wembley Stadium in November 1979. Sealing his conversion to Islam, the concert caused almost as much tumult as Ayatollah Khomeini's overthrow of the shah in Iran's Islamic revolution that same year. Commentators were scathing in their criticism of Yusuf and the religion that attracted him. Music lovers were distressed that a major talent had been forever lost.

The news of Yusuf's conversion was widely reported in the Muslim world, making him an instant celebrity from Morocco to Malaysia. Kings, prime ministers, and students wanted to meet him. He found a new and important role talking to a different audience, but it had also turned him into a lamb surrounded by zealous Muslim wolves eager to pounce on him in the cause of their particular Islamic ideology. The Saudis pulled him in one direction, emphasizing the literalist tradition of Islam, demanding that he disavow music of any kind because God disapproves of music. The Iranians pulled him in another direction, demanding in their exuberance that all Muslims fall in line behind their revolution that had shaken the world. When Ayatollah Khomeini issued the fatwa, or pronouncement, condemning Salman Rushdie to death, many Iranians insisted that other Muslims demonstrate their support for such edicts. Confused, Yusuf Islam made statements that seemed to imply he approved of the fatwa against Rushdie.

It was about this time that Yusuf Islam visited me in Cambridge. I was struck by the gentility of his soul but surprised to see how he conducted himself. He had driven up in a van with his daughters, who were all wrapped up in white sheets and crammed into the back, which had no seats. As our party walked into the University Centre for lunch, he created a minor sensation with his white Muslim clothes and long, straggly beard— greeted by many with a sly look and the nudging of elbows. I hoped that he would find his way back to his true self.

Yusuf's emphatic rejection of his previous identity, his strident association with a hard-line Islam in the early days after his conversion, and his appearance convinced many in the West that he was lost to Islamic fundamentalism. I suspect this impression was what landed him on the lists of officials charged with ensuring the security of the United States. In September 2004, on a flight from London to the United States to meet the singer Dolly Parton, the security agencies struck. The flight was diverted to Canada, and Yusuf was escorted off the plane and put on the next flight back to London. U.S. intelligence had construed his recording session as a "threat" to national security.

Yusuf has now gone back to his music. He admits that abandoning a gift from God may not have been a wise decision in the first place. He uses the power of his music to bring people of all religions together. His concerts prove that he is as popular as ever, with stars like Paul McCartney happy to share the stage with him.

The Philosophical Allure of Text-Based Islam

The reasons why most white males convert to Islam are rarely as dramatic as those of Hamza Yusuf and Yusuf Islam. Most are mainly searching for universal truths through intuition, scholarship, and reason. The exceptions to this trend, such as John Walker Lindh and Adam Gadahn, young men searching for identity who took to the hills of Afghanistan to fight along-side the Taliban against their own country, are few and far between.[5] Even more rare are white female converts like the blue-eyed and blonde Colleen LaRose, originally from Texas, who called herself "Jihad Jane" and was "desperate to do something somehow to help" the suffering Muslim people.

An earlier generation of white male converts came to Islam via the same path as those today. One of America's leading journalists at the end of the nineteenth century, the Scots-Irish Alexander Russell Webb, became interested in Islam while serving as U.S. consul to the Philippines in 1887. He had moved gradually from his Presbyterian faith to Buddhism and finally to Islam, which he felt was an ideal religion for Americans in that it allowed them to fulfill their ideals of liberty and equality. Speaking out against the mob violence and lynchings of the period, Webb observed such acts would be "impossible" in Muslim societies and predicted that in America Islam would "ultimately work a revolution in our social system."[6] He was greatly influenced by the Aligarh school of Islam, the writings of Sir Sayyed Ahmad Khan, and the tales of Muslim Spain told by Washington Irving.

Webb founded the first Muslim institution in the United States, the American Mission, and became the main spokesman for Islam in America, lecturing to prominent Americans such as Mark Twain. Webb also wrote many books intended to introduce Islam to Americans, including *Islam in*

America, started the first Islamic press in the country, opened a mosque on Broadway in New York City, published a journal entitled the *Moslem World,* and served as Islam's representative at the 1893 World's Parliament of Religions in Chicago.[7] The Turkish government appointed Webb its honorary consul general in New York in 1901 and honored him with two Ottoman medals of merit.

Other Westerners drawn to Islam include British Shakespearean scholar Martin Lings, who wrote a widely acclaimed biography of the Prophet. Muslims consider it to be one of the most authentic representations of the Prophet and early Islam. Another was Muhammad Asad, born Leopold Weiss in what was then the Austro-Hungarian Empire and descended from a long line of rabbis. Asad served as one of the first Pakistani ambassadors to the United Nations and is also known for his translation of the Quran, which is still widely read. Britain's Marmaduke Pickthall published a translation as well, considered a classic for the beauty of its language. Among his admirers were literary giants D. H. Lawrence, H. G. Wells, and E. M. Forster.

Johann Wolfgang von Goethe, one of the most celebrated intellectuals in the history of the West, who could include among his fans Darwin, Nietzsche, Mozart, Beethoven, and Napoleon, was also fascinated by Islam, especially by Rumi and Hafiz. Goethe's famous collection of poems, *West-östlicher Diwan* (West-East Divan), is a declaration of love for the Prophet of Islam. In the poem "Mahomet's Song," from an unfinished opus to the Prophet, Goethe wrote of the Prophet's mission to unite all the peoples of the world of all races and ethnicities into a "timeless mighty ocean."[8] There was "no doubt" in Goethe's mind that "in Islam we all live and die," and he did "not reject the suspicion" that he might himself "be a Muslim."

In America, scholar T. B. Irving also became absorbed in Islam and converted in 1952, taking the name Al-Hajj Ta'lim Ali Abu Nasr. Born in Ontario, Canada, in 1914, Irving was educated at the University of Toronto and received a Ph.D. in Near East Studies at Princeton University in 1940. He became particularly concerned about Muslim youth and devoted his time to producing a readable version of the Quran for American Muslims. His translation was finally published in 1985, the first American version of the Quran.

Another Irving drawn to Islam even earlier was Washington Irving, who lived in the early part of the nineteenth century and was probably the first major internationally known literary figure from the United States, writing stories including "Rip Van Winkle" and "The Legend of Sleepy Hollow."

As far as is known, he did not convert to Islam but clearly had a soft spot for the religion, writing a biography of the Prophet Muhammad.

Intellectual reasons were not the sole motivation for male conversion, however. In a San Diego Salafi mosque, Jonathan and Frankie interviewed a white male convert in his twenties "with tattoos covering his body" who cited sociological reasons. A former drug user, he had been attracted to Islam by the discipline it brought into his life, which was "out of control." Without Islam, he would "still be using drugs." Coming to the mosque five times a day gave him "discipline" and kept him "out of trouble." Prayers in the morning and at night took him to the mosque with other believers, so he was no longer sitting in his apartment "with nothing to do." Islam was unlike Christianity, he believed, in that "it sets out a process for the entire day, every day." In Christianity, "you don't actually follow anything; you just say you're a Christian."

Latino Converts

I was first alerted to the existence of Latin American Muslim converts when Zeenat and I visited Monterrey, Mexico, in 2007. Disembarking from the plane, we were surprised to see a small group of distinctly Muslim-looking people waving excitedly at us, among them a woman in a hijab and men with beards. They were welcoming us at the airport on behalf of the Council for a Parliament of the World's Religions, which was holding its annual conference in Mexico, and we quickly became friends. Over the next few days, I discovered that Mexico is home to a number of committed Muslims. The woman complained about being called a terrorist because of the way she dressed, and I realized that whether immigrant, white, or Latino converts, Muslims faced equal prejudice on the American continent.

Remembering Andalusia

Statistics on Latino converts to Islam in the United States are hard to come by, but it is estimated that there are some 200,000, or about 3 percent of American Muslims, and that women account for the majority of Latino converts.[9] Our team met and interviewed Latino converts in Texas, California, and Florida, a population that is not given much attention by either Muslims or Americans in general. Because Latinos form the largest minority in the United States, with some 50 million people, and one of four Americans by the middle of this century will be Latino, Latino Muslim converts will be playing an influential role in the future in bringing better understanding for Islam.

Latinos face similar challenges as whites, but their cultural background is different. While some women we interviewed cited sociological "push" factors having to do with shame and honor—for instance, a Colombian female Muslim in Miami mentioned the "machismo" of the Latino culture—most Latino converts, both men and women, came to Islam in search of a deeper meaning to life than they felt their Catholic faith could give them. Many women considered becoming nuns before they converted. When asked about American identity, they replied that they loved America because this was where they discovered Islam. All spoke about Islam with a religious fervor, and nearly all the women wore the hijab. Many of the bilingual converts said they intentionally spoke Spanish in public to let Latinos as well as mainstream Americans know they are Latino and Muslim, and proud to be both.

Could this Latino pride in Islam have a distant connection with Muslim Spain? I wondered how much of Muslim culture the Spaniards brought to the Americas, and how much of their memories of Islam remained, if in the subconscious. Andalusía, the heart of Muslim Spain, had a culture in which Jews, Christians, and Muslims flourished together and created impressive art, architecture, and literature.

Khadija Rivera

I hoped to find some answers in my meeting in 2009 with Khadija Rivera, a prominent Puerto Rican convert, who was fifty-nine years old. I asked Khadija why Latinos in particular would be so comfortable with Islam. Latino converts, she felt, look at their roots, which are embedded in Islamic history in Granada, Cordova, Seville, and Andalusía: "For 700 hundred years it was ruled by Muslims, and people coexisted in this time." She pointed out that "Spanish family life is very strong, and since it is so strong in Islam, it's not something alien. It's not so much a religion as a way of life because it's from the morning until night. I think it is very important to see that when we come to Islam, there is not a major difference." Khadija felt the family was not as strong as it used to be in American society, whereas Latinos "are always very close-knit. I think what's great about being a Muslim in America is that we try to keep that extended family a part of us. It's part of our way of life, to take care of our grandparents and our uncles and our cousins."

Khadija had driven across the state of Florida to meet us in Miami after an exhausting flight from the United Arab Emirates, where she had been received with dignity and even affection. Dressed in traditional Arab attire with a full black abayya, she spoke of her conversion with animation and cheerfully said that she had taken the name of the Prophet's wife. With a fiery gleam in her eyes, she recounted the days after 9/11 when people spat at her and pulled her hijab off. Her colleagues were so rude that she had to leave Miami. This did not deter Khadija from proclaiming her identity: "Many women were encouraged to take off their veils for safety, but I refused. I saw it as a sign of defeat. But I didn't do anything; none of the people I knew had anything to do with what was going on. So I felt like it was sort of a challenge."

Born and raised in Puerto Rico, Khadija was very spiritual growing up and even thought about becoming a nun. She was always searching for a deeper meaning in life. In the 1970s she went to the New York Institute of Technology and was introduced to all of the liberal ideas of the day, yet still felt drawn to God, no matter how much she denied Him. She said she would pray, "'God, oh God, help me with this.' There was always God, even though I said, 'Oh I don't believe in God. I don't believe in the statues.' I did everything thinking it was the right path, but that search was over with Islam because tranquility was found when I came to Islam."

Khadija converted in the early 1980s just after college. She married an Egyptian and had three children with him, divorcing in 1997. Her two older children are Christian, she said. She raised her children in the American style and school system while still trying to teach them Islamic values, but "they are not as devout as I would wish them to be." She finds that they are too steeped in American culture, but "they do pray, they do go to the mosque, and they do fast." But life in America still poses problems: "Either Muslims can isolate themselves and raise their children as proper Muslims, or they can acculturate to a certain degree, but they are going to have to still work with the child very hard on Islam. And what happens is they get to be either Salafi or like the peaceful Pakistani brothers who are Tabligh. In the Muslim world I was able to learn a middle way. Islam is not a fanatical religion. I think it brings dignity, self-esteem, honor, a sense of humility that is not spiteful or boastful, but it brings you to realizing who you really are. I am very comfortable with myself. I know who I am, and I think that Islam brings that to us. The sense of why we are here, what is coming afterward, the hereafter is very important in my life."

She also found that immigrant Muslims from South Asia and the Middle East have "a little arrogance" in their criticism of American Muslims:

"Someone will tell me, 'That's *haram*, which means sinful. I mean what made them the authority? Did they read this? Did they study this? What is the root of this, or is it because they were born into the culture and they believe this is it, you know? So I decided I need to read and study and go overseas and ask questions, not just read the books. I do think we tend to say, 'This is what I do in Pakistan' or 'This is what I do in Arab countries,' but we need to know what is correct." Because Khadija felt that the national Muslim organizations "don't understand Latinos," she decided to found a national Latino Muslim women's outreach group, Piedad (meaning piety), established in 1988.

The organization has three missions, she explained. "One is *dawah*, or outreach, to Latinos and women, meaning that women can be American also and be with us." A second is "dawah training either for us or the community. The third is community service, and that's where we feed the homeless, do interfaith work, and do a lot of work for the community, whether volunteering for the mosque or the school. We are very much intertwined in the community, so that sometimes you don't know where each ends, which is where we want it to be." Later in the same year that we had met her, we learned of Khadija's sad and unexpected demise. A courageous American leader had passed away and we mourned for her.

Latinos converting to Islam are also reflecting the crisis in their own community. We glimpsed some of the problems in Riverside, California, at the Arlington Regional Learning Center. There we met Latino youth who were gang members or were in trouble with the law. After addressing a class, I called for questions. As the team passed out our questionnaires, Alex, a seventeen-year-old half Mexican and half Native American asked Hailey if she had "any kids." Hailey replied that she was still too young and asked him the same question. "One-and-a-half months, a girl," Alex said with pride. As for his daughter's mother, "Oh my baby mama? No, I don't care about her." His friend behind him made a joke to which Alex replied, "Yeah man, you can have her!" Taken aback, Hailey rebuked Alex, "The mother of your child? You are just going to leave her like that?" Alex's friend jumped in with, "Yeah, it's America, land of the free. We can do whatever we want!"

The Cuban Muslims of Miami

At the local Council on American-Islamic Relations (CAIR) office in Miami, an American city with a majority Cuban population, Frankie and Craig met a group of Cuban Muslims eager to talk about their Islamic faith. Yahya Rivero, a dark-skinned Cuban in his mid-twenties with a small beard and black skullcap, discovered Islam in a Miami high school after he developed an infatuation for a Muslim girl in a hijab. He went online to start learning about Islam, where he came across the work of Malcolm X, which "really caught my attention." Rivero had taken his *shahada* (declaration of belief) just before his conversation with the team. His family had been expelled from Cuba by Fidel Castro in 1980 and joined a mass exodus of Cubans to the United States. Cubans of this generation had experienced a "loss of religion," focusing instead on "society and politics" because of Castro's revolution.

Rivero was finding that his Catholic faith did not satisfy him. It seemed "weird" that Catholicism had multiple gods in the Trinity, or "idol worshiping. . . . It's been a discomfort for me since I was young, like 'Pray to the saint for this particular thing, or another saint for something else.' I always told myself, 'This cannot be true.'" The more Rivero learned about Islam, the more he felt drawn to it, especially its way of prayer: "It wasn't . . . about just putting their hands together, but it was *bowing* to your Lord. It really touched me. I started attending this mosque in Miami. I was going for a while, for a year or so. I was a little hesitant to take my shahada, but finally something told me to just do it. I don't know what I was waiting for. My wife, she did it two or three days after I did. She's Cuban as well. There was just something about the shahada, there is no God but Allah, saying there is only one God. I just felt that in my heart."

Rivero instinctively took to Islam, he said, because of the similarities between Cuban and Muslim culture. In both cultures, for example, "men are supposed to take care of their wives and treat them well." Yet his Cuban family did not respond in a rational way, and "totally freaked out" and "thought Islam meant terror." Much of the friction, he said, had to do with cultural matters like food, which is very important for Cubans: "You can imagine telling a Cuban that you don't eat pork when that's all they cook. They even offered me a pig leg once. Cuban bread is made with pig lard, even the frosting on cakes!" Yet his family has now "accepted" the new Muslim-Cuban-American family he has begun.

In contrast to the recently converted Rivero, Roraima Aisha Kanar had been Muslim for thirty-three years. Her father was a general in Batista's army, which was defeated by Castro during the 1959 revolution. She got a job in Miami working in the airline industry, where she met several people from Saudi Arabia and Syria who piqued her interest in Islam. She was impressed by their "kindness, hospitality, and the love I would feel when I visited them in their countries." Like Rivero, she had a strong Catholic background, and like Khadija she dreamed of becoming a nun: "I was a very devout Catholic and went to a Catholic school, a nuns' school, until twelfth grade. I loved God and I wanted to serve God, but I wanted to be a nun, and my mother freaked out because she wanted me to have children, and nuns can't have children. So then I told her I wanted to be a missionary in Africa, which was worse. I talked to my friends about it, and they gave me a Quran and I started reading. In Catholic school we learned about every religion you can think of in theology class, but never Islam. I thought it was like Buddhist or Hindu or something strange, because we knew nothing. But once I started reading, I saw it was just our Christian faith from before, or even the Jewish faith, taken to a higher level. It was bringing all the prophets together, all the teachings. I loved the Quran, I couldn't put it down once I started reading it. And here I am thirty-three years later."

In Catholicism, she said, praying is not part of one's daily life. "You just go to church on Sunday and pray to someone when you want something. That's as far as it goes." But in Islam, any act, large or small, even giving someone a glass of water, is accompanied by the word *bismillah,* in the name of God, "which means you're doing it for His sake and His pleasure is what you're seeking. It's out of this world—it's such a rush to feel that."

Like Rivero, Kanar hoped her family would see the similarities she saw between her life as a Cuban Catholic and as a Cuban Muslim. Coming from a strict military family that did not like her to dress improperly or wear skimpy clothes, she thought her new way of life would make them happy, but it was very difficult: "My mother always told me I would go back to being one of them, and thank God I didn't. Once I got married and had children, she understood the happiness and respect I had. I didn't know the value of these things until I became a Muslim. The example I was setting as a mother and a daughter, I think before she died my mother finally realized how much I had grown closer to God. I tried to get her to become Muslim, but she said she was too old to change, which is very Cuban."

Kanar works in what she called "corporate America" for a Jewish-owned company that specializes in landing gear for airplanes. She says she has a good relationship with everyone at work and does not have problems wearing the hijab: "My coworkers respect me so much, and it feels so good to know that you are respected as a person, not for what gender you are."

LALMA

While in Los Angeles, the team spent a day at the Omar ibn al-Khattab Mosque talking to Muslim Latinos who belonged to the largest Latino

Muslim organization on the West Coast, the Los Angeles Latino Muslim Association (LALMA), founded in 1999. Madeeha interviewed LALMA's president, Marta Khadija Galedary, who identified herself as a "Mexican-born American Muslim now." She came to the United States in 1982 and converted to Islam in the same year. American identity, she responded enthusiastically, "is very important to me. I am American, I'm Mexican and a Muslim. The three identities in one, let's say. It's like asking who you love more, your mother or your father. I identify myself as an American because this country has given me the freedom to practice Islam. And I'm Mexican because of my skin color, my features—that's never going to go away. And I'm Muslim because now I pray more and I fast more. That makes my identity."

Marta explained the establishment of LALMA as a "natural phenomenon," arising because of the lack of information about Islam in Spanish. With probably 48 percent or more of Latinos speaking only Spanish, she noted, there was a real need for someone who could talk to them about Islam in the Spanish language. Since its founding, LALMA has held classes for about two hours every Sunday "to promote the understanding about Islam among the Hispanic community, so that we counteract the Islamophobia that is going on right now, especially after 9/11."

Relations between LALMA and other Muslim groups, including the Islamic Society of Orange County, have been good. Since 2001 LALMA has also been doing interfaith work with Latino Catholics through the Archdiocese of Los Angeles. Because of the confusion surrounding a religion that purportedly "sent to heaven somebody who's going to kill innocent people," the archdiocese contacted the Islamic Center of Southern California, asking if someone could talk to its parishioners about Islam in the Spanish language. "So we sat down with them for eight hours," said Marta, and "since then we go every year when they have their special biblical studies, for they include a section about Islam. And we have done the same thing with the United Methodist Church. These are the two Hispanic non-Muslim communities that we have dialogue with. We open the doors to the Hispanic neighborhood, particularly every year during Ramadan celebrations. We talk to them about the meaning of Ramadan, the meaning of fasting during Ramadan."

Marta first learned about Islam in the United Kingdom while studying there and converted not long afterward. The decision greatly upset her family, especially her mother, for little was known about Islam in her community at the time. "But something very interesting happened," recounted Marta. Her mother, a very devout Catholic, went to a priest in a small town southwest of Mexico City and asked, "Father, my daughter says she is a Muslim—what does that mean?" The priest replied, "Don't worry about your daughter. She is on the right path. Islam is a very old religion." The priest did not go into more detail but certainly had an understanding of Islam, according to Marta. "The priests study comparative religion, and they study Islam also. But his answer gave my mother peace in her heart that I was not following some kind of cult. So that was a major discovery that my mother had. After that when I visited Mexico everything was fine, thanks to this priest that opened her eyes and her heart."

While Madeeha interviewed LALMA's president, Hailey talked to Silvia Navela, a middle-aged woman from Guatemala living in Los Angeles. Speaking in Spanish, Silvia said she had married a Moroccan but chose not to convert and instead pressured him to convert to Catholicism. Yet she did convert to Islam after asking the Prophet Muhammad for his help following a tragedy in her country, and she believed he gave her the help she had asked for. Feeling ashamed, she told her husband, "This is what happened. I need the road of Islam." He told her to go to a mosque, find out more, and when she began looking for more information, she met Marta. She then studied Islam for a year in America and during that year took the shahada.

Arabs "confuse the religion and culture a lot," whereas Silvia sees more of "the reality of the Quran," says her husband, who was born a Muslim but feels she knows more about Islam than he does. Silvia wears the hijab only in the mosque, she explained, "as the hijab is cultural and not religious. It's not embarrassment. It's that it is in your heart . . . and you should not confuse religion and culture."

Silvia is contented to be in America, which she admires for its opportunities and openness for everyone: "The Americans are good people. They work hard. They don't abuse their workers. The pay is good. Americans are good. My profession is 'babysitting' for a Jewish American family. They know I'm a Muslim, but I always have said that I don't confuse my work with my religion. And I respect their religion."

Hailey also interviewed Antonia Descorcia in Spanish, a Mexican who has lived in the United States for eight years. Like Silvia, she is married to a Muslim, in this case an Algerian, and has three children. But unlike Silvia, Antonia converted before meeting her husband. In America, she said, she is grateful she can learn about Islam "more fully than in Mexico." The rest of Antonia's family is Catholic.

Antonia came to Islam when she found herself alone in the United States following the death of her father and met a Muslim woman. Although she had the "impression" that American identity was "a culture of whites"—which she described using the Spanish slang guero—in "reality America is something very multicultural in languages and ways." In her case, her children are American but have Mexican and Arab blood. "America has opened its doors to everyone in many situations," she noted, even to people without education, but she saw perhaps too much materialism here: "It's all fast, fast, fast, and there's no time to take a rest with your family to breathe a bit. And enjoy life. It's all run, run, run."

Antonia also felt Americans see the worst in Hispanic immigrants and do not take time to understand their culture: "I'm an immigrant, and I can say the immigrants have a wonderful culture that is very centered around the family." She also finds America "declining in its brotherhood," which perhaps never existed because the culture has its "higher and lower" levels and divisions between religions and races. When she sees conflict, as with gangs in her neighborhood, she tries to teach them to respect others, "to be humble and not see differences in trivial things like clothes. And if we have something to give another, we should help."

The Perception of Islam in the Latino Community

Latino converts have to deal with pressure and prejudice from two cultures: that of mainstream America and that of their native background, be it Mexican, Cuban, or some other kind. Eddie Jose Sin Cione, a young Dominican Muslim and son of a Major League Baseball player, summed up the problem when we met him in Miami: "There is a lack of information, period, in the Spanish language media about Islam. Most Latin families have children who are English-speaking, who will watch English news. A lot of the ideas with reference to Islam among Latinos come from the English media or are communicated by English-speaking friends who watch that media and communicate those ideas to Spanish speakers. But there really is a dead silence in the Spanish media about Islam."

Indeed, many Latinos we interviewed were bemused when asked about such an alien subject as Islam. A young Mexican woman working at a Schlotzsky's deli in Austin, Texas, told Frankie she had "no idea" what Islam is. In Los Angeles, a Latino high school student asked me if I, as a Muslim, "worshipped rats." Given the widespread indifference and hostility to Islam, many Muslim converts even had difficulty communicating their new faith to their families.

For converts like Luz Abulkheir, a forty-four-year-old Colombian woman wearing the hijab, however, Latino perceptions of Islam are driven in part by their situation in America. They arrive with the idea of making money, and are busy with that: "Latinos don't think here in America. They are concerned with entertainment and paying the mortgage, credit cards, and banks. So knowledge is set aside. They don't want to learn, they don't want to see what is happening on the other side of the world."

Abulkheir, who defined the "war on terror" as a "war on Islam," blamed the perception of Islam on "the Jews" who "own the networks" and "scare people," influencing the Latinos who do seek knowledge about the religion: "This is something that nobody talks about. Last week they had a pro-Israel rally in South Florida. They had a Christian Latino lady, hardly speaking English, saying that 'I am a Christian, I am here for Israel because Israel is the people of God.' I was thinking, 'Come on, Muslims are not people of God?' People have no knowledge whatsoever. How can people who are so in love with Jesus come to a rally to support Israel? How come the Latino Christians support people who don't recognize Jesus to kill people that do believe in Jesus and respect Jesus? It doesn't make sense to me."

Looking for Shame and Honor in American Society

Because concepts of shame and honor seem to be so important in the conversion of so many white and Latino converts to Islam, it is necessary to discuss these elusive notions here. Shame and honor evoke strong feelings among Muslims, especially those living in countries with a strong tribal tradition, from West Africa to Central Asia. Shameful behavior leads to a loss of honor in both men and women, which can damage the reputation of the individuals concerned and that of their extended families. These concepts are tied to the Quranic notion of modesty but in society are interpreted to mean the dress, appearance, and actions of women. That is why moral and cultural boundaries are so important in Muslim society.

Khushal Khan Khattak, one of Pashto's most celebrated poets, wrote: "Honor, the very word drives me insane with passion." In the extreme, this passion has led to the notorious honor killings, which are unacceptable in Islamic law and modern Islamic societies. These brutal actions are an expression of a distorted, almost obsessive desire to maintain form and decorum. Muslim communities in America are not immune, as was evident in the 2008 slaying of two teenage girls by their Egyptian father in Texas because he thought they had compromised the family's honor.

Muslims see America as they do because their notions of shame and honor are fundamental to their very social, religious, and psychological being. When McDonald's and the Marriot Hotel are bombed in Pakistan, when streets in Indonesia are flooded with protestors infuriated by the local publication of *Playboy,* when nightclubs in Bali are blown up—these acts are partly an expression of anger directed at the immorality Muslims see in American culture and the threat it poses to their local societies. For Muslims, a society without shame and honor is dangerously hollow as it lacks a moral foundation.

Americans, on the other hand, see concepts of shame and honor differently. The majority we met on our journey looked puzzled as to what we meant. Some found the concepts quite alien, as reflected in one suggestion that wars in the Muslim world might be won by introducing "titty bars" so Muslims would appreciate American culture. American society not only consists of a vast array of communities but is constantly changing its definitions of these very concepts. For one person, shame and honor may be linked to women's sexual behavior, for another it means hard and honest work, for yet another a soldier's duty abroad. American soldiers are widely believed to be upholding and embodying the honor of the nation. As we were departing from Omaha to fly back to Washington, several soldiers got off the plane we were about to board and the entire terminal broke out in applause, men took off their hats, and women put their hands to their hearts. After the opening night of my play, *Waziristan to Washington,* at Theater J in Washington, D.C., March 2009, the audience broke into spontaneous applause when they learned that a group of army officers from the Old Guard regiment based in Arlington, Virginia, was among them.

At a White House meeting during the Bush administration, I was called in with other so-called experts on Islam to suggest ways to win hearts and minds in the Muslim world. One of those present proposed that America export videos like *Baywatch* to the Muslim world. As I was the only Muslim present, I tried in vain to explain that Islamic culture finds the exploitation of women reprehensible and that such initiatives would be counterproductive. They needed to promote the vision of the Founding Fathers and *their* ideas of freedom—not just civil and religious rights and a free press, but also civility, decorum, honesty, concern for one's neighbor, and a respect and quest for knowledge. It is a vision that resonates with Muslims everywhere.

For Muslims, the behavior of American troops who humiliated Muslim prisoners sexually and religiously in Guantánamo and other prisons was symptomatic of a lack of honor. Once stories from those prison camps leaked out, the violence in Afghanistan and Iraq surged. Al Qaeda's appeal had less to do with ideology than the desire for revenge against those who had shamed and dishonored Muslim people. What Muslims failed to recognize was that these American soldiers were from a culture that looks at shame and honor differently. That is why some American commentators dismissed the events at Abu Ghraib as "frat pranks," failing to see the impact on Muslim society. Eventually, the U.S. Defense Department did bring charges against several soldiers involved with the Abu Ghraib scandal, followed by convictions. Two, Specialist Charles Graner, and his former fiancée, Lynndie England (see chapter 3), were sentenced to ten years and three years in prison, respectively.

Changing Society in America

It was not always like this. For the founders of Plymouth, modesty, shame, and honor were of primary consideration, and women were considered their very embodiment. Their honor reflected that of the community. In other words, original American identity was directly linked to shame and honor. Edward Winslow and John Winthrop were instruments of the church, which demanded complete obedience from the community in both Plymouth and Jamestown. The penalties for failing to attend church twice daily in Jamestown were the withholding of food for the day, whipping for a second offense, "six months in the gallows" for a third.[10] Adultery, sodomy, rape, and incest, all these carried the death penalty.

But white society was not uniform in the behavior of, and attitudes toward, women. When Anglican missionary Reverend Charles Woodmason, introduced in chapter 2, visited the Scots-Irish in the Carolina backwoods in the eighteenth century, he noted disapprovingly, "Indeed Nakedness is not censurable or indecent here, and they expose themselves often quite Naked, without Ceremony." He also noted that they "sleep altogether in Common in one Room, and shift and dress openly without Ceremony. . . . the Indians are better Cloathed and Lodged." Rates of prenuptial pregnancy were unusually high, and in 1767 Woodmason calculated that 94 percent of backcountry brides whose marriages he had performed in the past year were pregnant on their wedding day. He attributed this tendency to local customs: "Nothing more leads to this Than what they call their Love Feasts and Kiss of Charity. To which Feasts, celebrated at Night, much Liquor is privately carried, and deposited on the Roads, and in Bye Paths and Places. The Assignations made on Sundays at the Singing Clubs are here realized."[11]

Frontier society's notions of morality were different from those at Plymouth and were more about honor, clan loyalty, and expressions of courage and revenge among men. In time, this aspect of Scots-Irish culture would become normative American culture, as reflected in Benton Ward's motto: "A man's word is his honor" (see chapter 3). When asked about the *Girls Gone Wild* phenomenon, Benton replied: "The husbands of those girls and women are dishonored. It's not my problem."

For those who believed in American pluralist identity, questions of morality, modesty, and shame were matters of personal choice. As long as these choices did not infringe on the law, the Founding Fathers had little to say about them and instead focused their attention on the high ideals of freedom, civil liberty, and democracy. Morality was private business. That is how the advocates of Thomas Jefferson would explain his relationship with Sally Hemings, or others would view Washington's reputation as something of a "lady's man" and Benjamin Franklin's as the life and soul of the party in London and Paris. Meanwhile predator identity has always been more concerned with drawing boundaries around the entire community against outside threats than in judging the morality of its individuals.

The Swinging Sixties and the Start of Excess

Although the 1920s was a period of high materialism and excess, it was restricted to the American elite. In the 1960s, materialism and indulgence began to permeate general society. The current age thus truly began in the 1960s. Muslims who started to arrive in America from that decade onward watched the rapid cultural changes with a mixture of admiration and unease. It was the decade of the Kennedys, the Beatles, Martin Luther King Jr., and the moon landing, not to mention the burgeoning of television, the birth control pill, and the sexual revolution, with their impact on ideas about sex and marriage. Today's younger generation appears to show little interest in history and culture before this period. Walking with Hailey and Madeeha through the crowded lounge of our hotel in Las Vegas, I pointed to a picture of Dean Martin, who had performed there a half a century ago and was one of the most popular singers then, and both girls shook their heads, saying they had never heard of him.

Susan, Hailey's mother, saw America change from this period onward. Susan believed the sexual revolution started in the 1960s: "The sexual revolution was in full swing and I had roommates that had completely gone wild." It was, Susan said, "like taking the lid off a pressure cooker. . . . Suddenly what had been socially unacceptable behavior became acceptable and tolerated. Women were being told that if men could do it, then women could do it too, and that included *everything*. And so there were quite a few people who did not know how to handle this new freedom. I think the churches are trying harder to adapt to the changes and face the reality, but I don't really see that they've been able to have much impact on it."

Elvis Presley, the king of rock and roll, symbolized the new era of drugs, alcoholism, and sex. By the time Michael Jackson emerged as the king of pop in the 1980s, the moral boundaries had receded even further. I would like to believe that both Elvis and Michael Jackson were intelligent and sensitive human beings. Though they may not have intended to do so, their lifestyles helped to move the nation toward unchecked self-indulgence and consumerism. The tragic nature of their deaths simply confirms that something had gone horribly wrong. If the king was in trouble, so was the kingdom.

By the 1990s the different American identities had folded into one vast national identity defined by consumerism. To be American, of whichever identity, meant to be part of the most powerful, self-indulgent, and affluent nation on earth. Few social taboos and red lines remained. The prevailing attitudes to morality were exemplified in the presiding figure of that decade, Bill Clinton, who when asked to explain his affair with Monica Lewinsky, said he did it "because I could." It was clearly a time to "party."

Today, with half of the marriages in America ending in divorce, a large percentage of children are growing up in single-parent homes and are often lonely. Barely able to cope with their jobs, parents find it difficult to bring up their children and believe the best way to express affection is to overindulge them. They find it impossible to say no. So do young girls in school, where a virgin denotes an unattractive and unpopular girl. Normative behavior dictates that these girls aim to have a "hot" body so they can attract as many boys as possible and have as much "fun" as possible. In desperation, young Americans look for role models in the lives of celebrities, some search on the Internet, a few cannot sustain the pressure and resort to violence.

In the May 2009 *Reader's Digest,* an article titled "Parent Alert: Teens and Porn" begins with the seven-year-old son of the author, Judith Newman, using her cell phone's Internet capability to look up his favorite website, "juggworld.com." As she put it, this did "not involve earthenware." She also discussed the rapidly growing phenomenon of "sexting," that is, posting risqué photos of themselves transmitted over their cell phones or the Internet. According to Newman, 20 percent of young teenagers, boys and girls, engage in this practice (although studies suggest figures are much higher). "There is a me-me-ME quality to blogging, Facebooking, Twittering, and the like," she notes. "And what could be more attention-grabbing to a teenager than taking your clothes off?"

Girls Gone Wild

The sad fate of girls like Natalee Holloway and Amanda Knox is a commentary on the culture that produced them. Media interest in both cases has been intense (a new film on the former called *Natalee Holloway* was released in 2009). In both cases, drugs, alcohol, and sex led to violence. This was *Girls Gone Wild* resulting in death.

In 2005 Natalee Holloway, then eighteen, was in Aruba with her classmates a week after their high school graduation. Like many American students on vacation, she was, in the words of Aruba police commissioner Gerold Dompig, involved in "wild partying, a lot of drinking, lots of room switching every night. We know the Holiday Inn told them they weren't welcome next year. Natalee, we know, she drank all day every day. We have statements she started every morning with cocktails—so much drinking that Natalee didn't show up for breakfast two mornings."[12]

In the midst of the excessive drinking, Natalee told her friends that she was going to find a "guy" that night. She met up with three local young men, Joran van der Sloot and brothers Deepak and Satish Kalpoe. She was last seen driving away with them. She was announced missing later that day and has not been seen since.

The mystery and suspense mounted as American commentators declared that Aruba should be boycotted. Natalee's parents searched the entire island on foot for all of America to see. Her mother, Beth, emerged as a heroic figure, determined to get to the bottom of the mystery surrounding her daughter's fate. Van der Sloot, now back in Holland and still free though under suspicion, was the center of a sting operation for a reality show. He was tricked into confiding in someone and confessing what had happened before a hidden camera. Natalee was apparently on the beach with Van der Sloot and under the influence of drugs and alcohol. As they were kissing, she allegedly suffered a seizure and began foaming at the mouth. Van der Sloot called a friend who had a boat, and the two took Natalee's body on board. The as yet unidentified friend dumped Natalee, still alive, in the ocean. Van der Sloot referred to her in several interviews as a "bitch" and a "slut."

Natalee was by all accounts a model all-American girl. She had blonde hair and blue eyes, was on her school's dance team, graduated with honors, and had a full scholarship waiting for her at the University of Alabama. Her parents were divorced in 1993, and she was raised by her mother, Beth, who was remarried in 2000 to a prominent insurance broker. They lived in the affluent suburb of Mountain Brook outside Birmingham, Alabama.

Jonathan, who is from Huntsville, Alabama, described the area as "old money and very Christian."

In 2007 Amanda Knox, studying at the University of Washington in Seattle, came to Italy for a study program. Like Natalee, she was a good student with leadership qualities, and her parents too, like those of Natalee, were divorced. Amanda developed a reputation for bringing boys back to her room, which caused some problems with her British roommate Meredith Kercher. It was not long before Amanda and an Italian boyfriend were accused of sexually assaulting Meredith and stabbing her to death at the climax of a drug-induced sexual orgy. After being found guilty of the murder, Amanda is serving a prison term in Italy.

The cases of Natalee and Amanda are tragic in many respects, not only because of the nature of the incidents that led to the loss of lives, but also because they are the unwitting victims of a culture without limits or boundaries. For all the chauvinistic fury of the U.S. media and the denunciation of the foreign authorities by the families of the girls, never once did I hear anyone ask, "What was Natalee doing at 2 a.m., on drugs and drunk, with strange men on a lonely beach?" Or "Why was Amanda so drugged and drunk as to have little memory of either the night spent in group sex or the murder that came at the end of it?"

Mardi Gras

Perhaps the answers to these questions, as we discovered, can be found on a visit to Bourbon Street in New Orleans during Mardi Gras. Revelers—mainly tourists representing a cross section of society as to sex, age, and color—told us there were no boundaries for sexual or excessive drunken behavior, and that the definition of American identity today was precisely the freedom to indulge yourself. They had drunk enough to reveal their inner thoughts. What gave them the confidence to speak to the camera without concern about who might see or hear them was the knowledge that the traditional constraints of shame and honor did not apply to them.

In the early hours on Bourbon Street, Frankie and Craig asked people what American identity meant to them. An inebriated African American girl with bunny ears and short shorts looked straight at our camera and with a big smile said that American identity "means get fucked up, and just get fucked up!" As if to drive home her point, she added, "And have great sex and eat hot-wings." For her, Mardi Gras meant "Booooooobs and booty, boobs and booty. You see nekkid women running around boobs all out painted. There's a lot to see here, shit you never seen before, so you better come down here and see it!" She was not enthusiastic about Muslims: "Hell, yeah, we don't like the Muslims. That's all. They don't believe in our Jesus; they believe in their own freaking Jesus."

Another smiling girl said being American means having "as much sex as possible." The high point of the festivities came with the traditional "bead ceremonies," when girls lift up their blouses to show their breasts and receive a string of beads for every time they do so from the bystanders. Girls walked around with an air of triumph, fingering their garlands of beads as if they had received a recognized award for a notable feat. It was rumored that men, too, were now involved in a similar exercise. A young white man looking happily at the scenes of merriment said, "We really have no limits. Think about a lot of other countries—they can't do shit like this, ya know?"

At this point, a large young white man from Louisiana who had lost his job as an oil worker peered into the camera and asked Craig aggressively if he was a Muslim. When Craig hastily replied that he was not, the man muttered that was good; otherwise he would have to "kick you in the nuts." This was a threat delivered in earnest. He went on to describe Muslims as "sand niggers."

Many American girls become unwitting players in the consumerist culture that they find so seductive. On Bourbon Street, Frankie and Craig met the producer and founder of the Girls Gone Crazy company, who said he had also produced DVDs, including *Beach Bum Fighting*. His filming method was simple: "Girls in Mardi Gras will flash us. We catch them acting natural. And then we produce and manufacture DVDs and sell them all over the world. Don't get us confused with *Girls Gone Wild*. We've been doing this for eighteen years. *Girls Gone Wild* films underage girls—we don't make those kinds of mistakes."

Through the din of the merriment, Frankie asked the producer what he would say to those who thought he was doing something immoral. His unfazed reply was "To each his own—it's the general population. Everyone has their own choice. What are most people down here doing? It's the festival of Bacchus, Mardi Gras. Who was Bacchus? The patron of sex and everything else. You have people going crazy for what? For beads. They're going around flashing. Why not put it on film for everybody else to see? What we're doing is good for the economy and it boosts morale. A lot of our stuff goes over to the troops and keeps their morale up."

Girls Gone Wild videos that are advertised after 10 p.m. on cable are a prime example of the attitude of no limits to behavior. Joe Francis, the founder of *Girls Gone Wild* and the subject of a lengthy profile in the *Los Angeles Times* by Claire Hoffman, had a succinct explanation for the popularity of his product: "Sex sells everything."[13] Still in his mid-thirties, Francis is now planning to move into mainstream American culture with his Girls Gone Wild brand. He is planning a feature-length film, ocean cruises, an apparel line, and a chain of restaurants. He has an eye on mass-market retail outlets such as Walmart.

In the *Times* article, Claire Hoffman accompanied Francis to a club with his camera crew. There a young girl jumped at the sight of Francis, saying she wanted to be on *Girls Gone Wild*. When Hoffman asked why, the young girl answered, "I want everyone to see me because I'm hot. . . . You want people to say, 'Hey, I saw you. . . .' Getting famous will get me anything I want. If I walk into somebody's house and said, 'Give me this,' I could have it. . . . Most guys want to have sex with me and maybe I could meet one new guy, but if I get filmed, everyone could see me. . . . If you do this, you might get noticed by somebody—to be an actress or a model." To Francis, the girls' rationale is simple: "It's empowering, it's freedom." Hoffman's conclusions revealed that *Girls Gone Wild* was now symptomatic of American mainstream youth culture: "Whether it's 13-year-olds watching a Britney Spears video, 16-year-olds getting their pubic hair waxed to emulate porn stars, or 17-year-olds viewing videos of celebrities performing the most intimate acts, youth culture is soaked in sexuality." For men like Francis, *Girls Gone Wild* confirms the freedom that characterizes America and makes it "great" and "unique."

Liza—The Predator in Las Vegas

Like Mardi Gras in New Orleans, Las Vegas has become another byword for excess and indulgence in America today. The excited visitors milling about in the lounge of the Sahara hotel in Las Vegas seeing Hailey and myself on our way to meet a stripper would have been forgiven for thinking we were two visitors looking forward to the evening's entertainment. They would have been mistaken. Accompanied by my trusty assistant, both of us dutifully clutching our notebooks, I was on an anthropological mission to study the natives in their natural habitat. And who better to capture the culture and spirit of Las Vegas than an authentic stripper? I had spent time with a bishop and several imams, but if asked who best represents Vegas—these men of God or a stripper—the American public would not hesitate to name the latter. That is why we found ourselves face to face with a young lady whom I call Liza.

Liza had bleached blonde hair and pale white skin and was sporting a Gucci purse and matching shoes. Agitated when we told her the purpose of our meeting was to discuss Muslims and American identity, Liza wondered whether it was a joke. She felt she was wasting her time, rang her agency, and complained. The agency said that this was an unusual request, but we said that we were keen to talk to as diverse a range of Americans as possible, that Liza was an important addition to our list of respondents, and we asked the agency to make an exception in our case. When I explained our project to Liza, as was customary in these interviews, she showed not even the slightest curiosity. I could have been from Mars, and she probably would not have been interested—I was wasting her time. In the end, Liza talked to us, but with little joy. She fidgeted, rolled her eyes from time to time, and kept looking at her watch.

We began chatting in the lobby, essentially an extension of the casino, and when she said she was born in Dallas, Hailey said she was from the same city. But there was no sign of the usual camaraderie when two people from the same town meet. Liza had moved to Las Vegas for money and was now part of a lucrative business. She had been a dental assistant in California, had a high school diploma, a vocational school degree, and an associate of arts degree in business management.

Hailey asked Liza why she had become a stripper. Liza's joyless answer summed up her character and profession: "I'm rich." She described her three houses, the largest of which cost $2.3 million. Her daughter attends a private school and "can have anything she wants." When asked, Liza gave her age as twenty-three, then added, "Caucasians don't age well," perhaps noting Hailey's skeptical look. Liza confessed to plastic surgery: "I had my breasts reduced and lifted, a tummy tuck, lipo on my hips and thighs."

Liza sees her job like any other: she works eight to ten hours a day, seven days a week. She gets two to three calls a day and typically takes in $1,000 to $1,500 a day during the week and $2,000 to $2,500 on the weekends. Some strippers spend it all on drugs or alcohol. "I'm too pretty for that," she said, with an artificial laugh.

Like a CEO clinically surveying the operation of a company, Liza described her typical client: the businessman in town for conventions or "dumb guys" in town for a weekend of hedonism. "They have fun, spend money, do drugs, and gamble their life away," she said. "They are young, old, rich and poor—everyone calls for girls. It's the ho capital of the world." I wondered if her job was dangerous, and how she protected herself. She said her company had it down to a science. Before sending any girl to a client, they traced calls, confirmed room numbers, and had a service structure in place. If anyone attacked her, they would risk their normal lives outside Las Vegas—"families, mortgages, jobs."

Asked exactly what she did for her clients, she balked: "I don't have sex for money. I sell dreams. It's a hustle." She would come for up to an hour to strip in the client's room, and then if he liked what he saw, he could buy more time with her. Usually, she said, the clients were on drugs or drunk, and she could easily take them for more money. "You can practically refinance your home at the cage [the casino downstairs], so I take them down there and get as much money as I can from them. They gamble their whole life away." For Liza, men were witless and without willpower, and she had no remorse for what she did to them: "If I didn't do it, someone else would."

Liza had set certain standards for herself. She would not meet African Americans, or "Indians," by which she meant South Asians, Arabs, whom she called "Middle Easterns," or, in fact, any other minority. They are all "cheap," she said, and "suck." She was openly and unapologetically racist. She complained about "black girls." She said not only was there no demand for them, but they "steal." White girls, she said, were by far the most in demand. Asked why, she said, "White is beautiful. We paint our walls white."

What did American identity mean to her, then? "Gee, that's an interesting question. . . . That's deep. I dunno." I urged her to try answering it. "Well," she began, "I voted, I pay taxes. But everything has a price. Anything can happen. If you dream it, and you know the right people, have enough money, anything can happen. Especially in Las Vegas."

To Liza, what is shameful behavior among women is "doing stuff for free." She was contemptuous of the "dumb, young, and drunk" girls in *Girls Gone Wild:* "It's totally inappropriate. It never dawned on me to do something like that. They've lost their minds." Her role model was her grandmother, and for the first time during our conversation, her eyes showed a glimmer of emotion and spirit. "She's the best, she knows everything," she smiled. But her grandmother does not know about her life. In fact, "no one knows that I do this. I live in a nice white neighborhood. I have a nice life."

"Well, I'm sure this profession has an expiration date. What are your dreams after all of this is over?" Hailey asked. "I want to buy something—I mean I want to own my own business, . . . be the boss. I'll probably buy a nice salon. Everything here is about beauty—nails, hair, skin, body. I can also charge more here for everything than outside. I can charge like $2,000 per treatment where in other places it can cost like $200. Everything is better here."

Liza's Protestant work ethic and capitalistic spirit made her the perfect example of a successful businesswoman who saw an opportunity and took it. De Tocqueville had noted the importance of wealth—and its accumulation—to Americans, an attitude that differed from that of Europeans, who equated wealth with "servile cupidity," while in America it is "not stigmatized" but "is honored." This penchant, which "general reason and the universal conscience" would find condemnable, is in accord with American needs, said de Tocqueville: "To clear, to make fruitful, to transform the vast uninhabited continent that is his domain, the American needs the daily support of an energetic passion; that passion can only be love of wealth."[14]

Hailey found Liza disturbingly "empty and savage." The entire time Hailey felt repulsed by Liza, partly because of her profession and partly her coldness: "She was calculating, manipulative, and devoid of compassion. I would even go so far as to say she was evil. She was a part of destroying people's lives, and for what? So that she could, as she said, 'buy something.'"

For all her confidence, Liza obviously lived in fear of losing her looks and thus her source of income. Yet she could not be considered a victim of a heartless system. She knew exactly what she was doing. Because she preyed on the foolish and the vulnerable for profit, loathed those of color, showed no pity for the poor and weak, she could be said to be another face of American predator identity.

Americans React to Girls Gone Wild

Many young educated Americans are concerned about social trends. We found just as many college students repelled by *Girls Gone Wild* behavior as those who considered it socially acceptable. Female students interviewed at the College of William and Mary felt that girls who did behave that way were suffering from "low self-esteem." Anna Hayden had never heard of *Girls Gone Wild*. Anna, in her mid-twenties, works at Vanderbilt University Medical Center, is an Anglican, and attended Tennessee's University of the South. The "individualism" of American culture, which she linked to a loss of morality, was eroding the sense of community: "On the one hand, individualism is the quality that has made us great, but it's potentially dangerous. It hurts community. It's about advancing your own interests over and against everyone else's. Secondly, it is self-absorption. People don't care about larger issues as long as they are not directly affected."

Craig was struck by the vast difference between the appearance and behavior of white female converts to Islam like Nicole Queen and that of some of the young people he knew: "Meeting Nicole Queen and her tremendous amount of self-respect for her mind and body is something very admirable and is a character trait that American women and men can learn from.

In high school and college, I spent a lot of my social time with my fraternity brothers. . . . I saw that women were often verbally disrespected and treated as sexual objects. Men, on the other hand, were more interested in pursuing women for their bodies rather for their mind, soul, and love." He now sees a twofold beauty in women: "It's physical beauty but also depth of character, sense of self-respect, and a sense of honor for mind, body, and soul."

Blake Underwood, an American University student who joined my team after fieldwork, describes himself as an atheist, joining some 35 million other adults in the United States who say they are atheist or agnostic, and those who profess no religion. Blake says he is part of the "punk rock and hardcore subculture" and practices a philosophy called "straight edge," which leads him to abstain from the "college cocktail" of drugs, alcohol, and promiscuous sex in order to "avoid the pitfalls" that so often accompany those kinds of vices. "My community and my aspirations are too important for me to be sidetracked by frivolous indulgence that can so easily have devastating consequences."

Scholars Explain Girls Gone Wild

Because of the rapidity with which society has been changing and the uncertainty about its directions, even American scholars are not sure how to explain the *Girls Gone Wild* phenomenon. Sheikh Hamza Yusuf had a philosophic explanation: "Nietzsche talks about Dionysian and Apollonian impulses, and when a society is healthy there is a balance between these two. When societies deviate in the Apollonian, it becomes like Nazism, where the Dionysian is eliminated by force. Or they deviate in that kind of Dionysian culture where the Apollonian is suspended. Apollonian is order and rule based and the Dionysian is the free flow of the Bacchanalian type, . . . a 'let me dance beneath the diamond sky with one hand waving free silhouetted by the sea circled by the circus sand with all memory and faith buried deep beneath the waves; let me forget about today, until tomorrow.'" He felt that *Girls Gone Wild* is a degraded expression of a desire to escape the world, "a desire for ecstasy, to get out of one's state—to get out of the madness of the world by going mad." He found it troubling that people express that desire in such ways but understood "where the impulse comes from" and had some sympathy for it.

At the same time, the sheikh thought shame and honor could still be seen in American society today, for honor is deeply rooted in all cultures and is "one of the great virtues, like dignity and shame." Although not entirely shameless, American society is in many ways losing its sense of human dignity, which he finds disturbing. Yet as Charles Dickens might have said, "It is the best of times and the worst of times." On the honorable side, Barack Obama and his family have shown immense grace and dignity, which people recognize and respect when they see it, and "there are still many, many, profoundly dignified people in this culture. So I can sit here like an increasingly middle-aged man and lament the loss of the past, which is something people at my age start doing."

When anthropologist Roxanne Euben of Wellesley College, just outside Boston, spoke to us, she attributed the *Girls Gone Wild* phenomenon to today's era of postfeminism. This movement is a reaction to the feminism of the 1960s, with figures like Madonna setting trends through their "self-exploitation." The modern generation thinks being a woman entails the use of sexual power, but, says Euben, it is "profoundly misguided." Postfeminism has instead devolved into a crude commitment to the idea that "I'm a woman and I can do anything a man can do." Women want to be free from the shackles of the former "repressive" male-dominated society, and they repudiate the purity and asceticism they see in the women of the past. Today women are saying, "Who are you to tell me that I'm being exploited? I'm making this choice, and no one else." This has resulted in exaggerated expressions of sexuality. Porn stars speak of their pride in their liberated, sexual power.

Euben believes that women growing up in the postfeminist society are exploited, although they are not aware of it, and yet gain power and instant success because of it. They are entirely self-made and do not want to debate the subject. Society appears engaged in a broad, deliberate, systematic attempt to make women's bodies into a commodity, a process accelerated by free trade and globalization. Girls who grow up seeing Hooters and Gucci models "from the cradle . . . become desensitized to the comodification of their bodies." Women who have "sexy bodies have power, which is highly valued in this society. It is no wonder that they grab the chance to get free advertising on *Girls Gone Wild*."

The problem, according to Euben, is that women *will* hit a glass ceiling and will not understand why. They have the spirit of, and desire for, equality but no knowledge or idea of history or the resources to make sense of what is happening to them. Euben also finds the behavior of men shameful, citing the sexuality of American men in college fraternities and in places like Abu Ghraib and even Guantánamo Bay, where attempts were made to "feminize, animalize, shame, and sexually humiliate." *Reviving Ophelia*, by clinical psychologist Mary Pipher, diagnoses the problem among young women as a loss of their true selves, a breakdown of the family, and young girls' reliance on a hypersexualized culture for guidance and validation.[15]

In his class on pornography, anthropologist Lawrence Rosen of Princeton University draws observations about the larger picture of shame and honor in American society from examples such as the reaction to President Clinton's escapades—"No one cared." Thus any "red lines" in American society are actually the lines between public and private debate and concern infringing on individual rights. He asked his class on pornography to define the red line, that is, to name what is totally unacceptable in society. He was taken aback to find that the *only* thing his students could think of was sexual and physical abuse of a child because it would be infringing on the rights of that child before they could freely consent to anything. He says that he tries to shock his class, but "nothing works."

These cultural changes and trends have not gone unnoticed. Tom Wolfe's *I Am Charlotte Simmons* depicts the struggles of a young girl trying to maintain her sense of self among the elite children of America in an Ivy League university.[16] The novel shows a generation steeped in superficiality, selfishness, entitlement, and sexual promiscuity. When asked in an interview why this was happening, Wolfe quoted Nietzsche: "God is dead."

Morris Berman, in *Dark Ages America*, believes that society is disintegrating and atomizing.[17] His subtitle, *The Final Phase of Empire*, sums up the gloomy thesis. Berman links the collapse of morality to the broader collapse of society itself. In what other context would one find reality shows on TV, such as *Survivor*, "in which screwing the other person is the name of the game, and which millions find vastly entertaining?"[18] With unrelenting pessimism Berman concludes: "It seems clear enough that when you put money (or commodities) at the center of a culture, you finally don't *have* a culture."

Christianity and Social Excess

If Christians are converting to Islam because they see a lack of clarity and control over social behavior on earth, what does the church have to say about it? Throughout our journey, we visited many churches and many denominations, including Mormons (see chapter 8), and spoke with pastors and their congregations, asking for their views on current American culture and its social boundaries, as well as the church's response to the challenges of consumerism. We found no consensus, only intense debates on issues such as abortion, gay rights, family, and marriage. I was left

Akbar Ahmed observing a Sunday service at Houston's Lakewood Church, the largest church in America. Pastor Joel Osteen and his wife, Victoria, lead the service in a building that was once the Houston Rockets' stadium, holding up to 16,000.

looking for "mainstream Christianity" amid the plethora of Christian sects that have proliferated in the United States.

Lakewood Church

While in Houston, Hailey and I visited Lakewood Church, which we believed is as close to "mainstream Christianity" as you can get in America today. Said to be the largest house of worship in the country, with seating for 16,000 people, the building was once an arena, home to the Houston Rockets basketball team. The faces of its pastors, Joel and Victoria Osteen, Lakewood's glittering stars, adorn bookstores across the country (they are best-selling authors) and are fixtures on television.

We were among the thousands gathered for Sunday service conducted by the Osteens themselves. The church was full of well-turned-out, mostly middle-class people, about half of whom were African American or Latino. Particularly striking was the complete absence of statues, pictures, paintings, or signs of Jesus. Even the name, Lakewood, was different from the traditional names of churches, which usually reflected the denomination. Bands played on the stage, and the crowd joined in clapping and dancing as they stamped to the beat of the band. It was like a rock concert, but there was no doubting the sincerity of the worshippers

The size and scale of the church, the efficiency of the information desks, and the armies of earnest, well-scrubbed, and well-dressed young men and women who greeted every visitor with a brochure and an artificial smile conveyed the impression of a well-planned multimillion-dollar business. A prominent feature of their promotional material was the motto "Find the champion in you." Their brochures demanded only three actions from the flock: come early to church, be faithful in your giving, and invite your family and friends to come.

I was impressed by the well-oiled manner in which everything was being conducted, but I was still left looking for Jesus. I knew something of Jesus. I loved and revered him as part of my Islamic tradition. Besides, I was brought up in educational institutions run by European Catholics and American Protestants and had spent many years in Cambridge, England, and therefore could see Jesus through the eyes of my Christian teachers and friends. The Jesus I had come to know was the embodiment of love, compassion, humility, simplicity, and austerity, all of which I saw in my Christian teachers. They would often remind me of the sayings of Jesus, such as "It is easier for a camel to go through the eye of a needle than for a rich man to enter the kingdom of God" (a saying found in the Gospels of Matthew, Mark, and Luke). I was truly inspired by Jesus' commandment to love everyone, regardless of race or religion. I appreciate that the majority of those who go to church are inspired by their faith to be decent human beings and citizens. In spite of these good folk, as the media and the statistics reveal, society is rife with fundamental problems that need urgent redress. While I felt the rhythm and singing in Lakewood Church added something to Christian worship, the true spirit and message of Jesus was lost in the noise, music, and pageantry in the arena.

At one end of the arena, Joel and Victoria Osteen shared the stage with gigantic flower arrangements, fake waterfalls, a large rock band, a choir, and a massive rotating golden globe. At the other end stood a huge American flag brightened by a spotlight. The band played vaguely Christian rock music for the first twenty minutes of the service. It looked and sounded very professional. The congregants participated in the service by dancing and singing, some approaching a state of ecstasy. Then Joel Osteen stepped forward.

With his immaculately groomed thick, black hair, his dazzling smile and perfect teeth, elegant suit and slim form, Osteen resembled a successful young executive. He offered a short prayer that sounded like a motivational speech, rallying the company faithful with repeated phrases like "I feel victorious today." He exhorted the congregation to feel like a "victor, not a victim." He emphasized "standing strong" and asked everyone to turn to their neighbor and declare, "I'm still here. I'm standing strong." He reminded the audience that God "forms a bloodline against your enemies and protects you." He encouraged everyone to "fight the 'good' fight" for God. He told a story of a king who was in the middle of battle and prayed for victory. The battle instantly turned in his favor. Osteen thus encouraged his congregation to pray for peace in the midst of battle. The metaphor of battle was delivered with a sweet smile and soothing voice, and without a hint of aggression.

Osteen's sermons—seen by 7 million Americans weekly and broadcast to about 100 nations—are mainly about business and the need to listen to God, personal intuition, and other matters. In one story, he said his "head" was telling him to go into business with someone, but his "heart" told him not to. God then gave Osteen "inside information," and the man turned out to be a fraud. God, he told his congregation, sees the "big picture," and if you feel disquiet, God is sending you a message. In your "car, your house, your promotion, your spouse," God gives you "inside information." "God will make sure you come into the right opportunities, meet the right people, and get the right breaks." There was little to no scripture reading during the service.

Osteen's wife Victoria matched his interpretation of Christianity, which seemed to emphasize appearance. On Daystar, the television network that broadcasts Osteen's sermons, infomercials advertise a "nonsurgical face-lift kit," whose results are "just like plastic surgery." Female pastor Paula White said that women who bought the kit should do so "for God and for your ministry" as "your body is a temple," and we are the "ambassador of the most high God" who wants women to "renew their skin" until it "glistens."

For all their charisma, the Osteens are the targets of much criticism. In a 2009 cover story, *The Atlantic* magazine suggested Osteen and his "prosperity gospel" were to blame for the economic crash, noting the "growth of the prosperity gospel tracks fairly closely to the pattern of foreclosure hotspots."[19] It also found that the prosperity gospel "has spread exponentially among African American and Latino congregations."

The Osteens looked good, spoke well, and ran everything properly and on schedule. I could not help making some mental comparisons between these Christian preachers and the imams we had met. The Lakewood preachers were of mixed gender, engaging, always smiling, and seemed accessible. Their presentation, with its rock band and slick public relations, was part of contemporary culture. There was no ritual, and the service looked more like entertainment. The speakers' metaphors and rhetoric reinforced the idea that their message was aimed specifically at people facing problems today. Audience members were constantly reminded of the consumerist culture in which they lived. They were asked to "buy" the message of this church in the "free market" of churches. The congregants were welcomed by young, smiling greeters, who said "God bless you."

In contrast, Muslim religious leaders are almost always male. Too many of them tend to be inaccessible, aloof, and unsmiling. Services take the form of a strict orthodox ritual that reinforces tradition. Even the khutba, or sermon, is delivered in full or in part in Arabic, and in a highly stylized format. The success of the imam depends on adhering to tradition, with the result that those who become adventurous soon find themselves in trouble with the community. The purpose and atmosphere of the mosque encourage the shutting out of the world and thus enable the worshipper to pray directly to God without distraction. Visitors will find no young men or women to greet them, instead may be met with indifference or even hostility.

Although Lakewood does not represent all of Christianity, it helps delineate the substantive differences between mosque and church. The mosque allows the worshipper space and time to be alone with God. Every prayer therefore has the potential to be deeply meaningful. By its very act, it reinforces both the larger ideological frame of Islam and the more immediate "dos and don'ts." Despite the diversity of political and ideological opinion within the Islamic community, there is unanimity about the content of the prayer and its format. The service is unchanging and uniform across the land and cannot be altered at the whim of the imam. It also creates a sense in the worshipper of being anchored. The worshipper touches the forehead to the ground in prostration before God and sits on the floor in humility during the service. Prayers reinforce the belief that God is eternal and omnipotent, which reassures worshippers.

Lakewood has its critics within Christianity. Father Donald Nesti of Houston called it "Christianity lite." For Hailey, another Catholic, "visiting the Lakewood Church is more like going to a concert than communing with God. There was no self-reflection, no talk of sacrifice, and no culpability for one's sins. They repeated that we should 'move on' and have God as a positive role in our lives. It seemed to me watered-down, self-centered, and driven by money rather than faith. For all the communal, participatory, and even ecstatic elements, I felt that I had not attended a truly religious service. It felt intangible and amorphous—good but empty."

Finding Jesus on Bourbon Street

While the Osteens bask in the glow of the ardor of their followers, other more humble Christians plunge directly into the midst of those who are in their eyes sinning. Craig and Frankie met two white men on Bourbon Street during Mardi Gras late at night preaching about Jesus. One of them was holding a large white cross, and only the other man spoke throughout. Probably in his forties, he was thin and tall, with a short light beard. He described Mardi Gras as "literally a Pagan celebration," with all the foreign gods "that somehow got incorporated into what was supposed to be a Christian celebration." The whole world finds it enticing, he winced, "but it's really filled with sin, lust, and debauchery." He himself used to party, used to deal drugs and "be into all kinds of stuff," while his companion was sentenced to forty years in prison. But he was able to change "through the cross of Christ."

The United States, he said, "was founded on the providence of God," and those who arrived at Plymouth "had a covenant with God to establish this land and bring the gospel back to the four corners of the earth." Today, however, "Hollywood dictates everything, all the agendas, all the movies; it's all very against God with the liberality, anything goes. Generations have grown up believing you aren't created in God's image, you evolved out of some primordial slime."

For him, America meant "having the freedom to do what should be done, not necessarily the freedom to do what you want to do." Societies in which people did what they wanted imploded—"pagan Rome is typical of that." Being American also meant that he could come out to Mardi Gras and "shine the light of truth in the midst of darkness. America was founded on the gospel of Jesus Christ. These people matter to God; this is a river of souls going each way down the street. But these people here are lost, they don't know the truth."

Asked what he thought of Muslims, he found them by and large like most Christians, that is, "not real fervent in their beliefs." In his view, "the big difference is Jesus said to love your enemies. Islam has contradictions. Those that we call the radicals, they're not a bunch of lunatics, they're following their book. I follow our book. I don't blame them for following their book. Their book tells them to kill; that's why they're doing it." Furthermore, as an American, he is free to reach out to the lost folk "without an AK-47" in his back: "I can do this without a sword chopping my head off. I know a lot of people died to give me the right to do this. I am thankful for those who had the vision and the courage to found this nation and to fight for it and to fight to retain the freedom that we have."

Our questionnaires, however, reflected some uncertainty about America being a Christian country: while 42 percent of our respondents said that it is a Christian country, 44 percent said that it is not, and 8 percent said that it "sort of" is. When we correlated the answers with the different faiths, we found the highest percentage of affirmative responses—55 percent versus 28 percent saying no—among the Mormons. Surprisingly, Protestants had the lowest affirmative figure at 37 percent, which was even lower than the atheists' 38 percent affirmatives. Of the Muslims questioned, 41 percent said yes and 45 percent no. Jewish people said that America is a Christian country at a slightly higher rate: 47 percent yes versus 40 percent no. Many respondents made their feelings emphatically clear: "absolutely not," "of course," and even "unfortunately, yes."

Jonathan felt that American Protestant churches are more concerned with "the kingdom of heaven" than "the world." They are thus "conceding that you could do anything you wanted within the law and not be shamed in America, but in God's Kingdom, there are rules and no relativism." That means "there is a concept of right and wrong and what we are calling shame and honor in God's kingdom. The churches can't and won't try to control what is going on in the 'wicked' world. The church is driven by the concept of grace—being forgiven, although there is some theological debate here, for your sins. I think this idea shows up across American society: if you go out and flash yourself on *Girls Gone Wild*, or sleep with a bunch of people, you may be punished in the church, or in your office or school, but eventually you can be forgiven and work your way back into an honorable reputation."

Hailey thought American mainstream churches presented Christianity in a way that is "disconnected from reality and consequences." She recalled being asked by a Baptist church to sign a piece of paper "declaring our Lord and Savior to be Jesus Christ. If we did that, then any sin could be absolved because He died for our sins."

I wondered what preachers like Joel Osteen might have to say to girls like Natalee Holloway, Amanda Knox, and indeed Liza. Would they have talked about the dangers of crossing the red lines that involve sex, alcoholism, and drugs, about when to say no, and how to say no? Would they have explained that while "I" is important, "you" and the others around you are equally important? Would they have warned these young girls not to rely so much on their looks and appearance? Would they have talked of humility, piety, and austerity—the core message of Jesus himself? As our visit to Lakewood suggested, the answers to these questions would probably be in the negative, leaving these girls to search for instruction and guidance on their own, with the possibility of tragedy hovering over them.

"Too Much Freedom"

Muslims of every background that we met commonly complained that there was "too much freedom" in America, which they identified as "the greatest threat" to the country. For them, *Girls Gone Wild* symbolized the problem. Nicole Queen, who had been a part of this culture, believed *Girls Gone Wild* reflected the dominant value system of today's American women: "In America you are taught, as a woman, you need to look and be hot, and that's how you are going to be on TV and be somebody." Although she said that people make a "big deal" out of "brilliant girls," they are "not as glamorous as the girl who has a better body, is on TV because she takes her clothes off, or is in the shower with another girl. This is America—it is sick, it's embarrassing, that's what people around the world think when they think of us. When they see *Girls Gone Wild*, which is all over the Internet, that's what they think—'This is what teenage girls do in America; they get on a bus and let someone film them.'"

In New Orleans, especially, this theme was prevalent perhaps because of Mardi Gras and its rowdy party atmosphere. A Tulane University student from Saudi Arabia believed "people abuse their freedom," and this would "destroy" America. He recalled with palpable distaste the binge drinking and other immoral activities that went on in the dorms when he was a freshman at Tulane: "I couldn't sleep there, I had to sleep at the mosque so I wouldn't see it. They act worse than animals, and these people will lead this country one day, in politics, business."

An African American Muslim elder at a mosque told my team that "everything is acceptable in society; there are no guidelines." Another African American Muslim in New Orleans said that while freedom can be good, "there is a price tag for freedom. It will cost you your life." Whereas New Orleans locals "have too much honor to take their clothes off," he added, visitors have "wild perverted sex on the streets. Couples throw out their rings and their vows, which then "mean nothing . . . Satan is whispering to all of them, 'Come on, try me out.'" They would not dare act like this in their own homes, but in New Orleans "people dishonor themselves, the little boy comes out." He called it a "subliminal seduction." He lamented the fact that Muslim foreigners were getting caught up in the scene, taking off their Muslim clothes once in New Orleans and "trying to fit in but looking like a fool."

Sharwi, an Egyptian cab driver in New Orleans, found Mardi Gras "evil" and "disgusting." Drunken people often vomit and urinate on themselves in his cab. Islam forbids even speaking to a drunk person, he said. If he sees people who look drunk, he will not pick them up. "I ask people why they drink, and they say they have problems. So what? I have problems. Why don't they go to church or ask their father?" Revolted by their antics, Sharwi said these Christian revelers were not those mentioned in the Quran as being close to Muslims and called "people of the book."

Quadir Habeeb, whom we met in Buffalo (see chapter 4), recited a rap for us he had written about the challenges faced by his African American community. It focuses on the vulnerability of girls, and I include some lines to convey its flavor:

Man she was lost in the street,
Often found in the club shaking fast to the beat,
Used to get shook now she always getting beat.
Once a strong girl now she's always feeling weak.
She thought happiness was chillin' in the Jeep,
While her man out wild 'n killing in the streets. . . .

Twisted, young girl on her own,
Sixteen years old screaming out 'I'm grown!'
Sneaking in night club with the fake ID,
Now she laying with a thug getting HIV. . . .

If you put God first, good things occur.
It can always get bad, when it seems the worst.
Gucci necklace, watch and jeans and purse,
Don't mean a dang thing when you in the hearse.

Bridging the Clash of Cultures

Despite the seemingly critical tones of this chapter, its purpose has been to understand why some Americans convert to Islam and thereby reject certain parts of their own culture. There is clearly a relationship between the two, a case of cause and effect. The discussion has also revealed what Muslims see when they look at America, when they turn on the TV and see *Girls Gone Wild* infomercials, shows like *The Real World*, *Flavor of Love*,

The Girls Next Door, and *The Bad Girls Club,* when they hear that their son at Tulane University has been sleeping in the mosque rather than the dorm room, when they learn of rapes and murders on the local news, when they see the excesses of Tiger Woods with his mistresses, Michael Jackson with his little boys, and the scandals of Britney Spears—in short, when they see a society without shame or honor and one that is breaking down.

For Muslims, alarmed at what they consider a lack of shame and honor in society, dangers lurk in the most harmless cultural activity, and they tend to isolate their families to protect them. Meanwhile, Americans tend to be suspicious of anyone who would refuse to enjoy harmless national celebrations such as a Fourth of July barbeque. They do not think anyone would be offended by the beer in everyone's hand, the pork on the grill, and the women in tank tops and summer skirts. For a white woman like Nicole Queen in a hijab to decline such an invitation would be almost traitorous.

We can conclude on the basis of our fieldwork findings, corroborated by various American commentators and scholars, that the three American identities I have outlined are now more or less neutral to the idea of women's sexuality, however they define shame and honor. These three identities also abhor the conversion to Islam of someone like Nicole Queen. Pluralist identity sees her as regressing into a world of irrationality and violence that offers no rights to women. The other two identities condemn her for betraying her ethnic and cultural heritage. A white woman in a hijab is perhaps an uncomfortable reminder of the once powerful concept of miscegenation. That is why white Americans might denounce Nicole as a "whore." By contrast, the three American identities remain largely indifferent to non-white races, like Latinos, converting to Islam.

Not surprisingly, Muslims see Nicole as a luminous role model and visible proof of Islam's innate superiority and inevitable triumph over other faiths. Hence Muslim converts have become a metaphor in the larger clash of civilizations between Islam and the West.

But it is important to remember and celebrate the American tradition of religious pluralism, which presupposes the right to choose one's faith. Americans therefore need to remind themselves that it is because of the vision of the Founding Fathers that they can find the faith best suited to them without the death threats other seekers face in many Muslim lands. Ironically, although the Quran categorically states "there is no compulsion in religion" (Surah 2:256), Muslims who convert to other faiths often find themselves facing persecution. So even if Americans do not approve of someone's choice, in the spirit of the freedom and religious liberty promised them in the Constitution, they must accept that person's decision.

Nicole Queen is thus vindicating the pluralist vision of the Founding Fathers as much as she is bringing her American heritage of courage, independence, and the search for truth to her Islam. For Nicole, conversion to Islam allows her to reaffirm her American identity. Once the heat and noise subside, it is American converts like her who can play an effective role in interpreting mainstream Americans and Muslims to each other. By doing so, they are ideally placed to counteract the idea of a clash between the two.

PART THREE
Adjusting and Adapting

SEVEN

Jews and Muslims: Bridging a Great Divide

JUDEA PEARL'S LOVE of his son Danny is intense, and he mentions him frequently. As we settled down to talk to Judea and his wife, Ruth, in their modest home in Encino, a beautiful part of Los Angeles with gentle rolling hills, we saw heartbreaking reminders of an eternally young and always smiling Danny everywhere. Danny represented the best of America and Judaism, Judea said, and he recounted how much his son was enchanted by the Founding Fathers, studying their biographies for hours.

Danny's understanding of America differed from his, noted Judea, citing an unexpected example: "Danny showed more trust in people. . . . I remember walking with him in one of the dark alleys of Berkeley when a homeless person came out from one of the alleys and said, 'Hey, have you got a dime?' I retreated. But Danny just smiled at him and said, 'Yes, here's a dime. Have a nice evening.' I looked at him, and he said, 'Dad, you're racist. Come on.'" I asked Judea why Danny had said that.

"The man was black," Judea explained. "You know it was dark, it was evening. For Danny, color didn't make a difference. The fact that the man was homeless, and could be a criminal, didn't make a difference. He was just a man. They saw eye to eye. We are all creatures put here on this earth to enjoy it and make each other happy."

Danny's own identity made the tragedy of his death in Karachi even heavier: he was the embodiment of American pluralist identity. Raised in California, married to a Buddhist, and yet rooted in his American Jewish identity, he was working in the Muslim world to help explain it to American readers.

357

Danny's American and Jewish identities complemented each other. He was reflecting a strain in the larger Jewish community, whose members first arrived in America in the 1650s, and who in time came to exemplify the struggle for democracy, tolerance, and fair play. They thus became the strongest supporters of the vision of the Founding Fathers. Its leadership and vision in promoting this idea of America, not just for Jews but for other groups as well, would make the Jewish community American pluralists par excellence.

Promoting Jewish–Muslim Dialogue

No two religions have more in common than Judaism and Islam. And no two religions are so far apart today. The paradoxes underlying the complicated relationship between Jews and Muslims result from their shared genealogical history: both these Abrahamic peoples claim descent from an eponymous ancestor. Their conflict can be understood in what anthropologists call agnatic rivalry, or the competition between a father's brother's sons for social and political dominance.

Both have challenged American identity in profound ways. Jews have had to face long periods of virulent anti-Semitism, which has now faded but not entirely disappeared. Muslims have encountered Islamophobia, especially after 9/11. It is each group's response to America that is so different. American Jews have confronted American predator identity by forcefully working within the system to reinforce and bring to the fore American pluralist identity. They have been strong advocates of the Founding Fathers and the nation's founding principles. Muslims, in contrast, have either met predator identity head-on or gone to the other extreme and pretended to be invisible. Neither of these strategies has been beneficial to the Muslim community, which could learn from the Jewish experience, especially because the two religions have so much in common in their theology and culture.

Despite the similarities, the valiant efforts of Jews and Muslims to create harmony between their faiths are challenged at every turn by each group's fear and distrust of the other. To my mind, few things are as urgent as building bridges between Jews and Muslims, and the United States is perhaps the best country in the world for this to happen.

These were some of my thoughts as I sat on stage with Judea Pearl to promote Jewish-Muslim understanding in honor of Danny. We were in Pittsburgh on a chilly night in 2003 before a large audience, and the cold outside foreshadowed the frosty reception inside. Most in the audience were Christians and Jews (the latter having turned out in large numbers

Judea Pearl, father of slain journalist Daniel Pearl, and Akbar Ahmed at a public dialogue in San Francisco to promote Jewish-Muslim understanding. They were in the city to receive the inaugural Purpose Prize given in 2006.

because of our host, the American Jewish Committee), but there was also a sprinkling of Muslims, including the president of the Islamic Council of Greater Pittsburgh.

The event had been described on the front page of the local paper and on TV news. The Muslim community in Pittsburgh and elsewhere had debated the merit of holding such a forum. Many felt that the victimization and killing of Muslims around the world provided no reason to talk to the "Jews." Others pointed out that the Pearl family was associated with Israel, and therefore no dialogue or reconciliation could take place unless the Palestinian problem was resolved. Still others distrusted such attempts at dialogue because they had been let down too many times in the past. Such skepticism translated into countless negative responses that I had received.

Judea, whom I had met briefly once before, and the audience were interested in only two questions, which they aimed at me again and again like missiles: Did the Quran preach violence and instigate Muslims to murder and mayhem? and Where, if at all, were the "moderates" in Islam who condemn "Islamic terrorism"? I answered the first question with a "no," and tried to go into some detail, and the second by asking the audience to look more closely at the Muslim world. They would be surprised at the number of moderates who bravely challenge terrorism. I kept coming back to what was common between us: the idea of a monolithic, all-powerful, invisible God; the shared affection and reverence for the great prophets like Abraham, Moses, and David; the dietary laws; the practice of fasting; the emphasis on family, education, and charity; and even circumcision; and, of course, the Ten Commandments. I did note points of difference to be confronted—minor ones such as the drinking of alcohol, because Muslims are forbidden alcohol, as well as perhaps one of the most formidable, the difficult relationship between Israelis and Palestinians.

But emotions were high that night, and there was little interest in pursuing serious discussion in a cool manner. We were trying to accelerate a relationship that did not exist. What was I to say to a man whose son was so cruelly killed in the city where I had grown up, and at the hands of those belonging to my own faith?

Not long after Danny's death in February 2002, his father had approached me on a quest to talk with a Muslim. A renowned scientist and humble man, Judea loved nothing better, I later discovered, than spending his time with his priceless collection of first-edition books and articles. These included Galileo's *Discorsi e Dimostrazioni Matematiche* (1638), Newton's *Opticks* (1704), and Einstein's seminal paper on relativity published in 1905. As an ardent supporter of Israel, he also has the first edition of the book said to be a catalyst to the founding of the nation of Israel, Theodor Herzl's *Der Judenstaat* (1896).

As a scientist, Judea said, he wanted to understand better the religion and world of those who put his son to death. And as a father, he wanted to avenge that death by attacking the hatred that had led to it. He also gave another reason later, during our public exchange in Pittsburgh: he sensed my own empathy for the besiegement that many societies feel in the contemporary world, spanning both Muslim and Jewish communities.

From that first meeting in my office at American University grew a series of dialogues to promote understanding between Muslims and Jews. Judea and his wife, Ruth, now faced the challenge of converting the death of an only son into a platform for dialogue and understanding.

I agreed to go to Pittsburgh in order to express my support to the Pearl family for creating in Danny a bridge and a symbol of compassion. As a Muslim, I felt it would also allow me to express my deep sympathy for Danny's death while encouraging people to think of those thousands of innocent victims—Muslims and non-Muslims—who in different places, in different societies, were being unnecessarily and brutally killed. But I knew if I wanted to get through to Judea, I had to talk to him as a grieving father, to share in his sorrow. I knew that Pakistanis had neither publicly apologized nor reached out to him to express remorse.

With this in mind, I had invited two Pakistani friends to Pittsburgh to speak briefly from the stage. After their remarks, Umar Ghuman asked for forgiveness from the Pearl family, and Faizan Haq said his one regret was that his body had not been between Danny Pearl and his killers.

The effect of their words was dramatic. The atmosphere changed in an instant. Eyes were moist and faces looked lost in thought. A new chapter in Jewish-Muslim dialogue was opening.

Rabbis on American Pluralism

There is no more an authentic American representation of pluralist identity than my friend Senior Rabbi Bruce Lustig, who heads the Washington Hebrew Congregation. Asked about his role model, he replied: "The most formidable influence on me in my early years and even to this day is my mother, a Holocaust survivor, narrowly escaping in 1939 from the clutches of Nazi Germany. . . . My mother's approach to what happened to her has been most inspirational to me . . . the things that she faced, horrible things that no human being should ever have to witness, and yet . . . I grew up with this woman who was so loving, caring, and as an artist, could take colors and paint a canvas and make the world look so beautiful."

For the rabbi, American identity could be summed up as "opportunity, hope, and promise. We have the Founders and the Framers of our Constitution who were brilliant men, and those that have come after them have really seized the opportunity. Sometimes when we challenge the status quo, that is the greatest strength of America, whether it is Martin Luther King or American Muslims today who ask their country to be more sensitive and more caring, whether it is Christians who don't want to be stereotyped in one way or the other, or Jews, these are all lessons in our society that are forever important and are the great strength of American democracy."

I met Rabbi Lustig by chance—or as some of the Abrahamic faithful would say, by divine design—a few days after 9/11 when I was invited to a dinner in Washington, D.C., one cold and foggy fall evening, soon after I had arrived to teach there. My newness combined with the generally hostile media speculation about Muslims made me feel lonely and unwelcome. I did not recognize any of the guests at the dinner, who must have numbered over a thousand. I sat next to Amy Lustig, who was surprised that I had not heard of her husband, and she turned to introduce him. A friendship quickly grew between us that would include Bishop John Chane, the Episcopal bishop of Washington, whose office is in the magnificent National Cathedral, and our wives, Amy, Karen, and Zeenat. Together we formed the First Abrahamic Summit, which would create and contribute to interfaith dialogue in the nation's capital.

In those bleak days when the media were pouring out vitriol about Muslim terrorism and implying that every Muslim by definition was a potential terrorist, Rabbi Lustig's moral clarity and courage became a beacon of humanity. I heard him on several occasions publicly and forcefully condemn the human rights violations against the Muslim community. As he often told me, he must, as a rabbi, fight for the rights of everyone, not just those of his community.

The following spring, Rabbi Lustig invited me and my family to a special interfaith Passover seder with members and clergy of his congregation. I decided at the last minute to bring along some visiting Muslim orthodox religious leaders from India after they said they had never been to a synagogue. Rabbi Lustig began the celebration by reading from a special Haggadah text, developed especially for this interfaith seder. The readings included biblical and contemporary Jewish, Christian, and Muslim references. Martin Luther King Jr. and Archbishop Desmond Tutu were part of it. There was a reference to the suffering of the Jews but also to the suffering of others—including Muslims.

We Muslims participated in the ritualistic feast but adapted with our own customs. For example, while others drank wine, we sipped apple juice, which had been provided for this purpose. We felt wonderfully familiar with the stories that we heard of our common ancestors as the evening wore on. The themes of suffering, faith, freedom, and the importance of compassion were repeated throughout the evening.

My conversation with Bruce Lustig, who had been raised in the American South, made me curious about how Jewish communities today are operating in that region. To find out, I traveled to Memphis, Tennessee, to meet with a senior rabbi at Temple Israel, the oldest and largest synagogue in the state, tracing its origins back to 1854. Rabbi Micah Greenstein exemplifies the very struggle against injustice and inhumanity that occurred in the place where much of the battle for civil rights was fought and won. The Reverend Martin Luther King Jr. was martyred there, and today the hotel where he was shot has been converted into a museum, with the balcony and hotel room preserved exactly as they were at that fatal moment.

Educated at Cornell and Harvard, lean and fit in a smart dark gray business suit with a white shirt and blue striped tie, Greenstein exuded a glow of goodwill when he came to have breakfast with me early in the morning at my hotel. The rabbi exudes American pluralism. "You forfeit the right to worship God when you denigrate the worship of God in another human being," he told me, and American identity means "to be passionate about pluralism, justice, freedom, tolerance, and democracy" and the "quest to realize them." The greatest threat to America is indifference: "The opposite of hate is not love, it is indifference. The opposite of injustice is also indifference. Where in the Bible does it say to be indifferent to other human beings?"

I asked Greenstein what advice he would have for the Muslim community. As the rabbi had been speaking to Muslim groups in Memphis, he understood their plight. "More unites us than divides us," he replied, adding that Muslim communities needed to reach out and become less isolated, to "get across that they are not all fanatics. They are heart surgeons, teachers, and your neighbors."

The Holocaust Museum: A Lesson for Our Time

This spirit of healing is surely the inspiration for the Holocaust Memorial Museum in Washington, D.C., which bears testimony to man's inhumanity to man. I was honored to be the first Muslim speaker to give a public lecture at the museum on June 22, 2006. I explored anti-Semitism, Islamophobia, and anti-Americanism and their relationship to each other.

Beneath the shattering human tragedy depicted at the museum are disturbing and fundamental questions, which are not far removed from those raised in this book: How do we define ourselves? Is our definition based upon race, religion, or nation? Do we have to hate those who are not like us? And how can we learn to live together in harmony and with compassion for each other?

The evil in Nazi Germany and the lessons to be learned for global human society have still not been fully appreciated among Muslims. One-third of the world's Jews and two-thirds of those living in Europe during World War II were sent to their deaths. Altogether, more than 6 million Jews and 4 million others, including gypsies, homosexuals, dissenters, and Poles, were killed by the Nazis, and all are commemorated by the museum.

An exhibition I visited, "Deadly Medicine: Creating the Master Race," establishes the links between ideas of racial superiority and state-sponsored ideology and the disastrous consequences for humanity. The chilling connection between pseudoscientific ideas and modern science is brilliantly documented. Even before Germany's defeat in World War I, scholars had been writing about racial hygiene, or eugenics, maintaining that by keeping the "unfit" alive to reproduce and multiply, modern medicine interfered with what Charles Darwin, borrowing from Herbert Spencer, had called the "survival of the fittest" (see chapters 1 and 2). These scholars decried that members of the "fit" groups were marrying late and also using birth control methods. The result was a "biological degeneration" of the population. The solution was "a positive government policy" to sterilize genetic "inferiors." In the United States, many proponents of primordial and predator identity were exploring these ideas as well, as noted in chapter 2.

Adolph Hitler, in *Mein Kampf,* had laid down the philosophy of Nazism: "The *völkisch* [national ethnic German] state . . . must set race in the center of all life. It must take care to keep it pure. . . . It must see to it that only the healthy beget children. . . . It must put the most modern medical means in the service of this knowledge."[1]

Nazism was "applied biology," as stated by Hitler's deputy, Rudolf Hess. During Hitler's Third Reich, Nazi policy created a platform of anti-Semitism as an extreme form of eugenics. The regime projected the "Nordic race" as the eugenic ideal and excluded anyone who was "racially foreign." In the end, the years of pseudoscientific hatred led to the concentration camps and gas chambers. During this period, widely respected scholars talked openly and approvingly of Hitler's message: "I do not characterize every Jew as inferior, as Negroes certainly are . . . but I reject Jewry with every means in my power, and without reserve, in order to preserve the hereditary endowment of my people," wrote anthropologist Eugene Fischer in 1939.[2]

As the "final solution to the Jewish question" evolved, it came close to annihilating the Jewish population of Europe. The horrors of Auschwitz, where about one million Jews from German-controlled countries perished, were compounded by the use of adults and children as guinea pigs in sterilization experiments and genetic research conducted at the camp. After the war, few of the scientists and experts who helped in these inhuman experiments were ever indicted or brought to a moral accounting for their actions. Many continued in their professional careers.

Nazi ideas challenge the core tenets of the Abrahamic faiths of Judaism, Christianity, and Islam—all rooted in notions of caring and compassion. Yet critics of Islam have compared the Quran to *Mein Kampf.* Such remarks reflect ignorance about Islam and the failure of Muslim leadership to convey the message of Islam. The Quran stresses that God has created different tribes, races, and nations, but that their peoples are to be judged only on the basis of their deeds. And, as we know, in his last address to his followers in the early seventh century just before he died, the Prophet of

Islam specified that no difference exists between Arab and non-Arab or between black and white—that goodness resides in one's charitable acts.

The lesson of the museum is heartbreaking but also heartwarming as it yields a sociological maxim: the stronger the pressure on the community, the stronger the will to survive, and the stronger the sense of identity and cohesion. The Jews—the forebearers of the Abrahamic faiths who brought the humanist message of one God and the commandments and the preachings of the great prophets and their revelations—have borne a heavy price for their faith. Their suffering is the suffering of all humanity. With them, humankind must now say, "Never again."

Jews as American Pluralists

When Rabbi Lustig invokes Jewish notions of compassion, justice, and freedom and Rabbi Greenstein quotes his heroes like Martin Luther King Jr., one would expect such words to strike a chord with America's minority groups who have struggled to be accepted as full Americans. Yet many Muslims assume that a dichotomy exists between Americanness and Jewishness, and that mainstream Americans and Christians are "not so bad" except for being "misguided" by the Jews. What this notion overlooks is how tightly woven the threads of Jewish theology and culture are into the fabric of America. One has only to glance at the list of contributors to *I Am Jewish*, written in honor of Danny Pearl's life and last words, and edited by his parents.[3] Every part of American life is represented—political, academic, entertainment, and religion. It is like a Who's Who of the United States that includes actor Kirk Douglas, columnist Thomas Friedman, economist Milton Friedman, TV commentator Larry King, historian Bernard Lewis, radio host Michael Medved, economist Lawrence Summers, and author Elie Wiesel, to name but a few.

Talented and artistic individuals from many groups thrived in the open and competitive culture offered by the United States, but the Jewish contribution to American science stands out and includes world famous figures such as John von Neumann and J. Robert Oppenheimer. The most famous is Albert Einstein, who fled persecution in Europe and is a globally recognized example of the type of intellect and learning embraced by American culture.

According to Jewish writer Joel Stein, all eight major film studios in the United States are owned or run by Jews.[4] The Jewish presence in the American media goes beyond Hollywood. The presidents of NBC, CBS, and the Disney Corporation, which owns ABC, the publisher of the *New York Times*, and the president of MTV are all Jewish Americans.

The contrast in influence between the Jewish and Muslim communities in the United States is best illustrated by the numbers of those actually running the country—the members of Congress. While the two populations are roughly of a similar size in the United States—anywhere between 6 million and 7 million—thirty-two members of the House of Representatives and thirteen members of the Senate are Jewish, while only two members of the House of Representatives are Muslim.

The Jewish Diaspora Comes to America

President George Washington set the tone for the Founding Fathers in the warm reception he gave the Jewish community, which he addressed as "the Stock of Abraham" in a letter to the Hebrew Congregation in Newport, Rhode Island, in 1790.[5] The Jews responded in kind. Uriah Phillips Levy, a Jewish U.S. naval officer, for example, purchased Thomas Jefferson's debt-ridden property of Monticello and preserved it as a museum for posterity. In spite of the attitude of the Founding Fathers, however, anti-Semitism did not disappear.

The Jews coming to America consisted of two broad subgroups, Sephardic and Ashkenazi, each having distinct customs and forms of religious practice. The majority of the first American Jews in the seventeenth and eighteenth centuries, such as those who first arrived on the *Sainte Catherine* in 1654, were Sephardim, Jews from Mediterranean regions who had memories of towering figures from their community in science, philosophy, and politics. These included the philosophers Maimonides and Spinoza. Those with ancestors who had lived in a Muslim-dominated society had notions of Islam and some understanding of Muslim culture.

Sephardic Jews originated in Andalusia, or Moorish-ruled Spain. Expelled in 1492 by King Ferdinand and Queen Isabella, they dispersed across North Africa and the Middle East. Many made their way to countries with more liberal policies toward Jews such as the Netherlands, and from there they came to America, primarily New Amsterdam, Holland's major New World prize.

In contrast to the Sephardim, Ashkenazi Jews, who now vastly outnumber Sephardim, arrived later. The first waves initially came from Germany in the nineteenth century and were joined by a flood of Jewish emigrés fleeing persecution in Eastern Europe and Russia by the end of the century. The earliest Ashkenazi congregation, Philadelphia's Rodeph Shalom, was established in 1795. A major challenge for these arrivals early on was the barrier to their entry in an institution that itself symbolizes American identity, the U.S. military. At the dawn of the Civil War in 1861, President Lincoln's Scots-Irish secretary of war, Simon Cameron, had rejected an application by a Jew to be a military chaplain on the grounds that he was not Christian.[6] American Jews, now growing in numbers and strength, lobbied the president, who overruled Cameron, instituting Jews as full army chaplains for the first time.

This would not be the last time Lincoln would contradict a top official over the treatment of Jews. In 1862 Major-General Ulysses S. Grant, of Scots-Irish and English origin, issued General Order No. 11, which expelled all Jews in his military district, comprising areas of Tennessee, Mississippi, and Kentucky, as a way to crack down on black market cotton from the South, which he was convinced was being run "mostly by Jews and other unprincipled traders."[7] His order gave the Jews twenty-four hours to leave. One of the expelled Jews, Cesar Kaskel, gained an audience with President Lincoln just days after the passage of the Emancipation Proclamation. Lincoln was outraged by the order and immediately revoked it. The conversation between Lincoln and Kaskel became famous in American Jewish mythology, with many Jews proudly recounting the story in this allegorical way:[8]

> Lincoln: And so the children of Israel were driven from the happy land of Canaan?
>
> Kaskel: Yes, and that is why we have come unto Father Abraham's bosom, asking protection.
>
> Lincoln: And this protection they shall have at once.

A few days later a Jewish delegation led by a Cincinnati rabbi called on Lincoln at the White House to express the community's gratitude. Lincoln told those present that "to condemn a class is, to say the least, to wrong the good with the bad. I do not like to hear a class or nationality condemned on account of a few sinners." But men such as Lincoln were few and far between at that time.

The large numbers of Jewish immigrants arriving at the turn of the century provoked anti-Semitism and contributed to the rebirth of the Ku Klux Klan, which had largely faded by then. In the span of a decade, the KKK would go from single-digit membership to more than 4 million, spurred in part by an episode that unfolded in Atlanta, Georgia. Leo Frank, a Jewish Cornell University graduate, managed a pencil factory there, and on April 26,

1913—celebrated locally as Confederate Memorial Day—one of his factory workers, thirteen-year-old Mary Phagan, was raped and murdered. Frank was convicted and sentenced to death for the crime. While Frank awaited execution, new evidence emerged casting serious doubt on his conviction. His sentence was commuted to life in prison as further deliberations began.

Enraged by the court ruling, a group of close to twenty-eight men, calling themselves the Knights of Mary Phagan, broke into the prison on August 17, 1915. They seized Frank, drove him 240 miles to Mary Phagan's hometown, and lynched him. The Knights included the son of a senator, a former governor, lawyers, and a prosecutor. The rope was provided and noose tied by a former local sheriff. Joined by elderly members of the original KKK, the Knights of Mary Phagan met on Stone Mountain outside Atlanta, declaring the birth of a new KKK and vowing to target not only blacks but also Jews and Catholics.[9]

Throughout the South, postcards featuring pictures of Frank's dead body were widely circulated, and pieces of clothing torn off his body were sold as souvenirs, along with sections of the rope that was used for the hanging.[10] Close to 15,000 people came to view Frank's body, and townspeople took "pilgrimages" to the site of his lynching, where they "hugged" and "patted" the tree while "praying."[11] Jews in the South were soon panic-striken. Half of Georgia's 3,000 Jews fled that state alone.[12]

U.S. lawmakers, responding to public anger and prejudice, passed the Immigration Act of 1924, which effectively barred Jews from entering the United States. The legislation was shaped by Madison Grant, a leading figure in the eugenics movement whose book on race Hitler called his "Bible" (see chapter 2). The act had far-reaching consequences: as the Holocaust gained strength in the mid- to late 1930s, America turned away boats full of Jews fleeing Europe. Rabbi David Sandmel told us in Chicago that unless someone had relatives to act as sponsor or was a well-known artist or scientist, it was virtually impossible to gain entrance into the United States during this period.

Another, more spiritual struggle faced the Jewish immigrants: how to balance their religious traditions with the secular language and temperament of their new home. Samuel Schulman, a leading New York rabbi, writing in 1913, reflected on the dilemmas of maintaining a religious identity in a land claiming to be secular:

> We, of course, want to keep religion, Bible reading, hymn singing out of the public schools. Jews make a mistake in thinking only of themselves and assuming always a negative and critical attitude. They

must supplement that negative attitude with a constructive policy. Otherwise, they will soon be classed in the minds of the Christian men and women in this country with the free-thinkers and with those who have no interest in the religious education of the youth. That, of course, is undesirable both because it is contrary to our genius as Jews and also contrary to the real spirit of Americanism, which while not ecclesiastical, and separates Church from State, has always been religious.[13]

In the era before and after World War I, proponents of primordial identity such as Theodore Roosevelt and Woodrow Wilson who veered toward predator identity warned of the dangers posed by "hyphenated Americans" (see chapter 2). Their anxieties resulted in anti-immigrant legislation, including the Espionage Act of 1917 and Sedition Act of 1918. Many Americans suspected Eastern European Jews of sympathizing with the Russian Revolution of 1917 and the newly established Bolshevik government and worried that they might resort to acts of terrorism. Thousands of Jews and Catholics were caught up in federal dragnets like the Palmer Raids, which netted more than 4,000 people in thirty-three cities on a single night in 1920.[14] In response, organizations such as the newly formed American Civil Liberties Union demanded that the U.S. Constitution be honored, but their cries were met with indifference. "There is no time to waste on hairsplitting over infringement of liberty," declared the *Washington Post.*[15]

Despite the government crackdowns, American Jews continued their public activism against a host of issues, from dangerous work conditions to the practice of child labor in America's factories. And for many of these workers the lure of communism, with its promise of worker rights and equality, remained high. Much to their ire, white, Anglo-Saxon business owners now had to contend with a large-scale labor movement among immigrant workers making increasingly bold demands that held up production. This led to further accusations by people such as Henry Ford that the Jews were subversive anarchists and that their unions were "anti-American."

Ford could get away with openly anti-Semitic prejudices in that period. By 1930 one in every 1.3 American households had a car, so the American public was eager to read what Ford had to say, and much of what he proclaimed were anti-Semitic views in his own newspaper, the *Dearborn Independent,* particularly a series of writings later published in pamphlet form as *The International Jew.* He also published the fictitious anti-Semitic polemic *Protocols of the Learned Elders of Zion.* Ford's opinions of Jews so impressed Adolph Hitler across the Atlantic in 1923 that he described Ford "as the leader of the growing Fascist movement in America."[16] Parts of Hitler's *Mein Kampf,* published in 1924, are identical to passages in *The International Jew,* and in 1938 Hitler, who hung a large portrait of Ford beside his desk, presented Ford with the Grand Service Cross of the Supreme Order of the German Eagle, the highest award the Nazis could give to a foreigner.[17] Although Ford apologized for his anti-Semitism, the damage to his reputation had been done.

Anti-Semitism was like a contagious disease. Even the country's top universities were not immune, with Harvard and Yale implementing stringent Jewish quotas. In 1935 the dean of Yale's medical school issued precise directions to his admission staff: "Never admit more than five Jews, take only two Italian Catholics, and take no blacks at all."[18]

Father Charles Coughlin, a Catholic priest, built a vast national following through regular radio broadcasts of his anti-Semitic remarks. He condemned Roosevelt's "Jew Deal."[19] Coughlin was, *Fortune* magazine said in 1934, "just about the biggest thing that ever happened to radio."[20] As late as 1941, famed aviator Charles Lindbergh blamed the Jews and the British for pulling America toward war. Even Franklin D. Roosevelt, of English and Dutch descent and often accused of being soft on the Jews, was not immune from expressing sentiments in keeping with primordial identity, as in this statement made shortly after Pearl Harbor to Secretary of the Treasury Henry Morgenthau, a Jew, and Leo Crowley, a Catholic: "You know this is a Protestant country, and the Catholics and Jews are here under sufferance."[21]

Recognizing that the authorities could not always be relied on to provide security, the Jewish community established its own defense mechanisms through organizations such as the Anti-Defamation League and other vehicles that echoed the ideals of the Founding Fathers who had espoused religious tolerance. One such vehicle was the comic book and the idea of the superhero that have become part of American culture. These fictional heroes, developed by Jewish American cartoonists, fought for truth, justice, tolerance, and "the American way." They included Batman, Spiderman, the X-Men, and perhaps the character that most embodies American virtues and primordial values, Superman. An alien from another world, Superman is adopted as a baby by a white family in the Midwest and given the English name Clark Kent. These primordial connections give Superman legitimacy in terms of American identity. The idea of Superman, thus, is to reinforce the ideals of pluralist America through his strength, resolve, and integrity.

After World War II, anti-Semitism subsided somewhat. With the defeat of the Nazis and the revelations of the scale and tragedy of the Holocaust, followed by the creation of Israel, many Americans began to view the Jews in that country as a plucky little community, fighting for survival against hostile and backward forces, not unlike their own first settlers in the seventeenth century. Not long afterward, America was caught up in another kind of conflict, the cold war, which often seemed to make Jews its victims as well because of lingering beliefs that they were sympathetic to communism. The hysteria of this postwar period was captured by the Jewish playwright Arthur Miller in his play *The Crucible*, set during a Puritan witch-burning frenzy in Massachusetts in the decades following King Philip's War, a period in which an atmosphere of fear and paranoia prevailed (see chapter 2). It is difficult not to see Miller's main point: once again, the white Protestants were burning witches, and this time the Jews were the victims.

From Hollywood's early era through much of the twentieth century, anti-Semitism was a constant fixture in "Tinseltown," mirroring the situation in the country at the time. Jewish studio bosses had to get their films approved by Joseph I. Breen, an Irish Catholic who was the driving force behind the Motion Picture Production Code that censored the content and image of Hollywood films. Breen has frequently been described as an anti-Semite who repeatedly called Jews "lice" and "the scum of the scum of the earth."[22] A 1938 poster reproduced by Thomas Doherty in the *Jewish Daily Forward* in 2007 graphically sums up several tactics used by proponents of American predator identity against minorities like the Jews.[23] The poster (see next page) is a rallying call to the majority population to fight the minority (the Jews making the movies) by boycotting the films. The poster's arguments reflect those used against the black population, and its depiction of a lynching rope and coffin, along with the Star of David, is as explicit and crude a call to violence as is possible.

Changing one's name for a role in Hollywood was not unusual, but for many Jews it was essential. Warner Brothers Pictures, for example, was probably more acceptable to Americans than Wonskolaser Brothers Pictures, the original name of the family. The co-founder of Twentieth-Century Fox, Darryl Francis Zanuck, whose name reflects his Dutch descent, was so incensed when he was denied membership at an elite Los Angeles club on the suspicion he was Jewish that he decided to make a movie about anti-Semitism. To Zanuck's surprise, a group of powerful Hollywood Jews, including Sam Goldwyn (born Schmuel Gelbfisz), told him not to make the film. "We're doing fine," they told Zanuck. "Why stir up trouble?"[24] Besides, they argued, Zanuck would never get his film past Joseph Breen.

Zanuck ignored their advice and made *Gentleman's Agreement* (1947), starring the Catholic actor Gregory Peck. The film turned out to be a success, winning the 1947 Oscar for best picture and best director. Despite his agent's advice not to take the role (because it will "hang around your neck" and "people are going to think you're a Jew for the rest of your career"), Peck felt compelled to do it.[25]

Yet the words of warning Zanuck received from the Jewish moguls proved prophetic. In the same year the film was released, the House Un-American Activities Committee (HUAC) began looking for communist infiltrators in Hollywood. A prominent committee member from Mississippi, John E. Rankin, who was Scots-Irish, had referred to a Jewish journalist as "a little slime-mongering kike" on the floor of the House of Representatives. He was convinced the investigation into Hollywood would reveal "one of the most dangerous plots ever instigated for the overthrow of the government."[26] Zanuck was called before the committee, as were many of the film's actors. Some were blacklisted, not to be seen again in films for years afterward. American predator identity, led by figures like Senator Joseph McCarthy, was ravenous for victims.

Two Identities, Two Films: High Noon *and* Rio Bravo

One of the most celebrated Hollywood cowboy films of all time, *High Noon* (1952), did not escape the vigilant eye of the predator. When I first saw it in the 1960s as a university student in England, I could not believe that a cowboy film could be so rich in allegory, nuance, and metaphor. It was shot in black and white, which captured its bleak mood. The film has enduring appeal and is ranked twenty-seventh on the American Film Institute's list of great films.

High Noon presented the classic dilemma faced by the man of conscience: does he back down from a difficult situation and compromise or stand up to face almost certain destruction? The appeal of *High Noon's* theme is universal as everyone at one time or another has had to confront this kind of choice. Looking ill and tired, Gary Cooper was perfectly cast as Marshal Will Kane, a man at the end of his tether who must fight four gunmen sworn to kill him. Everyone, including his Quaker wife, played by a fresh-faced Grace Kelly, abandons him. Kane eventually triumphs but expresses his disgust at the moral cowardice of the local people by throwing his sheriff's star in the dirt and leaving town.

I was not entirely surprised to learn that the film's director, Fred Zinnemann, writer, Carl Foreman, and producer, Stanley Kramer, were Jewish. As a Muslim, I understood their Abrahamic compulsion to stand up against tyranny and injustice. These Jewish artists perhaps had Hitler in mind and the lack of sympathy the world showed to the Jews as they were led to the gas chambers. What I did not fully realize, when I first saw the film, was how courageously these men were promoting the idea of a pluralist America.

Unlike *Gentleman's Agreement*, *High Noon* was still being written when the federal government intervened to launch an investigation. Foreman, a former member of the Communist Party, was called before the HUAC. Facing unrelenting pressure from the government, studio moguls, journalists, and Hollywood luminaries, including legendary Scots-Irish cowboy actor John Wayne, Foreman fled the country and was blacklisted.

When *High Noon* was finally released, John Wayne expressed his distaste, calling it "the most un-American thing I've ever seen in my whole life."[27] His friend Howard Hawks, who had directed him in many famous cowboy films, was also offended, saying he could not believe that Marshal Kane, played by Cooper, would "go running around town like a chicken with its head off asking for help."[28] Hawks traced his descent on his father's side to English settlers who had arrived in America in 1630 and was known to have publicly made anti-Semitic remarks. The two saw the film as an attack on America and responded in characteristic fashion.

In 1959 the two made *Rio Bravo,* in which John Wayne plays the sheriff. It had music, glamour, humor, and was in glorious Technicolor. This time, the sheriff exuded manly courage and wry humor, was loved by an admiring community, and was more than a match for the villains; they stood as much chance of stopping him as a snowball of surviving in hell. *Rio Bravo* was make-believe Hollywood at its best. I must admit I enjoyed it too.

Jews in Camelot

The Jews found another natural ally in John F. Kennedy, who included two in his cabinet, more than ever before in American history. American Jews also appreciated Kennedy's support for Israel, which Kennedy called a "beacon of inspiration to all free men everywhere."[29] Kennedy felt Israel was founded on the same ideals as the United States and shared with the West "a tradition of civil liberties, of cultural freedom, of parliamentary democracy, of social mobility."[30]

Yet Kennedy was also concerned about the situation in the Middle East and adamant that the United States should pursue a policy of "friendship" with the Arabs, which would turn the Middle East into a land of "strength and hope."[31] He warned that if the United States forced its hand in the Arab world militarily, "the very sands of the desert would rise to oppose the imposition of an outside control upon the destinies of these proud peoples."[32]

When Kennedy was assassinated in 1963, Jews mourned the president as one of their own. In New York City's Congregation B'nai Jeshurun, over 1,000 Jews recited a mourner's *kaddish,* a sacred prayer uttered for the deceased. Clutching a copy of Kennedy's *Profiles in Courage* at the synagogue's pulpit, Rabbi Joel Geffen of the Jewish Theological Seminary compared the slain president to the ancient Jewish patriarch Jacob, who dreamed he saw a ladder leading to Heaven and the Lord standing above it. Like Jacob, Kennedy had dreams of equal rights for all mankind and world peace, said the rabbi, quoting Kennedy's vision of a world "where the weak are safe and the strong are just."[33] Inspired by Kennedy, many Jews would emerge to lead the rapid cultural changes of the 1960s and civil rights struggle that his election, and also his assassination, helped set in motion.

Notes on Anti-Semitism from the Field

Kennedy notwithstanding, the relationship between Jews and Christians is a complicated one, and over it hang 2,000 years of history. One of my Jewish friends said to me in a long interview on the subject, "We cannot take our present close relationship with the Christian majority for granted." He was right. Although the popular Christian evangelist rhetoric of love for Jews and Israel has buried the anti-Semitism, Chris Hedges, a religious scholar and son of a Presbyterian pastor, points to some disturbing facts regarding the place of the Jewish community in Christian America.

Hedges cites the *The Institutes of Biblical Law* by R. J. Rushdoony, written in 1973 and a seminal book for the Christian Reconstructionism movement, which "calls for a Christian society that is harsh, unforgiving, and violent." Rushdoony, notes Hedges, "draws heavily on the calls for a repressive theocratic society laid out by Calvin in *Institutes of the Christian Religion,* first published in 1536 and one of the most important works of the Protestant Reformation. Christians are, Rushdoony argues, the new chosen people of God and are called to do what Adam and Eve failed to do: create a godly, Christian state." Because they neglected to fulfill God's commands in the Hebrew scriptures, Jews have "forfeited their place as God's chosen people and have been replaced by Christians." Rushdoony also calls for the death penalty "not only for offenses such as rape, kidnapping and murder, but also for adultery, blasphemy, homosexuality, astrology, incest, striking a parent, incorrigible juvenile delinquency, and, in the case of women, 'unchastity before marriage.'" Hedges comes to the conclusion that for these Christians, "The world is to be subdued and ruled by a Christian United States. Rushdoony dismissed the widely accepted estimate of 6 million Jews murdered in the Holocaust as an inflated figure, and his theories on race often echo those found in Nazi eugenics, in which there are higher and lower forms of human beings. Those considered by the Christian state to be immoral and incapable of reform are to be exterminated."[34]

It was this philosophy that shaped the views of James Wenneker von Brunn, an elderly white Christian who in the summer of 2009 walked into the Holocaust Memorial Museum in Washington, D.C., with a loaded gun and began to fire, killing an African American security guard. Police later found extensive hate literature in von Brunn's belongings. A handwritten note in his car claimed, "The Holocaust is a lie" and "Obama was created by Jews." It later emerged that he had lived in Hayden Lake, Idaho, where Pastor Richard Butler was based (see chapter 2), that he opposed the Iraq War, and felt that the September 11 attacks were an "inside job." When the police raided his house, they uncovered paintings of Hitler and Jesus.

As the Holocaust Museum shooting proves, anti-Semitism still exists, and the challenge of racial and religious prejudice is far from over. Frankie experienced it firsthand on his way to a wedding. His cabdriver, a white man in his forties, asked him what he did: "I told him I worked at American University. He then asked me plainly: 'Are you Jewish?' Startled, I told him I wasn't, to which he said 'Ah, good' and launched into a tirade. He said I should know what the Jews are doing to 'destroy the United States.' He accused Jews of hijacking the U.S. for their own nefarious aims and pointed specifically to the Middle East."

The suicide bombings in Palestine, he told Frankie, were "actually arranged by Jews." He reached into his glove compartment and pulled out a stack of papers containing photos and website addresses that he told Frankie would prove what he was saying and asked him to "spread the word" about the Jewish threat. "When we arrived," said Frankie, "I left him my ID card while I went to the ATM. He examined the photo and suddenly started screaming, 'Martin, Martin that's . . . that's a Jewish name!' I replied that it was actually Irish, which seemed to calm him down a bit, but only just."

We witnessed or heard about other examples of anti-Semitism on our journey, including that of an inebriated young white girl during Mardi Gras in New Orleans who said that the greatest threat to America was the Jews. She believed Barack Obama was supported by the Jews, to the detriment of America. A Jewish woman in her mid-twenties from Chicago spoke of the swastika painted on her garage door when she was a child after neighbors observed her selling small Easter bunnies. For other Jews, stereotyping and teasing can also cause discomfort and reinforce their "otherness." A nineteen-year-old Jewish female college student at DePaul University said she had experienced "all the typical jokes about Jews having curly hair, big noses, and being frugal with money. It is always in jest, but I still find those stereotypes offensive." A fourteen-year-old Jewish female at Burroughs High School in St. Louis who listed "books about the Holocaust" as her favorites, said, "People have told me that I'm going to hell because I'm Jewish . . . which is odd because we don't believe in hell."

Jan Lund, a sixty-year-old woman of Russian Jewish descent who grew up in Council Bluffs, Iowa, said that when she was in high school her "greatest dream was to go abroad as an exchange student" but was shocked when she was told by the chairman of the committee that her town could not send a Jew to represent the school. To a twenty-three-year-old female at the Jewish Theological Seminary, problems emanate from the fact that "unfortunately too much Christianity comes into the public domain and into government."

A fifty-five-year-old Jewish woman, born in New York City, said that Americans view her religion "highly negatively," so she often feels as though she has to overcompensate with those who have had limited experience with Jews "to counteract many stereotypes of Jews." As a young professional, she was surprised to be at the receiving end of anti-Semitic remarks. "I was taken aback," she said. "These incidents have stayed with me."

"A Very Frightened Country"

My conversations with Jewish friends and colleagues have yielded similar stories of anti-Semitism—of harrowing experiences in schools and on playing fields, of having to run home swiftly after school to escape bullies bent on beating them. It is difficult to imagine such assured and successful figures as scholar Noam Chomsky, Rabbi Bruce Lustig, or college dean Louis Goodman being bullied and abused when they were at school. But this is exactly what happened.

We arranged to talk to Noam Chomsky with this in mind. His views on American capitalism, Israel, and U.S. foreign policy are well known and were not the subject of our interview. We were more interested in discovering Chomsky's own experience as a Jewish American growing up at a difficult time and learning to engage with American identity. In our interview, we uncovered a rarely glimpsed side of this world-famous philosopher and writer.

We interviewed Chomsky in his office at the Massachusetts Institute of Technology in Cambridge. His gentle, slightly disconnected professorial persona belies his critical intellectual faculties. To sense the pain of Noam Chomsky, whom the *New York Times* called "arguably the most important intellectual alive," is an unnerving experience. One does not expect a global guru to feel emotional stress—or heat or cold—like ordinary mortals. The anguish in Chomsky's voice was barely concealed as he recounted the brittle anti-Semitism he faced when growing up in Philadelphia and Boston. He tried to rationalize the prejudice as part of a historical process, that each wave of immigrants is harshly treated until members of that group make their way into society, and then a new wave from a different group comes along. And the Jews were no different.

In Boston, Honorary Consul General of Pakistan Barry Hoffman and renowned intellectual Noam Chomsky stand with Akbar Ahmed before a portrait of Chomsky's hero, Lord Bertrand Russell. Identity has been a "crucial issue" for America from its founding, says Chomsky, largely because it is a nation of immigrants.

Even Harvard, the oldest and most established university of the United States, was not immune to anti-Semitism, as Chomsky recounts: "Harvard is changed now, but in the early 1950s when I was there, you could cut the anti-Semitism with a knife. There were virtually no Jewish faculty. The Jewish students, like me, were kind of out of everything; there was this whole life going on that we didn't know about." Chomsky also related his childhood fear of Catholics, who, also harassed by the prevailing dominant Protestant culture, took out their anger on the Jews, as well as blacks and other groups.

The undercurrents of anti-Semitism, however, did not stop those with talent and drive from rising to the top. Paul Samuelson, Chomsky said, obtained his doctorate from Harvard but could not get tenure so he joined the more welcoming MIT: "One of the reasons MIT is a great university is because Jews couldn't get jobs at Harvard. So they came to the engineering school down the street, which didn't have the same class bias. This is now all deep in the past. And it's been true of, as I say, the Irish a century ago."

For Chomsky, it is not the idea of freedom or democracy that lies at the heart of America, but fear. A sense of fear and threat permeates every aspect of society, he explained to us: "It's a very frightened country. Unusually so, by international standards, which is kind of ironic because [we're] at a level of security that nobody's ever dreamed of in world history. You find it's been studied in popular literature, literature for the masses. Now it would be television or movies or something, but for a long time, it was magazines and novels. The theme is we're about to be destroyed by an enemy, and at the last minute, a super weapon is discovered or a hero arises, Rambo or someone, and somehow saves us. The Terminator or high school boys hiding in the mountains defending us from the Russians."

"And a lot of mythology was created, as is typical for nations," continued Chomsky, looking beneath the surface. "Nations are myths so they have founding myths, identity myths, and so on. And if you look back at the original colonists, . . . they were religious fanatics, who were waving the holy book calling themselves the children of Israel returning to the holy land slaughtering the enemy, following the Lord's wishes, the Amalekites being the native population." Chomsky noted, "The hysteria today about illegal immigration is just a replica of what's been going through American history. . . . We were all regarded as degenerates and it goes right to the present."

"To survive," said Chomsky, "every man and woman needed to be familiar with a musket or a sword. . . . The Bible provided spiritual comfort, but what was needed to protect the family and community from the many real dangers around them—hostile natives, lawless men bent on mischief, and even wild animals—was a gun. That is why the community looked up to the strong man who could till the land, build a log cabin, and protect his family." Chomsky believes that building up the "enemy" as a threat became a mechanism to allow white settlers and later other white parties to justify their actions against minority groups. "So in the early years, the great enemy was the Indians. . . . Then it was the black slaves. There's going to be a slave uprising, all they want to do is rape white women and so on and so forth. And then, you go later on in the century and it was the Chinese. You think they're coming in here to start laundries, but in fact they're planning to take over the country and destroy us. Progressive writers like Jack London were writing novels about how we have to kill everyone in China with bacteriological warfare to stop this nefarious plot before it goes too far, then the Hispanics, and now it is Muslims."

Chomsky went on: "The paranoia is very real. You see it with populist leaders. Lyndon Johnson, a man of the people close to the public mood, made some very interesting speeches during the Vietnam War to American soldiers. He said, 'Look, we're fighting for our lives. . . . There are a 150 million of us and 3 billion of them'—you know, the rest of the world—'and if might makes right they'll sweep over us, take all that we have. So, therefore we have to stop them in Vietnam.'"

As to his views on American identity, Chomsky noted that the United States is a country of immigrants, originally mostly English, but then German, Scots-Irish, Swedish, southeastern European, and eastern European. The fact that it is a melting pot made creating an identity "a crucial issue" from the very beginning. "If you look over American history," reflected Chomsky, "each wave of immigrants at first was very harshly repressed so in the Boston area where we are, there was a big Irish immigration after the Irish famine and so on. But the Irish were barely a cut above blacks. I think the average lifespan for an Irish male in Boston in the late nineteenth century was about forty years. . . . There were signs, 'No dogs or Irish allowed.' They gradually over time worked themselves into the political system, the social system, and became a part of it. The Jewish immigration was pretty similar. My father worked in a sweatshop. Jews were the criminals, Murder Incorporated was run by the Jews. Finally, they worked themselves up and became school teachers and the most privileged minority in the country. And it's happened with wave after wave of immigrants."

"The greatest threat to the United States," felt Chomsky, "is somebody like Rush Limbaugh, who would be something other than a mere cynic and would really be aiming for power. As long as he's just a cynic trying to make money, ok, it's not that serious. But if someone comes along, who's the Hitler type, who really wants power and who plays his cards right, it could be a major threat."

Proponents of militant Christianity, Chomsky believes, are preparing to battle imagined enemies, Muslim and non-Muslim. He mentioned a rally for Sarah Palin in Minnesota during which the crowd started shouting "Kill them" and other slogans. He noted that the meeting opened with a prayer inciting those present to vote for John McCain as a means to "protect Christianity from the Hindus, the Buddhists, the Muslims, whoever it is, who are trying to destroy Christianity." This type of call "goes right back in American history all the way to the colonists defending Christianity from the heathens," Chomsky concluded.

Negotiating Plymouth

Chomsky was not the only Jewish intellectual decrying the fanaticism among the Plymouth settlers. For Louis Goodman, dean of American University's School of International Service, the settlers "were crazy, religious zealots, who left England because they wanted to practice their own brand of religion." So Plymouth was a "pedigree": "The white Anglo-Saxon Protestants would trace their roots back to the *Mayflower* and encourage everyone else to assimilate and be like them."

Rabbi Greenstein of Memphis maintained his cheerful mood when I asked what Plymouth meant to him. (I had found that the question tended to agitate those who were not of English descent and Protestant.) The Rabbi answered in measured tones: "These settlers were coming to a land of opportunity. They were escaping from tyranny and religious persecution." While he noted they were not tolerant, he mentioned the exceptions such as Roger Williams, expelled from Plymouth for his belief in what the rabbi called "multiculturalism."

Michael Chertoff, the former secretary of homeland security, who is Jewish, incorporated his identity with the American identity that Plymouth represents. He understood the significance of Plymouth and offered a way for minorities to associate with it and become fully American while still retaining their own identity. Interestingly, Chertoff believes that a Muslim can be president of the United States if he or she is able to accept Plymouth and what it stands for: "To me, Plymouth means the desire of people who left the old world to find a place in a new world where they could build a foundation of their own choosing, and build it with their ideals, which are the ideals of freedom and toleration. And I recognize that there's a little bit of ambiguity, that some were more tolerant than others, but at least they articulated the ideals that are the foundation of this country. I think those were formed at Plymouth Rock, and to me we are descendents of the early Americans not because of the passage of blood or the fact that we're literally children of their loins, but because we have embraced their spirit. And that in America to me is all that is required to be a full American. And that's equally true with Muslim Americans, and I think there will no doubt come a time that we'll have a Muslim president."

Challenging Anti-Semitism and Islamophobia

Michael Chertoff's optimism about Muslims is a far cry from the time after World War II when the Jewish community confronted Muslims in America for the first time. The two did not get on well together. The Jews saw little of merit in Muslims and knew virtually nothing about them except that they seemed to be bent on destroying the recently created state of Israel. The African American Muslims saw the Jews as unsympathetic landlords and shop owners, and the immigrants associated Jews with the policies of Israel. As a consequence, the levels of Islamophobia in Jewish society and of anti-Semitism among Muslims remain high. Acts of commission and omission—actively attacking the other side, or, alternatively, doing nothing about it—mark the relationship between the two.

I define anti-Semitism and Islamophobia as racial and religious hatred against Jews and Muslims, respectively, but hasten to add a caveat—these terms are bandied about too frequently and too often with little justification. Criticism of Israeli policy or pointing to the plight of the Palestinians is not anti-Semitism; threatening to wipe Israel from the map or claiming the Holocaust never happened is anti-Semitism. Asking whether Islam encourages violence or why more Muslims do not speak out against terrorism is not Islamophobia; to single out Muslims in an airport queue or to claim that every Muslim is by definition a potential, if not a fully formed, terrorist is Islamophobia. Perhaps few are as guilty of these prejudices as Muslims and Jews themselves.

In their defense, Muslims will claim they cannot be accused of anti-Semitism because they share Islam with Arabs, who are also Semites. They will argue that Jews are oversensitive about Israel, which, after all, is just another country, not fully appreciating the special significance of Israel in the lives and history of Jews everywhere. In their defense, Jews will say they are raising legitimate questions regarding Muslims that are of concern to everyone. They will argue that Muslims are oversensitive about Islam and see every question about it as an attack, without appreciating the strong association Muslims everywhere feel with their own religion, whether as theology or culture.

Muslim Perceptions of Jews

Across the length and breadth of the United States, we saw evidence of the gap between Jews and Muslims and the consequent resilience and diffusion of different strains of anti-Semitism. We heard professors, imams, community leaders, and ordinary Muslims express doubts and reservations about the relationship between Jews and Muslims.

One of our first discussions on this issue was with the distinguished professor M. Cherif Bassiouni of DePaul University Law School in Chicago, a respected figure in the Muslim community. In an interview with Frankie, Bassiouni asked him if he could recall an important event in 1972. Before Frankie could answer, Bassiouni said the correct response was the Munich Olympic massacre, after which the Israelis launched a campaign to kill all Palestine Liberation Organization (PLO) terrorists involved. The Israelis, said Bassiouni, immediately began making contacts in the American FBI and Department of Justice, creating a database of Palestinians in the United States and, with this, tracking terrorist activity in the country.

Bassiouni claimed that Jews in Hollywood then activated a campaign to depict Palestinians as terrorists. Organizations in Israel like the Jaffee Center, he said, began to "reconfigure" America's thinking, and the definition of terrorist soon was expanded from Palestinians to all Muslims. Americans were constantly told to be worried about a "Muslim bomb" in two respects, a nuclear bomb and a population bomb. Bassiouni felt that it was Israel that successfully got the West to see Islam as a threat. He had evidence, he said, of a task force in the Department of Justice that sought to portray Islam as a terrorist religion. This continued in the late 1990s and early 2000s, stated Bassiouni, when the Israelis succeeded in convincing Americans that the physical threat Israelis faced from the Palestinians was the same that Westerners faced from Islam as a whole. This was partly accomplished, he said, through an alliance between Jews and the Christian Right in America, a relationship that has continued with the Neoconservatives.

For Imam Siraj Wahhaj of the Masjid At-Taqwa in New York City (see chapter 4), "our misguided foreign policy toward Israel" is the greatest threat facing America, and he asked why he could not criticize it in public in America. Mohamed Al-Darsani, the Syrian imam in Fort Myers, Florida (see chapter 5), was bitter about America, which he predicted would "soon be a Nazi country." He accused Christians of being "more Zionist than the Jews themselves. The Christians are . . . a bigger threat to Islam because they are motivated by the coming of Christ and Armageddon."

Ordinary Muslims also connected the dots for themselves between their predicament and the Jewish community. A seventy-two-year-old unemployed Pakistani in Fort Myers said, "Muslims are being slaughtered everywhere in the world. There is death everywhere. The USA backs Israel and India to kill Muslims."

An African American student at the mosque at Tulane University in New Orleans spoke approvingly of his right to make choices in America. And he raised the question of Abrahamic affinity: "Why are the Christians so close to the Jews? They don't believe in Jesus but we do; they should be closer with us!" A Palestinian student at the same mosque accused Jonathan and Frankie of being "biased toward Israel." He also complained that America remained silent on the "destruction to Palestine" and predicted that there would be a price to pay for this negligence. The Filipino-Hawaiian Muslim grave digger at the Colorado Muslim Society in Denver saw a Jewish hand in American law: "You know, its called the 'Jew-dicial' system. There are hardly any Jews in prison."

According to a nineteen-year-old female Egyptian student in Dearborn, Michigan, the greatest threat to America is the "Jewish hand in the media and continuous American support for Israel," despite Israel's "murder on an everyday basis." She considered Israel a "terrorist" state that with the help of America is conducting a "blood massacre" of Muslim civilians. Asked if she had ever met a Jew or a Christian and if those interactions changed her, she replied: "To be honest, I do not think my views on Jewish people will ever change regardless of who I meet."

At the Islamic Center of New Orleans, two cabdrivers, an Egyptian and a Pakistani, raised a topic that came up again and again on our journey: Who was really responsible for 9/11? The cabdrivers repeated a well-worn conspiracy theory, helping each other finish sentences and ideas: "Five hundred Jews were absent from the World Trade Center on the morning of 9/11. It's there on the Internet. The footage of the planes hitting the towers was shot by Jews, which proves that there was a conspiracy." These same conspiracy theories are shared by the younger generation of Muslims, as we found at the Palestinian school in New Orleans (chapter 5) and in conversation with a boy in New York's Little Pakistan (chapter 3).

In San Diego, at the Salafi-dominated Masjid AL-Ribat AL-Islami, an Egyptian and a Palestinian Jordanian also blamed the Jews for current conflicts: "Jews in America control the media—there are powerful Jewish interests in America. The Jews are engineering the animosity between Christians and Muslims. America's ideology must change; otherwise the wars will be continuous."

Dawud Walid, a prominent African American who heads the Council on American-Islamic Relations (CAIR) in Detroit, spoke about the troubled relationship between the Jews and the blacks in American history: "Many of the costumes blacks wear, including pimp clothes, come from Jews who gave the blacks the clothes they didn't want. They gave them 'clown clothes.' Jews came to the U.S., became 'white,' and then began to oppress the blacks. They moved into black neighborhoods and extracted wealth without giving back." Anti-Jewish sentiment is also widespread among followers of the Nation of Islam but was renounced by Imam W. D. Mohammed when he took his followers concurrently into Sunni Islam and American pluralism.

These Muslim perceptions of Jews are fed by the actions and words of some members of the Jewish community such as the militant Jewish Defense League (JDL), which plotted to bomb the King Fahad Mosque in Culver City, California. Jonathan and Frankie, who found the marble mosque most impressive, interviewed its imam, Mustafa Umar, on what was his first day of work. At twenty-seven, he had just completed his training at Nadwat-ul-ulema, the second largest Islamic school in India after Deoband. He had also studied in Egypt and France, as well as at the University of California, Irvine.

The mosque was financed by King Abdul Aziz Fahad of Saudi Arabia, who hosted its opening in November 1998. Three years later, in the aftermath of 9/11, the JDL targeted the mosque, as well as the offices of U.S. Representative Darrell Issa, a Lebanese Christian. Through a sting operation, the FBI foiled the plot and moved in, arresting two men, Irv Rubin and Earl Krugel. Krugel had been taped telling an FBI informant that Arabs needed a "wake-up call."[35] In the raid, the FBI confiscated five pounds of explosive powder, fuses, pipes, dozens of loaded rifles, and various handguns.[36] Imam Umar told Jonathan and Frankie that this episode once again convinced members of the Muslim community of the innate hostility of the Jews.

The JDL sees itself as the defender of the Jewish community and is ready, if necessary, to launch attacks on perceived enemies. The symbol of the JDL is a right-hand fist, and the organization's website shows a young man wearing a *yarmulke* with his left arm stretched out, also with fist clenched. [37] The organization was founded in 1968 by Meir Kahane, a Brooklyn-born Orthodox rabbi who would go on to be elected to the Israeli Knesset. Kahane preached that America's Jews were about to undergo a "second Holocaust" and that major Jewish organizations in the United States had failed to protect them from anti-Semitism, which he saw as "exploding" all over the country. Rabbi Kahane proved a popular figure among young American Jews searching for an identity, including singers and songwriters Bob Dylan and Arlo Guthrie, whose mother, a Jew, had married Woodie Guthrie, Dylan's troubadour Scots-Irish idol.[38] Kahane was assassinated in New York in 1990 by El Sayyid Nosair, an immigrant from Egypt associated with Brooklyn's Al-Farooq Mosque (see chapter 5). The rabbi still commands a following both in Israel and around the world.

Unlike Culver City's community, some Muslims showed more nuance in their remarks about Jews. In Atlanta the Sufi imam Salahuddin Wazir (see chapter 5) wanted Muslims and non-Muslims alike to be responsible and responsive, and to tell their lawmakers that "we don't want our tax money to go to mercilessly slaughter women and children." He mentioned specifically the Israeli bombing of a UN school in Gaza and places of worship in the Gaza war of 2009. He condemned the rocket attacks of both the Palestinians and the Israelis. "Stand up," he exhorted Americans. "Don't let your tax dollars fund this support for the Zionist state," which has cost billions of dollars and the lives of thousands. The actions of the Israeli Defense Force, he believed, were pushing young Muslims toward violence: "Are we going to continue to let Israel live in fear and the Palestinians in imprisonment? We are told that the kids killed are future terrorists. They might be one day, without hope. They are easy recruits for violence because they are living in fear."

Some Muslims praised the Jewish contribution to American pluralism. A seventy-one-year-old man of Lebanese descent in Cedar Rapids, Iowa, said that the United States is considered a Christian country by "evangelicals but will never be because the Jewish community stands in its way. I give them credit for this." Others disagreed: when asked if the United States is a Christian country, a thirty-two-year-old Turkish man in Houston saw "too much Jewish impact" and felt "like Jews supersede Christians, or Jews are ruling the country."

Jewish Perceptions of Muslims

The hatred between Jews and Muslims was highlighted for me when I suggested in an article in 2003 that Muslims need to be involved in dialogue with everyone, including those they think are hostile to them, like commentator Daniel Pipes. My general point was that "one of the challenges facing America after September 11 is how to deal with Islam. There is a need to understand the Muslim community, its history and its traditions. Who is better placed to act as a bridge than the scholar of Islam? What better challenge for Daniel Pipes than to assist in creating genuine dialogue with the Muslim community?"[39]

Muslims took this to mean I was endorsing the critics of Islam personified by Pipes, and my article unleashed a ferocious barrage of conversations, telephone calls, and e-mails condemning me. A headline in one of Pakistan's leading newspapers read "Dr Akbar S Ahmed Lone Muslim Voice in Favour of Daniel Pipes Nomination."[40] The article that followed accused me of "supporting a person who has said and written some extremely poisonous things about Islam and Muslims."

The intense Muslim rage that I faced indicated the problem was more serious than I had thought, the gap between Muslims and Jews bigger than I had imagined. I was bombarded with arguments that a toxic Islamophobia was being spread across the land by prominent Jews, including media personalities. Muslims saw this as part of a global Jewish conspiracy against Islam and thought the so-called Neocon movement, then playing a prominent role in the George W. Bush administration, was being led and defined by the Jewish community. Neoconservatives—such as columnist Charles

Krauthammer, writer Bill Kristol, defense official Paul Wolfowitz, and presidential adviser Richard Perle—were constantly on television and radio and writing articles on blogs and in newspapers arguing Islam was a threat to Western civilization. It was a shrewd strategy, Muslims figured, for Jews to divert Christian animosity toward Islam, given their own history with Christianity in Europe. It explained, they thought, why Jewish voices were so prominent in the Neocon movement.

In terms of my models of American identity, these media personalities present a paradox. Because they are not white Protestants, it seems more in their interest to promote and defend American pluralism. Yet here was a small group almost fanatically identifying with American primordial and predator identities, thereby negating a belief in pluralism as did non-Protestant Christians cited in chapter 3. Sometimes the fissures showed. In a column highlighting Howard Dean's reference to "guys with Confederate flags in their pickup trucks," Charles Krauthammer called white southern Protestants "rebel-yelling racist redneck[s]," "yahoos," and "white trash." Krauthammer's comments infuriated the Scots-Irish senator Jim Webb, who called them "the most vicious ethnic slur of the presidential campaign."[41] Increasingly after 9/11, figures like the eternally somber Krauthammer became the voice and face of American predator identity.

At times, Jews responded to our questionnaires with harsh words for Muslims and spoke of the dangers posed by "radical Islam." According to a sixty-six-year-old man from Arkansas, the best way to improve relations with Muslims was to "educate the 90 percent . . . who are only educated vis-à-vis the Koran, give Muslim women freedom and equality, and bomb the nuclear facilities in Iran." A woman in her fifties working the desk at the Sahara Casino in Las Vegas described Islam as "slavery" and said that Muslims "don't value families." An elderly Jewish woman of Romanian descent in Philadelphia told us her husband wants to expel all Muslims from the United States and bar any from entering the country, a sentiment she did not dispute. The Founding Fathers may have welcomed both Jews and Muslims, she allowed, "but that was before they wanted to kill us."

A fifty-one-year-old Jewish Theological Seminary student in New York believed the war on terror is a struggle "against radical Muslims who are opposed to Western values," while a seventeen-year-old student in Boston thought that in Islam "girls are treated like shit." At Temple Israel in Omaha, a seventy-one-year-old woman born in Jerusalem was disturbed that "there has been no public Muslim denunciation of 9/11 and other attacks." A sixty-six-year-old man from Arkansas felt that Muslims can be Americans, but "until we have a better example of American Islamics, I wouldn't vote for one."

Some Jews admitted they had no contact with Muslims at all. A woman in her forties at the Jewish Theological Seminary said, "I live on the Upper East Side. I listen to NPR and go to the deli, where sometimes I see what I think are Muslims working there. Actually, I know nothing about Muslims and have never met one, although we read about them in the newspapers all the time. We're really scared of the Nation of Islam, though. It is a natural reaction to be scared of people who have expressed hatred of Jews—hence our apprehension about Obama. But in our guts we know this is wrong."

For Jews who have been involved in interfaith dialogue, however, it is often a different story. A sixty-one-year-old woman in Omaha who attends the interfaith mission headed by Rabbi Aryeh Azriel expressed a change of heart. When asked who represents Islam today, she answered, "It was the terrorists; now it's people I've met through Tri-Faith."

Muslims tended to focus only on what they heard from the Neocon perspective and failed to recognize other public voices with a Jewish background that reflected a pluralist America. Amy Goodman on radio and Bill Maher and Jon Stewart in their television comedy shows have courageously and consistently exposed hypocrisy and injustice and thereby challenged Islamophobia while giving free access to Muslim voices on their shows.

Zionism

There is considerable controversy and debate about Zionism among Muslims, who see it as a source of Islamophobia. I asked Stephen Stern, a Jewish leader in interfaith dialogue in Washington, D.C., to define it: "Zionism," he replied, "is the profound modern-day act of rescue and redemption for a Jewish people through creation of the state of Israel—a historical necessity and I am an adherent. But it is impossible for me not to recognize that it came at the cost of the dispossession of the Palestinian Arab people. There are many contending explanations and many sources of shared blame—the Arab political order and the actions of international powers among them. Israel came to be through acts of rescue responding to millennia of ongoing siege against Jews. But the genius that allows it to survive was the Jewish leadership's acceptance of partition in the late 1930s, however tactical or military were its motives. Two states for two peoples. Intertwined stories that must be painfully and compassionately addressed. The arc of history is toward partition. May it be fulfilled in our time."

The matter gets complicated owing to the internal divisions within the Jewish community. Stern alerted me to what he called "the rule of thirds" among the Jews. By this, he meant that "one-third of the Jewish 'mainstream leadership,' while it might disagree in some particulars, knows that dialogue is necessary to secure the Jewish and Israeli future. Another third knows there needs to be some sort of conversation—but is buffeted by any harsh criticism, by any alternative narrative—toward thoughts of millennia of Jews under siege. The final third is unremittingly hostile (I hope it will be proved to be far less than a third)—the iron wall of protection against the siege of Jews and Israel must stand intact from all assaults, all self-criticism leads to catastrophe."

Israel also complicates the relationship with the Muslims. The grim situation on the ground for the Palestinians—the constant killings and counterkillings, the seeming hopelessness—induces despair. This is one of the world's most intractable problems because two peoples with potentially so much in common are linked in a cycle of death and destruction. Yet all the Jewish people I met, including Israelis, agreed with me that nothing is more important than peace between the two, which rests on the formation of a homeland for the Palestinians so that both peoples can finally live in security side by side as good neighbors, creating harmony and peace in the region. If that happens, and I pray it does soon, Israel will be able to live at peace with the Muslim world.

The Sephardic Warrior for Peace

David Shasha of Brooklyn, an Orthodox Jew introduced in chapter 3, writes and lectures about the experiences of Jews and Muslims in Spain over half a millennium ago, when they lived together and art, architecture, and scholarship flourished. David sees himself as a defender of the Sephardic Jews who were the inheritors of the Spanish legacy. He is the director of the Center for Sephardic Heritage and publishes the "Sephardic Heritage Update," a newsletter about his community supporting dialogue and understanding.

David Shasha told us that he is inspired by a "Medieval Judaism" coming from Andalusia. His family is originally from the Syrian and Iraqi Orthodox communities that moved to Mumbai, India, and then to the United States. David began his heritage center on a shoestring budget to keep the idea of Andalusia alive and to bring the "Andalusian model of religious humanism," as he called it, to the United States. This idea, he told us, has been considered "dangerous" to others in his community, and he has been deliberately ostracized. Yet he argues that historically Jews in Europe and Germany also appreciated the Andalusian model, one that harks back to Muslim Spain during the period known as La Convivencia, when Jews,

Christians, and Muslims developed a culture and environment in which each group could contribute to the whole. It was here that the identity and culture of the Sephardim matured, producing one of the greatest rabbis of all times, the legendary Maimonides. Muslim history connects Maimonides with none other than the equally legendary Muslim ruler Saladin.

My feeling on meeting Sephardim such as David, as well as Rabbi Susan Talve in St. Louis and Rabbi Aryeh Azriel in Omaha, was that of someone reconnecting with long-lost family. Their appearance, manner, and style hinted at the centuries they once shared with Muslims in Muslim lands. They were more informal and more insistent on hospitality, reminding me of Muslim adab, or etiquette.

David himself is an idealist yearning for a time long gone, a time of interfaith harmony and creativity. Sitting alone in an empty house full of books, David captures something admirable and noble, even as he clings to a cause that some would consider hopeless. His sense of isolation is accentuated by the unsympathetic attitude of the Ashkenazi Jews who dominate his neighborhood. Even though he had grown up and lived in Brooklyn, he complained, the majority of his Ashkenazi brethren never let him forget his Sephardic background. For his part, David described the Orthodox way of life in New York as being antithetical to today's world, with its precise rituals and traditions making a modern lifestyle nearly impossible. The community is plagued by poverty, he noted, as the men do not have jobs and read the Talmud all day. Modernity, too, worked against them, and all Jews in Europe: "Mercedes produced Auschwitz," he told us bluntly. David made the case that the Ashkenazi Jews in Europe "lived an unremitting existence of persecution" for centuries. For those living in America and Europe today, their perspective comes from this history, colored by the specter of Auschwitz and the hope offered by Israel's founding in 1948.

David's comment on his own isolation within the broader Jewish community also reflects the difference in attitude toward Muslims in that community. Because Ashkenazim do not share a history with Muslims, as do Sephardim, they tend to be more hostile toward Muslims. At the same time, Sephardim, who find more in common with Muslim culture, are few in number and thus have little influence on majority opinion in the Jewish community.

Stephen Stern, an Ashkenazi, notes other differences between Sephardic and Ashkenazi Jews, especially in relation to Israel: "The creation of Israel was largely under Ashkenazi nonreligious Jewish leadership. The founding of the state was followed by an influx of practically the entire Sephardic population from Arab nations—which is the narrow majority of Jewish-Israeli population today." But the irony, he points out, is that the Ashkenazim "have been the leaders of the 'peace process,'" not the Sephardic majority, which retains memories of long-settled communities from which they were uprooted. They are often the "most bitter about 'the Arabs,'" he remarked, and "have fueled a lot of the Greater Israel Likud and far right nationalists."

David Shasha is unsparing as to what he thinks damages relations between Muslims and Jews. The documentary *Obsession: Radical Islam's War against the West* (2006) directed by Wayne Kopping and produced by the Clarion Fund, a group representing Ashkenazi Orthodox interests, was very much on his mind when we met him. Alarmed at what he saw in *Obsession*, David wrote a strongly worded rebuttal in his newsletter.[42] He also told us that his exchanges "with the most ardent and hateful Zionists in the Jewish community" helped him understand better than most that "the obsessions of *Obsession* have been designed to cut us off from the rationality of history and culture." The cure for this hatred, David asserts, is an understanding of the past. If Jews, Muslims, and other Americans would learn about their rich shared history, there are better chances of understanding each other. Unfortunately, he sighed, the history that people are taught is "confrontationist" and does not solve any problems.

When we went out to dinner that night, David kept looking over his shoulder and saying, "I shouldn't be here." Hailey wondered "if a fellow Orthodox Jew has this much trouble here, how would outsiders, especially Muslims, feel in this community?" It made her realize that "all communities—whether Christian, Muslim, or Jewish—have their own internal contradictions and debates to resolve, which others need to understand before we can move forward toward dialogue and peace."

After dinner, David, Zeenat, Hailey, Craig, and I walked a few blocks to what was called Little Pakistan (see chapter 3). Within a few yards, the signs went from all Hebrew to all Urdu. Although David was intrigued, he did not venture into this part of the neighborhood often. He did not come into the mosque we were visiting and seemed in a hurry to return to his home, but wished us well.

"The Top of the Food Chain"

Anyone wishing to rub shoulders with seriously wealthy members of the American Jewish community needs to visit Palm Beach, Florida, in January. It is cold in the northern states, and that is when many of these "snow birds" migrate to the sun and beaches of the Sunshine State. The residents here have reached the top of the highly competitive American pyramid. They are the Darwinian victors in the hard-fought race for the survival of the fittest. They also constitute a different strain in predator identity. In this case, individuals have outgrown loyalty to America, and their only loyalties are to themselves, their businesses, and staying on top of the economic pyramid.

From their heights, the rich and powerful have their own peculiar way of looking at the world. On our journey, we had a glimpse into their lives when I was invited to speak to organizations at two of the most prestigious island retreats in America. The first was at the Forum on Sanibel Island, off Florida's western coast, and the second at the World Affairs Council in Palm Beach on its eastern coast. Both events drew capacity audiences—the president of the council at Palm Beach said this was the largest gathering to date.

The reality of America is reflected in the ethnic composition of the community. The original residents of Palm Beach were distinctly white and Protestant, arriving from the north, having made millions in a variety of enterprises and creating their own social cocoon. A resident in Palm Beach still recalled with a shudder of excitement the social turmoil when the Catholic Kennedys first moved there half a century ago. While Palm Beach remains largely Christian, there is a growing Jewish presence. Jews have recently asserted themselves by creating their own clubs in the face of the snobbery of the older residents. Some jokingly refer to Palm Beach as the "Gaza strip," because different ethnic groups live separate lives side by side.

African Americans and Muslims are barely visible. Embarrassed white hosts told me stories of police discreetly following black guests arriving at their homes. The local gendarmerie did not expect black people to be driving expensive cars and making social calls on these islands. The one Muslim I knew in Palm Beach became a friend. Nasser Kazeminy had migrated from Iran decades ago, and he and his American wife blend in with the surroundings. We had lunch at Donald Trump's club, Mar-a-Lago, and had a pleasant chat with him. Later, we also met Edwina Sandys, the granddaughter of Winston Churchill, and had an inspiring session on interfaith relations with leading Jewish and Christian figures from Palm Beach, which was joined by the Hanifs, a pleasant African American Muslim couple who drove over from the mainland. And we had tea at the legendary Breakers Hotel, a symbol of the grand vision and energy of those who were building America in the Great White American Century.

The conversation during the formal dinner following my talk to the World Affairs Council gave us insights into high society, with plenty of references to those whom the patrons knew: Bernie Madoff, Oprah Win-frey, and Rush Limbaugh. While my table was restricted to pleasantries, Frankie sat at one where diners engaged in sharp exchanges, and these threw light on our study. Frankie was seated next to a prominent Jew-ish professional originally from New York who had served in George H. W. Bush's administration. A boisterous dinner companion, speaking and chewing at the same time, he declared he was convinced that all Muslims "enslaved" their women and were inherently undemocratic and had always been that way, according to Frankie's account. He told the table that crime has gone up on the island because of the influx of "Obama-types." He kept repeating the phrase "I'm at the top of the food chain!" and declared that no one in Palm Beach "cares about America, just their own interests."

When Frankie mentioned he had traveled in the Muslim world, his din-ner partner cut him off. He did not like any Muslim country he had visited, and he was convinced Obama was a Muslim because he had "gone to a Muslim school" in Indonesia. When asked how Palm Beach had changed over the years, he said the biggest change was that there "aren't as many WASPs anymore," because they had moved slightly farther south and created their own white Protestant enclaves. And why had they moved? "Because the 'Js' came," he said, meaning Jews.

Frankie noticed a difference between persons he spoke with on Sanibel Island and those in Palm Beach: on Sanibel, "everyone was telling me how lucky I was to accompany Dr. Ahmed, but here people were asking me why Muslims wanted to destroy us. It was interesting that Sanibel was dominated by Christians and Palm Beach by the Jewish community. There seemed to be a correlation."

Hailey's experience in Palm Beach was similar: "In Palm Beach I met an older Jewish woman at an interfaith breakfast. She took me aside to 'warn' me of the real motives of Muslims and to beware of the violence they are capable of. I told her about some of my positive experiences, and she cut me off, saying, 'Have you seen *Obsession?* It's so true and so important. Everyone should see it.'"

This response did not come as a surprise to Hailey. She found after her travels to the Muslim world in 2006 that some Jewish friends questioned the purpose of her trip: "They were not only skeptical of the progress but hostile to even speaking with Muslims. Many of them criticized me for traveling there and trying to create peace. I was surprised that so many of my genera-tion had that view, something I equated with an older, less 'enlightened' generation, but they have grown up in an environment of intifadas in Israel and stalled peace negotiations. . . . Things seem to be deteriorating for the younger generations of these two groups rather than improving."

Toward Bridging the Divide

Viewing the gap between Jews and Muslims and the sometimes virulent exchanges between them, I am reminded of Matthew Arnold's "Dover Beach":

> And we are here as on a darkling plain
> Swept with confused alarms of struggle and flight,
> Where ignorant armies clash by night.

Weighing both the challenges and the possibilities of friendship, I believe it is imperative for every thoughtful Jew and Muslim to look into his or her heart and change the nature of the relationship. I am hopeful because of the Jewish people I have personally come to know who are involved in Jewish-Muslim dialogue. I can say with confidence that these are among the most impressive people I have met in their learning, compassion for humanity, and vision. They are concerned about the poor relations between Jews and Muslims and are prepared to extend their hand of friendship in order to help repair the damage. I met them all after 9/11, and in each case, they took the initiative to reach out to me and begin a process that resulted in friendship and mutual respect.

One of them was someone who has since become a mentor and teacher, Sir Jonathan Sacks, the chief rabbi of the United Kingdom and now a member of the House of Lords. In his book *The Dignity of Difference,* Sacks observes that Judaism gave rise to two other monotheisms, Christianity and Islam. Together these faiths represent more than half of the 6 billion people alive today. "There is much in common in the ethics of these three faiths," he notes, "though each speaks in its own distinctive accent."[43] Sacks asks the reader to think of the poor and the asymmetry in the world, pointing out that its three richest individuals have more assets than the 600 million who make up the poorest nations. The top 358 billionaires are collectively richer than almost half of the entire planet's population. One-sixth of that population—a billion people—live on less than a dollar a day and cannot meet their most basic human needs. In *To Heal a Fractured World,* he deals with one of the strongest driving forces in Judaism, that is, *tikkun olam,* or the impulse to heal the world.[44] Ever since hearing the phrase and appreciating its philosophic meaning, I have felt that it could be the perfect motto, not only for Jews, but also for all of us interested in creating a better and more harmonious world.

On our journey we came across many inspiring examples of Jewish leaders reaching out to Muslims and challenging the anger and hatred that threaten to keep the two apart. Berny Stone, the former vice-mayor of Chicago, told us that he had more support among Muslims than Jews. He had won the heart of the Muslim community by naming a street in Chicago after Mohammed Ali Jinnah, the revered founder of Pakistan. Another example is provided by my friend Barry Hoffman, the honorary consul general of Pakistan in Boston. He has remained a genuinely popular avuncular figure among Pakistanis, especially Pakistani students, since the time I first met him when I was at Harvard in 1980. His love for Pakistanis came through when he was describing the predicament of a four-year-old Pakistani child who needed a heart operation and could not get a visa after 9/11. Barry's eyes welled up with tears, his voice choked, and try as he might, he could not speak any more. Barry's story and humanity affected all the team members as we shared his anguish.

Through discussion and dialogue with my Jewish friends, I have learned about Jewish history and culture and how these shape Jewish identity— the destruction of the Temple in Jerusalem, the trauma of the Diaspora, and the tragedy of the Holocaust, which remains a dark and troubling cloud over the history of all humankind. I also learned of the deep attachment that Jews feel toward the city of Jerusalem and the land of Israel, which is more than a country for the Jewish people. It is an expression of their religious and cultural identity. Becoming friends with Jews allowed me to view the Israeli narrative from their perspective. In this way, while they saw and hopefully understood my Muslim narrative, I tried to understand theirs.

"An Open Letter"

Concerned about the "negative and destructive tensions" between Jews and Muslims, several prominent Muslims wrote an open letter in February 2008 as "A Call to Peace, Dialogue, and Understanding between Muslims and Jews." It was initiated by Amineh Ahmed Hoti, the first director of the only Muslim-Jewish center in the world, the Centre for the Study of Muslim-Jewish Relations, which is affiliated with England's Cambridge University, and her colleague Edward Kessler, who helped to establish the center. As a father, I was particularly proud of the initiative Amineh was taking, and as someone who believed in interfaith dialogue, I was privileged to sign the letter. Perhaps there is no better ending to a chapter on Jewish-Muslim relations than the sentiments that prompted this letter:

> Many Jews and Muslims today stand apart from each other due to feelings of anger, which in some parts of the world, translate into violence. It is our contention that we are faced today not with "a clash of civilizations" but with "a clash of ill-informed misunderstandings." Deep-seated stereotypes and prejudices have resulted in a distancing of the communities and even a dehumanizing of the "Other." We urgently need to address this situation. We must strive towards turning ignorance into knowledge, intolerance into understanding, and pain into courage and sensitivity for the "Other."
>
> For many centuries our communities co-existed and worked together fruitfully and peacefully such as in the Iberian Peninsula. As Muslims and Jews we share core doctrinal beliefs, the most important of which is strict monotheism. We both share a common patriarch, Ibrahim/Abraham, other Biblical prophets, laws and jurisprudence, many significant values and even dietary restrictions. There is more in common between our religions and peoples than is known to each of us. It is precisely due to the urgent need to address such political problems as well as acknowledge our shared values that the establishment of an inter-religious dialogue between Jews and Muslims in our time is extremely important. Failure to do so will be a missed opportunity. Memories of positive historical encounters will dim and the current problems will lead to an increasing rift and more common misunderstandings between us.

The letter includes a subsection, "Jews and Muslims as One Umma: Reflecting Briefly on Early Muslim-Jewish Encounters," which reminds its readers that there was a time in history when Jews and Muslims constituted a united body, which Arabs call the ummah and is today associated exclusively with Muslims. In the spirit of Islam's emphasis on compassion and respect for all humanity, one vignette from the Prophet Muhammad's life reveals how a Jewish funeral procession passed before him, at which the Prophet stood up as a sign of respect. His companions asked him why he stood up for a Jewish funeral. The Prophet dismissed this attitude with: "Is he not a human being!"[45]

When the Prophet died, his shield was mortgaged with a Jew to show that Muslims are permitted to trade with Jews. Also, the Prophet's married daughter, Hazrat Fatima, who was very close to her father, worked for a Jew—she would spin for him in return for grain. More significant, one of the Prophet's wives, Safia, was a Jewish woman who was considered by God "a mother of the believers." Jealous, the other wives mocked Safia by calling her "a Jew" in a derogatory manner, and upset by this, Safia complained to her husband. The Prophet responded that she need only proclaim to the others: "My father [Moses] was a Prophet and my uncle [Aaron] was a Prophet and I am the wife of a Prophet!"

Chief Rabbi Sacks, on the inauguration of the Centre for the Study of Muslim-Jewish Relations, emphasized the importance of learning from each other. "Islam's strength of faith is remarkable," he intoned. "We can all learn from Islam this strength of faith. And that is something immensely positive. If I wanted to suggest what Muslims can learn from Jews today, I would say how to survive as a minority in a culture that does not share your values. We have to learn from one another."

The open letter struck a chord. Many individual Jews and organizations responded, among them the prominent rabbi and scholar David Rosen, the president of the International Jewish Committee for Interreligious Consultations in New York City, a body that represents world Jewry to other world religions. Rabbi Rosen wrote:

> I wholeheartedly welcome this most important initiative on the part of Muslim scholars and representatives. The striking commonalities of Islam and Judaism and those historic periods and places of remarkable cooperation and cross-fertilization between the two faith communities, have been tragically overshadowed and even hijacked by modern politics. The benefits from respectful dialogue and cooperation between the Muslim and Jewish communities can be a blessing not only to the communities themselves; but can have a profound impact on wider even global relations between religions and peoples, contributing to the well being of human society as a whole.

These wise words echo those of other rabbis and secular thinkers, both Sephardic and Ashkenazi, and demand reconciliation between Jews and Muslims. Because the agnatic rivalry between Jews and Muslims burdens not only their larger family but directly or indirectly draws in peoples from other parts of the world, every avenue must be explored to find the path to peace. To proceed, both communities must mutually change the present paradigm of confrontation and prejudice that defines their relationship. This paradigm has failed and is responsible for the loss of countless innocent lives on both sides of the conflict, as well as away from it, as in the case of Danny Pearl. Perhaps the way forward toward bridging the gap is to build on the commonalities and then tackle the more difficult issues dividing the two.

It is for this reason that American pluralist identity is of such relevance to these Abrahamic children. Rabbi Bruce Lustig captured this sentiment beautifully when he presented me with the 2008 Rumi Peace and Dialogue Award on behalf of the Rumi Forum on Capitol Hill: "I'd like you to think about the following. In the Caucus Room of the Canon Building, a first-generation Holocaust survivor who is a rabbi in Washington, presents, at a Rumi Forum honoring a brilliant Islamic scholar mystic through the generosity of the Turkish people, an award to a scholar of Islamic studies, and a world-renowned anthropologist. Only in America can such things happen."

EIGHT

Mormons and Muslims: Getting to Know You

PERHAPS NO TWO religious communities in America are as dissimilar as Mormons and Muslims and yet invite so many comparisons. The former community is homegrown, the latter the classic outsider, bringing with it a thousand years of poorly understood history. Yet both boast adherents of about 7 million, have faced similar prejudices, and can justifiably draw some interesting historical parallels.

Because of the English ethnicity of their founders, Mormons trace their roots to Plymouth, are authentically American, and have absorbed American identity in its entirety, with its attendant contradictions. Through those roots, they identify with primordial identity, but they are also vocal proponents of American pluralism because of their minority status and universal mission, and as self-defined "true Americans," many would identify with the actions and thoughts of predator identity in order to keep the country safe and secure. For example, during his presidential run Mitt Romney was in favor of keeping Guantánamo Bay open for detainees, "where they don't get the access to lawyers they get when they're on our soil. I don't want them in our prisons, I want them there. Some people have said we ought to close Guantánamo. My view is we ought to double Guantánamo." U.S. Representative Jason Chaffetz of Utah suggested that undocumented immigrants convicted of crimes should be held in "tent cities" surrounded by barbed wire. This complex frame of American identity defines the Mormon relationship with Muslims.

A minority community in the United States whose experience is similar to the Jewish one, Mormons may have important lessons for Muslims. I was therefore surprised to find that none of the Muslim guests at Faizan Haq's dinner in Buffalo (see chapter 5) appeared to have visited nearby Palmyra, where the Mormon faith was born. Perhaps these Muslims were blissfully unaware of how much they could learn from the Mormon experience.

Palmyra: "Where It All Began"

Responding to the plight of the Muslim community after 9/11, many compassionate, sincere, and committed Jews and Christians made genuine attempts to understand Islam. Interestingly, Mormons had already been reaching out to Muslims from the birth of their religion. Upon meeting my first Mormons at Palmyra, I felt as if I was a long-awaited visitor. The Mormons appeared truly happy to see us, their influential leaders showing us around with zest and constantly pointing to the similarities between our faiths with some pride. Perhaps the attacks on the Muslims had struck a nerve among the Mormons. After all, the Prophet Muhammad, from the earliest days, was attacked by Christians as a failed priest, an errant bishop, and even the Antichrist. The mainstream Christian reaction to the founder of the Mormon faith, Joseph Smith, was somewhat similar, and even the terminology conveyed the same opposition and vitriol.

The Mormons that we met on our journey reminded me of my neighbors and friends in the small rural village in Cambridgeshire, England, where I lived in the 1990s. In their features, skin color, the way they dressed, and even names, they appeared English: Ben and Susan Banks, Jeffrey Clark, Daniel Peterson, and Holly Tuttle. If Mormonism's first leaders, Joseph Smith and Brigham Young, could have been magically transported to a nineteenth-century English home at teatime, they would surely have been received without the raising of an eyebrow. Further, to confirm the Mormon link with their English primordial ancestry, one need go no further than the U.S. Census Map of Ethnicity (2004), which shows the entire state of Utah dominated by the English in a belt extending west into Nevada and north into Idaho and Wyoming.

We visited Palmyra on a clear autumn Sunday morning in late October. The air was translucent as we were far from big cities and their pollution. It was my first exposure to the Mormon Church, or, as it is officially known, the Church of Jesus Christ of Latter-day Saints (LDS). As we entered the Mormon house of worship, called the meetinghouse, the service had just begun. Senior officials were waiting to receive us and usher us in. Their wives greeted Zeenat and Madeeha like long-lost sisters. The reception committee included Jeffrey Clark, president of the "Stake," which is like a diocese or branch of the church. The men had short haircuts and wore ties and suits, and the women were dressed modestly. They appeared healthy and well turned out. "Squeaky clean" was the phrase I used to describe the community. Later, in Salt Lake City, Elder Ben Banks pounced on it, quoting it back to me several times with a chuckle, adding, "That is exactly how the Mormons see themselves."

The Mormon priesthood is strictly male, but other officials may be of either sex. We noticed the titles "sister" and "elder" on the nametags affixed to members' jackets. The presiding bishop spotted us as we settled into the pews and specifically welcomed us, singling out the Muslims in the team. This would be the pattern in all our meetings with the Mormons: a general welcome, with specific interest and affection for the Muslims.

Although the title of bishop sounds grand, especially if one thinks of either a Protestant or Catholic personage of this rank, among Mormons this person is more of a first among equals. As part of the service, water and bread were passed around. The absence of wine at communion had puzzled me and was immediately noted by Hailey, one of the Catholics on the team, who said their church rituals were not complete without wine.

The meetinghouse was stark, modern, and airy. There were no pictures and no statues inside the sanctuary. The ceremony itself resembled a town hall meeting more than a religious service. The chapel's hymnbooks as well as hymns written by Mormons included both "God Save the King" and "The Star-Spangled Banner." The royal anthem was obviously a relic of a bygone time when Americans declared loyalty to the king of England. The irony of displaying it alongside America's ultimate symbol of independence may have escaped those who compiled the hymnbook, or they may have been emphasizing their links with the English origins of colonial America.

Looking around, I saw eager worshippers of all ages. All were white except for one young black male. The atmosphere was not intimidating and bordered on the informal. Husbands had their arms around their wives, while children in the back rows moved about restlessly and were sometimes heard above the speeches.

There were several speakers, including some the community wished to honor. Their themes were honesty, accountability, responsibility, and forgiveness. Several teenagers spoke briefly and were described by the elders as the "priesthood of children," which underscored the importance of the young among Mormons. Each one talked about the tests to their faith in their daily lives and how they overcame them.

Mormon Theology

After the service, President Jeffrey Clark and the church elders took us to three of their holiest sites: the cabin in which Joseph Smith lived; the nearby "Sacred Grove" where in 1820, according to Mormon mythology, God and his son, Jesus, revealed themselves to Smith, and he received "revelations" and saw "light"; and the Hill Cumorah, where Smith was led by the Angel Moroni to the "golden tablets" that would form the basis of the *Book of Mormon.* Smith was just seventeen when he was visited by Moroni, who had lived in North America 1,500 years earlier. After Smith translated the tablets, Moroni took them away. Smith published the revelation as the *Book of Mormon,* and his followers became known as Mormons, after Mormon, the father of Moroni, although adherents of the faith prefer to be identified as members of the Church of Jesus Christ of Latter-day Saints.

Smith's cabin, located on a 100-acre farm, was rebuilt to resemble its appearance in Smith's time. Descended from English immigrants, Smith's family had clearly done reasonably well in the new country. This is "where it all began," the elder said. Inside the cabin, President Clark emphasized the similarities with Islam, and one of the elders present told us that he had bought a copy of the Quran on his visit to Jordan and found much in it that he could empathize with. They all talked about their admiration for the Prophet of Islam and expressed their regard for Islam at every opportunity. It was, observed Hailey, a "lovefest."

The essence of Mormonism is to be found in the Thirteen Articles of Faith, which place the religion in the context of American history and geography, expressing a belief in the "literal gathering of Israel and in the restoration of the Ten Tribes" and stating that "Zion (the New Jerusalem) will be built upon the American continent; that Christ will reign personally upon the earth; and, that the earth will be renewed and receive its paradisiacal glory." The belief in religious freedom is entrenched in the founding tenets of the faith: "We claim the privilege of worshipping Almighty God according to the dictates of our own conscience, and allow all men the same privilege, let them worship how, where, or what they may." For Mormons, man can be elevated beyond prophethood and become a god. In some ways—in the location of the "New Jerusalem," the belief in religious freedom, and egalitarian ethos—Mormonism seems the quintessential American religion.

Mormons believe they are restoring the true faith of Christianity. After all, they told us, Jesus came to America to spread his word. He did so because his original message—the Old and New Testaments—was exclusively aimed at those in the Middle East. That is why they describe their faith as the Restoration of the Gospel of Jesus Christ. They assert that all Christian texts after the death of Jesus were false, as are organizations like the Roman Catholic Church, and that it was only through the revelations of Joseph Smith that the faith was set straight.

According to Mormons, the inhabitants of America arrived here from the Middle East 600 years before Christ's birth and were divided into the warring Nephites and Lamanites. God favored the pale-skinned Nephites over the Lamanites, who God had cursed with dark skins. The former are described as "white," "exceedingly fair and delightsome," and "industrious" people who labored "with their hands," and the latter as having a "skin of blackness," and being "idle people, full of mischief and subtlety." Miscegenation between Nephites and Lamanites was forbidden by God: "Cursed shall be the seed of him that mixeth with their seed; for they shall be cursed even with the same cursing."[1]

It is said that Jesus came to North America shortly after the Resurrection and succeeded in his mission to bring peace between the two groups, so for a few hundred years there was harmony in the land. Then the "dark," "filthy," and "loathsome" Lamanites reverted to "unbelief and idolatry."[2] Wars between the two tribes culminated in the Lamanites slaughtering all 230,000 Nephites in the year AD 400 except for one survivor, Moroni, son of the Nephites' heroic leader, Mormon. Moroni would return fourteen centuries later and reveal the location of the sacred tablets at Palmyra to Joseph Smith. This Mormon "victory" was expected to inaugurate the reign of Christ.

With the aid of a social mechanism known to anthropologists as the creation of fictitious genealogy, the Mormons were able to incorporate the Native American tribes into their own system. In this regard, they differed from the leading proponents of primordial identity, who regarded Native Americans as irredeemable savages and heathens. Even Indians who converted to Christianity were considered hostiles, as illustrated by the Scots-Irish massacres of Christian Indians in Pennsylvania that so incensed Benjamin Franklin (see chapter 2).

Unlike the English and Scots-Irish who sought to destroy and dislocate the natives, the Mormons sought to absorb them. They certainly could not ignore the Native Americans as they pushed westward. Smith's solution was to assume that Native Americans were once white, had changed to a darker color, and would revert to white once they became Mormons and therefore find redemption. In this way, Smith bridged the gap between primordial identity and the Native Americans.

Like African Americans rediscovering Islam, Native Americans were returning to a religion that their ancestors practiced on that very soil. Indeed, we found a strong Mormon presence among native communities, and conversely a genuine Mormon acceptance of Native Americans. George, our Navajo guide in Arizona mentioned in chapter 3, said a great number of the Navajo, whose vast reservation surrounded that of the Hopi we were visiting, had embraced Mormonism. According to him, about 40 percent of Navajo are strict Mormons, 20 percent follow both Mormonism and traditional culture, and 20 percent retain their traditional ways. The rest found solace in different belief systems.

This idea of theological "reversion" could also apply to Mexicans, Pacific Islanders, and other native peoples around the world. Our host in Salt Lake City, Elder Ben Banks, referred to both Native Americans and Pacific Islanders as having "believing blood." Just outside Honolulu, Brigham Young University operates a satellite campus that links the Mormon Church with the native population.

The Exponential Growth of—and Resistance to— the "American Religion"

Mormonism was born at the dawn of what I have called the Great White American Century, when American identity was defined as being white and Protestant (see chapter 2). This was the era of Andrew Jackson, the Scots-Irish ascendency, and mob rule. Pluralist voices were few and far between, and it would not be until the Lincoln years that prominent Americans would plead for tolerance toward Mormons. Despite the Mormons' English background and white appearance, nineteenth-century proponents of primordial and predator identity sought to suppress and even eradicate them, as they would other minorities such as the Jews and Irish Catholics.

The Scots-Irish, in particular, resented Mormon theology for deviating from their Protestant faith, as well as the Mormon view of authority and hierarchy, which was the exact opposite of the Scots-Irish democratic and egalitarian impulse. As the Scots-Irish gained dominance in the U.S. government, the full force of the state and military descended on the Mormons like a sledgehammer. The U.S. Constitution provided Mormons little protection, as it was enforced by members of the dominant ethnic group. Eventually, the Mormons would journey beyond the jurisdiction of the United States to create in Utah, or Deseret as they called it, their own island in a sea of hostile American Protestants. There they would become the law, putting behind them the blood-soaked days of ferocious frontier mobs baying for their blood.

Joseph Smith was not the century's only religious reformer wishing to advance his religion in new ways and threatening the established order. Mirza Ghulam Ahmad in India and Bahá'u'lláh in Persia, both born in the Muslim faith, set out to reform Islam, establishing the Ahmadiyya and Baha'í faiths, respectively, while Theodor Herzl launched Zionism, which drew its inspiration from Jewish history and the idea of a homeland for the Jews in the Holy Land. And outside the Abrahamic tradition, Swami Dayananda in India founded the Arya Samaj, a Hindu reformist movement. The fervor of these movements was matched by the resistance of the local majority population, which saw them as dangerous and heretical influences.

Indeed, it was a century of extraordinary social and political upheaval. The forces unleashed by industrialization, colonization, and mass migration challenged people to think about old problems in different ways. In America, the Second Great Awakening was well under way, with itinerant Protestant preachers and visionaries spreading new religious ideas throughout the country. Meanwhile, Mormonism was experiencing exponential growth against all the odds. The reason was perhaps twofold: whites and non-whites alike were "reverting" to a purer form of American Christianity; and Mormonism provided an optimistic theology in an era of hope and promise. Unlike the austere and puritanical preachings of Calvinism, Mormonism offered what scholar Fawn Brodie called an "ingenious blend of supernaturalism and materialism, which promised in heaven a continuation of all earthly pleasures—work, wealth, sex, and power."[3]

Many in the Jacksonian age would have found Mormonism attractive. As Americans pushed westward, those disillusioned by the frontier chaos found refuge in the Mormon Church. Among them were some 30,000 freshly arrived Scandinavians wanting a new life in America who settled in Utah between 1850 and 1880.[4]

Unlike their white brethren, most Mormons headed west not with the aim of conquering territory and extending the United States, but in search of a new homeland where they could live in peace and safety. Yet as the Mormons moved westward from Palmyra in the 1820s and 1830s, they faced mob violence wherever they attempted to settle. In Missouri they were driven out by bloodthirsty crowds and a Scots-Irish governor who ordered that the Mormons "must be exterminated." Eager for hardworking settlers, the state of Illinois was initially sympathetic to their plight and allowed Smith to set up a largely autonomous city-state in which the church council declared Smith "King, Priest, and Ruler over Israel on Earth."[5] In Illinois the Mormons grew in strength, with the settlement of Nauvoo rivaling Chicago in size. Soon Smith was at the head of his own well-trained and fully armed cohort, the Nauvoo Legion, with half as many men as the army of the United States.[6] In the 1844 presidential elections, only fourteen years after establishing his church at Palmyra, Smith was confident enough to run for the office.

But trouble was not long in coming. In 1844, five months before the election, a mob killed Joseph Smith, then thirty-eight years old, and his brother, an action for which all who took part were acquitted. A succession crisis now befell the movement. The LDS leadership in Illinois passed to Brigham Young, although some believed that it should have come down through the blood descendants of Joseph Smith. The Reorganized Church of Latter-day Saints (RLDS) advocated the rights of Smith's descendants to leadership and its first prophet was Joseph Smith's eldest son, Joseph Smith III, who headed the sect until 1914. The RLDS, known after 2001 as the Community of Christ, has a membership of 130,000 in the United States and small satellite communities abroad, including 10,000 in the Pacific and 25,000 in Africa. The controversy surrounding succession in the Mormon Church is similar to that between Sunnis and Shias in Islam, the latter believing that the descendants of the Prophet should have been officially recognized as the leaders of Islam.

Opting Out of America

With the ascendancy of the charismatic Brigham Young, the Mormon faith and its relationship with American identity changed. Unlike Joseph Smith, who ran for president of the United States, Young wished to opt out of America altogether. In 1846 Young led his community from Illinois and arrived in Utah in 1847, then part of Mexico, to start what was essentially a new nation with him at its head. Under Young, the Mormon Church took the form and structure it is known by today.

During this period, the LDS was transformed from an obscure and embattled sect to essentially a powerful state within a state. After Mexico ceded Utah to the United States in 1848, the federal government, with enough problems on its hands, found it politic to allow the Mormons a degree of autonomy to run their own affairs. Young was declared governor and given a free hand, with the Mormons left to practice their religion according to their own vision. Young took as many as fifty-seven wives, roughly ten to fifteen more than his predecessor. His position on slavery was also much more conservative than that of Smith, who opposed it on moral grounds and had ordained an African American as an elder in the Mormon priesthood in 1836. A supporter of the Confederacy in the Civil War, Young justified the enslavement of blacks by referring to them as the "children of Ham" in the manner of proponents of American primordial identity.[7] Only in 1978 did the LDS reverse the ban on black priests.

Mormons consider Utah the "Promised Land," having been led there by Young, the "American Moses." In one of the many similarities with Islam observed on our trip to Salt Lake City, the Mormons called their migration to Utah the *hijra,* taking a leaf from the life of Prophet Muhammad when he left Mecca to go to Medina in 622, the year from which Muslims count their calendar. Hence, Salt Lake City became known as the Mormon Mecca.

The Mormons had named their territory Deseret, a neologism from the *Book of Mormon* meaning "honeybee," which struck Brigham Young as an apt symbol of Mormon industry and belief that personal freedom should yield to the welfare of the collective whole. In Salt Lake City, we saw many beehive pictures and signs, especially on the highways. But Congress refused to call the territory Deseret, instead naming it Utah Territory after the Ute Indians who populated the region.

The migration to Utah did not stop attacks against the community, however. In 1857 the Scots-Irish president James Buchanan, incensed at rumors of polygamy, ordered Young to step down as Utah's governor. Young refused. The U.S. government then declared the area in rebellion, and the Utah War followed. At the same time, Young respected the Founding Fathers, as they were "the voice of the Lord inspiring all those worthy men who bore influence in those trying times, not only to go forth in battle, but to exercise wisdom in council, fortitude, courage, and endurance."[8] He accused the "opposers" of Mormons like Buchanan of having "broken their own laws" and having "trampled" on the Constitution. He predicted that when the Constitution "hangs, as it were, upon a single thread," it will be the Mormons who will "save it from utter destruction."

As expected in the context of the discussion in this book, Lincoln's policy toward the Mormons differed from that of his predecessors, and he articulated it by alluding to his family's history of farming: if the Lincolns encountered a log in a field that was "too hard to split, too wet to burn, and too heavy to move," they simply "plowed around it."[9] After the Civil War and Lincoln's assassination, relations once again changed, to the detriment of the Mormons.

Once the intercontinental railroad that ran through Utah connected the east and west coasts in 1869, new settlers poured into the territory, and it saw greater integration into the American economy and political system. Yet polygamy prevented Utah from being admitted into the Union. In 1890 the LDS Church relented, releasing "The Manifesto," which instructed Mormons to obey the law of the land. Statehood followed in 1896, and Salt Lake City was declared the state capital. Polygamy did not quite die out, but by then the authorities were too busy elsewhere to pay much attention to Utah. Besides, neighboring Canada and Mexico beckoned to those Mormons with polygamy on their minds.

Although both Palmyra and Salt Lake City play a central role in Mormon history and tradition, they differ greatly in what they mean in the Mormon narrative. Palmyra is the fountainhead of the faith but has little significance beyond that. Salt Lake City is the living testimony to the power and glory of the church today. Its buildings and centers and its university in nearby Provo all testify to the presence of the Mormon Church. At Palmyra, the Mormons were a tiny persecuted minority struggling to survive against primordial and predator identity; in Salt Lake City, they became a powerful majority in "opting out" of America altogether. At Palmyra, the aim was to formulate the faith; in Salt Lake City, it was to convert the world to the Mormon vision. Palmyra has all the hallmarks of a small, rural community; Salt Lake City is heavy with the gravitas of a church, supported by state-like structures whose very mention puts people on guard.

As we prepared to leave Palmyra, President Clark gave us a farewell blessing: "I am so grateful for your efforts in making an attempt to bridge that gap, to break down those walls, to introduce us to each other in a way that is nonthreatening and encourage us to seek out the best in our respective cultures and marry them together in one larger world culture. I applaud you and hope that you have great success."

The Team Responds to the Mormons

The differing reactions of the team to meeting the Mormons are of some interest. For Muslim member Madeeha Hameed, the experience brought "a new understanding of this faith, regardless of what the media portrays." In Palmyra, Madeeha struck up a friendship with a woman named Holly Tuttle, who, she wrote, "introduced me to a whole new aspect of American life that I did not know much about."

What touched Madeeha in particular was that everyone the team met "went out of their way to reach out to Muslims like me and Ambassador Ahmed just to show support of the struggles and challenges Muslims are going through currently." After our visit to Palmyra, Madeeha remarked,

"Wow, these are the nicest Christians I've ever met!" However, the Christian members of the team protested, "I'm not sure these are Christians." While Zeenat, Madeeha, and myself—the Muslims in the group—were duly impressed with the sympathy shown to us by the Mormons, the others had questions and doubts despite their cordial feelings for our "sincere," "really nice," and "extremely religious and devout" hosts.

Initially, Hailey thought that the Mormons were "bizarre" but changed her mind after meeting more in Salt Lake City and getting to know them better. Craig was outraged at some of the things he saw. "To claim this as the true command of God," he kept whispering in an indignant tone, "not possible, not possible." When Craig heard one of the guides explain that Mormons believed keeping long hair and beards was "dirty," he was upset because he had long hair and a beard. "Jesus had both," he said indignantly. Used to the openness with which they had been received in different houses of worship on our journey, Jonathan, Craig, and Frankie were disappointed when we were not allowed to enter a temple near the meetinghouse we had just visited. As we stood outside the temple, we did have a conversation with the Mormon elders, which Craig filmed:

Ahmed: When you say that God and Jesus have a physical body, what does that mean?

Elder: Yes, but they are immortal, whereas you and I are mortal. But they are in a resurrected condition whereby their body has been perfected.

Ahmed: What heaven or place do they inhabit?

Elder: They inhabit a place in the universe. At times they have been on this earth and Jesus Christ has lived on this earth, so I suppose they travel some, they get around some. But they have a place of habitation in the universe.

Jonathan: Do they live on a different planet?

Elder: Yes.

Ahmed: Do we know which planet?

Elder: I would not be able to point to it in the sky, would you Elder Weston? But we know that they do live in a heavenly realm in the universe. They created the universe; the Father created the universe through working with his Son.

Ahmed: Is it the same time period, the six days of the Bible?

Elder: Yes, but when it says six days, really that means six time periods. So it would not be the same as one day for us on the earth. In six time periods, as described in the book of Genesis, and on the seventh day they rested.

Jonathan: When you pass from this earth, do you go to where God is? Is it a heaven?

Elder: We believe that the heaven that we pass to when we die is on this earth, and it is in a different dimension. So we pass just like walking from one room to another into a different dimension. But it varies according to the righteousness of the people: there are places that are more desirable and favorable than others.

Frankie: So there are different levels?

Elder: Yes, different levels.

Jonathan: Based on behavior on earth?

Elder: That is correct.

The elder explained the significance of the temple and its connection with the generations that have passed before, a cardinal feature of the faith: "We believe that not only can these ceremonies be done on behalf of ourselves, we may do them on behalf of ancestors, and that is why this church has the largest and finest genealogical library in the world in Salt Lake City." The Founding Fathers as well as their descendants had been baptized into the Mormon Church so that they could ascend to a higher level in heaven, the elder said, proudly claiming they are now Mormon. He was anxious to point out that Mormons are no different from other religious sects when it comes to concern about their ancestors: "The Catholics, for example, they like to light candles and have masses, special things hoping to affect their ancestors."

Normally polite, the team began to show signs of impatience, now and then rolling their eyes, sighing, shuffling their legs, or emitting a long "hmmm." Members were skeptical about the possibility of Jesus visiting America or everyone on the continent being white and then Native Americans being cursed and given dark skins. With the talk of people living in different dimensions, husbands and wives being "sealed" and "melded" forever in union in preparation for the next life, and God being a man who lived on another planet, it seemed time for me to move our group to the next phase of the program.

The unease of the team's Christian members stemmed from their faith's different version of these matters. Although much was familiar to them, a great deal also appeared to be an accretion and a distortion. The problem is that the Mormon Church and the older Christian churches are not quite antipodal. They do share the central figure of Jesus, for example—but the differences are all too evident. Polygamy, for instance, is anathema to Americans, many of whom think the conduct of the Mormons and their clandestine rituals are inherently un-American. Many also consider the Mormon faith a cult and doubt the verity of its claims.

Hailey made a valiant attempt to understand the Mormons, although she approached the subject from the perspective of her Catholic faith. She had never met a Mormon before and had only read about the faith in Jon Krakauer's book *Under the Banner of Heaven,* which is not a very flattering account.[10] Although impressed by their openness and friendliness, she was "almost repulsed" by the statues of God: "It was so strange to me, especially Him standing arm and arm with Jesus like identical twins. I was also taken aback by all of the depictions of Jesus appearing to the Mayas and Incas. I found it hard to accept that someone could actually believe this."

For me, as a Muslim, it did not much matter whether there was a statue of Jesus or God—it was all outside the boundaries of Islam. But why not accept the Mormons on their own terms: appreciate their culture rather than focus on their theology? Yet I understood the sentiments of the Christian members of my team. Mainstream Muslims from Pakistan or Saudi Arabia, for instance, would respond in similar fashion to the movement of Mirza Ghulam Ahmad, referred to as the Ahmadiyya after the founder. Muslims accuse the Ahmadiyya of challenging the cardinal principle of Islam, the finality of the Prophet Muhammad, by attributing prophethood to Ahmad. The government of Pakistan has declared the Ahmadiyya non-Muslim, and no one can obtain a passport without first signing a statement declaring the Ahmadiyya to be non-Muslim. The Ahmadiyya are unfairly victimized and have become strangers in their own homes.

Salt Lake City: Living among Mormons

Flying into Salt Lake City to meet our Mormon hosts was like arriving in familiar territory. Although I had never been there before, I found nothing but friendliness. This is the center of the Mormon faith today, and it is where Thomas Monson, the prophet of the Mormon Church, resides.

The Mormon presence is everywhere in the city, at the heart of which is a 35-acre complex of Mormon buildings and the imposing and dramatic Salt Lake Temple, opened in 1893 after four decades of construction. The city itself is set amid snow-covered mountains and reflects the cleanliness and tidiness of the Mormon community. Its airport bathrooms were probably the cleanest I had ever seen in any airport in the world, its facilities sparkling as if they had just been scrubbed. In my travels, I have found that as a broad indicator, the cleaner the public bathrooms, the better managed the community.

The demographic pattern of Salt Lake City is a telling comment on the Mormon faith itself. It is 67 percent white, 22 percent Latino, and a mere 4 percent black. A considerable number of Pacific islanders who have adopted the Mormon faith have also settled here. Although Mormons account for less than 50 percent of the population of Salt Lake City, they are in a strong majority in the rural municipalities with the LDS population at 90 percent in some towns.

Elder Ben Banks, director of church hosting, who had ascended to the top LDS rank of Presidency of the Seventy, and his wife, Susan, were our hosts and guides. Although semiretired and senior figures in the church, they took us around as diligently as scoutmasters on a trek with their cub scouts. The team was taken with their cordiality and appreciated their willingness to join our free-flowing discussions about everything under the sun. With regard to the Mormon belief in the End Times, for example (elements of which they share with some American Protestant sects), Elder Banks told us that "three months of food are kept in their houses at all times by Mormons," but he himself keeps a year's worth because "you never know what could go wrong." Joseph Smith taught that "the hour is nigh,"[11] and the LDS instructs all Mormons to prepare for the apocalypse, which will mark the return of Jesus to America, by storing food. Frankie admitted to being perplexed when Banks explained that "Christ created the world and all the planets" and then contradicted himself by saying, "the world was created before Christ."

Elder Banks and Susan took us to the Family History Library, with its famous genealogical collection, and to the LDS Humanitarian Center, which Frankie found "truly a marvel with its scale, organization, efficiency, and capacity for rapid mobilization. . . . The State Department," he said thoughtfully, comparing the activities of the center to those of organizations like the U.S. Agency for International Development, "with its interest in winning Muslim 'hearts and minds,' would be jealous of the kind of slick operation the Mormons run."

Visiting BYU

Elder Banks and Susan drove us to neighboring Provo for a delightful visit to Brigham Young University (BYU), which has about 30,000 students from 120 countries. Throughout our visit, on a spectacular November day with a clear blue sky, snow on the mountains in the distance, and autumn leaves ablaze with red, brown, and gold, it was apparent that the Mormons prized education. We met Daniel Peterson, the vice president of BYU, visited the Missionary Training Center, and met scholars who were overseeing the translation of classic Arabic literature into English. We concluded with my address to a full house of faculty and students, followed by an interesting and sympathetic question-and-answer session.

Daniel Peterson, like many Mormon fathers, had what for Americans is a large family—in his case, six children. He is the very embodiment of the best of the Mormon Church: imposing in his presence, open and scholarly in his conversation, and reaching out to others in intelligent interfaith exchanges. He talked affectionately of Muslim friends in Jordan whom he "dearly loved" and considered "brothers." Like others we met, he felt Mormons found it much easier to talk to Muslims about their faith than to other Christians.

Peterson, whose background is part English and part Scandinavian, recognized the "multiple identities" of Americans. "Through our religion we embrace the world," he said. For Peterson, American identity related to freedom and democracy. His experience in the military had left him with an appreciation of the significance of the Stars and Stripes. His eyes moistened: "When I see the flag raised, a chill goes up and down my spine."

I asked Peterson a question that had been puzzling me, especially in light of the discussion in chapter 6. How do young Mormons resist the temptations surrounding them in the permissive atmosphere of a campus? It was, Peterson replied, a combination of different tactics and strategy. Drinking and drugs are not allowed, nor is coffee or any substance containing caffeine. The dormitories are not coed. Students are expected to be back in their rooms by 9:30 p.m. and to be in bed by 10:30. They rise at 6:30 a.m., and their first task is to read the *Book of Mormon*. If students violate rules, they are put on probation, and if they break them again they are asked to leave. It was a combination of positive incentives—public recognition and trips abroad—and negative or punitive action implemented through family, friends, community, and church that kept individuals within the fold.

Walking about the campus, I saw no students with long hair or beards and noticed the girls dressed neatly and modestly. I also saw virtually no black or brown faces. It seemed a snow-white university composed of white faculty and white students, although I did come across a Pakistani student who turned out to be the son of a friend of mine, now a judge in the Supreme Court of Pakistan.

The Missionary Training Center, not an official part of the university but affiliated with it, trains annually 20,000 dedicated young people, male and female, to go abroad and eagerly spread the faith's ideas from its 334 missions around the world. Fifty languages are available for instruction. At nineteen, Mormon males are asked to serve abroad for two years. Girls must wait until they are twenty-one and serve for only a year and a half. Between 50,000 and 60,000 Mormon missionaries are currently abroad in about 120 countries, following in a tradition begun in 1837 when the first Mormon missionaries were sent to Great Britain. Prophet Monson himself writes to each student, announcing his or her selection. The young Mormon sees this duty as an honor.

We talked to several classes, including a group of young men and women learning foreign languages. The men wore dark suits with ties and white shirts. Although they looked American, they included some German and Swiss students. Having picked up some Chinese when his father was posted to the American embassy in Beijing, Frankie spoke to a young man learning Chinese and was impressed by the student's flawless diction.

A high point of the visit to the university was a discussion with scholars working on translations of some key Arabic texts, to be published together with the original. About twenty members of the faculty, all devout Mormons, joined us and seemed knowledgeable and sincere in their study of Islam. Here, in the middle of America, in a most unlikely setting, some of the rarest books of Islam are being translated for a wide readership. Yet few Americans even know about this important initiative.

The books already published are of a high caliber. Take the exquisitely produced *The Niche of Lights* by Abu Hamid Al-Ghazali, a parallel English-Arabic text translated, introduced, and annotated by David Buchman.[12] A product of the prestigious Islamic Translation Series, which is edited by Peterson with Islamic scholars such as William Chittick and Seyyed Hossein Nasr on the advisory board, it is a small gem. When we arrived back in Washington, D.C., we found a large package waiting for us, BYU's gift of the full series, including works by Islamic scholars such as Averroës and also non-Muslims such as the great Jewish sage Maimonides—both stars of Muslim Spain. It appeared the Mormons were trying to promote the kind of interfaith dialogue and exchange of ideas that characterized Muslim Spain centuries ago.

Akbar Ahmed and Mormon elders sit with Muslims after Friday prayers at the Utah Islamic Center in Salt Lake City. Of the roughly 20,000 Muslims in Salt Lake City, many call it "the best place for Muslims in America" because of Mormon kindness to them and the similarities between the two faiths.

Muslims in Salt Lake City

As if to confirm Mormon acceptance of other faiths, Salt Lake City has six mosques, five Sunni and one Shia. I met two of the city's leading imams when they attended a public lecture I gave at the University of Utah. Both were immigrants and involved in various public controversies surrounding the lack of organization and leadership in the Muslim community (see chapter 5). The community itself is surprisingly large, with a population of 15,000 to 20,000 of various ethnic backgrounds: Bosnian, Somali, South Asian, and Arab. Those we met repeatedly told us: "This is the best place in the United States for Muslims—it's the best-kept secret." The Mormons had clearly been good to them. The Mormon Church had even donated $25,000 toward the building of the Utah Islamic Center. To be fair, it gave a similar sum to the Hindu temple and houses of worship of other faiths.

Imam Shuaib-ud-din of the Utah Islamic Center, one of the Sunni imams who had come to my talk, felt that Mormons, like Muslims, are very family-oriented: "And their values are very conservative. Probably the best place for a Muslim to raise his family is Utah." He praised the Salt

Lake City clothing store Modest by Design, which caters to LDS people. At the same time, he recognized their fundamental theological differences and also noted relations have remained cordial since 9/11.

Shuaib-ud-din's family is originally from India, but he was born in Milwaukee. He was the first imam at the largest mosque in Salt Lake City and found himself much in demand in the media, he said, until members of the board became jealous and maneuvered his removal. Shuaib-ud-din described himself as a Deobandi, having trained in a Deobandi madrassah in Pakistan and in England. My team immediately became interested because they had visited Deoband and it was one of the models of Islamic expression in our previous study. The imam did express great respect for Aligarh, the Muslim modernist university and another of our models, and has visited there to pay homage. He felt, however, that imams who had studied in Deoband were the most qualified to speak on behalf of Islam. Religion, he said disapprovingly, "has a place" in Aligarh lives but "does not dominate it." He told us that he was the first Muslim born in the United States to study in a madrassah in India and complained that 90 percent of the imams who have come from abroad do not speak English, with the result that foreign imams cannot relate to the American youth.

We also talked to Imam Muhammed Shoayb Mehtar, a South African of South Asian background who became an imam shortly after 9/11. Shoayb recalled his days in Africa, where he often went backpacking. He emphasized that he was educated in the Western tradition, learning about science and technology.

Although Imam Shuaib-ud-din was born in the United States, it was Imam Shoayb who seemed more "liberal" in his views. Both of their mosques were open to Mormons, but Mehtar pointed out that some seventy to eighty of them came to his every Friday. He talked of Mormons and his "open-door policy" with the LDS enthusiastically. Mehtar was not as effusive about his own community. Muslims held onto the culture of their original homes, he complained, constantly referring back to their places of birth. Mehtar believed that any possible "perception problems" between Muslims and non-Muslims are "all the Muslims' fault!" Muslims must contribute, the imam said, "and stop going for a 'free ride' in the United States. Islam must help America, just as Muslims made Spain great with art and literature. Muslims can do this in America as well and make it a great country."

He was more hopeful about the next generation, "the ideal Muslims and Americans," and felt "the young people are different because they embrace Islam, but with a 'secular appeal.' Muslims should embrace

American democracy, as the Prophet himself was elected." The threat, said the imam, lies within the Muslim community, which needs to redefine its global image.

A bearded young man in Imam Mehtar's mosque who spoke with the team was excited about the similarities between Mormons and Muslims: "They say that if they weren't Mormon they'd be Muslim because Islam and Mormonism have almost the exact same belief system, you know. . . . With me, it was just that I felt that I could be more myself here than I could anywhere else, even in a Muslim country because over here . . . if you're different it's not viewed as bad. I feel really at home here, more than anywhere else."

"Yankee Mahomet"

A thoughtful, charismatic man, seeking answers in a time of change; an angel that brings revelations of the word of God; a small but dedicated community that acknowledges the coming of a new prophet; a prophet who takes multiple wives; controversy around and persecution of the community and escape to a distant place where it sets up a government that in time begins to grow; and finally, today, a community that has a world presence—this is the Mormon's story. It is also the Muslim's story. The similarities between the two faiths were picked up early in Mormon history. When Joseph Smith declared his faith, mainstream America described him as a "Yankee Mahomet" or "backwoods Mahomet." As early as 1842, the *New York Herald* editorialized that Joseph Smith "indicates as much talent, originality, and moral courage as Mahomet, Odin, or any of the great spirits that have hitherto produced the revolutions of the past ages."[13] In an 1853 speech, Brigham Young, the second prophet of the Mormons, compared Joseph Smith to the Prophet Muhammad, a comparison still made among Mormon scholars.[14]

Thus from Mormonism's birth, its founder was compared to the Prophet of Islam—approvingly by Mormons and dismissively by their critics. This was, however, still an American exercise in comparative religion. The man who changed all that was Sir Richard Burton. Fearless, strong-willed, a brilliant linguist, a perceptive anthropologist (though expelled from Oxford), and officer of the East India Company, Burton tormented the straight-laced, humorless Victorian elite with exotic and erotic stories based in eastern societies and customs, which he collected on his travels. His works created a sensation, making the prudish all the more eager to see him ostracized from public life. The color and excitement he brought to the study of "other cultures," his critics said, was nothing more than titillation.

Burton is best known for his translation of *The Book of the Thousand Nights and a Night,* commonly called *The Arabian Nights.* Its stories have given American culture widely recognized names such as Aladdin and Sinbad the Sailor. Less well known are his other translations, such as *The Perfumed Garden* from Arabian literature and the *Kama Sutra of Vatsyayana* from Sanskrit. To many of Burton's Victorian contemporaries, the former was considered an erotic Arab sex manual, and the latter its equivalent from ancient Hindu culture.

Arriving in Salt Lake City in 1860 when it was barely settled, Burton sensed an anthropological find. Rumors of harems and plural wives would have piqued Burton's interest. Being a bold man who had traveled to the forbidden city of Mecca disguised as a Muslim, his curiosity would have been aroused by stories comparing the Mormons to Muslims. Burton managed to meet Brigham Young, and the two got along famously. In *The City of the Saints,* which Burton published one year after his visit to Utah, he acknowledged that Young's critics saw him as a "hypocrite, swindler, forger, murderer."[15] But, wrote Burton, "no one looks it less." Burton's book introduced the idea that Mormons and Muslims had many parallels, which quickly spread through his network of Orientalist scholars and admirers.

Mormon Scholars Compare Their Faith to Islam

Mormon scholars have been quick to pounce on Burton's idea. "Having discovered the Muhammad–Joseph Smith comparison while reading up on Mormonism but familiar with Islam as none of the American clergymen were, Burton agreed that there were indeed a number of bona fide similarities," writes the Mormon historian Arnold H. Green. Burton, said Green, found that both claimed "to be a restoration by revelation of the pure and primaeval religion of the world." Furthermore, Burton suggested that Mormons, a "spontaneous agglomeration of tenets . . . are Muslims," in their belief in a literal resurrection, their practice of polygamy, and "in their views of the inferior status of womenkind." Brigham Young's title, "Lion of the Lord," Burton added, "was literally borrowed from El Islam."[16]

"Why did God reveal books specifically to the Jews and the Christians while leaving the Arabs and the Americans without their own special scriptures?" asks Green. He answers by quoting the German historian Eduard Meyer: "The solution was the same in both cases. . . . Joseph Smith brought forth a Bible for America; a Bible for the Arabs is what Moham-med longed for and received bit by bit." Thomas B. Marsh stated in 1838 that he overheard Joseph Smith warn that "he would yet tread down his enemies, and walk over their dead bodies; and if he was not let alone, he would be a second Mohammed to this generation, and that it would be one gore of blood from the Rocky Mountains to the Atlantic Ocean; that like Mohammed, whose motto in treating for peace was 'the Alcoran or the sword,' so should it be eventually with us, Joseph Smith or the sword." The late Mormon scholar Spencer J. Palmer, former director of the Reli-gious Studies Center at BYU and editor of *Mormons and Muslims,* devotes an entire chapter to similarities between the two faiths.[17] Appropriately, he quotes Meyer: "Without the least exaggeration, we may designate the Mormons as the Mohammedans of the New World according to their origins and their manner of thinking. There is hardly a historical parallel which is so instructive as this one; and through comparative analysis both receive so much light that a scientific study of the one through the other is indispensable."[18]

Mormon professors have prepared handouts for their students that identify similar rituals and daily practices between Mormons and Mus-lims. In the handout for his geography class, for example, BYU's Chad F. Emmett lists twenty-one similarities. However, the handout also points out the differences between Mormons and Muslims, including Islam's lack of a priesthood and the Muslim belief that Jesus was a great prophet but not the Son of God and that Muhammad was the "seal of the prophets," meaning there would be no prophets after him.

Clearly, while the similarities are significant, the differences cannot be ignored. Green argues for caution in emphasizing parallels between the two faiths:

> Muhammad transformed an essentially pagan and polytheistic com-munity into a strictly monotheistic one, whereas Joseph Smith intro-duced among Christians a "restored" version of Christianity having pluralistic tendencies. Also, in a sociological sense Muhammad was vastly more successful than Joseph Smith in both the religious and the political roles. Within Muhammad's own lifetime virtually all the Arabs were reconstituted into an Islamic state under his leadership, whereas Joseph Smith, at the time of his death, had merely created a comparatively small religious movement ignored or despised by most Americans, and although he aspired to national political leadership he died as mayor of Nauvoo.[19]

Because of the position in which Mormon scholars find themselves in relation to Islam and America simultaneously, they can provide a unique perspective on the mindset of both. Daniel Peterson, for example, traces the resentment in Muslims to a "deep hypocrisy" they perceive in Americans, who "seem to care about Israeli Jewish suffering, [while] they turn a blind eye (at least in much Arab and Muslim opinion) to the suffering of Palestinian Muslims." In Muslim eyes, that hypocrisy is in the tradition of the "colonialism and imperialism and oppression that they have endured," not to mention that of American colonists, who were "themselves repressive." Americans, observes Peterson, want democracy at home yet "seem perfectly comfortable with repression abroad" and with "supporting undemocratic regimes" in pursuit of their foreign policy. "And, of course, blaming others—the Zionists, Israel's Mossad, the CIA—serves the interests of more than a few failed governments in the Islamic world: it distracts popular attention from the poverty and tyranny that characterize the region." Peterson also notes the dramatic change in Muslim attitudes toward Jews since the establishment of Israel in 1948: "Where the Jews were once held in rather benign contempt, they are now commonly held in bitter awe as a race of malicious supermen."

Many Muslims, adds Peterson, are of much the same mind as medieval Europeans who saw "malevolent demons behind the actions of their enemies." He attributes this lack of reformation to Muslims' inability to "live alongside adherents of other faiths as full equals—as Europeans were gradually forced, very reluctantly, to do." Thus it is entirely up to them to restore their "historic place in world culture." [20]

Listening to Mormon Voices

Of all the religious or cultural groups we surveyed on our journey into America, the Mormons had the most positive opinion of Muslims. For example, 98 percent of Mormons said they would vote for a Muslim for public office. A twenty-two-year-old female Mormon of Northern European descent from Webster, Texas, stated, "I feel that Muslims are almost more God-fearing than most Christians—so I would almost be more inclined to vote for them."

Although not obliged to do so, a very high percentage of Mormons put their names on the questionnaires, thereby indicating a degree of confidence both in themselves and in the project. One of our questions asked respondents to rank four social categories in order of importance: their religion, nationality, political beliefs, and ethnic heritage. For 96 percent of Mormons, religion was number one. This figure was higher than for any other group, including the Muslims, 85 percent of whom placed religion first. Mormons ranked nationality second, followed by political beliefs and ethnic heritage in similar numbers. When asked to choose between religion and law if they were in conflict, 69 percent of Mormons answered religion, higher than for any other group. Kiri Redford, a twenty-two-year-old white female Mormon student, ranked religion first but then qualified her answer: "I would put religion first, but my religious beliefs *include* my love for this country. My ethnic loyalties and heritage and my religious beliefs strongly feed my political beliefs so they're all number one for me."

One of our most sensitive and illuminating questions was, "What is the biggest threat to America?" Mormons said "ourselves," followed by "immorality," "the economy," and "breakdown of the family." Mormons were by far the most concerned about immorality and breakdown of the family. A Mormon student at Salt Lake Community College, for example, named pornography as the greatest threat to America, calling it "the root of a lot of evil." Others named "same-sex marriage." Answers to "Is America a Christian Country?" were generally divided evenly across religious groups, with 55 percent of Mormons answering in the affirmative, the highest of any group, and 28 percent saying no. In other words, more Mormons saw America as a Christian country than did either Protestants or Catholics.

It is common practice to apply the term "Judeo-Christian" to American and Western values, but we found Mormons including "Muslim" in their description of American identity. For example, M. William Richards, a twenty-four-year-old Mormon of British descent, said that the greatest threat to America was "if Judeo/Christian/Muslim morals are replaced by progressive liberal ones; then God will cease to support this nation." He felt America "used to be" a Christian country but is "losing our Christian identity because liberal Americans are forcing anti-Christian values on the majority Christians."

Unlike other American groups, Mormons appeared to be familiar with Islam and invariably knew Muslims personally and had even visited them in their homes and mosques. A high percentage of Mormons interviewed and responding to our questionnaires indicated that they had a Muslim friend who introduced them to Islam. Some actually attended prayers at mosques. They were therefore not hostile to Muslims.

The Mormons were unambiguous in their devotion to America. A high number of Mormon respondents defined an American as someone who "loves" America. Like most Americans, Mormons also revere the U.S. military. A twenty-year-old white female Mormon said her greatest role model is "any war hero because it's amazing what people have done for our country." A twenty-one-year-old Native American female Mormon who was a senior at BYU identified "a failing sense of patriotism" as the biggest threat to America. Her role models were Ronald Reagan, Jesus, and the Prophet Muhammad, the Prophet because he "brought peace to a people and fought for goodness."

For Mormons, a love for America and a respect for Islam seemed to go hand in hand, although not all Mormons had the same views on terrorism. Some respondents reflected the American predator identity. A twenty-two-year-old Mormon, a man of Irish descent, said the war on terror is a "war to stop attacks on innocents. The enemy is fundamentalist terrorists. It is succeeding." He also cryptically said that the best way to improve relations with the Muslim world was the Monroe Doctrine, the purpose of which was to ensure the supremacy of the United States in the sphere of the American continents and to keep it isolated from outside powers.

Many Mormons told us that they often experienced prejudice on their mission trips, both in the United States and abroad. A forty-year-old white male with a Ph.D. said he experienced prejudice from evangelicals who "suppose they 'know' what I believe as a Mormon and who feel it is their duty to 'fix' me, or set me straight."

When asked how they believed others saw their religion, Mormons responded with an array of unflattering terms: "a cult," "an oddity," "extreme," "crazy," "out there," "unknown," "creepy," "backwards," "they think I'm foolish for believing my religion is correct," "boring," "robotic," "arrogant," "untrustworthy," "false," "polygamist," "strange," "close-minded," "uptight," "devilish," "hypocrites," "not Christian even though we are," "odd," and "over the top." A twenty-year-old white female claimed, "No one likes Mormons."

However, some believe Americans have a positive view of their faith. One said that people view Mormons positively for the "good they achieve," and several others said that Mormons are perceived as "good people." One noted: "The people who have actually had contact with Mormons always tell me how impressed they are with the genuine love and service they have seen come from Mormons." A twenty-three-year-old male Mormon lamented that people view his community as either "maddeningly heretical or terribly conservative. We're like the bats in Aesop's fable of the war between the birds and the mammals."

Mormon role models frequently include Prophet Thomas Monson, Prophet Gordon Hinckley, Jesus Christ, Joseph Smith, and Captain Moroni. Unlike respondents in the rest of the country, barely any Mormons listed Barack Obama as a role model except one or two Mexican Mormons. We frequently heard Mormons saying that they would like to ask Prophet Monson for advice on a religious issue, and it is apparent they have a high level of trust in, and respect for, him.

When asked the best way to improve relations between Muslims and non-Muslims, Mormons by and large called for dialogue, or a change in foreign policy. Arturo Fuertes, a twenty-four-year-old Mexican and Native American Mormon said: "The U.S. needs to not let Israel get away with so much crap; it needs to stop giving most of our international aid to Israel. That I think is a slap in the face to the Muslim world that we look at the Arab-Israeli conflict as a religious conflict when it is not." He told us that he has had "pretty frequent interactions and friendships with several Muslims. I love them and think there is something *very* special about them. I have met some Jews—not too impressed by them." Joshua S. McKinney, a twenty-seven-year-old white Mormon from Louisiana, agreed: "We shouldn't back Israel so much." Heath Dowers, a twenty-six-year-old convert, said the best way to improve relations is to "allow our Church in Middle Eastern countries."

Critics of Mormons: "The Most Un-American Thing Possible"

However hospitable and open our hosts, it was hard not to notice the controversy surrounding the Mormon community in Salt Lake City. In private conversations at the University of Utah, non-Mormon academics referred to Mormons as "fascists" and "exclusivists." They said the Mormons were responsible for leaving the Native Americans "crippled, irrelevant, sad, and spaced out on drugs and drinks. In short, finished."

Jonathan was surprised to hear non-Mormons complain about the "exclusive" attitude of Mormons and their reluctance to interact with those outside the faith. Non-Mormons, he observed, felt excluded not only religiously but also socially and economically in Utah, and he saw the fact that Mormons felt this way when white Protestants composed the majority everywhere else in the country. In Utah, the best way to integrate, as outsiders saw it, was to become Mormon. Another frustration of non-Mormon state residents was that Mormons would not associate with someone who does "bad things like drinking or smoking." Unlike other communities, noted Jonathan, Mormons excluded people solely on the basis of behavior, whereas many others exclude on the basis of race, ethnicity, or other factors.

The team's visit to Salt Lake City coincided with a storm of protests over the role of the LDS in mobilizing funds and support for California's

Proposition 8, which banned gay marriage in that state. On a frigid November night, Jonathan, Frankie, Craig, and Madeeha attended a noisy rally protesting the decision outside Temple Square in order to speak to some of the thousands of Mormon critics who had descended on Salt Lake City from around the country. They chanted and waved slogans such as "Sep-a-rate church and state" and "No more Mr. Nice Gay."

A man outside Temple Square with a swastika sign to indicate what he thought of Mormons, told Jonathan that the Mormons were now approaching "Nazi" status: "It's illegal, it's wrong, it's immoral, and it's un-American. It's the most un-American thing possible." What the Mormons had done, he said, was flaunt "our founding laws" in the Constitution, which the "whole country is based on." Another protestor felt his definition of American identity conflicted with that of the Mormon Church: "Everybody should have equal rights. Gay, straight, transgendered, whether you're black, white, Asian. Whoever you want to love you should be able to love."

A contingent of Mormons was also present at the protest, standing protectively outside their large central temple. One claimed that it was unfair to blame the LDS for the California vote because it was just part of democracy: "The Mormon Church is less than 2 percent of the population of California, and yet all of this is against the Mormon Church. It's totally misguided. I have gay friends, but I don't support the gay agenda."

Another young male Mormon said that Mormons supported Proposition 8 because "they feel very strongly . . . that there's nothing more beautiful than man and woman together, and to encourage, or allow, or suggest that it's OK for a man and man to be together, woman and woman to be together, is kind of contrary to what makes society so beautiful. So, it goes against the grain of what a lot of people believe, not just members of the church."

After watching the huge crowd of both gay and straight protesters expressing their views, and watching a similar protest a week later in San Francisco, both peaceful, it made Jonathan realize how proud he himself was to be an American: "One of the things we've heard over and over from the people across the country, when we ask them about America, is the pride that people have in the First Amendment. The right to free speech and to congregate and protest peacefully is part of American identity—people from every ethnicity, religion, age, and gender say proudly. While in Utah the protest was directed at the LDS, there were a lot of other religious groups and denominations that supported the proposition as well."

At the same time, Jonathan found it difficult to comprehend the position of the Mormon Church, which "so boldly proclaims" the message of

Jesus: "I didn't see the Jesus I know—I just didn't see compassion and love in the words and speech of the church in this particular instance. I saw intolerance, and not just intolerance but discrimination—the same kind that once, not too long ago, used similar justifications to prohibit marriage based on race."

Similarly, mainstream America retains lingering doubts about the Mormon faith and practices, as reflected in Krakauer's *Under the Banner of Heaven*. The Mormon community found the book disquieting. The title was drawn from an 1880 address by John Taylor, the third president of the LDS, in which he defended plural marriages: "God is greater than the United States, and when the Government conflicts with heaven we will be ranged under the banner of heaven and against the Government. The United States says we cannot marry more than one wife. God says different." To the Mormons, the content and tone of the book were hostile and mischievous, and the barb of its subtitle, *A Story of Violent Faith,* seemed aimed at the very heart of their religion. Mormons were not amused by the many examples of Krakauer's contempt for their faith, often conveyed through quotations such as Mark Twain's reference to the *Book of Mormon* as "chloroform in print." In an unsparing description of Joseph Smith, the reader is reminded that Smith married at least thirty-eight women and probably as many as forty-eight, and that his youngest wife was fourteen years old. In 1826 he was tried by the state of New York and found guilty of being "a disorderly person and an imposter."[21]

Krakauer concludes that Mormon belief predisposes members of the church to commit acts of violence. In short, the fault lies not so much with ordinary Mormons as with the theology that shapes them. It is an argument familiar in post-9/11 America because it has been widely used in the media in the case of Muslims and Islam. Krakauer draws on Islam freely in building his picture of the Mormons. Although he is referring to the Fundamentalist Church of Latter-day Saints (FLDS), he gives the general impression that they represent the real Mormon faith, encouraging the organization of small communities that bear "more than a passing resemblance to life in Kabul under the Taliban."[22] By drawing parallels between the anarchy and violence that are associated with the Taliban and the Mormons, and between Joseph Smith and the Prophet of Islam as men of violence and war, Krakauer was, in one stroke, swiping at both Islam and the Mormon Church.

The Mormon Church took the book seriously enough to publish a rebuttal, pointing out its inaccuracies and flaws. The church leadership's reaction to the book was understandable. Most people coming across a

"Mormon story" are not likely to distinguish between the faith's different branches. They all seem alike. In fact, the main church, the LDS, had banned both polygamy and the idea of vengeance and teaches Mormons to have only as many children as can be supported. The FLDS, on the other hand, sees the larger branch as the errant one and itself as more orthodox and so has preserved and promoted the banned practices. FLDS Mormons follow not the LDS's Monson but the FLDS prophet, Warren Jeffs, a direct blood descendant of Joseph Smith, currently in federal prison for the rape of young girls after being on the FBI's Ten Most Wanted list alongside figures such as Osama bin Laden.

There are said to be about 30,000 FLDS polygamists living in the United States, Canada, and Mexico, although some believe this number could be as high as 100,000. Utah County, Utah, a stronghold of both the LDS and the FLDS, has the highest birthrate in the United States, higher than that of Bangladesh.[23]

Krakauer devotes one chapter to the Elizabeth Smart case, in which a millionaire's blonde, fourteen-year-old daughter was abducted from her house by a Mormon fundamentalist—but not an "official" member of the FLDS—named Brian David Mitchell who took her as one of his wives. The nation became transfixed by her case, and when she was located, her father received a call from an elated George W. Bush, then planning the imminent Iraq invasion in the wake of 9/11.[24] Preaching to his FLDS adherents, Warren Jeffs had called the attacks a cause for celebration and a sign of the End Times and of the imminent return of Christ. Canadian FLDS compounds reportedly posted 9/11 images everywhere.

Mainstream American media continues to cast the spotlight steadily and cruelly on the Mormons. The 2007 film *September Dawn* is based on the alleged slaughter of 120 settlers on September 11, 1857, by Mormons on their way to California. Mormon leaders, including Joseph Smith and Brigham Young, are shown as sinister, murdering fanatics who constantly utter phrases like "curse and kill these dogs of gentiles, the children of Satan." At one point, Young intones "any miserable soul who comes to our Zion, cut his throat." There is a disclaimer at the film's end stating that Mormons, to this day, deny they ever took part in such a massacre.

Film critics picked up the allusion to Islam in the film, with some criticizing it for equating "the institution of the Mormon church with Islamic extremism at every opportunity." Others, however, declared the "fact-based" and "historical" film a "pulse-pounding movie experience reminding us that a terrorist act can happen anywhere, anytime, by anyone."[25] Like

Krakauer, Hollywood was singling out the Mormons as potential threats to the United States.

Mormons, Muslims, and American Identity

As this chapter explains, the dilemmas facing the Mormons and the Muslims in the United States are significantly similar. Both Mormons and Muslims consciously cling to their religious and cultural practices in the face of a larger encroaching American culture. Moreover, both Mormons and Muslims have much in their tradition that mainstream American culture can pick on and reduce to caricature. Polygamy among Mormons and Muslims—although Mormons officially banned it in 1890 and Muslims do not insist on it as citizens of the United States—is a frequent target of ridicule.

The relationship Mormons and Muslims have with mainstream Americans calls to mind terms such as "tense," "distrustful," "angst-ridden," and "uneasy." Too rarely does one hear words like "harmony" or "acceptance." Both communities have reason to be apprehensive. The founders of the Mormon faith in the nineteenth century were hounded and killed. Even though there could be no more "American" Americans than the Mormons—coming as they do from a Christian, white, and English background—a cloud of distrust and hatred still hangs over them. The slightest scandal, usually linked to issues of polygamy, opens up old prejudices. Similarly, the Muslims, who are so different from the Mormons in their religious and ethnic background, have had an uneasy presence in the United States, which has been exacerbated since 9/11.

Where do Mormons stand in terms of the three American identities? Clearly, they are the beneficiaries of pluralist America, and they recognize their debt to its Founding Fathers by elevating them to prophethood. Throughout our journey Mormons indicated that "the American Founding Fathers were prophets—they formed a country where we have freedom of religion." After the first turbulent decades, Mormons merged into and flourished with American pluralist identity.

If, in the context of this book, color is such an important factor in defining groups and the interaction between them, how does one explain the white U.S. government's predatory attack in the mid-nineteenth century on a community that was descended from the first white settlers and emphasized its "Americanness?" The answer is that while there is no doubt that the founders of the Mormon faith are descended from English immigrants, their aim of creating a centralized, powerful, and even secretive organization structured like a state within a state challenged the U.S. establishment. That is why governors and senior officials cheerily joined in the attacks on the Mormons. No government, however sympathetic or understanding, will allow a minority to appropriate its authority, especially when that minority sets up alternative, state-like organizations.

The harsh response to the Mormons is therefore rooted in statecraft and the American policy of zero tolerance to any challenge to its authority. Still, the administration was not quite as brutal to the Mormons as it was to the Native Americans and the slaves, for by contrast it allowed Mormons to set up their semiautonomous structure in Utah and live the way they wished.

In the twentieth century, Mormons compensated for their earlier status as not fully American or even fundamentally un-American by unreservedly identifying with America and Christianity. The stereotype of the blue-eyed, blond, clean-cut, and conservatively dressed Mormon is also an image of America itself, which is comforting to those who equate it to primordial identity. They vote Republican in the main, wave the Stars and Stripes at every opportunity, and work for the federal government in large numbers. Their skills in language training and experience abroad combine with their patriotism to give them an advantage in joining the intelligence services.

Mormonism appears to have a bright future. It is the fastest-growing religion in the Western Hemisphere. Mormons now outnumber Episcopalians or Presbyterians in the United States, and there are more Mormons than Jews in the world. Elected Mormon officials hold high office in the United Kingdom, Brazil, Mexico, and Japan. Mormonism seems likely to become a major world religion, the first to emerge since Islam, according to some scholars.[26] Sociologist Rodney Stark predicts that the LDS will have 300 million members by the end of the twenty-first century.

From a Muslim point of view, the arguments laying out the similarities between Mormons and Muslims are gratifying, especially as Muslims find themselves in need of friends in a post-9/11 America. Still, it is important to remind oneself that God, divine revelation, and prophethood do not mean quite the same thing to Muslims as they do to Mormons. Perhaps the way forward in the relationship between adherents of the two faiths is not to be bogged down in religious discussions and debates. That will lead nowhere. What can bring the communities together is the mutual appreciation of two minority groups with much in common and a desire to live as good neighbors and good friends. Sociology rather than theology needs to define relations between Mormons and Muslims and their place in American identity.

NINE

The Importance of Being America

THE UNITED STATES that we have come to know in our travels is indeed a nation of multiple identities, both divided and wondrously united. As the ethnographic data of the preceding chapters indicate, the divisions occur between and within communities and at times put serious strain on the overall unity of any of these. Of wide concern at present are the stresses that have arisen with the growth of America's Muslim community and its unfortunate association with 9/11. Increased and intense dialogue that leads to understanding seems the obvious way to reduce these stresses, but it can only be achieved through mutual appreciation, beginning perhaps with a deeper understanding of the founders of both the United States and Pakistan, a major Muslim nation—keeping in mind the different time periods, continents, and cultures in which they lived.

Founding Fathers: Jefferson and Jinnah

Just as Thomas Jefferson represents the former, Mohammed Ali Jinnah embodies the latter. Yet when Americans discuss Muslim leaders, they usually think of figures who have been cast as stereotypes: Saddam Hussein, tyrant; Muammar Qaddafi, mad tyrant; Ayatollah Ruhollah Khomeini, religious fanatic; Hamid Karzai and Asif Ali Zardari, corrupt and incompetent heads of state; and Hosni Mubarak and Pervez Musharraf, corrupt military dictators. Rarely if ever do they mention leaders such as Jinnah, the founder in 1947 of Pakistan, then the largest Muslim nation on earth. In fact, most Americans have never heard of this revered Muslim leader.

Similarly, when Muslims speak of American leaders, they usually refer to those of recent history, George W. Bush, Dick Cheney, and Donald Rumsfeld, who they see as arrogant and morally perverted leaders of a war on Islam. Other American leaders, such as Bill Clinton and Barack Obama, are seen as either too flawed or too weak. Muslims are aware of the American Founding Fathers such as George Washington, Thomas Jefferson, Benjamin Franklin, and those who lived and died to uphold their vision, Abraham Lincoln and John F. Kennedy, but still know little about them. And while some American Muslims have a genuine affection for Jefferson, he is virtually unknown in the Muslim world.

On September 11, 2001, the worlds of Jefferson and of Jinnah collided.[1] The events of that day would impact both societies in ways that their respective founding fathers could not have imagined. But after so many years, many Americans and Muslims still view each other as an oddity, failing to understand how much each shares with the other.

Jefferson is the quintessential founding father of the United States. He is at the core of the American political universe, just as Isaac Newton is at the core of Western intellectual development explaining the laws of modern science.[2] Through what he said and did, Jefferson symbolizes the American ideal. An early biographer wrote of him, "If Jefferson was wrong, America is wrong. If America is right, Jefferson was right."[3]

Similarly, Jinnah *is* Pakistan. For Pakistanis, he is, as the title of a biography suggested, *The Modern Moses*.[4] An eminent Englishman who had worked in British India described Jinnah as the Pakistani equivalent of the king-emperor, the archbishop of Canterbury, the speaker, and the prime minister, all rolled into one.[5]

Both Jefferson and Jinnah were heads of state and made a permanent contribution to the definition of their nations. The American Declaration of Independence is one of the most eloquently written political texts in history, and Jefferson's contribution to it makes him the preeminent interpreter of the American vision. Jinnah also left behind a memorable and eloquent testament in his first speeches to the Constituent Assembly of Pakistan in August 1947. The flavor is captured in these lines that narrow-minded Pakistani leaders have tried unsuccessfully to erase from history: "You are free; you are free to go to your temples, you are free to go to your mosques; or to any other place of worship in this State of Pakistan. . . . We are starting in the days when there is no discrimination, no distinction between one community and another, no discrimination between one caste or creed and another. We are starting with this fundamental principle that we are all citizens and equal citizens of one state."

There are other parallels as well. The two men were born subjects of the British Empire, yet both led a successful revolution against the British. Both were religious in a general, broad sense, and were humanists, and neither was dogmatic or what today is called fundamentalist. The two were self-made men not belonging to any aristocratic lineage; both found it difficult to have comfortable personal relations with people around them, yet were strongly conscious of speaking on behalf of "the people." Both were involved in relationships that raised eyebrows (Jefferson with his slave mistress; Jinnah with a bride half his age); both were accused by their critics of inconsistency (Jefferson for not being robust in defending Virginia from an invading British fleet with Benedict Arnold in command; Jinnah for abandoning his role as ambassador of Hindu-Muslim unity and becoming the champion of Pakistan). Both were cerebral men and have been cast in heroic terms by followers as fathers of their nations, and they attract people from across the political spectrum. Each is remembered in national monuments on the must-see list of tourists—the Jefferson memorial in Washington, D.C., and Jinnah's mausoleum in Karachi. Not quite from the upper reaches of the aristocracy in terms of lineage, they nonetheless lived and behaved as aristocrats. Both married women who belonged to the aristocracy. One of the paradoxes of politics is the popularity of both Jefferson and Jinnah in the public mind in spite of being intellectual and somewhat elitist in appearance.

As lawyers, Jefferson and Jinnah revered the guarantee of the rule of law and of certain citizens' rights, as embodied in a constitution that reflects the finest of human reason and civilization. Both their nations were born out of revolution, murder, and mayhem, as well as out of great hope. Jefferson's love of education helped him to establish the University of Virginia, which he continued to support after his presidency and which still honors his name. And he always maintained his affection for the College of William and Mary, which he entered in 1760. Jinnah, too, would keep in close touch with several educational institutions, including the Sindh Madrassah in Karachi where he was educated. He had a close relationship with Aligarh University, and Aligarh students were his most loyal supporters in the struggle for Pakistan. When his will was disclosed after his death, people were surprised to see that he had left his fortune to colleges in Delhi and Bombay, which were not in Pakistan but in India. He had not changed his will, even after leaving India for Pakistan.

No man in public life is free of controversy. Not even a genuine founding father. Both Jefferson and Jinnah continue to arouse controversy well after their deaths. There is little doubt that Jefferson, who had a general respect for humanity, nonetheless reflected the prejudices of his time. While his views on slavery cannot be condoned, sometimes commentators go to absurd lengths to criticize him. His support of the French Revolution is well documented,[6] but this has inspired some to compare him with apologists for the murderous tyrants Stalin and Mao. Several Christian denominations, including the Presbyterian Church, have attacked Jefferson for possessing the "morality of devils," and others have referred to him as an "arch-infidel."[7]

The criticism of Jinnah was as complex, and many orthodox Muslims condemned him as a kafir, or nonbeliever. Some called him "the greatest kafir." Contemporary Muslims continue to criticize Jinnah for not being "Islamic" enough. "Jinnah Defies Allah" was the subtitle of a special feature on Jinnah with the title "Mohammed Ali Jinnah Exposed!" in the December 1996 issue of the Hizb-ut-Tahrir magazine *Khilafah* (London). Jinnah's sin, the article complained, was that he insisted on saying that Islam stood for democracy and supported women's and minority rights.

Jefferson's ideas are a product of the European Enlightenment, and he was influenced by Greek philosophers such as Aristotle and Plato. Jinnah, too, may be said to be a product of the European Enlightenment, considering his education at Lincoln's Inn, the law college in London, and how impressed he was by London's Westminster, which symbolizes parliamentary democracy. However, he looked beyond the European Enlightenment, to the origins of Islam. Both men, each inspired by his own tradition, had concluded that human society was best organized and conducted when individual liberty, religious freedom, and universal education were guaranteed. In short, the study of Jefferson and Jinnah is more than an examination of two historical figures. The similarities between these two men provide a useful corrective to the flawed but influential idea of the "clash of civilizations."

While few Americans I asked knew Jinnah, many American Muslims, of every background and age, expressed admiration for Jefferson. In a private conversation with me, even the head of the Islamic Circle of North America (ICNA), one of the continent's most orthodox Islamic organizations, talked of his appreciation of Jefferson (in chapter 5). These Muslims saw Jefferson as a man so "Islamic" in his ideas that some even suggested he was a Muslim in all but name. They attributed the Islamic nature of the founding documents to Jefferson. In their eyes, the highest ideals of the United States and those of Islam are compatible: both emphasize justice, the rule of law, respect for knowledge and education, family, and human rights. Perhaps the Muslim love for Jefferson is best summed up by the simple but sincere tribute of a Nigerian man in Houston: "Jefferson is at the top of my heart. I love him." The Founding Fathers, he felt, were guided by God. "They had genius to give freedom. They were not perfect; they were human, but good men." He described America as the "best hope for the world."

In spite of the towering status—and relevance—of Jefferson and Jinnah, it appears that some young American Muslims are inspired by neither. Their guides and role models are men who preach violence, and their actions have caused confusion and turmoil within the community and in mainstream America.

Homegrown Terrorists

One such individual was Major Nidal Hasan. Not long after he gained notoriety in 2009 for killing thirteen fellow soldiers and wounding thirty more in Fort Hood, Texas, I was interviewed on CNN by the well-known newscaster Wolf Blitzer. His questions astonished me. Their tone confirmed what I feared—that Islam remained a mystery to Americans, who continued to conflate Islam with terrorism. Here was a top media personality asking me if there was a "perverse" school of Islamic thought that required Muslims to go to "strip clubs and enjoy lap dancing, while at the same time getting ready to kill." Blitzer finally asked me if Hasan was an "Islamic jihadist terrorist" or just someone who had gone "berserk." The debate about Muslims had gone on for years, yet this latest combination of terms proved that Americans were nowhere close to understanding Muslims, and Muslims to explaining themselves satisfactorily.

Consider the last months of 2009 when many cases in the news, including the Fort Hood incident, involved Muslims accused of terrorism. An African American convert, Sheikh Luqman Ameen Abdullah, was shot and killed by the FBI, and John Allen Muhammad, a Nation of Islam member who had terrorized the nation's capital region in 2002, was executed. Adam Gadahn, a white American convert, issued a tape on behalf of al Qaeda, once again threatening America. While these cases were still being discussed, another Muslim story captured attention. Five basketball-loving young men, American Muslims from Northern Virginia, were arrested in Pakistan for alleged terrorist-related activity.

Also in the fall of 2009, President Obama announced his intention to deploy another 30,000 troops to Afghanistan, and the violence in Pakistan brought on by the Taliban reached new heights. At the end of the year, as Americans settled down for a brief respite, a young Muslim from Nigeria flew into Detroit on Christmas Day carrying a deadly present. Strapped onto Umar Farouk Abdul Mutallab's body were enough explosives to blow up the plane.

Almost instantly every type of Islamic expert and commentator in America was back in the media warning of the Islamic peril and the homegrown terrorist. To complicate matters, the perpetrators were diverse—African American, white converts, and immigrants from across the Muslim world. They included men with full beards and those like the Christmas Day bomber, with barely a hint of a beard and a fascination for Western culture. Adding another dimension to the problem, in early 2010 the first white female convert, a blue-eyed blonde originally from Texas, was singled out as a potential terrorist.

Connecting the Dots

These events confronted America with the reality of its deepest anxiety: the homegrown terrorist, the citizen who is prepared to commit murder and mayhem without regard to his or her own life or that of others. The United States is becoming uncomfortably aware that its adventures overseas are creating complications at home. Muslim leadership in the West still remains in a state of denial.

But I also knew how difficult it was for Americans to understand what was happening in the Muslim community. While cases linking American Muslims to terrorist plots appeared in the media with increasing frequency, and the words "homegrown terrorists" became common currency, there were no satisfactory explanations for what this meant. Few of the reports connected the dots.

Why are young Muslims who are born and bred in America opting to commit terrorist acts against their own homeland? There are many reasons, the cumulative effect of which pushes them toward, and sometimes over, the brink. Their religion, Islam, while categorically rejecting violence, places a great deal of emphasis on the need to fight injustice and tyranny, and interpreted in a certain way, it provides a ready-made reference for violence. This is on the minds of many American converts who have been involved in terrorism-related cases.

Although Islam teaches Muslims to stand up for justice, it does not support any kind of unprovoked aggression, and its rules of war include protection for women, children, priests, and even vegetation. However, the Afghan war against the Soviet Union in the 1980s has had an incalculable effect on how contemporary Muslims now define holy war, or jihad. It was the mujahideen in the field who defeated the Soviet forces with their courage and sacrifice, not those Muslims protesting at the United Nations. This lesson was not lost on the new generation, and one expression of it was the rise in suicide bombings and indiscriminate killing after 9/11—acts that should be unequivocally condemned. Although some Muslims participate in this kind of violence, it is neither an Islamic response nor a humanist one.

What is pervasive, however, is the concept of the ummah, or the world community of Muslims, and Muslims everywhere point to the unresolved problems and suffering of its members: Palestinians, Kashmiris, Chechens, Uighurs, and others. These proud and ancient peoples have been made second-class citizens in their own homelands. If they protest, they are labeled "terrorists" and crushed. While being aware of their potential power—one out of four people in this world is Muslim—Muslims feel helpless and frustrated.

Some Muslims are affected by U.S. actions taken in response to 9/11, which led to arrests and deportation, prompting others to flee the country. This has reinforced the sense of being a mistrusted community. Others resent the Islamophobia they see in the media. Commentators on all the major networks have generally fed into the idea of Islam as an inherently violent religion and of Muslims, especially those living in America, as potential terrorists or supporters of terrorism.

The influential pastor Rod Parsley argues that "America was founded, in part, with the intention of seeing this false religion [Islam] destroyed" and that the sole purpose of Christopher Columbus in sailing to the New World in 1492 was to discover enough wealth there to defeat Islam. The Prophet Muhammad, Parsley writes, "received revelations from demons and not from the true God," which makes Islam an "anti-Christ religion."[8] For Parsley, all Muslims are the same and there is no such thing as an extremist to be distinguished from the mainstream. Parsley called for a new crusade to eradicate the religion. Even senior political figures in America have not been immune to the views of men like Pastor Rod Parsley. During the 2008 presidential campaign, John McCain called Parsley his "spiritual guide."[9]

The Islamophobia continued unabated even though America's Muslim community had demonstrated its aversion to terrorist acts. It had immediately and roundly condemned Major Hasan after the Fort Hood incident and had tipped off the FBI in Virginia about the five young would-be militarists seeking training in Afghanistan. In their case and in that of the Nigerian apprehended in Detroit, it was the parents who mustered the moral courage to alert the authorities. In the latter, the intelligence and security officials did not follow the lead.

The Islamophobic nature of covering Muslim stories also prevents the media from reporting the sacrifices Muslims are making for America. The greatest challenge for a Muslim is to join the American army and to be sent to a Muslim land to fight against fellow Muslims. Yet this is precisely what Muslims are doing, as we witnessed in a solemn visit to Arlington National Cemetery. Among those buried in section 60, reserved for American soldiers killed after 9/11, is Humayun Khan, killed in Iraq and awarded the Purple Heart. And he is but one example of Muslim soldiers who have sacrificed their lives.

Muslims complain that American media ignore the scale of Muslim losses, and that this implies Muslim lives have no value. This sentiment is captured by the plea of an Iraqi man who survived a 2007 incident in which employees of a military contractor, Blackwater, opened fire on civilians, leaving seventeen dead: "What are we—not human? Why do they have the right to kill people? Is our blood so cheap? For America, the land of justice and law, what does it mean to let criminals go?"[10]

American Greg Mortenson, coauthor of *Three Cups of Tea,* which chronicles his praiseworthy charitable work in Afghanistan and Pakistan, has worked extensively with Muslims in the very regions where America is conducting a war. He notes that "the worst thing you can do is what we're doing—ignoring the victims. To call them 'collateral damage' and not even try to count the numbers of the dead. Because to ignore them is to deny they ever existed, and there is no greater insult in the Islamic world. For that, we will never be forgiven."[11]

The scale of the killing and disruption has been staggering. In Iraq over 1.1 million people have been killed, nearly 5 million have been displaced, and 5 million children orphaned.[12] Although few figures are available for Afghanistan, it is estimated that 50,000 died in the year after 9/11 alone.[13] Since 9/11 about 26,000 Pakistanis have been killed, and 3 million have been displaced.[14] In 2009 American drone strikes killed more than 700 Pakistanis, mostly women and children. As a result of the chaos in Somalia since a U.S.-backed invasion in 2006, some 80,000 have died, and about 2 million have been displaced.[15] More than half the population of Somalia is in need of immediate food aid in order to survive and is facing what the United Nations calls a "humanitarian catastrophe."[16]

Such lopsided casualty figures, resulting from U.S. incursions, are rooted deep in the American psyche and the policy of zero tolerance. Recall General William Shafter's admission that "it may be necessary to kill half of the Filipinos in order that the remaining half of the population" may adopt American ideals (see chapter 3).[17] From the dropping of the atom bomb on

The grave of Captain Humayun Khan, a decorated Pakistani American soldier killed in the Iraq War. He is buried in section 60 at Arlington Cemetery, where soldiers killed in action after 9/11 are laid to rest.

Japan to the deaths of over 3 million people in Vietnam, the tendency of the predator to pursue victory at any cost is evident.

From my position in Washington, D.C., watching the drama unfold from the front row, it was clear to me in the years following 9/11 that proponents of predator identity inside and outside the U.S. government were contemplating the invasion of other Muslim countries after Iraq, including

Syria and Iran. What stopped them was a combination of fierce resistance from Muslim tribes, incompetent planning of the Iraq and Afghan invasions, and breathtaking ignorance of local cultures, as well as a fierce, if belated, pluralist backlash at home to their excesses. The definition of "success" in the current Muslim wars, after so many years, still remains elusive.

Muslims from these countries are quick to point out that not one of the nineteen 9/11 terrorists came from their lands. If the billions of dollars poured into these catastrophic wars in these Muslim countries were diverted into education and relief, they say, there would be many more people looking to America with affection than loathing. In the meantime, the chorus of Muslim voices condemning terrorism is ignored and the sacrifices of these Muslims remain unacknowledged while Americans continue to ask, "Where are the moderates?" I am constantly asked why Muslims do not condemn violence, and I try to explain that thousands of so-called moderate Muslims have sacrificed their lives to the violence perpetrated by the extremists. I give the example of people like Benazir Bhutto who, whatever her politics and reputation, went back to Pakistan to promote democracy and lost her life in the bargain.

Indeed, major Muslim capitals like Cairo and even Tehran that had poor relations with the United States roundly condemned what happened on 9/11, as did thousands of individuals and organizations. Moreover, every Muslim organization continues to make its position clear with each new controversy or scare. An Internet search will yield tens of thousands of statements and press releases emphatically condemning terrorism. Yet few of them appear in the Western media, and any that do are drowned in the flood of Islamophobic sentiment.

Inasmuch as the subject of the homegrown terrorist has focused attention on Muslim societies in the West, clues to these societies can be found by comparing Muslims in the United States and in Europe. I have lived among European Muslims for many years and now live among American Muslims. The fact of the matter is that neither of these Muslim communities is a monolith, and both are riven with ideological, ethnic, sectarian, and generational divisions. The experience of each Muslim community in Western countries is in one sense similar and in another different.

In countries like Britain, Muslims are more concentrated in certain enclaves and therefore able to preserve their ethnic culture, whereas in America they are more dispersed. In Britain the vast majority of Muslims come from South Asia, and they dominate the Muslim discourse, whereas in America Muslims have more diverse backgrounds. Furthermore, the African American Muslim community has a unique history of its own.

Some commentators argue that Muslims are better assimilated in America, but others claim this is more likely the case in Europe. Both sides have their supporters. Some say that because America has had no colonial experience in Muslim lands, has nurtured religious freedom, and is a nation of immigrants itself, it is more welcoming to its newer Muslim immigrants; others note that a dozen members of Parliament in the United Kingdom are Muslim, whereas the number in the U.S. Congress has only reached two. In other fields, a Pakistani has been the captain of England's cricket team, and several top commentators for the BBC are from Pakistan. Americans, however, could point to the Afghan who became a key member of President Bush's inner circle after 9/11, and to the often overlooked fact that America has a large African American Muslim population, which is as American as the proverbial apple pie and has produced figures such as Muhammad Ali, Malcolm X, and Imam W. D. Mohammed.

A new, holistic, intelligent, long-term strategy, which includes both internal and external action, is needed to keep the nation safe and its communities in harmony. Western administrations need to work with national, community, and interfaith leaders to involve Muslims and make them feel they are valued citizens. The homegrown terrorist is a symptom of the failure of several communities and their leaders to work together to prevent future terror and change the way the young are thinking. Although the Muslim community is overwhelmingly patriotic, all it will take to ruin relations with the majority population for a long time to come will be a major incident or two involving just a few young Muslims. A new chapter fraught with tension and danger may have just opened in the history of Western societies, and there is little time to lose if they are to avert disaster.

What Is American Policy toward Its Muslims?

In order to proceed, Americans need an adequate answer to this question, yet a satisfactory one remains elusive. When Barack Obama became president, Muslims had high hopes. So it was ironic that the first black president in U.S. history within a year of taking office officially sanctioned the profiling of people from thirteen Muslim nations out of a list of fourteen. (Cuba, the only non-Muslim country, was included because it is invariably an American favorite for this kind of action.) In the immediate aftermath, stories of open discrimination against Muslims at U.S. airports, especially against women wearing the hijab, were widely reported in the media. Critics protested that profiling violates the United Nations Declaration of Human Rights, which prohibits any kind of discrimination based on religion. Obama went on to disappoint when he extended the life of the Patriot Act by one year.

Almost without notice, the very foundation of American identity—including the U.S. Constitution—was being challenged. Torture was discussed in the media, and many sections of society supported it with gusto. An entirely new vocabulary—words like "extraordinary rendition" and "enhanced interrogation"—was created to deal with this penumbral subject. While the head of Blackwater, as mentioned in chapter 5, was pursuing his vision of "eliminating Muslims and the Islamic faith from the globe," the U.S. government was instituting measures against Muslims in Guantánamo Bay and in CIA "black sites" around the world that "constituted torture," according to the Red Cross.[18] In addition to sanctioning tactics such as waterboarding, sexual humiliation, confinement with insects in coffinlike boxes, and bashing detainees against walls, or "walling," the U.S. government looked the other way when Muslim prisoners were killed. In early 2010, for example, *Harper's Magazine,* in an investigation conducted with NBC News, concluded that the United States had four years earlier tortured to death three Guantánamo detainees whose deaths American officials had claimed were suicides.[19] Prominent U.S. military commanders like four-star general Barry McCaffrey affirmed that the military and the CIA had "murdered" and "tortured people unmercifully."[20]

To President Bush, however, American methods were in keeping with international law: "Common Article III (of the Geneva Conventions) says that, you know, there will be no outrages upon human dignity. It's like—it's very vague. What does that mean, 'outrages upon human dignity?'"[21]

According to Secretary of State Colin Powell's chief of staff, Colonel Lawrence Wilkerson, Bush, Cheney, and Secretary of Defense Donald Rumsfeld were fully aware that the majority of Muslims sent to Guantánamo "were innocent." The indefinite detention of these Muslims, including 12-year-old children and 93-year-old men, who had been "sold" to the Americans by Afghan and Pakistani authorities for up to $5,000 each, was deemed "justified by the broader War on Terror." Cheney's rationale was simple, according to Wilkerson: "If hundreds of innocent individuals had to suffer in order to detain a handful of hardcore terrorists, so be it."[22] Unlike the early Americans, observed by de Tocqueville, who could take an Indian nation "like a brother by the hand and lead it to die outside the country of its fathers" and yet maintain the fig leaf of the law, Cheney believed that the Americans of this generation had the right to dispense with the law altogether.[23]

I wondered how a panel of judges that comprised George Washington, Thomas Jefferson, and Benjamin Franklin would have conducted itself in the post-9/11 cases. George Washington had ordered his army to maintain the moral high ground at all costs by *not* torturing British prisoners, even though Americans had been tortured by the British—"Treat them with humanity and Let them have no reason to Complain of our Copying the brutal example of the British army."[24] Jefferson believed that government "shall not have power . . . to prescribe torture in any case whatever."[25] Benjamin Franklin's instructions to the American navy during the American Revolution were that even if they came across Captain James Cook, a senior officer in the British navy, they were to treat him and "his People with all Civility and Kindness . . . as common Friends to Mankind."[26]

But, in the heated atmosphere after 9/11, arguments on behalf of the vision of the Founding Fathers took a hammering, as few were ready to heed Benjamin Franklin's warning: "What'er's begun in anger ends in shame."[27] The country seemed to be heading back to square one, with the CIA promising to "avenge" the killing of seven of its operatives in Afghanistan in December 2009, and in the end killing eleven Afghan children. Revenge had also motivated Humam al-Balawi, who blew himself up along with the CIA agents. In a prerecorded interview, the Jordanian doctor told Hakimullah Mahsud, Baitullah Mahsud's successor as head of the Taliban in Pakistan, that he would take "revenge" for the death of Baitullah caused by American drones. These encounters were sounding like tribal wars of revenge.

Religion, too, colored the way people looked at each other. While fair and impartial justice is a crucial bulwark in a society with many religions competing for status and power, we discovered that for large sections of America the laws of religion are as important as the law of the land. Many believe that civil law is corrupt, man-made, and ever changing, but that religion, being made by God, is infallible and should take precedence. Asked if they had to choose between their religion and the law, a large proportion of our respondents answered religion: close to 57 percent of Christians, 40 percent of the Protestants, 43 percent of the Catholics, 69 percent of Mormons; 59 percent of Sunni Muslims, 38 percent of Shia Muslims; and only 24 percent of Jews. The sense of being watched and judged may have had something to do with the fact that 17 percent of Muslims refused to answer this question.

As most Americans are confused and unsure about U.S. policy toward Muslims, many Muslims are convinced that in the event of another major attack within the United States with a large number of fatalities, Americans would round them up and send them to internment camps. Some we met were sure that the camps already existed in light of the camps in remote desert locations during World War II to intern innocent Japanese and German civilians.

Internment camps for Muslims, in fact, had been discussed after 9/11. In December 2001 Attorney General John Ashcroft told a group of leaders from the Dearborn Arab community, who complained that their civil liberties were being violated, that they should be "thankful" they had not been sent to internment camps like the Japanese.[28] Ashcroft's views on Islam had by then become public. "Islam is a religion in which God requires you to send your son to die for him. Christianity is a faith where God sent his Son to die for you," he told a radio interviewer a few weeks preceding the meeting with the Arabs.[29] Then in summer 2002 the media revealed that the U.S. Department of Justice was drafting plans to build "military internment camps" to hold "enemy combatants" in which U.S. citizens would be subjected to "indefinite incarceration."[30] Also that summer a Bush appointee to the U.S. Commission on Civil Rights had told Arab American leaders in Detroit in July that another terrorist attack against the United States could lead to Muslim internment camps, which would have the widespread support of the American people. If a new attack came "from a certain ethnic community or certain ethnicities that the terrorists are from," the official said, "you can forget about civil rights in this country."[31] Adding to Muslim concerns was a statement made soon after the 9/11 attack by Saxby Chambliss, Republican representative from Georgia, chairman of the House Subcommittee on Terrorism and Homeland Security, and candidate for the Senate. He had instructed Georgia law enforcement officials to "just turn [the sheriff] loose and have him arrest every Muslim that crosses the state line."[32] He won the election and is currently serving as senator from Georgia.

A few years later, in 2006, Muslims were understandably alarmed when the U.S. Army announced that Halliburton subsidiary Kellogg Brown and Root (KBR), which had been active in New Orleans after Katrina, had been given $385 million to build temporary detention facilities in the United States for "immigration" purposes. The *New York Times* quoted an army spokesperson as saying "the centers could be at unused military sites or temporary structures and that each one would hold up to 5,000 people."[33]

Simple solutions like internment will not be possible for the Muslim community: it is too large, numbering some 7 million, and it has too many connections with countries important to America in Africa and Asia. Moreover, such a move would inflame public opinion throughout the world, especially in areas where Americans are posted. It would also become the best possible recruiting tool for groups like al Qaeda and the Taliban, who have long been arguing that America is the enemy of Islam. And it would compromise the core ideals of American pluralist identity. It is not difficult to conjecture what the Founding Fathers would have thought of the mass internment of innocent citizens.

If Americans cannot use a sledgehammer to forcefully solve the Muslim problem, then they need to develop a viable alternative. At present they have no visible or coherent policy to improve relations between mainstream Americans and Muslims and thus make American society stronger and more cohesive. Every fresh incident involving a Muslim like Major Hasan or Mutallab opens the already raw wounds on both sides. Many Americans believe their country is locked in a cosmic war with Islam, which they cast as "the greatest threat."

Colonel David Kilcullen on "The Greatest Threat"

The "intelligence" and "security" community has shown little intelligence and much insecurity. Along with the so-called Neocons, its members are— with some honorable exceptions—the cheerleaders of the hate and fear-mongering directed against Muslims. This community of experts has been consistently wrong on Afghanistan, Iraq, Pakistan, and Somalia. Despite its poor understanding of American Muslims, its spokespersons regularly issue "Muslim alerts" in the media. After a decade of their expert advice, America is neither safer nor assured of safety in the future.

These experts must ultimately take some responsibility for the billions of dollars and the hundreds of thousands of lives lost in the implementation of their flawed advice. Most of their opinions—and much of what they say is little more than that—are rejected by genuine experts in the field like Lieutenant Colonel David Kilcullen, General David Petraeus's top adviser in Iraq and Afghanistan, the intellectual architect of the Iraqi "surge," and "one of the world's leading experts on guerrilla warfare."[34]

Rejecting the idea that Islam is the greatest threat, Kilcullen told us during an interview at American University that "the threat to our identity, the existential threat, is our reaction toward the outside world and ways that take us away from our true nature that is the United States." By way of example, he cites a scenario in which a nuclear weapon is about to go off in a major American city: "Some people will say that under those circumstances it is OK to do whatever you want, you can torture people and you can execute people and so on." Such an event would indeed be "the most grievous blow America would have ever suffered, but it wouldn't destroy

America. If we start torturing people to stop that from happening, that would destroy America, and we would get to the point where whatever we might do to keep our people and buildings safe, we would ultimately destroy what makes us American." In other words, Kilcullen emphasizes, the nation's biggest threat is "our reaction to terrorism and the way that it has caused us to treat people within our own society and people in the rest of world society."

Kilcullen's suggestions for improving relations between America and the Muslim world need to be heeded, beginning with a "genuine" dialogue between people with real authority in the Muslim community and leaders of mainstream America, both in Congress and the executive branch. Second, the enemy must not be defined too broadly. When Kilcullen's team studied radicalism in Indonesia, it was told that madrassahs are hotbeds of extremism. Upon close study, however, it became clear that only about 300 of the country's 30,000 or more madrassahs gave any suggestion of ever being involved in terrorism. And of the nearly 200 million Muslims in Indonesia, less than half of 1 percent have ever been associated with violent extremism.

Kilcullen correctly believes that "justice is a very important concept for Muslims . . . that we need to start paying a little more attention to." That concept accounts in part for grievance in the Muslim world over the issue of Palestine: "This is about reaching a just solution to a problem that has been around for sixty years. I think if we can put a man on the moon, we ought to be able to sit down and solve a problem that is so earth bound as this one."

Questionnaire Data

Kilcullen's views coincide with our own findings, which challenge conventional wisdom in America. Our statistics indicate, for example, that John McCain was not speaking for most Americans when in 2007 he said he would not vote for a Muslim, preferring instead "someone who I know who has a solid grounding in my faith."[35] Ninety-five percent of those questioned for our study said that they would vote for a Muslim for public office. Muslims predictably said yes almost 99 percent of the time, but Mormons followed close behind with almost 98 percent. The lowest among the different religions were the Jews, but at 90 percent the number was still high. Although these statistics convey a more optimistic picture than we found in our interviews, many of the respondents qualified their answers with a "yes, if . . ." or a "yes, but . . ."

For our respondents, both Muslim and non-Muslim, ignorance was the greatest threat to the United States. Close behind was "intolerance" of other cultures and races. For Muslims, the media and lack of knowledge of Islam were also major threats. Terrorism was a major threat primarily among non-Muslims in white "conservative" areas such as Catholics in California and Mormons in Utah. However, many people, for example in Vermont, answered "terrorism" only because they believed the foreign policy of the United States had increased terrorism, so the number of people believing in a kind of existential threat from Muslim terrorists is lower than it appears.

Latinos in Los Angeles also named "terrorism" as a threat but seldom included a reason or caveat for their answer. Some expressed "gung-ho" sentiments toward fighting terrorists in answer to the question regarding solutions to the threat. This could be because Latinos are part of American culture yet remain outside the "mainstream," so they believe the greatest threat is what is depicted in the media. Another factor may be that many of them are in the military and are fighting Muslims overseas. It is, I suspect, very much an "insider/outsider" perspective.

African Americans were among the populations expressing the lowest number of "terrorism" answers. Not one of sixteen queried in the Northeast College Preparatory School in Rochester, New York, which is nearly all African American, mentioned "terrorism" as a threat, for example. African Americans were more concerned with internal problems such as drugs, violence, poverty, and the economy.

We asked Americans if Muslims could "be American." Many Muslims and non-Muslims were insulted by the question, but it was one we had to ask. Almost 99 percent said yes, as did 99 percent of Muslims and 98 percent of Christians and Jews. Giving us hope for the future, the questionnaires revealed a striking respect for the similarities between the three Abrahamic faiths—Judaism, Christianity and Islam. We asked if Jews, Christians, and Muslims worship the same God. In all, 73 percent of those questioned said yes. Looking at the three Abrahamic faiths separately, we received yes responses from 88 percent of the Mormons, 77 percent of the Muslims, 73 percent of Christians and Jews, and 65 percent of atheists and agnostics. When Muslims were divided by sects, 76 percent of Sunnis and 89 percent of Shia answered yes.

Recommendations for the Coming Time

Our findings from the field bring both bad news and good news. The bad news is that every one of the major Muslim categories—African Americans, immigrants, and converts—has been involved in recent violence-related cases in the United States. In view of the bankruptcy of Muslim leadership and American failure to truly understand the Muslim community, it is not difficult to predict that violence will increase in both frequency and intensity. The good news is that American and Muslim leaders alike are now conscious of the problem of terrorism and its scale and are actively discussing the position of Muslims in America. Their methods, however, require some fine-tuning. Leaders of both communities need to build on what is common and binds them together. It is in this spirit that I offer the following recommendations.

The first and most important recommendation is that American leaders help to change the tone of the discussion of Islam. Too many Americans consider Islam a pestilence, and their dislike of it has become almost an obsession. American Muslim leaders, too, need to face the crisis in their community rather than recoil in the customary defensive manner. At present, Muslim leaders are paralyzed by fear of informants (especially in mosques), indecision (regarding whether to support Republicans or Democrats, for example), and compromise (putting aside parts of their own identity in order to ingratiate themselves with the majority). Muslims, especially the young, are also frustrated with the corruption and ineptitude of Muslim leaders in Muslim countries, and further frustrated by the support these individuals receive from the United States. These leaders appear out of touch even with those cases that require ordinary human compassion. For example, Muslims have not been heard condemning the atrocities in Darfur, or the too-often-repeated attacks on Christians in Egypt and Pakistan or on the Baha'í in Iran.

New Muslim voices need to be heard in the media. Even after so many years since 9/11, commentary on Islam is given mainly by men of the older generation of immigrants whose heavy accents and poor grammar betray their background and who lose their case the moment they open their mouths. When they do speak, they do little more than intone "Islam is a religion of peace" and "We love America." It is time to encourage them to take up American pastimes like sailing and long mountain treks so that they are kept busy and out of public sight. The Neocons and security experts, too, should rediscover these American pastimes. It may help them become more self-reflective and develop much needed humility.

Already well known in the Muslim media, religious leaders like Sheikh Hamza Yusuf and Imam Hassan Qazwini need to be heard by mainstream America. I would also like to see articulate and charismatic community leaders like Imam Fateen Seifullah, Najah Bazzy, and Nicole Queen explaining Islam in the media. An African American, a Detroit-born Arab, and a white female convert, respectively, they are ideally placed to act as credible links between the two cultures in which they reside.

Articulate Muslim "moderates" with a popular media personality are already appearing in the media and making an impact, notably Fareed Zakaria, Irshad Manji, Reza Aslan, and Eboo Patel. However, the Muslim community is not entirely comfortable with them, complaining that they are either self-consciously "secular" (promoting the views of the government of India and, as an Indian Muslim, gratuitously bashing Pakistan to show he is more loyal than the king, in the case of Zakaria) or from minority Islamic sects (the last three). In either case, the community, largely Sunni and still traditional, believes that these media Muslims are too eager to say what Americans would like to hear.

Non-Muslim voices that understand Islam and the Muslim community also need to be heard. Though familiar in their own communities, many in this category have not yet gained the attention of the national media. These include scholars like Lawrence Rosen and Tamara Sonn; interfaith leaders like Bishop John Chane, Ambassador Doug Holladay, and Rabbi Bruce Lustig; and those who know the Muslim world like Joanna Herring, Lee Baca, and Barry Hoffman.

Because Muslim leadership is divided and because Islam does not have central figures of authority like an archbishop or a senior rabbi, self-reflection and self-criticism in the community are crucial to set future directions. Muslim leaders need to look to the African American experience for pointers on how to improve their community's self-image. One of the earliest steps in the reawakening of the African American community was the leadership's campaign to convince its members that "black is beautiful" after generations of being demonized and degraded. Similarly labeled worthless, violent, and even inhuman, many Muslims are exhibiting signs of self-loathing. Some even wish to distance themselves from Islam altogether. Alas for them, history teaches that nothing will change unless a society changes from inside and challenges the negative stereotypes. Muslims must launch a sustained campaign to create pride in the community. Perhaps "Islam is awesome"?

If they are able to resurrect and explain their genuine heroes, Muslims will help not only themselves but also the larger community. Whenever I have talked of Jinnah and his struggle to create a modern Muslim nation against all odds, for example, it has resonated with Americans. In Jinnah they see a leader who is unlike the usual stereotype. The Muslim world has produced other men and women of stature like Jinnah—Miss Fatima Jinnah, Muhammad Abduh, Allama Muhammad Iqbal, King Hussein bin

Talal of Jordan, to name a few—and articles, books, and films about their lives need to be produced and circulated.

Muslim leaders in America need to vigorously support programs for their young. So far Muslims have focused on careers that make money. The community has to encourage its younger generation to participate more extensively in occupations that will generate not the highest income but scholars and thinkers so that it will no longer be bereft of the capacity to define itself. At the moment, it is being defined by those who are hostile to it or know little of it.

Young people who wish to improve the world should be encouraged to return to the countries of their family's origins and join specially designed programs along the lines of the Peace Corps, bringing doctors and teachers to rural areas. They would thus become both angels of mercy to the people of Somalia or Afghanistan and ambassadors for America. If the five young Virginians apprehended in Pakistan in search of jihad had been persuaded to spend time in the rural areas of that country helping villagers, they would have been a credit to America and Islam.

Muslims also need to invest time, effort, and resources to a serious study of both their own community and larger American society. They are not living in a vacuum, and the two are interconnected. I found the lack of curiosity among Muslims we met on the journey dispiriting. Again and again, when I would invite them to ask me about the purposes of my journey into America—or about any aspect of it—the response was meager. If they did raise questions, it would be to inquire whether the FBI had anything to do with our questionnaires. There was little intellectual or philosophic curiosity about examining the Muslim community in America. This was not entirely surprising. Their lack of interest reflects a larger problem in the Muslim world. The state of education and the treatment of scholars in Muslim societies today are abominable. In the absence of knowledge, the worst kind of ethnic, sectarian, and political conflicts have paralyzed these societies. Abandoning their own principles, Muslims have drifted into a world of materialism and consumerism without appreciating its dangers. Constantly on the defensive, some believe that violence is necessary to implement the Islamic message.

This is why American Muslims need to overhaul the management of the mosques, which are an important religious and social center of community life, and provide a long-term policy for training American imams. Without a wise and well-informed imam, the community is like a ship without a rudder. Today, too many imams are the focus of controversy. Some imams are reduced to being little more than puppets in the hands of the board running the mosque that hires them. Some have been trained in Egypt or Pakistan and seem out of tune with their congregation and its cultural context. In either case, the community has little respect for their opinions. Everyone we met was conscious that the imam was being scrutinized by his own community and the agencies. Thus their turnover rate is high just when the mosque is in desperate need of stability. That is why some young Muslims are seeking religious advice on the Internet from radical imams overseas.

Traditionally, Americans can effect change and make their government take notice in two ways: either assault it physically or work within the system. The first has been tried many times without much success. Americans will respond with everything at their disposal to any challenge they see as a form of threat. The homegrown Muslim terrorist has attempted and failed in this tactic several times in the recent past. Working within the system tends to take time but has invariably succeeded, the best example being the approach of Martin Luther King Jr. and the civil rights movement, which changed the fate of African Americans and the shape of America, paving the way for a black president. Muslim leaders need to explain the principles of how the American system works so that angry young Muslims wanting to be heard can do so within the system rather than plan to blow up buildings.

To this end, Muslims need to become more deeply involved in American electoral politics—especially at the local level (joining school boards, planning commissions, and the like). Nowhere do Americans pay so much attention to one another than in elections, and nowhere do compromise and common cause show themselves better. Surely the history of other immigrant groups in the United States is defined in no small part by their involvement in electoral politics—and nowhere have blacks been discriminated against more. Muslim leaders must encourage the community to enter politics at the local level so that Americans can see them with increasing frequency in the public realm.

From the Mormon and Jewish communities Muslims can learn to balance their religious and American identities, and strong alliances need to be built with them. Many Mormons have discovered a semblance of themselves in Islam, while we saw Jews throughout the land devising impressive initiatives to reach out to Muslims—whether Rabbi Bruce Lustig's First Abrahamic Summit; Rabbi Susan Talve's launching of our journey into America in St. Louis; Rabbi Steve Jacobs's prayers with a Muslim congregation at the Islamic Center of Southern California in Los Angeles, during which he bowed and kneeled along with the rest of us; or Rabbi Hillel Levine's giving us his home during our field trip to Boston, even though he was out of town.

The federal government and its agencies have much to do also. They need to actively engage and absorb Muslims, especially the youth, so that the future generation will think of building rather than destroying America. Muslims need to be visible in the administration, media, and public life. Unless the Muslim community is integrated into the mainstream, it will remain alienated and prey to anxiety and indignation. The so-called homegrown terrorists come from disaffected parts of the Muslim community. The government needs to cultivate sources within it. Unfortunately, Americans rely far too much on technology, which alone cannot provide security, and far too little on human intelligence. A working relationship between the intelligence agencies and the Muslim communities cannot be achieved without mutual trust and respect.

Yet the trends appear to be in the opposite direction, and relations between government agencies and the Muslim community have reached new lows. Muslim trust in the agencies has been eroded "as more and more communities feel they are being treated not as partners but as objects of suspicion."[36] Even foreign newspapers like Israel's *Hareetz* were openly doubting the methods of the American agencies in dealing with issues of Muslim terrorism.[37] By December 2009 Muslim frustration had driven the Council on American-Islamic Relations (CAIR) to plead with President Obama to address the "alarming level of Anti-Islam hate." Even as well-adjusted and happily assimilated a Muslim as my daughter Nafees became nervous when she first heard the news about the Christmas day flight to Detroit and began praying, "Please, please let it not be a Muslim."

Equally important, America needs to learn about Muslim culture, especially about the seminal figures of Islam like the Prophet of Islam. Most Muslims we met—old or young, male or female, black or white—named the Prophet as their most inspiring figure. In keeping with Muslim tradition, many added the words "peace be upon him" as a blessing every time they mentioned his name. Women had tears in their eyes when they spoke of him and his compassionate and merciful nature. Like Muslims the world over, many African Americans who converted to Islam after hearing stories of the Prophet and his concern for the poor and the dispossessed took the name Muhammad as a mark of affection. White converts saw in him an answer to the spiritual problems of the world.

Hence if the American aim is to win Muslim hearts and minds, it is not wise strategy to hurl abuse against the Prophet. Granted that the provisions and traditions of free speech allow Americans to express their opinions, there is something to be said for common civility and courtesy, as the Founding Fathers advocated. Significantly, George Washington's only book, based on a collection of his papers, was titled *Rules of Civility and Decent Behavior in Company and Conversation.*[38] It is no coincidence that L.A. County's Catholic sheriff Lee Baca, who added the words "peace be upon him" every time he mentioned the Prophet, is such a trusted and popular figure in the Muslim community.

At the same time, it is well for Muslims to remind the community that Americans feel the same intense loyalty toward America as Muslims do toward Islam. Although many Americans we spoke to expressed greater attachment to their Christian faith than symbols of the nation, the vast majority saw the flag as the key symbol of their identity. That is why Muslims need to keep in mind that when they desecrate the American flag they hurt and anger Americans in much the same way that Americans hurt and anger them when they flush the Quran down the toilet. Just as the Quran is the divine word of God for Muslims, the flag is almost a sacred symbol for Americans. It is essential to be sensitive to what a society holds dear if there is to be any hope of mutual respect and friendship. Muslims should reach out to average Americans, learn about their culture and history, and break their own pattern of isolation.

Our respondents in the field recognized the need for better understanding between the United States and the Muslim world. At the end of each interview and questionnaire, we asked "What do you believe are the best steps toward fostering greater understanding and bridging relations between the United States and the Muslim world?" In all, 41 percent of the respondents said the path to better relations was "education and understanding." It also scored highest for each of the faiths. Meanwhile 26 percent said "dialogue" was the best method, and it scored highest among atheists and agnostics (at 40 percent), and second highest among Jews. Muslims favored "education and understanding," with dialogue a close second. The third most popular answer, chosen by 20 percent overall, was a change in U.S. foreign policy, and it was cited most often among Muslims. Other answers of note called for changes in the "media" or indicated that Muslims here and overseas needed to do a better job of representing themselves. Most respondents expressed a clear desire to learn about and enter into dialogue with one another.

Heeding Americans

Dialogue was uppermost in the minds of my students in my last honors class of the semester in December 2009 when Maya Soetoro-Ng, the sister of Barack Obama, spoke to them.[39] With its assortment of Jewish, Christian,

In Honolulu, team members met with Maya Soetoro-Ng, sister of President Barack Obama. Soetoro-Ng represents the pluralist identity of America.

and Muslims students—it also had an American soldier from Guam who had served in Iraq—the class was a microcosm of American society.

No one in the class could consider him- or herself more American than Maya, yet her American identity rested on many different cultures. Maya was born to an Indonesian Muslim father and a white Unitarian mother from Kansas who was of Scots-Irish background with some Cherokee blood. Maya lives in Hawai'i, is married to a Malaysian-Chinese-Canadian, and is a Buddhist. Her name comes from the Sanskrit word for "illusion." Maya's world embraces the adhan, the Muslim call to prayer, on the one hand, and Latino salsa music, on the other. She recalls the adhan as the "most beautiful sound to me" from her childhood in Indonesia, when she would hear one call fading, another starting, followed by a third, each one drifting into the other.

Maya shares certain characteristics with her brother, most notably eloquence, a scholarly frame of analysis, and self-deprecating humor (the students enjoyed her description of Obama's first reaction on seeing her as a baby: "incredibly ugly"). Brother and sister owe these qualities to their extraordinary mother, Ann Dunham. An anthropologist, Ann married first a Muslim Kenyan, the father of Barack, and then a Muslim Indonesian, Maya's father. Like Dorothy from *The Wizard of Oz*, the other famous girl from Kansas, Ann loved to travel to exotic lands and meet wonderfully different people. Ann's character, curiosity about the world, and poetic vision shaped a president of the United States and his equally remarkable sister.

In Maya's view, patriotism is something more than an American flag-pin on a lapel (an indirect reference to the controversy surrounding Obama for not dutifully displaying it). It is pride in one's identity. Unfortunately, Maya pointed out, many people are "afraid" of diluting what they think is their identity. America's greatest gift to its citizens, she told the class, is its willingness to allow them to "name" the identity they cherish most of the several that every individual carries. Being curious about other cultures and respecting their peoples creates a spiritual balance in and around us. In Hawai'i, this is called the Aloha spirit.

It is reflected in Representative Keith Ellison's definition of American identity, which is about "principles," not color or language: "American identity is rooted in a system of ideas. Our cultural ethos is fairness, rule of law, freedom of expression. These are American ideas." Ellison also thinks Americans have "a certain sense of optimism," of being able to solve problems, whereas people from other parts of the world are more fatalistic. The American attitude is "Well, if it's not right what are we gonna do about it?" That is one reason he is proud to be an American: "Has there ever been a country in the rest of the world that started out taking the land from the Indians, dragging Africans to do the work, denying the right of half the population of women to participate in civic life, and then within a few hundred years solving these problems internally? It wasn't easy, people lost their lives, people lost their careers, there were prices paid. But now we live in a time when a black man is president."

Ellison's colleague in the House, Representative André Carson, had some useful tips for the Muslim community, one being to take control of its own image: "We can't let others define who we are. We need more Muslims in public office, we need more Muslim women in public office, with or without hijab. I think it's critically important because there is this image of Muslim women being oppressed. This is not true." Carson also hoped that Americans would recognize Muslims are a part of the American fabric: "Muslims love America and want to see it grow and improve . . . and want to make great contributions to our economic situation, our educational system."

Sheriff Lee Baca had sympathetic if tough advice for Muslims in America, urging them to develop a greater presence in the media. He suggested approaching some of the wealthiest Muslim nations in the world to fund a Muslim-owned cable TV station based in the United States. This would free up the discourse, allowing broadcasts of programs, talk shows, and news reflecting a more objective Muslim view. Muslims, he said, do not point to what is extreme in the Old or New Testaments and say this is what Christianity is about. If anything, noted Baca, the one religion that has caused human tragedy more than any other is Christianity. Baca also suggested that CAIR publish in Jewish journals "some complete revocation and opposition to terrorists that are Palestinians." This might help in part to defuse American society's negative view of Muslims. That view is also fed by Westerners' inability to understand a culture that appears to condone suicide: "We cannot even comprehend what this is. This is the ultimate sin in our way of thinking and therefore the leadership of all Muslim organizations in America . . . cannot leave that issue unaddressed."

The greatest victim of suicide bombers, added Baca, is not the Americans or those who have been killed, but the Quran and the Prophet: "Never use the Quran, never use the Prophet, peace be with him, for your own criminal deeds, including killing yourself. It is totally unacceptable in the eyes of God." Before any "windows of light" are likely to open up, however, Muslims will have to feel the same level of disgust that Americans did over 9/11, concluded Baca.

Joanne Herring of Houston is a good example of a "true blue" American representing primordial identity. Her solution to improving relations between Muslims and non-Muslims emphasizes compassion and respect: "Muslims value their traditions, just as we southerners do—we don't want to give our traditions up. I never saw anything from any Muslim that wasn't something that I could relate to. It was loving and kind. Christians and Muslims have many things that we agree upon. We mustn't separate ourselves. . . . We need to understand one another's religion and one another's traditions. I like to think of it as a basket. We are all weavers of this basket. Everybody puts their little straw where it has to be flexible for the next one. Flexibility is what makes a basket strong. We have to say we respect and admire you and honor your religion and hopefully you will respect and admire and honor ours."

The Team's Recommendations

For Jonathan, the first step is for the government to "get in the field. The intelligence community, or anyone else for that matter, will learn nothing without traveling from mosque to mosque and community to community and approaching them with respect and dignity. It seemed unbelievable that no government agencies are out in the field building relationships as we did. There seems to be some confusion as to which government agency would be responsible for this kind of endeavor. The FBI builds cases, not relationships; the National Counterterrorism Center and the Office of the Director of National Intelligence analyze intelligence but do not gather it; and the Department of Homeland Security inspects containers and secures American airports and borders. Those that even try to engage with the community do not get an accurate picture because they rely on who they wrongly believe are its leaders."

"The Muslim community," Jonathan believes, "is still on shaky ground, even nine years after 9/11." At this point, he would "fear for Muslims in America if another attack happened, as I'm not convinced the government would know who to turn to as a liaison with the community. However, Americans would be more sympathetic to Muslims now than after 9/11."

In terms of our models, Jonathan estimates that the Muslim community is 50 percent modernist, about 40 percent literalist, and the rest mystics—percentages that the rest of the team broadly agrees with. The major trends Jonathan sees within the Muslim community are "isolation both from each other and from the non-Muslim communities, on several levels concurrently, and grouping within ethnicity, nationality, and ideology. For example, the literalists are separating themselves both from non-Muslims and from the modernists and mystics. Somalis, for instance, would naturally gravitate to other Somalis unless they had a different interpretation of the religion. This occurs primarily in the older generation. Freshly arrived immigrants of the younger generation are more adept at mixing with other nationalities and ethnicities."

At the same time, Jonathan senses a threat lurking in the community: "A significant percentage of modernists that we met would, I think, be very sympathetic to the literalists where conversations on terrorism were occurring. In that way, those modernists could be influenced to become aggressive, perhaps like Major Hasan in Texas, though still in small percentages. A young modernist might be tempted to go to the Internet for answers and be exposed to the same kinds of debates that we observed in Salafi mosques, but with the saner voices drowned out. One man we spoke to who is close to the Salafis said that though he doesn't agree with them, he doesn't think of them as a terrorism threat on their own, unless given orders from above. He then made a vague reference to the Saudis."

Therefore Jonathan recommends creating specific positions that would entail visits to mosques. These people could be based in cities around the country and connected to a university or research center. "They should be knowledgeable (know what they are looking for)," Jonathan advises, "but should be there to listen, not engage in arguments or propaganda. The culture and dynamics of a community are constantly changing so the leadership is changing as well. As we have learned, the communities, even the most conservative ones, enjoy America for the freedom of religion and believe it is in their own self-interest to ensure the government and intelligence services see an accurate picture of the larger Muslim community." That, he concludes, is the only way to build a relationship based on trust and honor.

"You can't prevent the next terror attack if you do not understand the community that it will come from," Frankie emphasizes. He found it frustrating that the government failed to appreciate the importance of this kind of work to the security of the United States: "We just scratched the surface of the kind of information these agencies could be getting. When the agencies do go into the field, they should pay attention to the intra-Muslim tensions, such as the tensions between Sufis and Salafis." Muslims themselves could benefit from learning more about the American Muslim community "as even the Muslim leaders often do not understand it," noted Frankie. "Both should ask the kinds of questions our team was asking."

"Most Muslims in America would never dream of committing violence against the United States," Frankie maintains, "despite the widespread revulsion in the Muslim community to aspects of U.S. foreign policy. Yet we were aware of an active debate over violence and the interpretation of Islam. For a young kid from Somalia, for example, I can imagine the pressures in deciding which mosque to go to, which websites to visit, who to listen to, especially with ongoing U.S. involvement in his home country. If someone like this ends up in a Salafi mosque, for example, and falls under the sway of those advocating an offensive, aggressive Islam, violence could result."

Indeed, Frankie feels that "nowhere is this debate over violence as intensely conducted as in Salafi mosques. Americans may fear Muslim violence against the United States, but it is the Muslims in America who seem closer to violence against other Muslims, many of whom are petrified that violence such as that directed against Farhan Latif in Dearborn (see chapter 5) will get out into the mainstream and further stereotype them. We found Muslims like Farhan across America in the thick of these battles to define Islam and its place in the country, inside and outside the Salafi community. Organizations like the Anti-Defamation League and the Southern Poverty Law Center should become more involved in condemning Muslim violence against other Muslims—in addition to attacks on Muslims by non-Muslims—as hate crimes against fellow Americans. The U.S. government should be enabling and helping American Muslims to challenge and isolate extremists, not tying their hands. To do this, it must have an unambiguously clear image of what is happening."

For Hailey, "Islam is not the problem. There is much more to the story, and we are not at war with a great religion, but a few who have hijacked it." Although the media and policymakers should know better, and often profess that they do, "their language tells a different story," notes Hailey: "Every time we hear them talk, they say 'Islamic radicalism.' This leads to an exacerbation of the fury felt in the Muslim world on behalf of their identity and creates unnecessary enemies for America."

"I am seeing three main trends," says Hailey. "The first is an atomization of groups. I saw this in Dearborn when I visited the ACCESS site in the now mainly Yemeni neighborhood. The women were all wearing niqabs and the signs were all in Arabic. It was like I was in another world. Secondly, I am seeing the modernist model as strong but dumb. They are proud to be Muslim and American, proud to accept both traditions, etc., but they do not know the greater problems surrounding them, and they would not know what to do if they did. Thirdly, I am seeing a new American culture of Islam developing. This is an active, engaged, and reinvigorated Islam. I see it in the African Americans who help in the communities; I see it in the political organizations like MPAC and ISNA; I see it in the architecture of the new mosques that are also youth centers, offer classes, and feed the poor. There is a new power given by the American spirit of hard work and the do-it-yourself attitude that has affected Islam here, and I see that as very positive."

She, too, detects problems in the community, especially "with the younger generation, maybe fifteen and younger, a pattern evident throughout the country. Kids who have suffered the stigma of being called 'terrorist' in school while their religion is attacked daily or their families injured will not be stable. This is a problem that needs to be addressed now, both culturally in the greater American community and in the Muslim community."

Hailey believes a new paradigm is needed to build bridges, "a broad education program to teach media folk and policymakers about Islam, the political issues, and what is going on in the world." This would replace the old "clash of civilizations" thinking with new ways of grasping the problem. Hailey also recommends a broad effort to help Muslims attain greater access to Islamic learning and encourage real Islamic scholarship: "Educate the young generation—and I mean young. Those who are most genuinely proud of who they are and what they believe are the best leaders and best

American Muslims. Create and support a network of leaders across the United States that encourages dialogue and debate."

For their part, advises Hailey, Muslims should try to discover the best of American culture: "hard work, generosity, openness, optimism, order, and, above all, freedom in the best and purest sense." Fuse those values with the "best of Islam," she urges: "Many of the Muslim women I have met are incredible role models for the American spirit, and the refugees from Somalia, Bosnia, and Kurdish Iraq often the most patriotic." Hailey suggests that to improve its image to Americans, the Muslim community needs a "public relations army." Instead of going on vaguely about "Islam is peace," Muslims need "a sustained and coherent campaign that explains who they are in terms that are appealing to Americans, shows that they are patriotic, and that gets across their point of view."

Listening to Muslims was the best way of understanding the Muslim community, Craig concluded after the field trip. Furthermore, Islam in America must not be treated as a monolith. It is as diverse here as it is throughout the world, Craig emphasized. Hence "going into a mosque or an Islamic center with preconceived notions of Muslims in America will have a negative impact on your conversation. Respect, dignity, and honor are the only ways to win the hearts and minds of Muslims. Before entering the mosque, one must understand its rules; this will let them know that you are respecting them."

Craig urges government officials to let Muslims in America know that Islam is not under threat. Inasmuch as one-fourth of the world's population is Muslim, Craig believes that Americans cannot afford to be ignorant of Islam: "American educational systems must teach subjects relating to Islam in elementary, middle, and high schools, as well as college. This simple curriculum initiative would show Muslims in America that the United States is out to learn about Islam and its amazing achievements throughout history rather than fight it."

Craig also warns against viewing madrassahs in a negative light: "We visited madrassahs in Chicago, Atlanta, and Houston (among other cities), and they were as 'American' as you could get. Madrassahs in America are not teaching 'radical Islam' or preaching hatred against America. They are simply a way for children to retain their Islamic heritage while simultaneously being more fully integrated into the American social fabric to ensure a brighter future in this country."

Craig believes that "the biggest challenge for the Muslim community is being under the microscope of the media and the ideologically driven commentary of the 'culture warriors,' Fox especially. One thing that became clear to me as the journey progressed was that some of the best Americans are Muslim. It is completely illogical to claim that Islam is at war with the United States or incompatible with American values. I would argue the exact opposite, that Islam is at peace with the United States."

My daughter Amineh found a resonance in the approach and work of the team when she joined us in Texas: "For a Muslim woman like myself who has engaged in interfaith dialogue with the *Ahl-e-kitaab* (People of the Book: Jews, Christians, and Muslims) in the United Kingdom, I see mutual respect and deeper understanding as vital for improving relations between communities. I am therefore grateful to God and also to my father for giving my own children the opportunity to join the team on a journey dedicated to this end." Amineh remarked on the success of our project, as was clear from the team's own transformation in learning to walk in the shoes of "the Other." She saw "a dynamic group of young Americans seeking knowledge through ethnographic fieldwork and participant observation and only then drawing informed conclusions that are ethically sound and sensitive, and through this strategy becoming sources of building bridges between cultures, religious groups, and nations. I saw this as a gift of compassion, a legacy of responsibility, an ideal model not only for the benefit of America but for all who care for humankind's shared and diverse world."

The Importance of Being America

"America is Michael Jackson," said television host Bill Maher a few weeks after Jackson's death in June 2009. Both were "fragile, overindulgent, childish, in debt, on drugs, and over the hill" and both were resting on their laurels, which included the moonwalk decades ago. It was a cruel comparison, but was echoed by the sagacious Gore Vidal: "The Republic is broken."[40] A more recent critique of America, its foundational myths, and ideological assumptions comes in James Cameron's *Avatar* (2009), the costliest and most technologically advanced film in history. It is about soulless, arrogant, and murderous white colonists out to deplete the planet Pandora's natural resources and in the process destroy its tribal population.

Cameron is eclectic in his cultural references. The colonists' military commander is the predatory native-hating Colonel Miles (Myles Standish from the *Mayflower* and the first commander of the Plymouth Colony?). He calls the natives "savages" and "roaches" (the former commonly used by the Plymouth settlers and the latter by U.S. troops in Vietnam). Cameron neatly reverses the American usage of the word "alien" by depicting the colonists as aliens from the point of view of the natives. Not all colonists are bad. If Miles represents American predator identity, Jack Sully, a paraplegic former marine, and Dr. Grace Augustine personify the best of American pluralist identity. In the end the natives survive only because of them.

While I may not agree with these somewhat extreme and pessimistic positions, I believe America is on the verge of facing some fundamental problems. My assessment is based on both my fieldwork and many years of experience in dealing with Western and Muslim societies.

Consider the big idea: while the Darwinian struggle has brought America to the top of the pyramid, the consumerism and hedonism of this present generation will make it difficult to remain there without some change in the way Americans conduct their lives. In the nineteenth century Americans were a self-confident people driven by a sense of adventure, discovery, advancement, and learning. In their race to colonize the far reaches of the continent, they began transforming a newly found nation into a world power. The future was theirs. As surely as the Protestant work ethic brought America to world prominence, the "let's have a good time and spend as much as we can while having it" ethic promises a decline. Besides, China and India have now joined Russia on the world stage in a new version of the survival of the fittest. America's wars have driven its debt to China to almost two trillion dollars. Indebtedness on this scale to another superpower that has already begun challenging America defies common sense and is far from sensible foreign policy.

To ignore the cause and effect in the destinies of nations is to invite peril. American statesmen have been warning society of its excesses for the past few decades. In his presidency, Jimmy Carter tried to stem the tide of consumerism and selfishness by calling for the development of alternative energy and a foreign policy that conformed to the principles of the Founding Fathers. He saw a crisis looming that would "destroy the social and the political fabric of America" if the nation once devoted to "hard work, strong families, close-knit communities, and our faith in God" continued to "worship self-indulgence and consumption."[41] There is no way, Carter said, that we can "avoid sacrifice." But America was not ready to listen to Carter, and henceforth "greed is good" would become the American philosophy and way of life.

These Americans were ignoring not only Carter but also Pope Gregory the Great, who in the sixth century warned Christians about the seven deadly sins, the deadliest being greed and pride—and Gregory was only amplifying the preaching of Jesus. In short, in their embrace of Darwinism, Americans had cast aside the lessons of the biblical teachers, an important source of inspiration for the Founding Fathers. It is well to remember Jefferson, who described Jesus as surpassing all others in "inculcating universal philanthropy, not only to kindred and friends, to neighbors and countrymen, but to all mankind, gathering all into one family, under the bonds of love, charity, peace, common wants and common aids."[42]

Americans—like the rest of the world—are living in a time of rapid change and turmoil. Technological developments baffle and dazzle them. Never before has the world been so interconnected, and never before have individuals been so awash with information, most of it blindingly superficial and crudely commercial. Television, the Internet, e-mail, Twitter, Facebook, and MySpace are drowning everyone with information and images. Yet individuals have never been so isolated as they are today. They nonetheless take pride in the fact that they are "connected" and believe that is what makes them "hip" and "cool." This tidal wave leaves them yearning for peace and quiet. As thinking, sentient beings, people need time to themselves to reflect, yet they rarely escape this flood of information. Modern life is bereft of the sound of silence and the place to contemplate with true humility and love. Even its "retreats" are extensions of life with one's family or friends.

As a result, people have lost the capacity for self-reflection and find it difficult to see the majesty and mystery of life. In today's cynical, noisy, iconoclastic, and materialistic world of consumerism, even its heroes and role models provide little more than temporary entertainment. The public builds them up high so that pulling them down becomes that much more pleasurable. Whether they are politicians like Bill Clinton, performers like Michael Jackson, or sportsmen like Tiger Woods, they end up as fodder for everyone's entertainment.

It is perhaps an awareness of this predicament at various levels that makes Americans, in spite of consuming a disproportionately large share of the world's wealth, among the unhappiest people on earth while obsessively insisting they are happy.[43] Americans have much to be unhappy about: the incidences of suicide and depression are abnormally high, especially among their students and soldiers; their jails are the fullest compared with those of any other nation, their rates of obesity the highest, their marriages more in danger of breaking up, and more Americans claim to have been abducted by aliens than any other nationality. A foreigner may be forgiven for assuming Americans perpetually oscillate between two primary emotions, those of anger and fear, all the while proclaiming that their country is the greatest and best in history.

Osama bin Laden, aided and abetted by George W. Bush and Dick Cheney, ignited the deep-rooted American sense of fear. Americans live in fear—of flying, of the next terrorist plot, of their Muslim neighbors, of the economy, and of the loss of optimism. Americans remain fearful of potential threats to their security, and they blame Muslims directly or indirectly for much of their anxiety. They are not sure how to proceed with the Muslim world, and that is why they appear to be giving generously with one hand while slapping it with the other.

This unhappiness and fear generate the almost irrational outbursts of anger that are on display in American society ranging from TV commentators who appear to be frothing at the mouth to ordinary citizens whose emotions are so easily whipped up in what is called road rage. Examples are reported on an almost daily basis in the media: a father —and even a mother—murdering his family, a child shooting and killing other children in his school, and random violence inflicted on a homeless person or in an assault on a female. The invasion of Afghanistan, and to an extent Iraq, was partly motivated by this consuming American rage.

Even Obama, who once seemed the messenger of hope, appears increasingly inept, and his supporters pray that his golden promises do not turn into lead. American prestige abroad has taken a battering, and the nation's continued military involvement in Iraq, Afghanistan, Pakistan, and Somalia ensures that the recruiting lines for those who would do America harm will remain long and full.

All this has left Americans bewildered, fearful, and angry—and searching for reasons for their predicament, often with paranoia and suspicion. That is why so many yearned for the past, their nostalgia exacerbated by the colors, cultures, and languages that make up the United States today. Even scholars in their ivory towers are not immune to these anxieties.[44] The atmosphere has been thick with conspiracy theories and encourages a depressing lack of self-confidence and self-flagellation. The self-criticism is almost irrational, reducing America to a caricature. In this atmosphere of uncertainty, messianic figures like Glenn Beck play to the fear and anger among Americans effectively and thereby find a following.

If Osama bin Laden's objectives were to damage America economically as well as psychologically while putting a dent in its global reputation, he has succeeded beyond his wildest dreams. America is now deep in debt and spending nearly 800 billion dollars a year on defense, exceeding the military budgets of the next twenty-five highest-spending countries combined. Its banking, trading, and credit systems are teetering, millions are out of work, its airline industry has not recovered from the effects of 9/11, and air travel, with its constantly changing restrictions and delays, bad-tempered cabin crews, jumpy passengers, and smelly toilets, has become an unpleasant exercise in unrelieved tedium. It is heartbreaking to recall the friendly, clean, and efficient flights and airports before 9/11, which I was certain were the best in the world.

A Pakistani American girl participates in the festivities of the Muslim Day parade on Madison Avenue in New York City in October 2008 and shows her patriotism with a veil of the Stars and Stripes.

Yet American critics need to see American society as complicated, diverse, and changing, but still influenced by its history. This was illustrated for us when we joined the New York City Muslim Day Parade in October 2008. A river of red, white, blue, and green flags fluttered and flowed down Madison Avenue on that crisp, clear, and cold afternoon. Shouts of "Allahu Akbar" mingled with "God bless America." Black, brown, and white men and women, Muslims in police uniforms, boy scouts, school groups, female activists, women in niqabs and hijabs, and bearded imams marched with an air of self-conscious festivity. Young Muslim girls wore head coverings patterned with the Stars and Stripes. Jews and Christians were prominent in the parade, showing solidarity with Muslims. The Muslim leaders of the parade, including Imam Shamsi Ali, saw us standing on the side watching the proceedings and invited us to join.

As we walked down the avenue aglow with friendship and brotherhood, the parade abruptly seemed to have entered a zone of pandemonium. On our right a small group of white men and women was demonstrating with placards proclaiming that the Prophet of Islam was a "pig" and "child-killer" and shouting abuse. Opposite this group stood another group, equally vociferous in its criticism of the parade, but they were Muslims who believed what they were seeing was too "American." The balloon of festivity had been punctured. Tempers were running high, and the groups were shouting at each other across the avenue. They were separated by some burly-looking and impassive New York policemen.

In the midst of this seemingly irreconcilable clash of cultures and ideas, we saw clearly displayed, in the freedom of speech and the right to assemble, a respect for the Constitution. Here, too, we saw America's policemen, like the countless law enforcement officers keeping watch in other circumstances, ensuring that these rights would be upheld. Such Americans have sworn to uphold the Constitution and live—and often die—to do so, whatever their personal opinions. The parade also brought out America's great capacity to self-correct. The very community that had been at the center of suspicion and distrust, like so many other immigrant communities before it, had began participating in an expression of Americanness. It all ended appropriately with a group of young Muslim girls wearing the hijab singing "The Star-Spangled Banner." They were slightly off-key, but their enthusiasm carried the day.

The critics—including Maher, Vidal, and Cameron—too easily miss the "goodness of America." This is the only country with the morality, muscle, and willingness to play a global role that can make a difference in trying to prevent man-made ravages (genocide in the Balkans) or to rush aid to those suffering from natural ones (earthquakes in Pakistan and Haiti and tsunamis in Indonesia). These traits are precisely what define America as a global leader. That is why John F. Kennedy preparing to welcome immigrants in the 1960s and Ronald Reagan welcoming Afghan mujahideen at the White House in the 1980s can be said to reflect the best of American identity. This book's discussion of American identity shows precisely that *Avatar*'s Colonel Miles is only one face of America.

Striving for Knowledge

Although this book attempts to present neat and tidy analytic models of identity, in the end I must point to the "messiness" of the exercise. Take my own case, in which a vast array of influences have been at work. I was born when the British Empire was dying, and now, in my twilight years, I live in the capital of the United States, a nation many call the wealthiest and most powerful empire in history. I saw one empire fold almost overnight like a gigantic circus tent, and I am, I suspect, witnessing the start of the decline of another empire. Born in Allahabad in India, by the banks of the Ganges, which is holy to the Hindus, to a Pathan mother descended from warriors and aristocrats and a father who came from Muslim sacred lineages, I was educated by Catholic priests at Burn Hall, a boarding school in the hills of Pakistan, and by American Presbyterians at Forman Christian College in the city of Lahore. Growing up, I spent my long winter vacations in Bangkok and fell in love with the gentility and artistic expression of Buddhist culture. Later, I served as an administrator in the hills and among the tribes of the border districts between Afghanistan and Pakistan. I obtained a doctorate in anthropology from the University of London and taught at Princeton, Harvard, and Cambridge Universities. East and West, Islam, Christianity, Judaism, Hinduism and Buddhism, in one form or another, in small or big ways—all influenced me.

"To Strive, to Seek, To Find, and Not to Yield"

At Burn Hall I developed a passion for English literature, and "Ulysses" by Lord Tennyson was one of my favorite poems. Whenever I got the chance, I would climb the hill behind school at sunset to recite poetry, and I knew this one by heart. Shrewd Ulysses recognized that without knowledge, he could not know himself or the world around him. The following lines in particular would come to me on these recent journeys as well:

Yet all experience is an arch wherethro'
Gleams that untravell'd world, whose margin fades
For ever and for ever when I move. . . .

To follow knowledge, like a sinking star,
Beyond the utmost bound of human thought. . . .

To strive, to seek, to find, and not to yield.

Americans have always had an abundance of the spirit of Ulysses. It was the same impulse that drove the *Mayflower*'s travelers across the Atlantic, their descendants across the expanses of America, and their offspring to the moon, and that propelled my young American team on the journey into America. The same spirit is captured in the documents and wise sayings bequeathed to the nation by its Founding Fathers. For men like Washington, Jefferson, Adams, and Franklin, few things were as important as knowledge, and Washington spoke of it both in his first State of the Union speech and in his farewell address. For Jefferson, "Knowledge is power . . . knowledge is safety . . . knowledge is happiness."[45]

The Founding Fathers believed that only through knowledge could peace and charity prevail. Thus Washington's sincere wish was "peace with all the world."[46] Jefferson saw that "nature hath implanted in our breasts a love of others, a sense of duty to them, a moral instinct, in short, which prompts us irresistibly to feel and to succor their distresses."[47] And Franklin believed that "to relieve the misfortunes of our fellow creatures is concurring with the Deity; 'tis godlike."[48]

I found an echo of "Ulysses" in the Islamic concept of *ilm*, or knowledge. Muslim tradition encourages learning above all else because that, in turn, promotes *ihsaan* (compassion) and *adl* (justice) in society. Recall the Prophet asking his followers to go to China to seek knowledge in the belief that "the ink of the scholar is more sacred than the blood of the martyr." Some three hundred times, the Quran asks its readers to look at the heavens and ponder its mysteries. The Muslim scholars who have inspired me—like Al-Beruni, Ibn Battuta, Ibn Khaldun—traveled to distant lands in search of knowledge.

Do They Hate Us?

I have often thought of the question American commentators asked after 9/11: "Why do they hate us?" It seemed a logical question on the surface. America, which had been attacked by Muslims, was now pumping billions of dollars in aid into their countries. Yet Americans are so disliked there that they cannot wander about in the bazaars and suburbs because of security concerns. The image of Danny Pearl just before his throat was slit remains in the minds of American travelers to these lands.

George W. Bush's answer, "because they hate our freedoms," was as vague as the phrase that defined his presidency, "war on terror." Bush's phrase was empty but evocative. It spawned a language of hatred all its own that Muslims found grossly inaccurate and offensive—Islamofascism was one example—and created a culture of fear. In that environment, commentators, looking for answers to "why do they hate us?" suggested it must be because the enemy's religion preaches hatred of nonbelievers. It is a pathological condition, a fundamental flaw in Islam, they said, that Muslims cannot overcome. The problem with this line of thinking, now widely accepted in the West, is that it is contradicted by personal and historical evidence. Muslims have responded with affection to non-Muslims when they recognized their worth.

My parents, good decent Muslims with ancient lineages in Islam, respected our teachers, the Catholic priests from Europe, to a fault and even sided with them in all school-related matters, even if the priests were wrong, often admonishing me with "How can you complain about these wonderful fathers who have dedicated their lives to educate you?" I stood no chance of convincing them that the charges for breakages in my bills, for example, were fictitious, and that all the boys saw them as a kind of tax to help with the construction of a new building. I had never broken a window or a chair, yet found these items frequently on my bills. Many of my classmates were similarly "taxed," while their parents, too, sided with the priests.

My American Presbyterian teachers at Forman Christian College in Lahore were living examples of American pluralist identity. Generous with their time, advice, and friendship, they were never judgmental and accepted us as we were. Their only concern was to give us what they believed was the best college education in Pakistan. Their only complaint was that we insisted on proceeding to England for further education rather than America. "Come to America," they would say. "You would love it there." Because Muslims respect education and those who provide it, the college is today, in spite of all the anti-American feelings in the region, still run by the American Presbyterians. It remains a prestigious center of education and has produced several presidents of Pakistan.

Now for the historical evidence. The openness of Muslim peoples, especially those with a tribal background, is evident in the works of writers familiar with the British Raj, whether Rudyard Kipling or John Masters. In spite of their colonial associations, some of the British officers in charge of these tribes were so liked that the towns named in their honor were not changed after Pakistan became independent—as in the case of Jacobabad in Baluchistan, after John Jacob, and Abbottabad in the North-West Frontier Province, after James Abbott. So popular was Jacob, the story is told, that when he died, the major Baluch tribes almost went to war over who would have the honor of burying him in their territory. After Pakistan achieved independence, Jinnah, the head of state, asked Sir George Cunningham to return from Scotland to retake his old position as the governor of the North-West Frontier Province. Mrs. Cunningham recounted the excitement of her husband on receiving Jinnah's telegram and ordering her to pack without delay. He came back to find a rousing welcome among his beloved tribes. After Cunningham's tenure, Pakistan offered the same post to Sir Ambrose Dundas, another Scotsman.

As a parenthesis, and with reference to the discussion in this book, when these Scotsmen saw the Muslim clans and heard of their tribal codes of "honor," "courage," "hospitality," and "revenge," they were reminded of their own background and felt an immediate empathy with them. Unlike the severe and unbending Scots-Irish opponents of the Indian tribes in America, their kinfolk in South Asia proved to be sturdy, principled, and fair administrators with a marked respect for the tribes.

Cunningham and Dundas were not the only British officers asked to return to serve in a postindependence Pakistan. Can one even imagine, Americans need to ask themselves, Iraqis asking Paul Bremer to return and run Baghdad, as the Pakistanis did in the case of Cunningham, Dundas, and others?

Even decades after the British left, some tribal elders remembered the administrators with nostalgia. When I visited a remote part of Quetta Division as commissioner, I was welcomed by a grand *jirga* (assembly) of Pathan tribal elders. One of them, white-bearded and straight as a lance in spite of his years, stood up and praised me as the best commissioner since the time of the British. Knowing that this was nothing more than a standard greeting, I asked him what I could do for his people. "Sahib," he said without a trace of irony, "bring back the British officers to administer justice to us. They were foreigners, but they were fair people."

It is this fairness and sense of justice that Muslims find missing in Americans. That is why the very tribes who saw Westerners with a degree of affection and respect are now suspected of harboring the most wanted men on America's terrorist list: Osama bin Laden, Mullah Omar, and the al Qaeda leadership.

To complicate matters further, relations between Islam and America are bedeviled by paradoxes on each side that baffle, exasperate, and infuriate the other side. American society is anchored in democratic principles, yet the United States has consistently supported Muslim military dictators; America prides itself on human rights and civil liberties, yet has let itself be tarnished by its treatment of prisoners and by legislation like the Patriot Act. Something has gone awry with American nobility and common sense.

My own comment on some of the cases involving Muslims in America is based on my experience as a first-class magistrate trying cases in Pakistan, though I hasten to add that the judiciary there has come under attack with the arbitrary removal of the Supreme Court's chief justice, accusations of corruption, and other issues. The fundamental principle of my court was to discover the truth and establish justice. Hearsay, it had been drummed into me by those who taught me law, was no basis for evidence, and justice delayed was justice denied. On these principles alone, I would have dismissed the bulk of the suspected terrorist cases I have read about in the American media. To me, most of these young men look as if they cannot be trusted with the simple act of posting a letter, let alone implementing a complicated scheme to blow up a city, an airport, or shopping malls.

The team pays homage to the Statue of Liberty in New York City, the symbol of a pluralist and open America.

On the Muslim side, Islam emphasizes knowledge, yet Muslim countries have among the lowest literacy rates and worst track records for education. Contradictory, too, is the struggle to establish rights for women in Muslim countries alongside reports of savage crimes against women, including honor killings. It is also incongruous that a society inspired by its vision of a compassionate and merciful God can produce individuals who subscribe to acts of violence and terror. Paradoxically, when Benjamin Franklin berated the Scots-Irish who slaughtered innocent Native Americans, he reminded fellow Americans that this "Christian" behavior contrasted poorly with Muslims' consistent generosity to the enemy, as noted in chapter 2. Through Islam, Franklin reminds America to become a nobler and better version of itself.

America at a Crossroads

America is at a crossroads. Will it continue down the path it has taken since 9/11, or will it alter its course? Will it be able to resolve its internal contradictions and tensions? In one way or another, the world has a stake in the answer. It looks to the United States for leadership. This is not because of America's economic strength. China and India are doing very well on that score. Nor is it because of America's democracy. India is the largest democracy in the world. Rather it is because of America's unique vision of society formulated by its Founding Fathers and encapsulated in its founding documents. That vision is truly universal in spirit and therefore attracts the world—recall Jefferson's statue at the entrance to the University of Virginia that proclaims "Religious Freedom, 1786" and bears the names of God from the Abrahamic and even non-Abrahamic faiths.

However grand and sweeping the American founding vision, it is flawed in leaving out the original inhabitants of the land and those forcibly brought from Africa. For the white settlers arriving from Europe, America was the gateway to the Garden of Eden, but for the native tribes and those brought on the slave ships from Africa, it was the entrance to hell. Yet while there is no America without Plymouth, America with Plymouth is difficult to accept.

The only way to resolve this contradiction is to forge a new American identity from the old by looking at history beyond Plymouth and reconciling the narratives of the Wampanoag and the white settlers, of Massasoit and Winthrop, and learn lessons from both. This would not only preserve the mythology of Plymouth but also enhance and transcend it. Indeed, it is time to reexamine American history and culture with a view to rediscovering and redefining its guiding maxims and shibboleths, such as Manifest

Destiny, zero tolerance, and Darwinian fitness. In short, America needs more of the true spirit of Jesus and less of Darwin.

All three American identities need to work as an integrated whole if America is to play its role on the world stage with any degree of success. The task calls for the faith, drive, and order inherent in primordial identity; the humanity, compassion, and knowledge of pluralist identity; and the commitment, patriotism, and resolve of predator identity. Each of the three identities needs to rediscover and rekindle the true spirit of the Founding Fathers who defined and managed the reconciliation of American identity. Without that effort, every form of American identity remains incomplete and Americans will continue in a state of confusion and uncertainty, lurching toward one expression of identity and then another.

The Founding Fathers had no doubts as to how to organize American society. After citing Prophet Muhammad as one of history's "sober inquirers after truth," John Adams wrote that "the definition of a republic is an 'empire of laws and not of men.'"[49] Opposed to this view of the organizing principles of society, Dick Cheney, in a bunker following the 9/11 attacks, declared: "We will probably have to be a country ruled by men rather than laws in this period."[50] Cheney and the cabal around Bush proceeded to suspend, twist, and override the law. While the pedigree for Adams's thought traces itself to the roots of Western civilization nourished by Aristotle, the Bible, Saint Augustine, and Saint Aquinas, that of Cheney, who would subordinate the law to political will, reflects the thinking of men like Machiavelli.

Americans need to make a choice. It is either the Founding Fathers or men like Dick Cheney. It is a clear-cut question of either/or; it cannot be a bit of one and a bit of the other. Either Americans can be true to the Founding Fathers' concept of America or to the post-9/11 vision of leaders like Bush and Cheney. But the former America cannot coexist with an America that compromises the Constitution and the values of the Founding Fathers. On such clarity does the fate of civilizations rest.

Of course, being a democracy, American citizens can vote for a different kind of America, and Congress can ratify it. The new America could order the faces of Bush and Cheney carved on Mt. Rushmore and those of Washington and Jefferson, two of the Founding Fathers, removed. But that America, in certain aspects—by suspending human rights, compromising civil liberties, and setting aside certain laws—would be closer to regimes in the Muslim world run by ruthless dictators. If that happens, the triumph of Saddam Hussein and bin Laden will be complete and the loss to the world of modern history's oldest democracy incalculable. That is why America cannot compromise being true to itself. The stakes are too high.

It may end up not only losing its own soul but also the chance of saving the planet.

America needs to find a different way of looking at the world, not through the chauvinistic, almost tribal lens of Republicans or Democrats, conservatives or liberals, blacks or whites, Christians or Muslims, but through a rediscovery of the true American spirit formed by the Founding Fathers and forever couched in the frame of universal humanism. This can only begin when Americans end their entanglement with the Muslim world.

If that were to happen, the Muslim world would be responsive. But Muslims, too, need to rediscover their own central traits resting in notions of ilm, ihsaan, and adl, which many have forgotten. Muslim leaders and commentators also need to recognize the positive role they can play in the world crisis by promoting true understanding between different peoples through a closer look at Quranic verses such as "O mankind! We created you from a single (pair) of a male and a female, and made you into nations and tribes, that ye may know each other (not that ye may despise each other). Verily the most honored of you in the sight of Allah is (he who is) the most righteous of you" (Surah 49: 13).

Just as the different American identities need to coalesce and work together, so must the three Muslim models. The mystics with their universal acceptance, the modernists and their vision of living in the world community of nations, and the literalists with their passion for their faith must work as a coordinated whole. These are the Muslims who will provide bold, wise, and caring leadership and stand shoulder to shoulder with other world leaders.

This coordination will only be possible if Americans and Muslims cultivate a genuine philosophic curiosity about themselves and each other, and thereby discover the infinite variety of the human race. While maintaining the integrity of their own identity, they need to see each other not as stereotypes but as individual identities that constitute an important piece of the greater whole. Perhaps then they will create and sustain the capacity to feel compassion for, and understanding of, each other—which is, after all, what makes the human species so unique.

Like infants, we, Muslims and non-Muslims alike, are easily distracted by the clamor and color that surround us. We resolutely ignore the monumental challenges that threaten our very survival—environmental issues, poverty, and ethnic and religious wars. We fail to recognize the importance of America in that it alone has the capacity to mobilize the world to tackle these daunting tasks. But it cannot do so without resolving the question of its identity. The challenge of Islam is to help America find that identity and enable it to fulfill its destiny.

Appendix

PERSONAL REFLECTIONS ON THE FIELDWORK

AT OUR JOURNEY'S end, I asked my team to give me their reflections on their fieldwork experience and how it changed them. Jonathan recalled arriving from Alabama five years earlier to become my assistant: "Suddenly I was meeting ambassadors, going to the White House and State Department. As if it was not enough to go along with Dr. Ahmed, he would ask me to advise him on what he should say, and he would call on me to offer advice to some of these decisionmakers." Jonathan found his assignments "completely different from working in other offices, where you are simply told what to do—staple this, file that. . . . The journeys were an example of this—we constructed the whole exercise as a team. I learned so much from having this responsibility placed on me."

The journey into America was educational for Jonathan in a wider sense as well: "I have a much more nuanced understanding of what America means to me and of where I fit in and what I know to be true of my home country. The Muslim community was mostly happy to see us and to hear what we are doing. We were embraced and thanked for allowing people to speak for themselves instead of someone else from some other religious community speaking about them. The community acted as a protector of our team, and I constantly was told, 'Take care of this man. Do not let anything happen to Dr. Ahmed.' With an arm around my shoulder, looking directly into my eyes, an African American in New Orleans told me to make sure that Dr. Ahmed is safe so that he can continue the work that he is doing. As might be expected, many Pakistanis said this to me, but the more I heard it, the more I was amazed. From evangelical Christians to a Muslim member of Congress to an Israeli diplomat, people of all

473

backgrounds were shaking my hand or grabbing me by the arm and saying, 'Jonathan, I'm serious, look after Dr. Ahmed.'"

Frankie, one of my honors students, had been with me the longest, starting from the time he took my class on Islam in 2003, just after the United States invaded Iraq. For Frankie, the scope of our travels has been "epic": "It has taken me from the heart of the Muslim world to the heart of America, risking danger in isolated towns and villages, meeting presidents and prime ministers on the world stage, and spending hours with ordinary people from the Middle East to the Midwest."

"Under the tutelage of Dr. Ahmed," Frankie wrote, "I have grown from an underclassman recently out of high school to someone, I hope, who is aware of the real world, its problems, and its possibilities. Dr. Ahmed always tried to get me to realize my potential by playing to my strengths and to be aware of my vulnerabilities. He never stopped instilling in me the importance of knowledge, and of always asking the most important question, 'why?'"

For Frankie, it was not only a journey of self-discovery but also "a kind of rediscovery of my own country." He felt he could now say he was American "with a pride and awareness that I did not have before, as through Dr. Ahmed's teaching and all our fieldwork and research, I have a better idea what that actually means." Frankie is optimistic about Islam in America after seeing Muslims who have found a way to be Muslim and also American—"ostensibly by clinging to and reviving the Founding Fathers' philosophy as compatible with their religion at a time when many non-Muslim Americans seem to be losing it. However, Muslim society is very divided."

Hailey, another of my honors students, had been with me on both my long field trips and projects. Her experiences, she wrote, taught her "how to be more empathetic, how to interact with other communities in America, and to see different communities through their own eyes." Having grown up in a mainly white suburb of Dallas, Hailey said she had not realized how much "WASP perspective was ingrained in me" until she traveled with our team: "All of our biases and worldviews were exposed at one time or another. I would find myself agreeing with the primordial identity often in the back of my mind, although I consciously, and still do, think, that the ideal America is the pluralist vision set forth by the Founding Fathers."

Hailey felt somewhat less hopeful than Frankie about the chances of promoting dialogue, mainly because of the "breakdown of our society in America—a loss of civility and respect and a loss of community." At the same time, she felt an important personal transformation had occurred during our journey: "Ambassador Ahmed taught me how to know myself.

If you know yourself, you are in control. That is something that I think America, too, can learn from this book. Because we do not know who we are, we can no longer respond clearly. He taught me restraint, grace, and patience. Despite a death in his family or being ill himself, he always put the project and the team first. I have grown mentally and spiritually simply by being around him. He has been so generous to me with his time, patience, and knowledge. He taught me that it is not what you are, but who you are, that makes a person great. He is one of the truly great men alive today, and I am honored to have been given the chance to work with him for so long."

Craig, another student of mine and the newest member of the field team, also felt the trip had changed him, making him more proud "that the Founding Fathers of this country had an open and pluralistic vision that can incorporate people of all walks of life and faith." The trip changed his perception of Muslims as well, leading him to see them as "some of the best citizens in the country" and to be "very optimistic with the direction the Muslim American community is heading in." He was particularly struck by Muslim views on violence: "Practically ALL Muslims in America condemn terrorism and acts of violence. We entered the most conservative mosques in the whole country, and even there they mentioned how the Quran forbids killing innocent people, women and children, and even trees and the environment."

The educational rewards were equally important for Craig: "Professor Ahmed has taught me that the search for ilm (knowledge) is one of the highest virtues for human beings. Most important, he continues to inspire me to try to build rather than burn bridges wherever I step foot. Rather than responding to violence with more violence (which only continues the vicious cycle of revenge), Professor Ahmed has shown me that our greatest challenge as human beings is the tackling of issues that often motivate violence. One of these issues, and perhaps the most influential, is ignorance. Only through learning and open dialogue, as he has suggested countless times, can human beings overcome this evil."

ACKNOWLEDGMENTS

IN VIEW OF the scope and scale of this project, with its rigorous and lengthy fieldwork, I could not have successfully completed it without the help of many people and institutions. I owe all of them a debt of gratitude.

The biggest challenge was to obtain funding for travel and accommodations for myself and my team for the duration of our work in the field. Eventually, funding came through, though I was acutely aware that we would be operating on a shoestring budget. The project was officially sponsored and backed by American University and had the support of both Dean Louis Goodman of the School of International Service and President Cornelius Kerwin. The university not only granted me a year-long sabbatical but also helped financially. My colleagues on campus, especially Quansheng Zhao, Michelle Egan, Nanette Levinson, and Brian Forst, consistently provided me good cheer and support; so did the Brookings Institution, where I am a nonresident senior fellow. I still needed funds to allow the team to join me, and one of the earliest positive responses arrived from the Berkley Center at Georgetown University, which provided Hailey Woldt, a former Georgetown student, a base. I am grateful to Thomas Banchoff and Melody Fox of the center for their consistent and enthusiastic support. The Dar-Al-Islam organization in New Mexico supported Craig Considine's travel, the College of William and Mary sponsored Madeeha Hameed, and the Case Foundation provided hand-held cameras and a computer. We also received support from the Kingdom Foundation headed by Prince Al-Waleed bin Talal, a member of the Saudi royal family known for his active role in interfaith dialogue and understanding, and for his support of Harvard and Georgetown Universities.

Several individual Muslims—Munir Akthar Chaudry, Hamid Malik, Aitizaz (Bob) Din, and Adnan Khan—also helped us financially, and Rauf Ahmed obtained discounted rates at hotels for us. Countless other individuals provided us with transport, housing, and other assistance. In addition, universities and institutions throughout the journey provided honoraria, accommodation, meals, and local hospitality and sponsored events. These included the University of St. Thomas, DePaul University, Colgate University, Harvard University, University of Utah, University of Texas, Creighton University, Randolph College, St. Michael's College, Vanderbilt University, the Institute for Social Policy and Understanding in Michigan, the East-West Center in Honolulu, Wayne State University, University of Colorado–Denver, Park Avenue Christian Church, BIG Arts Forum on Sanibel Island, and the World Affairs Council in Palm Beach, Florida, and St. Louis, Missouri.

During a strategy session on the project with Dean Goodman, he suggested I contact the Department of Homeland Security (DHS), since it had launched a series of major research projects on Muslims in America based at the University of Maryland's START Center. I applied for funding on the condition that they agree unconditionally to my request for academic freedom and editorial, intellectual, and fieldwork independence. This they did, and the START Center provided funding for the project through DHS Grant 2008-ST-061-ST-0004 to American University, which operated it. I would like to express my appreciation to Professor Kathleen Smarick, the center's director. In keeping with the spirit of transparency, the DHS officially acknowledged our independence: "The views and conclusions contained in this document are those of the authors and should not be interpreted as necessarily representing the official policies, either expressed or implied, of the U.S. Department of Homeland Security." True to their word, no one interfered with the shaping of ideas, opinions, and conclusions of the book. Furthermore, neither the DHS nor indeed any of the other funders of the project at any point asked us for the interviews we conducted or the questionnaires that we gathered during the field trip. We believe that the findings will help not only the DHS but also anyone concerned with seriously appreciating and understanding the Muslim community in the United States.

This project would not have been possible without the commitment, faith, and hard work of my indomitable team. Jonathan Hayden, Frankie Martin, and Hailey Woldt were with me on my previous project and were joined for the journey into America by Craig Considine for the entire period of fieldwork, by Madeeha Hameed for three months, and intermittently by Celestine Johnson. At various stages, the team was assisted by other American University students. Aja Anderson, Catharine Robinson, and Kaitlan Peterson worked in the office in advance of the fieldwork. Blake Underwood and Elise Alexander assisted in the research for and editing of the manuscript in its final stages, along with Lillian Cicerchia. The contribution of my team is amply displayed in the text, and I am deeply grateful to each and every one of them. Bob Faherty at Brookings Institution Press and his excellent colleagues, especially Janet Walker and Vicky Macintyre, were as supportive and efficient as they were for my previous book.

My wife Zeenat joined me for part of the fieldwork and, as always, worked selflessly and tirelessly in helping me finish the manuscript even if awakened in the early hours of the morning. I have dedicated this book with love and prayers to Anah, our lovely granddaughter, who was born in the fall of 2009 after she joined me on the field trip with her mother earlier in the year. Her name means perseverance and patience—the two virtues that will be vital in order for her and the people of this century to understand and cope with the world in which they live.

Chapter One

1. Akbar Ahmed, *Journey into Islam: The Crisis of Globalization* (Brookings, 2007).

2. Winston S. Churchill, *Never Give In: The Best of Winston Churchill's Speeches* (New York: Hyperion, 2003), p. 199.

3. Chris Hedges, *American Fascists: The Christian Right and the War on America* (New York: Free Press, 2006) pp. 189–90.

4. David Kilcullen, *The Accidental Guerilla: Fighting Small Wars in the Midst of a Big One* (Oxford University Press, 2009).

5. General Stanley McChrystal, "Gen. McChrystal's Speech on Afghanistan," *RealClearPolitics*, October 1, 2009 (www.realclearpolitics.com/articles/2009/10/01/gen_mcchrystals_address_on_afghanistan_98537.html [March 1, 2010]).

6. Rayford W. Logan, "Estevanico, Negro Discoverer of the Southwest: A Critical Reexamination," *Phylon* 1, no. 4 (1940): 305–14.

7. Samuel S. Hill, Charles H. Lippy, and Charles Reagan Wilson, eds., *Encyclopedia of Religion in the South* (Mercer University Press, 2005), p. 394.

8. Michael A. Koszegi and J. Gordon Melton, eds., *Islam in North America: A Sourcebook* (New York: Garland, 1992), p. 3.

9. Comments like that of Father Donald Nesti and other respondents throughout the book are based on interviews, mostly on camera, conducted during fieldwork for purposes of this study.

10. Ambassador Michael Oren, personal communication, 2009. See also Michael Oren, *Power, Faith, and Fantasy: America in the Middle East, 1776 to the Present* (New York: W. W. Norton, 2007).

11. Alexis de Tocqueville, *Democracy in America*, edited and translated by Harvey C. Mansfield and Delba Winthrop (University of Chicago Press, 2000), p. 227.

12. Fredrik Barth, ed., *Ethnic Groups and Boundaries: The Social Organization of Cultural Difference* (Prospect Heights, Ill.: Waveland Press, 1998); Akbar S. Ahmed, *Resistance and Control in Pakistan* (Abingdon, Oxon: Routledge, 2004).

13. See Joseph Ellis, *American Creation: Triumphs and Tragedies in the Founding of the Republic* (New York: Vintage, 2008); David Hackett Fischer, *Albion's Seed: Four British Folkways in America* (Oxford University Press, 1989); Walter Russell Meade, *Special Providence: American Foreign Policy and How It Changed the World* (New York: Routledge, 2002); Sarah Vowell, *The Wordy Shipmates* (New York: Riverhead Books, 2008).

14. Morris Berman, *The Twilight of American Culture* (New York: W. W. Norton, 2001); Diana Eck, *A New Religious America: How a "Christian Country" Has Now Become the World's Most Religiously Diverse Nation* (San Francisco: HarperCollins, 2001); Hedges, *American Fascists*; and Samuel P. Huntington, *Who Are We? The Challenges to America's National Identity* (New York: Simon and Schuster, 2004).

15. See Howard Zinn, *A People's History of the United States: 1492–Present* (New York: HarperCollins, 2003); Noam Chomsky, *Hegemony or Survival: America's Quest for Global Dominance* (New York: Metropolitan Books, 2003), and *Terrorizing the Neighborhood: American Foreign Policy in the Post–Cold War Era* (Stirling, Scotland: AK Press, 1991); Larry Schweikart and Michael Patrick Allen, *A Patriot's History of the United States: From Columbus's Great Discovery to the War on Terror* (New York: Sentinel, 2007).

16. De Tocqueville, *Democracy in America*.

17. Ibid., pp. 234, 244.

18. Ibid., pp. 191, 242.

19. Ibid., p. 379.

20. Ibid., pp. 249, 265, 310.

21. Ibid., p. 306.

22. Jane I. Smith, *Islam in America* (Columbia University Press, 1999); and Karen Isaksen Leonard, *Muslims in the United States: The State of Research* (New York: Russell Sage Foundation, 2003).

23. Paul M. Barrett, *American Islam: The Struggle for the Soul of a Religion* (New York: Picador, 2008); Dilara Hafiz, Yasmine Hafiz, and Imran Hafiz, *The American Muslim Teenager's Handbook* (New York: Atheneum Books for Young Readers, 2009); Yvonne Yazbeck Haddad, Jane I. Smith, and Kathleen M. Moore, *Muslim Women in America: The Challenge of Islamic Identity Today* (Oxford University Press, 2006); and Jamillah Karim, *American Muslim Women: Negotiating Race, Class, and Gender within the Ummah* (New York University Press, 2009); Evelyn Shakir, *Bint Arab: Arab and Arab American Women in the United States* (Westport, Conn.: Praeger, 1997); Abdo A. Elkholy, *The Arab Moslems in the United States: Religion and Assimilation* (New Haven, Conn.: College and University Press, 1966); Alia Malek, *A Country Called Amreeka: Arab Roots, American Stories* (New York: Free Press, 2009); John Tehranian, *Whitewashed: America's Invisible Middle Eastern Minority* (New York University Press, 2008); Robert Dannin, *Black Pilgrimage to Islam* (Oxford

University Press, 2002); and Sherman A. Jackson, *Islam and the Blackamerican: Looking toward the Third Resurrection* (Oxford University Press, 2005).

24. Aminah Beverly McCloud, *African American Islam* (New York: Routledge, 1995), and *Transnational Muslims in American Society* (University Press of Florida, 2006).

25. Imam Hassan Qazwini, *American Crescent: A Muslim Cleric on the Power of His Faith, the Struggle against Prejudice, and the Future of Islam in America* (New York: Random House, 2007); and Asma Gull Hasan, *American Muslims: The New Generation* (New York: Continuum, 2002).

26. Steven Emerson, *American Jihad: The Terrorists Living among Us* (New York: Free Press, 2002); and Robert Spencer, *Onward Muslim Soldiers: How Jihad Still Threatens America and the West* (Washington: Regnery, 2003).

27. For a review by Jonathan Benthall, the former director of the Royal Anthropological Institute, see "You'll See How Big We Are: *Journey into America,*" *Anthropology Today* 25 (October 2009): 23; Asif Ismail, "The American Odyssey," *Khaleej Times,* August 5, 2009; John Milewski, "In Search of the Muslim World," *Huffington Post,* July 2, 2009; and Saleem H. Ali, "Islamic Identity in America," Doha Network, July 17, 2009.

28. De Tocqueville, *Democracy in America,* p. 64.

29. Vowell, *The Wordy Shipmates,* p. 127.

30. "U.S. Population Hit 300 Million This Week," Progressive Policy Institute, October 18, 2006 (www.ppionline.org/ppi_ci.cfm?knlgAreaID=108&subsecID=9 00003&contentID=254082 [March 1, 2010]); John Donnelly, "Alarm Sounds on U.S. Population Boom: Report Says Growth Threatens Resources," *Boston Globe,* August 31, 2006.

31. Ragnar Carlson, "Aloha Akbar," *Honolulu Weekly,* December 3, 2008.

32. De Tocqueville, *Democracy in America,* p. 28.

33. Charles Darwin, *The Origin of Species* (New York: Gramercy, 1995).

34. Kurt Vonnegut, *A Man without a Country* (New York: Random House, 2007), p. 98.

35. Nathaniel Philbrick and Thomas Philbrick, eds., *The Mayflower Papers: Selected Writings of Colonial New England* (New York: Penguin, 2007), p. ix.

36. Robert S. Wistrich, *Laboratory for World Destruction: Germans and Jews in Central Europe* (University of Nebraska Press, 2007), p. 370.

37. Ahmed, *Journey into Islam*; W. E. B. Du Bois, *The Souls of Black Folk* (New York: Penguin, 1996); Lawrence Rosen, interview on camera, October 2008. For works on caste in India, see Declan Quigley, *The Interpretation of Caste* (Oxford: Clarendon Press, 1993); Louis Dumont, *Homo Hierarchicus: The Caste System and Its Implications* (Oxford University Press, 1988); C. J. Fuller, ed., *Caste Today* (Oxford University Press, 1996); M. N. Srinivas, *Village, Caste, Gender and Method: Essays in Indian Social Anthropology* (Oxford University Press, 1996).

38. Kamran Khan, personal communication, Chicago, 2008.

39. Huntington, *Who Are We?*

40. David G. Savage, "Secret Service Investigates Obama Poll on Facebook," *Los Angeles Times*, September 29, 2009.

41. John L. Perry, "Full Text of *Newsmax* Column Suggesting Military Coup against Obama," Talking Points Memo (www.talkingpointsmemo.com/news/2009/09/full_text_of_newsmax_column_suggesting_military_co.php [March 2, 2010]).

42. Alexander Nehamas and Paul Woodruff, translated and introduction, *Plato: Phaedrus* (Indianapolis: Hackett, 1995), p. 44.

Chapter Two

1. Nathaniel Philbrick. *Mayflower: A Story of Courage, Community, and War* (New York: Viking, 2006), p. 356.

2. Ibid., p. 350.

3. George McKenna, *The Puritan Origins of American Patriotism* (Yale University Press, 2007), p. 46.

4. Philbrick, *Mayflower*, p. 354.

5. Ibid., pp. 355–56.

6. Ibid, p. 52.

7. Jon Meacham, *American Gospel: God, the Founding Fathers, and the Making of a Nation* (New York: Random House, 2006), p. 53.

8. Sarah Vowell, *The Wordy Shipmates* (New York: Riverhead Books, 2008), p. 37.

9. Howard Zinn, *A People's History of the United States: 1492–Present* (New York: HarperCollins, 2003), p. 14.

10. Vowell, *The Wordy Shipmates*, p. 77.

11. Ibid., p. 126.

12. Ibid., p. 146.

13. Ibid., p. 136.

14. For Williams's comment on the treatment of the natives, see ibid., p. 127. On Williams's desire for a "hedge or wall of separation between the Garden of the church and the wilderness of the world," see Meacham, *American Gospel*, p. 54.

15. Robert M. Utley and Wilcomb E. Washburn, *Indian Wars* (New York: Mariner Books, 2002), pp. 53–54.

16. Philbrick, *Mayflower*, pp. xiv, 345. For an in-depth discussion of the *Seaflower* and Puritan debates about slavery, see Jill Lepore, *The Name of War: King Philip's War and the Origins of American Identity* (New York: Vintage, 1999), pp. 150–72.

17. Philbrick, *Mayflower*, p. 252.

18. Ibid., pp. 263, 296.

19. Daniel Webster, *The Works of Daniel Webster*, vol. 2 (Charleston, S.C.: BiblioBazaar, 2008), p. 527.

20. Kipling's poem, "The White Man's Burden," was published in 1899 with the subtitle "The United States and the Philippine Islands."

21. Samuel P. Huntington, *Who Are We? The Challenges to America's National Identity* (New York: Simon and Schuster, 2004), p. xvi.

22. David Hackett Fischer, *Albion's Seed: Four British Folkways in America* (Oxford University Press, 1989).

23. Robert Bellah, "Civil Religion in America," *Daedalus, Journal of the American Academy of Arts and Sciences* 96 (Winter 1967): 1–21.

24. Elaine Dundy, *Elvis and Gladys* (University Press of Mississippi, 2004), pp. 13, 14, 21.

25. James G. Leyburn, *The Scotch-Irish: A Social History* (University of North Carolina Press, 1989), p. 109.

26. Fischer, *Albion's Seed*, p. 613.

27. Leyburn, *The Scotch-Irish*, p. 328.

28. Richard J. Hooker, ed., *The Carolina Backcountry on the Eve of the Revolution: The Journal and Other Writings of Charles Woodmason, Anglican Itinerant* (University of North Carolina Press, 1953), pp. 52–53.

29. Fischer, *Albion's Seed*, pp. 641, 654.

30. June Banks Evans, *The Blackwells of Blackwell's Neck: An Inferential Genealogy Based on Material Available* (New Orleans: Bryn Ffyliaid, 2004), p. 67.

31. Carlton Jackson, *A Social History of the Scotch-Irish* (Lanham, Md.: Madison Books, 1993), p. 59.

32. Saul Cornell, "Aristocracy Assailed: The Ideology of Backcountry Anti-Federalism," *Journal of American History* 76, no. 4 (March 1990): 1151–53.

33. Fischer, *Albion's Seed*, p. 841.

34. James Webb, *Born Fighting: How the Scots-Irish Shaped America* (New York: Broadway Books, 2005), p. 202.

35. Ibid., p. 12.

36. Angela Brittingham and G. Patricia de la Cruz, "Ancestry: 2000, Census 2000 Brief" (www.census.gov/prod/2004pubs/c2kbr-35.pdf [February 26, 2010]), p. 8.

37. Meacham, *American Gospel*, p. 102.

38. Jean M. Yarbrough, *The Essential Jefferson* (Indianapolis: Hackett, 2006), p. 125.

39. Paul Leicester Ford, ed., *The Works of Thomas Jefferson*, vol. 12 (New York: G. P. Putnam's Sons, 1905), p. 270.

40. Meacham, *American Gospel*, pp. 245–46.

41. Ibid., p. 103.

42. J. R. Pole, ed., *The Revolution in America, 1754–1788: Documents and Commentaries* (Stanford University Press, 1970), p. 394.

43. Meacham, *American Gospel*, p. 11.

44. Ibid., p. 62.

45. Joyce Appleby and Terence Ball, eds., *Jefferson: Political Writings* (Cambridge University Press, 1999), p. 501.

46. Joseph J. Ellis, *American Creation: Triumphs and Tragedies at the Founding of the Republic* (New York: Vintage, 2008), p. 55.

47. Martha Lou Lemmon Stohlman, *John Witherspoon: Parson, Politician, Patriot* (Philadelphia: Westminister Press, 1976), p. 75.

48. Morton Borden, *The Antifederalist Papers* (Michigan State University Press, 1965), p. 28.

49. Walter Isaacson, *Benjamin Franklin: An American Life* (New York: Simon and Schuster, 2004), pp. 111–12.

50. Alan Taylor, *American Colonies: The Settling of North America* (New York: Penguin, 2002), p. 436.

51. Ibid.

52. Patrick Griffin, *The People with No Name: Ireland's Ulster Scots, America's Scots Irish, and the Creation of a British Atlantic World, 1689–1764* (Princeton University Press, 2001), p. 169.

53. Ibid., pp. 169–70.

54. J. A. Leo LeMay, ed., *Franklin: Writings* (New York: Literary Classics of the United States, 1987), pp. 545–56.

55. Peter Silver, *Our Savage Neighbors: How Indian Wars Transformed Early America* (New York: W. W. Norton, 2009), p. 204; Griffin, *The People with No Name*, p. 171.

56. Griffin, *The People with No Name*, p. 171.

57. Eric Burns, *Infamous Scribblers: The Founding Fathers and the Rowdy Beginnings of American Journalism* (New York: Public Affairs, 2006), p. 342.

58. Geoffrey R. Stone, *Perilous Times: Free Speech in Wartime from the Sedition Act of 1798 to the War on Terrorism* (New York: W. W. Norton, 2004), p. 35.

59. Robert V. Remini, *Andrew Jackson* (New York: HarperCollins, 1999), p. 32.

60. R. B. Bernstein, *Thomas Jefferson* (Oxford University Press, 2003), pp. 181–82.

61. Alexis de Tocqueville, *Democracy in America*, edited and translated by Harvey C. Mansfield and Delba Winthrop (University of Chicago Press, 2000), p. 325.

62. Andrea Smith, "Rape and the War against Native Women" in Inés Hernández-Avila, ed., *Reading Native American Women: Critical/Creative Representations* (Lanham, Md.: AltaMira Press, 2005), p. 65.

63. Derrick Jensen, *The Culture of Make Believe* (White River Junction, Vt.: Chelsea Green Publishing, 2004), p. 313.

64. Chip Berlet and Matthew N. Lyons, *Right-Wing Populism in America: Too Close for Comfort* (New York: Guilford Press, 2000), p. 41.

65. John Ehle, *Trail of Tears: The Rise and Fall of the Cherokee Nation* (New York: Doubleday, 1988), p. 220.

66. Walter R. Borneman, *1812: The War That Forged a Nation* (New York: HarperCollins, 2004), p. 152.

67. Jon Meacham, *American Lion: Andrew Jackson in the White House* (New York: Random House, 2008), p. 204.

68. Amy H. Sturgis, *The Trail of Tears and Indian Removal* (Westport, Conn.: Greenwood Press, 2007), p. 2.

69. Sean Patrick Adams, ed., *The Early American Republic: A Documentary Reader* (Hoboken, N.J.: Wiley-Blackwell, 2009), p. 17.

70. Zinn, *A People's History of the United States*, p. 128.

71. Edward G. Lengel, *General George Washington: A Military Life* (New York: Random House, 2007), pp. 311–12.

72. Appleby and Ball, eds., *Jefferson*, p. 194.

73. Brett F. Woods, ed., *Thomas Jefferson: Thoughts on War and Revolution* (New York: Algora Publishing, 2009), p. 163; Joseph J. Ellis, *American Sphinx: The Character of Thomas Jefferson* (New York: Vintage, 1998), p. 238.

74. Jerry Holmes, ed., *Thomas Jefferson: A Chronology of His Thoughts* (Lanham, Md.: Rowman & Littlefield, 2002), p. 186; Saul Kussiel Padover, ed., *The Complete Jefferson: Containing His Major Writings Published and Unpublished, Except His Letters* (New York: Duell, Sloan and Pearce, 1943), p. 408.

75. "Our Relations with Mexico," *The American Review: A Whig Journal of Politics, Literature, Art, and Science* 4 (July 1846): A14.

76. Merritt B. Pound, *Benjamin Hawkins, Indian Agent* (University of Georgia Press, 2009), p. 99.

77. Mark Twain, *The Adventures of Tom Sawyer; Tom Sawyer Abroad; and Tom Sawyer, Detective*, edited by John C. Gerber, Paul Baender, and Terry Firkins (University of California Press, 1980).

78. Kenneth Silverman, *Edgar A. Poe: Mournful and Never-ending Remembrance* (New York: HarperCollins, 1992), p. 265; Kent Ljungquist, "The Poet as Critic," in *The Cambridge Companion to Edgar Allan Poe*, edited by Kevin J. Hayes (Cambridge University Press, 2002), p. 15.

79. Margaret Fuller, *Woman in the Nineteenth Century and Other Writings*, edited by Donna Dickenson (Oxford University Press, 1994).

80. Vowell, *The Wordy Shipmates*, p. 25.

81. Ronald C. White Jr., *A. Lincoln: A Biography* (New York: Random House, 2009), p. 313.

82. Josiah Strong, *Our Country: Its Possible Future and Its Present Crisis* (Charleston, S.C.: BiblioBazaar, 2008).

83. Ibid., p. 178.

84. Ibid., p. 175.

85. Ibid., p. 171.

86. Charles Darwin in Strong, *Our Country*, p. 170.

87. Strong, *Our Country*, p. 172.

88. Theodore Roosevelt, *The Winning of the West*, vol. 4: *Louisiana and the Northwest 1791–1807* (University of Nebraska Press, 1995), pp. 1, 2.

89. Christine Rosen, *Preaching Eugenics: Religious Leaders and the American Eugenics Movement* (Oxford University Press, 2004), p. 10.

90. Meacham, *American Lion*, p. 356.

91. Roosevelt, *The Winning of the West*, vol. 4, pp. 98, 196, 217.

92. Ibid., pp. 98, 196.

93. Ibid., p. 98.

94. Ibid., pp. 271, 280.

95. Theodore Roosevelt, *The Winning of the West*, vol. 1 (Charleston, S.C.: BiblioBazaar, 2008), p. 104.

96. Ibid., p. 103.

97. Roosevelt, *The Winning of the West*, vol. 4, p. 53.

98. Ibid., p. 17.

99. Ibid., p. 316.

100. Ray Batchelor, *Henry Ford: Mass Production, Modernism, and Design* (Manchester University Press, 1994), p. 30.

101. McKenna, *The Puritan Origins of American Patriotism*, pp. 98, 99–100.

102. Michael Medved, *The 10 Big Lies about America: Combating Destructive Distortions about Our Nation* (New York: Three Rivers Press, 2008), pp. 103–04.

103. David M. Kennedy, *Over Here: The First World War and American Society* (Oxford University Press, 2004), p. 87.

104. Laurence Bergreen, *Capone: The Man and the Era* (New York: Simon and Schuster, 1994), p. 190.

105. Ibid., p. 191.

106. James Gill, *Lords of Misrule: Mardi Gras and the Politics of Race in New Orleans* (University Press of Mississippi, 1997), p. 153.

107. "Chief Hennessy Avenged," *New York Times*, March 15, 1891.

108. Rosen, *Preaching Eugenics*, p. 5.

109. H. G. Wells, *Anticipations* (Charleston, S.C.: BiblioBazaar, 2007), pp. 183, 184, 194.

110. Christopher Cumo, *Science and Technology in 20th-Century American Life* (Westport, Conn.: Greenwood Press, 2007), p. 67.

111. Lynne Curry, *The Human Body on Trial: A Handbook with Cases, Laws, and Documents* (Santa Barbara, Calif.: ABC-CLIO Inc., 2002), p. 124.

112. Paul Popenoe and Roswell Hill Johnson, *Applied Eugenics* (New York: Macmillan, 1920), pp. 75, 184.

113. Edwin Black, *War against the Weak: Eugenics and America's Campaign to Create a Master Race* (New York: Thunder's Mouth Press, 2003), p. 249.

114. Ibid., p. 276.

115. Madison Grant, *The Passing of the Great Race or the Racial Basis of European History* (New York: Charles Scribner's Sons, 1916), pp. 45, 228; Max Wallace, *The American Axis: Henry Ford, Charles Lindbergh, and the Rise of the Third Reich* (New York: St. Martin's Press, 2003), p. 97.

116. Grant, *The Passing of the Great Race*, p. 95; and Black, *War against the Weak*, p. 35.

117. Kwando Mbiassi Kinshasa, *Black Resistance to the Ku Klux Klan in the Wake of the Civil War* (Jefferson, N.C.: McFarland, 2006), p. 228.

118. Thomas Dixon Jr., *The Clansman: An Historical Romance of the Ku Klux Klan* (New York: A. Wessels, 1907), p. 326.

119. *Nazi America: A Secret History*, History Channel, 1999.

120. Robin Aitken, "Trying to Explain McVeigh," BBC.com, May 12, 2001 (http://news.bbc.co.uk/2/hi/programmes/from_our_own_correspondent/1325650.stm [March 10, 2010]).

121. George M. Fredrickson, *White Supremacy: A Comparative Study in American and South African History* (Oxford University Press, 1982), p. 104.

122. Ibid., pp. 104–05.

123. Harriet Beecher Stowe, *Uncle Tom's Cabin: Authoritative Text, Backgrounds and Contexts, Criticism*, edited by Elizabeth Ammons (New York: W. W. Norton, 1994).

124. Lee E. Williams and Lee E. Williams III, *Anatomy of Four Race Riots: Racial Conflict in Knoxville, Elaine (Arkansas), Tulsa, and Chicago, 1919–1921* (University Press of Mississippi, 1972), p. 60.

125. Scott Ellsworth, *Death in a Promised Land: The Tulsa Race Riot of 1921* (Louisiana State University Press, 1982), pp. 71–72.

126. Walter F. White, "The Eruption of Tulsa," *The Nation*, June 29, 1921, pp. 909–10.

127. Nicholas J. Santoro, *Atlas of Slavery and Civil Rights: An Annotated Chronicle of the Passage from Slavery and Segregation to Civil Rights and Equality under the Law* (Lincoln, Neb.: iUniverse, 2006), p. 125.

128. Charles L. Lumpkins, *American Pogrom: The East St. Louis Race Riot and Black Politics* (Ohio University Press, 2008), p. 2; Mia Bay, *To Tell the Truth Freely: The Life of Ida B. Wells* (New York: Hill and Wang, 2009), p. 310.

129. Susan M. Chambré, *Fighting for Our Lives: New York's AIDS Community and the Politics of Disease* (Rutgers University Press, 2006), p. 81.

130. James Baldwin, *Notes of a Native Son* (Boston: Beacon Press, 1984), p. 38.

131. Thomas A. Guglielmo, *White on Arrival: Italians, Race, Color, and Power in Chicago, 1890–1945* (Oxford University Press, 2004), p. 163.

132. Gregory Kane, "Dispatch from Bodymore, Murderland," *Washington Examiner*, June 15, 2009.

133. "Editorial: Terror in a Flash," *Philadelphia Inquirer*, March 23, 2010.

134. Anthony Walsh and Kevin M. Beaver, eds., *Biosocial Criminology: New Directions in Theory and Research*, (New York: Routledge, 2009), p. 144.

135. U.S. Department of Justice, Bureau of Justice Statistics, "Criminal Victimization in the United States, 2006 Statistical Tables," table 42, NCJ 223436, August 2008 (http://bjs.ojp.usdoj.gov/content/pub/pdf/cvus06.pdf [February 13, 2010]).

136. U.S. Department of Justice, Bureau of Justice Statistics, "Criminal Victimization in the United States, 2005 Statistical Tables," table 42, NCJ 215244, December 2006 (http://bjs.ojp.usdoj.gov/content/pub/pdf/cvus05.pdf [February 13, 2010]).

137. Premdatta Varma, *Indian Immigrants in USA: Struggle for Equality* (New Delhi: Heritage, 1995), p. 114.

138. *United States v. Bhagat Singh Thind*, 261 U.S. 204 (1923).

139. Paul Spickard, *Japanese Americans: The Formation and Transformations of an Ethnic Group* (Rutgers University Press, 2009), p. 107.

140. Juan F. Perea, "'Am I an American or Not?' Reflections on Citizenship, Americanization, and Race," in *Immigration and Citizenship in the 21st Century*, edited by Noah M. J. Pickus (Lanham, Md.: Rowman and Littlefield, 2002), p. 58.

141. Zinn, *A People's History of the United States*, pp. 430–31.

142. Irene Bloemraad, *Becoming a Citizen: Incorporating Immigrants and Refugees in the United States and Canada* (University of California Press, 2006), p. 32.

143. John Fitzgerald Kennedy, *Public Papers of the Presidents of the United States: John F. Kennedy, Containing the Public Messages, Speeches, and Statements of the President* (Washington: Office of the Federal Registrar, National Archives and Records Service, 1964), p. 502.

144. David Talbot, *Brothers: The Hidden History of the Kennedy Years* (New York: Free Press, 2007), p. 353.

145. Thurston Clarke, *The Last Campaign: Robert F. Kennedy and 82 Days That Inspired America* (New York: Henry Holt and Co., 2008), pp. 46–47.

146. Irving Bernstein, *Promises Kept: John F. Kennedy's New Frontier* (Oxford University Press, 1991), p. 42.

147. Robert F. Kennedy, *Rights for Americans: The Speeches of Robert F. Kennedy*, edited and with commentary by Thomas A. Hopkins (Indianapolis: Bobbs-Merrill, 1964), p. 17.

148. *The Papers of Martin Luther King Jr.*, edited by Clayborne Carson, with volume editors Susan Carson, Susan Englander, Troy Jackson, and Gerald L. Smith, vol. 6: *Advocate of the Social Gospel, September 1948–March 1963* (University of California Press, 2007), p. 472.

149. James M. Washington, ed., *A Testament of Hope: The Essential Writings and Speeches of Martin Luther King, Jr.* (New York: HarperCollins, 1991).

150. Malcolm X, *Malcolm X on Afro-American History* (New York: Pathfinder Press, 1970), p. 30.

151. Thomas Hauser, *Muhammad Ali: His Life and Times* (New York: Simon and Schuster, 1992), pp. 65, 189.

152. Muhammad Ali with Hana Yasmeen Ali, *The Soul of a Butterfly: Reflections on Life's Journey* (New York: Simon and Schuster, 2004), pp. xxiv, 160.

153. J. C. Beaglehole, *The Life of Captain James Cook* (Stanford University Press, 1974), p. 365.

154. Michael Fry, *How the Scots Made America* (New York: Thomas Dunne Books, 2003), p. 223.

155. Francis Fukuyama, "The End of History?" *National Interest*, no. 16, (Summer 1989): 3–18.

156. Robert Frank, "Plutonomics, The Wealth Report," *Wall Street Journal*, January 8, 2007.

157. Joe Bageant, *Deer Hunting with Jesus: Dispatches from America's Class War* (New York: Crown Publishers, 2007), p. 204.

158. Harriet B. Braiker, *The September 11 Syndrome: Anxious Days and Sleepless Nights* (New York: McGraw-Hill, 2002), p. 47.

159. Michael Savage, on Talk Radio Network's *The Savage Nation*, August 21, 2009.

Chapter Three

1. The Knights Party, USA, "About National Director Pastor Thomas Robb" (www.kkk.bz/nationalleaders.htm [March 10, 2010]).

2. The Knights Party, USA, "Obama Alert" (www.kkk.bz/Obamalert.htm [March 10, 2010]).

3. Craig Baker, personal communication, 2009.

4. John Howard Griffin, *Black Like Me* (New York: Signet, 1996).

5. Jessica Ravitz, "Muslim in America: A 'Voyage of Discovery,'" CNN.com, February 9, 2009 (www.cnn.com/2009/LIVING/wayoflife/02/09/muslims.america/index.html [January 24, 2010]).

6. "Virginia Paper Drops Columnist Malkin," *Editor and Publisher*, November 22, 2004.

7. Mark Shanahan, "Making Waves," *Boston Globe*, September 1, 2007.

8. David E. Stannard, *American Holocaust: The Conquest of the New World* (Oxford University Press, 1993), pp. 126, 127.

9. Fred Anderson and Andrew Cayton, *The Dominion of War: Empire and Liberty in North America, 1500–2000* (New York: Viking, 2005), p. 336.

10. Peter Matthiessen, *In the Spirit of Crazy Horse* (New York: Penguin, 1992), p. 107.

11. Mahmood Mamdani, *Good Muslim, Bad Muslim: America, the Cold War, and the Roots of Terror* (New York: Three Leaves Press, 2005), p. 143.

12. Alexis de Tocqueville, *Democracy in America*, edited and translated by Harvey C. Mansfield and Delba Winthrop (University of Chicago Press, 2000), p. 177.

13. Allan J. Lichtman, *White Protestant Nation: The Rise of the American Conservative Movement* (New York: Atlantic Monthly Press, 2008).

14. Isaac Baker, "American Muslims Live in Fear of Govt," Antiwar.com, February 19, 2005 (www.antiwar.com/ips/baker.php?articleid=4891 [February 18, 2010]).

15. Dave Eggers, *Zeitoun* (San Francisco: McSweeney's Books, 2009).

16. Jesse Hyde, "Texas Woman Fights Abuse at the State's Schools for the Mentally Retarded: Her Son Was Beaten Up by an Angry Caregiver at Denton State School," *Houston Press*, July 31, 2008.

17. Ibid.

18. U.S. Department of Justice, "Federal Judge Hands Downs Sentences in Holy Land Foundation Case," May 27, 2009 (www.justice.gov/opa/pr/2009/May/09-nsd-519.html [December 1, 2009]).

19. Ibid.

20. Personal communication, 2010. See also Jonathan Benthall and Jerome Bellion-Jourdan, *The Charitable Crescent: Politics of Aid in the Muslim World* (London: I. B. Tauris, 2009).

Chapter Four

1. Yusuf Progler, "Reading Early American Islamica: An Interpretive Translation of the 'Bilali Diary,'" *Al-Tawhid: A Journal of Islamic Thought and Culture* 16, no. 3 (Autumn 2000): 5–43.

2. Imam Al-Hajj Talib Abdur-Rashid, "We Came before Columbus: The Pre-Columbian Presence of Muslim Africans in America Is No Myth!" December 1, 2005 (www.mosqueofislamicbrotherhoodinc.org/page/page/4985846.htm [March 10, 2010]).

3. Alexis de Tocqueville, *Democracy in America*, edited and translated by Harvey C. Mansfield and Delba Winthrop (University of Chicago Press, 2000), pp. 305, 327.

4. Mattias Gardell, *In the Name of Elijah Muhammad: Louis Farrakhan and the Nation of Islam* (Duke University Press, 1996), p. 43.

5. Ibid.

6. Abul Pitre, *The Educational Philosophy of Elijah Muhammad: Education for a New World* (Lanham, Md.: University Press of America, 2007), p. 3

7. James Baldwin, *The Fire Next Time* (New York: Vintage International, 1993), pp. 50–51.

8. "Yakub" (www.thenationofislam.org/yakubabraham.html [February 18, 2010]).

9. Malcolm X with Alex Haley, *The Autobiography of Malcolm X* (New York: Ballantine Books, 1992), p, 181.

10. "Yakub."

11. Sulayman S. Nyang, "The Transformer-in-Chief," *Islamic Horizons*, November/December 2008, p. 16.

12. Malcolm X with Alex Haley, *Autobiography*, p. 371.

13. Ibid., p. 183.

14. Ibid., pp. 371–72.

15. Susan Saulny, "Prayers and Criticism in Wake of Detroit Imam's Killing by F.B.I.," *New York Times*, October 30, 2009.

16. Imam Abdullah El-Amin, "FBI Kills Muslim Imam—What Really Happened?" Muslim Media News Service (MMNS), Muslim Alliance in North America (www.mana-net.org/pages.php?ID=activism&NUM=1178 [March 31, 2010]).

17. Michael Waller, "Alamoudi, Islamists, and Muslim Chaplains," Testimony before Senate Judiciary Committee, Subcommittee on Terrorism, Technology, and Homeland Security, October 14, 2003 (www.freerepublic.com/focus/f-news/1039743/posts [February 18, 2010]).

18. Ibid.

19. "Why Did National Public Radio Turn Down an Interview with President Bush?" Foxnews.com, September 25, 2007 (www.foxnews.com/story/0,2933,297890,00.html [February 19, 2010]).

20. Karen Isaksen Leonard, *Muslims in the United States: The State of Research* (New York: Russell Sage Foundation, 2003), p. 8.

21. Malcolm X with Alex Haley, *Autobiography*, p. 183.

Chapter Five

1. See Gallup poll, "Muslim Americans: A National Portrait," 2009 (www. muslimwestfacts.com/mwf/116074/Muslim-Americans-National-Portrait.aspx [February 26, 2010]). For economic disparity, see pp. 74–75, for demographics, p. 21.

2. Mark Mazzetti and David Johnston, "Bush Weighed Using Military in Arrests," *New York Times*, July 24, 2009.

3. Steven Waldman, "Jesus in Baghdad: Why We Should Keep Franklin Graham Out of Iraq," *Slate*, April 11, 2003 (www.slate.com/id/2081432/ [February 23, 2010]).

4. "Erik Prince and the Last Crusade," *The Economist*, August 6, 2009.

5. Mohammed Ismail Memon Madani, *Hijab: Islamic Commandments of Hijab*, translated by Mohammed Sadiq (Alexandria, Va.: Al-Saadawi, 1996).

6. Sheikha Fariha Fatima al-Jerrahi, a female convert who is a mystic, is discussed in chapter 6, and Maryam Kabeer Faye, a Jewish female convert tells her story in Faye, *Journey through Ten Thousand Veils: The Alchemy of Transformation on the Sufi Path* (Clifton, N.J.: Tughra Books, 2009).

7. Muhammad Hisham Kabbani, *Angels Unveiled: A Sufi Perspective* (Chicago: Kazi, 1995); *Pearls and Coral: Secrets of the Sufi Way* (Fenton, Mich.: Islamic Supreme Council of America, 2005); and *Illuminations: Compiled Lectures on Shariah and Tasawwuf* (Fenton, Mich.: Islamic Supreme Council of America, 2007).

8. "Intellectuals," *Prospect*, 2009 (www.prospectmagazine.co.uk/prospect-100-intellectuals/ [February 24, 2010]).

9. Jane I. Smith, "Patterns of Muslim Immigration, Muslim Life in America" (State Department, Office of International Information Programs) (http://infousa. state.gov/education/overview/muslimlife/immigrat.htm [February 20, 2010]).

10. For example, Diana Eck's guide was "a minister at Littlefield Presbyterian Church in Dearborn": Diana Eck, *A New Religious America: How a "Christian Country" Has Become the World's Most Religiously Diverse Nation* (San Francisco: Harper San Francisco, 2001), pp. 248–49.

11. Saleem Ahmed, *Islam: A Religion of Peace?* (Honolulu: Moving Pen Publishers, 2009).

12. Debbie Schlussel, "Radical Muslim Fine Whine of the Week," August 23, 2005 (www.debbieschlussel.com/271/radical-muslim-fine-whine-of-the-week/ [February 20, 2010]).

13. Haneef James Oliver, *The 'Wahhabi' Myth: Dispelling Prevalent Fallacies and the Fictitious Link with Bin Laden* (Toronto, Ont.: TROID, 2004).

14. Lawrence Wright, *The Looming Tower: Al-Qaeda and the Road to 9/11* (New York: Vintage, 2007), p. 15.

15. Shaykh Aboo Nasr Muhammad ibn 'Abdullaah ar-Raymee, "The Illumination of Darkness in Unveiling the Evils and Uncertainties of Elections," Masjid At-Tawheed: With the Understanding of the Salafis Saalih (www.masjidattawheed. net/Articles/elections.pdf [March 5, 2010]).

16. See Akbar S. Ahmed, *Postmodernism and Islam: Predicament and Promise* (London: Routledge, 1992), and *Living Islam: From Samarkand to Stornoway* (London: BBC Books, 1993).

17. Imam Hassan Qazwini, *American Crescent: A Muslim Cleric on the Power of His Faith, the Struggle against Prejudice, and the Future of Islam in America* (New York: Random House, 2007).

18. Ahmed, *Living Islam.*

19. Kirk Semple, "A Somali Influx Unsettles Latino Meatpackers," *New York Times.* October 16, 2008.

20. Ann Corcoran, "Old Article Sheds More Light on Hispanic/Somali Culture Clash in Meatpacking Plants," January 8, 2009 (http://refugeeresettlementwatch. wordpress.com/2009/01/08/old-article-sheds-more-light-on-hispanicsomali-culture-clash-in-meatpacking-plants/ [February 24, 2010]).

21. Dilara Hafiz, Yasmine Hafiz, and Imran Hafiz, *The American Muslim Teenager's Handbook* (New York: Atheneum Books for Young Readers, 2009), p. 81. See also chapter 10, "The Four Ds," which begins with an appropriate Quranic verse: "They ask you concerning wine and gambling. Say, 'In them is great sin, and some profit, for men; but the sin is greater than the profit'" (Surah 2:219).

22. Akbar Ahmed with Gustaaf Houtman, "Swat in the Eye of the Storm: Interview with Akbar Ahmed," *Anthropology Today* 25, no. 5 (2009): 20–22.

Chapter Six

1. Yvonne Yazbeck Haddad, "The Quest for Peace in Submission: Reflections on the Journey of American Women Converts to Islam," in *Women Embracing Islam: Gender and Conversion in the West,* edited by Karin van Nieuwkerk (University of Texas Press, 2006), p. 20.

2. Haifaa Jawad, "Female Conversion to Islam: The Sufi Paradigm," in *Women Embracing Islam,* edited by van Nieuwkerk, p. 154.

3. Alexis de Tocqueville, *Democracy in America,* translated and edited by Harvey C. Mansfield and Delba Winthrop (University of Chicago Press, 2000), pp. 563, 564.

4. Amy Sullivan, "Church-Shopping: Why Americans Change Faith," *Time,* April 28, 2009.

5. Young men such as Lindh and Gadahn show some confusion in their understanding of the concept of jihad, which for them became a military struggle. In converting to Islam they were attracted to the idea of fighting on behalf of the oppressed ummah against tyranny. Lindh, in Pakistan and feeling empathy for the

ordinary people, "wanted to help them one way or another." After he was captured by American troops, he apologized for fighting alongside the Taliban against the Northern Alliance, confessing, "had I realized then what I know now . . . I would never have joined them," and saying he "never understood jihad to mean anti-American or terrorism." On the other hand, Gadahn, a heavy metal fan raised in a conservative Christian household, was an outsider in his home and community. He ended up as an al Qaeda spokesman and sees himself as a warrior in a war against America. For more on both of these cases, see "John Walker Lindh Profile: The Case of the American Taliban," CNN.com (www.cnn.com/CNN/Programs/people/shows/walker/profile.html [February 20, 2010]), and Brendan Bernhard, *White Muslims: From LA to New York . . . to Jihad?* (Hoboken, N.J.: Melville House Publishing, 2006), pp. 54–55.

6. Umar F. Abd-Allah, *A Muslim in Victorian America: The Life of Alexander Russell Webb* (Oxford University Press, 2006), pp. 136, 137.

7. Alexander Russell Webb, *Islam in America: A Brief Statement on Mohammedanism and an Outline of the American Islamic Propaganda* (New York: Oriental Publishing Co. and Acton Press, 1893).

8. Fred Dallmayr, *Dialogue among Civilizations: Some Exemplary Voices* (New York: Palgrave Macmillan, 2002), pp. 150, 152, 153.

9. Amy Green, "More US Hispanics Drawn to Islam," *Christian Science Monitor,* September 28, 2006; Pew Forum on Religion and Public Life, U.S. Religious Landscape Survey, February 2008 (http://religions.pewforum.org/pdf/report-religious-landscape-study-full.pdf), p. 44. See also Rachel Martin, "Latinas Choosing Islam over Catholicism," NPR.org, September 24, 2006.

10. Jon Meacham, *American Gospel: God, the Founding Fathers, and the Making of a Nation* (New York: Random House, 2006), p. 43.

11. Richard J. Hooker, ed., *The Carolina Backcountry on the Eve of the Revolution: The Journal and Other Writings of Charles Woodmason, Anglican Itinerant* (University of North Carolina Press, 1953), pp. 32–33, 61, 99–100,

12. Bryan Burrough, "Missing White Female," *Vanity Fair,* January 2006.

13. Claire Hoffman, "Baby, Give Me a Kiss," *Los Angeles Times,* August 6, 2006.

14. De Tocqueville, *Democracy in America,* p. 594.

15. Mary Pipher, *Reviving Ophelia: Saving the Selves of Adolescent Girls* (New York: G. P. Putnam's Sons, 1994).

16. Tom Wolfe, *I Am Charlotte Simmons* (New York: Farrar, Straus and Giroux, 2004).

17. Morris Berman, *Dark Ages America: The Final Phase of Empire* (New York: W. W. Norton, 2007). See also Robert D. Putnam, *Bowling Alone: The Collapse and Revival of American Community* (New York: Simon and Schuster, 2001).

18. Berman, *Dark Ages America,* pp. 41, 77. See also Christopher Lasch, *The Culture of Narcissism: American Life in an Age of Diminishing Expectations* (New York: W. W. Norton, 1991).

19. Hanna Rosin, "Did Christianity Cause the Crash?" *The Atlantic,* December 2009.

Chapter Seven

1. Gretchen E. Schafft, *From Racism to Genocide: Anthropology in the Third Reich* (University of Illinois Press, 2004), p. 72.

2. Susan D. Bachrach and Dieter Kuntz, eds., *Deadly Medicine: Creating the Master Race* (Washington: Holocaust Memorial Museum, 2004), p. 12.

3. Judea Pearl and Ruth Pearl, eds., *I Am Jewish: Personal Reflections Inspired by the Last Words of Daniel Pearl* (Woodstock, Vt.: Jewish Lights, 2005).

4. Joel Stein, "Who Runs Hollywood? C'mon," *Los Angeles Times*, December 19, 2008.

5. Jon Meacham, *American Gospel: God, the Founding Fathers, and the Making of a Nation* (New York: Random House, 2006), pp. 260–61.

6. Albert Isaac Slomovitz, *The Fighting Rabbis: Jewish Military Chaplains and American History* (New York University Press, 2001), p. 16.

7. Michael Feldberg, ed., *Blessings of Freedom: Chapters in American Jewish History* (Hoboken, N.J.: KTAV, 2002), pp. 118–19.

8. Jonathan D. Sarna, *American Judaism: A History* (Yale University Press, 2005), p. 121.

9. John Moffatt Mecklin, *The Ku-Klux Klan: A Study of the American Mind* (Whitefish, Mont.: Kessinger, 2006), p. 4.

10. Leonard Dinnerstein, *The Leo Frank Case* (University of Georgia Press, 2008), p. 143.

11. Ibid., pp. 144, 145.

12. Athan G. Theoharis and John Stuart Cox, *The Boss: J. Edgar Hoover and the Great American Inquisition* (Temple University Press, 1988), p. 45.

13. Meacham, *American Gospel*, p. 149.

14. Michael Foley, *American Credo: The Place of Ideas in U.S. Politics* (Oxford University Press, 2007), p. 195.

15. Geoffrey R. Stone, *Perilous Times: Free Speech in Wartime from the Sedition Act of 1798 to the War on Terrorism* (New York: W. W. Norton, 2004), p. 224.

16. Neil Baldwin, *Henry Ford and the Jews: The Mass Production of Hate* (New York: PublicAffairs, 2003), p. 185.

17. Edwin Black, *The Transfer Agreement: The Dramatic Story of the Pact between the Third Reich and Jewish Palestine* (New York: Carroll and Graf, 2001), p. 27; Baldwin, *Henry Ford and the Jews*, p. 284.

18. Gerard N. Burrow, *A History of Yale's School of Medicine: Passing Torches to Others* (Yale University Press, 2002), p. 107.

19. Meacham, *American Gospel*, p. 157.

20. Ibid., p. 142.

21. Ibid., p. 157.

22. For more details about Breen's attitude, see Mick LaSalle, *Complicated Women: Sex and Power in Pre-Code Hollywood* (New York: Thomas Dunne Books/ St. Martin's Press, 2000), pp. 192–93; and Thomas Doherty, *Hollywood's Censor:*

Joseph I. Breen and the Production Code Administration (Columbia University Press, 2007), p. 199.

23. Thomas Doherty, "Was Hollywood's Famed Censor an Antisemite?" *Jewish Daily Forward*, December 14, 2007.

24. Lynn Haney, *Gregory Peck: A Charmed Life* (New York: Carroll and Graf, 2005), p. 149.

25. Peck took on another controversial role, as Atticus Finch in *To Kill a Mockingbird*, which addressed racism against African Americans. The actor's pluralist sensibilities would get him blackballed by many Los Angeles clubs. These same clubs in the 1960s extended invitations to Peck to join, but he repaid them the "compliment" and refused. See ibid., pp. 154–55.

26. Otto Friedrich, *City of Nets: A Portrait of Hollywood in the 1940's* (University of California Press, 1997), p. 299.

27. Ronald L. Davis, *Duke: The Life and Image of John Wayne* (University of Oklahoma Press, 1998), p. 142.

28. Randy Roberts and James S. Olson, *John Wayne: American* (University of Nebraska Press, 1997), p. 439.

29. Herbert M. Druks, *John F. Kennedy and Israel* (Westport, Conn.: Praeger Security International, 2005), p. 28.

30. Ibid., p. 29.

31. Ibid., p. 30.

32. Ibid., p. 28.

33. Robert B. Semple Jr., ed., *Four Days in November: The Original Coverage of the John F. Kennedy Assassination by the Staff of the New York Times* (New York: St. Martin's Press, 2003), p. 215.

34. Chris Hedges, *American Facists: The Christian Right and the War on America* (New York: Free Press, 2006), pp. 12–13.

35. David Rosenzweig, "Ex-JDL Official to Plead Guilty in Bombing Plot," *Los Angeles Times*, February 1, 2003.

36. Greg Krikorian and Richard Winton, "JDL Leader Accused in Mosque Bomb Plot," *Los Angeles Times*, December 13, 2001.

37. "Never Again," Jewish Defense League (www.jdl.org/ [March 10, 2010]).

38. Clinton Heylin, *Bob Dylan: Behind the Shades Revisited* (New York: Harper Collins, 2003), p. 328; Peter Doggett, *There's a Riot Going On: Revolutionaries, Rock Stars, and the Rise and Fall of the '60s* (New York: Canongate, 2007), p. 391.

39. Akbar Ahmed, "Scholarship about Islam in America," *Religion News Service*, July 2, 2003.

40. Khalid Hasan, "Dr. Akbar S Ahmed Lone Muslim Voice in Favour of Daniel Pipes Nomination," (Lahore) *Daily Times*, July 26, 2003.

41. Charles Krauthammer, "The Perfect Liberal Storm," *Washington Post*, November 7, 2003. See also James Webb, "Secret GOP Weapon: The Scots-Irish Vote," *Wall Street Journal*, October 23, 2004.

42. David Shasha, "Uncovering the Obsessions of 'Obsession,'" Center for Sephardic Heritage—Tikun Olam: Make the World a Better Place, October 27, 2008

(www.richardsilverstein.com/tikun_olam/2008/10/27/david-shashas-obsession-review/ [February 19, 2010]).

43. Jonathan Sacks, *The Dignity of Difference: How to Avoid the Clash of Civilizations* (New York: Continuum International, 2002), p. 13.

44. Jonathan Sacks, *To Heal a Fractured World: The Ethics of Responsibility* (New York: Schoken Books, 2005).

45. As recorded in *Sahih al-Bukhari,* a collection of statements and traditions, or hadiths, by and about the Prophet Muhammad; see the section titled "Standing Up in Respect of a Jewish Funeral" in the *Book on Funeral Procession.*

Chapter Eight

1. *Book of Mormon,* Second Book of Nephi, Chapter 5: 21; 4 Nephi: 10; 2 Nephi 5:17; 2 Nephi 5:21; 2 Nephi 5:24; 2 Nephi 5:23.

2. Ibid., Mormon 5:15.

3. Fawn Brodie quoted in Jon Krakauer, *Under the Banner of Heaven: A Story of Violent Faith* (New York: Anchor Books, 2004), p. 115.

4. Leonard J. Arrington and Davis Bitton, *The Mormon Experience: A History of the Latter-day Saints* (University of Illinois Press, 1992), p. 142.

5. Krakauer, *Under the Banner of Heaven,* p. 108.

6. Ibid.

7. See ibid., p. 209; and G .D. Watt, ed., *Journal of Discourses by Brigham Young, His Two Counselors, the Twelve Apostles and Others,* vol. 2 (Whitefish, Mont.: Kessinger, 2006), pp. 172, 184, 216.

8. Watt, ed., *Journal of Discourses,* pp. 170, 171, 182.

9. Arrington and Bitton, *The Mormon Experience,* p. 170.

10. Krakauer, *Under the Banner of Heaven.*

11. *The Doctrine and Covenants of the Church of Jesus Christ of Latter-day Saints,* 29: 9, 10.

12. Abu Hamid Al-Ghazali, *The Niche of Lights,* translated, introduced, and annotated by David Buchman, Islamic Translation Series (Brigham Young University Press, 1998).

13. Arnold H. Green, "The Muhammad–Joseph Smith Comparison: Subjective Metaphor or a Sociology of Prophethood?" in *Mormons and Muslims: Spiritual Foundations and Modern Manifestations,* edited by Spencer J. Palmer (Brigham Young University, Religious Studies Center, 2002), pp. 112, 114.

14. Ibid., p. 112; Arnold H. Green, personal communication, 2008, BYU.

15. Richard F. Burton. *The City of the Saints, and across the Rocky Mountains to California* (New York: Harper and Brothers, 1862), p. 240.

16. Green, "The Muhammad–Joseph Smith Comparison," p. 114.

17. Spencer J. Palmer, "Comments on Common Ground," in *Mormons and Muslims,* edited by Palmer, pp. 87–91, 113, 116,

18. Eduard Meyer, quoted in ibid., p. 88.

19. Green, "The Muhammad–Joseph Smith Comparison," pp. 128–29.

20. Daniel C. Peterson, "Understanding Islam," in *Mormons and Muslims*, edited by Palmer, p. 41.

21. Krakauer, *Under the Banner of Heaven*, pp. 5, 58, 59, 70, 252.

22. Ibid., p. 11.

23. Ibid., pp. 5, 80.

24. Ibid., pp. 43–44, 323.

25. Chris Gladden, "'September Dawn' a Grotesque Western," *Roanoke Times*, August 25, 2007; Pete Hammond, "September Dawn," *Maxim* (www.maxim.com/movies/movie-reviews/33283/september-dawn.html [March 24, 2010]).

26. Krakauer, *Under the Banner of Heaven*, pp. 4, 324.

Chapter Nine

1. For a fuller discussion, see Akbar S. Ahmed, "Jefferson and Jinnah: Humanist Ideals and the Mythology of Nation-Building," in *The Future of Liberal Democracy: Thomas Jefferson and the Contemporary World*, edited by Robert Fatton Jr. and Rouhollah K. Ramazani (New York: Palgrave Macmillan, 2004).

2. In the film *Mindwalk* (1990), an actor playing an American presidential candidate compares Jefferson to British physicist Isaac Newton.

3. R. B. Bernstein, *Thomas Jefferson* (Oxford University Press, 2005), p. 197.

4. E. H. Enver, *The Modern Moses: A Brief Biography of M. A. Jinnah* (Karachi: Jinnah Memorial Institute, 1990).

5. Alan Campbell-Johnson in the documentary *Mr. Jinnah: The Making of Pakistan* (London: Café Productions, 1997).

6. Conor Cruise O'Brien, "Thomas Jefferson: Radical and Racist," *The Atlantic*, October 1996. See also O'Brien's *The Long Affair: Thomas Jefferson and the French Revolution, 1785–1800* (University of Chicago Press, 1996).

7. Gary Scott Smith, *Faith and the Presidency: From George Washington to George W. Bush* (Oxford University Press, 2006), pp. 71, 74.

8. Rod Parsley, *Silent No More: Bringing Moral Clarity to America . . . While Freedom Still Rings* (Lake Mary, Fla.: Charisma House, 2005), pp. 90, 91, 96.

9. Hannah Strange, "John McCain Told to Dump Spiritual Guide in Row Over 'War' on Islam," *The Times* (London) March 13, 2008.

10. The man was reacting to a U.S. court ruling exonerating the contractor. See Timothy Williams, "Iraqis Angered as Blackwater Charges Are Dropped," *New York Times*, January 1, 2010.

11. Greg Mortenson and David Oliver Relin, *Three Cups of Tea: One Man's Mission to Fight Terrorism and Build Nations . . . One School at a Time* (New York: Viking, 2006), p. 294.

12. Tina Susman, "Civilian Deaths May Top 1 Million, Poll Data Indicate," *Los Angeles Times*, September 14, 2007; "Only 4 Percent of Iraqis in Syria Plan to Return Home," UN News Centre, April 29, 2008 (www.un.org/apps/news/story.

asp?NewsID=26494&Cr=iraq&Cr1 [February 16, 2010]); "Occupation's Toll: 5 Million Iraqi Children Orphaned," Alternet, December 18, 2007 (www.alternet. org/world/70886/?page=entire [February 16, 2010]).

13. Jonathan Steele, "Forgotten Victims," *Guardian,* May 20, 2002.

14. "Fatalities in Terrorist Violence in Pakistan, 2003–2010," Institute for Conflict Management, New Delhi, South Asia Terrorism Portal (www.satp.org/satporgtp/countries/pakistan/database/casualties.htm [February 16, 2010]); "Over 700 Killed in 44 Drone Strikes in 2009," (Karachi) *Dawn,* January 2, 2010; "Number of Displaced Persons Exceeds Three Million," (Karachi) *Dawn,* May 30, 2009.

15. Frank Nyakairu, "Somali Refugees Pour into Kenya by the Thousands," Reuters, June 4, 2009. The United Nations has given a figure of 1.5 million internally displaced in Somalia; see "Half of Somalia's Population Could Go Hungry, UN Warns," UN News Centre, August 25, 2009 (www.un.org/apps/news/story. asp?NewsID=31848 [February 16, 2010]). In addition, "hundreds of thousands" of Somalis have fled the country as refugees, according to Nyakairu.

16. "Urgent Food Aid Needed to Avert Humanitarian Catastrophe in Somalia," UN News Centre, September 4, 2009 (www.un.org/apps/news/story.asp?NewsID= 31953&Cr=somali&Cr1 [February 16, 2010]).

17. Fred Anderson and Andrew Cayton, *The Dominion of War: Empire and Liberty in North America, 1500–2000* (New York: Viking, 2005), p. 336.

18. Joby Warrick, Peter Finn, and Julie Tate, "Red Cross Described 'Torture' at CIA Jails," *Washington Post,* March 16, 2009.

19. Scott Horton, "The Guantánamo 'Suicides': A Camp Delta Sergeant Blows the Whistle," *Harper's Magazine,* January 2010.

20. Scott Horton, "The Bush Era Torture-Homicides," *Harper's Magazine,* May 2009.

21. Mark Danner, "US Torture: Voices from the Black Sites," *New York Review of Books,* vol. 56, no. 6, April 9, 2009.

22. Tim Reid, "George W. Bush 'Knew Guantánamo Prisoners Were Innocent,'" *The Times* (London), April 9, 2010.

23. Alexis de Tocqueville, *Democracy in America,* edited and translated by Harvey C. Mansfield and Delba Winthrop (University of Chicago Press, 2000), p. 325.

24. David Hackett Fischer, *Washington's Crossing* (Oxford University Press, 2004), p. 379.

25. Merrill D. Peterson, ed., *The Political Writings of Thomas Jefferson* (University of North Carolina Press, 1993), p. 50.

26. Larzer Ziff, ed., *The Portable Benjamin Franklin* (New York: Penguin, 2005), p. 391.

27. Benjamin Franklin, *Wit and Wisdom from Poor Richard's Almanac* (Mineola, N.Y.: Dover, 1999), p. 3.

28. Paul M. Barrett, *American Islam: The Struggle for the Soul of a Religion* (New York: Picador, 2008), p. 46.

29. Aladdin Elaasar, *Silent Victims: The Plight of Arab & Muslim Americans in Post 9/11 America* (Bloomington, Ind.: Authorhouse, 2004), p. 15.

30. Anita Ramasastry, "FindLaw Forum: Why Ashcroft's Plan to Create Internment Camps for Alleged Enemy Combatants Is Wrong," CNN.com, September 4, 2002 (http://archives.cnn.com/2002/LAW/08/columns/fl.ramasastry.detainees/ [March 15, 2010]); Jonathan Turley, "Camps for Citizens: Ashcroft's Hellish Vision," *Los Angeles Times*, August 14, 2002.

31. Robert E. Pierre, "Fear and Anxiety Permeate Arab Enclave Near Detroit," *Washington Post*, August 4, 2002.

32. Mohammed Nimer, *The North American Muslim Resource Guide: Muslim Community Life in the United States and Canada* (New York: Routledge, 2002), p. 150.

33. Rachel L. Swarns, "Halliburton Subsidiary Gets Contract to Add Temporary Immigration Detention Centers," *New York Times*, February 4, 2006.

34. David Kilcullen, *The Accidental Guerrilla: Fighting Small Wars in the Midst of a Big One* (Oxford University Press, 2009).

35. "McCain: I'd Prefer Christian President," Associated Press, September 30, 2007.

36. Paul Vitello and Kirk Semple, "Muslims Say F.B.I. Tactics Sow Anger and Fear," *New York Times*, December, 17, 2009.

37. Amira Hass, "Did FBI Informant Actually Inspire Bronx Synagogue Plot?" *Hareetz*, June 15, 2009.

38. George Washington, *George Washington's Rules of Civility and Decent Behaviour in Company and Conversation* (Bedford, Mass.: Applewood Books, 1989).

39. Elise Alexander, "Learning to Name: An Afternoon with Maya Soetoro-Ng," *Pakistan Link*, December 18, 2009.

40. Gore Vidal, interview with Amy Goodman, *Democracy Now*, May 14, 2008.

41. Andrew J. Bacevich, *The Limits of Power: The End of American Exceptionalism* (New York: Metropolitan Books, Henry Holt and Company, 2008), pp. 33, 35.

42. E. M. Halliday, *Understanding Thomas Jefferson* (New York: HarperCollins, 2001), p. 206.

43. Daniel M. Haybron, *The Pursuit of Unhappiness: The Elusive Psychology of Well-Being* (Oxford University Press, 2008), pp. 217–21.

44. Samuel P. Huntington, *Who Are We? The Challenges to America's National Identity* (New York: Simon and Schuster, 2004).

45. Jennings L. Wagoner Jr., *Jefferson and Education* (University of North Carolina Press, 2004), p. 93.

46. Stephen Lucas, ed., *The Quotable George Washington: The Wisdom of an American Patriot* (Madison, Wisc.: Madison House Publishers, 1999), p. 68.

47. Halliday, *Understanding Thomas Jefferson*, p. 201.

48. H. W. Brands, *The First American: The Life and Times of Benjamin Franklin* (New York: Doubleday, 2000), p. 220.

49. J. R. Pole, ed., *The Revolution in America, 1754–1788: Documents and Commentaries* (Stanford University Press, 1970), pp. 394–95.

50. Ron Suskind, in "Cheney's Law," PBS *Frontline*, October 16, 2007.

INDEX

Abayya (traditional dress), 115, 116f, 117, 289, 307, 308, 322

ABCD (American-Born Confused Desi). *See* Muslims—in America

Abdullah, Luqman Ameen (imam), 183–85, 433

Abdulla, Kasar (Kurdish-American student), 288, 289

Abdul-Rahman ("prince among slaves"), 170

Abdur-Rashid, Talib (imam), 162, 169, 210–11, 257

Abrahamic faiths, 25–28, 129–32, 445

Abudiab, Daoud (director, Islamic center), 137–38

Abu Ghraib (prison; Baghdad, Iraq), 112, 133–34, 330–31, 342

Abyssinia, 1–2

ACCESS. *See* Arab Community Center for Economic and Social Services

Ackroyd, Steve, 244, 305

ACLU. *See* American Civil Liberties Union

Adab (traditional etiquette), 6, 101, 273

Adams, John (president; Founding Father): Alien and Sedition Acts and, 64; background of, 60; Prophet Muhammad and, 59, 471; religious tolerance of, 59; view of the Pilgrims, 42

Adams, John Quincy (secretary of state), 66

Afghanistan: American troops in, 6, 125, 433; Carter and, 124; Herring, Joanne, and, 124; killing and disruption in, 436; Muslims and, 261, 434–35; protection of Muslims in, 8; refugees from, 289–91; Soviet invasion of, 230. *See also* Taliban

African Americans: African American imams, 186–94; Catholics and, 86; Christianity and, 82; civil rights movement and, 89; crime and violence by, 87; culture of, 160; drugs and, 160; Jews and, 384; Muslims and, 83–84; in Palm Beach, Fla., 392; prejudices against, 28–30; in prison, 200; sexual insecurities and, 84–85; struggle for humanity of, 84–87; syphilis and AIDS in, 85–86; the system and, 181–85, 202; whites and white culture and, 29, 30, 82–83, 86–87, 160, 180–81; World War II and, 89. *See also* Color; Ethnic, minority, and racial issues; Islam; Sapelo Island; Slaves and slavery

African Americans—Muslims: early Muslim awakenings, 169–73; identity of, 160–61, 174; immigrant Muslims and, 208–13, 214–15, 236, 381–82; Muslim organizations and, 269; Muslim traditions on Sapelo Island, 165–66

503

CPSIA information can be obtained
at www.ICGtesting.com
Printed in the USA
LVOW08s1623100717
540843LV00001B/317/P